PEERS, POLITICS AND POWER

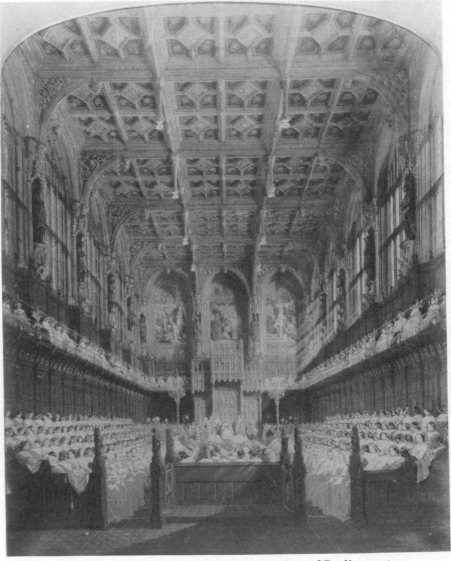

1. Queen Victoria at the State Opening of Parliament,
3 December 1857.

*Gouache by Joseph Nash, by courtesy of the House of Lords
Record Office.*

Queen Victoria and Prince Albert are seated awaiting the Commons. The
Lords had been in their new chamber since 1847.

PEERS, POLITICS AND POWER:

THE HOUSE OF LORDS,

1603-1911

EDITED BY

CLYVE JONES
AND
DAVID LEWIS JONES

THE HAMBLEDON PRESS

LONDON   AND   RONCEVERTE

Published by the Hambledon Press 1986

35 Gloucester Avenue, London NW1 7AX (U.K.)

309 Greenbrier Avenue, Ronceverte
West Virginia 24970 (U.S.A.)

ISBN 0 907628 78 8

History Series 56

British Library Cataloguing in Publication Data

Peers, politics and power: the House of Lords,
    1603-1911.
    1. Great Britain, *Parliament, House of Lords*
    — History
    I. Jones, Clyve II. Jones, David L.
    328.41'071'09   JN621

Library of Congress Cataloging-in-Publication Data

Main entry under title:

Peers, politics, and power.

    Bibliography: pp. xvii-xxix.
    Includes index.
    1. Great Britain. Parliament. House of Lords —
    History — Addresses, essays, lectures.
    2. Great Britain — Politics and government —
    Addresses, essays, lectures.
    I. Jones, Clyve, 1944-
    II. Jones, David Lewis, 1945-
    JN621.P39   1986   328.41'071 85-31722
    ISBN 0 907628 78 8 (U.S.)

Printed by WBC Print Ltd., Bristol
Bound by WBC Bookbinders Ltd., Maesteg

CONTENTS

Notes on Contributors viii
List of Illustrations ix
Acknowledgements x
Preface xi
General Introduction xiii
Bibliography xvii

I. THE EARLY STUARTS (1603-1641)

Bibliographical Note 2

1 The Nature of Opposition in the House of Lords in the 5
Early Seventeenth Century: a Revaluation
Jess Stoddart Flemion

2 The Dissolution of Parliament in 1626: a Revaluation 23
Jess Stoddart Flemion

3 The Struggle for the Petition of Right in the House of 31
Lords: the Study of an Opposition Party Victory
Jess Stoddart Flemion

4 The Peers, the People, and Parliamentary Management 49
in the First Six Months of the Long Parliament
Paul Christianson

II. THE FIRST AGE OF PARTY (1689-1750)

Bibliographical Note 77

5 Divisions in the House of Lords on the Transfer of the 79
Crown and Other Issues, 1689-94: Ten New Lists
Eveline Cruickshanks, David Hayton, Clyve Jones

6 The Defeat of the Occasional Conformity Bill and the 111
Tack: a Study in the Techniques of Parliamentary
Management in the Reign of Queen Anne
Henry L. Snyder

7 Godolphin, the Whig Junto and the Scots: a New 133
Division List from 1709
Clyve Jones

8 The Hamilton Affair of 1711-1712: a Crisis in Anglo- 151
Scottish Relations
Geoffrey Holmes

9   Hanover, Pensions and the 'Poor Lords', 1712-13   177
       Edward Gregg, Clyve Jones

10   The Impeachment of the Earl of Oxford and the Whig   185
      Schism of 1717: Four New Lists
      Clyve Jones

11   The Origin of the Leadership of the House of Lords   207
      J.C. Sainty

III. THE AGE OF REVOLUTION AND REFORM (1750-1850)

Bibliographical Note   230

12   The Decline of the 'Party of the Crown' and the Rise   233
      of Parties in the House of Lords, 1783-1837
      David Large

13   Bishops and Scottish Representative Peers in the House   261
      of Lords, 1760-1775
      William Curtis Lowe

14   The Scottish Peerage and the House of Lords in the Late   283
      Eighteenth Century
      Michael W. McCahill

15   The Scottish Representative Peers and Parliamentary   309
      Politics, 1787-1793
      G.M. Ditchfield

16   The House of Lords and Parliamentary Reform in the   327
      Seventeen-Eighties
      G.M. Ditchfield

17   The House of Lords and Parliamentary Patronage in   355
      Great Britain, 1802-32
      James J. Sack

18   The House of Lords and Ireland in the Age of Peel,   373
      1832-50
      David Large

19   Peerage Creations and the Changing Character of the   407
      British Nobility, 1750-1850
      Michael W. McCahill

20   Peers, Patronage and the Industrial Revolution, 1760-1800   433
      Michael W. McCahill

IV. THE GROWTH OF DEMOCRACY (1860-1911)

Bibliographical Note   459

21   Salisbury and the Lords, 1868-1895   461
      Corinne Comstock Weston

22   The Liberal Leadership and the Lords' Veto, 1907-10   489
      Corinne Comstock Weston

23   Lord Newton, the Conservative Peers and the Parliament   519
      Act of 1911
      David Southern

24   The 'Judas Group' and the Parliament Bill of 1911   527
      Corinne Comstock Weston; Patricia Kelvin

Index   541

NOTES ON CONTRIBUTORS

Clyve Jones is an assistant librarian at the Institute of Historical Research in the University of London.

David Lewis Jones is deputy librarian in the House of Lords Library.

Paul Christianson is a professor of history at the Queen's University, Kingston, Canada.

Eveline Cruickshanks is editor of the 1690-1715 section of *The History of Parliament*.

G.M. Ditchfield is a lecturer in history at the University of Kent at Canterbury.

Jess Stoddart Flemion is a professor of history at San Diego State University.

Edward Gregg is a professor of history at the University of South Carolina.

David Hayton is research assistant on the 1690-1715 section of *The History of Parliament.*

Geoffrey Holmes is emeritus professor of history at the University of Lancaster.

Patricia Kelvin is an archivist for the General Synod of the Church of England.

David Large is a senior lecturer in history in the University of Bristol.

William C. Lowe is a professor of history at the Mount St. Clare College, Clinton, Iowa.

Michael W. McCahill is director of studies at the Brookes School, North Andover, Massachusetts.

James J. Sack is a professor of history at the University of Illinois at Chicago.

J.C. Sainty is the Clerk of the Parliaments.

Henry L. Snyder is dean of the College of Humanities and Social Sciences in the University of California, Riverside.

David Southern is a barrister and sometime lecturer in politics and European studies at the University of Kent at Canterbury.

Corinne Comstock Weston is a professor of history at the Herbert H. Lehman College of the City University of New York.

LIST OF ILLUSTRATIONS

1   Queen Victoria at the State Opening of   ii
     Parliament, 3 December 1857

2   The State Opening of Parliament, 17 March 1628   30
     (detail)

3   The 'abdication and vacancy' resolution of the   *between*
     Commons on 28 January 1688/9, showing the   81 and 82
     proposed amendment by the Lords.

4   William III enthroned in an imaginary House   *between*
     of Lords, 1689   81 and 82

5   The House of Lords in 1741-42   232

6   External view of the House of Lords from   346
     Old Palace Yard, 1826-34

7   Passing the Reform Bill, 1832   372

8   The Home Rule Debate in the House of Lords, 1893   488

ACKNOWLEDGEMENTS

The articles reprinted here first appeared in the following places and are reprinted by the kind permission of the original publishers.

1   *Albion* 8 (1976): 17-34.

2   *English Historical Review* 87 (1972): 784-90.

3   *Journal of Modern History* (University of Chicago Press) 45 (1973): 193-210.

4   *Journal of Modern History* (University of Chicago Press) 49 (1977): 575-99.

5   *Bulletin of the Institute of Historical Research* 53 (1980): 56-87.

6   *Bulletin of the Institute of Historical Research* 41 (1968): 172-92.

7   *Scottish Historical Review* 58 (1979): 158-74.

8   *English Historical Review* 77 (1962): 257-82.

9   *Parliamentary History* 1 (1982): 173-80.

10   *Bulletin of the Institute of Historical Research* 55 (1982): 66-87.

11   *Bulletin of the Institute of Historical Research* 47 (1974): 53-73.

12   *English Historical Review* 78 (1963): 669-95.

13   *Journal of British Studies* 18 (1978): 86-106.

14   *Scottish Historical Review* 51 (1972): 172-96.

15   *Scottish Historical Review* 60 (1981): 14-31.

16   *Bulletin of the Institute of Historical Research* 54 (1981): 207-25.

17   *Historical Journal* 23 (1980): 913-37.

18   *Irish Historical Studies* 9 no. 36 (1955): 367-99.

19   *English Historical Review* 96 (1981): 259-84.

20   *Journal of British Studies* 16 (1976): 84-107.

21   *Historical Journal* 25 (1982): 103-29.

22   *Historical Journal* 11 (1968): 508-37.

23   *English Historical Review* 96 (1981): 834-40.

24   *English Historical Review* 99 (1984): 551-63.

PREFACE

The purpose of this collection of reprinted essays is to provide the reader with a selection of the most important recent writings on the history of the House of Lords. While the mediaeval Lords are the subject of a magisterial survey by Enoch Powell and Keith Wallis, *The House of Lords in the Middle Ages* (London, 1968), there are few monographs on the later period but a larger number of valuable articles. Because there has been little academic work on the Tudor House of Lords, the editors decided to limit the coverage of this collection to the period from the accession of James I in 1603 to the Parliament Bill of 1911.

The editors resolved to exclude from the present collection all those articles which cover the procedure and the judicial work of the House. This was done in the belief that the political history of the Lords is more central to the teaching and the research currently in progress on parliamentary history. The constraint of space was an additional reason for thus limiting the choice of articles.

A bibliography of writings in the twentieth century on the House of Lords 1603-1911 is included as a guide to the historical research available on the House. With one exception, no. 158 in the bibliography, studies of the art and architecture of the Palace of Westminster have been excluded. The bibliography also confines itself to those studies whose entire content, or the major part of the content, is solely concerned with the House of Lords. General studies of political history and of Parliament as a whole will inevitably include references to the upper House. University dissertations are listed in the bibliography although the general reader may have difficulty in consulting them but the editors decided to include them as an indication of the trend of research on the history of the House. No additions were made to the bibliography after 1 October 1985.

The editors wish to thank the authors and the original publishers of the articles included for their generous permission to reprint them. The Institute of Historical Research kindly provided very necessary assistance. Martin Sheppard gave much help and encouragement at all stages of the publication of this volume. Finally, the editors are grateful to Alasdair Hawkyard for compiling the index.

C.J.
D.L.J.

GENERAL INTRODUCTION

[The numbers in brackets refer to items in the bibliography, below pp xvii-xxix. Chapter numbers refer to the essays printed below.]

An early landmark in the study of parliamentary history was the survey produced as part of the *Reports on the Dignity of a Peer* (1820-29). This reflected the general attitude in the nineteenth century when historians were more concerned with the history of the peerage than with the study of the House of Lords as an institution. The result was the publication of a number of handbooks to the peerages which culminated in the invaluable compilation, *The Complete Peerage,* edited by G. E. C. (13 vols. 1910-40). Before 1900, there was only one serious study of the House, *A Constitutional History of the House of Lords from Original Sources* by L. O. Pike (1894), and this is a book for constitutional lawyers rather than for historians.

Interest in the legislative powers of the House grew as a result of the controversy over the Parliament Bill of 1911. As a contribution to this debate, C. H. Firth wrote a monograph on the House during the Civil War which includes a study of its abolition and its restoration during the Protectorate (56). Two years later, A. S. Turberville published *The House of Lords in the Reign of William III* which was the first in a series of books and articles on the history of the House from the Restoration to the early nineteenth century (77, 93, 112, 131, 138-43, 147, 151). When he died in 1945, at a relatively early age, Turberville was working on a history of the House in the nineteenth century. This was later published as an appendix to another work (131) and his notes were deposited in the Library of the House of Lords. While Turberville's work is limited in the range of sources he used, he laid an important foundation and his studies, especially of the eighteenth century (112), are still valuable.

Turberville worked in a period when access to the essential records was difficult. This situation changed rapidly after 1945 when the papers of aristocratic families were either listed by the National Register of Archives or were deposited in national or local record offices. The records of the House itself were placed under the charge of a new archive, the House of Lords Record Office. Since 1950, this office had issued a number of useful memoranda (3, 7, 8, 10, 14, 18-21); continued the calendar of the House of Lords manuscripts up to 1718 (16); and published, under the editorship of Maurice Bond, the valuable *Guide to the Records of Parliament* (London, 1971).

This archival activity has been answered by an increased interest in the House among historians in Britain and the United States. The decline in the influence of the Whig, and then the Namierite, schools, both of which regarded the Lords as largely irrelevant, has contributed significantly to the emergence of a group of historians interested in the Lords. This has been led by American historians. The tradition in the United States in parliamentary history has been largely one of producing superb editions of documents, mainly diaries covering the early seventeenth century. This magnificent project based at Yale University gradually led to the writing of a significant number of monographs on individual parliaments. These works of necessity have looked at the Lords as well as the Commons. The most recent result of the widening of research to cover both Houses is the establishment of a new journal specifically devoted to the history of British parliaments. Since 1982, *Parliamentary History: a Yearbook* has been publishing the work of both established and younger historians. Its editorial structure also represents both the British and American traditions in parliamentary history

Partly due to the strong American contribution to early seventeenth century parliamentary history, the early Stuart parliaments are perhaps the best endowed with detailed works – particularly on the procedure and the organisation of the House of Lords. Elizabeth Read Foster, in a number of articles (30-31, 37-38, 60, 74) and in a monograph (29), has made a definitive study of these aspects of the upper House. Foster has also edited the proceedings of the Parliament of 1610; the first volume covers the Lords (39). A similar edition has been prepared for the Parliament of 1628 (49) and there is room for such works on other seventeenth century parliaments. The political role of the House in this period has been studied in some detail by, among others, Jess Stoddart Flemion (chapters 1-3).

While there are a number of studies on specialised topics, as, for example, the trial of Strafford (70-73), there has been no comprehensive study published on the House during the Civil War and Interregnum since Firth (56), although there are two recent university dissertations on the period (64-65). The House during the reign of Charles II has also been the subject of a number of dissertations and a brief monograph (78-82). Richard W. Davis has published three interesting studies including a note on divisions (83, 85-86). The period after 1689 is rich in division (and other types of parliamentary) lists. Sainty and Dewar produced an essential tool in their list of officially recorded divisions 1685 to 1857 (11), while Hayton and Jones edited a compilation of all known parliamentary lists (including the Lords) from 1660 to 1761 (9). There has been a flowering of work on the lists from the reigns of William III, Anne and George I (107, 109, chapters 5-7, 10) and this work has used the analysis of the information within the lists to draw wider implications for the development of politics in the Lords. The reign of Anne is also well covered by the magnificent survey of party development by Geoffrey Holmes (99) and the recent edition of the *London Diaries of William Nicolson, Bishop of Carlisle, 1702-1718* (edited by Clyve Jones and Geoffrey Holmes) which is the best unofficial source for the House of Lords in the early eighteenth century (98).

Work on the House during the reign of the first two Georges has been meagre so far, although there are two interesting articles which discuss Walpole's management of the House with particular reference to the bishops (121-22). On the other hand, the reign of George III has been well covered especially in the works of Lowe for the earlier part of the reign (125, 127-28, chapter 13) and of McCahill (132, chapters 14, 19-20) and Ditchfield (135, chapters 15-16) for the later period of the reign. David Large has written an important account of the rise of political parties during the reigns of George III and his sons (chapter 12).

We still rely largely on Turberville for the history of the House in the early nineteenth century. A number of useful dissertations have been written on the Victorian House of Lords but it is regrettable to note that very little of this work has been published (150, 153-54, 156, 161, 163-65, 169, 171). A valuable survey of the Victorian House may be found in Le May's excellent study of the Victorian constitution (162).

The legislative work of the Lords has been neglected except for Large's examination of the Lords and Irish legislation. He also includes a list of peers with Irish estates (chapter 18). The membership of the house has been studied by Pumphrey, Anderson and Phillips (169, 170, 159, 172).

The standard account of the struggle between the House of Lords and Asquith's government is the elegant account by Roy Jenkins (176). In a series of studies, Phillips has portrayed the right-wing opposition to the Parliament Bill (179-81). Weston, Kelvin and Southern have revised the work of Jenkins and Phillips (chapters 22-24).

Although this volume of reprinted essays concerns itself with the political development of the House of Lords, it should be noted that the judicial work of the House has not been neglected by historians.

Horstman has written a careful study of the judicature in the seventeenth century, especially in the 1620s (53-54). J. S. Hart broke new ground in his study of the years 1640-43 (65-67) and Maclean has surveyed the impact of Scots law on the House after the Union (103). The most impressive study in this field is, however, by Robert Stevens in his thorough survey of the appellate jurisdiction between 1800 and 1976 (25).

The major area of the working of the Lords which has not yet received much attention is that of legislation. Geoffrey Elton and some of his students at Cambridge are working in this field for the sixteenth century but, as yet, there is little evidence of anything appearing in print for the later period.

The last thirty years have seen a rapid growth in interest and consequent publication of work on the House of Lords. The recent availability of a forum for new work with the appearance of the journal, *Parliamentary History,* can only serve to sustain interest in the House of Lords as a subject for serious historical study.

BIBLIOGRAPHY

GENERAL

1   Weston, Corinne Comstock. *English constitutional theory and the House of Lords, 1556-1832*. London: Routledge & Kegan Paul, 1965.

2   Wagner, *Sir* Anthony; Sainty, J.C. 'The origin of the introduction of peers in the House of Lords'. *Archaeologia* 101 (1967): 119-50.

3   Sainty, J.C. *A list of representative peers for Scotland, 1707 to 1963, and for Ireland, 1800-1961*. Memorandum no. 39. London: House of Lords Record Office, 1968.

4   Fergusson, *Sir* James. *The sixteen peers of Scotland: an account of the elections of the representative peers of Scotland, 1707-1959*. Oxford: Clarendon Press, 1960.

5   Lassiter, John C. 'Defamation of peers: the rise and decline of the action for Scandalum Magnatum, 1497-1773'. *American Journal of Legal History* 22 (1978): 216-36.

6   Adair, Edward Robert; Evans, Florence May Greir. 'Writs of assistance, 1558-1700'. *English Historical Review* 36 (1928): 356-72.

7   Sainty, J.C. *Leaders and whips in the House of Lords, 1783-1964*. Memorandum no. 31. London: House of Lords Record Office, 1964.

8   Sainty, J.C. *The origin of the office of Chairman of Committees in the House of Lords*. Memorandum no. 52. London: House of Lords Record Office, 1974.

9   Hayton, David; Jones, Clyve. *A register of parliamentary lists, 1660-1761*. Leicester: Leicester University, History Department, 1979. [A supplement was published in 1982.]

10 Sainty, J.C. *Parliamentary functions of the sovereign since 1509*. Memorandum no. 64. London: House of Lords Record Office, 1980.

11 Sainty, J.C.; Dewar, David. *Divisions in the House of Lords: an analytical list 1685 to 1857*. House of Lords Record Office Occasional Publications no. 2. London: H.M.S.O., 1976.

12 Powell, J. Enoch. 'Proxy voting in the House of Lords'. *Parliamentary Affairs* 9 (1955-56): 203-13.

13 Sainty, J.C. 'Proxy records of the House of Lords, 1510-1733'. *Parliamentary History* 1 (1982): 161-65.

14   House of Lords Record Office. *The journals, minutes and committee books of the House of Lords.* Memorandum no. 13. London: House of Lords Record Office, 1964.

15   Mallaber, Kenneth A. 'The House of Lords sessional papers'. *Journal of Librarianship* 4 (1972): 106-14.

16   'Calendar of House of Lords manuscripts' [1450-1678]. In Historical Manuscripts Commission. *1st-9th Reports.* London: H.M.S.O., 1874-1910. Continued by *The manuscripts of the House of Lords, 1678-1693; new ser., vol. 1-v. 12, 1693-1718.* London: H.M.S.O., 1887-1977. [The first series of the continuation was published by the Historical Manuscripts Commisssion as appendices to the *11th-14th Reports*; the new series was published by the House of Lords Record Office.]

17   Johnson, David J. 'The House of Lords and its records , 1660-1864'. In *Parliamentary history, libraries and records: essays presented to Maurice Bond*; ed. by H.S. Cobb. London: House of Lords Record Office, 1981.

18   House of Lords Record Office. *The private bill records of the House of Lords.* Memorandum no. 16. London: House of Lords Record Office, 1957.

19   Sainty, J.C. *Officers of the House of Lords, 1485-1971: a list.* Memorandum no. 45. London: House of Lords Record Office, 1971.

20   Sainty, J.C. *Clerks in the Parliament Office, 1600-1900.* Memorandum no. 22. London: House of Lords Record Office, 1960.

21   Sainty, J.C. *The Parliament Office in the seventeenth and eighteenth centuries: biographical notes on clerks in the House of Lords, 1600-1800.* London: House of Lords Record Office, 1977.

22   Bond, Maurice. 'Clerks of the parliaments, 1509-1953'. *English Historical Review* 73 (1958): 78-85.

23   Bond, Maurice. 'The office of Clerk of the Parliaments'. *Parliamentary Affairs* 12 (1958-59): 297-310.

24   Bond, Maurice; Beamish, David. *The Gentleman Usher of the Black Rod.* London: H.M.S.O., 1976. 2nd impression (with additions), 1981.

25   Stevens, Robert. *Law and politics: the House of Lords as a judicial body, 1800-1976.* London: Weidenfeld & Nicolson, 1979.

26   Gibb, Andrew Dewar. *Law from over the border: a short account of a strange jurisdiction.* Edinburgh: W. Green, 1950.

27   Furneaux, Rupert. *Tried by their peers.* London: Cassell, 1959.

28   Seaman, R.D.H. *The reform of the Lords.* London: Arnold, 1971.

1603-1714

29 Foster, Elizabeth Read. *The House of Lords, 1603-1649: structure procedure and the nature of its business.* Chapel Hill: University of North Carolina Press, 1983.

30 Foster, Elizabeth Read. 'Procedure and the House of Lords in the seventeenth century'. *Proceedings of the American Philosophical Society* 126 no. 3 (1982): 183-87.

31 Foster, Elizabeth Read. 'The painful labour of Mr. Elsyng'. *Transactions of the American Philosophical Society* 62 pt. 8 (1972): 1-69.

32 Mayes, Charles Ray. 'The sale of peerages in early Stuart England'. *Journal of Modern History* 19 (1957): 26-37.

33 Britton, Angela H. *The House of Lords in English politics, 1604-14.* DPhil dissertation, Oxford University, 1982.

34 Dawson, D. Jean. *The political activity and influence of the House of Lords, 1603-29.* BLitt dissertation, Oxford University, 1950.

35 Mayes, Charles Ray. *The early Stuarts and the English peerage, 1603-1649.* PhD dissertation, University of Minnesota, 1955.

36 Beatty, John Louis. 'Committee appointments in the House of Lords in early 17th century England'. *Huntington Library Quarterly* 29 (1966): 117-26.

37 Foster, Elizabeth Read. 'Procedure in the House of Lords during the early Stuart period'. *Journal of British Studies* 5 no. 2 (1966): 56-73.

38 Foster, Elizabeth Read. 'Staging a parliament in early Stuart England'. In *The English Commonwealth, 1547-1640: essays in politics and society presented to Joel Hurstfield,* ed. by Peter Clark, Alan G.R. Smith and Nicholas Tyacke. Leicester: Leicester University Press, 1979.

39 *Proceedings in Parliament, 1610,* ed. by Elizabeth Read Foster. Vol. 1: House of Lords. New Haven: Yale University Press, 1966.

40 Price, J.T. *The House of Lords, 1625-9.* MPhil dissertation, University of Nottingham, 1977.

41 Stoddart, Jessie Lucinda. *Constitutional crisis and the House of Lords, 1621-1629.* PhD dissertation, University of California, Berkeley, 1966.

42 Flemion, Jess Stoddart. 'The nature of opposition in the House of Lords in the early seventeenth century: a reevaluation'. *Albion* 8 (1976): 17-34.

43 Sharpe, Kevin. 'The Earl of Arundel, his circle and the opposition to the Duke of Buckingham, 1618-1628'. In his *Faction and Parliament: essays on early Stuart history.* Oxford: Clarendon Press, 1978.

44   *Notes of the debates in the House of Lords officially taken by
         Robert Bowyer and Henry Elsing, clerks of the parliaments, A.D.
         1621, 1625, 1628*; ed. by Frances H. Relf. London: Royal
         Historical Society, 1929. (Camden Series, 3rd ser., 42).

45   Bard, Nelson P. 'Losing the initiative in the House of Lords: 1621'.
         Journal of the West Virginia Historical Association 2 (1978): 41-55.

46   Villiers, Lady E. de. 'The Hastings journal of the Parliament of
         1621'. *Camden Society* 3rd ser., 83 (1953) otherwise *Camden
         Miscellany*, 20.

47   Snow, Vernon F. 'The Arundel case, 1626'. *The Historian* 26 (1964):
         323-49.

48   Flemion, Jess Stoddart. 'The dissolution of Parliament in 1626: a
         revaluation'. *English Historical Review* 87 (1972): 784-90.

49   *Proceedings in Parliament, 1628. Vol. 5: Lords proceedings, 1628*; ed. by
         Mary Frear Keeler, Maija Jansson Cole, and William B. Bidwell. New
         Haven: Yale University Press, 1983. [Vol. 6. contains the index.]

50   Relf, Frances H. 'Debates in the House of Lords, 1628'. *Transactions
         of the Royal Historical Society* 4th ser., 8 (1925): 38-55.

51   Fraser, Ian H.C. 'The King's letter to the House of Lords, 12 May
         1628: its original purpose and authorship'. *Notes & Queries* 201
         (1956): 384.

52   Flemion, Jess Stoddart. 'The struggle for the Petition of Right in
         the House of Lords: the study of an opposition party victory'.
         Journal of Modern History 45 (1973): 193-210.

53   Horstmann, Allen Henry. *Justice and peers: the judicial activities
         of the seventeenth-century House of Lords.* PhD dissertation,
         University of California, Berkeley, 1977.

54   Horstmann, Allen Henry. 'A new *curia regis*: the judicature of
         the House of Lords in the 1620s'. *Historical Journal* 25 (1982):
         411-22.

55   Flemion, Jess Stoddart. 'Slow process, due process, and the High
         Court of Parliament: a reinterpretation of the revival of the judic-
         ature in the House of Lords in 1621'. *Historical Journal* 17 (1974):
         3-16.

56   Firth, *Sir* Charles. *The House of Lords during the Civil War.*
         London: Longmans, Green, 1910.

57   Farnell, James E. 'The aristocracy and the leadership of Parliament
         in the English civil wars'. *Journal of Modern History* 44 (1972): 79-86.

58 Cope, Esther S. 'The Earl of Bedford's notes on the Short Parliament of 1640'. *Bulletin of the Institute of Historical Research* 52 (1980): 255-58.

59 Cope, Esther S. 'Lord Montagu and his journal of the Short Parliament'. *Bulletin of the Institute of Historical Research* 46 (1973): 209-15.

60 Foster, Elizabeth Read. 'The Journal of the House of Lords for the Long Parliament'. In *After the Reformation: essays in honour of J.H. Hexter*; ed. by Barbara C. Malament. Manchester: Manchester University Press, 1980.

61 Russell, Conrad. 'The authorship of the bishop's diary of the House of Lords in 1641'. *Bulletin of the Institute of Historical Research* 41 (1968): 229-36.

62 Christianson, Paul. 'The peers, the people, and parliamentary management in the first six months of the Long Parliament'. *Journal of Modern History* 49 (1977): 575-99.

63 Hirst, Derek. 'Unanimity in the Commons, aristocratic intrigues and the origins of the civil war'. *Journal of Modern History* 50 (1978): 51-71.

64 Crummett, J.B. *The lay peers in Parliament, 1640-4.* PhD dissertation, Manchester University, 1972.

65 Hart, J.S., Jr. *The House of Lords and the reformation of justice, 1640-3.* PhD dissertation, Cambridge University, 1985.

66 Hart, J.S., Jr. 'The House of Lords and the appellate jurisdiction in equity, 1640-43'. *Parliamentary History* 2 (1983): 49-70

67 Hart, J.S., Jr. 'Judicial review in the House of Lords, 1640-43'. *Journal of Legal History* 5 (1984): 65-78.

68 Jones, G.F. Trevallyn. 'The peers' right of protest in the Long Parliament'. *Bulletin of the Institute of Historical Research* 31 (1958): 211-15.

69 Maddison, Raymond E. 'Passes for travel abroad granted by the House of Lords during the time of the Long Parliament'. *Notes & Queries* 200 (1955): 191-95, 296-301.

70 Timmis, John H., III. *Thine is the kingdom: the trial for treason of Thomas Wentworth, Earl of Strafford, first minister to King Charles I, and last hope of the English Crown.* Alabama: University of Alabama Press, 1974.

71 Timmis, John H., III. 'Evidence and Eliz. I, cap. 6: the basis of the Lords' decision in the trial of Strafford'. *Historical Journal* 21 (1978): 677-83.

72   Christianson, Paul. 'The "obliterated" portions of the House of
     Lords journals dealing with the attainder of Strafford, 1641'.
     English Historical Review 95 (1980): 339-53.

73   Russell, Conrad. 'The theory of treason in the trial of Strafford'.
     English Historical Review 80 (1965): 30-50.

74   Foster, Elizabeth Read. 'The House of Lords and ordinances,
     1641-1649'. *American Journal of Legal History* 21 (1977): 157-73.

75   Hart, Mercy C. *The Upper House during the protectorates of
     Oliver and Richard Cromwell.* MA dissertation, London University,
     1929.

76   Fitzgerald-Uniacke, R.G. 'The Protectorate House of Lords
     commonly known as Cromwell's "Other House", 1657-1659'.
     Complete Peerage Vol. 4: 585-648.

77   Turberville, A.S. 'The House of Lords under Charles II'. *English
     Historical Review* 44 (1929): 400-17; 45 (1930): 58-77.

78   Leamy, A.R. *The relations between Lords and Commons in the
     reign of Charles II.* MA dissertation, Leeds University, 1966.

79   Schoenfeld, Maxwell P. *The restored House of Lords.* Studies in
     European History, 9. The Hague: Mouton, 1967.

80   Herr, Elmer Frances. *The House of Lords under Charles II.* PhD
     dissertation, University of Wisconsin, 1957.

81   Vincent, William Allen. *Politics and the Restoration House of
     Lords, 1660-1685.* PhD dissertation, Yale University, 1974.

82   Swatland, A.C. *The House of Lords in the reign of Charles II,
     1660-85.* PhD dissertation, Birmingham University, 1985.

83   Davis, Richard W. 'Recorded divisions in the House of Lords,
     1660-1680'. *Parliamentary History* 1 (1982): 167-71.

84   Swatland, Andrew. 'Further recorded divisions in the House of
     Lords 1660-1681'. *Parliamentary History* 3 (1984): 179-82.

85   Davis, Richard W. 'Committee and other procedures in the House
     of Lords, 1660-1685'. *Huntington Library Quarterly* 45 (1982):
     20-35.

86   Davis, Richard W. 'The "Presbyterian" opposition and the emergence
     of party in the House of Lords in the reign of Charles II'. In *Party
     and management in Parliament, 1660-1784,* ed. by Clyve Jones.
     Leicester: Leicester University Press, 1984.

87   Roberts, Clayton. 'The impeachment of the earl of Clarendon'.
     Cambridge Historical Journal 13 (1957): 1-18.

88 Jones, G.F. Trevallyn. 'The Bristol affair, 1663'. *Journal of Religious History* 5 (1968): 16-30.

89 Davies, Godfrey; Klotz, Edith L. 'The Habeas Corpus Act of 1679 in the House of Lords'. *Huntington Library Quarterly* 3 (1940): 469-70.

90 De Beer, Esmond. 'The House of Lords in the parliament of 1680'. *Bulletin of the Institute of Historical Research* 20 for 1943-45 (1947): 22-37.

91 Haley, K.H.D. 'A list of the English peers, c. May 1687'. *English Historical Review* 69 (1954): 302-05.

92 Hosford, David H. 'The peerage and the Test Act: a list, c. November 1687'. *Bulletin of the Institute of Historical Research* 42 (1969): 116-20.

93 Turberville, A.S. *The House of Lords in the reign of William III.* Oxford: Clarendon Press, 1913.

94 Cruickshanks, Eveline; Hayton, David; Jones, Clyve. 'Divisions in the House of Lords on the transfer of the crown and other issues, 1689-94: ten new lists'. *Bulletin of the Institute of Historical Research* 53 (1980): 56-87.

95 Simpson, Alan. 'Notes of a noble lord, 22 January to 12 February 1688/9'. *English Historical Review* 52 (1937): 87-98.

96 Holdsworth, *Sir* William. 'The House of Lords, 1689-1783'. *Law Quarterly Review* 45 (1929): 307-42, 432-58.

97 Hall, Michael Garibaldi. 'The House of Lords, Edward Randolph and the Navigation Act of 1696'. *William and Mary Quarterly* 14 (1957): 494-515.

98 Nicolson, William. *The London diaries of William Nicolson, Bishop of Carlisle, 1702-18*, ed. by Clyve Jones and Geoffrey Holmes. Oxford: Oxford University Press, 1985. [Includes a detailed introduction on the House; most of the diary entries relate to proceedings in the Lords.]

99 Holmes, Geoffrey. *British politics in the age of Anne.* London: Macmillan, 1967. [Includes a valuable chapter on parties in the House of Lords.]

100 Jones, Clyve. 'Seating problems in the House of Lords in the early eighteenth century: the evidence of manuscript minutes'. *Bulletin of the Institute of Historical Research* 51 (1978): 132-45.

101 Snyder, Henry L. 'The defeat of the Occasional Conformity Bill and the Tack: a study in the techniques of parliamentary management

in the reign of Queen Anne'. _Bulletin of the Institute of Historical Research_ 41 (1968): 172-92.

102 Jones, Clyve. 'Debates in the House of Lords on "The Church in Danger" 1705, and on Dr. Sacheverell's impeachment, 1710'. _Historical Journal_ 19 (1976): 759-71.

103 Maclean, A.J. 'The 1707 Union: Scots law and the House of Lords'. _Journal of Legal History_ 4 (1983): 50-57. Reprinted in _New perspectives in Scottish legal history_, ed. by Albert Kiralfy and Hector L. Macqueen. London: Cass, 1984.

104 Jones, Clyve. 'Godolphin, the Whig Junto and the Scots: a new division list from 1709'. _Scottish Historical Review_ 58 (1979): 158-74.

105 Downie, J.A.; Woolley, David. 'Swift, Oxford and the composition of Queen's speeches, 1710-1714'. _British Library Journal_ 8 (1982): 121-46.

106 Szechi, D. 'Some insights on the Scottish MPs and peers returned in in the 1710 election'. _Scottish Historical Review_ 60 (1981): 61-68.

107 Jones, Clyve. 'The division that never was: new evidence on the aborted vote in the Lords on 8 December 1711 on "no peace without Spain" '. _Parliamentary History_ 2 (1983): 191-202.

108 Holmes, Geoffrey. 'The Hamilton affair of 1711-1712: a crisis in Anglo-Scottish relations'. _English Historical Review_ 77 (1962): 257-82.

109 Jones, Clyve. ' "The Scheme Lords, the Neccessitous Lords, and the Scots Lords": the Earl of Oxford's management and the "Party of the Crown" in the House of Lords, 1711-14'. In his _Party and Management in Parliament, 1660-1784_. Leicester: Leicester University Press, 1984.

110 Gregg, Edward; Jones, Clyve. 'Hanover, pensions and the "poor lords", 1712-13'. _Parliamentary History_ 1 (1982): 173-80.

111 Holmes, Geoffrey; Jones, Clyve. 'Trade, the Scots and the parliamentary crisis of 1713'. _Parliamentary History_ 1 (1982): 47-77.

1714-1832

112 Turberville, A.S. _The House of Lords in the XVIIIth century._ Oxford: Clarendon Press, 1927.

113 McRedmond, Louis. 'Irish appeals to the House of Lords in the 18th century'. _Analecta Hibernia_ 23 (1966): 245-55.

114 MacDonagh, Michael. 'The battle of the Upper Houses'. *Irish Ecclesiastical Review* ser. 5, 25 (1925): 373-88.

115 Beckett, J.V.; Jones, Clyve. 'Financial improvidence and political independence in the early eighteenth century: George Booth, 2nd Earl of Warrington (1675-1758)'. *Bulletin of the John Rylands University Library* 65 (1982): 8-35.

116 Jones, Clyve. 'The impeachment of the Earl of Oxford and the Whig schism of 1717: four new lists'. *Bulletin of the Institute of Historical Research* 55 (1982): 66-87.

117 Naylor, John F. *The British aristocracy and the Peerage Bill of 1719.* London: Oxford University Press, 1968.

118 Turner, E.R. 'The Peerage Bill of 1719'. *English Historical Review* 28 (1913): 243-59.

119 Sainty, J.C. 'The origin of the leadership of the House of Lords'. *Bulletin of the Institute of Historical Research* 47 (1974): 53-73.

120 Walters, P.C. *Politics in the House of Lords in 1733.* MPhil dissertation, University of Leicester, 1977.

121 Kendrick, T.F.J. 'Sir Robert Walpole, the Old Whigs and the Bishops, 1733-1736: a study in eighteenth-century parliamentary politics'. *Historical Journal* 11 (1968): 421-45.

122 Taylor, Stephen. 'Sir Robert Walpole, the Church of England, and the Quakers Tithe Bill of 1736'. *Historical Journal* 28 (1985): 51-77.

123 McCahill, Michael W. 'Peerage creations and the changing character of the British nobility, 1750-1850'. *English Historical Review* 96 (1981): 259-84.

124 McCahill, Michael W. 'Peers, patronage and the industrial revolution, 1760-1800'. *Journal of British Studies* 16 (1976): 84-107.

125 Lowe, William Curtis. *Politics in the House of Lords, 1760-1775.* PhD dissertation, Emory University, 1975.

126 Lowe, William Curtis. 'Bishops and Scottish representative peers in the House of Lords, 1760-1775'. *Journal of British Studies* 18 (1978): 86-106.

127 Lowe, William Curtis. 'The House of Lords, party and public opinion: opposition use of the protest, 1760-1782'. *Albion* 11 (1979): 143-56.

128 Lowe, William Curtis. 'Archbishop Secker, the bench of bishops and the repeal of the Stamp Act'. *Historical Magazine of the Protestant Episcopal Church* 46 (1977): 429-42.

129 Bargar, B.D. 'Chatham's first debate in the House of Lords'. *Journal of Modern History* 29 (1957): 361-2.

130 Rea, Robert R. 'Anglo-American parliamentary reporting: a case study in historical bibliography'. *Papers of the Bibliographical Society of America* 49 (1955): 212-29. [On Chatham's speech in the Lords, 20 Jan. 1775.]

131 Turberville, A.S. *The House of Lords in the age of reform, 1784-1837; with an epilogue on aristocracy and the advent of democracy, 1837-1867.* London: Faber, 1958.

132 McCahill, Michael W. *Order and equipoise: the peerage and the House of Lords, 1783-1806.* London: Royal Historical Society, 1978

133 Large, David. 'The decline of "the party of the Crown" and the rise of parties in the House of Lords, 1783-1837'. *English Historical Review* 78 (1963): 669-95.

134 Ditchfield, G.M. 'The House of Lords and parliamentary reform in the seventeen-eighties'. *Bulletin of the Institute of Historical Research* 54 (1981): 207-25.

135 Ditchfield, G.M. 'Dissent and toleration: Lord Stanhope's bill of 1789'. *Journal of Ecclesiastical History* 29 (1978): 51-73.

136 McCahill, Michael W. 'The Scottish peerage and the House of Lords in the late eighteenth century'. *Scottish Historical Review* 51 (1972) 172-96.

137 Ditchfield, G.M. 'The Scottish representative peers and parliamentar politics, 1787-1793'. *Scottish Historical Review* 60 (1981): 14-31.

138 Turberville, A.S. 'Aristocracy and revolution: the British peerage, 1789-1832'. *History* 26 (1942): 240-63.

139 Turberville, A.S. 'The House of Lords as a court of law, 1784-1837'. *Law Quarterly Review* 52 (1936): 189-219.

140 Turberville, A.S. 'The House of Lords in the early nineteenth century'. *Leeds Philosophical & Literary Society Proceedings, Literary & Historical Section* 5 pt. 6 (1943): 357-66.

141 Turberville, A.S. 'The Scottish and Irish representative peers, 1783-1837'. *Leeds Philosophical & Literary Society Proceedings, Literary & Historical Section* 6 pt. 1 (1944): 19-40.

142 Turberville, A.S. 'The episcopal bench, 1783-1837: the episcopal bench in the House of Lords in the revolutionary period'. *Church Quarterly Review* 123 (1937): 261-85.

143 Turberville, A.S. 'The younger Pitt and the House of Lords'. *History* 21 (1937): 350-55.

144 Richards, Gerda C. 'The creation of peers recommended by the younger Pitt'. *American Historical Review* 34 (1928): 47-54.

145 Sack, James J. 'The House of Lords and parliamentary patronage in Great Britain, 1802-1832'. *Historical Journal* 23 (1980): 913-37.

146 Snow, Vernon F. 'The reluctant surrender of an absurd privilege: proctorial rep esentation in the House of Lords, 1810-1868'. *Parliamentary Affairs* 29 (1976): 60-78.

147 Turberville, A.S. 'The House of Lords and the Reform Act of 1832'. *Leeds Philosophical & Literary Society Proceedings, Literary & Historical Section* 6 pt. 2 (1945): 61-92.

148 Davis, Richard W. 'Deference and aristocracy in the time of the Great Reform Act'. *American Historical Review* 81 (1976): 532-39.

149 Hawkins, Gary J. *Speaking in the House of Lords on the Reform Bill of 1832*. PhD dissertation, Ohio University, 1964.

1833-1914

150 Sweeney, J.M. *The House of Lords in British politics, 1830-41*. DPhil dissertation, Oxford University, 1973.

151 Turberville, A.S. 'The House of Lords and the advent of democracy, 1837-67'. *History* 29 (1944): 152-83.

152 Jones, David Lewis. 'The House of Lords and the Chambre des Pairs: an exchange of books, 1834'. In *Parliamentary history, libraries and records: essays presented to Maurice Bond*; ed. by H.S. Cobb. London: House of Lords Record Office, 1981.

153 Sachar, A.L. *The Victorian House of Lords*. PhD dissertation, Cambridge University, 1923.

154 Fraser, Robert Smythe. *The House of Lords in the first Parliament of Queen Victoria, 1837-1841*. PhD dissertation, Cornell University, 1967.

155 Large, David. 'The House of Lords and Ireland in the age of Peel, 1832-50'. *Irish Historical Studies* 9 no. 36 (1955): 367-99.

156 Mullen, R.F. *The House of Lords and the repeal of the corn laws*. DPhil dissertation, Oxford University, 1973.

157 Dewar, David. *The financial administration and records of the Parliament Office, 1824-1868*. Memorandum no. 37. London: House of Lords Record Office, 1967.

158 Bond, Maurice. *Works of art in the House of Lords*. London: H.M.S.O., 1980.

159 Anderson, Olive. 'The Wensleydale peerage case and the position of the House of Lords in the mid-nineteenth century'. *English Historical Review* 82 (1967): 486-502.

160 Heuston, R.F.V. 'The Wensleydale peerage case: a further comment'. *English Historical Review* 83 (1968): 777-82.

161 Collieu, E.G. *The radical attitude towards the monarchy and the House of Lords, 1868-85.* BLitt dissertation, Oxford University, 1936.

162 Le May, G.H.L. 'The House of Lords and the "doctrine of the mandate" '. In his *The Victorian constitution: convention, usages and contingencies.* London: Duckworth, 1979.

163 Harris, Marc Anthony. *Gladstone and the House of Lords: a study in political conflict, 1860-94.* MA dissertation, Stephen F. Austin State University, 1978.

164 Zaring, Philip Brewer. *In defense of the past: the House of Lords, 1860-1886.* PhD dissertation, Yale University, 1966.

165 Williams, J.E. *The Liberal party and the House of Lords, 1880-95.* MA dissertation, University of Wales, 1961.

166 Slater, Douglas. 'Beaconsfield: or Disraeli in Elysian fields'. In *Parliamentary history, libraries and records: essays presented to Maurice Bond*; ed. by H.S. Cobb. London: House of Lords Record Office, 1981.

167 Weston, Corinne Comstock. 'Salisbury and the Lords, 1868-1895'. *Historical Journal* 25 (1982): 103-29.

168 Fair, John D. 'The Irish Disestablishment Conference of 1869'. *Journal of Ecclesiastical History* 26 (1975): 378-94.

169 Pumphrey, Ralph E. *The creation of peerages in England, 1837-1911.* PhD dissertation, Yale University, 1934.

170 Pumphrey, Ralph E. 'The introduction of industrialists into the British peerage: a study in the adaptation of a social institution'. *American Historical Review* 65 (1959): 1-16.

171 Brown, Susan Elizabeth. *Gladstone and the House of Lords, 1880-94.* PhD dissertation, University of Toronto, 1980.

172 Phillips, Gregory D. 'The Whig Lords and Liberalism, 1886-1893'. *Historical Journal* 24 (1981): 167-73.

173 Sainty, J.C. 'The Edmunds case and the House of Lords'. In *Parliamentary history, libraries and records: essays presented to Maurice Bond*; ed. by H.S. Cobb. London: House of Lords Record Office, 1981.

174 Stevens, Robert. 'The final appeal: reform of the House of Lords and Privy Council, 1867-76'. *Law Quarterly Review* 80 (1964): 343-69.

175 Cosgrove, Richard A. 'The Judicature Acts of 1873-1875: a centennial reassessment'. *Durham University Journal* 68 (1976): 196-206.

176 Jenkins, Roy. *Mr. Balfour's poodle: an account of the struggle between the House of Lords and the government of Mr. Asquith.* London: Heinemann, 1954. New edn. London: Collins, 1968.

177 Cromwell, Valerie. 'The House of Lords crisis, 1906-11'. In *Herrschaftverträge, Wahlkapitulationen, Fundamentalgesetze*; ed. by Rudolf Vierhaus. Göttingen: Vandenhoeck und Rupprecht, 1977.

178 Le May, G.H.L. 'The crisis of the constitution, 1904-1914'. In his *The Victorian constitution: conventions, usages and contingencies.* London: Duckworth, 1979.

179 Phillips, Gregory D. *The diehards: aristocratic society and politics in Edwardian England.* Cambridge, Mass.: Harvard University Press, 1979.

180 Phillips, Gregory D. 'The "diehards" and the myth of the "backwoodsmen"'. *Journal of British Studies* 16 (1977): 105-20.

181 Phillips, Gregory D. 'Lord Willoughby de Broke and the politics of radical Toryism, 1909-1914'. *Journal of British Studies* 20 (1980): 205-24.

182 Fanning, Ronan. ' "Rats" versus "Ditchers": the die-hard revolt and the Parliament Bill of 1911'. In *Parliament and community*, ed. by A. Cosgrove and J.I. McGuire. Belfast: Appletree Press, 1983. (*Historical Studies*, 14.)

183 Weston, Corinne Comstock. 'The Liberal leadership and the Lords' veto, 1907-10'. *Historical Journal* 11 (1968): 508-37.

184 Weston, Corinne Comstock; Kelvin, Patricia. 'The "Judas group" and the Parliament Bill of 1911'. *English Historical Review* 99 (1984): 551-63.

185 Southern, David. 'Lord Newton, the Conservative Peers and the Parliament Act of 1911'. *English Historical Review* 96 (1981): 834-40.

186 Watson, Steven. 'The budget and the Lords: the crisis of 1909-11'. *History Today* 3 (1953): 240-48.

187 Clarke, Peter. 'Edwardian Britain: peers versus people?' *History Today* 31 (1981) no. 11: 26-30.

THE EARLY STUARTS
1603 – 1641

BIBLIOGRAPHICAL NOTE

THE EARLY STUARTS (1603-1641)

[The numbers in brackets refer to items in the bibliography, above pp xvii-xxix. Chapter numbers refer to the essays printed below.]

The historiography of Parliament during the early Stuart period is in a state of great flux. Most of the current controversy, however, surrounds the House of Commons, though the sea swell of argument and counter-argument washes over into the somewhat calmer lagoon of the writings of the House of Lords.

The four articles reprinted here represent two of the major themes tackled in the recent writings on the early seventeenth-century Lords. Jess Stoddart Flemion in her three articles examines both the nature and functioning of opposition to the King's government in the upper House. In her more general study of opposition (chapter 1), Flemion looks at the traditional interpretation of a personal source of opposition and concludes that with the loss of the appointment of the leadership of the House and the consequent loss of loyalty of the peerage, the King lost his already precarious authority. In a more detailed study of the dissolution of the 1626 parliament, 'the most acrimonious of the parliaments of the decade', Flemion shows that it was the precarious position of Buckingham in the Lords and not the Commons' remonstrance over supplies that caused Charles I to dissolve Parliament; indeed, Charles may have deliberately provoked the remonstrance to cover his real motive upon realising that he had lost control of the Lords (chapter 2). The case of the Earl of Arundel (see Snow, no. 46) and the control of proxy votes was central to this loss of royal control. Finally, Flemion (chapter 3) analyses the tactics used by the opposition to push the 'Petition of Right' through the Lords in 1628. Its passage was most important in proving that the royal dominance over the House could be neutralised.

Christianson (chapter 4) portrays the early events in the House of Lords during the Long Parliament as a sustained effort of an aristocratic network of peers and their clients, friends and relations in the Commons to carry through a moderate reform of church and state. This reveals the importance of the Lords in the context of the hierarchical nature of early Stuart society and Parliament. James Farnell reaches similar conclusions (57).

Christianson and Farnell, together with Mark Kishlansky, 'The emergence of adversary politics in the Long Parliament', *Journal of Modern History* 49 (1977): 617-40, and Conrad Russell, 'Parliamentary history in perspective, 1604-1629', *History* 61 (1976): 1-27, have been labelled 'revisionist' in their position. They have been criticised by J. H. Hexter, 'Power struggle, Parliament and liberty in early Stuart England', *Journal of Modern History* 50 (1978): 1-50, who rejects the central contention of Christianson and Farnell that political conflict in the Commons can be reduced to faction fights between aristocratic puppets. Hexter reasserts that the conflict during the period 1603 to 1642 is essentially one of liberty between the kings as the antagonists and the Commons as the main protagonist. Another critic, Derek Hirst (63), while agreeing that the aristocracy needed rescuing from obscurity, contends that Christianson and others ignore the importance of other public loyalties and social groups within the complexity of personal connections.

It could be argued that the interdependence of the two Houses was more crucial under the early Stuarts that at any other time covered by this volume of essays. Consequently, it is a little strange that so much concentration of effort has been focused on the Commons to the detriment of the Lords, for little has been written on the *politics* of the upper House in the early seventeenth century. The paucity of these 'Lord-lookers', as Hexter has called them, are placed in historiographical context in a long article by Hexter, 'The early Stuarts and Parliament: old hat and the *Nouvelle Vague'*, *Parliamentary History* 1 (1982): 181-215. This surveys the historiography of the early seventeenth-century Parliament from S. R. Gardiner to 1981 and ought to be the starting point for any study of the subject. Four other works which also ought to be consulted are by Conrad Russell: *The Crisis of Parliaments: English History, 1509-1660* (Oxford, 1971); the more detailed *Parliaments and English Politics, 1621-1629* (Oxford, 1979); the article in *History* referred to above; and, his summary of the present position designed mainly for sixth-formers and undergraduates, 'The nature of Parliaments in early Stuart England' in *Before the Civil War: Essays on Early Stuart Politics and Government*, edited by Howard Tomlinson (London, 1983).

Finally, a glance at the bibliography (27-55) shows, and Hexter in *Parliamentary History* 1, p.190 on 'Lord-lookers' confirms, that much of the work published on the Lords has been on procedure, an essential prerequisite to a full understanding of political developments.

Also, there has been much effort expended on the publications of diaries and debates, which has placed before the student the raw materials for a study of the upper House. Pre-eminent among these publications is the work of Elizabeth Read Foster (29-31, 37-39, 74) who in 1983 produced the definitive work on the procedure of the early Stuart House of Lords (29).

1

THE NATURE OF OPPOSITION IN THE HOUSE OF LORDS IN THE EARLY SEVENTEENTH CENTURY: A REVALUATION

JESS STODDART FLEMION

The growth of an opposition party in the House of Commons is a primary reason given for the altered distribution of power within the government of England in the early seventeenth century. While historians are not unaware that opposition also emerged in the Upper Chamber of Parliament, little serious investigation of this phenomena has been undertaken since it has not been viewed as essential to an explanation of the growing constitutional crisis within England. Consequently, the nature and extent of noble dissidence continues to be a subject of vague generalization including no small amount of contradictory assumptions and conclusions. The traditional interpretation may be termed the "personalist" view of opposition in the House of Lords and has been dominant at least since Samuel Rawson Gardiner's massive study of England in the early seventeenth century.[1] This explanation, which still prevails among historians, asserts that opposition was based on little more than personal rivalries and jealousies over power and status among the members of the peerage. Indeed it is argued that monarchs encouraged "government by division" as a major weapon in the maintenance of their own authority. Those who view noble opposition in this manner usually assert that it had no important ideological or philosophical underpinnings, little continuity or organization of the type associated with the rise of opposition in the Commons, and minimal constitutional impact and significance.[2]

[1] One searches long and hard to find anything beyond the "personal grievances of the Peers" in Samuel Rawson Gardiner, *History of England from the Accession of James I to the Outbreak of the Civil War*, 10 vols. (London, 1883-1884), IV:39.

[2] David Willson, one of the historians of recent decades whose research interests led him to consider the nature and impact of noble opposition, could nonetheless conclude that "opposition there [the House of Lords] was not a serious matter." David Willson, *The Privy Councillors in the House of Commons, 1604-1629* (Minneapolis, 1940), p. 155. Robert Zaller, in his recent study of the 1621 parliament reiterated the widely held attitude that opposition from within the nobility was not very significant when he wrote of "the weakness of the Upper House as a staging ground for parliamentary opposition." Robert Zaller, *The Parliament of 1621* (Berkeley, 1971), pp. 123-24. Robert Ruigh spoke of it being "axiomatic that the seventeenth century king ruled through division—pitting one court faction against another." Robert Ruigh, *The Parliament of 1624* (Cambridge, Mass., 1971), p. 258.

The most recent restatement of this view can be found in Robert Ruigh's excellent study of the 1624 parliament in which he states that "since preferment at court was chiefly channeled through the favorite, there was a tendency for all opposition groups to define themselves negatively. They were against Buckingham and his entourage rather than for any particular policies or principles.... Jacobean politics were intensely personal."[3]

In recent years, some historians have raised questions about the validity of the "personalist" interpretation. The leading exponent of what may be called an "ideological" view of opposition in the House of Lords is Perez Zagorin who has applied his "Court versus Country" thesis to the upper as well as the lower legislative chamber. According to Zagorin, "the Country was the first opposition movement in English history whose character transcended that of a feudal following or faction."[4] Moreover,

> the Country was not constituted as a system of dependency under the personal authority of great men who aspired to a preponderant share in the prince's favor and the shaping of his policy. Fundamentally, it consisted rather, of a loose collaboration or alliance of men in the governing class, peers and gentlemen of assured position and often of substantial fortune, alienated for a variety of reasons from the court.[5]

An investigation of the functioning of the opposition party in the Upper House during its most active phase, the parliaments of the 1620's, reinforces the conclusion that noble opposition by that date was of a unique sort based on important ideological foundations. The best evidence of this is the wholehearted support of the prince and the favorite which the opposition provided during the 1624 parliament when their views on foreign policy coincided. A study of the daily workings of the opposition party also reveals that the traditional assertion that opposition was unorganized and sporadic is erroneous. Its victories were, in fact, made possible only because of conscious and thorough planning.

This essay proposes to examine the principal tactics and strategy by which opposition nobles achieved a number of permanent changes in their legislative body during the third decade of the century, winning control of their house during the two critical parliamentary sessions of 1626 and 1628. Rather than centering upon the tangible victories of the opposition—the most important of

[3]Ruigh, p. 258.
[4]Perez Zagorin, *The Court and the Country* (New York, 1970), p. 74.
[5]Ibid., pp. 74-75.

which have been detailed elsewhere[6]—it will concentrate upon the mechanics employed to form and maintain a successful opposition faction within the Upper House over the decade. Examination of the way in which the opposition group actually became an alternative leadership indicates that the popular peers understood from the outset that the achievements of their compatriots in the Commons did not rest solely on an ability to exploit issues. Like their colleagues, the opposition nobility saw that control over the deliberations of the body was also essential. The peers therefore combined their ideological attacks upon royal policy with an organizational program aimed at controlling the daily debate and committee activities of their chamber. Imitation of what was, in fact, the successful model of the House of Commons, brought considerable success to the popular peers in the House of Lords as well with permanent consequences for the internal workings of the upper house and the Crown's traditional methods of dealing with it.

The opposition accomplished this goal by setting forth not only their alternative views of foreign and religious policy, of prerogative and revenue issues, but also by making optimum use of a number of other issues relatively unimportant to the members of the House of Commons. Among them were the inflation of honors, the sale of titles of nobility, the Crown's interference in the deliberation of the House of Lords, the decline of the political influence of the nobility and the upper house, and the replacement of the older system of governance by the rule of favorites. These concerns agitated many peers who were indifferent to the larger constitutional debates of the day. Over a period of time, the opposition leaders were able to translate their championship of such causes into respect and support for their parliamentary leadership. Trust of their abilities and integrity would, by the end of the decade, carry over into broader ideological disputes with the Crown, in the form of support in the House of Lords by many of the rank and file members.

---

[6]See my investigations of the victories of the opposition in "The Dissolution of the Parliament of 1626: A Revaluation," *English Historical Review,* 87 (1972): see below, 23-9; "The Struggle for the Petition of Right in the House of Lords: The Study of an Opposition Party Victory," *Journal of Modern History,* 45 (1973): below, 31-48; and "Slow Process, Due Process, and the High Court of Parliament: A Reinterpretation of the Revival of Judicature in the House of Lords in 1621," *The Historical Journal,* 17 (January 1974):3-16. See also Vernon Snow, "The Arundel Case, 1626," *The Historian,* 26 (1964):332-47.

The way in which the opposition built this following is revealed by the types of battles in which the opposition figured prominently in the parliaments which met between 1621 and 1629. The popular peers raised the first complaints over the effects of the sales of titles of nobility.[7] In fact, the drafting of the first petition against foreign nobility took place after private meetings in the homes of two prominent opposition peers, the Earls of Southampton and Dorset.[8] Opposition members provided the leadership in every clash between the House of Lords and the Crown concerning royal control over and interference in the deliberations of their body. A number of permanent internal reforms resulted, the proxy reforms of 1626 constituting the most substantial victory in this area.[9]

The dissidents also took the lead in channeling the desire of their colleagues for greater influence in the parliamentary system into several successful reforms. Their first move in this direction occurred during the opening days of the parliament of 1621 when the peers selected the Earl of Huntingdon, who would become a principal opposition leader, to chair a committee to investigate the ancient rights of the baronage. The results of this investigation led to the first set of permanent standing orders for the body and also contributed to the resumption of judicial authority in the House of Lords, the greatest expansion of constitutional authority for the upper house since its inception.[10] This acquisition of original criminal jurisdiction in the form of impeachment and appellate civil jurisdiction by petition also revealed how well the opposition groups in each house were already organized to coordinate activities of

[7] The first outburst of discontent took the form of a petition against the precedence extended to holders of non English titles of nobility. Nearly every member of the opposition signed this petition. February 1, 1620/1, Thomas Locke to Dudley Carleton, SP/14/119/99.

[8] Vernon Snow, *Essex the Rebel, the Life of Robert Devereaux, Third Earl of Essex, 1591-1646* (Lincoln, Neb., 1970), p. 105.

[9] Professor Snow says that Viscount Say and Sele introduced the proposal for reform of the proxy system and was immediately seconded by the Earls of Essex, Mulgrave, Pembroke, and Hertford as well as by Lord Russell. Ibid., p. 153. Other reforms of the decade included the right of a peer to a writ of summons, the right of peers to attend parliament unless charged with a specific crime, and the right of peers to freely choose their proxy. The Bristol and Arundel cases of 1626 established the first two of these rights while the third was part of the report on proxies voted into law during the same parliament. April 25, 1626, *The Journals of the House of Lords 1509 to 1847*, 79 vols. (n.d.), III:472; February 25, 1625/6, ibid., III:507.

[10] Before the House of Lords undertook what was for them a most novel role in criminal judicature, both Edward Coke, the leading constitutional lawyer of the day, and King James appeared before them to cite ancient legal precedents which were said to prove that the upper house had played a judicial role in the middle ages.

mutual concern.[11] During the same parliament, the House of Lords created the first two standing committees of its body, the Committee for Customs and Privileges and the Committee for Petitions. Each became dominated by opposition peers and both committees played a crucial role in opposition victories and in the expansion of the influence of the house. The impact which the leadership of the opposition made upon the sensibilities of other colleagues by championing these causes made it possible for the popular peers to move into a natural role of leadership in the struggles over the Earl of Arundel's case and the Petition of Right.

The abuses of the normal governmental processes of English government produced by the dominance of the royal favorite, the Duke of Buckingham, constituted the single most important issue alienating nobles from the Crown in the 1620's. The personalist interpretation is not incorrect in emphasizing its significance. But, as an issue, it was more than a reflection of personal jealousies on the part of other noblemen as so often has been suggested. The dissident peers attacked abuses of power which had serious consequences for the processes of government. Their challenge took many different forms during the decade. As early as 1621 they launched the first investigations into Buckingham's excesses in high office with their attacks upon monopolists, with the Bacon impeachment and the Yelverton affair. Each, in part, aimed at exposing the corruption of the favorite's rule.[12] The attempt to raise

---

Helen Relf, ed., *Notes of the Debates in the House of Lords, 1621...1628,* Camden Society, 3d series, 32 (London, 1929): XIV-XV; March 10, 1620/1, King's Speech to House of Lords, Lady Elizabeth de Villiers, ed., *The Hastings' Journal of the Parliament of 1621,* Camden Society, 3d series, 83 (London, 1953):27-29; March 15, 1620/1. Wallace Notestein et al., eds., *Debates in the House of Commons in 1621,* 7 vols. (New Haven, 1935), VI:383. For a complete description of the resumption of this authority see my article in *The Historical Journal,* 17:3-16.

[11] *The Historical Journal,* 17:3-16. See also the recent study by Colin C. G. Tite, *Impeachment and Parliamentary Judicature in Early Stuart England* (London, 1974).

[12] The investigation into the monopolists is certainly linked to the favorite since the first monopolist tried and convicted by the upper house, Sir Giles Mompesson, was a kinsman of Buckingham. Two of his brothers also held monopolies under question. Moreover, the king felt it necessary to defend Buckingham's role in the granting of these patents before the upper house on March 10. E. de Villiers, *Hastings' Journal,* pp. 27, 29. The Yelverton affair struck even more directly at Buckingham for Yelverton, the former attorney general, openly declared before the House of Lords that he could do nothing about the granting of the patents because "he feared the power of the Lord of Buckingham, he who was ever present at His Majesty's elbow ready to hew him down." May 2, 1621, Samuel Rawson Gardiner, *Notes of the Debates in the House of Lords Taken by Henry Elsing...in 1621,* Camden Society, 103 (London, 1870):54-56. Finally, while the attack upon Bacon was part of a larger inquiry into

questions about the governance of Ireland in the House of Commons after the spring recess also appears to have been orchestrated by opposition noblemen who hoped that the Commons could develop this matter into a direct attack upon Buckingham's ineptitude. In every case where these issues reached the floor of the House of Lords, popular peers led the debates, urging their colleagues on to reform abuses and punish all wrongdoers.[13] Their attacks frightened the favorite sufficiently that Buckingham had spies watching and reporting on the movements and contacts of several of his principal antagonists in the upper house during that spring.[14]

Opposition in the Lords had little chance to flourish in the sessions of 1624 and 1625 although for differing reasons. In the former session, the policies pursued were precisely those desired by the opposition leadership and it worked closely with the government to bring about the breaking of the treaties for the marriage of Prince Charles to the Spanish Infanta and for the settlement of the Palatinate. In the latter session, business was so confused in the lower house due to the lack of preparations for the parliament on the part of the new king that hardly any business came before the upper house during the brief session. However, during both of these sessions, the strategy employed by the peers to assure control of the daily business of the chamber continued to develop unabated and it brought important victories in 1626. The constitutional triumph of the House of Lords in the Arundel case, the impeachment trial of

the courts of justice, the fact that Buckingham was Bacon's patron and that he attempted to ameliorate the lord chancellor's punishment was hardly overlooked by the favorite's opponents in the upper house nor by contemporary observers. Katherine D. Bowen, *Francis Bacon, the Temper of the Man* (Boston, 1963), p. 209; Gardiner, *History of England*, IV:85-86.

[13]The Yelverton and Bacon cases illustrate the role of opposition leaders in the debates of this parliament. The Earl of Southampton and Lords North and Sheffield each argued strongly against the assertion of the Crown's spokesmen that Yelverton's accusations had touched upon the king's honor and that therefore the culprit should be left to the sovereign for punishment. Gardiner, *Lords' Debates, 1621*, pp. 56-59. These peers sought a "charitable" explanation of Yelverton's remarks. May 8, 1621, *House of Lords Record Office*, MS Minute Book, unfoliated. When Yelverton was censured by the house Viscount Say and Sele, the leading debater of the popular faction, left the chamber rather than participate. May 15, 1621, ibid. It was the Earl of Southampton who led the debate to investigate Bacon's activities as a judge. It was opposition peers who later argued for a public confession by the now disgraced lord chancellor and who took a stand for the most severe punishment possible. April 17, 1621, Gardiner, *Lords' Debates, 1621*, p. 1; ibid., pp. 13-14, 20-22.

[14]May 21, 1621, Sir Anthony Ashley to the Marquis of Buckingham, *Cabala, Sive, Scrinia Sacra, Mysteries of State and Government in the Letters of...Great Ministers of State...in the Reign of Henry VIII to King Charles* (London, 1691), pp. 307-8.

the Duke of Buckingham, and the proxy reforms reveal the importance of organization as the key to leadership of the deliberations of the house.[15]

The paralysis of political life which resulted from the divisions between Charles and his peers in 1626 plunged the monarchy into financial chaos and new constitutional abuses. These events, in turn, led to the greatest constitutional debate of the decade. In 1628 the popular faction obtained passage of the Petition of Right. The Crown expected easy defeat of the measure in the upper chamber but, instead, found its representatives out-debated and out-maneuvered at every turn.[16] Its expectation that the Crown's position would receive the unquestioned loyalty of the nobility on an issue touching the prerogative power proved false. The Petition's passage revealed beyond doubt that the majority of peers accepted the leaders of the dissident faction in their house as spokesmen equal in stature to the royal officials.

The constitutional impact of these events should not be underestimated. Opposition efforts provided the deciding factor in the key constitutional triumphs of the decade. While these victories, and the alterations which came with them, could not have occurred without unique issues to exploit among the majority of non-politically oriented peers, and while no one would deny the importance of the blunders of the Crown nor deemphasize the importance of Buckingham as an issue drawing support to the popular peers, yet these factors alone did not guarantee the extraordinary success of the small opposition faction. These victories were won on the floor of the house by the extensive preparation of a highly skilled and experienced leadership. Such disciplined organization demanded considerable ideological agreement on a number of general issues and goals. Without it, the creation of such a tightly knit group capable of coordinating strategy over a ten-year interval would have been impossible. And, in the long run, it was this assiduous attention to the mechanics of parliamentary machinery by the opposition which provided the crucial margin of difference between success and failure. Their newly acquired leadership status was the basis for the successful challenge of the Crown. However, their practical, daily dominance of the workings of their chamber is what provided the basis of that leadership. Investigation of the means by which they achieved the latter provides an insight into opposition obtainable by no other means.

[15] Flemion. "Dissolution of 1626."
[16] Flemion. "The Petition of Right."

The men who carried through this decade of struggle against the Crown in the House of Lords do not fall into simple categories.[17] Although not all members of the group which formed the nucleus of organized opposition professed puritanism; sympathy for Calvinist religious views (which at this time were still diffuse), a desire to alter the organization or the tone of the English church (especially after the Laudian influence began to prevail), and the desire for an active protestant foreign policy, both anti-Catholic and anti-Spanish in character, provide the key reference points linking the noblemen in this faction.[18] The group who formed the dissident party include nearly every kind of peer—ancient and new minted,[19] great and insignificant,[20] rich and poor,[21] leader and follower.[22] Many were

[17]Modern investigaors seem generally agreed in naming the Earls of Bedford (Lord Russell until 1628), Bolingbroke, Clare, Dorset, Essex, Hertford, Huntingdon, Lincoln, Mulgrave, Oxford, Salisbury, Southampton, Stamford, and Warwick; Viscount Say and Sele; and Lords Kimbolton, North, Pagett, Robartes, and Spencer as members of the dissident group.

[18]Nine of these men are said to be almost certain puritans—Bedford, Essex, Huntingdon, Lincoln, Salisbury, and Warwick along with Viscount Say and Sele and both Lords Spencer. Many of the others showed sympathy toward the political and religious positions espoused by puritans at that date. Indeed, only two members of the nobility thought to be puritans were not members of the opposition faction. Lord Montague was never associated with it while the Earl of Pembroke did occasionally assist their efforts with his massive electoral and political influence. His motivation seems based primarily on his dislike of the favorite, Buckingham, however. Perhaps what is best concluded about the influence of puritanism on political dissent among the nobility is contained in the observation of Perez Zagorin that the puritanism which did exist in the nobility was heavily concentrated in this small group in the peerage. Zagorin, p. 96.

[19]The Earl of Oxford held the oldest title, dating back to 1124. About half of the titles dated from before the Stuart succession although this figure includes some who had no titles at James' accession to the throne but who had them restored shortly afterward. This includes two of the most prominent oppositionists, the Earls of Essex and Southampton. The Earls of Bolingbroke, Clare, Mulgrave, and Stamford, along with Viscount Say and Sele all represented elevations from lower titles during the 1620's. Robartes and Kimbolton acquired titles late in the 1620's.

[20]Probably the most illustrious of the peers were Essex, Southampton, and Warwick. The first two carried particularly famous names associated with dissent in the Elizabethan era and both had substantial entourages of followers who looked to their patrons to provide leadership in the protest against Stuart abuses. Southampton was also a privy councillor at the outset of the decade.

[21]Lawrence Stone has provided information on the estimated income of peers in the century prior to the civil war. According to his tables, only the Earl of Dorset ranked among the wealthiest peers in 1603 and he may have fallen from that state by the 1620's since he was noted for his profligate life. Hertford and Salisbury were both among this wealthiest classification in 1640. Only one of the dissident peers fell into the category which Stone viewed as representing impoverishment. That was the Earl of Oxford. It is certain that the fortunes of the Earldom of Oxford were in such straits as to warrant a discussion in parliament and a request to the Crown that the earldom be provided with sufficient revenues to maintain it in dignity. Somthing must have

allied by marriage or business connections.[23] For most of them, the motive for opposition seemed primarily ideological.[24] For others, some personal factors also shaped their decision to join in the challenge of royal policies.[25] Although the opposition exploited to good advantage the disgust of many peers at the idea that honor could be acquired for gold, several members of the group purchased titles or elevations during the decade.[26] Amongst all this variety, one tie bound these men together—a deep and continuous desire to find a way to express their disapproval of the thrust of Stuart government. Many of the more important of these leaders had worked to alter the course of policy at court; but, with the coming of the supremacy of Buckingham in the affairs of the council and

been done for the title is listed with an income of £6,600 in 1640. The statistics generally suggest that opposition to the Crown had no notable effect upon the economic fortunes of these noblemen and that most of them had average incomes for their class at the time of their dissent. Stone, *The Crisis of the Aristocracy, 1558-1641* (Oxford, 1965), Appendix VIII, pp. 760-61.

[22]By virtue of their titles, wealth, and associations, Essex and Southampton were the recognized leaders of the group. The most active and skillful parliamentarian however, was Viscount Say and Sele, a tireless and fearless debater. Of all the earls, Lincoln took the least active political role in parliament.

[23]There were substantial marital ties to the opposition in the Commons and amongst this group of peers. Kimbolton and Robartes were married to daughters of the Earl of Warwick; the Earl of Bedford's daughter married Lord Brooke (an oppositionist peer who succeeded to his title in 1630). Viscount Say and Sele's daughter married the Earl of Lincoln and Essex's sister married the Earl of Hertford. Southampton's daughter married William, Lord Spencer. The business connections of these peers were most prominent in colonizing ventures. Among those more actively involved were Warwick, Say and Sele, Robartes, Kimbolton, and Southampton. Zagorin, p. 101. For a detailed account see A. P. Newton, *The Colonizing Activities of the English Puritans* (New Haven, 1914).

[24]The prominence of puritan beliefs among these peers has already been noted. Southampton, Essex, Oxford, and others also had strong attitudes on the proper foreign policy for the monarchy to pursue in the 1620's and all of them served in the armies of the protestant Elector of the Palatinate during the decade. Snow, *Essex*, p. 118.

[25]Probably the best examples of opposition which stemmed, at least in part, from personal reasons are to be found in the careers of Essex, Hertford, Clare, Salisbury, and Kimbolton. Essex was publicly humiliated by the annulment of his marriage to Frances Howard so that she could marry the royal favorite, the Earl of Somerset. Hertford had been forced into exile over his marriage to Arabella Stuart. Ibid., p. 70. Bitterness at their failure to achieve just reward for their services certainly played a role in the discontent expressed by Clare and Salisbury. C. R. Mayes, "The Sale of Peerages in Early Stuart England," *Journal of Modern History*, 29 (1957):24. Kimbolton's forced marriage to a kinswoman of Buckingham did nothing to attach him to the royalist cause. One cannot really separate these motivations from others since every peer probably had several reasons for his actions and which one may have weighed most heavily at any given time is impossible to say.

[26]Members of the group who are known to have purchased their peerages include Warwick, Clare, and Robartes. Stone, p. 106.

kingdom, these peers found the House of Lords their best remaining forum to express alternative points of view on the content and course of national policy.[27]

The investigations of the past century have turned up about twenty regular adherents to the opposition in a House of Lords which ranged over the decade from an initial membership of 95 in 1621 to 127 in 1629.[28] A comparison with the remaining Catholic nobility (after a half century of recusance laws) shows how numerically insignificant the popular group appeared. The Catholics outnumbered the dissidents by at least ten.[29] Even the addition of a half dozen or so other peers who occasionally augmented the opposition or who were driven into its ranks periodically by the hostility of the monarch or favorite raises the size of the popular party to no more than fifteen percent of the membership of the house.[30] The individuals within this group, unlike their recusant colleagues, acquired an extraordinary ability to influence affairs in their chamber by developing into the most active and skilled parliamentarians of the age.

The first notable characteristic of the parliamentary activity of these lords is the regularity of their attendance at parliament. It

---

[27] The best examples of peers who frequented the Court before turning to overt opposition are the Earls of Clare, Essex, Salisbury, Southampton, and Warwick.

[28] Add to this figure the twenty-six episcopal seats to get the full membership of the upper house.

[29] Approximately thirty peers or seventeen percent of the nobility still espoused the old faith. The Catholic nobility included the titles of Abergavenny, Arundel of Wardour, Audley, Brudenell, Eure, Viscount Montague, Morley, Petre, Rivers, Rutland, Sandys, Savage, Shrewsbury, Stafford, Stourton, Teynham, Vaux, Weston, Wotton, and Winchester. Possible Catholic titleholders during the period include the Earl of Banbury, Viscount Dorchester, the Earl of Exeter, and Viscount Purbeck. Minors holding titles included male members of the Dormer and Wharton families. In addition, two other peers appeared on a list of suspected papists in 1624 although no further reference to them as Catholics appeared. These are the Barons Herbert and Scrope. May 20-21, 1624, *Lords' Journals*, 3:393-94. A principal source of information on Catholic recusants comes from the petitions against them drawn up by the House of Commons at various times in the decade. One from the 1624 session included the names of eleven peers, Ibid. References to other Catholic nobility are scattered through many secondary works on the period such as David Mathews, *The Jacobean Age* (London, 1938); Martin Havran, *The Catholics of Caroline England* (Stanford, 1962); and George Anstruther, *Vaux of Harrowden: A Recusant Family* (Newport, Mass., 1953). Licenses given to Catholic noblemen to exempt them from the penalties of recusancy can be frequently found in the State Papers as well, such as that of [Oct.?] 1626 for Lord Arundel of Wardour. SP/16/38/96.

[30] These others include the Archbishop of Canterbury who opposed the religious policies of Charles and Laud, and Bishop Williams of Lincoln and Hall of Exeter. Two who may be described as driven into opposition during part of the decade are the Earls of Arundel and Bristol.

contrasts sharply with the behavior of the average member and most of the Crown's supporters. Bedford, Bolingbroke, Clare, Essex, Mulgrave, North, Pagett, Salisbury, Say and Sele, Stamford, and Warwick each served in every session of the 1620's. The Earl of Dorset and Lord Spencer attended all meetings before their deaths. Only the Earl of Huntingdon had a poor record of attendance which, in his case, was necessitated by financial difficulties which forced him to live quietly (and inexpensively) in the country.[31]

Viscount Say and Sele provides the best example of the parliamentary activity typical of opposition leadership. He attended about ninety percent of all daily meetings and acted as the faction's most outspoken debater in the house. Spencer, Pagett, Southampton, and Lord Russell (later Earl of Bedford) often led the debate against the Crown's managers also. After Clare joined the group, he too, became a principal spokesman. As Table I indicates, nearly all of these men attended better than two out of every three sessions, a record above average for the membership as a whole.

An examination of committee service among this group reinforces the picture of the opposition leadership as unusually active. Three of the peers, (see Table II), Bedford, Say and Sele, and William, Lord Spencer, were among the ten most active committee men in the house and the first two of these peers attended all sessions. Perhaps more important in terms of the long-range impact of the opposition, of this entire group, only three—Lincoln, Salisbury, and Kimbolton failed to place with the upper half of the nobility in this form of legislative service. It was collective participation on this scale which gave the small band of dissidents a voice and impact quite disproportionate to their numbers. Indeed, only a selected group of royal managers have records of attendance and committee service to rival these and an unusual number of royal activists were spiritual, not lay, peers (see Tables III and IV).

Developments within both houses in the preceding century had made the committee system the key element in the machinery of parliament. In the upper house the opposition's views on the constitutional issues of the day probably acquired their greatest impact at the committee level for the faction held nearly twice as many seats as its numbers in the house would warrant. Working majorities

31All others have special circumstances to explain their absence. Oxford died in 1625. Southampton was ordered to stay away from the second session of 1621, Hertford did not become politically active until 1626 after his marriage to a sister of the Earl of Essex. Kimbolton and Robartes received their peerages too late in the decade to become politically significant.

on the two standing committees, the Committee for Customs and Privileges and the Committee for Petitions, increased the oppositions' influence at the committee level also. Many important political issues filtered through these two committees before reaching the floor of the house. The former committee was responsible for involving the peers in one of their chief constitutional struggles with the Crown during the period by challenging the grounds on which Charles justified the removal of the Earl of Arundel from the house in 1626.[32] The successful outcome of the dispute reinforced the right of peers to political independence by making it more difficult for the monarch to remove a member from the House of Lords on the pretext of a personal affront to the sovereign. Similarly, the Committee on Petitions played a key role in the acquisition of an almost unlimited judicial authority by the upper house during the same decade.

In the Commons the development of an organization and alternative political program culminated quickly in the permanent loss of royal control over that body. In the House of Lords, the opposition party did not supplant the Crown. The difference in outcome is not explained by lack of skills, zeal, or sustained purpose but rather in the special controls which the monarch still retained over the House of Lords. The proxy system,[33] the control of episcopal votes,[34] the Crown's essential role as the fountain of all rewards,[35] and its punitive power[36] all placed the members of the

[32]March 20, 1625/6, Samuel Rawson Gardiner, *Notes of the Debates in the House of Lords...1624 and 1626*, Camden Society, 2d series, 24 (1879):127-35.

[33]Opposition peers held only eleven proxies (about five percent of the total) during these years while the favorite alone held nineteen percent of the proxies.

[34]Forty-one men were elevated to the bench in the 1620's representing a turnover of fifty percent in the decade. After 1625 when churchmen who favored the views of Charles and Laud filled most of the vacancies, the clerical block formed the most secure source of royalist votes left in the upper house—more loyal than the Privy Council itself. The bishops who were politically active (thirty-five in all) averaged attendance of eighty-four percent which was better than twenty percent above the average of lay attendance. Their committee participation showed less unusual levels of activity due to the custom of balancing the various ranks within the house on each committee. Traditionally, most committees had twice as many barons as bishops or earls.

[35]Additions to the peerage were a major form of reward. C. R. Mayes, "The Sale of Peerages in Early Stuart England," p. 30; most of the royalist faction in the 1620's came from the nobility who, as James once put it, were "made by me." March 10, 1621, E. de Villiers, *Hastings' Journal*, p. 28. The studies of Lawrence Stone have revealed that the Crown nearly bankrupted itself, giving away lands and rents worth £1 million between 1603 and 1640, to a group of thirty noblemen. Lawrence Stone, *The Crisis of the Aristocracy*, pp. 475, 493.

[36]A good example of the punitive exercise of royal power was James' removal of the office of Captain of the Isle of Wight from the Earl of Southampton along with

peerage in a very different relationship to the sovereign than that experienced by the vast majority of the members of the Commons. These restraints acted as a strenuous political rein on disobedience among the nobility. Moreover the peerage was, almost by definition of its place and role in English society, a politically conservative group.

At the same time, it is also obvious that these controls, natural and otherwise, failed to maintain the usual dominance of the Crown over the House of Lords. A central reason for this is that, while James and Charles continued to employ the traditional techniques of political control, they totally disregarded the cultivation of the peerage. The neglect of this responsibility made the Crown incapable of dealing with the new environment which emerged in the upper house as opposition strategy and tactics began to bear fruit. Each attempt to reimpose control through new measures such as the creation of peers for political purposes and the attempts to deny writs to opponents alienated additional members of the house. Indeed, events of this decade reveal clearly that one of the Crown's most serious political errors was its failure to realize that, in the long run, the strongest tie which bound most of the nobility to the Crown was neither threat nor reward but the sense of reciprocity of interest. This tie had bound the bulk of peers who rarely lived at court, had little expectation of high office or large reward, and who preferred their manor houses and country life to the intrigue of the court and national politics to the Crown's goals in previous times. These peers constituted the great swing vote in the House of Lords as well, and, during the 1620's, that vote over and over again swung away from the Crown and toward the views represented by the opposition.

How to measure accurately the opposition's successes in the House of Lords is not a simple matter. Some accomplishments were immediate and tangible. The proxy reforms, the acquisition of judicial power, the victories in the Arundel case and in the Petition of Right struggle clearly fit this category of victory. Other achievements were more indirect yet sometimes more far reaching. The neutralization of the Crown's power in the House of Lords for-

---

the £3,000 pension the earl had been granted. These moves were undertaken to punish Southampton for leading the opposition's attack in the first session of 1621. They effectively silenced the earl and caused him to submit to banishment from the second session of that parliament called in the fall. Charlotte Stopes, *The Life of Henry, Third Earl of Southampton* (Cambridge, 1922), pp. 406, 417.

ced the monarchy to reverse much of the callous treatment of the nobility characteristic of the preceding two decades. After 1629 Charles assiduously cultivated his peers. Moreover, the rule of favorites, such an important issue with the nobility, ended with the assassination of Buckingham in 1628. The processes of government returned to a more normal pattern. The sales of titles of nobility ceased as well. Even so, these actions did not reverse completely the damage done to the Crown's traditional relationship with the House of Lords. Undoubtedly many opposition leaders would have liked greater independence for the house than achieved through their efforts. Many would also have wished for more success for the views they expressed on foreign policy and religion. Yet though their achievements here were more limited than in the House of Commons, the success of the opposition movement left a substantial constitutional legacy in the upper house. For the first time, the opposition established a second locus of leadership within the House of Lords held together by long-range ideological issues rather than short-term personal jealousies. The "aristocratic opposition" of an earlier decade, described by Professor Snow so largely in terms of a personal following around the Earl of Essex, had grown into something far more mature, complex, and dangerous. A political party had been created which would remain in force when parliament met again in 1640. Equally important, the idea that the Crown should not have exclusive control over the scope of deliberations or the leadership of the House of Lords had become imbedded in the political environment of that chamber. The two changes together constituted little less than a revolution for when the Crown lost the exclusive right to determine the leadership of the House of Lords and the programs and policies which would be discussed by that body, and when it also lost the certain loyalty of the peerage, the last remnant of traditional parliamentary management upon which the Stuart monarchy depended for its precariously balanced authority had been destroyed.

Table I

Daily Attendance Figures for Opposition Peers*

	Percentage of Attendance	Number of Sessions**
Henry, Earl of Southampton	90	2
William, Viscount Say and Sele	88.5	6
Oliver, Earl of Bolingbroke	88	6
Robert, Earl of Essex	87.8	6
William, Earl of Hertford	86	2
Richard, Earl of Dorset	84.1	3
William, Lord Spencer	82	2
Dudley, Lord North	80	6
Francis, Earl of Bedford	78.7	6
William, Lord Pagett	78	6
Theophilus, Earl of Lincoln	74.6	6
John, Earl of Clare	69.5	6
William, Earl of Salisbury	69.2	6
Robert, Lord Spencer	64.5	5
Robert, Earl of Oxford	62.7	3
Robert, Earl of Warwick	59.2	6
Edmund, Earl of Mulgrave	55.6	6
Henry, Earl of Stamford	55	6
Henry, Earl of Huntington	48.6	4
Edward, Lord Kimbolton	37.7	2
Richard, Lord Robartes	9.7	3

*The attendance of all peers averaged 62 percent in the 1620's.

**No daily attendance records exist for the 1629 session. These figures are based on the six preceding sessions.

Table II

Committee Participation of Opposition Nobility

	Percentage of Committees*
Francis, Earl of Bedford	45
William, Lord Spencer	40
Dudley, Lord North	39.5
Robert, Lord Spencer	39
Edward, Earl of Mulgrave	37
William, Viscount Say and Sele	36.5
John, Earl of Clare	36
Henry, Earl of Southampton	35
William, Lord Pagett	34
Henry, Earl of Huntingdon	27
Richard, Earl of Dorset	21
Robert, Earl of Essex	19.5
Robert, Earl of Oxford	16
Richard, Lord Robartes	16
Oliver, Earl of Bolingbroke	15.5
Henry, Earl of Stamford	14.5
William, Earl of Hertford	13.5
Robert, Earl of Warwick	13
William, Earl of Salisbury	6
Edward, Lord Kimbolton	5
Theophilus, Earl of Lincoln	3

*These figures are based upon the number of committees during the sessions of parliament in which each of the individuals participated. Thus, Bedford sat on 45 percent of the committees of all seven sessions of parliament between 1621 and 1629 while William, Lord Spencer, sat on 40 percent of all committees created during the two sessions of 1628 and 1629 which he attended.

Table III

Daily Attendance of Royal Managers*

	Percentage of Attendance	Number of Sessions
John Williams, Bishop of Lincoln	96.5	4
William Laud, Bishop of St. Davids and of Bath and Wells	89	6
Richard, Lord Weston	87	1
Henry, Earl of Manchester	86.3	6
Thomas Morton, Bishop of Coventry and Litchfield	83	6
Philip, Earl of Montgomery	78.2	6
John, Bishop of Winchester	75.8	6
James, Earl of Marlborough	71.3	4
Thomas, Earl of Arundel	70	6
William, Earl of Pembroke	66.8	6
Thomas, Lord Coventry	65	2
William Harsnet, Bishop of Norwich and Archbishop of York	63.6	6
Edward, Earl of Worcester	61.3	5
George, Duke of Buckingham	52.4	5
George Montaigne, Bishop of Lincoln, Durham, London	52	6

*The difficulty in characterizing members of the house over the entire decade is apparent from this table. Listed among the Crown's managers are three men who, at one point or another, aided the opposition in the House of Lords. These three are Bishop Williams, the Earl of Arundel, and the Earl of Pembroke.

Peers, Politics and Power

Table IV

Committee Service of Royal Managers

	Percentage of Committees
William Harsnet, Bishop of Norwich, Archbishop of York	60.5
Henry, Earl of Manchester	48.5
Thomas Morton, Bishop of Coventry and Litchfield	42.5
William Neile, Bishop of Winchester	39.5
Thomas, Earl of Arundel	31.8
William, Earl of Pembroke	29
James, Earl of Marlborough	26.5
Richard, Lord Weston	26
William Laud, Bishop of St. Davids and of Bath and Wells	20
George Montaigne, Bishop of Lincoln, Durham, and London	19
John Williams, Bishop of Lincoln	14
Edward, Earl of Worcester	14
Philip, Earl of Montgomery	14
George, Duke of Buckingham	12
Thomas, Lord Coventry	7

2

THE DISSOLUTION OF PARLIAMENT IN 1626:
A REVALUATION

JESS STODDART FLEMION

THE parliament of 1626 has always been considered an important milestone in the constitutional struggles of the early Stuart era. It was probably the most acrimonious of the parliaments of the decade and the impeachment of the duke of Buckingham, the trial of the earl of Bristol, the 'Arundel case', the proxy reforms, and the Commons' remonstrance against Buckingham crowd one another for the attention of the student of this parliament. Of all of these events, however, the attack on Buckingham, the royal favourite, remains the centre of interest. The conclusion of this matter by means of an abrupt dissolution on 15 June, widened the rift between the Crown and important political groups within the nation to an extent which could hardly be bridged in the future. While the upper house was especially active during 1626, the attention of historians has largely concentrated upon the lower house and the standard explanation of the dissolution of the parliament is that the remonstrance presented by the house of commons on 14 June, which asked that Charles remove Buckingham from his counsels and presence whatever the outcome of his impeachment trial, caused the king to terminate the meeting. The decision was taken despite the fact that it cost Charles the five subsidies which the Commons had promised him and in spite of the objections of the entire privy council (except for the duke) and both houses of parliament.[1]

The view that Charles dissolved parliament in order to save Buckingham is fundamentally correct. However, the reasons for this royal decision appear to be more complex than are commonly thought. It is not surprising that both earlier historians and contemporary ones have accepted the Commons' remonstrance as the cause for the ending of the 1626 parliament. The king himself offered a public explanation for his decision in a carefully-worded addition to the message of dissolution which he sent to the house of

---

1. This is the interpretation found in S. R. Gardiner, *The History of England from the Accession of James I to the Outbreak of the Civil War* (10 vols.; London, 1883–1884), vi. 116–20 and followed with only minor shifts in emphasis by subsequent historians. See also C. H. Firth, *The House of Lords during the Civil War* (London, 1910), pp. 43–47; Harold Hulme, *The Life of Sir John Eliot, 1592–1632* (London, 1957), p. 149; and Godfrey Davies, *The Early Stuarts, 1603–1660* (Oxford, 1937), p. 35. Several of the textbook surveys consulted gave such a vague explanation of the course of events surrounding the dissolution of 1626 as to leave a serious confusion in the mind of the reader.

lords on 15 June. In it he assured the peers that the termination had not come 'for any cause gyven by your l[ordships], but proceeding from the Commons'.[1] Why then, at this date, should there be any reason to doubt the accuracy of the accepted interpretation based on the king's own words?

The reconsideration of another well-known event of this parliament sheds new light upon the motives for dissolution and suggests that it was the house of lords which the king feared most in mid-June of 1626. Professor Vernon Snow published an article on the Arundel case of 1626 seven years ago in which he proved that the arrest of the earl of Arundel and his imprisonment for most of the session was not for the reason stated by King Charles but for a quite different one. Snow showed that Arundel was incarcerated when it became plain to the king that the earl intended to side with the popular opposition in the upper house against Buckingham.[2] Since some kind of attack upon the favourite was certain to emerge from the house of commons during the meeting, Charles decided that Arundel was too dangerous to be allowed to remain in the house of lords. He represented a threat in parliament not because he possessed any unusual gifts of leadership or a following but simply because he controlled five proxy votes.[3] Thus he had six votes which he could cast against the duke of Buckingham in the upper chamber. Because of Snow's discoveries, the Arundel case and the impeachment of Buckingham can now be seen as inextricably linked in the political struggles of that parliament.

The proxy system had long been a major part of the methods by which the Crown maintained tight control over the house of lords. While the peers apparently accepted the system without too much resentment, many had become increasingly angry when it came to be employed as a vehicle for the personal aggrandizement of the favourite. Buckingham held thirteen proxies that session, nearly one half of the votes of all absent nobles,[4] and, with the likelihood that no more than sixty members would be present on any given

1. 15 June 1626, *Journals of the House of Lords, 1509–1847* (79 vols.; n.d.), iii. 682. (Hereafter cited as *L.J.*)

2. Vernon Snow, 'The Arundel Case, 1626', *The Historian*, xxvi, iii (May, 1964), 323–50. Arundel was supposedly placed under arrest for his participation in arranging a clandestine marriage between his son and a royal ward. By law, wards of the Crown could not marry without the king's permission. Although Gardiner noted the bad feeling which existed at this date between Arundel and Buckingham, he accepted this reason as the cause of the earl's incarceration. Gardiner, vi. 71–72.

3. He held the proxies of the marquis of Winchester, the earl of Shrewsbury, and Lords Arundel of Wardour, Petre, and Windsor.

4. *L.J.* iii. 490–1. Most accounts state that Buckingham held eleven proxies yet the Journal clearly lists thirteen proxies in his name: the earls of Bath, Cumberland, Exeter, Newcastle, Northumberland, Rivers, and St. Albans; Lords Darcy, Eure, Noel, Robartes, St. John de Basing, and Teynham. Of the forty proxies licensed for the session, twenty-nine were lay proxies.

day, fourteen votes in the hands of one man represented a block of enormous political power. Thus hostility to Buckingham emerged early in the session in the form of a report in favour of reforming the proxy system.

The peers had sat for barely three weeks when, on 25 February, four reforms were presented to the house and passed. The most important of these limited a peer to a maximum of two proxy votes.[1] Arundel was a member of the committee which recommended the reform and it seems certain that he cast all of his votes in favour of it.[2] This, according to Snow, was Arundel's real crime.[3] The king interpreted the vote as final proof that the earl would side with the opposition against Buckingham in the upper house. While proxy procedures did need review and change, the king saw the reform in the same light as did most contemporaries, such as the writer who drew the conclusion that: 'Last week the Duke had one feather plucked from his wing in the Upper House in the matter of proxies'.[4] Shortly afterward Arundel was removed from the council table and placed under arrest.[5]

Arundel's absence soon raised a constitutional issue of major importance. Peers of the realm had the special right of personal attendance at parliament except under some fairly well-defined circumstances. The reason given for Arundel's imprisonment, a personal offence to the king, was not among these. The earl's absence was officially brought to the attention of the house within a week after his removal and, from the outset, members of the opposition championed his return.[6] At first the peers attempted to use the ordinary procedures of their house to secure Arundel's release; they petitioned the king. However, Charles engaged in deliberate evasion for a period of nearly two months so that the lords failed to achieve any satisfaction on this matter between 5 April, the date of their first petition, and 2 June.[7] The king's callous indifference to the privileges of the house and the liberty of one of its members can now be understood in light of the relationship of the case to Buckingham's security. At the time, its immediate consequence was that it led the nobility to take an extremely radical

1. 25 Feb. 1626, *L.J.* iii. 507.

2. Snow, *ubi supra*, p. 332. 3. *Ibid.* p. 334.

4. 7 Mar. 1625/6, John Chamberlain to Dudley Carleton, Norman Egbert McClure (ed.), *The Letters of John Chamberlain* (2 vols.; Philadelphia, 1939), ii. 630.

5. Arundel was sequestered one week after the vote. While impeachment proceedings would not begin in the lower house for another week, the Commons had already begun an extensive investigation into Buckingham's conduct as lord admiral. Gardiner, vi. 67, 76.

6. 14 Mar. 1626, S. R. Gardiner, *Notes of the Debates in the House of Lords . . . 1624 and 1626*, Camden Society, 2nd ser., xxiv (1879), p. 126.

7. See the Journal for the series of actions taken by the peers on the case between 5 Apr. and 2 June. *L.J.* iii. 552–653.

step. On 3 June the house voted to refuse to proceed with any other business – including the impeachment trial of Buckingham which had opened in their house in May – until the Arundel matter had been concluded to their satisfaction.[1] Faced with a complete deadlock on this issue, Charles relinquished Arundel and allowed him to return to the upper house on 8 June, one week prior to the dissolution.[2] Snow's investigation terminated at this point and although he examined in great detail the direct relationship between Arundel's imprisonment and the attack on Buckingham, he did not go on to consider the consequences of Arundel's return for the prevailing political situation.

Snow did feel that the return of Arundel made the conviction of Buckingham a certainty in the upper house.[3] Yet there is a serious problem with such an interpretation for, if it were true, there is no way to explain logically why the house of commons presented the king with a remonstrance against the favourite prior to the termination of the trial. One would have to presume that the Commons knew nothing of the state of affairs in the upper house and this is obviously false. There is more evidence of co-operation between the opposition in the two houses for this session than for any preceding one in the decade.[4] The decision to draft a remonstrance does suggest that the popular party in the Commons still had doubts about the outcome of the trial and feared that Buckingham might manage an acquittal. To cope with this possibility, the leaders of the lower house turned to the idea of petitioning for the favourite's removal whatever the outcome of the criminal charges against him and made the passage of the subsidies dependent upon a satisfactory conclusion of this matter. With the remonstrance serving as a supplemental measure to the articles of impeachment, the Commons

---

1. 2 June 1626, *ibid.* p. 653. 2. 8 June 1626, *ibid.* p. 655.
3. Snow, *ubi supra*, p. 348.
4. The primary evidence of increased co-operation between members of the two houses is to be found in several letters from Sir James Bagg, a crony of the favourite, to Buckingham, written in March and April of 1626. Bagg accused the earl of Pembroke of secretly arranging for the election of a substantial number of the members of the house of commons who had been most forward in the attack upon the favourite in 1625 and who were again leading the impeachment proceedings in the 1626 parliament. Among those whom he cited as placed by Pembroke were Sir John Eliot, Sir Robert Mansell, Sir Francis Stuart, Clipsley Crew, and Dr. Turner. Bagg also accused Abbott, archbishop of Canterbury, Viscount Say and Sele, and Lord Cavendish (who succeeded to the earldom of Devonshire in 1626) of placing men in the lower house who were professed enemies of Buckingham. Bagg later wrote to Buckingham in April linking the earl of Warwick with Sir John Eliot, the foremost leader of the attack on the favourite in the house of commons with the vague statement that the two 'continue in their ways'. [Mar. 1626], Sir James Bagg to the duke of Buckingham, P.R.O.S.P. 16/523/77; 23 Apr. 1626, same to same, P.R.O.S.P. 16/61/36. David Willson in his *The Privy Councillors in the House of Commons, 1604–1629* (Minneapolis, 1940), pp. 179–89, provided a detailed discussion of opposition co-operation before and during the 1626 session based on the Bagg letters and other materials.

could afford to be uncertain about the outcome of the trial. Charles could not chance such a mistake. The security of the man who had become something near an alter ego of the king hung in the balance.

Charles had ample reason to fear that Buckingham might now face conviction in the upper chamber. On 8 June, Arundel brought back six votes for the opposition while the duke's party lost from one to three that same day when Buckingham voluntarily departed from the house until his trial had concluded.[1] There is extensive evidence from the preceding month that six votes may have been enough to unbalance the political strength of the two sides. Buckingham himself told one henchman who asked for a vacant office that he would have to wait, for the favourite dared not 'distemper a vote'.[2] On a crucial motion early in his impeachment, whether to sequester Buckingham during his trial, the duke's supporters carried the day by only four votes.[3] The king immediately created three new peers 'to weigh down . . . the balance on the Duke's side'.[4] There were rumours of further creations although none occurred.[5] The cause was still so precarious in late May, however, that Buckingham personally engaged in intensive efforts to lobby the earl of Clare and other peers for their support or neutrality.[6] His friends were trying at the same time to get some of the proxies held by Arundel released by their owners and transferred into the hands of safe supporters of the favourite. Finally, it is clear that Buckingham went to unusual lengths to guarantee that all of his reliable supporters would be in town and present for the critical conclusion of his trial.[7] With the return of Arundel all of those preparations may not have been sufficient, for the peers that the Crown could be certain would vote to acquit the duke may have been less than a majority of six.

1. 8 June 1626, *L.J.* iii. 667.
2. 8 Sept. 1626, Viscount Wimbledon to the duke of Buckingham, P.R.O.S.P. 16/524/130. The date of this letter is misleading for Wimbledon's letter makes it clear that he approached Buckingham about a vacant office during the parliament of the preceding spring and received the quoted answer.
3. 25 May 1626, Meade to Stuteville, B[ritish] M[useum], Harleian MS. 390, fo. 64.
4. *Ibid.* The new peers were Baron Kimbolton, married to a niece of Buckingham; Lord Tregoze (Lord Grandison in the Irish peerage), Buckingham's chief Irish adviser; and Sir Dudley Carleton, a chief royal spokesman in the house of commons.
5. Four other names were rumoured as likely candidates for peerages. All received them before the fall of 1628. *Ibid.* The creation of new peers for political purposes could easily backfire on Charles, however, straining his relations with older members of the nobility. This is probably why it was disregarded as a possible tactic to shore up the ducal party after 8 June. It was also rumoured that if additional creations occurred some peers would being a resolution into the upper house that any further peers created that session should not be allowed to vote. Gardiner, vi. 115.
6. 29 May 1626, Edmund Bolton to the duke of Buckingham, P.R.O.S.P. 16/524/19; May 1626, Salvetti Correspondence, H.M.C., *The Manuscripts of Henry Duncan Skrine, Esq., Salvetti Correspondence* . . . (London, 1887), pp. 64–65.
7. 20 May 1626, Meade to Stuteville, B.M., Harleian MS. 390, fo. 60.

There are other reasons as well to believe that the remonstrance was not the real cause for Charles' decision. Undoubtedly the king viewed the remonstrance as another vicious and unwarranted attack on his friend. Nevertheless, he could have delayed at least a few days in hearing or answering this complaint – at least long enough to let the upper house complete its trial. The remonstrance asked for Buckingham's removal on grounds completely apart from the articles of impeachment, basically for the 'good of the nation' as the Commons interpreted it and not for any criminal offence. The king could not have had a better way of handling a reply to the remonstrance than to have been able to say that he would not abandon a servant whom the peers of the realm had just tried and found innocent of all charges raised by the lower house. Perhaps Charles would have lost the five subsidies with such a negative reply; he lost them anyway by his decision to dissolve the parliament. Thus, the only explanation of this dissolution which encompasses all of the circumstances surrounding it points to a crisis in the house of lords.

Perhaps a doubt concerning the king's motives lingered in the minds of some peers after the house of lords sent a delegation asking for only one or two more days to finish the trial and received the brusque reply, 'not a minute'.[1] If any such suspicions entered the minds of members of the upper house, the addition to the message of dissolution was well designed to assuage them. Whatever its effect upon its audience at the moment, historians throughout the centuries have accepted the king's declaration as conclusive evidence that he terminated his second parliament as an angry reaction to the remonstrance of the house of commons.

One question remains: why did Charles insist that the remonstrance caused his decision if it did not? Given the relationship of the king to the two houses of parliament at this time, his deviousness is not difficult to understand. Charles had already reached the conclusion that the house of commons was determined to encroach upon his traditional powers. As his attitude toward the Commons hardened, he realized the imperative need to maintain the loyalty of the upper house if he were to preserve his authority from further challenge. He cultivated close relations with the house of lords whenever possible. During a joint address to parliament on 29 March, he pointedly thanked the lords for their good offices toward him and their care and consideration of the nation's security. Turning to the Commons, he bluntly remarked that in their case he had called them into his presence to tell them of their errors.[2] In general, it can be said that the Crown's relations with the upper house

---

1. Gardiner, vi. 121.   2. [29 Mar.] 1626, B.M., Lansdowne MS. 491, fo. 150.

were good, although not so harmonious that Charles could have interfered with the impeachment trial of Buckingham at its close in mid-June without irreparable damage to his relations with a large number of the nobility. At the same time he could not allow the trial to conclude. So the remonstrance really provided him with a fortuitous excuse for dissolving the session before the trial ended. One can even question how fortuitous this latter event really was. Arundel and his six votes returned to the house of lords on 8 June. Only days remained before the vote on Buckingham. The day following Arundel's return, Charles commanded the house of commons to vote him supplies within a week or he threatened to use 'other resolutions'.[1] No royal command would be more calculated to anger the house of commons than a peremptory demand for immediate money. The Commons responded with the remonstrance against Buckingham, a reaction which may not have been unexpected. Rather, the king's action seems perfectly designed to produce the result which followed; that is, some sort of confrontation between the Commons and himself which could serve as an excuse for dissolution.

1. Gardiner, vi. 116.

Cancellary sedes in

2. The State Opening of Parliament, 17 March 1628 (detail)
Anonymous engraving, by courtesy of the Ashmolean Museum.

Charles I is enthroned in the old House of Lords, originally built as a private apartment by Henry III for his Queen and used by the Lords from the reign of Henry VIII until 1800. On the king's right is Sir Thomas Coventry, the Lord Keeper, and on his left, the Earl of Marlborough, the Lord Treasurer. Around the throne are the Great Officers of State. The bishops are on the extreme left; the peers on the extreme right; and, judges sit on the wool-sacks in the centre. Behind the table in the centre sit the four Masters of Chancery with the four clerks kneeling behind them. Immediately in front of the bar are more peers while below the bar stand the Commons.

3

THE STRUGGLE FOR THE PETITION OF RIGHT IN
THE HOUSE OF LORDS:
THE STUDY OF AN OPPOSITION PARTY VICTORY

JESS STODDART FLEMION

More than fifty years ago, Frances Helen Relf demonstrated the compromise nature of the passage of one of England's most famous constitutional documents in her study of the Petition of Right.[1] She showed how Charles I forced the House of Commons to give up an attempt to pass a statute on this subject and to resort to a special form of petition. Her work, like that of most scholars who deal with the parliamentary and constitutional issues of this era, concentrated upon the maneuvering between the House of Commons and the king.[2] The only account of the passage of the Petition viewed from the perspective of the House of Lords was written prior to Relf's account by Charles Firth in a study of the House of Lords during the Civil War.[3] His interpretation predicated the existence of three parties in the Upper Chamber of Parliament: the court party, the opposition, and the "middle party"; and Firth concluded that the middle party played the key role in the passage of the Petition in that House.[4] As he stated it, "after its [the middle party's] attempts at compromise had failed, it decided in favour of the Commons, and not, as it usually had done, in favour of the Crown."[5] Such an interpretation, which posits an organized faction of moderates who worked from the outset for a compromise statement, incorrectly shifts attention from the two prime protagonists in the Upper House—the court and opposition factions. It also obscures much of the political significance of this victory over the Crown.

To be sure, there was at all times a third group within the nobility—peers who are not known to have been regularly attached to either of the

[1] Frances Helen Relf, *The Petition of Right* (Minneapolis, 1917) (hereafter cited as Relf, *Petition*).

[2] Two more recent works since Relf have also concentrated their attention upon the passage of the Petition in the Lower House (see Harold Hulme, "Opinion in the House of Commons on the Proposal for a Petition of Right, May 6, 1628," *English Historical Review* 50 [April 1935]: 302–6; and E. R. Adair, "The Petition of Right," *History* 5 [July 1920]: 99–103).

[3] Charles H. Firth, *The House of Lords during the Civil War* (London, 1910) (hereafter cited as Firth, *House of Lords*). Samuel Rawson Gardiner's great study, *The History of England from the Accession of James I to the Outbreak of the Civil War, 1603–1642*, 10 vols. (London, 1896), also contains a lengthy account of the Petition's passage through both of the Houses (see Gardiner, *History of England*, 4:230–89, passim).

[4] Firth, *House of Lords*, p. 52.

[5] Ibid.

two factions. They could be called a middle group of sorts, but it is difficult to describe these men as anything except a number of politically indistinguishable noblemen about whom almost nothing is known. To designate this amorphous body of peers as a party or faction in the sense of the other two groups distorts the political complexion of the House of Lords at the time. In fact, Firth's narrative concentrated upon the activities of the other two groups and only alluded to the middle party in a concluding, undocumented generalization.[6]

Firth was most correct about these men when he implied that they held the balance of power in the House since opposition objectives could never be achieved without their votes, and the court party used their votes to augment its dominance of the House. While they usually sided with the Crown, on this occasion they gradually came to accept certain propositions—that the Petition was a r' :essary guarantee of the rights of the subject, that it ought to pass basically as it had come from the House of Commons, and that it did not need any special reservations within it to protect the royal prerogative in its legal uses. Such were the conclusions of the majority after two months of discussions. But these conclusions are not a middle-party position; rather, they reflect the arguments advanced by the opposition spokesmen from the first day of debate. Consequently, it is far more accurate to view the opposition as the key to the success of the passage of the Petition of Right through the House of Lords. The decisive factor was the opposition's ability to delay a decision on the Petition until it had time to win the uncommitted members of the House away from an early inclination to support the royal wishes. Seen in this light, the passage of the Petition becomes the greatest victory of the small body of opposition nobles in the House of Lords during the era before the Civil War. Only the closest cooperation with the opposition leadership in both Houses achieved this remarkable feat. And, since the Petition itself was quickly sabotaged by the king after its acceptance, its greatest immediate importance lay in the way this struggle had tested the value of pursuing a parliamentary strategy involving the coordination of tactics in both Houses.

It could be argued, correctly I believe, that such an approach had been

---

[6] Ibid. Firth probably followed Gardiner's interpretation here for the latter also alluded to a middle party, although he named only the Earl of Arundel as one of its leaders (Gardiner, *History of England*, 6:288). Firth implied that Arundel was part of the opposition (Firth, *House of Lords*, p. 49). The Earl's political status in 1628 is difficult to ascertain. Early in the decade he had been a leading member of the court faction. After falling out with the favorite, however, he allied himself with the popular peers and felt the royal displeasure to such a degree that he became the focus of a constitutional dispute between Charles and the Upper House in 1626. He remained confined to his country house until shortly before the opening of the 1628 Parliament. Since he collaborated with Lord Weston, a leading royal spokesman in the House of Lords, on an addition to the Petition of Right in May, it is doubtful that he was the leader of any recognizable party of moderates, or in opposition.

tried during the impeachment of the Duke of Buckingham in 1626. However, a full test of this type of cooperative effort was precluded when Charles dissolved the Parliament rather than face possible defeat on the issue of his favorite.[7] In 1628 Charles could have dissolved the Parliament again or refused to sign the Petition. He probably could even have forced its rejection in the House of Lords if he had exerted extreme pressure on the nobility or created enough new peers.[8] But Charles did not react strongly against the statement of liberties at its initial introduction into Parliament because he did not believe personal intervention necessary. He was confident that the House of Lords would reject the statement for him. The Crown party, composed of royal officials, bishops, personal friends and supporters of the king and Buckingham, and the proxy votes of absent peers, usually attracted a numerical majority of the entire nobility.[9] In contrast, the opposition party in the House of Lords rarely numbered more than two dozen peers.[10] Thus the Upper House was the logical place for Charles to block a measure he disliked.

The use of the Upper House for such purposes was the nearest thing to a parliamentary policy developed by James and Charles in the 1620s. This

[7] The culmination of the 1626 Parliament would also suggest that the opposition leaderships in the two Houses were not well coordinated. The House of Commons decided to pass a remonstrance against the Duke of Buckingham at the very time when his impeachment trial was nearing completion in the House of Lords. Charles used the remonstrance as an excuse to dissolve the Parliament which caused the work of the opposition peers to convict the favorite to end in failure (Jess Stoddart Flemion, "The Dissolution of Parliament in 1626: A Reevaluation," *English Historical Review* 87 [October 1972]: 784-90) ; see above, 23-9.

[8] Charles created four new peers in mid-April—Lord Howard of Escrick, Lord Weston of Nyland, Lord Goring, and Lord Mohun. All attended regularly after April 15 as far as can be determined from the attendance records in the *Journal* (which abruptly end on May 6). All appear to have been safe adherents of the royal cause. Howard was the nephew by marriage of Buckingham, Weston was Chancellor of the Exchequer and soon to become Lord Treasurer of England, and Goring was a notorious courtier and favorite of the queen. Mohun seems to have been elevated for his wealth and local connections in the West, and he may have purchased his title. One other peer created during the session, Viscount Campden, never took his seat. Campden, a wealthy London merchant, paid heavily for his honor. The sum, as much as £20,000, may have tided Charles over his financial difficulties that spring when the House of Commons refused to pass its subsidies until the Petition of Right had been accepted.

[9] In the 1628/29 Parliament I have identified 38 lay peers who, by reason of their offices or connections, were likely adherents to the Crown faction. These 38 also held 21 proxies. Among the bishops, at least 16, holding 9 proxies, can be considered as royal supporters. This gives a total of 84 possible members of 124 persons eligible to attend the Upper House. While this figure is undoubtedly too high, even a reduction of one quarter would still leave the court party in numerical control of the Upper House.

[10] The principal members of the opposition were given in a letter of May 3, 1628 from Meade to Stuteville, British Museum, Harleian MS 390, fol. 400. The names listed are the Earls of Bristol, Bolingbroke, Clare, Devonshire, Essex, Lincoln, Mulgrave, Sussex, and Warwick; Viscount Say and Sele; Archbishop Abbot of Canterbury, Bishops Williams of Lincoln and Harsnett of Norwich; Lords Pagett and Spencer, and "the more ancient nobility."

policy, though essentially negative and sterile, suited the Crown's purposes perfectly when it wished to halt a controversial measure without directly confronting the Commons. The Petition of Right was precisely such an issue. The passage of the Petition, indicating that the opposition in Parliament could upset the Crown's control of the House of Lords, is an event of enormous significance in the struggles to limit royal power which marked the early seventeenth century. The tactics which won this victory have been well documented for the House of Commons. But the more difficult execution of this task came in the House of Lords and requires a detailed examination of the way in which popular peers maneuvered the Petition of Right through their House in April and May of 1628.

The most important constitutional issue raised in the Petition was that of the imprisonment of subjects by the king and Privy Council without a stated cause. However, since the issue arose from specific incidents of imprisonment for refusal to pay illegal taxes, the statement on imprisonment cannot be completely separated from the portion of the Petition which dealt with nonparliamentary taxation. The precipitating issue was *Darnell's Case* (1626) resulting from refusals to pay the forced loan of 1626. The Privy Council imprisoned many, but only five dared challenge the legality of their restraint. The order for their commitment stated no specific cause—only that the men were restrained by the special command of the king. The prisoners applied to King's Bench for a writ of *habeas corpus*. The issue was not whether the king could arbitrarily imprison, for most lawyers agreed that the royal prerogative included this power under special circumstances; rather, the counsel for the prisoners submitted that the defendants had the right to bail. Otherwise, the effect on them was a kind of perpetual imprisonment for an unstated crime. Later, these men could be released without ever having been charged and with no legal recourse available to them. Their lawyers argued that this was a dangerous and illegal maneuver to punish men for unpopular but not unlawful acts. The king's counsel disagreed, and the judges refused the request for the writ or for bail and remanded the petitioners to prison.[11]

When the subject arose in Parliament, the general belief was that the judges had given a final ruling in favor of the Crown's position that it could commit without stating the cause. The popular leaders from both Houses who met in London to plan and coordinate their parliamentary strategy before the opening of the session in March 1628 agreed that the passage of a statement of the liberties of the subject should take precedence over all other business.[12] The issue was first raised in the Lower House, for there the popular leadership could count on an overwhelmingly

[11] Relf, *Petition*, p. 11.
[12] Ibid., pp. 2-3, 11, 19.

sympathetic reception. Most spokesmen desired to proceed by bill, the strongest and clearest affirmation of rights, despite the tactical disadvantage that bills did not ordinarily receive the royal assent until the end of a session. A delay in the voting of subsidies, the principal source of leverage available to the Lower House, might be less effective in such circumstances. Although Charles eventually forbade any bill on the subject, he did so only after his supporters were unable to quash the business completely in the House of Lords. Charles anticipated a complete victory for the Crown on this matter and did not reveal his antipathy to the bill when the issue was first presented to the Upper House because he expected the lords to reject the Commons' request quickly and decisively. Royal strategy was predicated upon this belief during both the bill and the petition phases of the struggle. In view of this, there can be no doubt that the passage of the Petition by the House of Lords represented a singular victory for the opposition peers over the Crown faction which normally dominated that House.

Throughout the struggle, debate centered on one central dispute: would the prohibition against imprisonment without stating a cause infringe upon the royal prerogative and weaken the Crown's ability to protect the realm? The Crown's supporters consistently maintained that the statement of liberties emasculated the king's legal powers and would lead to disastrous results. Later, after the king issued a reassurance that he would respect all traditional liberties his predecessors had recognized and gave a specific pledge never again to imprison subjects for refusing to lend him money, his supporters insisted that nothing further was necessary to prevent any abuse of the prerogative. Despite these arguments and the potential strength of the Crown party,[13] the Petition passed almost unaltered in late May. The longer the final decision was delayed, the more the number of royal adherents shrank and the weaker became the new proposals for amending the statement of liberties.

While the opposition peers could not have triumphed without the aid of their friends in the Commons, the reverse is equally true. The strategy of the opposition in the Upper House can best be described as the performance of a successful holding action followed by a superb counteroffensive. Time became the chief ally. All parliamentary business except the statement of liberties ceased in April and May. With the legal aid of the Commons' lawyers, the opposition nobles were able to counter the arguments presented by the Crown's many legal counselors in the House

---

[13] Apart from the direct control which the Crown wielded over peers such as the royal officials and the bishops, the king had considerable indirect power over the nobility in general through his ability to extend or withhold the many varied forms of patronage upon which the nobility thrived.

of Lords. They employed the device of delay, calling for frequent conferences with the Lower House and making these time-consuming negotiations their chief tactic. The court group, most powerful at the outset, made
its moves early in each of the two phases of the struggle. Both times the
opposition forced it into a settlement far different than had been expected.
The superior forces of the Crown were turned back by a combination of
parliamentary maneuvering, superior debating skills, and sheer tenacity.

The careful coordination of the opposition leadership in both Houses is
evident from the way in which the leaders of the Lower House
accommodated their actions to the needs of the opposition leadership in
the House of Lords. The Commons showed unusual willingness to seek the
cooperation of the Upper House as well as incredible patience in debating,
repeatedly and at length, every point raised against the Petition in the
Upper House. It engaged in free conferences on the subject, something
which the Lower House had refused to do since the early years of the century when the Earl of Salisbury had used them to run Parliament from the
House of Lords. Time and time again the opposition peers persuaded the
uncommitted nobility to agree not to conclude any matter without first
allowing the Lower House a new hearing. The Commons argued for this
same consideration in all of its conferences and often sent special messages of thanks to the peers for their willingness to continue these extensive hearings. While the opposition peers had the onerous task of
persuading their colleagues that the Crown had nothing to fear from the
Petition, the leaders of the Commons had the equally difficult responsibility for countering the arguments of the Crown's legal experts in the House
of Lords[14] and convincing their own membership to proceed in such a
spirit of sincere goodwill that they would gradually assuage the doubts of
the conservative nobles and secure their acceptance of the Petition. Fire-
brands such as Sir John Eliot chaffed at this strategy which gave unaccus-
tomed reverence to the doubts of the House of Lords, but most members
followed the leadership of more realistic leaders such as Sir Thomas
Wentworth who stated categorically "that the Lords join with us, else all is
lost."[15]

The bill phase of the struggle, from April 7 to April 28, opened when the
House of Commons presented the House of Lords with four resolutions
against arbitrary imprisonment and taxation. At the first conference,
Attorney General Sir Robert Heath argued the Crown's case on the
legality of imprisonment without cause shown. It is doubtful that many

---

[14] Aside from the Crown's legal counsel who served as assistants to the House of Lords,
Lord President Manchester and Lord Treasurer Marlborough had both been Chief Justices
of the King's Bench. Two other prominant spokesmen on the royal side were also
lawyers—Lord Keeper Coventry and Chancellor of the Exchequer Weston.

[15] Gardiner, *History of England*, 6:283.

lords could follow the legal intricacies of the arguments; moreover, Relf concluded that all of the precedents on both sides were discredited eventually. However, in this opening debate, Heath was able to score two devastating points for the Crown. First, he cited an opinion of a famous Elizabethan jurist, Sir William Stamford, Judge of the Common Pleas, which he asserted supported the Crown's case. It was far more embarrassing to the Lower House, however, when Heath revealed that Sir Edward Coke, the constitutional expert of the Commons, had held the same opinion in 1616 when Chief Justice of the King's Bench. Coke, unable to deny it, could only say that he had changed his mind now that the power to commit was abused.[16]

The first clash in the House of Lords occurred on April 12, following Heath's presentation. Supporters of the prerogative power wished to have him followed immediately by the judges, expecting that their testimony would cement the Crown's position irrevocably in the Lords. They planned to follow this testimony with a snap vote. Lord Treasurer Marlborough, Lord President Manchester, Lord Steward Pembroke, the Duke of Buckingham, and the Earl of Bridgwater all spoke in favor of hearing the judges. These peers, along with Lord Keeper Coventry and Chancellor of the Exchequer, Lord Weston, were the Crown's chief spokesmen during the following two months, while Lords Say and Sele and Spencer, the Earl of Clare, and the Bishops of Lincoln and Norwich led the supporters of the Petition. In this debate the opposition sought a delay by asking for another conference with the Commons. Their only hope was that the Commons' lawyers could answer Heath's arguments.[17] But Heath had been very effective, so much so that one observer from the Commons reported that some "conceived in our house that the Lords . . . might possibly give sentence in the cause without calling for a conference."[18]

The supporters of the Crown had their way, and the judges appeared before the Upper House on April 14. However, these royal servants administered a serious setback to the Crown's supporters. The general understanding of the decision in *Darnell's Case* was that a final judgment favorable to the Crown had been returned. Heath had asserted this in his arguments before the House. But now the judges stated that their order had not been a final decree in favor of either side but merely a temporary return of the prisoners to confinement while the judges sought knowledge

[16] April 12, 1628, *Journal of the House of Lords, 1509 to 1847*, 79 vols. (n.d.), 3:735–36 (hereafter cited as *L.J.*).

[17] April 12, 1628, British Museum, Additional MS 40091, 29 (hereafter cited as Add. MS). This is a scribbled book kept by the Clerk of the House of Lords in 1628.

[18] April 14, 1628, Sir Francis Nethersole to the Queen of Bohemia, Public Record Office, State Papers Domestic, Charles I, 16/101/4 (hereafter cited as P. R. O. S. P.).

of the cause of imprisonment.[19] The importance of this revelation to the pro-Petition forces in the Lords cannot be overestimated. Sir Francis Nethersole, a member of the Lower House, wrote afterward that "there is, therefore, much hope conveyed that the matter will not be delivered against the subject in the Upper House."[20]

On the next day, the court faction, with Buckingham leading, still pressed for a quick conclusion. But uncertainty had been planted in the minds of many peers. Even such a firm royalist as the Earl of Dorset thought that the House should "take it into consideration how to preserve the prerogative . . . *and* to secure the subject in his person and goods."[21] The opposition peers dominated debate again, arguing that another conference with the Lower House was necessary to clarify these matters before any vote. In a second important setback for the Crown party, the majority of the House agreed.[22]

The conference lasted two full days, after which three days of debate in the Upper House ushered in a critical phase of the struggle. Although it appeared that the king's supporters still had a safe majority, Charles took no chances and strengthened his forces on April 15 by creating four new peers. Howard, Goring, and Mohun apparently provided votes only. Chancellor of the Exchequer Thomas Weston, however, was a valuable addition to the debating strength of the royal party. The king's move disheartened some of the members of the House of Commons who saw the court faction as already numerous and now increasing,[23] so the prospects for an opposition victory in the Lords did not look promising. On the first day the House decided that the king and Privy Council could imprison subjects but that they ought to have cause. It was left for the next day's debate—presumably the final one on the matter—whether that cause should be expressed in the arrest warrant. On April 22, the Lords debated this question all day and, as one writer vividly recorded, such "tongue-combat was never heard in the Upper House."[24] Lord Say and Sele, the most vigorous spokesman among the opposition, opened the day with a carefully prepared speech arguing that the law of the land guaranteed due process, which was all that the statement sought to protect. The right of a subject to know what crime he was charged with or to be bailed until his trial was inherent in the concept of due process, he argued. He further declared that "there is not one precedent that doth say negatively that a man committed merely upon . . . [the order of the king] that prayed a bail-

[19] April 14, 1628, *L. J.*, 3:738.
[20] April 14, 1628, Nethersole to the Queen of Bohemia, P. R. O. S. P. 16/101/4.
[21] April 14, 1628, Add. MS 40091, 34.
[22] Ibid.
[23] Thomas Birch, *Court and Times of Charles I*, ed. R. F. Williams, 2 vols. (London, 1848), 1:351.
[24] May 3, 1628, Meade to Stuteville, British Museum, Harleian MS 390, fol. 400.

ment upon a *habeas corpus* was denied it."[25] Royal spokesmen, including Lord Keeper Coventry, Weston, and Buckingham, all insisted that the Petition would destroy the king's necessary power to secure the persons of men deemed dangerous to the safety of the state. They argued for its need particularly in cases of conspiracy against the Crown and reminded the House that the reigns of the preceding two monarchs had both been troubled by such plots. The allusion to such events as the Gunpowder Plot had a strong effect upon the peers, and the debate appeared to be going badly for the opposition. It was estimated that a vote at this point would have favored the Crown by at least ten.[26] The opposition maneuvered to forestall a vote, which the Duke of Buckingham and others repeatedly called for during the course of debate, by asking to hear the opinions of the judges on the meaning of the term "the law of the land." In so doing, they sought clarification of the legal distinction between the king's ordinary and extraordinary powers but also sought the delay which such an appearance of the judges would require. They argued for further postponement of the decision until after another conference with the Lower House.[27]

While the debate continued, leaders of the Commons made a crucial tactical decision. The Lower House sent a message asking for a conference before the Lords voted anything if the Upper House were not entirely satisfied with the earlier arguments. A member of the Commons noted: "It having sufficiently appeared by yesterday's debate that the plurality of voices in the Upper House would be fore the King our House this day sent to them desiring that if they had any scruple of the truth of our resolutions they would give us a conference for the clearing of all doubts before they concluded."[28] The crucial timing of this offer was obvious, for the writer continued: "This message was delivered in the very heat of debate and had it not come so seasonably they say for certain the Lords had voted our questions and the plurality would have been against our determinations."[29] The close cooperation of the leaders of both Houses, begun even before Parliament opened, makes most implausible any interpretation of this act as coincidental. It is especially so since the popular leaders were known to have meetings in the evenings. Moreover, it was common practice for men from the Commons and servants of peers to congregate in the chamber next to the Upper House and occasionally even to stand in the doorway of the House itself listening to debate. Under such

[25] April 22, 1628, House of Lords Record Office, Main Paper Series, Minute Book, March 17, 1627/8 to October 20, 1628, unpaginated (hereafter cited as MS Minute Book, 1628).
[26] Ibid.; April 22, 1628, Nethersole to the Queen of Bohemia, P. R. O. S. P. 16/101/54; May 3, 1628, Meade to Stuteville, British Museum, Harleian MS 390, fol. 400.
[27] April 22, 1628, MS Minute Book, 1628.
[28] April 22, 1628, Nethersole to the Queen of Bohemia, P. R. O. S. P. 16/101/54.
[29] Ibid.

circumstances, nothing transpired in the House of Lords without being immediately reported to the leaders of the Commons.[30] Earlier in the decade an opposition peer had even been accused of using the ante-chamber of the House to meet with members of the Commons and plot strategy to thwart the policies of the Crown.[31] Undoubtedly, the leaders had decided the evening before that if debate continued to favor the royal position, on the following day they would intervene to try to keep a final vote from occurring.

The message gave the supporters of the resolutions the opportunity they needed to argue against an immediate and adverse vote. A long debate followed on whether to have a vote first and a conference afterward or the other way around. The royal spokesmen took the former position but it was very difficult to maintain since a vote before the conference would ob-viate the purpose of the meeting. The pro-liberties peers spoke one after another in favor of another conference, and Lord Say and Sele stated that if the final question were put at this time, "We who shall dissent . . . may . . . enter a protestation."[32] Although the Crown's spokesmen insisted that another conference was time consuming and unnecessary, a majority finally agreed to go along with the pleas of the popular peers. The royal supporters had expected, with good reason, to conclude the matter promptly and successfully that day. The decision to continue debate was a major turning point for the opposition in its struggle against the court party.

The vote on April 22 to continue discussions was a major setback but hardly a total defeat for the Crown. The peers soon gave up attempts to reword the original resolutions and decided to draft a set of their own. The five proposals eventually presented to the Lower House varied greatly from those of the Commons and indicated the continuing tendency of most of the nobility to take a very cautious approach to any matter that involved the royal prerogative. The fifth resolution in particular was explicitly against the spirit of the Commons' statement, for it declared: "In case, for the security of His Majesty's royal person, the Common safety of his people, or the peaceable government of his kingdom, His Majesty shall find just cause, for reason of state, to imprison or restrain any man's person, His Majesty would graciously declare, that, within a convenient time, he shall and will express a cause of his committment."[33]

---

[30] David Willson, *The Privy Councillors in the House of Commons, 1604-1629* (Minneapolis, 1940), p. 54. On several occasions debates in the House of Commons prove decisively that the speaker was aware of the exact words used by a peer in the Upper House (see Gardiner, *History of England*, 6:280-81).

[31] Examination of the Earl of Southampton, British Museum, Harleian MS 161.

[32] April 22, 1628, MS Minute Book, 1628.

[33] April 28, 1628, *L. J.*, 3:772.

Judging from the Arundel case of the previous Parliament,[34] a phrase such as "convenient time" was a weak defense against arbitrary royal action. But at this point the pro-Petition peers could make little further progress against the overwhelming conservatism of their colleagues. Their success in drawing out the matter, however, forced the king into his first direct intervention in the matter three days later. He called the two Houses before him and issued a message on the liberties of the subject which closely paralleled the first four resolutions of the House of Lords. These had been rejected already by the Commons as vague and useless, so it was not surprising that the Commons continued to frame its own resolutions into a bill. This drove Charles farther from his original plans, for he sent word on May 1 that he would have no bill which did more than confirm ancient rights. Even an explanation of these rights would "hazard an encroachment" he said.[35] Charles knew that his position was completely unsatisfactory to the Commons but he expected the order to remove their only legal means to bind the Crown. He wanted to force them to accept his earlier verbal promise as the only guarantee they could obtain. Undoubtedly, he expected the House of Lords to support him in this position since his statement had so closely echoed their resolutions. But Charles had not reckoned with the innovative ability of the famous common-law theoretician, Sir Edward Coke. Coke persuaded the Lower House to drop the bill and adopt a new procedure called "a petition of right."[36]

The private petition of right was a form of plea previously used in the courts of law but not in Parliament. The petition form used by Parliament was the petition of grace, or a request, whereas the petition of right was a public affirmation of an already existing right. According to Coke, such a petition of right, passed by Parliament, would be binding on the judges in the courts and could guarantee an end to present abuses.[37] It was supposedly a petition to the king from both Houses acting in their judicial capacity as the High Court of Parliament and supreme judicial authority of the realm. It is of the greatest importance that the Petition of Right was conceived of as a judicial act of Parliament by Coke and other leaders of

---

[34] See Vernon Snow's article, "The Arundel Case, 1626," *Historian* 26 (May 1964): 323–50.

[35] May 2, 1628, king's speech, *L. J.*, 3:772; king's letter to the House of Commons, cited in Relf, *Petition*, p. 34.

[36] The use of a petition of right had been broached twice before in the House of Commons. Only a few weeks earlier, on April 26, Sir Dudley Digges had suggested its use. The bill had not yet been rejected by Charles, however, and no further mention was made of this possibility until Coke revived it (Harold Hulme, *The Life of Sir John Eliot* [London, 1957], pp. 213–14). The first suggestion for its use came in the Lower House in 1624. This discovery was made recently by Professor Vernon Snow. I am indebted to him for this piece of information and for the use of his manuscript article on the subject: T. B. Clendinen and Vernon Snow, "Prelude to the Petition of Right: A Debate on Procedural Activities in the 1624 Parliament."

[37] Relf, *Petition*, p. 36.

the Commons. As such it was not legal without confirmation by both Houses. Unless the Upper House joined in it, the Petition would have no legally binding authority.

The presentation of the new statement of liberties to the peers on May 9 inaugurated the second phase of the struggle. After two readings and some debate in the Committee of the Whole, the Petition was committed to ten members, six of whom were opposition men.[38] The committee recommended some minor changes but left the principal issue of imprisonment to the full debate of the lords. In one sense the peers were back at the same point that they had occupied one month earlier. But, in fact, the Crown had lost ground, for the Petition was a stronger statement of liberties than the bill had been and the reservations of the majority of the peers on the subject had lessened. Yet once again the Crown pressed a strategy predicated on quickly squelching the new attack on its powers. Charles attempted to use the Upper House to force the Commons into a compromise by sending the lords a letter promising that he would never again commit anyone for refusing to lend money.[39] At the same time he reiterated his complaint that an absolute prohibition upon imprisonment without showing cause was detrimental to the security of the state and an infringement upon the prerogative such as no sovereign had ever suffered.[40] After receiving this message the lords voted to request the Lower House to alter its Petition to meet the objections raised by the king. It appears that this step by the House of Lords, so favorable to the royal desires, was accomplished only by a snap vote taken after a number of peers had gone home believing that a decision on the matter had been put off until the next day. Lord Grey of Warke went so far as to say that the business was not "fairly carried."[41] However, the full House reconfirmed the decision the following day.

If the Commons had acquiesced in the request it would have meant victory for Charles, so it seems doubtful that the king expected this. More likely, he had hit upon the letter as a tactic to divide the Houses. If the Commons refused the request of the Lords the division might prove fatal to the Petition. But the opposition leaders immediately recognized this

[38] Initial membership on the committee included Coventry, Manchester, Arundel, and Weston, Crown supporters; and Bedford, Bristol, Say and Sele, Pagett, and Bishops of Norwich and of Lincoln of the opposition (May 9, 1628, *L. J.*, 3:787). A committee appointment book indicates that six more peers were added to the committee that same day. Of these, four were Crown supporters: Buckingham, Pembroke, Dorset, and Norwich; and two were opposition peers: Clare and the Archbishop of Canterbury. If all remained, that would make the committee evenly balanced between the parties (May 9, 1628, House of Lords Record Office, Committee Appointment Book, March 20, 1627/8 to June 23, 1628, 27).
[39] May 12, 1628, king's letter to the House of Lords, *L. J.*, 3:789.
[40] May 12, 1628, Add. MS 40091, 62.
[41] Ibid., 63.

and altered their own tactics accordingly. Previously, the Lower House had initiated almost all proposals concerning the statement of liberties. It had been willing to accommodate the Upper House with as many reiterations of the legal arguments of the Commons as the peers requested. But now the Commons insisted that the Upper House must assume the initiative in proposing further changes to the statement. If the lords still had objections, then it was up to them to make new proposals or to reframe the Petition in a mutually satisfactory way. While the leaders of the Commons moved into this intransigent posture, refusing any substantial alteration of their work at this point, the pro-Petition group increased its offensive in the Upper House to win passage of the Petition without alteration.

From the middle of May onward all progress toward a satisfactory solution had to come from the House of Lords. It was indicative of how well the opposition had accomplished its task that, by now, a majority of peers seemed convinced that some statement on liberties was necessary. But they found themselves in an almost impossible situation when they tried to alter the Petition's section on imprisonment without changing its substance. For two days they debated this problem without resolving anything. They finally decided to write an accommodation to be attached to the Petition, but not before the opposition won a clear guarantee that if the accommodation were unacceptable to the House of Commons it would not automatically mean that the lords would reject the entire Petition. [42] Once this understanding was achieved they acquiesced in the formulation of an additon, undoubtedly realizing that the Commons would have no fear of rejecting the proposal if it were not crucial to the passage of the Petition in the Upper House.

At least two additions were presented to the House of Lords in the third week of May. The one finally submitted to the Commons was the work of the Earl of Arundel and Lord Weston. [43] Despite its coauthorship by a chief royal spokesman, the addition represented a much weaker statement than the resolutions penned by the Upper House a month earlier. [44] On May 17, it, along with several further wording changes, was sent to the Commons. The most important wording alteration sought was the removal of the term "unlawful" and its replacement with the softer phrase, "not warrantable by the laws and customes of the realm." [45] Discussion of the changes provides crucial evidence of the changed attitudes in the House by

[42] May 14, 15, 19, 21, 1628, ibid., 68–83.
[43] Gardiner, *History of England*, 6:278–79.
[44] The clause stated, "We humbly present this petition to your Majesty, not only with a care of preserving our own liberties, but with due regard to leave entire that sovereign power wherewith your Majesty is trusted for the protection, safety, and happiness of your people" (May 17, 1628, *L. J.*, 3:801).
[45] May 17, 1628, Add. MS 40091, 67–68.

this date. The diminished court group took the position that both the addition and the word change must be accepted. But apparently more peers considered the word change as the most important obstacle left in the path of settlement. The growing popularity of this view reflected the success of the opposition spokesman in playing down the need for a specific protection for the prerogative within the Petition, something which the court forces insisted upon. The number who desired the wording change was very large, however, and the opposition nobles must have communicated this fact to their colleagues in the Commons; for, after initially rejecting the change, the Commons reversed itself and sent a message accepting the alteration. At the same time, however, it rejected the proposed addition. [46] The Petition's friends in the Upper House now had their strongest line of argument for the final days of debate—that the two Houses had labored too long and were too close to agreement for the Petition to be lost merely for a saving clause that many felt nonessential.

The court's spokesmen had only one final argument to employ. The rejection of the addition caused Buckingham to insist that the only alternative was a separate statement of liberties from their own House. He stated his case on the final day of debate, May 24, arguing, "If we now depart from our addition we do in a manner depart from ourselves." [47] And he concluded, "The addition to be either in the preamble or in the body or the conclusion [for] if it be no where I cannot give my vote to it." [48] It is clear that by this date most peers felt more inclined to the attitude expressed by an opposition nobleman, Lord Pagett, when he told the House that he hoped it would "not let it depend upon any nice and thin distinction which one amongst a hundred doth not understand." [49] There was some desultory discussion of penning still another statement in hopes that it might prove satisfactory to the Commons, but most peers now recognized the futility of trying to add something to the Commons' Petition which would still leave its substance unaltered. And, in their attempt to persuade the Lower House to accept their original addition, the spokesmen for the House of Lords had already done much to undermine remaining belief that such a clause was necessary. Court spokesmen as well as others all but argued that the Lower House should accept the addition because it meant nothing. [50]

The popular peers now used this damaging suggestion to argue against any breach with the Commons for the sake of the addition. They hammered away at the argument that the Lower House had given repeated

[46] May 20, 1628, *L. J.*, 3:804.
[47] May 24, 1628, Add. MS 40091, 91.
[48] Ibid.
[49] May 21, 1628, ibid., 81.
[50] Gardiner, *History of England*, 6:279.

assurances that it intended no infringement upon the legal prerogative; that, in fact, the Commons had made a solemn declaration to that effect only the day before.[51] Finally, a nobleman who had rarely spoken before in debate, Lord Maynard, returned to a suggestion made earlier by the opposition peer, the Earl of Bristol. Bristol had suggested that the Lords leave the Petition unchanged but have it "duly mended by word of Mouth" when delivered to the king.[52] Now Maynard suggested a declaration "clearing the prerogative," as he put it, to be drawn up for their House such as the one passed in the House of Commons the previous day.[53] It was hardly what Buckingham intended when he insisted upon a saving clause, but it immediately found favor with most of the other lords. It was a perfectly acceptable position for most of the Petition's early proponents to take for the declaration would come only from the Upper House and have no legal relationship to the Petition. For those peers who had remained undecided, the new suggestion seemed to provide the only resolution to what had been a total impasse at the opening of the day's discussion. Buckingham tried to hold out, insisting upon a saving clause within the Petition itself or total rejection. However, most peers, including many from the court faction, supported the other suggestion. Only Lord Say and Sele among the opposition lords continued to insist for a time that there was no need for either kind of saving statement.[54] After one final attempt by Buckingham to raise support for a separate petition, he then also agreed to support the majority view.[55] With this capitulation the struggle was over. The House agreed to accept the Petition as it stood with a separate declaration to be delivered to the king at the time of the presentation of the Petition. The Petition which the House passed on May 26, stated: "Be it now enacted that noe free man shall be committed by the command of the King or the Privie counsell but the cause ought to bee expressed and the same beeing returned upon a habeas corpus hee shall be delivered or bailed, and wheras by the common lawe, and statutes every free man hath a proprietie in his goods and estate as no tax, tallage etc. Bee it now enacted that noe tax, tallage, loane, shall be levied, etc. by the King or anie minister without act of parliament and that none bee compelled to receive anie soldier into his house against his will."[56] The accompanying declaration from the lords stated that their intention in

---

[51] May 24, 1628, Add. MS 40091, 90–91.
[52] May 20, 1628, ibid., 79.
[53] May 24, 1628, ibid., 91.
[54] Ibid.
[55] May 24, 1628, Frances Helen Relf, *Notes of the Debates in the House of Lords, 1621 . . . 1628*, Camden Society, 3d series, vol. 32 (London, 1929), pp. 194–98.
[56] The Petition of Right from *The True Relation*, Massachusetts Historical Society, in Relf, *Petition*, appendix B, p. 63.

presenting the Petition was not to lessen any authority of the Crown which, by their oath of supremacy, they had sworn to defend. [57]

This conclusion to the struggle for the Petition of Right was definitely not a victory of the moderates. It was clearly a victory of the opposition, for the position which emerged as the majority opinion on May 24 was almost everything which the pro-Petition forces had labored for from the outset. To paraphrase Sir Edward Coke on another occasion, "The live child was theirs"—for the small piece of excess apparel it wore was legally irrelevant. [58]

Since its passage was the most significant victory against the Crown's arbitrary activities during the decade, the Petition of Right has not lacked the attention of a number of the most prominent historians over the last century. It would seem that everything to be known about the passage of the Petition had already been written. The current interpretation, still based on Frances Relf's book, stresses the compromise which had been forced upon the Commons by Charles. Yet the compromise forced upon Charles should not be forgotten. The latter required a victory in the Upper House as well as in the Lower. While the well-planned maneuvering of the Commons leaders which achieved this success in the House of Commons has been thoroughly documented, the courageous fight of the pro-Petition peers has gone largely unrecognized due to the emphasis of Gardiner and Firth upon a nonexistent compromise party. In fact, every step along the way opposition leaders in the two Houses coordinated their strategy and tactics, thereby saving the Petition from the fate intended for it in the House of Lords. The victory is ultimate proof that the opposition peers deserve to stand alongside their better-known colleagues in the Commons for their superior abilities as parliamentary tacticians.

The same day that the Petition was presented to the king, Charles agreed to restore all peers out of favor to mark the auspicious occasion. It was significant, and perhaps symbolic, too, that the list of those out of grace read like a list of the leadership of the pro-Petition forces in the Lords; including Archbishop Abbott of Canterbury; Bishops Williams of Lincoln and Harsnet of Norwich; the Earls of Bristol, Essex, Lincoln, and Warwick; and Viscount Say and Sele. Most of these lords had refused the forced loan which had initiated the train of events now ending in victory.

Charles's acceptance of the Petition on June 2 (and his fuller reply on June 7) was not to be the end of the Petition of Right during this session of Parliament. Less than three weeks later, disagreement over its interpretation helped to provoke the prorogation on June 26. Since the Crown and Commons clashed almost immediately over the interpretation of a

---

[57] May 26, 1628, *L. J.*, 3:824.
[58] April 22, 1628, Nethersole to the Queen of Bohemia, P. R. O. S. P. 16/101/54.

document, the intent of which was to clarify the proper division between the liberties of the subject and the extent of the royal prerogative, one may well wonder what had been accomplished. Legally, very little had been won for the immediate future. Charles had publicly accepted that imprisonment for refusing to lend money was an abuse of the prerogative, and he never again resorted to a forced loan. The most obvious forms of extra-parliamentary taxation would seem to be illegal now as well, although this did not hinder the raising of a great amount of money by the prerogative power in the next decade. Only the judges could end such quasi-legal extortions, and they were dependent on the Crown. The return of peace reduced the immediate importance of the Petition's protection against the billeting of soldiers on the civilian populace. As for imprisonment, the judges had already assured Charles that he could continue to imprison men without stating the cause. [59] Far more than any of these particulars, however, the great legal weakness of the Petition lay in its unenforceability. That was precisely why Charles had refused an act of Parliament on the subject. The opposition leaders may have believed that this special form of petition possessed binding legal sanction on the Crown. But ultimately the enforcement and interpretation of the Petition depended upon the king and his judges in a manner that statutes did not. Only a willingness to uphold the protections granted, and only basic agreement on the content of these liberties, could assure what Parliament desired. Charles might have been willing to do the former but only so long as he had complete independence on the interpretation of the Petition. And nothing more widely separated Parliament and the Crown than the question of the rights of the subject and the limits of royal power. Three weeks after acceptance of the Petition, the Commons realized that its victory was largely an empty shadow. As in the struggle for the Magna Carta four centuries earlier, so also in this case it would be posterity that would find the Petition of Right an immortal legal protection.

That is not to say that the Petition had no deep contemporary significance. This importance was more political than legal or constitutional, however. It was a particularly crucial event in the development of techniques for organizing opposition to royal policies in Parliament. Such organization was still in its adolescent stage, and the term "party" as it would be understood in the late seventeenth century has no place in the 1620s. Nonetheless, opposition had been forming in Parliaments for several decades, although primarily on the basis of independent activities in each House with only the loosest contact between the two leaderships. Perhaps this was due to the difference in the numerical size of the two oppositions, perhaps to the rapidly altering balance of power between the

[59] May 1628, Opinion of the Judges, P. R. O. S. P. 16/105/93.

Houses or to the traditional conception of the Houses as absolutely equal and independent of one another. Whatever the reasons, it was obvious that these tactics had not achieved many positive results in recent years. In 1628, for the first time, the statement of liberties provided the opportunity to attempt a fully integrated strategy. It proved more effective, perhaps, than any of the opposition could have hoped. A new stage of party organization resulted, at least temporarily. And this presaged something even more politically portentous for the future.

The Stuart monarch had lost the precious initiative in policy direction in the Commons and with it adequate control of that House. From this loss much of the conflict of the period stemmed. What kept the Parliaments of these years from mounting even more damaging attacks upon the authority of the king, such as in the highly controversial area of the control of foreign policy, was the Crown's use of the House of Lords as a buffer between itself and its opponents in the Lower House. The success of royal policy by the 1620s required a House of Lords safely dominated by men completely loyal to the Crown. When the opposition won passage of the Petition through the House of Lords in 1628 it proved that royal dominance over that House could be neutralized in the same way that it had been in the House of Commons for some time. This meant that the Crown's most important protection within the structure of Parliament had been shaken as never before and the constitutional crisis between the Stuarts and their Parliaments had entered a new and critical stage of development.

4

THE PEERS, THE PEOPLE, AND PARLIAMENTARY MANAGEMENT IN THE FIRST SIX MONTHS OF THE LONG PARLIAMENT * *PAUL CHRISTIANSON*

For more than a century, historians have characterized the events of 1640–60 as the "Puritan Revolution" or the "English Revolution." Both terms spring from the assumption that some sort of revolution—whether the limited one of S. R. Gardiner or the wide-ranging one of Lawrence Stone—preceded the outbreak of civil war in England. Such an event logically required long-term constitutional, religious, and social causes such as the "rise of the middle class" and its corollary, the "winning of the initiative by the House of Commons." Few, if any, historians interpret the earlier Scottish and Irish rebellions within the same framework, but blame them instead upon the policies of Charles I. Recently, a growing group of historians have demonstrated their dissatisfaction with these traditional categories of explanation by writing about the "Great Rebellion" or the "English Civil War." This paper argues that the English civil war began as a rebellion led by what contemporaries called the greater and lesser nobility. It hypothesizes that the hierarchical nature of Stuart society carried over into the working of Parliament and, therefore, that peers exercised a strong, if not predominant, influence upon affairs. From this point of view, it appears that the aristocracy of seventeenth-century England, unlike their counterparts in the French and Russian revolutions, never lost political control and that gentry replaced peers as managers of the parliamentarian network only under the changed conditions of civil war. One could entitle it "The Nobles, the People, and the Constitution," had not another historian already used this title for a brilliant article some twenty years ago.[1] While the scope of this essay will not

* An earlier version of my article was delivered as a paper at the conference on Puritanism in Old and New England held at Thomas More College in April 1975; I would like to thank Dr. Frank Bremer for inviting me to give that paper. In addition, I would like to thank Dr. John K. Gruenfelder, Dr. Caroline Hibbard, and Mr. Conrad Russell for their comments on a later draft. The errors that remain are mine.

[1] Brian Manning, "The Nobles, the People, and the Constitution," *Past and Present* 9 (1956): 42–64; for the two basic approaches, see Lawrence Stone, *The Causes of the English Revolution, 1529–1642* (London, 1972), and Conrad Russell, ed., *The Origins of the English Civil War* (London, 1973). A full-scale critique of the assumptions of the old interpretation and an attempt to put forward a new one appear in my article, "The Causes of the English Revolution: A Revaluation," *Journal of British Studies* 15 (1976): 40–75. Gardiner pointed out: "In the English Revolution . . .

permit a full demonstration of the interpretation put forward above, it should indicate the powerful part played by peers in the crucial opening months of the Long Parliament.

When the Long Parliament assembled in November 1640, it contained many gentlemen charged with feelings of grievance and expectation. In the previous decade, men of substance protested the policies of the Crown in word and deed—for example, many refused to pay ship money and attacked the Laudians, while the Lords refused to sit as a Great Council at York and, thereby, forced King Charles to call a Parliament. Men of lower degree expressed themselves in direct action—for example, when seamen and apprentices attacked Lambeth palace or when soldiers killed their Catholic officers or tore down altars, images, and communion rails on their way north to fight the Scots. An aristocratic network of political friends, relations, and patrons and clients came to Westminster ready to channel these feelings into action.[2] The Earl of Clarendon later named the leaders of this grouping without, however, spelling out the ties which connected them together: "In the Lords' House the Earls of Essex, Bedford, Warwick, the Lords Say and Kimbolton, were the governing voices, attended by Brooke, Wharton, Paget, and such like. In the House of Commons Mr. Pym, Mr. Hampden, Mr. St. John, Mr. Holles, and Mr. Fiennes, absolutely governed, being stoutly seconded upon all occasions by Mr. Strode, Sir John Hotham. . . , Sir Walter Earle, young Sir Henry Vane, and many others of the same tempers and dispositions. . . ."[3] Historians still have not worked out all of the relationships between these

---

the essence of the movement [was] that the authority of the King should be restricted." Stone quotes a definition of revolution as " 'a sweeping, fundamental change in political organization, social structure, economic property control, and the predominant myth of a social order, thus indicating a major break in the continuity of development' " (S. R. Gardiner, *Constitutional Documents of the Puritan Revolution, 1625–1660* [Oxford, 1906], p. x, see pp. ix–xi; and Stone, p. 48, see pp. 47–54).

[2] Patron-client relationships occurred between persons of unequal power or degree, those of political friendship between men roughly equal, and those of kinship between relatives by blood or marriage. All operated on a principle of reciprocity, were basically private and anchored only loosely in public law, but stood planted in community values in the long run. Since these represented dyadic, interpersonal relationships based upon the mutual interchange of favor, they varied considerably from person to person and over time. All members of Parliament held positions near the peak of the hierarchy in local or county communities; as a result, master-servant relationships with their greater social distance rarely applied there. For this sort of political model, see Christianson, pp. 62–64; Robert R. Kaufman, "Patron-Client Concept and Macro Politics: Prospects and Problems," *Comparative Studies in Society and History* 16 (1974): 285, 284–308; and Matthias Gelzer, *The Roman Nobility*, trans. Robin Segar (Oxford, 1969).

[3] Edward Hyde, Earl of Clarendon, *The History of the Rebellion and Civil Wars in England*, ed. W. Dunn Macray (Oxford, 1888), 1:263n.

men—for example, Conrad Russell has shown that their economic ties extended well beyond the confines of the Saybrook, Providence Island, and Massachusetts Bay companies—and they have displayed a marked tendency to ignore one of the most obvious rules of patron-client politics, the precedence of patron over client.[4]

Great differences of wealth and prestige, such as those between the Earl of Bedford and John Pym, made for relationships of full clientage. When the social distance narrowed, like that between the Earl of Warwick and Sir Thomas Barrington or Harbottle Grimston, so did the precedence of patron over client. And when the gap became so small as to approach a situation of rough equality, like that between Viscount Say and Sele and John Hampden, then the relationship became one of political friendship. The leaders of the Commons listed by Clarendon—and many more—sat as the clients, relatives, and friends of peers. It appears that members of the reform network forged a working alliance in the 1620s, strengthened it in the 1630s, and carried it into the management of the Long Parliament in the 1640s.[5] Although Bedford and Pym, Say and Nathaniel Fiennes—his son, came prepared and eager to take office, the network as a whole derived its strength from a loosely shared religious and political philosophy and program.

A key aim binding together the leaders of the reform network and helping them gain wide support sprang from their desire to defend Reformed religion, especially from the innovations of the Arminian or Laudian group within the Church of England. The attempt to punish the Arminians and to prevent them from gaining positions of

[4] Russell, pp. 110–12; he has shown also that the Earl of Bedford used John Pym as his spokesman in the Commons. Robert Ruigh has established a similar relationship between the Earl of Pembroke and Sir Benjamin Rudyard (see Robert E. Ruigh, *The Parliament of 1624* [Cambridge, Mass., 1971], p. 178, n. 38). Most historians of Tudor and early Stuart Parliaments, however, have rested content with tracing relationships between individual peers and members of the Commons only at election time. It seems rather incredible to assume that such carefully nurtured ties did not extend into the session itself. Such connections deserve careful examination, especially over time, since their reciprocal nature could make for instability. For the purposes of this article, it suffices to extend those electoral ties noted in standard secondary works into the sitting of Parliament.

[5] See James E. Farnell, "The Aristocracy and the Leadership of Parliament in the English Civil War," *Journal of Modern History* 44 (1972): 79–86; Jess Stoddart Flemion, "The Nature of Opposition in the House of Lords in the Early Seventeenth Century," (1976); see above, 5–22; Russell, "Introduction" and "Parliament and the King's Finances," pp. 1–31, 91–116; Vernon Snow, "Essex and the Aristocratic Opposition to the Early Stuarts," *Journal of Modern History* 32 (1960): 224–33, and *Essex the Rebel* (Lincoln, Nebr., 1971); Christopher Thompson, "The Origins of the Politics of the Parliamentary Middle Group, 1625–1629," *Transactions of the Royal Historical Society,* 5th ser. 22 (1972): 71–86; and Perez Zagorin, *The Court and the Country* (London, 1969), chap. 4.

influence started in the 1620s and continued into the 1640s. It grew
even more pressing after the Duke of Buckingham seemed to renounce John Preston at the York House Conference of 1626 and to
throw his weight behind the promotion of men like Bishops Neile
and Laud. Christopher Thompson has clearly shown how this crucial
issue brought together Warwick, Say, and Pym at an early date.[6]
The attempted impeachment of Buckingham in 1626 seems no coincidence. Despite some success in Parliament, however, they lost the
battle both at court and in the church hierarchy by the end of the
1620s. With Laud ascendant in the 1630s, their prophecy that the
Arminians would plot to bring England back under the mantle of
Rome—of the popish antichrist—appeared to come true. During this
decade, the battle moved out into many parts of the countryside.
Much against the will of prominent laymen, Laudian bishops en-
forced changes in church ceremonies and practices. They disciplined, suspended, deprived, or drove into exile those reformed
pastors who refused to conform to their new definition of Anglican
orthodoxy. The Earl of Warwick put up a tenacious defense of his
stable of puritan preachers, but even he—a powerful peer with
prestigious allies in the country and a brother at court—could not
protect such divines as Hugh Peter, Jeremiah Burroughs, and William Greenhill. All were forced into exile.[7]

The beliefs of members of the network spanned a considerable
portion of the Protestant spectrum, ranging from moderate Episcopalians like Bedford, Essex, and Pym, through root and branch
enemies of episcopacy like Say and Fiennes, all the way to Congregationalists who sympathized with the separatist sects like
Brooke. Warwick's religious patronage mirrored this very diversity.[8]
Such inclusiveness, far from being a source of weakness in 1640,
continued the common front of the 1630s and enhanced a wide range
of religious opinion with aristocratic respectability. As yet, few
Englishmen held rigid positions on worship or church government.
The small number who did were themselves divided among the *jure*

[6] Thompson, pp. 74–80.

[7] Kenneth W. Shipps, "Lay Patronage of East Anglian Clerics in Pre-Revolutionary
England" (Ph.D. thesis, Yale University, 1971).

[8] See William Fiennes, Viscount Say and Sele, *Two Speeches* (London, 1641), wing
S796; Robert Greville, Lord Brooke, *A Discourse Opening the Nature of That Episcopacy Which Is Exercised in England* (London, 1641); and the speeches cited in n. 33
below. Say's speeches survive in numerous editions, but are improperly dated in
most; he delivered the first on March 6, 1641 and the second most probably on June
4, 1641 (see Bishop Warner's diary of the Lords for 1641, British Library, Harleian
Manuscripts 6424, fols. 43r–44v, 71r; and John Nalson, ed., *An Impartial Collection
of the Great Affairs of State* [London, 1682–83], 2:265).

divino: Episcopalians, the root and branch opponents of prelacy (embracing both Presbyterians and Congregationalists), and the dedicated Congregationalists (mostly separatists or exiles returned from the Netherlands and New England). The divisive debates of the 1640s, however, still lay largely in the future and most reformers wished first to redress the grievances of the past. Ironically, the English primate contributed to their coalition by providing all of the Reformed with a common enemy; his methods bound the leaders of the reform network more firmly together and created a large constituency who came to heed their warnings. Laud and his colleagues, by branding every supporter of Reformed (or Calvinist) theology as a dangerous "puritan" and by pressing a program deliberately designed to step on many toes, alienated even those who worshipped the Elizabethan tradition.[9]

In an age which valued precedent above all else, members of the network got wide support for their attack upon the Arminians. As Nicholas Tyacke has so forcefully pointed out: "In terms of English Protestant history the charge in 1640 that King Charles and Archbishop Laud were religious innovators is irrefutable."[10] No wonder few spokesmen defended the Laudians in print, pulpit, or Parliament during the first year of the Long Parliament. To ensure that the wavering would see the light, Warwick and others came well equipped with preachers to make the point. Stephen Marshall, Warwick's client and one of the foremost clerical politicians of the 1640s, stood in St. Margaret's pulpit, paired with Cornelius Burges, for the first of an important series of fast sermons to the recently assembled Commons on November 17, 1640.[11] Lay puritans from the greater and lesser nobility—the peers and the gentry—commanded their network of religious and political friends, clients, and relations in the autumn of 1640, just as naturally as they came to

[9] See Nicholas Tyacke, "Puritanism, Arminianism and Counter-Revolution," in Russell, pp. 119–43; Mervyn James, *Family, Lineage and Civil Society* (Oxford, 1974), chap. 6; and Huntingdon County Record Office, Manchester Papers, ddM/32/5/15 (a letter from John Williams, Bishop of Lincoln). A personal friend of such network peers as Bedford and Essex, Williams rightly claimed to have suffered for opposing the "innovators" in print; he was also clearly ambitious to return to power. I wish to thank Conrad Russell for drawing this letter to my attention.

[10] Tyacke in Russell, p. 143.

[11] For the fast sermons and their impact, see Paul Christianson, "From Expectation to Militance: Reformers and Babylon in the First Two Years of the Long Parliament," *Journal of Ecclesiastical History* 24 (1973): 225–44, and the works cited therein. For Marshall's relationship with Warwick, see Shipps, p. 209, and Stephen Marshall, *A Coppy of a Letter* (London, 1643), wing M761. The patronage of preachers by individual peers and gentry needs systematic study before historians can reach a full understanding of religious disputes in Stuart England.

command the armies and navy of Parliament in 1642.[12] If in church affairs they stood at first as enemies of Laudian innovations, in those of state they started out as defenders of the Ancient Constitution of England against the recent abuse of power by evil advisers of the Crown.

In general terms, the leaders of the network seem to have believed in an Ancient Constitution which stretched from Anglo-Saxon times to their own with its fundamentals intact. They came to conceptualize this as a mixed monarchy of king, Lords, and Commons—representing the estates of monarchy, aristocracy, and democracy—each holding the other in check and combining together as a sovereign king-in-Parliament. This amalgam of the Polybian and English common law traditions found favor with sixteenth-century writers like Sir Thomas Smith and Bishop John Aylmer, received bulky support from Sir Edward Coke in the early seventeenth century, apparently received the approval of the Lords in the Short Parliament, and provided the basis for the king's answer to the Nineteen Propositions in June 1642. It helps to explain why Sir John Culpepper and Viscount Falkland, who wrote the latter, worked in cooperation with the leaders of the reform network for most of the first year of the Long Parliament.[13] While others sounded variations on the theme, Viscount Say expounded a brief and cogent version in a letter to John Winthrop, the governor of Massachusetts, dated July 9, 1640. ". . . I do judge and think I can maintain by good reason," Say wrote, "that to be the best form of government which hath in it the good of all three [i.e., monarchy, aristocracy, and democracy], so fitly limiting each other, and thereby preventing the evils of either, that being equally poised one by the other, they shall all yield what is good, in either, for the settling and preserving of common right and liberty, to all and every particular." To Winthrop, he emphasized the necessity of a "power in a state to reward virtue hereditarily and for disservice to lay a punishment that shall extend to posterity," adding that "there is no danger in such different degrees (which will be found necessary), so long as they are always

[12] Clive Holmes, *The Eastern Association in the English Civil War* (Cambridge, 1974); and Snow, *Essex*, chaps. 12–17.

[13] See Zera Fink, *The Classical Republicans* (Evanston, Ill., 1945); R. W. K. Hinton, "Constitutional Theories from Sir John Fortescue to Sir John Eliot," *English Historical Review* 75 (1960): 426–43; M. J. Mendle, "Politics and Political Thought, 1640–1642," in Russell, pp. 219–45; J. G. A. Pocock, *The Ancient Constitution and the Feudal Law* (Cambridge, 1957); and Corrine Comstock Weston, *English Constitutional Theory and the House of Lords* (London, 1965). J. P. Kenyon, *The Stuart Constitution, 1603–1688* (Cambridge, 1966), pp. 21–23, prints the relevant portions of the king's answer.

accountable to Parliaments consisting of estates united yearly, and having in that union *supremam potestatem.*"[14] One can hardly overstress the vital role of the Lords in such a scheme. Say underlined the natural need for a hereditary aristocracy in his letter to Winthrop, a notion almost demanded by the hierarchical world view of contemporaries. Many years later, he developed this point and the significance of the Lords more specifically in a letter to Lord Wharton: ". . . The peers of England, and their power and privileges in the House of Lords, they have been as the beam keeping both scales, king and people, in an even posture, without encroachments one upon another to the hurt and damage of both. Long experience hath made it manifest that they have preserved the just rights and liberties of the people against the tyrannical usurpation of kings, and have also as steps and stairs upheld the Crown from falling and being cast down upon the floor by the insolency of the multitude from the throne of government."[15] Of course, only a properly led and constituted House of Lords could fulfill this crucial function, which explains why Say wanted to unseat the bishops in 1640–42 and refused a summons to the "other house" of the Protectorate in 1657. Mixed monarchy stood not only as a political theory, however; it also provided the foundation for a practical program of reform. The Crown appeared to extend its power too far in the 1630s and, thereby, to overbalance the Ancient Constitution. In such a situation, peers and people naturally joined forces to resist such dangerous innovations, to punish those lords and commoners—even to their posterity—who offered "evil" advice to the monarch, to replace them with trustworthy men of stature, to assure that the sovereign power of king-in-Parliament met at frequent intervals, and, by these measures, to restore the balance of the Ancient Constitution.

While the leaders of the reform network worked out some sort of general strategy during the 1630s, they still had to decide upon specific tactics once Parliament started to meet. They lacked full agreement on detailed religious and political reforms. For example, Viscount Say and Lord Brooke stood committed to annual Parliaments and to the abolition of episcopacy, while the Earl of Bedford placed a heavy emphasis upon the role of the privy council and wanted to maintain a "primitive" church hierarchy. Say and

---

[14] *Collections,* Massachusetts Historical Society, ser. 5, no. 1 (Boston, 1871), p. 302; see Mendle in Russell, pp. 226–28.

[15] C. H. Firth, ed., "A Letter from Lord Saye and Sele to Lord Wharton, 29 Dec. 1657," *English Historical Review* 10 (1895): 106–7; cf. [William Fiennes and Nathaniel Fiennes], *Vindiciae Veritatis* ([London], 1654), wing F884.

Brooke almost emigrated to New England in 1636 and three years later took the radical step of refusing to swear the oath of allegiance to Charles I proffered to all peers at York upon the opening of the first Bishops' War.[16] Shortly after Parliament opened, the reform peers met together in London with their clients, friends, and relatives in the Commons to fix a set of tactics. In his unpublished memoirs, the then Lord Mandeville gives us a glimpse of these proceedings:

> The grievances of the kingdom, having been fully enumerated and declared, some of the members of both Houses had private meetings and consultations how to direct their parliamentary resolutions, in order to present redress and future security; and it was conceived by them to be the most certain way, and most consistent with the duty and allegiance of subjects, to fix their complaints and accusations upon evil counsellors, as the immediate actors, in the tragical miseries of the kingdom, rather then upon the personal failings and maladministrations in the king. Therefore it was resolved, that the House of Commons, as the grand inquest of the kingdom, should draw up such a remonstrance, as might be a faithful and lively representation to his majesty, of the deplorable estate of his kingdom, and might point out unto him, those that were most obnoxious and liable to censure; owning still such a due regard to his royal authority, as not to mention his name but with honour; and in the deepest sense of their former grievances, to render him thanks for the calling of this Parliament, as the happy omen to their present hopes of future redress and establishment.[17]

Peers and people would cooperate—each in their proper sphere—to reform the ills of the commonwealth. By preserving King Charles from aspersions, the network leaders hoped to preserve the proper place of the Crown in the theory of mixed monarchy, to gain the support of members who were not firmly allied with them, and to fill the places vacated by punishment of the Crown's evil servants. Old Parliament hands, they set to work at once.

In the Lords, reform peers registered their proxies, secured appointment to all important committees, renewed old and forged new political friendships, and made some preliminary moves, within their jurisdiction, against the clerk of the privy council and the secretaries of state.[18] In the Commons, a more dramatic debate on grievances

[16] Russell, p. 111; Thomas Hutchinson, *The History of the Colony and Province of Massachusetts-Bay*, ed. Lawrence S. Mayo (Boston, 1936), 1:410–13; and Marc L. Schwarz, "The Making of a Roundhead Peer: The Opposition of Viscount Saye and Sele in Pre–Civil War England," *Duquesne Review* 18 (1973): 19–33, and "Viscount Saye and Sele, Lord Brooke and Aristocratic Protest to the First Bishops' War," *Canadian Journal of History* 7 (1972): 17–36.

[17] Nalson, 2:689. Nalson prints other portions of Manchester's memoirs as well; see 2:206, 209, 272, 427.

[18] *Journals of the House of Lords* (London, 1767+), 4:86–89 (hereafter cited as *L.J.*); also see C. H. Firth, *The House of Lords during the Civil War* (London, 1910),

opened on Saturday, November 7, when Arthur Capel, a client of the Earl of Salisbury, presented a petition from Hertfordshire which listed a large number of abuses in church and state from the previous decade. One of the first of a new breed, it gathered a large number of specific grievances together under a few distinct points and purported to represent the views of the majority of the landed proprietors of the county. Many more would follow in the next two years. Once the theme was sounded, Harbottle Grimston—a client of Warwick, Sir Francis Seymour—a nephew of the Earl of Hertford and brother-in-law of Essex, and Sir Benjamin Rudyard—a client of the Earl of Pembroke—enlarged upon the grievances of other parts of the country in lengthy, powerful speeches.[19] Bedford's spokesman in the Commons, John Pym, summed up and gave a focus to this assault by espying in the events of the previous decade "a design to alter the kingdom both in religion and government." In religion, the Arminians had plotted at "a union between us and Rome." In government, there was "no imputation to be laid upon the king for any irregular actions, but upon them that he entrusted." Evil advisers corrupted the courts of justice, separated the king from his people, brought on a war with Scotland, kept Parliament from meeting, and molded "the Irish government into an illegal course, with intent to do [the same] here. . . ."[20] That afternoon, Sir John Clotworthy—a client of Warwick and a relative of Pym by marriage—enlarged upon the woes of Strafford's Ireland. Pym's interpretation of the 1630s as a period in which the ministers of the Crown attempted to introduce popery and arbitrary government sounded a theme that played repeatedly during the next two years and beyond.[21] It brought events into a coherent pattern, linked them

---

chap. 3; G. F. Trevallyn Jones, *Saw-Pit Wharton* (Sydney, 1967), chap. 4; and Snow, *Essex,* chap. 10. Bishop Warner's diary does not indicate the use of proxies for any crucial vote during the first six months of the Long Parliament; I, therefore, have not spelled out who held whose proxy for this period.

[19] Wallace Notestein, ed., *The Journals of Sir Simonds D'Ewes* (New Haven, Conn., 1923), pp. 4–7. Alderman Pennington presented a similar petition on November 9; city radicals learned the new techniques quickly (Notestein, p. 16). See Valerie Pearl, *London and the Outbreak of the Puritan Revolution* (Oxford, 1961), pp. 102, 108–9, 174–75, 210–11. Large numbers of petitions against individual clergymen also poured into Parliament. See Margaret Spufford, *Contrasting Communities* (Cambridge, 1974), pp. 232–38, for that against Bishop Wren and *Historical Manuscripts Commission,* 4th report, pp. 27 ff. (hereafter cited as *HMC*), for individual notices. Only a few of these broke into print.

[20] Kenyon, pp. 204–5; cf. John Pym, *A Speech Delivered in Parliament* (London, 1641), wing P4284.

[21] Notestein, p. 13. Pym repeated this theme in speeches at the impeachments of Strafford and Laud and at the summation of Strafford's trial in Westminster Hall (see John Pym, *Two Speeches* [London, 1641], wing P4302, *The Speech or Declaration*

to the prophecies made by puritan protesters in the 1620s and 1630s, and pointed the way to remedy those abuses so strongly felt by most members of the political nation. No spontaneous utterance, Pym's speech set the tone for the reform program in the Long Parliament.

The initiative seized by members of the network in the Commons on Saturday continued during the next week. On Tuesday, the House struck a committee of twenty-four to draw up a declaration on the state of the kingdom. On the next day, they appointed a smaller committee to prepare charges against the Earl of Strafford and sent Pym to the Lords to move the impeachment of Strafford for treason. The Lords not only obliged, but ordered his imprisonment in the Tower. An examination of the membership of these two important committees of the Commons reveals just how much members of the two Houses worked together. Originally, that for the impeachment of Strafford encompassed two clients of Bedford, Pym and Oliver St. John; one of Warwick, Sir John Clotworthy; a friend of Essex, William Strode; the eldest son of the Earl of Bristol, George Lord Digby; and a son of the Earl of Clare, Denzil Holles. All of these peers joined the anti-Buckingham faction in the 1620s. As proceedings against Strafford got under way, Grimston replaced Holles and two additional members joined their colleagues: Sir Walter Earle, a relative of Say by marriage; and John Hampden, an independent member of the network. These formed a cozy group. Pym, St. John, and Hampden had worked together recently on the ship money case; Pym and Clotworthy, and Earle and Strode were related by marriage.[22] All but Clotworthy had considerable experience in the Commons. Familiar faces also appeared when, on

---

[London, 1641], wing P4295, and *Mr. Pymms Speech to the Lords* [London, 1641], wing P4297; cf. Kenyon, pp. 206–7, 213–16).

[22] *Journal of the House of Commons* (London, 1742+), 2:26–27 (hereafter cited as *C.J.*); also see Mary Frear Keeler, " 'There are no remedies for many things but by a Parliament'; Some Opposition Committees, 1640," in *Conflict in Stuart England: Essays in Honour of Wallace Notestein,* ed. William Aiken and Basil Henning (London, 1960), pp. 134–35, 145, for the membership and importance of these committees. Rushworth reports that John Maynard, Geoffrey Palmer, John Selden, and Bulstrode Whitelocke were added to the impeachment committee on January 23, 1641. While they undoubtedly joined the committee, I was unable to trace the precise date in either D'Ewes's diary or in the *Journals;* it may represent the ellipsis in the latter on that date. The connections derive primarily from Mary Frear Keeler, *The Long Parliament, 1640–1641* (Philadelphia, 1954); D. Brunton and D. H. Pennington, *Members of the Long Parliament* (London, 1954); and John K. Gruenfelder, "The Election to the Short Parliament, 1640," in *Early Stuart Studies: Essays in Honor of David Harris Willson,* ed. Howard S. Reinmuth, Jr. (Minneapolis, 1970), pp. 180–230; the last of these systematically traces and estimates the patronage of individual peers. I would like to thank John Gruenfelder for his help in tracing and verifying such connections.

December 3, the Lords established a small committee to take preparatory examination of witnesses in the impeachment case. It consisted of the Earls of Bath, Bedford, Essex, and Hertford, Viscount
Say, and Lords Brooke, Mandeville, Robartes, Savile, and
Wharton—all members of or allied to the network at this time.[23]

Everyone on the Commons' impeachment committee except Holles and Strode also sat on the committee of twenty-four. Several
independent members joined the larger committee—Sir John Culpepper, John Crew, George Peard, and John Selden—but a host of
clients and relatives of peers filled out its ranks: Henry Bagshaw, a
client of Savile; Sir Thomas Barrington, a client of Warwick; Henry
Belasyse, a son of Viscount Fauconberg; Capel; Sir Miles Fleetwood, a client of Lord Cottington; Sir Robert Harley, a friend of
Essex who solicited his support in the election; Sir Peter Heyman, a
client of the Earl of Northumberland; Edward Kirton, a client of Sir
Francis Seymour; William Pierrepont, a son of the Earl of Kingston;
Rudyard; Seymour; Sir John Strangways, a client of Bristol; and Sir
Thomas Widdrington, a client of Strafford. Significantly, all but two
of the sixteen members singled out by Mary Frear Keeler as managers of the Commons in 1640 sat on the committee of twenty-four.
The exceptions were Sir Christopher Wray, an independent member
married to a Cecil and father-in-law to Sir Henry Vane the younger,
and Geoffrey Palmer, a vigorous lawyer who possibly sat as a client
of the new Earl of Exeter.[24] Aside from Cottington and Strafford,
the noblemen named above pursued the policies of the network in
the early stages of the Long Parliament, if not before. Some proved
very shaky allies in time. The most recent converts, Fauconberg,
Kingston, Northumberland, Pembroke, and Salisbury, had personal
reasons for hating either Strafford or the policies of the 1630s.[25]

---

[23] *L.J.*, 4:103. Earlier a larger committee was established for this purpose, but the
smaller, more easily managed one superseded it (ibid., p. 99). Bishop Williams made a
long speech that justified cooperation between the Lords and the Commons in
examining witnesses; see John Hacket, *Scrinia reserata* ([London], 1693), pp. 151–53.

[24] The connections derive primarily from Keeler, Brunton and Pennington, and
Gruenfelder. Had not the second Earl of Exeter died in July 1640 and been succeeded
by his nephew, one could be almost certain that Palmer sat for Stamford as his client.
For the sixteen managers, see Keeler in Aiken and Henning, p. 144.

[25] Fauconberg and his son nurtured a long-standing hatred of Strafford. Kingston
was fined £2,000 in 1632 for refusing to pay coronation knighthood fees and Salisbury
was fined £20,000 in 1636—later reduced to £3,000—for his father's enclosures from
the royal forest in Brigstock Park. Northumberland and Pembroke were pro-French,
disliked the Scottish wars, and—most important perhaps—lusted to replace Laud and
Strafford in office and influence. See Clarendon, 1:161–62, passim; Brian Manning,
"The Aristocracy and the Downfall of Charles I," in his *Politics, Religion, and the
English Civil War* (London, 1973); Snow, *Essex*, pp. 205, 211, 239–40; Lawrence
Stone, *Fortune and Family* (Oxford, 1973), pp. 119–20; C. V. Wedgwood, *Thomas*

Bedford, Brooke, Essex, Hertford, Mandeville, Say, and Warwick—all network leaders but Hertford—ranked among those
twelve peers who, in August 1640, petitioned Charles I to call a
Parliament. Bristol, Savile, and Wharton added their weight to this
request at a later date. Bath, Clare, and Robartes voted for redress
of grievances before granting supply in the Short Parliament, thereby
showing public support for the network. Many of the ties stretched
back to the attempted impeachment of Buckingham in 1626—some
even further. If Bedford headed the "country" and Essex attached
courtiers to the cause, Say proved himself the master tactician time
and again.[26] As well as taking a lead, Bedford, Essex, and Say
collected long-standing political debts in the early stages of the Long
Parliament. They came not alone, but with those men they helped to
elect to the Commons. Within less than a month, the network
leaders seized the initiative in both Houses, dominated crucial committees, and began to put their program into effect.

Religious grievances stood high on the list. However, they posed a
thorny and potentially inflammatory issue that might arouse the lower
orders of society. When John Williams, Bishop of Lincoln, returned
from the Tower to take his seat at the request of the Lords, rejoicing
throngs of common people welcomed him. Led by the powerful in
their coaches and the established on horseback, even larger crowds,
however, turned out for the triumphal entry into London of those
more radical religious martyrs, Henry Burton and William Prynne.
Neither hostile nor friendly witnesses escaped the significance of the
latter event, for it more than symbolized the use of popular pressure
for religious reformation, a unity of upper, middle, and lower orders
in one cause.[27] On December 11, Alderman Pennington marched at
the head of a crowd of 1,500 people to present the London root and
branch petition to the Commons. Attached to this plea for abolition

---

Wentworth, First Earl of Strafford, 1593–1641: A Revaluation (London, 1961), pp.
106–7, 270–71, 886; and Zagorin, pp. 54, 70–71, 202, 211–12.

[26] Jones, appendix 1; also see Manning, *Politics*, pp. 37–51; Snow, *Essex*, chaps.
5–10; Vernon Snow, "The Arundel Case, 1626," *Historian* 26 (1964): 332–47; Lawrence Stone, *The Crisis of the Aristocracy, 1558–1641* (Oxford, 1965), chap. 3; and
Zagorin, pp. 90–104. One can exaggerate these differences; Bedford had contacts with
numerous court officials and Warwick's younger brother Henry Rich, Earl of Holland,
was a classic courtier. With some misgivings, I have not included Holland in the
network; although he sometimes cooperated with the reform peers, his actions in the
House strike me as too ambiguous to place him even in the category of an ally. For
the events of 1640–41, I draw heavily without specific reference upon Manning,
Zagorin, S. R. Gardiner (*History of England* [London, 1883–84], vol. 9), and C. V.
Wedgwood (*The King's Peace, 1637–1641* [London, 1955], and her *Strafford*).

[27] [William Prynne], *A New Discovery of the Prelates Tyranny* (London, 1641), pt.
2, *A Briefe Relation*, pp. 114–15; Clarendon, 1:246, 268–69; *HMC*, De L'Isle and
Dudley, 6:346; and *HMC*, 9th report, 2:499.

of the church hierarchy were some ten to twenty thousand signatures. Most men signed their names with gravity and a sense of commitment in the early 1640s, before repetition dulled their sense of responsibility in such things. The combination of written weight and active, orderly demonstration outside the Houses of Parliament ushered in a new, effective, organized mode of putting pressure on both Lords and Commons. At first, however, use of the "monster" petition and of popular demonstrations was confined to the radicals. The root and branch petition probably helped to produce one desired result. Within a week of its presentation, the Commons finally impeached Archbishop Laud for treason.[28] Nor could the matter of church reform lie dormant, for it contained political implications of great magnitude as well as eternal significance.

Although the reform lords gained the initiative in their House, a solid group of spiritual peers stood as an obstacle to their ascendancy, a bloc of votes which inclined toward finding Strafford innocent of treason. An attempt to transform the widespread dislike of the Arminians into an attack either upon episcopacy or upon the temporal powers of the bishops appeared tempting. Either course, if successful, removed the votes of the "prelates" from the Lords. Say and Brooke favored the former program, while Bedford and Essex supported the latter. The issue raised its head again in the Commons on January 13 when Sir Edward Dering presented a root and branch petition from Kent; Sir William Masham, one of Warwick's clients, a similar one from Essex; and Sir Philip Parker, one of the Barnardiston clan, a milder version from the ministers of Suffolk. The House, however, postponed debate on episcopacy to Monday, January 25, 1641. In anticipation, Sir Robert Harley introduced a more moderate petition and remonstrance on the morning of Saturday, January 23. Signed by nearly a thousand pastors, it called for considerable changes in the church hierarchy, but preserved the name and some of the traditional functions of the bishops.[29] Just as the alternative methods of reforming church government came before the Commons with considerable indications of support, King Charles decided to take a firm stand on religion and dashed any hopes for a smooth passage.

[28] The root and branch petition is printed in Gardiner, *Constitutional Documents*, pp. 137–44; see Pearl, pp. 212–16. The case against Laud was not yet complete, however.

[29] Notestein, pp. 244–50; Pearl, pp. 213, 215n.; and William A. Shaw, *A History of the English Church during the Civil Wars and under the Commonwealth, 1640–1660* (London, 1900), 1:15–26. Historians have given various interpretations to Dering's role; see Derek Hirst, "The Defection of Sir Edward Dering, 1640–1641," *Historical Journal* 15 (1972): 193–208, and the studies cited therein.

On the Saturday before debate on episcopacy was scheduled to open in the Commons, the king addressed members of both Houses in the banqueting house at Whitehall. According to Sir Simonds D'Ewes, who attended, he "spake very loud."[30] One wonders if he spoke very wisely. Charles opened by renewing his request for funds to pay the armies in the north and the navy. He continued by drawing attention to "distractions that are at this present occasioned through the connivence of Parliament," blaming these upon "some men that, more maliciously than ignorantly, will put no difference between reformation and alteration of government." Shrewdly, King Charles expressed a desire to reform all abuses in "church and commonwealth" by restoring "all things to the best and purest times, as they were in the time of Queen Elizabeth." Two "rocks" somewhat blocked the road to reformation and reconciliation, however, the triennial bill passed by the House of Commons and religious affairs, especially recent threats to episcopacy. The king believed that the bill trenched too strongly upon his prerogative, suggested that his councillors would produce a version more suitable to his honor, and promised to consent to a bill so amended. More adamant at removing the other "rock," Charles deplored disturbances of church services and lashed out against "some very strange (I know not what term to give them) petitions, given in in the names of divers counties, against the present established government of the church, and of great threatenings against the bishops, that they will make them to be but ciphers, or at least their voices to be taken away." In one blow, he cast aspersions upon both the root and branch petitions from the counties and upon the more moderate ministers' remonstrance and blamed malicious members of Parliament for raising these troubles. Protesting his willingness to redress past wrongs and even to place some limitations upon episcopal power, King Charles firmly drew the line beyond which religious reform must not pass. "But this must not be understood, that I shall any way consent that their voices in Parliament should be taken away; for in all the times of my predecessors, since the Conquest and before, they have enjoyed it, and I am bound to maintain them in it, as one of the fundamental constitutions of this kingdom."[31] Bishops must remain full members of the House of Lords, for in voices the king included votes.

Since the majority of the members of Parliament worked to restore the Ancient Constitution to its pristine purity, the king's stance

---

[30] Notestein, p. 279.
[31] Nalson, 1:735–36; also printed in Kenyon, pp. 19–20.

seemed to be planted on firm ground. In reality, however, Charles made a grave mistake. He staked out his position too firmly before debate opened in the Commons, cut down his field of maneuver very considerably by lumping moderate and radical reformers together, foolishly berated members of Parliament, and—by his timing and temerity—indicated in advance an unwillingness to listen to the advice of Parliament on this important issue. Not a radical by any means, Sir Simonds D'Ewes noted: "This speech filled most of us with sad apprehensions of future evils in case his majesty should be irremovably fixed to uphold the bishops in their wealth, pride, and tyranny."[32] For once, his reaction probably reflected that of the members of the Commons in general and of many Lords, as well.

On the following Monday, knights of the shire presented root and branch petitions from the counties of Bedford, Buckingham, Cambridge, Cheshire, Gloucester, Hertford, Suffolk, Surrey, Sussex, and Warwick. Countrymen had taken a lesson from London. This meant that at least eight hundred clergymen, nearly one-third of the counties in England, and thousands of London citizens had lent their weight to petitions which ran counter to the position taken by King Charles. So did the vast majority of those members who spoke in the Commons when debate over episcopacy opened a fortnight later. Not one defender of the bishops supported the Laudians or opposed commitment of the ministers' remonstrance. Instead, they expressed a willingness to cut the wealth and temporal power of the church hierarchy, a sentiment more vociferously pressed by supporters of the root and branch petitions. After two days of fiery debate, the House voted 180 to 145 to send both the London petition and the ministers' remonstrance to the committee of twenty-four, augmented for this purpose by Nathaniel Fiennes, Robert Holborne, Denzil Holles, Geoffrey Palmer, Sir Thomas Roe, and Sir Henry Vane the younger. The religious radicals gained, since Fiennes, Holles, and Vane outweighed the other three in both social prestige and political ability.[33] When church reform arose again in the Commons on March 10, the House voted overwhelmingly to prepare a bill which would remove the legislative and judicial power of the bishops in the Lords. On the next day, they decided unanimously to prohibit the exercise of any civil judicial power, including the commission of peace, by any clergyman. Eventually these provisions melded into a single bill passed unanimously by the Commons on the first of

[32] Notestein, p. 281.
[33] Ibid., pp. 282–83, 334–43, and *C.J.*, 2:80–81. Fuller accounts of some speeches appeared in pamphlets and were printed in Nalson, 1:748–72; and John Rushworth, ed., *Historical Collections* (London, 1659–1701), 4:170–86.

May.[34] While dissension in the Commons over episcopacy may well have augured the eventual breakup of the reform network and alliance, it had an even more profound immediate impact. The Commons, after all, firmly ignored the stand taken by King Charles and, united, pressed ahead to push through a major change in church government.

After the king delivered his banqueting hall speech, the reform lords faced a terrible dilemma. In order to keep peers and people together they had to ensure the conviction of Strafford and carry through a reformation of church and commonwealth. In order to gain office for themselves and for their clients, friends, and relations, they had to win the confidence of King Charles. Unless handled with the greatest of care, the one task jeopardized the success of the other. Moving cautiously but firmly, the Lords amended and passed the bill for frequent Parliaments on February 5, 1641, adding to it an obligation upon the lord chancellor, or keeper, and upon the Lords, or any twelve peers, to send out writs for a Parliament if the Crown failed to act in time. Thus they added two steps between the Crown and the sheriffs, an amendment which probably strengthened the original bill and one that certainly reflected the theory of mixed monarchy. In addition, they passed a subsidy to provide pay for the Scottish and English armies in the north. After some pressure, Charles appeared in the Lords on February 16, gave his assent to both bills, and used the occasion to deliver another rather impolitic speech.[35] Upon the initiative of the Commons, both Houses responded by asking the king to join with them in commanding the people to celebrate the passing of the triennial act "by public fires and ringing bells."[36] Shortly afterward, King Charles finally indicated some public confidence in the network leaders and their allies by naming the Earls of Bedford, Bristol, Essex, and Hertford, Viscount Say, and Lords Mandeville and Savile to his privy council on February 19. The Earl of Warwick joined his colleagues there just a few days later.[37] At last, it looked as though the careful tactics of the network would succeed. They removed one "rock" entirely, but three additional ones still stood, the impeachment of Strafford, the role of the bishops, and the establishment of peace with the Scots.

[34] Notestein, pp. 465–70, and *C.J.*, 2:131.

[35] Harleian MSS 6424, fols. 10, 12; *L.J.*, 4:145, 147, 150, 152; Conrad Russell, "The Authorship of the Bishop's Diary of the House of Lords in 1641," *Bulletin of the Institute of Historical Research* 41 (1968): 229; and Nalson, 1:776. Reform peers dominated the committee struck to make additions to the triennial bill.

[36] Harleian MSS 6424, fol. 22r, see 20–22. According to Rushworth, the bonfires were lighted and the bells rung (Rushworth, 4:192).

[37] Clarendon, 1:259; see Manning, *Politics*, p. 55.

King Charles attended the Lords on February 24, 1641, to hear formal charges read against Strafford; he indicated his sympathies when his servant appeared at the Bar by putting "off his hat graciously."[38] After the Commons' representatives had presented their articles of impeachment for treason, Strafford's counsel had answered each article, and the accused had withdrawn, "the king said that he had done him no wrong for ought he knew, and that he had spoken all truth, so far as concerned him. . . . And so the king telling the Lords that he would not be at their debate, but at the trials for treason, left them."[39] To overcome any initiative lost by this display, Viscount Say moved a repetition of the process and "the Lords, taking all that was done in the king's presence to be no act of the House, commanded the Earl of *Strafford* to be brought to the bar, and appointed the Lord Keeper to demand of him his answer in writing. . . ."[40] Before Strafford appeared a second time, however, Lord Mandeville moved that the bishops withdraw from the trial at this point. He received vigorous support from the Earls of Arundel and Manchester, Viscount Say, Lords Paget and Brooke, and "divers others," but the prelates stood upon their privileges. Most likely fearing that this thrust would lead to a full-scale attack upon the right of spiritual peers to sit in the House, Bishop Williams parried by suggesting that he and his colleagues withdraw voluntarily, "it being *in agitatione causae sanguinis*; and the lords the bishops said they would withdraw when the Earl of Strafford came in with his answer to the Bar."[41] By removing the episcopal bloc from the trial, Williams proved himself a valuable ally of the reform peers. Two days later, the Lords—upon a motion by the Earl of Warwick, supported by Lords Paget, Brooke, and Andover—sent a delegation to the king to request that all ecclesiastical offices of the Archbishop of Canterbury be sequestered. Three days after that, the House finally ordered the imprisonment of Laud on a charge of impeachment for treason and, upon a motion by Say, set up a large committee, chaired by Bishop Williams, to examine all innovations in religion. Williams was rewarded. Within a week he reciprocated by defending Say's religious orthodoxy in the

[38] Harleian MSS 6424, fol. 26r. For the trial of Strafford, see Clayton Roberts, *The Growth of Responsible Government in Stuart England* (Cambridge, 1966), pp. 77–119; Conrad Russell, "The Theory of Impeachment in the Trial of Strafford," *English Historical Review* 80 (1965): 30–50; and Zagorin, pp. 209–26.

[39] Harleian MSS 6424, fol. 39r; see *L.J.*, 4:171.

[40] *L.J.*, 4:171, and Harleian MSS 6424, fol. 52v.

[41] Harleian MSS 6424, fol. 39r; *L.J.*, 4:171; and Hacket, pp. 153–60. Originally raised in the Commons by Oliver St. John, this issue had come up earlier in the Lords, as well (see *L.J.*, 4:150, 165; Harleian MSS 6424, fol. 13; and *C.J.*, 2:26).

House.[42] On the day on which the Lords made final arrangements for the trial, some supporter of Strafford raised the question of whether or not the bishops could vote by proxy in the impeachment case, a move that ill accorded with the standing orders of the House since the proxy reform of 1626. Reform peers, however, dominated the committee struck to consider this and related problems; the House, following their advice, decided on March 20 that all lords would forbear appointing proxies for the trial.[43] Through careful maneuvering, the reform peers managed to remove the bishops, just as they earlier excluded all lords giving testimony in the case, from the ranks of those who would decide Strafford's fate. Having prepared the way for a verdict of guilty, they could feel quite secure when the trial formally opened on March 22, 1641 in Westminster Hall, a building large enough to accommodate the members of both Houses, with their clients, friends, and relatives from the Commons in attendance as added weight. However, the network leaders did not count upon the skill of Strafford or the conscience of King Charles.

As the trial proceeded, the network faced its first test under severe pressure and threatened to split apart. Strafford's defense caused a number of lords to waver in their resolve to find him guilty of treason. The king manipulated such changes of conscience by holding forth the alluring bait of office to those, including Bedford and Pym, who would assure his income, preserve episcopacy, and save the life of Strafford. In the mid-seventeenth century, the Lords still retained a great deal of latitude in impeachment cases, especially in fixing the sentence. Fearful that Strafford might escape death, Sir Arthur Haselrig created the first break in the network when he moved, on April 10, that attainder be substituted for impeachment. Despite the opposition of Pym, Hampden, Strode, and Earle at the first and second readings of this motion, the Commons followed Haselrig. Bristol and Digby, his son, broke with the reform alliance and opposed attainder even more vociferously, as did Savile. Faced by a serious loss of leadership in the Commons, Pym came reluctantly to support attainder, while St. John vigorously pushed it forward.[44] Having tasted power for a change, the radicals kept up their pressure outside Parliament.

[42] Harleian MSS 6424, fols. 39v–45r. It was upon the last of these occasions that Say delivered his vicious personal attack upon the character of Archbishop Laud.
[43] *L.J.*, 4:189–91; *HMC*, House of Lords, 10:8–9; and Snow, "Arundel Case" (n. 26 above). Snow discusses the proxy reform of 1626 and the changes to the standing orders of the House appear in the *HMC*, House of Lords.
[44] *C.J.*, 2:118–25; Sir Simonds D'Ewes, Diary of the House of Commons for

A great multitude of London citizens, led by three captains of the city trained bands, marched to Westminster and presented the Commons with a petition of grievances on April 21, 1641. Drawing attention to the fact that "incendiaries of the kingdoms and other notorious offenders remain unpunished, the affairs of the church—notwithstanding many petitions concerning it and long debate about it—remain unsettled, the papists still armed, the laws against them not executed, some of the more active of them still at court, priests and Jesuits not yet banished, the Irish popish army not yet disbanded," and trade decaying daily, the petitioners agreed that all of these things "make us fear that there may be practices now in hand to hinder the birth of your great endeavours, and that we lie under some more dangerous plot than we can discover." Rumors of plots were flying around London, but had made little impact on the members of Parliament, as yet. Addressed to both Houses, the petition claimed a subscription of 20,000 "men of good rank and quality."[45] In reaction, King Charles "immediately forbade the City authorities to countenance this petition or any other similarly subscribed."[46] The Commons, however, learned another lesson. On the same day, they passed the attainder of Strafford by a vote of 204 to fifty-nine. Within a fortnight, they petitioned the king to disarm papists, remove papists from court, and disband the Irish army and they passed the bill "to restrain bishops, and others in holy orders, from intermeddling with secular affairs," including voting in the Lords.[47] Pressures from above and below now centered upon the Lords, whose task of balancing king and people became extremely delicate.

The Lords delayed a first reading of the attainder bill until April 26. By then, Bedford and Hertford had joined Bristol and Savile in an attempt to preserve the life of Strafford in return for high office. Convinced that Crown and Lords should stand against the people to

---

1640–45, British Library, Harleian MSS 163, fols. 27r, 28r, 43r–53r; and Zagorin, pp. 220–22. It is apparent from D'Ewes's account that Pym and Hampden lost a number of crucial votes related to the attainder and that St. John joined those pushing for attainder quite early in the debate. In November 19, 1640, the Commons had established a committee "to search the record of attainder in the *King's Bench,* in such manner, and at such time, as they shall think fit, for the furtherance of the charge in hand against the Earl of Strafford" (John Rushworth, *The Tryal of Thomas, Earl of Strafford* [London, 1680], p. 7); I wish to thank Mr. Christian Norman for bringing this reference to my attention.

[45] *Petition of London to Parliament* (London, 1641), B.L. 669 f4.13; also in Rushworth, *Historical Collections,* 4:233–34. John Aston printed this petition and pirated editions of the protestation in May 1641. For its career in Parliament, see *C.J.,* 2:127–28, and *L.J.,* 4:226–27.

[46] Pearl, p. 216.

[47] *C.J.,* 2:125–31, and Zagorin, p. 222.

preserve the kingdom from terrible divisions, Bedford and Hertford tried to draw Essex to their new position, only to have Essex reply with the firm rebuff: "Stone-dead hath no fellow."[48] A group of peers, headed by Essex and Say, appeared willing to join with the people to force the execution of Strafford through the Lords and on King Charles. Despite the vociferous objections of Bristol and Savile, the bill of attainder had its second reading in the upper House on the next day. Adding tension to an already troubled situation, the king gave an equivocal answer to that request to remove all papists from court brought on by the London petition and he attempted to move extra troops into the Tower. Breaks in Bedford's clientage, apparent on the second reading of the attainder bill in the Commons, became more public on April 29 when, at a joint meeting of the committees of both Houses in Westminster Hall, Oliver St. John justified the legality of attainder for treason and vigorously called for the execution of Strafford.[49] On the same day, rioters gave a rude, negative reply to the king's speech on the dangers of popery by attacking the lodgings of the Spanish ambassador. On Saturday, May 1, 1641, King Charles tried to save Strafford in a speech to Parliament. Bedford—who favored an address by the king—suffered an attack of smallpox the night before and died on May 9. Unable to draw upon the Earl's advice for the content of the speech, Charles turned to Viscount Say and "old subtlety" apparently moved the king to say that he could not in conscience agree to the execution of Strafford.[50] By reducing the argument to inflexible, personal morality, Charles undermined the careful defense built up by Strafford and made an attempt to defeat the bill in the Lords much more difficult. On Sunday, Captain Billingsley ànd Sir John Suckling led a desperate attempt to rescue Strafford from the Tower. By giving his consent to this plot, King Charles provided the final weapon which would ensure the execution of his servant.[51] Over that same weekend, the peers who stood against Strafford most probably worked upon the conscience of John Pym to ensure success for their plan.

At this point, Pym occupied a precarious position in Parliament. During the past three weeks, his ascendancy in the Commons suffered several direct challenges and at least one serious loss. On the fateful day of the first reading of the attainder bill in the

[48] Clarendon, 1:320, see pp. 318–21. The Scots, of course, also wanted Strafford dead.
[49] Rushworth, *Tryal*, pp. 675–705; for the most striking passages, see pp. 702–3.
[50] Wedgwood, *Strafford*, p. 371.
[51] Manning, *Politics*, p. 64.

Lords—when Essex refused to support Bedford's compromise—Pym absented himself from the Commons. Indeed, he probably engaged in widespread negotiations throughout that week. Carefully laid plans, however, came to naught now that Bedford, his patron and the source of much of his power, lay dying. Unable or unwilling to face the consequences of throwing his lot with those who had gone over to the king, Pym at last joined with the adamant network peers, the city radicals, and the inflexible members of the Commons to force through the attainder.[52] Events moved quickly thereafter.

On Monday, May 3, crowds gathered at Westminster to "greet" members of Parliament, some lords rather roughly, and reminded them to execute "justice" upon "incendiaries." In the Commons, Alderman Pennington appropriately drew attention to the armed following of Suckling. The reliable Clotworthy followed to expand this disclosure into the unfolding of a widespread army plot.[53] Only after the House ordered the sergeant at arms "to suffer no man to go forth, without leave" and the speaker reported on the king's address, did Pym rise to the floor. Confident again, he delivered a powerful rebuke to King Charles's appeal for the life of Strafford, linked the army plot to his earlier plot theory of the 1630s, and concluded by suggesting that the Commons join together to express their "allegiance to the king's person and legal prerogative, and bind ourselves to maintain the liberties of the subjects."[54] Henry Martin, Strode, and Holles stood up in turn to underline this last suggestion and a committee, consisting of these four plus Barrington, Fiennes, John Glynne, Hampden, Harley, John Maynard, and Sir Philip Stapleton, withdrew from the House to compose the appropriate document. It reported back to the House and, after some discussion, met again with the addition of Lord Falkland, Selden, and John Vaughan.[55] This time the committee's report, the protestation, proved acceptable to the Commons.

[52] *C.J.*, 2:128. Without citing much evidence, Wedgwood variously dates Pym's renunciation of Bedford's patronage to April 27 or 28, 1641 (*Strafford*, pp. 369–70, and *King's Peace*, pp. 420–21). Since St. John held royal office, he could leave Bedford's clientage both earlier and more easily than Pym. Pym's vigorous actions on Monday point to a switch of position, and possibly of patron, over the weekend. He may have strengthened his long-standing relationship with Warwick, one not as close as that with Bedford. As late as July 8, 1634, Pym felt it necessary to give advice to Warwick indirectly by writing to Sir Nathaniel Rich; see Hunts R.O., ddM/28/7/31; I wish to thank Conrad Russell for bringing this point and source to my attention.

[53] Gardiner, *History*, 9:351.

[54] *C.J.*, 2:132, and *Verney Papers*, ed. John Bruce (Camden Society, London, 1845), 31:66–67.

[55] *C.J.*, 2:131–32, and *Verney Papers*, pp. 67–68. Glynne, Vaughan, Falkland, and Maynard look like independent members, but Stapleton was a cousin of Wharton. Falkland, of course, vigorously supported the attainder of Strafford.

All members present took the oath it contained:

I, A. B., do, in the presence of God, promise, vow and protest to maintain
and defend, as far as lawfully I may with my life, power and estate, the true
reformed Protestant religion expressed in the doctrine of the Church of
England, against all Popery and popish innovation within this realm, contrary to the said doctrine, and according to the duty of my allegiance, I will
maintain and defend His Majesty's royal person and estate, as also the
power and privilege of Parliaments, the lawful rights and liberties of the
subjects, and every person that shall make this Protestation in whatsoever
he shall do, in the lawful pursuance of the same; and to my power, as far
lawfully I may, I will oppose, and by all good ways and means endeavour to
bring to condign punishment all such as shall by force, practice, counsels,
plots, conspiracies or otherwise do anything to the contrary in this present
Protestation contained: and further, that I shall in all just and honourable
ways endeavour to preserve the union and peace betwixt the three kingdoms
of England, Scotland, and Ireland, and neither for hope, fear or any other
respects, shall relinquish this promise, vow and protestation.[56]

A masterly stroke, the rite of taking this oath in the face of an army
plot and of the king's breach of the privilege of Parliament in his
speech on the previous Saturday bound members of the Commons
together in what preachers would call a covenant with the Lord.
This compact tied members together at a time of extreme anxiety
and restored unity to the reform network. Its very language en-
visioned an extension of the oath to other people as well.[57] As a
final touch, the Commons added a preamble which laid out that
interpretation of the 1630s announced by Pym in his speech of
November 7, 1640. Pym regained his initiative in a dramatic way.

While the Commons sat behind closed doors, pondering the revelation of the army plot and taking the protestation, the Lords
concerned themselves with the crowds gathered outside. King
Charles, through them, commanded that "both Houses do take into
their consideration some speedy course, to settle peace, and prevent
these tumults."[58] Unable to hold a joint conference with the Commons on this matter and faced with vocal petitioners from London,

[56] Gardiner, *Constitutional Documents*, p. 156, see pp. 155–56. The combination of
the preamble, which gave a potted version of the network program, and the oath,
which committed those who took it to that program, made the protestation into a
marvelous propaganda device.

[57] For a wide range of contemporary reaction, see Robert Baillie, *The Letters and
Journals of Robert Baillie*, ed. David Laing (Edinburgh, 1841), 1:351–52; John Geree,
Vindiciae Voti (London, 1641); [Henry Burton], *The Protestation Protested* (London,
1641); *A Learned and Witty Conference Lately betwixt a Protestant and a Papist*
(London, 1641), wing L799; and *Certaine Queries of Some Tender Conscienced Chris-
tians about the Late Protestation* ([London], 1641), wing C1741. Baillie at first hoped
that it was "in substance our Scottish covenant," but on the next day reported: "The
bishops has put their hand to it, and we like it all the worse" (ibid.).

[58] *L.J.*, 4:232.

the Lords began to investigate the army plot. They heard the petitioners and commanded the Earl of Newport, as Master of the Ordnance, to take up his charge at the Tower and to carry out such further actions there as he deemed appropriate.[59] From Charles they wrung an acknowledgment that he had given Billingsley orders to enter the Tower with 100 men on the previous day. Giving in to pressure, the king commanded Newport to go to his post at the Tower and to discharge the men commanded by Captain Billingsley. Having grasped the initiative in military affairs, the Lords established a committee to investigate the recent events at the Tower.[60] Within a week, Parliament followed through by ordering the ports closed and by dispatching members from both Houses to various parts of the kingdom to scotch any attempt at a concerted army plot.[61]

On Tuesday, May 4, the upper House opened dramatically when the "Earl of Stamford wished the Bishops of Carlisle, Bristol, and Rochester to give God thanks for our great deliverance, which is greater than that from the Gunpowder Treason. . . . "[62] After hearing a report about the Tower, the Lords again debated the attainder of Strafford. Faced now with a bill to remove clergymen from all secular offices already passed by the Commons, Bishop Williams got the spiritual peers to agree not to vote on the attainder. In a joint conference, the Lords pointed out that the only hindrance to their passage of the attainder sprang from the crowds of people gathered outside—they would not even appear to give in to such threats. In turn, the Commons presented the protestation to the upper House. Assembled again, the Lords voted "*nemine contradicente,* that every lord of this House will take this protestation."[63] Protestant peers complied on the spot. Cornelius Burges then dispersed the throngs by reading the protestation to them and assuring them that the Lords and the Commons had taken its oath.[64] The protestation completed the demoralization of those lords who wished to save Strafford—many absented themselves shortly thereafter—and it kept Catholic peers away from the House for some

[59] House of Lords Record Office, Manuscript Journals of the House of Lords, 16:218–19.

[60] Ibid., 16:220–23, and Harleian MSS 6424, fols. 58–61.

[61] *L.J.*, 4:236–45, and *C.J.*, 2:136–43. Contemporaries feared an outbreak of armed conflict at this time. In an initiative coming from the Commons, both Houses requested Charles to make the Earl of Essex Lord Lieutenant of Yorkshire; since the king granted this favor, there was no militia dispute in May 1641.

[62] Harleian MSS 6424, fol. 58v.

[63] *L.J.*, 4:234, and Harleian MSS 6424, fols. 58v–61r.

[64] Rushworth, *Historical Collections*, 4:250, see pp. 240–50.

time.[65] Combined with the shock of the army plot, it provided the network leaders with an opportunity to regain a firm ascendency in Parliament, and that at a time when their initiative had nearly slipped away. The oath bound peers and people more closely together in one common cause. Soon it would spread through the parishes of London and eventually large numbers of men across the nation would subscribe their names in token of having taken the protestation.[66] It committed common people to the parliamentary cause on the eve of civil war.

The consequences of the renewed strength of the reform network made a more immediate impact in Parliament, however. It came in the passage of the attainder of Strafford and of the bill to prevent the dissolution of the Long Parliament without its own consent. Mobs, delegations from Parliament, and a backroom twisting of the king's conscience forced Charles to give his consent to both bills on May 10. Strafford went to the block on May 12, 1641, three days after the death of Bedford; before the end of that month Say became Master of the Court of Wards and Hertford governor of the Prince of Wales. In July, King Charles elevated Essex to the position of Lord Chamberlain. At last, it seemed the king had some good advisers.[67] Even before these things happened, however, the network leaders strengthened their grip of the management of Parliament by creating a joint committee, specifically sworn to secrecy, to investigate the army plot. On May 5, the Lords established a committee, consisting of the Earls of Bath, Essex, March, and Warwick, Viscount Say, and Lords Howard of Charlton, Howard of Escrick, Mandeville, Paget, and Wharton—or any four of them, to "take examinations upon oath of such persons as shall be presented to them by members of the House of Commons" as accomplices in the army plot.[68] To meet with these Lords, the Commons selected a committee consisting of Clotworthy, Fiennes, Hampden, Holles, Pym, and Strode—

---

[65] Catholic peers were allowed to take a modified form of the protestation on May 10, 1641, ironically just before the announcement of the royal consent to the attainder of Strafford (*L.J.*, 4:243). The *Journals* record many absences from May 5 onward.

[66] The Commons ordered the protestation printed on May 5, 1641, specifically to spread it across the countryside (*C.J.*, 2:134–35). On January 19, 1642, the speaker of the Commons sent out a letter to the sheriffs enjoining the taking of the protestation oath (*C.J.*, 2:389). Returns exist for more than half of the counties of England (*HMC*, 5th report, pp. 120–34). Almost all of the petitions addressed either to the king or to Parliament from 1642 contain references to or wording from the protestation. This is true of all of the fifty-two printed petitions from June through September 1642 that I have examined.

[67] Snow, *Essex*, pp. 267–68.

[68] *L.J.*, 4:235. On May 11, a committee was established to open and inspect all foreign letters (*L.J.*, 4:245).

Stapleton was added two days later.[69] No strangers here, it formed
an interlocking directorate of the network leaders. The Commons'
portion grew into the famous committee of six or seven which,
according to Lotte Glow, the reform leaders employed repeatedly in
their management of the House. One suspects that the Lords'
portion operated in a similar fashion.[70] As a whole, the committee
created an official forum where secret plans could be laid, tactics
mapped out, for keeping peers and people together.

If the outbreak of civil war in 1642 demonstrated the eventual
failure of the strategy and philosophy of the leaders of this aristocratic network, the reform legislation of 1641 stood as a tribute to some
of its members. The threat of violence almost broke up the network
in the spring of 1641—it detached allies like Bristol, but forced
through the attainder of Strafford. The execution of Strafford and
the revivification of the network in May 1641 created political debts
for future payment, as well as lasting hostility. The city radicals,
who whipped up popular demonstrations which helped to force the
hand of King Charles, expected religious reform of the root and
branch variety as their price. Such was one of the necessities of a
politics based upon reciprocal relationships. Those appeals to the
common people, taken up in petitions and enlivened by offering the
protestation oath in London, spread more easily to the countryside
when the printing of petitions and of the protestation began in
earnest in May 1641. These developments, however, belong to
another phase of the history of the Long Parliament. One hopes that
the present article has indicated that peers may well have led that
aristocratic network which gained the initiative in the first six
months of the Long Parliament, that the aims and actions of the
parliamentary leaders generally followed a moderate course in
1640–41, and that historians need not assume that a wide ranging
"revolution" took place—at least during the first six months of the
Long Parliament—to explain those events that led to the English
Civil War.

---

[69] *C.J.*, 2:135, 138. This joint committee was called the "Committee for the Defense
of the Kingdom" (*L.J.*, 4:246).

[70] Lotte Glow, "The Manipulation of Committees in the Long Parliament, 1641–
1642," *Journal of British Studies* 5 (1965): 31–52. Despite its title, her valuable article
deals only with committees in the Commons.

THE FIRST AGE OF PARTY
1689 – 1750

BIBLIOGRAPHICAL NOTE

THE FIRST AGE OF PARTY (1689-1750)

[The numbers in brackets refer to items in the bibliography, above pp xvii-xxix. Chapter numbers refer to the essays printed below.]

The historiography of parliamentary and political history for the late seventeenth and eighteenth century — the first age of party — is in a more settled state than that of the early Stuarts. This is largely due to the work of Geoffrey Holmes, whose *British Politics in the Age of Anne* was published in 1967, and to a lesser extent the work of Henry Horwitz in his *Parliament, Policy and Politics in the Reign of William III* published in 1977. Together, they mapped out the contours of Parliament from 1689 to 1714 which have been largely accepted, though much in-filling has gone on in recent years as illustrated by some of the articles reprinted here. Holmes devoted a whole chapter to 'The Court and the Parties in the House of Lords' (99) in which he laid down firm analytical foundations for future superstructures. Some of this later building has been erected by himself, together with Clyve Jones, in their edition of *The London Diaries of William Nicolson, Bishop of Carlisle, 1702-1718* (98). The long general introduction deals with many procedural topics and topographical problems which place the political history of the Lords in a firm context, while the introductions to the thirteen parliamentary sessions of the diaries give the most up to date narrative and analytical history of the politics of the House. The diaries themselves are, of course, the best unofficial source for the Lords in Anne's reign.

The period under review in this section was perhaps the most important in the history of the Lords — its 'golden age' (see Holmes (99) pp. 382-3; Jones and Holmes (98) pp. 62-9) — and the development of the two parties, Whig and Tory, out of the proto-parties of the reigns of Charles II and James II (see 77, 86-92) is one of the two major themes studied in recent years. The House of Lords was to prove important in the relatively smooth transfer of power during the Revolution of 1688-89 and the structures of the parties within the House were crucial to the offer of the Crown to William and Mary (chapter 5). The catalyst which finally forged strong and definable parties in the Lords was the abortive impeachment of four Whig peers by a Tory dominated Commons in 1701. The first major test for this new party structure was over religion, especially the defeats of the Occasional Conformity bills (chapter 6) and the 'Church in danger' scare of 1705 (102). The defeat of the Occasional Conformity bills also illustrates the second major theme of this period: the techniques of parliamentary management that both government and opposition, but particularly government, were developing for the control of the upper House. The government held most of the cards and under Harley, as Earl of Oxford, at the end of Anne's reign there developed a 'party of the Crown'. Based on the experience of earlier first ministers in managing the Lords through the leadership of privy councillors, it was to prove the basis for Walpole's later and more effective control of the Lords (109).

One element of this 'party of the Crown' — the sixteen Scottish representative peers who entered the Lords upon the Anglo-Scottish union in 1707 — has been extensively studied in recent years (chapters 7-8, nos 109, 111). The two other elements — the pensioners (109, chapter 9) and the crown servants (109) have received less attention, although their importance was delineated by Holmes (99). The bishops were not to form an important fourth element of the Crown's natural supporters until the 1720s under Walpole. Some details of their position in the Lords can, however, be found in William Nicolson's *Diaries* (98).

After the Hanoverian succession in 1714, the two party system was weakened by the gradual proscription of a large part of the Tory party who were tainted (falsely or not) with Jacobitism (for the recent controversy over this point, see E. Cruickshanks, *Political Untouchables: the Tories and the '45* (London, 1979) and L. Colley, *In Defiance of Oligarchy: the Tory Party, 1714-60* (Cambridge, 1982)). The increasing hegemony of the Whig party at Westminster was also weakened in 1717-20 by the split between the two chief rivals for power within the party — Sunderland and Walpole. Clyve Jones has looked at one aspect of this schism (chapter 10). Walpole and his followers returned to power in 1720 and not until the 1730s were serious defections from the party to affect the Whig administration of the Lords.

Towards the end of the first age of party, the growth of the party of the Crown and the increasing use of mangement techniques led to the development of more 'institutionalised' forms of management. John Sainty has led the way in the study of this aspect of the history of the Lords with his analysis of the origins of the office of the chairman of committees (8) and of the leadership of the House (chapter 11).

Recent work on this period has also pioneered the use of the sophisticated analysis of various types of parliamentary lists (chapters 5-7, 10, nos. 107, 109). The recent compilation by David Hayton and Clyve Jones of a register of such lists (9) ought to stimulate further research. It seems certain that the often feverish activity of the 'rage of party' was responsible for the sudden flowering of this type of documentation.

As yet, though much new work is in progress, there is no analytical study of the Lords covering the first half of the eighteenth century after Holmes (99) stops in 1714. The early work of Turberville (112) remains the only narrative history for the period and, while lacking in analysis, it remains a valuable starting point for any study of the Lords in the first age of party.

5

DIVISIONS IN THE HOUSE OF LORDS ON THE TRANSFER OF THE CROWN AND OTHER ISSUES, 1689-94: TEN NEW LISTS[1]

EVELINE CRUICKSHANKS, DAVID HAYTON, CLYVE JONES

FOR SOME TIME division lists, or more strictly parliamentary lists,[2] have exerted a fascination over students of politics under the later Stuarts. These documents have been seen as marker buoys charting the treacherous channel of party development in parliament, though historians have been quick to warn against using them in isolation. Most recent work on parliamentary lists has concentrated on the house of commons rather than the house of lords, partly because the study of the Commons has been more fashionable, and partly because of the dearth of such lists for the Lords.[3] For the whole reign of William III only five Lords' lists have been known, two of them on virtually the same issue.[4] The recent discovery among Lord Ailesbury's papers at the Wiltshire Record Office, of ten further lists (nine of divisions and one a forecast) for the period 1689–94 in a single volume of manuscripts is therefore little short of sensational.[5]

Of these ten new lists, the substance of which is printed below in tabular form, three are concerned with the crucial constitutional proceedings on the offer of the crown to William and Mary in 1689; they throw new light on the composition of the parties and the process by which William's supporters gained control of the House. Two more, also from 1689, deal with the bill to reverse judgment on Titus Oates, a party measure which caused a dispute between the two Houses. Four are from the session of 1692–3, two of them covering divisions on the place bill, which was of considerable political importance, and two the duke of Norfolk's divorce bill. The last dates from 1694 and is concerned with the private legal case of Montagu versus Bath. The nine divisions, and the one forecast, have been identified as follows.[6]

[1] We wish to thank the History of Parliament Trust, and particularly Mr. E. L. C. Mullins, for help and encouragement in the preparation of this article.

[2] The term 'division list' is strictly applicable only to a list recording the result of a particular vote. Other types of parliamentary list are forecasts, management lists and 'white' and 'black lists' published to influence public opinion, generally at elections.

[3] See, for example, *The Parliamentary Lists of the Early 18th Century*, ed. A. Newman (Leicester, 1973), the proceedings of a colloquium held in 1970, in which Lords' lists are not discussed.

[4] Four are printed in part in H. Horwitz, *Parliament, Policy and Politics in the Reign of William III* (Manchester, 1977), pp. 335–7; and one in its entirety in A. Browning, *Thomas Osborne, Earl of Danby and Duke of Leeds, 1632–1712* (3 vols., Glasgow, 1944–51), iii. 173–6. For a description of all known Lords' lists see *A Register of Parliamentary Lists, 1660–1761*, ed. D. Hayton and C. Jones (Leicester, 1979).

[5] We are grateful to the marquess of Ailesbury and the earl of Cardigan for permission to publish these lists, and the Wiltshire County Archivist for his kindness and help. This one volume, numbered 1300/856 in the Record Office's collections, also contains a Commons division list (printed in E. Cruickshanks, J. Ferris and D. Hayton, 'The house of commons vote on the transfer of the crown, 5 February 1689', *BIHR* (1979), 37–47). According to a catalogue of the manuscripts, compiled before their transfer to the Record Office, a further volume, not deposited and presumed lost, contained 3 more Lords' lists, on the 'Church in danger' motion of 6 Dec. 1705, a 'Question on the Register Bill, 1716' and the Septennial Act, 1716 ('Lord Bruce's Collections', i, items 12, 23 and 24).

[6] The lists were identified with the aid of *Divisions in the House of Lords: an analytical list, 1685–1857*, comp. J. C. Sainty and D. Dewar (House of Lords Record Office Occasional Pubns., ii, 1976) using the information contained in them, such as headings, numbers of voters (including proxies) and names of tellers.

OFFER OF THE CROWN

A1: 31 Jan. 1689: in committee of the whole House: to insert words declaring prince and princess of Orange king and queen.
contents 47 (teller Devonshire)
not contents 52 (teller Clarendon)

A2: 4 Feb. 1689: to agree with the Commons in the word 'abdicated'.
c. 51 (Devonshire)
nc. 55 (Thanet)

A3: 6 Feb. 1689: to agree with the Commons in the word 'abdicated', etc.
c. 65 (Oxford)
nc. 45 (Ailesbury)

OATES'S CASE

B1: 31 May 1689: to reverse judgments (main question).
c. 23 (Bridgwater)
nc. 35 (Ailesbury)

B2: 30 July 1689: to adhere to amendments.
c. 34 + 14 proxies = 48 (Jermyn)
nc. 32 + 6 proxies = 38 (Cornwallis)

PLACE BILL

C1: 31 Dec. 1692: to commit.
c. 48 (Ailesbury)
nc. 33 (Bridgwater)

C2: 3 Jan. 1693: to pass.
c. 42 + 3 proxies = 45 (Feversham)
nc. 40 + 7 proxies = 47 (Berkeley)

NORFOLK'S DIVORCE BILL

D1: forecast of the vote on 2 Jan. 1693 (D2).

D2: 2 Jan. 1693: to read.
c. 29 + 3 proxies = 32 (Howard of Effingham)
nc. 35 + 4 proxies = 39 (Monmouth)

MONTAGU V. BATH

E: 17 Feb. 1694: to reverse dismission.
c. 29 (Manchester)
nc. 32 (Bridgwater)

Thomas Bruce, 2nd earl of Ailesbury, among whose papers these lists were found and who compiled some if not all of them, was a prominent supporter of King James II. He had entered the house of commons in 1680 for Marlborough, his family's borough, which he represented in the second and third Exclusion parliaments, transferring to one of the county seats for Wiltshire in James's parliament and then to the upper House when he succeeded his father on 20 October 1685. An active member of the house of lords, he was a teller fourteen times between February 1689 and December 1692, more frequently than any other peer, and in May 1689, in the temporary absence of the acting Speaker, Lord Halifax, who had deserted the House without notice in order to attend an unexpected meeting of the privy council, Ailesbury was chosen to take the chair after the earl of Rochester and another peer had both refused to serve.[7]

A firm adherent of King James, Ailesbury spoke only once in the debates on the transfer of the crown in 1689, writing in his memoirs, 'the speaking in so great and honourable an assembly was never my genius, and a timidity ever overawed me, yet I furnished others that had talent with subject matters to enlarge on, and which were well accepted of'.[8] He also canvassed 'a great number of lords spiritual and temporal' against the abdication and vacancy, and claimed to have persuaded both his 'friend and kinsman' the earl of Chesterfield, and Bishop Barlow of Lincoln to vote against.[9] This is the most probable reason for his keeping division lists of votes on the transfer of the crown. His interest in the case of Titus Oates arose out of his having attended Oates's two trials for perjury in 1685, when he thought that Lord Chief Justice Jeffreys had behaved with uncharacteristic good temper towards Oates, the value of whose testimony on the Popish Plot Ailesbury compared to 'the barking of a dog', and that the sentences imposed had been too light for one who had caused the death of over thirty innocent people, particularly that of Lord Stafford. He now suspected that the disciples of the late Lord Shaftesbury were trying to revive the Popish Plot for political ends, and this probably explains why he recorded the two divisions on Oates's appeal.[10]

Ailesbury's conscientious attendance at the Lords was interrupted by his alienation from the new régime. He missed the spring session of 1690 entirely, and in July was one of those ordered to be arrested for high treason at the time of the threatened French invasion. Having gone into hiding and evaded capture, he was eventually able to make his peace with the government through the intercession of Queen Mary, and in December presented himself at the house of lords, took the oaths and resumed his attendance.[11] It was probably his Jacobite sympathies which drew him to assist the duchess of Norfolk, the daughter of a fellow Jacobite suspect Lord Peterborough, against her Protestant and whig husband and his bill of divorce in the parliamentary session of 1692-3. Ailesbury voted against this bill, as he had against the duke's first bill in 1691-2, and it is possible that he acted as one of the managers for the duchess in the House, since in his memoirs he mentions a few years later approaching her lover, John Germain, with a request for a favour on the grounds of 'friendship, and also by way of gratitude for a service of importance I had rendered him'.[12] Furthermore he says that he was 'often with' Germain during a stay in France in the spring of 1693, immediately after the defeat of the duke of Norfolk's bill.[13] Ailesbury also took a keen interest in the place bill, which the Lords were discussing at the same time as Norfolk's bill, acting as teller on 31 December 1692 in favour of the bill being committed in one of the divisions which he lists. The last division in the batch, that of 17 February 1694 in the case of Montagu versus Bath, probably concerned him as a friend of Lord Bath.[14] Thereafter Ailesbury was involved in

---

[7] Bodleian Library, MS. Ballard 45 fo. 39a, [Robert Woodward] to Arthur Charlett, 21 May 1689.

[8] *Memoirs of Thomas, Earl of Ailesbury, written by himself*, ed. W. E. Buckley (2 vols.,Roxburghe Club, 1890), i. 232.

[9] *Ibid.*, pp. 229–30, 233.

[10] *Ibid.*, pp. 50–2, 137–44.

[11] *Ibid.*, pp. 257–65; *Calendar of State Papers, Domestic, 1690–1*, p. 65; C. S. C. Brudenell-Bruce, earl of Cardigan, *The Life and Loyalties of Thomas Bruce* (1951), pp. 154–62; *Lords' Journals* (hereafter *L.J.*), xiv. 576.

[12] *L.J.*, xv. 25; *Ailesbury Mems.*, ii. 444–6.

[13] *Ailesbury Mems.*, i. 338.

[14] *Ibid.*, ii. 376.

3. William III enthroned in an imaginary House of Lords, 1689.

Engraving by Romeyn de Hooghe, by courtesy of the House of Lords Record Office.

With the accession of William III to the throne in 1689, there was a great deal of interest in the Dutch Republic concerning English parliamentary affairs and this imaginary depiction of the Lords is a product of that interest. It is incorrect in most of its detail, though the general layout is fairly accurate. Only two rows of benches ran down each wall of the chamber and there were no benches at the left-hand end of the room. The side of the chamber facing the viewer was the spiritual side where the bishops (not the peers) sat. The chamber is too wide and was not curtained off as part of a larger room. There were more cross benches. The clerks, by this time, were seated at their table. The impression is of an artist updating an earlier engraving of the House, possibly one showing Charles I (see above, p. 60).

Resolved &c. Luno 28° *Jan E*ij 1688

*That King James the Second haveing —
endeavoured to subvert the Constitution of
the Kingdome by breaking the Originall Contract
betweene King and People, and by the Advice
of Jesuites and other wicked persons haveing —
violated the fundamentall Lawes And —
haveing withdrawne himselfe out of this —
Kingdome has abdicated the Government
and that the Throne is thereby vacant.*

4. The 'abdication and vacancy' resolution of the Commons of 28 January 1688/9, showing the proposed amendment by the Lords.

By courtesy of the House of Lords Record Office.

See Chapter 5, pp. 82-85, and L. G. Schwoerer, *The Declaration of Rights, 1689* (Baltimore and London, 1981), p. 207.

Jacobite schemes until his arrest for high treason in March 1696.[15] After his release he spent the rest of his life in exile in Flanders, dying in 1741.

A Convention, designed to settle the kingdom after the flight of James II, assembled for the first time on 22 January 1689. It was not until the 28th that the constitutional issues were debated, James's supporters in the Commons having delayed matters there in order to pass the initiative to the house of lords, which was considered the more conservative of the two Houses. The Lords failed to take this opportunity, and on Monday, 28 January the Commons agreed, with a deceptive consensus of only three votes against, that James had broken 'the original contract', 'abdicated the government', and left the throne vacant. The House having approved this resolution, the initiative passed to the Lords.

Over the next nine days a battle developed in the Lords between the adherents of James II and those of William of Orange. James's supporters, after they had lost the motion for a regency on 29 January, were able to control the House until 6 February, during which time they managed to stave off pressure from the Commons to agree that James had abdicated and the throne was vacant. Eventually, however, this and the pressure of outside events proved too much, and following the defeat of the conservatives in a crucial vote on 6 February on agreeing with the Commons that James had abdicated, William and Mary were at last declared king and queen.

Three main groups of lords have been identified as vying for control of the House during this time: the 'loyalists', those who remained loyal to James; the 'Williamites', those who adhered to the prince of Orange and were ready to adopt the Commons' resolution of 28 January and install William (or later William and Mary jointly) on the 'vacant' throne; and a small group led by Danby, which supported the Princess Mary as James's sole and rightful successor. This last group has previously been considered as holding the balance in the House, and there is some evidence to show that contemporaries thought that Danby was 'very instrumental in this great settlement'.[16] Hitherto, because of the nature of the sources, it has not been possible to see more than a tentative outline of the composition of these groups, but with the discovery of the Ailesbury lists the picture becomes clear.[17]

On Tuesday, 29 January, the Lords in a committee of the whole House, with Danby in the chair, began consideration of the Commons' resolutions. The debate was long and heated, and the loyalists, probably as a further tactical move to gain time, brought in a motion for the establishment of a regency during James II's lifetime. This was rejected by 51 votes to 48, Danby's group voting against the motion.[18] The only previously known Lords' division list for the Convention is on this vote.[19] On the following day, Wednesday, 30 January, the

---

[15] *Cal. S.P. Dom. 1696*, p. 95.

[16] E.g. British Library, Egerton MS. 3346 fo. 14, [newsletter?], 7 Feb. 1689.

[17] For the sources previously used see H. Horwitz, 'Parliament and the Glorious Revolution', *BIHR*, xlvii (1974), 43–5.

[18] Bodl. Libr., MS. Rawlinson D 1079 fo. 4, a diary of proceedings in the Convention, states that the yeas included 'all the Bishops but two Vizt London & Bristoll: and all the Dukes but Norfolk'. Bodl. Libr., MS. Ballard 45 fo. 25, [Robert Woodward] to [George Smalridge ?], 31 Jan. 1689, agrees that the 'Lord of London and Bishop of Bristol were against the Rest of the Bishops but the Latter modestly withdrew when they came to vote'.

[19] It is in fact half a division list, showing only those who supported the regency, and is printed in *Correspondence of Henry Hyde, Earl of Clarendon*, ed. S. W. Singer (2 vols., 1828) (hereafter *Clar. Corr.*), ii. 256. It has been possible to identify the other side in the vote, and such a reconstructed list is printed in part in Horwitz, *Parliament, Policy and Politics*, pp. 335–7.

fortieth anniversary of the execution of Charles I, the House held an unprecedented afternoon sitting.[20] At this sitting, the loyalists, with the support of the group led by Danby, appear to have gained control of the House, carrying by 54 to 43 the substitution of the word 'deserted' for the word 'abdicated' in the Commons' resolution.

On Thursday, 31 January, there were two further loyalist victories, after a debate lasting till eleven o'clock at night.[21] A motion to declare the prince and princess of Orange king and queen was defeated, on the previous question, by 52 to 47, and the Commons' clause of 'vacancy' was thrown out, by 55 to 41. The first of the newly discovered division lists (A1) is concerned with the first of these votes, to declare William and Mary king and queen. It has previously been assumed that Danby's group supported the loyalists in both divisions.[22] The new list shows, however, that of those lords who were previously thought to constitute Danby's allies, Bishops Compton and Trelawny and Lords Northampton, Lindsey and Fauconberg, only Trelawny voted with the loyalists in opposing the offer of the crown to William and Mary.[23] It is probable that other members of the group did join with the loyalists on the second vote. The London nonconformist, Roger Morrice, who has left the fullest record of this day's debate, says that every bishop including Compton 'was of the opinion the Throne was not vacant'.[24] Northampton appears to have supported the motion, while a note in Ailesbury's hand at the end of his copy of the new division list for the first vote on the 31st gives Danby, Fauconberg and Compton as 'Lords for Crowning the Prince and Princess, and yet were against vacating the Crown'.[25] It was not illogical to want William and Mary as king and queen while opposing a vacancy, and Danby's position was that if the throne was not vacant but James had deserted it then Mary was the next successor (excluding the prince of Wales). On the other hand, if the throne was vacant then the Convention would have to elect a successor, who would certainly be William. The next votes in the Lords on this question occurred on the following Monday, 4 February, and it is with the first of these, 'to agree with the Commons in the word abdicated', that Ailesbury's second list (A2) is concerned. On the afternoon of the 4th, the two Houses held a joint conference on the previous Lords' amendments to the Commons' resolutions of 28 January. The Commons made it clear that they intended to stick to the original wording of their resolutions. After the conference was reported to the upper House there was a debate, and two votes ensued. The Lords resolved by 55 to 51, in the division recorded by Ailesbury, to maintain their substitution of the word 'deserted' for 'abdicated', and by 54 to 53 to reassert that the throne was not vacant. Again it has been assumed that

---

[20] This was the first sitting on the anniversary of Charles I's death since the statute of 1661 imposing a solemn fast on that day. The experiment was not repeated. See J. P. Kenyon, *Revolution Principles* (Cambridge, 1977), p. 69.

[21] Archives Nationales, Fonds Stuart, K. 1351/27.

[22] Horwitz, 'Glorious Revolution', p. 44.

[23] *Ibid.*, p. 45. It has also been thought that Lord Paget may have belonged to this group: A. Simpson, 'The Convention Parliament, 1688–9' (unpublished University of Oxford D.Phil. thesis, 1939), p. 144. The new lists show him to have voted consistently with the Williamites.

[24] Dr. Williams's Libr., Morrice MS. Q (hereafter Morrice MS. Q) pp. 451–2. Edward Harley, in discussing the 2 votes on 31 Jan., says that 'all the Bishops go one way so do the Naturals [royal bastards] and blew Garters except Norfolk, Oxford and Hallifax' (Brit. Libr., Add. MS. 40621 fo. 12, Edward Harley to Robert Harley, 2 Feb. 1689). It is not clear to which vote this refers, but it is more likely to be the second, on vacancy.

[25] Ailesbury's note also names 'The Lords that were for vacating the Crown and that Protested against the disagreeing with the house of Commons'. He identifies 38 protesters, while the *L.J.*, xiv. 113 lists only 36. The 2 extra are Northampton and Newport.

Danby's group sided with the loyalists on both these votes. In the first the actual question was whether to agree with the Commons in the word 'abdicated', so the loyalists voted not content. Though all of Danby's group are recorded in the *Lords' Journals* as present, two do not appear on the division list—Danby himself and Fauconberg.[26] Bishops Compton and Trelawny and Lord Lindsey voted with the loyalists, but Northampton voted content with the Williamites. Whatever Danby's reason for not voting in the first vote, there is evidence that he voted with the Williamites in the second. In a note in Ailesbury's hand at the foot of his copy of the division list is the sentence, 'Earle of Danby was content the last vote', i.e. he agreed with the Commons that the throne was vacant.[27] On this second vote Compton and Trelawny seem to have divided against him.[28]

At these two votes thirty-nine protests were entered, and afterwards a committee was appointed to draw up reasons for the Lords' adhering to their original amendments, to be offered the following day at a conference between the two Houses. On Tuesday, 5 February, after the conference, the Commons voted to reject both the Lords' first amendment, replacing the word 'abdicated' by 'deserted', and their second, to omit the words 'and that the Throne is thereby vacant'.[29] The following day, yet another inconclusive conference took place, lasting three to four hours, and principally managed for the Lords by Nottingham, Pembroke, Clarendon, Rochester and the bishop of Ely—all loyalists.[30]

Outside pressure was now exerted to break the stalemate. William, at a private gathering of lords which included Halifax and Danby, and which probably took place on the evening of 3 February, declared his intention to settle for nothing less than the crown in his own right, with Mary as joint sovereign.[31] On the 6th the Princess Anne, in a message delivered to the Lords by Lord Churchill, publicly waived her right to the throne should Mary predecease William.[32] Probably as a result of this message, the debate in the Lords (opened by an 'excellent' speech from Danby) on the reasons the Commons had offered in the conference earlier that day as to why they could not concur with the Lords' amendments, lasted only half an hour.[33] The question was then put whether to

[26] There is a curious story about Fauconberg in *Ailesbury Mems.*, i. 230. Ailesbury, whose account of this week, written years later, is too confused to be unscrambled, states that in one vote Fauconberg 'retired between the hanging and the door next to the Bishops' room'. If this is true it may well have happened on this vote, though Fauconberg's companion in hiding, Bishop Crew of Durham, is not recorded in the *LJ*. as having been present on the day.

[27] The full note reads, 'Earle of Berkley went out the second vote from the house. Earle of Danby was content the last vote'. There is some evidence that Danby made a last-minute decision about switching his support away from the loyalists to the Williamites, though the dating is uncertain. See Chatsworth House, 'Devonshire House' notebook, *sub* 'Abington, Ld'. This reference was assigned by Browning (i. 426) and Foxcroft (*The Life and Letters of Sir George Savile, Marquis of Halifax*, ed. H. C. Foxcroft (2 vols., 1898), ii. 49) to the vote of 29 Jan. on the regency, and by Horwitz ('Glorious Revolution', p. 46) to the vote of 6 Feb. It may be that it refers to the second vote on the 4th, and that Danby's change of mind came earlier than was supposed, possibly as a result of what he had heard from William's own lips at a private meeting of lords which may have taken place on the evening of 3 Feb. (see below, n. 31).

[28] Roger Morrice recorded that on this vote 'every Bishop in the House was against agreeing with the Commons' (Morrice MS. Q p. 456).

[29] See Cruickshanks, Ferris and Hayton, pp. 37–8.

[30] Bodl. Libr., MS. Ballard 45 fo. 27a, [Robert Woodward] to [Arthur Charlett?], 7 Feb. 1689; House of Lords Record Office, Willcocks collection, 6, Tweeddale letters, 20, Lord Yester to earl of Tweeddale, 7 Feb. 1689; W. Cobbett, *The Parliamentary History of England* (36 vols., 1806–20), v. 66–108. All but one of the Lords' managers for this conference were loyalists, the exception being Lord Oxford (*LJ*., xiv. 118).

[31] For the meeting, and its dating to 3 Feb., see Horwitz, 'Glorious Revolution', p. 46.

[32] *Ibid.*, and Bodl. Libr., MS. Rawlinson D 1079 fo. 13v.

[33] Bodl. Libr., MS. Rawlinson D 1079 fo. 13v; Morrice MS. Q p. 459.

agree with the Commons in the word 'abdicated', which was carried by 65 to 45.[34] After a futile rearguard action by one of the uncles of the Princess Mary (either Clarendon or Rochester), who urged that she be named first, it was decided by the Lords without a vote that the prince and princess of Orange be declared king and queen.[35]

It has long been known, principally from Clarendon's account,[36] that the crucial vote on 6 February to agree with the Commons in the word 'abdicated', was lost by the loyalists for three main reasons: deliberate abstentions and absenteeism on the part of some of their supporters; an increase in the Williamite vote by new recruits absent from earlier votes; and the final abandonment of resistance by Danby and his group.[37] The third new division list (A3) concerns this vote, and allows a more accurate assessment of the forces involved and the reasons for the loss of control of the House by the loyalists.

Clarendon was in no doubt why his party's change of fortune had come about:

Under one pretence or other, several Lords, who had hitherto voted for the King, being unwilling to change the government, were not in the House at putting the question. The Earl of Chesterfield, though at the conference, went away before the question; as likewise did the Bishop of Bristol [Trelawny], Lord Ferrers, and Lord Godolphin, the latter telling some of his friends, that he was to attend the Prince of Orange at the Treasury; an undeniable evidence certainly, that he had rather ingratiate himself with a new master, than support his old one, to whom he owed his present station in the world . . . The Lords Weymouth and Hatton did not appear today. The Earl of Yarmouth, the Lords Coventry and Crewe, who had always voted for the King, went away before the question.[38]

Other absentees listed by Clarendon were the bishop of Oxford and Lord Burlington, who 'was really very ill [and] had always voted with us'.[39]

An examination of the three new division lists shows that Clarendon was mistaken in stating that these eleven lords had consistently voted with the loyalists and had then absented themselves before or during the day's proceedings on the 6th. He was right about only five: Chesterfield and Ferrers had been in the House that day but did not vote, while Weymouth, Hatton and Burlington made no appearance (the latter also appears not to have voted on the 4th, though recorded as present). Previously all had voted loyally for King James. Of the remainder, four who had voted loyalist all along continued to do so on the 6th, contrary to Clarendon's statement: Bishop Trelawny and Lords Yarmouth, Crew and Godolphin. One, Bishop Hall of Oxford, who had not sat in the House before 5 February,[40] voted with the loyalists on the 6th. The last member of Clarendon's eleven, Lord Coventry, belongs to a small but highly significant group, the existence of which has previously been almost totally obscured by Clarendon's misleading account, who had voted consistently loyalist but now switched to the Williamites. As we shall see, this small group of loyalist

[34] Bodl. Libr., MS. Rawlinson D 1079 fo. 13 claims that there were 2 votes on the 6th, the first on the word 'abdicated' being carried by 3 voices and the second on the vacancy of the throne by 20, but according to the official records of the House only one vote took place on the 6th, on 'abdicated'.

[35] Lords R.O., Willcocks collection, 6, Tweeddale letters, 20, Yester to Tweeddale, 7 Feb. 1689; Bodl. Libr., MS. Rawlinson D 1079 fo. 13. Morrice (Morrice MS. Q p. 461) thought there would have been about 25 not contents had there been a vote.

[36] Both in *Clar. Corr.*, ii. 260–2 and in A. Simpson, 'Notes of a Noble Lord, 22 January to 12 February 1688/9', *Eng. Hist. Rev.*, lii (1937), 94–5.

[37] See Horwitz, 'Glorious Revolution', p. 46. It has been hinted above (n. 27) that Danby may have abandoned resistance as early as 4 Feb.

[38] Simpson, 'Notes of a Noble Lord', pp. 94–5.

[39] *Clar. Corr.*, ii. 261. The absentees named in this version were Chesterfield, Weymouth, Ferrers, Hatton, Godolphin, the bishop of Oxford, and Burlington.

[40] *LJ.*, xiv. 117.

deserters on the 6th were as important as Danby's group in the final collapse of the loyalist control of the House. Finally, to Clarendon's list of absentees can be added Anglesey, who is noted as absent by Ailesbury.[41]

Clarendon has also left us a misleading account of the lords who were brought into the House for the first time on the 6th to support William:

All imaginable pains were taken to bring other Lords to the House, who never used to come; as the Earl of Lincoln, who, to confirm the opinion several had of his being half mad, declared he came to do whatever my Lord Shrewsbury and Lord Mordaunt would have him. The Earl of Carlisle was brought upon his crutches: the Lord Lexinton, who came into England but three days ago; and the Bishop of Durham [Crew], who had been at the House but twice before, came to-day to give his vote against the King who had raised him. These four all voted against the King.[42]

The new division list confirms that all four voted with the Williamites on the 6th. It is also true that neither Lord Lincoln nor the bishop of Durham had attended before,[43] and Morrice noted on the 6th that Lincoln had supported William for the first time on that day. Lexington, however, had voted with the Williamites on the 4th (though he was absent on 31 January), while Carlisle had voted consistently with the Williamites in the three divisions covered by the new lists.

Lord Montagu was later to claim in a letter to William that he had been responsible for carrying over some of the new recruits,

bringing my Lord Huntington, the bishop of Durham, and my Lord Ashley [*recte* Astley], to vote against the Regency, and for your having the crown; which was carried but by those three voices and my own.[44]

It is not clear to which vote Montagu is referring, where there was a majority of four. The regency vote on 29 January had a majority of three, but neither Bishop Crew nor Lord Astley was then in the House. Their first recorded attendance was on 6 February when they did vote with the Williamites.[45] Huntingdon appears from the *Journals* to have been a fairly regular attender from as early as 22 January.[46] He was present on 29 January and voted against the regency,[47] and from the new lists he appears to have been absent on the 31st, and to have voted with the loyalists on 4 February and with the Williamites on the 6th. In the debate on the 6th, in Morrice's account, Huntingdon spoke in favour of crowning William and Mary, though he had not always been of this mind, the Commons having convinced him that the throne was vacant, while according to another source Huntingdon said 'my Lords, severall of the members have Declared in the Conference that they Did not Designe the Altering the Line by makeing the Throne vacant only for this Tyme'.[48]

---

[41] Ailesbury, in a note at the end of his copy of the division list for 6 Feb., gives the following as absent: Chesterfield, Anglesey, Burlington, Weymouth, Hatton and Ferrers.

[42] *Clar. Corr.*, ii. 261.

[43] Bodl. Libr., MS. Ballard 45 fo. 27a, Woodward to [Charlett], 7 Feb. 1689. For the reason why Crew had kept away until 6 Feb. see *Bishop Burnet's History of his own Time*, [ed. M. J. Routh] (6 vols., Oxford, 1833), iii. 398–9; *The Life and Times of Anthony Wood*, ed. A. Clark (5 vols., Oxford, 1891–1900), iii. 298.

[44] J. Dalrymple, *Memoirs of Great Britain and Ireland* (2 vols., 1771–3), ii, app. ii, p. 340, Lord Montagu to William III, 18 May 1694.

[45] *LJ.*, xiv. 117.

[46] *Ibid.*, pp. 101–17.

[47] Horwitz, *Parliament, Policy and Politics*, p. 336.

[48] Morrice MS. Q p. 460; West Sussex Record Office, Shillinglee MS. 482, [Ralph Chaplin?] to Sir Edward Turnour, 9 Feb. 1689 (we owe this reference to Miss P. E. Murrell). His switch to William is also noted by Woodward (Bodl. Libr., MS. Ballard 45 fo. 27a, to [Charlett?], 7 Feb. 1689). Forgetting Huntingdon's vote on 4 Feb. Clarendon states that he 'had all along voted against the King' (*Clar. Corr.*, ii. 262).

Of the six new recruits to William's cause who Clarendon and Montagu would have us believe were brought in to tip the balance, Huntingdon had attended the Lords from the first sitting and his idiosyncratic voting behaviour led him to oppose the loyalists on 29 January, support them on 4 February and then oppose them again on the 6th; Carlisle and Lexington had consistently supported William and had both voted earlier than the 6th. Only Bishop Crew, Lincoln and Astley voted for the first time on 6 February. To these three, however, can be added one more (from the evidence of the lists), Lord Howard of Escrick, who had been absent from the House until the 6th and who voted for William on that day.[49]

On the opposite side, nearly balancing this group of four new Williamites, were three loyalists, who appeared in the House for the first time on the 6th, or returned after a short absence, to vote for James. Bishop Hall of Oxford and Bishop Lloyd of St. Asaph voted for the first time on the 6th (though Lloyd is recorded as present but not voting on the 4th) and the duke of Beaufort reappeared, to vote loyalist as he had done over the regency vote on 20 January. None of these three was noted by Clarendon, apart from a misleading reference to Bishop Hall.

As to Danby's group, the lists are clear as to their voting on 6 February: Danby, described as 'in and in for the P[rince] and P[rincess]',[50] Fauconberg, Lindsey, Northampton and Bishop Compton all voted with the Williamites, while Trelawny voted loyalist. Morrice confirms the voting pattern of the two bishops, stating, 'its credibly reported that only the Bishop of Durham and the Bishop of London were fore the affirmative'.[51]

A final factor in the loyalists' loss of control of the House, in addition to absenteeism in their own ranks, the influx of new Williamites and the switch of Danby's followers, was the defection of a small group of loyalists. Until now the existence of this crucial group has been ignored, for Clarendon mentions only one lord who changed sides, Thanet, who was quizzed by Clarendon about his defection at the end of the sitting on 6 February. Thanet's reply is instructive and is likely to be the general reason why the loyalists finally lost control of the House. Clarendon wrote:

He told me he was of our mind, and thought we had done ill in admitting the monarchy to be elective; for so this vote had made it: but he thought there was an absolute necessity of having a Government; and he did not see it likely to be any other way than this.[52]

The new division lists reveal that there were three (and possibly four) others who made a last-minute change of allegiance. One, Coventry, has been mentioned.[53] Two others who went over were Carnarvon (Danby's brother-in-law) and Kent. The last, whose allegiance was doubtful, is Huntingdon. He had remained faithful to James until the second flight, and, although he was classed as a Williamite by Clarendon and had opposed the regency motion, his voting with the loyalists on the 4th probably reveals his true allegiance. This seems confirmed

[49] The lists reveal that Lords Bath and Morley were Williamites who appeared for the first time on 4 Feb.

[50] Bodl. Libr., MS. Ballard 45 fo. 27a, [Woodward] to [Charlett?], 7 Feb. 1689.

[51] Morrice MS. Q p. 461. Though it is probable that Morrice is here referring to the debate after the vote on the 6th, on whether to make William and Mary king and queen, it can fairly be taken as also referring to the vote itself. Morrice goes on to record that 'some adde [to Crew and Compton] Dr. Watson Bishop of St. Davids who certainly was in the House several dayes in the latter end of this weeke'. The lists show, however, that Watson voted consistently loyalist.

[52] *Clar. Corr.*, ii. 261–2.

[53] See above, p. 85.

by the reasons he was reported to have given for his vote on 6 February.[54] All five lords, Thanet, Coventry, Huntingdon, Carnarvon and Kent, are listed by Ailesbury as having deserted the loyalists, and in his copy of the list they are grouped together under the heading 'Went of[f]'.

What do the new division lists tell us about the parties in the Lords between 31 January and 6 February 1689? First, they enable us to name precisely the members of Danby's squadron. Far from comprising 'probably six (and certainly no more than eight)',[55] there are only three lords who appear to have followed Danby throughout in their voting: Fauconberg, Lindsey and Bishop Compton. Bishop Trelawny voted consistently loyalist, and Lord Northampton consistently Williamite. Secondly, the new lists show that the loyalists were probably in full control of the House by their own strength alone between 31 January and 6 February. On 31 January there were fifty-three loyalists voting, opposed by forty-six Williamites and Danby's group of four.[56] On 4 February the loyalists mustered fifty-two votes by themselves as opposed to fifty-one for William's supporters, and so would have carried the first vote that day, against agreeing with the Commons in the word 'abdicated', without the help of the two members of Danby's group who supported them.[57] We cannot be sure of the relative strengths of the parties on the second vote on the 4th, that the throne was not vacant. This was won by the loyalists by 54 to 53. There is evidence that Danby himself supported the Williamites, as we have seen, and that the loyalists had lost one vote at least (Lord Berkeley went out).[58] As the vote was on the vacancy of the throne it is possible that the other two members of Danby's group, Lindsey and Fauconberg, joined Compton in supporting the loyalists, in which case their votes were decisive,[59] though on the opposite side to Danby himself. On the final day, 6 February, deserters and absentees reduced the loyalist strength from their over-all majority of earlier in the week to a minority of forty-six, while the Williamites, swelled by new recruits, former loyalists and Danby's group, now numbered sixty-four.[60] When the loyalists were defeated on the 6th, Danby's four votes were of small significance compared with the six absent loyalists, five defectors and four new Williamite recruits who went to make up the decisive majority for William. The three new division lists show that, in parliament at least, Danby's role as a kingmaker has been exaggerated.

OATES'S CASE

The case of Titus Oates took up a great deal of time in the first session of the Convention, delayed the bill of rights and other more important matters, produced a deadlock between the Houses and raised issues of constitutional importance.

In an action for *scandalum magnatum* in 1684, Oates had been ordered to pay £100,000 damages for calling James, duke of York a traitor. After James's accession Oates had been tried twice more for perjury before Lord Chief Justice Jeffreys in 1685 and had been sentenced to be whipped twice in one week, once

[54] See above, p. 86.

[55] Horwitz, 'Glorious Revolution', p. 45.

[56] These figures are derived from Ailesbury's list, and not from the official record in the minutes of the House, in which error is possible (see below, p. 103).

[57] Again, these are Ailesbury's figures.

[58] See above, n. 27.

[59] See above, p. 83, for Compton's probable support for the loyalists.

[60] Ailesbury's figures.

from Aldgate to Newgate and once from Newgate to Tyburn, to be imprisoned and to stand in the pillory four times a year for life.[61] At the Revolution he had been released, probably because excessive fines and punishments had been declared illegal by the Declaration of Rights. On 11 March 1689 a petition from Oates was presented to the house of lords, setting out his services in defence of the Protestant religion, complaining of his having been browbeaten by Jeffreys and seeking redress for his sufferings.[62] On 4 April three writs of error were brought in to reverse the judgments of 1684–5, and five days later a petition from Oates was read praying for a hearing.[63] The ground was skilfully chosen, as this was a species of appeal which raised no question of fact.[64] Counsel for Oates pleaded, and, no counsel appearing on behalf of the Crown, the Lords ordered two of the presiding judges at the 1685 trials, Sir Richard Holloway and Sir Francis Wythens, to appear at the bar to give their reasons for their judgments.[65] They did so on 17 May when Holloway was reported to have made 'some foolish excuses', but Wythens was bold enough to say that he still thought Oates 'was a very Great Rogue and that he deserved the punishment Adjudged'. In the ensuing debate Danby, now marquess of Carmarthen, 'declared that he thought the best way to Reverse the Judgment was to Whipp him back to the place from whence he came'. Halifax too was said to have been 'very warm' against reversal.[66] Oates's reaction was a declaration that 'if he could not have justice in the Upper House, he hoped to have it in the lower'. Six days later a petition from him, seeking relief, was presented to the Commons. In this petition he publicly renewed his former accusations that, as lord treasurer, Danby had taken money from France to prorogue parliament and had tried to stifle the exposure of the Popish Plot. Oates also published a pamphlet entitled *The Case of Titus Oates*, reaffirming the veracity of his testimony on the Plot.[67] Appearing at the bar of the Lords on 25 May, Oates owned the pamphlet. Carmarthen then moved 'that Oates might again be set upon the Pillory', and after a debate in which all the bishops except Burnet spoke against him, the House resolved to send Oates to the King's Bench prison for breach of privilege.[68] Two days later, a petition from Oates was presented humbly begging their lordships' pardon. When he was brought to the bar on the 30th to make his submission, Ailesbury moved that he should be made to strike out the words 'doctor of divinity' from his petition. Though his supposed Salamanca degree had long been the butt of satirists from Dryden downwards, Oates refused to do so 'out of conscience', and was returned to prison.[69]

On 31 May, the occasion of the first division on Oates's case for which we have a list (B1), all the judges present were unanimous in their opinion that the

[61] *A Complete Collection of State Trials*, comp. T. B. Howell (33 vols., 1816–26), x. 126–47, 1079–1330. For Oates's career, see J. P. Kenyon, *The Popish Plot* (1972).

[62] Hist. MSS. Comm., *12th Rept.*, app. vi, pp. 47–9.

[63] *L.J.*, xiv. 167, 172; Hist. MSS. Comm., *12th Rept.*, app. vi, pp. 75–6, 80–1.

[64] Lord Macaulay, *History of England*, ed. C. H. Firth (6 vols., 1913–15), iv. 1656.

[65] Hist. MSS. Comm., *12th Rept.*, app. vi, pp. 76–7; *L.J.*, xiv. 193–4.

[66] Bodl. Libr., MS. Ballard 45 fo. 39a, [Woodward] to Charlett, 21 May 1689; Hist. MSS. Comm., *12th Rept.*, app. vi, p. 77; *Halifax Letters*, ii. 218; Simpson, 'The Convention Parliament', p. 226.

[67] *Commons' Journals* (hereafter *C.J.*), x. 144–5; *L.J.*, xiv. 219–20; Hist. MSS. Comm., *12th Rept.*, app. vi, p. 78; Morrice MS. Q p. 559; *To the Right Honourable the Lords Spiritual and Temporal, and to the Honourable the Knights, Citizens and Burgesses in this present Parliament assembled; the humble petition of Titus Oates, D.D.* (1689); *The Case of Titus Oates D.D. humbly offered to the tender Consideration of the Right Honourable the Lords Spiritual, and Commons, in Parliament assembled* (1689).

[68] Kenyon, *Popish Plot*, p. 175; *L.J.*, xiv. 219–21.

[69] Morrice MS. Q pp. 559, 562; *L.J.*, xiv. 221; *Ailesbury Mems.*, i. 144; *Poems on Affairs of State, 1660–1714*, ed. G. de F. Lord and others (7 vols., New Haven, 1963–75), v. 255.

judgments against him were erroneous, illegal and cruel. Morrice, who gives a full account of the proceedings, reported:

Suddenly after the Judges had thus delivered their opinions and gave their reasons a Lord said the judgement given against Oates was very erroneous and illegal and inhumane, and ought to be reversed, and much to this purpose and to this sense the Earl of Nottingham the Earl of Danby the Lord President, the Bishop of Salisbury and very many others spoack, and it seemed to be the sense of the whole house that the Judgement was erroneous, after a little intermission a Lord I think the Earle of Rochester desired the opinion of the Judges might be asked whether or not if the Judgement were reversed against Oates it tooke off his Perjury and set him *Rectus in Curia* and made him *vir probus et legalis* so that he might be a witnesse etc. Chief Justice Holt answered it did. Then divers of the Lords spoak to this purpose as the Earle of Rochester, the Bishop of Salisbury the Marquess of Halifax the Earle of Nottingham the Earle of Danby that this was a very great Case, and they must very well consider the Consequences of Reversing this Judgement. If Oates were thereby made capable of giving evidence . . . the Bishop of Salisbury said if such rascalls and perjured persons were capacitated to give evidence no honest man was secure of his life. Another said he thought there was no Lord Present but believed that Oates was really guilty of Perjury, and that it was the worst kind of perjury, and such as had taken away many persons lives.[70]

On the other side, the duke of Bolton spoke in favour of reversal, declaring 'he had raither be thought Dr. Oates his friend than King James's'.[71] The earl of Oxford stressed that the Lords were sitting in their judicial capacity and that all the judges had said the judgments were erroneous, while another lord exclaimed, 'what a great blemish it would be upon the Popish Plot that so many Parliaments and their Lordships themselves had so often judged to be reall and dangerous'. By a majority of twelve, including all the bishops, the Lords voted not to reverse their judgments. On 1 June, however, the Lords reversed the judgment for *scandalum magnatum* of 1684, thus removing the fine of £100,000 imposed on Oates.[72]

When, three days later, a bill was introduced in the Commons to reverse the two judgments for perjury of 1685, some tory members 'hissed', but it went through and the House went on to vote that there had been 'a Design to stifle the Popish Plot: And that the Verdicts given thereupon were corrupt'.[73] Probably in order to avoid a clash between the two Houses, and because he had been criticized by the king and by many lords 'for his violent carriage in Oates' business, which has damned the whole Popish Plott', Carmarthen on 6 June carried an address to their Majesties to grant Oates a pardon.[74] After sitting three days 'very close and long' on the Commons' bill, the Lords amended it on 12 July so as to make Oates incapable of ever being a witness again.[75] Ten days later, the Commons rejected the Lords' amendments, reaffirmed their belief in the veracity of Oates as a witness and voted that the juries who had convicted him were corrupt.[76] Several conferences between the Houses failed to produce agreement.[77]

[70] Hist. MSS. Comm., *12th Rept.,* app. vi, pp. 78–80; Morrice MS. Q pp. 562–3.

[71] Chatsworth, 'Devonshire House' notebook, *sub* 'Bolton, Duke'.

[72] *LJ.,* xiv. 228, 230; Morrice MS. Q pp. 263–4.

[73] *CJ.,* x. 176–7, 204, 206; A. Grey, *Debates of the House of Commons* (10 vols., 1769), ix. 286.

[73] *Halifax Letters,* ii. 218; Hist. MSS. Comm., *12th Rept.,* app. vi, pp. 125–6; *LJ.,* xiv. 234.

[75] *Correspondence of the Family of Hatton,* ed. E. M. Thompson (Camden new ser., xxii, xxiii, 1878), ii. 135; *LJ.,* xiv. 276–7.

[76] *CJ.,* x. 230–1.

[77] N. Luttrell, *A Brief Historical Relation of State Affairs from September 1678 to April 1714* (6 vols., Oxford, 1857), i. 563; *LJ.,* xiv. 292, 295; *CJ.,* x. 240–2; Simpson, 'Convention Parliament', pp. 235–8.

On 30 July, Morrice reported, the Lords avoided a vote on whether to agree with the Commons, as 'that would have led them into the debate of the merits of the Case', but divided on a motion whether to adhere or not to their own amendments. This was the second of the two divisions recorded by Ailesbury (B2). One earl, according to Morrice, 'upon some *capritio* or other was most zealous against Oates, though he has been of the Countreyside in all other matters throughout this Sessions'. This was probably Northampton, who had agreed with the Commons on the abdication and the offer of the crown in February, but now voted against Oates. Another who 'voted for him and was against adhearing', Morrice said, 'was the first man that spoake against Oates when his Case came into the House of Lords, and continued to speake against him all along': probably Burnet, who was the only lord who voted against Oates on 31 May but for him on 30 July. 'Of the four new Lords', Morrice concluded, 'Lansdowne only was present, Berkley, Sidney and Portland were absent, and my Lord Delamare and the Lord Ewer were not there, though they were sent to and desired to be present'.[78] Delamer, who was described as the 'patron of their perjured darling Oates',[79] in fact voted against adhering, and so did Eure. Of the proxies for adhering, Northumberland's and Rutland's were sent to Carmarthen, Huntingdon's to Ailesbury, and Barlow's and Beaw's to Bishop Compton. Ailesbury lists thirty out of thirty-two of the not contents and four out of six proxies on the same side. Mulgrave and Shrewsbury were recorded as being present on the day,[80] and they held the proxies of Chesterfield and Marlborough respectively. Though the first is unlikely to have supported Oates, Shrewsbury may have done so and cast Marlborough's proxy on the same side. The other not content proxy not recorded by Ailesbury could be either Bridgwater's cast by Bolton, or Clare's cast by Oxford.

The managers of a conference between the two Houses on the reasons why the Lords should adhere to their amendments, reported on 2 August: 'the Lords did not think it fit, that Oates should take Advantage of an erroneous Judgment, to destroy the Verdict'; 'the Persons who served Upon the Juries at Oates's Tryals, were Men of great Consideration in London, some of the first Form of Merchants; and to dispute their Verdicts was, in Effect, to attaint them'; 'they had looked upon Oates as perjured in other Matters; That he had accused the Queen Dowager of High Treason, in conspiring the Death of her Husband, at the Bar of the House of Commons, which nobody could believe of her'; concluding that Oates seemed to think he had 'a Right of creating Evidence, rather than delivering it; That it was not fit to encourage such Witnesses: That his Brain seemed to be turned: And that, when he was lately brought before the House of Lords, he seemed to hang his Rod over them' and that 'a Judgment that was erroneous in point of Form, might not be said to be illegal'. Immediately afterwards, the king's warrant to pardon Oates from all punishments attached to his sentences for perjury was read. On the 20th the Commons voted an address asking the king to grant Oates a pension. The same day the king prorogued parliament, and he later granted Oates £200 to pay his debts, and £10 a week for life.[81] This, together with another short prorogation of 19–24 October, put an end to the disputes between the Houses on Oates's case.[82]

---

[78] Morrice MS. Q p. 592; *L.J.*, xiv. 299–300.

[79] *Poems on Affairs of State*, v. 87.

[80] *L.J.*, xiv. 299.

[81] *C.J.*, x. 249–51, 270; *Halifax Letters*, ii. 236; Hist. MSS. Comm., *14th Rept.*, app. ii, p. 440.

[82] *Hatton Corr.*, ii. 136; Luttrell, *Brief Relation*, i. 594.

THE PLACE BILL

The place bill of 1692–3, or to give it its proper title the bill 'touching free and impartial Proceedings in Parliament', was the first in a series of bills introduced into parliament after the Glorious Revolution with the object of excluding placemen from the Commons, an essential element in the 'Country' campaign against Court influence. Had it passed it would have resulted in a substantial change in the relations between Crown and parliament. To its advocates it was a necessary measure 'to prevent corruption'; to its opponents a mine under the foundations of monarchy.[83] The bill was also important in the immediate political context. Having passed the Commons easily, it was defeated in the Lords only at the last hurdle, and then very narrowly, after considerable exertions on the part of the king and the Court interest; and while William was no doubt relieved at the outcome, the manner of the bill's defeat cannot have been at all gratifying to him. Such a close shave emphasized the ministry's weakness in parliament, a message driven home as the session went on by amongst other things the success of another 'Country' measure, the triennial bill. No sooner had the session ended than William, taking heed, began to change his ministers.[84]

The place bill had been presented to the Commons by Sir Edward Hussey, M.P. for Lincoln, on 13 December 1692, and had gone through all its stages there quickly and with little serious opposition.[85] Ten days later it was brought up to the Lords and read. The second reading was eventually fixed for Saturday, 31 December, 'all the Lords to be summoned then to attend'.[86] The bill as it then stood excluded from the Commons any member elected after 1 February 1693 who subsequent to his election accepted a 'place, office or employment of profit' under the Crown. A member so excluded would not be able to sit again until the next parliament, but would not then be disqualified from taking his seat if returned again, even while still a placeman, provided that his taking office antedated his election.[87] The purpose of the bill was to stop the Court 'corrupting' members who, when they had stood for election, had been free of any such taint. It did not exclude placemen as such, as Lord Mulgrave pointed out to the House, but in fact allowed them to sit, 'provided the electors know it first, and are not deceived in their choice'.[88] Nevertheless, William and his chief ministers were deeply hostile to the bill, and were prepared to use every weapon against it, including as a last resort the royal veto, which indeed was used in the following session when the bill was reintroduced.[89] There were probably at least a hundred placemen in the lower House, whose presence there was rightly considered vital to the government.[90]

[83] *The Parliamentary Diary of Narcissus Luttrell, 1691–3*, ed. H. Horwitz (Oxford, 1972), p. 336; Hist. MSS. Comm., *7th Rept.*, p. 212.

[84] J. P. Kenyon, *Robert Spencer, Earl of Sunderland, 1641–1702* (1958), pp. 254–5; Horwitz, *Parliament, Policy and Politics*, pp. 109–15.

[85] *C.J.*, x. 742, 744, 745, 747, 760–1; *Luttrell Parl. Diary*, pp. 328, 336; *Burnet's History*, iv. 189–90; Trinity College, Dublin, MS. 1996/251, George Tollet to [Bishop King], 22 Dec. 1692.

[86] *L.J.*, xv. 164, 165–6, 167.

[87] Hist. MSS. Comm., *14th Rept.*, app. vi, pp. 279–80.

[88] Cobbett, v. 750. This point has been missed by modern commentators, who have generally treated of the bill as designed to exclude all placemen from the Commons: see for instance B. Kemp, *King and Commons, 1660–1832* (1957), p. 54. D. Rubini, *Court and Country, 1688–1702* (1967), p. 100, departs from this assumption, but his summary of the bill is equally erroneous and misleading.

[89] Hist. MSS. Comm., *7th Rept.*, p. 212; L. von Ranke, *A History of England, principally in the 17th Century* (6 vols., Oxford, 1875), vi. 199.

[90] Hist. MSS. Comm., *7th Rept.*, p. 212; Horwitz, *Parliament, Policy and Politics*, p. 358.

On 31 December, after 'a long debate' and in spite of 'great endeavours . . . to throw it out', the bill was committed by a majority of fifteen, in the first of the two divisions listed by Ailesbury (C1), in which he was himself teller for the contents.[91] The only speech which survives from this debate is Mulgrave's, in support of the bill: a fierce harangue, which he subsequently published.[92] The principal speakers on the Court side were Carmarthen, Rochester, Portland, Nottingham and Devonshire.[93] Their arguments, according to Mulgrave, could be reduced to two main objections: that the bill was disrespectful to the king, in that it excluded from the Commons his 'servants and officers'; and secondly that it would probably 'by its consequence prolong this Parliament', the king being unlikely to surrender the advantage reserved to him in the bill in respect of those members elected before 1 February 1693. The first objection was answered by reminding the House of the exact provisions of the bill, that it only excluded such placemen as accepted office after being elected; the second by an expression of disbelief that William would ever follow such bad advice. 'The King', declared Mulgrave,

owes the nation entire freedom in chusing their representatives; and it is no less his duty, than it is his true interest, that such a fair and just proceeding may be used towards us.[94]

A foreign observer noted that, while the place bill produced something of a 'mélange des partis', the whigs were mostly in favour of the bill and the tories mostly against it, but Ailesbury's lists are evidence against any such generalization.[95] In the vote on 31 December whigs and tories appear in about equal proportions on each side of the question. In favour of the bill were whigs, high tories, Jacobites real or suspected, and some who were simply alienated from the Court, like Mulgrave, Halifax and Marlborough; against were the ministers, Carmarthen, Nottingham and Rochester, Court tories, Court whigs and a number of bishops. The possession of office was the important distinguishing feature of the whigs on the Court side, whether it was great office, as with Cornwallis (first lord of the admiralty), Devonshire (lord steward) and Dorset (lord chamberlain); some lesser post, as with Essex (gentleman of the bedchamber), who was also Portland's son-in-law, Howard of Effingham (governor of Virginia), Newport (cofferer of the household) and Scarbrough (gentleman of the bedchamber); a pension, as with Norfolk; or some local dignity, as with Bridgwater (lord lieutenant of Buckinghamshire). There were office-holders on the other side too: whigs like Monmouth (gentleman of the bedchamber), Montagu (master of the wardrobe) and Warrington, who according to Carmarthen in 1690 depended on his lord lieutenancy of Cheshire to 'support his popularity'; and among the tories, perhaps most remarkable of all, the lord privy seal, Pembroke, who was said by the Prussian envoy to be the bill's 'grand protecteur'.[96] But in the main the supporters of the bill, in contrast to its opponents, were lords without Court employment or Court connections.

The king and his managers had but two clear days in which to marshal their forces, a motion on the 31st to put the Lords into committee immediately having been defeated and the proceedings on the bill having been adjourned to the

[91] Brit. Libr., Loan 29/186 fo. 237, Robert Harley to [Sir Edward Harley], 31 Dec. 1692; *ibid.*, Add. MS. 34096 fo. 249, newsletter, 3 Jan. 1693.

[92] Printed in Cobbett, v. 748–51.

[93] Hist. MSS. Comm., *7th Rept.*, p. 212.

[94] Cobbett, v. 750.

[95] Hist. MSS. Comm., *7th Rept.*, p. 212.

[96] Browning, iii. 181; Ranke, vi. 200.

following Tuesday, 3 January 1693, when again all the lords were summoned to attend.[97] A great deal of activity ensued. Supporters of the bill were approached: if they could not be persuaded to change sides attempts were made to keep them away from the House. For instance, Lord Scarbrough took Pembroke out to dinner on the 3rd, apparently on the understanding that they would both be absent when the bill was debated, but then doubled back and presented himself at the House, though he does not appear to have been successful in registering his vote.[98] Some absentees reappeared, and others, who were unable to come up, gave in their proxies. The result of this strenuous campaigning was to close the gap between the two sides until there was very little between them.

On 3 January the Lords sat 'very late' on the place bill, and the bill's supporters maintained a narrow advantage throughout, until the very last vote.[99] There were speeches in favour of the bill from Montagu, Monmouth, Warrington, Marlborough and Vaughan; and from Lord Wharton, who according to an opposition whig 'spoke very well':[100] all except Marlborough were whigs. Most prominent on the Court side were Nottingham, Devonshire, Portland and the younger Lord Berkeley.[101] Carmarthen was on this occasion absent, perhaps unwilling to appear once more against a very popular measure, which three of his brothers-in-law, Abingdon, Carnarvon and Lindsey, had already voted for. In the committee of the whole House the opposition carried every vote against the Court bar one, by majorities of between one and seven. The exception was an amendment to strengthen the bill by including pensioners with the placemen, which was lost by 45 to 36. The bill was reported unaltered. After the third reading the House first voted by 42 to 40 that it should pass, but when the proxies were cast the Court was found to have squeezed home by 47 to 45.[102]

The bill's supporters were bitterly disappointed. Twenty-nine entered protests, a small group headed by Halifax, giving no reason, but the remainder, headed by the prince of Denmark and including Ailesbury, taking the opportunity to reiterate that they were 'very sensible of just occasion given for such an act' and to repeat their answer to the 'principal objection' raised against the bill, 'the great danger that might happen thereby of the too long continuing this present Parliament', that it was inconceivable that the king would ever take such advice.[103] Looking back on the fateful division, Ailesbury's terse comment was that the bill had been 'thrown out by two Dutch votes', meaning Portland's and

[97] *L.J.*, xv. 169.

[98] Ranke, vi. 199–200. Ailesbury's list on the final division of 3 Jan. includes a note on 7 lords 'that went away and for the bill' (marked in the table below as 'went off'), i.e. who had been for the bill but had now absented themselves from the vote, and a further 4 (St. Albans, Manchester, Willoughby of Parham and Bishop Stratford) now opposed to the bill 'that went of[f] from the vote the day before'.

[99] Brit. Libr., Loan 29/79/2, Robert Harley to [Sir Edward Harley], 3 Jan. 1693.

[100] Ranke, vi. 199; Brit. Libr., Loan 29/187 fo. 1, [Edward Harley] to Sir Edward Harley, 7 Jan. 1693.

[101] Hist. MSS. Comm., *7th Rept.*, p. 212.

[102] Before the proxies were cast there was a debate as to whether proxies entered on that day could be admitted, which was agreed after a division had apparently been 'challenged . . . but not insisted on'(Hist. MSS. Comm., *14th Rept.*, app. vi, pp. 280–1; *L.J.*, xv. 171–2). Since each side held one such proxy (Essex's and Huntingdon's), the point was academic.

[103] *L.J.*, xv. 172. Those who protested without giving a reason were (in order of signing) Halifax, Lindsey, Bishops Sprat, Trelawny and Watson, Abingdon, Bishop Hough, Monmouth and Crew; the other group comprised Prince George (as duke of Cumberland), Warrington, Mulgrave, Ailesbury, Thanet, Rivers, Denbigh, Marlborough, Stamford, Montagu, Longueville, Clifford of Lanesborough, Ashburnham, Vaughan, Cholmondeley (who appears in Ailesbury's second list of this division as 'Not at the vote but had leave to enter his protestation'), Fitzwalter, Weymouth, Arundell of Trerice, Sandwich and Carnarvon.

Schomberg's.[104] Others put the blame for the loss of the bill on the number of opposition absentees, the most notable of whom had been Shrewsbury, who was for the bill but had stayed in the country instead of coming up to vote.[105] The consensus of opinion, however, was that the bill had been defeated 'by the power of the Court, aided by the bishops'.[106] Ailesbury's lists enable us to see in detail how this power was exercised.

From the lists it is clear that the battle was won by the Court rather than lost by the opposition, whose vote in fact held up well between 31 December and 3 January. The crucial factor would seem to have been the number of new voters that the Court was able to mobilize for the final vote. Of those who had originally voted for the bill, seven changed sides on 3 January; six more, including Bishop Burnet, who had earlier spoken strongly for the bill,[107] 'went away' before the vote; and one other, Lord Cholmondeley, arrived too late to vote. But against these fourteen opposition losses could be set nine or ten gains: Craven, and possibly Denbigh,[108] won over from the Court side; and eight new voters, five in person and three by proxy. As well as Craven and Denbigh, the Court lost seven voters through absence, but more than made up for them with the seven who came over from the opposition and a flock of new voters. No less than twenty lords not appearing on Ailesbury's first list, which it should be noted is five short on the Court side, are recorded as having voted against the bill on 3 January, fourteen in person and six by proxy.

The vast majority of the Court gains were lords with some dependence on the Crown. Of the bishops, Stratford of Chester changed from opposition to Court; Burnet, as we have seen, 'went away'; and as many as eleven others appear as new voters on the Court side. Among the temporal lords who deserted the opposition were Bath, who was colonel of a regiment and enjoyed various governorships and county lord lieutenancies; his eldest son Lord Granville, who held the post of gentleman of the bedchamber and several local offices; Macclesfield, lord lieutenant of North and South Wales, who according to the Prussian envoy 'voulut plaire à la Cour et s'absenta'; Manchester, captain of the yeomen of the guard and lord lieutenant of Huntingdonshire; Lord Oxford, colonel of a regiment, gentleman of the bedchamber and lord lieutenant of Essex; St. Albans, an army officer; and four 'poor lords' in receipt of pensions from the king, Colepeper, Eure, Hunsdon and Willoughby of Parham.[109] And apart from the bishops, the Court's new voters included Hatton, who besides being Nottingham's brother-in-law was governor of Guernsey and *custos rotulorum* of Northamptonshire; Lovelace, captain of the band of gentlemen pensioners and chief justice in eyre south of the Trent; the soldiers Ormond and Schomberg; Derby, whose brother was a major-general and held a post at Court; and Sunderland, 'comme bon courtisan' to quote the Prussian envoy again.[110] In addition, Lexington, who came over to the Court for the last vote, probably did so in the expectation of imminent reward. On 29 December Luttrell had reported that Lexington 'stands fair to be secretary of state', and although he did

[104] Endorsement on the sheet containing lists C1–D2.
[105] Hist. MSS. Comm., *7th Rept.*, p. 212.
[106] Hist. MSS. Comm., *Portland MSS.*, iii. 511.
[107] Hist. MSS. Comm., *7th Rept.*, p. 212. Cf. *Burnet's History*, iv. 189–90.
[108] See below, n. 142.
[109] Browning, iii. 180–1; Ranke, vi. 200; *Calendar of Treasury Books*, x. 165, 167, 186; xvii. 521, 531, 570, 585, 682, 685; Hist. MSS. Comm., *13th Rept.*, app. v, p. 399; *idem, House of Lords MSS.* (new ser.), i. 92; *Halifax Letters*, ii. 209.
[110] Ranke, vi. 200.

not get so far he was made a gentleman of the bedchamber and a privy councillor in the following March.[111]

NORFOLK'S DIVORCE BILL

The several attempts of Henry, 7th duke of Norfolk, to divorce his erring wife by act of parliament, against stiff opposition from those anxious to protect her reputation and property, excited prurient interest and partisan sympathies. The eminence of the principals made the case sensational: the duchess was the only child of the earl of Peterborough, and her lover, John Germain, a Dutch soldier and gambler, was rumoured to be King William's illegitimate half-brother.[112] Accounts of the various proceedings were published, and even translated into Dutch.[113] Party politics intruded because of the respective allegiances and connections of the duke and duchess: he had conformed to the Church of England and was a strong whig, while she and her father were Catholics suspected of Jacobitism.

The bill rejected on 2 January 1693, on the division recorded by Ailesbury (D2), was the second that Norfolk had brought in. He had known of his wife's infidelity since 1685, when he had discovered her intrigue and had removed her to a convent in France, but it was not until 1691, after she had returned to London and had reunited herself with Germain, that he decided to divorce her.[114] His first bill was heard by the Lords in January and February 1692. It would not only have dissolved the marriage but would also have enabled him to remarry, which he could not have done had he been divorced in the usual way by an ecclesiastical court on grounds of adultery.[115] Although adultery was proved the House threw out the bill, insisting that the proof be first made out in a lower court.[116] Accordingly Norfolk brought an action against Germain in King's Bench for 'criminal conversation' with the duchess. He won his case easily, and then introduced another bill into the Lords, identical with the first except in that particular notice was now taken of the King's Bench judgment.[117] The bill was given its first reading on 29 December 1692 and its second four days later, on 2 January 1693. No witnesses were called. Instead, the King's Bench record and the opinion of Lord Chief Justice Holt were read, counsel heard and the matter then put to a vote.[118]

As listed by Ailesbury, the contents in this division were mainly whigs and the not contents mainly tories: the same alignment of parties as appears to have taken

[111] Luttrell, *Brief Relation*, ii. 657.

[112] On Germain see the *D.N.B.* and R. Sedgwick, *The House of Commons, 1715–54* (2 vols.; 1970), ii. 61.

[113] *His Grace the Duke of Norfolk's Charge against the Dutchess, before the House of Lords, and the Dutchesses Answer* (1692); *The Proceedings before the House of Lords . . . between the Duke and Duchess of Norfolk . . .* [1692], of which the only known copy is apparently at Arundel (*Arundel Castle Archives*, ed. F. W. Steer (3 vols., Chichester, 1968–76), iii. 69); *De Proceduuren Gehouden in't Hogerhuis tusschen de Hertog en de Hartogin van Norfolk* (Rotterdam, 1692); *The further Depositions and Proceedings in the House of Lords In the Affair of the Duke and Dutchess of Norfolk* (1692); *The Tryal between Henry, Duke of Norfolk, Plaintiff, and John Jermaine, Defendant . . .* (1692); *Het Proces tusschen Hendrik, Hertogh van Nortfolk . . . En Johan Germain . . .* (The Hague, 1693); *A true Account of the Proceedings before the House of Lords . . . between The Duke and Dutchess of Norfolk . . .* (1692[–3]), the 2nd edn. of which was entitled *A Vindication of her Grace Mary Dutchess of Norfolk* (1693). Further accounts were published at the time of Norfolk's third attempt at a bill of divorce, in 1700. See also *Poems on Affairs of State*, v. 316–22, 346, 398.

[114] Details of the story are in the evidence printed in the pamphlets listed above, and reprinted in *State Trials*, xii. 883–947.

[115] Hist. MSS. Comm., *14th Rept.*, app. vi, p. 17.

[116] Public Record Office of Northern Ireland, D.638/13/102, John Pulteney to Lord Coningsby. 26 Jan. 1692; Luttrell, *Brief Relation*, iii. 4.

[117] *State Trials*, xii. 927–47.

[118] *L.J.*, xv. 165, 170.

place over the duke's first divorce bill.[119] Norfolk was supported by his political friends and by those persuaded that it would be good for the Protestant interest if he were to remarry and produce a Protestant heir, his present marriage being childless.[120] On the other side were 'all that favoured the Jacobites', as Burnet would have it, including of course Ailesbury, together with some who were simply against the Court, William and Mary having earlier 'expressed a great deal of warmth for the duke'.[121] Votes across these political lines may have been prompted by pity, either for the duke as a wronged husband (it was said, perhaps seriously, that all the cuckolds in the House voted for him) or for the duchess as the wife of a rake who in fact had been 'the original introducer of all the bad company she kept, to her acquaintance'. The diarist John Evelyn wrote that Norfolk lost because he 'manedged it so very indiscreetely'.[122] There was also an element of family or local loyalty on the duchess's side. The earl of Monmouth, her cousin and Peterborough's heir presumptive, led a small squadron of her 'relations' who 'opposed the bill with great zeal and warmth'.[123] Ailesbury thought that Monmouth was himself in love with the duchess, but it is more likely that he was concerned about the vast Mordaunt estates in Northampton-shire which she stood to inherit and to which he also had a claim.[124] Later, when she had succeeded to the property, Monmouth pressed his claim against her in the courts, though admittedly this was after she had given evidence to parliament of his dealings with the Jacobite conspirator Sir John Fenwick.[125] Of her supporters in 1693, Leominster, Montagu and Rockingham had strong Northamptonshire connections, and the two former also protested against the passing of Norfolk's third and last divorce bill in 1700.[126] Another observation, made by Burnet, was that 'those who were thought engaged in lewd practices' opposed the bill on the duchess's behalf.[127] It is not clear who was meant by this, but two of her side, Devonshire and Vaughan, did indeed have bad reputations.[128]

For Burnet the most important feature of the vote was the split between 'all those [bishops] . . . made during the present reign', who were for the bill, and 'all the bishops . . . made by the two former kings', who were against it.[129]

---

[119] *Hatton Corr.*, ii. 170; *L.J.*, xv. 25, 78; Kent Archives Office, Chevening MSS. 78/17, enclosure, 'February 1690/1'.

[120] *State Trials*, xii. 923.

[121] *Burnet's History*, iv. 227–8; *Hatton Corr.*, ii. 170. William had attended incognito to listen to the witnesses examined in support of Norfolk's first bill but had felt constrained to withdraw because of the obscene nature of some of the testimony (Hist. MSS. Comm., *Portland MSS.*, iii. 488).

[122] Hist. MSS. Comm., *7th Rept.*, p. 211; *Burnet's History*, iv. 228; *The Diary of John Evelyn*, ed. E. S. de Beer (6 vols., Oxford, 1955), v. 127. The defeat of the duke's first bill in February 1692 was said at the time to have caused 'no small joy among the Amouretts of the Town, and no small pain to the Cornudos' (National Library of Wales, Brogyntyn MS. 1059, [Owen Wynne] to Sir Robert Owen, 17 Feb. [1692]).

[123] *Burnet's History*, iv. 228.

[124] *Ailesbury Mems.*, ii. 392. Monmouth had already been trying to lay hands on Peterborough's estates (Chatsworth, 'Devonshire House' notebook, *sub* 'Monmouth, Ld').

[125] *Charles Earl of Peterborow Appellant. Sir John Jermaine and the Lady Mary Mordant his Wife, Respondents. The Appellant's Case* (1702).

[126] *L.J.*, xvi. 540.

[127] *Burnet's History*, iv. 228.

[128] *Burnet's History*, ii. 84; *Remarks and Collections of Thomas Hearne*, ed. C. F. Doble and others (11 vols., Oxford, 1885–1921), ii. 74–5; F. Jones, 'The Vaughans of Golden Grove', *Trans. Hon. Soc. Cymmrodorion* (1963), pp. 134–5.

[129] *Burnet's History*, iv. 226, 228–9. This should be compared with a division in Jan. 1692 on Norfolk's first bill, when '4 Bpps were for the Dutchesse vizt London, Rochester, St Davids and another . . . The rest were for the Duke' (P.R.O. Northern Ireland, D.638/13/94, Pulteney to Coningsby, 12 Jan. 1692). It is interesting that the earl of Nottingham, a patron of many of William's bishops, also supported both the first and second bills (*Hatton Corr.*, ii. 170).

Ailesbury's forecast (D1) and division list substantially confirm this evidence as to the bishops' voting. Only two certain exceptions appear: Simon Patrick, bishop of Ely, and Gilbert Ironside, bishop of Hereford, both raised to the episcopal bench by William and Mary and both against the bill. Patrick's opposition was consistent, for he too protested against the passing of Norfolk's third bill in 1700. Ironside, though appointed in 1689, was closer in background and cast of mind to the older bishops, being a tory and the former head of an Oxford college who had earned his mitre by defying King James. The 'Bp L' who appears at the foot of Ailesbury's list of the contents might be another exception, but is more likely to be Tenison of Lincoln, whom Ailesbury had put down as a probable content, than Tenison's fellow Williamite appointee Lloyd of Lichfield or the older Bishop Beaw of Llandaff, neither of whom had been included in the earl's forecast.

Why the bishops divided in this way over Norfolk's bill is nowhere fully explained. One observer thought that those bishops who were for the bill were making it 'a point of conscience' to declare themselves against a flagrant adulteress.[130] Burnet says merely that he and the other new bishops gave their opinion to the House that 'a second marriage in that case was lawful and conformable both to the gospel and to the doctrine of the primitive church', while the others took the opposite view 'though some of them could not tell why'.

Here was a colour for men, who looked at things superficially, to observe that there was a difference of opinion, between the last made bishops and those of an elder standing; from which they inferred, that we were departing from the received doctrine of our church; and upon that topic the earl of Rochester charged us very vehemently.[131]

But the bill did raise another issue more pertinent to the growing conflict within the Church: whether the authority of the Church courts was to be maintained or diminished. Norfolk's bill would have derogated from that authority, and thus it offended conservative Churchmen. One of the reasons given for the protest against his third divorce bill in 1700 was that 'it is without Precedent, that a Bill of this Nature was ever brought into a Parliament, where the Subject-matter had not first been proceeded on in the Ecclesiastical Courts'.[132] The enactment of this last bill 'marked the beginning of the long process whereby the state took over the control of divorce from the church'.[133]

MONTAGU V. BATH

The case of Montagu v. Bath was one of the most expensive and long drawn out lawsuits of the century, involving estates worth £10,000 a year, and in which contemporaries took a great interest.[134] In 1675 General Monck's son, Christopher Monck, 2nd duke of Albemarle, who was childless, had made a will leaving most of his estates to his cousin Lord Bath and other members of the Granville family, and in a deed signed in 1681 had further stipulated that the 1675 will could not legally be revoked except by another will signed by six witnesses, three of whom were to be peers of the realm, and then only if the sum of sixpence changed hands at the time. In 1686, to his friends' surprise,

130 Hist. MSS. Comm., *7th Rept.*, p. 211.
131 *Burnet's History*, iv. 228–9.
132 *L.J.*, xvi. 540.
133 D. Ogg, *England in the Reigns of James II and William III* (Oxford, 1955), p. 78.
134 E. F. Ward, *Christopher Monck, Duke of Albemarle* (1915), pp. 340–6; *Evelyn Diary*, v. 246.

Albemarle took the post of governor of Jamaica, partly to help pay for his and wife's debts but mainly, it seems, in order to recover a sunken Spanish galleon, from which he obtained treasure worth £40,000. Under pressure from his duchess, who had always been proud and headstrong and was now mentally unstable, Albemarle made another will in 1687, leaving most of his estates to her and to Christopher and Henry Monck, sons of his illegitimate elder brother Colonel Thomas Monck. The second will did not meet the provisions of the 1681 deed, since three peers of the realm could not be found in Jamaica to witness it and no money changed hands. This was widely interpreted to mean that the duke did not intend the second will to stand.[135]

After Albemarle's death in 1688 and the mad duchess's return to England, her father the 2nd duke of Newcastle took up her claims under the second will, but on the first trial in 1690, judgment was given for the earl of Bath. The suit was complicated by the duchess's marriage in 1692, after her father's death, to one of the ablest, most unscrupulous, and most litigious men of the age, Ralph Montagu, 1st earl of Montagu. The circumstances of the marriage were bizarre: she was believed to have declared publicly that she would wed none but a reigning monarch, and to overcome this obstacle Montagu had disguised himself as 'the Emperor of China'. Montagu keenly pursued his wife's claim to the Albemarle estates, and, having lost his case in the court of chancery in 1693, appealed to the house of lords. The case was before the Lords almost continuously between 8 January and 19 February 1694, and public interest was such that both parties published their side of the case, and King William went to the House incognito to hear the debates. On the 17th, after a long debate, judgment was given for Bath by three votes. This final division is the one to which Ailesbury's list (E) refers. The argument which clinched the verdict, according to the Dutch envoy, was that if the deed of 1681 was set aside no property would be secure in England.[136] The division was not on party lines. Montagu's two brothers-in-law, Lords Thanet and Clare, who had married the other co-heiresses of the duke of Newcastle, voted on different sides: Thanet, a tory peer, voted for Montagu; Clare, a whig, who was said to have disapproved of Montagu's marriage to the mad duchess, as it made Montagu a rival claimant to the Newcastle estates, voted for Bath.[137] Montagu's cousin, the earl of Manchester, voted for him and acted as teller on his behalf. The case went on with appeals and counter-appeals, and was still not settled when Lord Bath died in 1701.

THE LISTS

The ten new Lords' lists are included in a large vellum-bound volume headed 'a book of loose papers starched in', begun as an account book by Thomas, earl of Ailesbury, and later used for the insertion of miscellaneous papers. All the lists are in Ailesbury's hand, and of each of the first three lists (A1, A2 and A3 in the table, concerned with the offer of the crown) there is an additional copy in the hand of Ailesbury's steward, Charles Beecher.[138] The lists consist of columns of names for and against, neatly set out, the lords named in order of precedence,

---

[135] Ward, pp. 340–6; F. Cundall, *The Governors of Jamaica in the 17th Century* (1936), pp. 109–17; *Horace Walpole's Correspondence*, ed. W. S. Lewis (39 vols., 1937–74), xxv. 564.

[136] Luttrell, *Brief Relation*, iii. 239, 244, 245–6, 270, 271–2; Hist. MSS. Comm., *House of Lords MSS.* (new ser.), i. 311–21; *The Case of Elizabeth, Duchess of Albemarle and Christopher Monke Esq., Appellants against John Earl of Bath and others Respondents* (n.d. [1694]); Brit. Libr., Add. MS. 17677 OO fos. 181–2, 185–6, L'Hermitage to the States General, 13/23 Feb., 20 Feb./2 Mar. 1694.

[137] Brit. Libr., Add. MS. 34096 fo. 150, newsletter, 13/23 Sept. 1692.

[138] For Beecher, see Cruickshanks, Ferris and Hayton, p. 39.

the bishops in order of consecration. Whether, in the case of the first three lists, Ailesbury copied Beecher or Beecher copied Ailesbury, cannot be determined: the general neatness implies the existence of earlier working drafts.

For the division on 31 January 1689 (A1) the columns in Beecher's copy are headed 'The Lords that were for Crowning the Prince and Princess of Orange' and 'The Lords that were against Crowning the Prince and Princess of Orange'. Ailesbury's has a similar heading. In both versions the lords on the content side number fifty (the official figure was forty-seven),[139] while the not contents number fifty-three (official figure fifty-two). Ailesbury's list is endorsed 'At the Vote of crowning the prince and P. Orange', and it also gives in figures the voting totals for each side: contents forty-eight, not contents fifty-three. In addition it gives the voting figures for the second vote on 31 January on the vacancy of the throne: contents forty-two, not contents fifty-six (official figures forty-one and fifty-five), and a note of the three lords who changed sides on this second vote—Danby, Fauconberg and Bishop Compton. Ailesbury's version also lists 'The Lords that were for vacating the Crown and that Protested against the disagreeing with the house of Commons', thirty-eight in all (thirty-six in the official record).[140]

Beecher's list of the division on 4 February 1689 (A2) has the two columns of names headed 'The Lords that were for agreeing with the house of Commons by leaving in the word Abdicated' and 'The Lords that were against agreeing with the Commons about the Incertion of the Word abdicated', while Ailesbury's has 'Against agreeing with the House of Commons who insist on the word abdicate' and 'For agreeing with the house of Commons to leave in the word Abdicated'. Both give the tellers. The number of names in each list is contents fifty-one, not contents fifty-four (official figures fifty-one and fifty-five). Ailesbury again gives the total for the vote in figures on his copy: contents fifty-two, not contents fifty-five (the last figure could be fifty-six). In addition he gives the total voting figures for the second vote on 4 February on the vacancy of the throne as contents fifty-two, not contents fifty-three (official figures fifty-three and fifty-four), and also the names of the tellers. Finally, this copy has the note, 'Earle of Berkley went out the second vote from the house. Earle of Danby was content the last vote'. The last sentence is repeated.

Beecher's list for the vote on 6 February 1689 (A3) has the two columns headed 'The Lords that were fore the Throne's being Vacant' and 'The Lords that were against the Throne's being vacant', and is endorsed 'List of the Lords at the abdicating vote'. Ailesbury, who was teller for the not contents, has the headings 'The Throne to be vacant' and 'The Throne not vacant'. Both versions total the contents and not contents as sixty-five and forty-five (the same as the official figures), but in both versions the actual names listed total contents sixty-four, not contents forty-six. Beecher's (but not Ailesbury's) names the tellers, and also marks eight lords in the not content column with a cross, giving the explanation, 'Observe that all the Lords (except those marked +) protested against the Throne's being Vacant'. The thirty-eight names unmarked agree with the official record.[141] Ailesbury's has two notes at the end of the columns of voters: under 'Absent' he puts the names of Chesterfield, Anglesey, Burlington, Weymouth, Hatton and Ferrers; under 'Went of[f]', the names of Kent, Huntingdon, Carnarvon, Thanet and Coventry.

The remaining lists are all in Ailesbury's hand. The two on Oates's case, which are on separate sheets, are neatly copied and arranged in order of precedence.

[139] The official figures, recorded in the MS. minutes of the House, have been published in *Divisions in the House of Lords.*

[140] *LJ.*, xiv. 113. The 2 extra names are Northampton and Newport.

[141] *LJ.*, xiv. 119.

The first (B1) is headed 'For reversing Oats Judgment' and 'Against reversing', and gives twenty-three contents, which accords with the official figure, but thirty-seven not contents, which exceeds the official figure by two. Originally there were thirty-eight not contents (this is the total marked in by Ailesbury) but the name of Lord North and Grey was subsequently erased. This discrepancy is the more curious since Ailesbury was himself the teller for the not contents. Both tellers are identified. The second list (B2), headed 'Against Oats bill' (the contents) and 'For Oats bill' (not contents), names forty-eight contents, including fourteen proxies, the holders of which are identified, but only thirty-four not contents, with four proxies identified, as compared with the official figures of forty-eight to thirty-six. Presumably two proxy-holders are missing. In this list the tellers are not named.

Lists C1 and C2, on the place bill of 1692–3, and D1 and D2 on the duke of Norfolk's divorce bill, are all on the same sheet of paper, endorsed 'Lords at the vote of comittment of the bill for impartiall proceedings in Parlament and it thrown out . . . And D. Norfolks bill'. All three divisions occurred within a space of four days, and these lists differ from the others in that some of them appear to be working lists. The first list on the place bill (C1) is not as neat a copy as the previous lists, being less carefully written and containing a few lapses from the strict order of precedence. The two columns appear under the headings 'For committing' and 'Against', and there are forty-nine contents (originally fifty, Lord Rockingham's name having been deleted) and twenty-eight not contents (Pembroke and Oxford were originally listed but their names were crossed out), which compare with the official totals of forty-eight and thirty-three, inserted by Ailesbury in his list. Ailesbury was again a teller here, though the tellers are not indicated on his list. The clarity of this list has been impaired by its having been put to a further use subsequently by Ailesbury, as a basis for a forecast of another vote (D1). Those listed are marked 'x' or 'o' and/or 'q', or left unmarked, the purpose being to assess two sides in a vote and a number of doubtfuls. In addition, three extra columns of names have been added at the bottom of the page, fourteen names in all, twelve of them marked with the 'x' or 'o' legend. This annotation produces two problems of interpretation: in the first place it is arguable that the additional names may have had some connection with the original place bill division, though in only two cases does this seem likely;[142] secondly, it is impossible to tell for certain whether the three deletions in the list (of Lords Rockingham, Pembroke and Oxford) are connected with the division or the forecast, or even the outcome of the forecast. What can be said with some certainty, however, is that the forecast is for the vote on the Norfolk divorce bill two days later. This is indicated by a comparison of the forecast, taking 'o' to be for the bill and 'x' against (which is how the marks have been represented in D1 below), with the actual list (D2) of the 2 January division. No one appears as having voted on the opposite side to that in which Ailesbury placed him; and the four lords who are assigned a definite position by the forecast but do not appear in the vote all conform in their general party allegiance and current political behaviour to the general pattern of the division, three of them actually appearing in the division list on the appropriate side only to be crossed out.[143] Moreover, it

---

[142] The names of Denbigh and Bedford appear close to the column of not contents, and may have been intended to belong to it. They have been marked as 'nc?' in the table of votes below; the other additions as 'a', meaning absent.

[143] The 3 who appear in the division list but are crossed out are Capel and Villiers on the content side, and Godolphin among the not contents. Bishop Kidder is forecast as content but not included in the division list. In addition, Bishop Tenison of Lincoln is forecast as content but not recorded for certain as having voted. However, he is most likely to be the 'Bp L' on the content side in the division list. See above, p. 98.

is highly unlikely that any other issue at the time would have given rise to such peculiar cross-party combinations; certainly the place bill did not, and the absence of any addition to the endorsement, although negative evidence, none the less reinforces still further the grounds for our assumption.

Overleaf from C1 and the superimposed D1 is list C2, on the final vote on the place bill, which took place the day after Norfolk's bill was thrown out. This list is clearly based on list C1, with the precedence order rearranged, extra names inserted, and finally, after the vote, the names of those who changed sides or absented themselves being moved over or deleted, and new voters added. That this was the way the list was compiled is shown by the headings of the columns of names, 'Commitment' and 'Nocommitment [*sic*]', which refer to the first vote, and by the numbers forty-eight and thirty-three, the totals in the first vote, at the foot of the two columns, erased and the new totals inserted. Forty-one contents are listed, plus three proxies, and forty-one not contents plus seven proxies (official figures forty-two plus three proxies and forty plus seven proxies respectively). There is a fair copy of this list on a separate sheet, corrected so as to agree with the official totals:[144] here Ailesbury has appended to a copy of the protest against the bill's defeat and a list of the protesters (written in a clerk's hand) a copy of the full division list, beginning 'For the bill The 29 Protesters' and naming their fellows in the vote, with a separate column of those 'Against the bill'. In neither the original list nor the fair copy are the names of the tellers given, but in the fair copy those who cast proxies are identified, and there are notes of 'Lords that went away and for the bill' and 'Lords that went of[f] from the vote the day before'. The fair copy is endorsed by Ailesbury, 'Reason given for Entering the dissent at the throwing out the bill for impartiall proceedings in parlament and List of the Lords'.

On the same sheet as the two place bill lists and the forecast is a list (D2), headed 'D Norfolk', of the division of 2 January 1692 on the divorce bill. It gives the thirty-five not contents recorded in the official minutes, and twenty-seven of the twenty-nine contents. The column of contents in fact tails off, the last two entries being 'Bp L' and 'Bp'. At the foot of each column are the official figures. The tellers are not mentioned, nor are proxy votes indicated, but from the proxy-holders listed it is possible to infer which proxies were cast on either side. Seven proxy-holders, holding between them eight proxies, are recorded as present in the *Journals*. Six are listed by Ailesbury: three not contents with four proxies between them (those of Brooke, Derby, Ferrers and Ormond), which correspond exactly to the number of not content proxies recorded—they have therefore been entered in the table of votes below within square brackets, thus [ncp]—and three contents, each with one proxy (of Hatton, Howard of Escrick and Archbishop Sharp). The latter probably correspond to the three content proxies in the division, but since the seventh proxy-holder present in the House, Bishop Lloyd of Coventry and Lichfield (who held Bishop Stillingfleet's proxy) may also have voted content, and may indeed have been the 'Bp L' in Ailesbury's list, the likely proxy votes on the content side have been entered in the table with a question mark, thus [cp?].

Finally there is the Montagu v. Bath list (E), a fair copy in Ailesbury's best hand, with the precedence order preserved and the tellers indicated. Endorsed 'Ld Bath and Ld Montagu', the list itself is headed 'To throw out Ld Montagues petition appeall', and the columns 'Against the appeall' and 'For the appeall'.

---

[144] Rockingham was added to the contents (his name may have been on the first list, which is torn), Scarbrough and Leominster removed from the not contents and Schomberg added (see Ranke, vi. 200).

The official totals are included but the list has one too many contents and is two short on the not content side.

It is likely that these lists were prepared either by an individual or by a team of peers, each contributing the names on one side or the other that he could remember. Possibly the two methods were combined to produce a more accurate list, one person compiling a rough draft (the most likely would be a teller, who would have firsthand information), and others helping to refine the draft by additions and subtractions. Apart from lists C2 and D1, which are discussed above, the lists in the Ailesbury papers are all fair copies, and as such reveal nothing of the method of their composition, beyond that they are arranged in precedence order, which suggests that the original drafts may have been compiled from published lists of those entitled to sit in the House, which were marked pro and con during the actual telling.[145] The fact that Ailesbury was himself a teller in three of the nine divisions strengthens this hypothesis.

A technical point: Ailesbury's lists contain voting figures which often do not correspond exactly with the official figures for the divisions. This is a not uncommon occurrence in this period. A good example, where there are six sets of unofficial voting figures, is the vote of the Lords on 29 January 1689 on the motion for a regency. Here only two of the unofficial totals tally with the clerk's record.[146] The official figures are those accepted by the House and written into the manuscript minutes by the clerk assistant, who received the figures from the two tellers. Though it is more likely that the official figures are the correct ones, it is not beyond the bounds of possibility that the clerk could make a mistake in entering them up. One such mistake is to be found in the entry for the vote on 6 February 1689, where the vote of 65 to 45 was originally entered as 65 to 44.[147] The process of telling was also open to error and even abuse, as in the famous case of the 'fat peer' counted as ten in the vote on the Habeas Corpus Act in 1679.[148] Finally, there is evidence that in February 1689 the House, probably because of the small majorities being recorded on crucial constitutional votes, was unhappy about the method of telling, which required the contents to withdraw below the bar while the not contents were counted *in situ*. On 5 February 1689 it was moved that 'when the House is to be told, the Lords shall go on each side the House to be exactly counted, and not go below the Bar'.[149] Nothing, however, seems to have come of this proposed change. Thus Ailesbury's figures, which in any case are usually very close to the official figures, may be taken as reliable, provided that allowance is made for the possible small margin of error.

[145] Printed lists of the Lords and Commons in 1698 and 1702, with manuscript annotations possibly indicating party allegiance or voting on a specific issue, are among Danby's papers in the British Library (Egerton MS. 3359 fos. 37–8, 45–6).

[146] The 2 contemporary unofficial sources which agree with the official figures are E. Bohun, *History of the Desertion* (1689), p. 126, and Hoffman, a German observer of the Revolution, quoted in O. Klopp, *Der Fall des Hauses Stuart* (14 vols., Vienna, 1875–88), iv. 357. Also the bishop of Ely recorded that there was a majority of 3 (R. Beddard, 'The loyalist opposition in the Interregnum: a letter of Dr. Francis Turner, bishop of Ely, on the Revolution of 1689', *ante*, xl (1967), 107). Other unofficial figures are 49–51 (*Clar. Corr.*, ii. 256); 49–52 (Bodl. Libr., MS. Rawlinson D.1079 fo. 4; see also Hist. MSS. Comm., *Portland MSS.*, iii. 425); 49–53 (Brit. Libr., Sloane MS. 4024 fo. 22, Robert Hooke's diary) and 51–54 (*Evelyn Diary*, iv. 619).

[147] Hist. MSS. Comm., *12th Rept.*, app. vi, p. 18.

[148] *Burnet's History*, ii. 256–7.

[149] Hist. MSS. Comm., *12th Rept.*, app. vi, p. 18. The 'Draft Journal' of John Browne, clerk of the parliaments, records, 'Ordered that when the cause of division upon a vote, the Lords are to divide within this house, and not to goe belowe the barr' (Lords R.O., Braye MS. 43 fo. 21v).

Offer of the crown:
A1: to declare William and Mary king and queen, 31 Jan. 1689.
A2: to agree with the Commons in the word 'abdicated', 4 Feb. 1689.
A3: to agree with the Commons in the word 'abdicated', etc., 6 Feb. 1689.

Oates's case:
B1: to reverse judgments, 31 May 1689.
B2: to adhere to amendments, 30 July 1689.

Place bill:
C1: to commit, 31 Dec. 1692.
C2: to pass, 3 Jan. 1693.

Norfolk's divorce bill:
D1: forecast of vote on 2 Jan. 1693 (D2).
D2: to read, 2 Jan. 1693.

Montagu v. Bath:
E: to reverse dismission, 17 Feb. 1694.

Symbols:
c = content
nc = not content
p = by proxy
q = q[uery] on list
a = does not appear on list [150]
+ = not recorded as present in the *Journals*[151]
went out = described on list as 'Lords that went away and for the bill'
d. = died
cr. = created
pr. = promoted
s. = succeeded

	Offer of the crown			Oates's case		Place bill		Norfolk divorce		Montagu v. Bath	
Name	A1	A2	A3	B1	B2	C1	C2	D1	D2	E	
Abingdon, 1st earl	nc	nc	nc	nc+	cp	c		c	a	a	a+	
Ailesbury, 2nd earl	nc	nc	nc	nc	c	c		c	nc	nc	nc	
Anglesey, 2nd earl	a+	nc	a+	a+	c							d. 1690
Arundell of Trerice, 2nd baron	nc+	nc	nc	nc	c	c		c	nc	nc	nc	
Ashburnham, 1st baron				a+	a+	c		c	q	a	nc	cr. 20 May 1689

[150] The normal voting procedure after 1675 was that the contents withdrew below the bar to be counted, while the not contents remained in the chamber. Abstentions were certainly allowed by the late 18th century. Lords who did not wish to vote withdrew to the woolsacks, where they were not counted. It is not clear when this procedure evolved, so that the lords who are tabulated with the symbol 'a' (i.e. do not appear on the list but are recorded as present in the *LJ*.) either abstained, or had left the House before the vote took place, or arrived for the first time in the House after the vote. For voting procedure see *Divisions in the House of Lords*, pp. 8–11.

[151] The lists to be found in the *LJ*. of those recorded as present each day in the House are, in certain respects, subject to error, and therefore cannot be totally relied upon. See C. Jones, 'Seating problems in the house of lords in the early 18th century: the evidence of the manuscript minutes', *BIHR*, li (1978), 139-41.

Name	Offer of the crown			Oates's case		Place bill		Norfolk divorce		Montagu v. Bath	
	A1	A2	A3	B1	B2	C1	C2	D1	D2	E	
Astley, 3rd baron	a+	a+	c								d. by 8 May 1689
Bath, 1st earl	a+	c	c	c	nc	c	went out	c	c	a	
Beaufort, 1st duke	a+	a+	nc	nc	c	a+	a+	a	a+	a+	
Bedford, 5th earl	c	c	c	c	a	nc?[152]	a+	c	c	a+	
Berkeley, 1st earl	nc	nc	nc	nc	c	a+	a+	a	a+	a+	
Berkeley, baron[153]				a+	nc	nc	nc	nc	a	c	cr. 11 July 1689
Berkeley of Stratton, 3rd baron	c	c	c	nc	a+	nc	nc	a	a	a+	
Bolingbroke, 3rd earl	c	c	c	c	nc	a+	c	a	a+	a+	
Bolton, duke (see Winchester)											
Bridgwater, 3rd earl	c	c	c	c	a+	nc	nc	c	c	nc	
Bristol, 3rd earl	c	c	c	a	a+	a+	a+	a	a+	a	
Brooke, 5th baron	nc+	nc	nc	a+	a+	a+	cp	a	[ncp]	a+	
Burlington, 1st earl	nc	a	a+	a+	cp	a+	a+	a	a+	a+	
Byron, 3rd baron	c	c	c	a+	a+	a+	a+	a	a+	a+	
Capell of Tewkesbury, 1st baron						nc	nc	c	a	a+	cr. 11 Apr. 1692
Carlisle, 2nd earl	c+	c	c	a+	a+						d. 23 Apr. 1692
Carlisle, 3rd earl						nc	a	c	c	a+	
Carmarthen, marquess (see Danby)											
Carnarvon, 2nd earl	nc	nc	c	nc	c	c	c	a	a	nc	
Carteret, 1st baron	c	c	c	a+	ncp	a+	a+	a	a+	nc	
Chandos, 8th baron	nc	nc	nc	nc	c	c	c	ncq	nc	a+	
Chesterfield, 2nd earl	nc	nc	a	a+	a+	c	c	c	c	a+	
Cholmondeley, 1st baron				a+	a+	c	a[154]	a	a	a+	cr. 10 Apr. 1689
Churchill, 1st baron (Marlborough, 1st earl)	nc	c	c	a+	a+	c	c	nc	nc	c	pr. 9 Apr. 1689
Clare, 4th earl	c	c	c	a+	a+	c	c	c	c	nc	
Clarendon, 2nd earl	nc	nc	nc								refused oaths
Clifford of Lanesborough, baron[155]				a+	c		c	a	a+	a+	cr. 16 July 1689

[152] See above, n. 142.

[153] Charles Berkeley, eldest son of the 1st earl of Berkeley (whom he succeeded in 1698); called in his father's barony of Berkeley 11 July 1689. He was known by his courtesy title of Viscount Dursley, and is so called in the division lists for the place bill and the Montagu v. Bath case.

[154] 'Not at the vote', but protested against the bill's defeat (see above, n. 103).

[155] Charles Boyle, 1st surviving son of the 1st earl of Burlington, called in his father's barony 16 July 1689, died *v.p.* Oct. 1694.

Name	Offer of the crown			Oates's case		Place bill		Norfolk divorce		Montagu v. Bath	
	A1	A2	A3	B1	B2	C1	C2	D1	D2	E	
Colepeper, 3rd baron	c	c	c	c	nc	c	nc	c	c	a	s. 27 Jan. 1689
Cornwallis, 3rd baron	c	c	c	c	nc	nc	nc	nc	nc	c	
Coventry, 5th baron	nc	nc	c	a	ncp	a+	a+	a	a+	a	
Craven, 1st earl	nc	nc	nc	nc	c	nc	c	ncq	nc	c	
Crew, 2nd baron[156]	a+	nc	nc	a+	nc	c	c	a	a	c	
Cumberland, duke[157]				a+	c	c	c	nc	nc	a	cr. 16 Apr. 1689
Danby, 1st earl (Carmarthen, 1st marquess)	c	a	c	nc	c	nc	a+	a	a+	a+	pr. 9 Apr. 1689
Dartmouth, 1st baron	nc	nc	nc	nc+	c						d. 1691
Delamer, 2nd baron (Warrington, 1st earl)	c	c	c	a+	nc	c		c	c		pr. 1690; d. 2 Jan. 1694
Delawarr, 6th baron	nc	nc	nc	a	nc	a+	a	a	a	c	
Denbigh, 4th earl	a+	a+	a+	a+	a+	nc?+[158]	c	c	c	a+	
Derby, 9th earl	c	c	c	nc	a+	a+	ncp	a	[ncp]	a+	
Devonshire, 4th earl	c	c	c	a+	a+	nc	nc	nc	nc	nc	
Dorset, 6th earl	c	c	c	a+	nc	nc	nc	q	a+	a	
Essex, 2nd earl	a+	a+	a+	a+	a+	nc	ncp	a	a	c	
Eure, 7th baron	c	c	c	c	nc+	c	nc	cq	c	nc	
Exeter, 5th earl	nc	nc	nc								refused oaths
Fauconberg, viscount (1st earl)	c	a	c	a+	a+	a+	a+	a	a+	a+	pr. 9 Apr. 1689
Ferrers, 1st baron	nc	nc	a	a+	cp	a+	cp	a	[ncp]	a+	
Feversham, 2nd earl	nc	nc	nc	nc	c	c	c	nc	nc	nc	
Fitzwalter, 18th baron	a+	a+	a+	a+	a+	a+	c	a	a+	c	
Godolphin, 1st baron	nc	nc	nc	nc	c	nc	a	nc	a	c	
Grafton, 1st duke	nc	nc	nc	nc	c						d. 1690
Granville, baron[159]					nc	c	went out	c	c	a	cr. 16 July 1689
Grey of Ruthin, 15th baron (Longueville, 1st viscount)	c	c	c	a+	c	c	c	c	c	c	pr. 1690
Grey of Wark, 3rd baron	c	c	c	c	a+	a+	a+	a	a+	c	
Griffin, 1st baron	nc	nc	nc								cr. 3 Dec. 1688; took seat 25 Jan. 1689; refused oaths
Halifax, 1st marquess	c	c	c	nc	c	c	c	nc	nc	a+	

[156] Brother of Nathaniel Crew, bishop of Durham, who succeeded him as 3rd Baron Crew.

[157] Prince George of Denmark, husband of the Princess Anne.

[158] See above, n. 142.

[159] Charles Granville, eldest son of the 1st earl of Bath (whom he succeeded in 1701); called in his father's barony 16 July 1689. He was known by his courtesy title of Viscount Granville of Lansdown, and is listed as Lord Lansdown in the second division on Oates's case, the 2 votes on the place bill and the division on Norfolk's divorce bill.

Name	Offer of the crown			Oates's case		Place bill		Norfolk divorce		Montagu v. Bath	
	A1	A2	A3	B1	B2	C1	C2	D1	D2	E	
Hatton, 1st viscount	nc	nc	a+	a+	cp	a+	ncp	a	[cp?]160	a+	
Herbert of Chirbury, 4th baron	c	c	c	c	nc						d. 1691
Howard of Effingham, 5th baron	a+	a+	a+	nc	a+	nc	a+	c	c	a+	
Howard of Escrick, 3rd baron	a	a	c	a+	a+	a+	a+	a	[cp?]160	a+	
Hunsdon, 7th baron						c	went out+	ncq	nc	c	s. 1692; took seat 26 Sept. 1692
Huntingdon, 7th earl	a+	nc	c	nc	cp	a	cp	a	a+	c	
Jermyn, 2nd baron	nc+	nc	nc	c	c	a+	a+	a	a+	a+	
Kent, 10th earl	nc	nc	c	nc	c	c	went out+	a	a	nc+	
Kingston, 4th earl	c	c	c	a+	a+						d. 1690
Leigh, 2nd baron	nc	nc	nc	a+	a+	c	c	nc	nc+	a+	
Leominster, 1st baron						nc	a	nc	nc	c	cr. 12 Apr. 1692
Lexington, 2nd baron	a+	c	c	c	cp	c	nc+	q	a	a+	
Lichfield, 1st earl	nc	nc	nc								refused oaths
Lincoln, 5th earl	a+	a+	c	a+	ncp						d. 25 Nov. 1692
Lindsey, 3rd earl	c	nc	c	nc	c	c	c	nc	nc	a+	
Longueville, viscount (see Grey of Ruthin)											
Lovelace, 3rd baron	c	c	c	a+	nc	a+	ncp	a	a+		d. 27 Sept. 1693
Lovelace, 4th baron										nc	
Lucas, 3rd baron	c	c	c	c	nc	a+	a+	a	a+	a+	
Lumley, 1st baron (1st viscount; Scarbrough, 1st earl)	c	c	c	a+	a+	nc	a	c	c	c+	pr. 9 Apr. 1689, and 1690
Macclesfield, 1st earl	c	c	c	c	nc	c	went out	nc	nc		d. 7 Jan. 1694
Macclesfield, 2nd earl										nc	
Manchester, 4th earl	c	c	c	a	nc	c	nc	a	a	c	
Marlborough, earl (see Churchill)											
Maynard, 2nd baron	nc	nc	nc	nc	c	nc	nc	nc	nc+	c	
Monmouth, earl (see Mordaunt)											
Montagu, 3rd baron (1st earl)	c	c	c	a+	nc	c	c	nc	nc	a	pr. 9 Apr. 1689
Mordaunt, 2nd viscount (Monmouth, 1st earl)	c	c	c	a+	a	c	c	nc	nc+	c	pr. 9 Apr. 1689
Morley, 15th baron	a+	c	c	a	a	a+	a+	a	a+	c	

160 See above, p. 102.

Name	Offer of the crown			Oates's case		Place bill		Norfolk divorce		Montagu v. Bath	
	A1	A2	A3	B1	B2	C1	C2	D1	D2	E	
Mulgrave, 3rd earl	c	c	c	nc	a	c	c	a	a	a	
Newport, 1st viscount	c	c	c	c	a+	nc	nc	ncq	a	a	
Norfolk, 7th duke	nc	c	c	nc	a+	nc	a+	a	a	a	
North and Grey, 5th baron	c	c	c	c	nc						d. 1691
Northampton, 4th earl	c	c	c	a+	c	c	c	c	a	a+	
Northumberland, 1st duke	nc	nc	nc	a	cp	a	a+	a	a+	a+	
Nottingham, 2nd earl	nc	nc	nc	nc	c	nc+	nc	c	c	c	
Ormond, 2nd duke	nc	nc	nc	nc	cp	a+	ncp	a	[ncp]	a+	
Ossulston, 1st baron	a+	a+	a+	a+	nc+	a+	a+	a	a+	a+	
Oxford, 20th earl	c	c	c	c	nc	c?161	a+	q?161	a+	c	
Paget, 7th baron	c	c	c	c	nc	a+	a+	a	a+	a+	
Pembroke, 8th earl	nc	nc	nc	nc	cp	nc?162	went out	ncq?162	nc	nc	
Portland, 1st earl				a+	a+	nc	nc	a	a+	a+	cr. 9 Apr. 1689
Radnor, 2nd earl	c	c	c	a+	nc	c	c	c	c	a+	
Rivers, 3rd earl	c	c	c	a+	nc	c	c	a	a+		d. 14 Feb. 1694
Rochester, 1st earl	nc	nc	nc	nc	c	nc	nc	nc	nc	nc	
Rockingham, 3rd baron				a+	c?+163	c	nc?163	nc	a+		s. 22 June 1968
Rutland, 9th earl	c	c	c	a+	cp	a+	a+	a	a+	a+	
St. Albans, 1st duke						c	nc	a	a+	a	cr. 1684, took seat 1691
Sandwich, 3rd earl	a+	a+	a+	a+	a+	a+	c	a	a	nc	
Say and Sele, 3rd viscount	a+	a+	a+	a+	cp	a+	a+	a	a+	a+	
Scarbrough, earl (see Lumley)											
Scarsdale, 3rd earl	nc	nc	nc	nc	c	c	c	nc	nc	c	
Schomberg, 1st duke				a+	ncp						cr. 9 May 1689; d. 1690
Schomberg, 2nd duke						a+	nc	a	a+		d. 1693
Shrewsbury, 12th earl	c	c	c	a	a	a+	a+	a	a+	a+	
Somerset, 6th duke	nc	nc	nc	c	nc	a	nc	nc	nc	a	
Southampton, 1st duke	nc	a+	nc	nc	c	a	a+	nc	nc	a+	
Stamford, 2nd earl	c	c	c	c	nc	c	c	a	a+	nc	
Strafford, 1st earl	a+	a+	a+	a+	a+	a	nc	a	c	nc	
Suffolk, 4th earl	c	c	c	a+	nc+						d. 1691
Sunderland, 2nd earl	a+	a+	a+	a+	a+	a	nc	a	a	a	
Sussex, 1st earl	c	c	c	a	nc	a	c	nc	nc	a	
Sydney, baron164				a+	a+		nc	a	a		cr. 11 July 1689

161 See above, p. 101.

162 See above, pp. 93-4, 101.

163 See above, p. 101.

164 Robert Sydney, eldest son of the 3rd earl of Leicester (whom he succeeded in 1698); called in his father's barony 11 July 1689. He was known by his courtesy title of Viscount Lisle, by which he is listed in the second vote on the place bill.

Name	Offer of the crown			Oates's case		Place bill		Norfolk divorce		Montagu v. Bath	
	A1	A2	A3	B1	B2	C1	C2	D1	D2	E	
Thanet, 6th earl	nc	nc	c	a+	a+	c	c	nc	nc	c	
Torrington, 1st earl				a+	a+	a+	a+	a	a+	nc	cr. 29 May 1689
Vaughan, 2nd baron[165]	c	c	c	c+	a+	c	c	nc	nc	c	
Villiers, 1st viscount						nc	nc	c	a	a+	cr. 1691
Ward, 2nd baron	c	c	c	c	nc	c	c	c	c	c	
Warrington, earl (see Delamer)											
Westmorland, 3rd earl	nc	nc	nc	a+	a+						d. 1691
Weymouth, 1st viscount	nc	nc	a+	a+	c	c	c	nc	nc	c	
Wharton, 4th baron	c	c	c	c	nc	c	c	a	a+	a+	
Willoughby de Eresby, baron[166]						nc	nc	c	c	nc	cr. 1690
Willoughby of Parham, 1st baron	a+	a+	a+	c	a+						d. 29 Feb. 1692
Willoughby of Parham, 2nd baron						c	nc	cq	c	a+	
Winchester, 6th marquess (Bolton, 1st duke)	c	c	c	c+	nc	a+	a+	a	a+	nc	pr. 9 Apr. 1689
Winchilsea, 3rd earl	c	c	c	a+	a+						d. 28 Aug. 1689
Yarmouth, 2nd earl	nc	nc	nc								refused oaths
Bishops											
Barlow of Lincoln	nc	nc	nc	a+	cp						d. 1691
Beaw of Llandaff	nc	nc	nc	nc	cp	a+	nc	a	c?[167]	a+	
Burnet of Salisbury				nc	nc	c	went out+	c	c	nc	cr. 31 Mar. 1689
Compton of London	c	nc	c	nc	c	a	nc	nc	nc	c	
Crew of Durham	a+	a+	c	a+	a+	a	nc+	a	a	c	
Cumberland of Peterborough						a	nc	c	c	nc	cr. 1690
Fowler of Gloucester						nc	nc	a	a	a+	cr. 1691
Frampton of Gloucester	nc	nc	nc								refused oaths; deprived 1690
Grove of Chichester						a+	a	a	a	a+	cr. 1691
Hall of Oxford	a+	a+	nc	a+	a+						d. 1690
Hough of Oxford						c	c	q	a	a+	cr. 1690
Humphreys of Bangor					c	nc	nc	c	c	a+	cr. 30 June 1689
Ironside of Hereford						nc	nc	a	nc	nc	cr. 1691
Ken of Bath & Wells	nc	nc	nc								refused oaths; deprived 1690
Kidder of Bath & Wells						a	nc	c	a	a+	cr. 1690

[165] Lord Vaughan was also 3rd earl of Carbery in the Irish peerage, and is listed as Carbery in the first vote on the place bill.

[166] Robert Bertie, eldest son of the 3rd earl of Lindsey (whom he succeeded in 1701); called in his father's barony 19 Apr. 1690.

[167] See above, p. 98.

Name	Offer of the crown			Oates's case		Place bill		Norfolk divorce		Montagu v. Bath	
	A1	A2	A3	B1	B2	C1	C2	D1	D2	E	
Lamplugh of York	nc	nc	nc	nc	c						d. 1691
Lloyd of St. Asaph (Lichfield)	a+	a	nc	nc	c	nc		nc	a	c?[167]	a+	pr. 20 Oct. 1692
Lloyd of Norwich	nc	nc+	nc								refused oaths; deprived 1690
Mews of Winchester	nc	nc	nc	nc	c	a		nc	nc	nc	a+	
Moore of Norwich						a		nc	c	c	a+	cr. 1691
Patrick of Chichester (Ely)	nc	nc	nc	a+	a+	nc		nc	nc?	nc	nc	pr. 1691
Sharp of York						a+		ncp	a	[cp?][168]	c	cr. 1691
Smith of Carlisle	a+	a+	a+	nc	c	a+		a+	a	a+	a+	
Sprat of Rochester	nc	nc	nc	nc	c	c		c	nc	nc	nc	
Stillingfleet of Worcester						a+		ncp	a	[cp?][168]	nc	cr. 13 Oct. 1689
Stratford of Chester						c		nc	c	c	nc	cr. 15 Sept. 1689
Tenison of Lincoln						a		nc+	c	c?[167]	nc	cr. 10 Jan. 1692
Tillotson of Canterbury						a		nc	a	a	a+	cr. 1691
Trelawny of Bristol (Exeter)	nc	nc	nc	a+	cp	c		c	nc	nc	nc	pr. 13 Apr. 1689
Turner of Ely	nc	nc	nc								refused oaths; deprived 1690
Watson of St. David's	nc	nc	nc	a+	c	a+		c	nc	nc	c	
White of Peterborough	nc	nc	nc								refused oaths; deprived 1690

[168] See above, p. 102.

6

THE DEFEAT OF THE OCCASIONAL CONFORMITY BILL AND THE TACK: A STUDY IN THE TECHNIQUES OF PARLIAMENTARY MANAGEMENT IN THE REIGN OF QUEEN ANNE

HENRY L. SNYDER

AMONG THE POLITICAL and religious controversies that dominated the reign of Queen Anne, none was more celebrated or crucial than that over the bill to prevent occasional conformity. The passing of this measure became the cherished goal of the high church party. The defeat of this bill was, therefore, the principal objective of the whigs, who were allied with the dissenters and the low church leaders. As the bitter contest over the bill caused a regrouping of political factions, it is a key to understanding the nature of political parties and alignments in the period. The defeat of the bill eventually resulted in the resignation or dismissal of the high church party leaders from the government. By driving them into opposition, the chief ministers, the duke of Marlborough and Lord Godolphin, began that long train of events which resulted in their own humiliation and the return of the tories to power in 1710.

In spite of the attention which this measure has received from students of the period, the details have not been fully revealed of how the ministry brought about its defeat on three successive occasions. Now that the nature of parliamentary management and with it the state of political parties in the augustan age is coming under closer scrutiny, the struggles over this bill appear to have even greater significance. The third and most famous contest occurred in November 1704, when the tories attempted to tack the bill on to the land tax in order to force its passage through the house of lords. New light was thrown on this episode a few years ago by the discovery of a list of M.P.s to be canvassed for their vote against the tack.[1] Drawn up by Robert Harley, Speaker of the Commons and a secretary of state, it gives us some understanding of the means the ministry employed to secure its objective. Now the discovery of a hitherto unknown volume of letters from Godolphin to Harley makes possible a detailed analysis of the manoeuvres of the ministers.[2] Fresh materials from the Blenheim archives, moreover, furnish evidence on the way in which the bill was defeated in the Lords during the two previous sessions. A re-examination then of the parliamentary contest over the occasional conformity bill utilizing these new sources

[1] Patricia M. Ansell, 'Harley's parliamentary management', *B.I.H.R.*, 35 (1961), 92–7.

[2] It is among the Harley papers in the muniments of the marquess of Bath at Longleat House, Warminster. Bound in contemporary calf, it bears the title 'Miscell. MSS.' on the spine. (It will be referred to hereafter as P.M.V.) I am indebted to Lord Bath for permission to consult his manuscripts and quote from them.

provides an insight into the techniques of parliamentary management in the early eighteenth century.

The occasional conformity bill was designed to safeguard the Anglican monopoly of offices secured by the corporation and test acts passed soon after the Restoration. The dissenters evaded the restrictions placed upon them by these measures by taking communion in the established church to qualify themselves for office, then returning to their own meeting houses and chapels for worship. During the reign of William III the tories were frustrated by their Calvinist sovereign from instituting stricter measures to keep the dissenters out of office. On the accession of Queen Anne, a strong supporter of the established church, the tories saw their chance. A bill entitled *An Act for preventing Occasional Conformity* was introduced in the Commons late in 1702 and passed quickly despite the opposition of the whigs.[1] Marlborough and Godolphin, though nominally tories, had no desire to see the bill become law, for it would alienate the whigs and their nonconformist supporters whose assistance they needed to carry on the war. By exacerbating the struggles between the two parties in parliament it would jeopardize the passage of essential government measures. They did not dare to oppose the bill openly, however, for fear of angering their tory colleagues.[2] Instead, they left it to the whigs to secure the defeat of the bill in the Lords. This was not easily achieved.

For some weeks the bill was the principal focus of attention for all parties. Bishop Burnet reports:

> Both sides took pains to bring up the lords that would vote with them, so that there were above an hundred and thirty lords in the house; the greatest number that had ever been together. The court put their whole strength to carry the bill. Prince George, who had received the sacrament as lord high admiral, and yet kept his chapel in the Lutheran way, so that he was an occasional communicant, came and voted for the bill.[3]

Afraid to risk a direct vote, the opponents of the bill added a series of amendments which they knew would be unacceptable to the Commons. There

[1] For an account of the bill and its course in parliament in all three sessions, see G. M. Trevelyan, *England under Queen Anne* (1930–4), i, *passim*. A good contemporary account with the details of all the amendments made to the bill is W[illiam] P[ittis], *The Proceedings of both Houses of Parliament, in the Years 1702, 1703, 1704, Upon the Bill to Prevent Occasional Conformity* (1710) (hereafter referred to as Pittis).

[2] 'The Duke of Marlborough, who endeavoured to hinder the bringing in of the bill, and "would have possessed the Archbishop [of York] with the ill consequences of it", yet added, "that let it come in never so often, he would give his vote for it, but he was afraid it would break us."' T. Sharp, *Life of John Sharp, Archbishop of York* (1825), i. 368–9. Marlborough is even said to have threatened Lord Lucas with the loss of his regiment if he did not come to town and vote for the bill. [J. Le Neve,] *Memoirs British and Foreign, of the Lives and Families of the Most Illustrious Persons Who dy'd in the Year 1711* (1712), p. 431.

[3] G. Burnet, *History of His Own Time* (Oxford, 1833), v. 53. The prince was ordered to vote for the bill by the queen, but as he passed into the lobby he remarked to Lord Wharton, whom he divided against, 'My Heart is vid you'. J. Oldmixon, *History of England* (1735), p. 299.

were several conferences between the two Houses in which each Chamber insisted on its own version of the bill. The final conference was held on 16 January, in the painted chamber. Burnet says that the room 'was the most crowded upon that occasion that had ever been known; so much weight was laid on this matter'. Following this meeting the Lords returned to their Chamber, where they held a series of divisions on each amendment. The vote was close in each instance. In Burnet's words, 'the lords were so equally divided, that in three questions, put on different heads, the *adhering* was carried but by one voice in every one of them; and it was a different person that gave it in all the three divisions'.[1] Bishop Nicholson, writing a summary of the debate in his diary, adds some more details.

Upon the Amendment to the Clause relateing to the Corporation Act the Votes were Equal; *Contents*, 64. *Not Contents*, 64. . . . Praesumitur pro Negante. The next was the Amendment to the penalty. Upon this the Bishop of O[xford] divided with the *Contents*; telling us that he could not agree to the Tempting an Informer with so much money as the Commons had baited him with. This made the Voices 65 against 63 and, being the Cardinal Question which Determined the Fate of the whole Bill, the rest of the points were given up without comeing to any Division.[2]

Among the managers for the whigs against the bill was Marlborough's son-in-law, Charles, 3rd earl of Sunderland, whose list of this key division, hitherto unprinted, is reproduced below. The general was criticized for his inability to control his relation in the House.[3]

The duumvirs (Marlborough and Godolphin) and the whigs realized that the bill would be brought up again the following session. During the time intervening between the two sessions the high church leader, the earl of Rochester, was dismissed from his post as lord lieutenant of Ireland. Although this encouraged the whigs, it increased the inveteracy of the tories. The best place to stop the bill, if possible, would be in the Commons, where it could be expected to originate again. In contrast to the previous year Godolphin was willing to work (though behind the scenes) for its rejection there.[4] On 9 November, the very day parliament opened, the treasurer wrote to the Speaker:

[1] Burnet, v. 53–4.
[2] MS. diary of William Nicholson, bishop of Carlisle, in the Tullie House Library, Carlisle. I am grateful to the librarian, Tullie House Library, for permitting me to publish extracts from it.
[3] Le Neve, *Memoirs . . . 1711*, p. 431.
[4] Besides his activity in securing votes against the bill, he commissioned the pamphleteer and economist Charles Davenant to write against it. Davenant's work, *Essays upon Peace at Home, and War Abroad*, appeared at the end of November. Pittis, p. 36; N. Luttrell, *Brief Historical Relation of State Affairs* (Oxford, 1857), v. 359; letter of Abel Boyer, 22 Dec. 1703, House of Lords Library, B.R.A. deposit, no. 833 (*House of Lords MSS.*, new ser., xi. 506); (J. Le Neve), *The Lives and Characters of the Most Illustrious Persons British and Foreign who Died in the Year 1712* (1714), pp. 335–6.

I have sent about severall of those you call orderly men. I have spoken to Mr. Lowndes[1] to ply his coffee house and to diffuse. I have spoken very thorowly to Mr. Howe,[2] myself; and to Mr. Bruer[3] this morning. All appear to bee very well convinced of the unseasonableness of this bill; but all seem to bee apprehensive, the matter is to farr engaged if once the bill comes into the house. And Mr. Bromley, by what I hear, is obstinate to the last degree.[4]

True to his fears, William Bromley (M.P., Oxford University) introduced the bill into the Commons on 25 November. It was carried after the first reading that day, committed after the second reading on 30 November, and passed on 7 December after the third reading. The day after its passage in the Commons the treasurer advised Harley:

The Whig Lords have been very industrious to gett proxy's and tell votes. They assure themselves of a majority of 5 or 6; some of them bragg of more.

Everybody sees, too late, wee were in the right that would have kept the bill at a distance. Like an unruly muskett it might serve to frighten those against whom it was presented, but not hurt any but those who give fire to it.

I wish sometimes the Land Tax bill were sent up before it came amongst us, but I don't see how that is possible, and sometimes I think quite otherwise, and wish you would enter upon the remainder of ways and means, and fix the funds in your house before Gentlemen are enraged by the obstruction their favorite bill will meet with in our house.[5]

The Lords had expected the bill to be presented to them on 8 December, the day after it had been passed in the Commons, and a full House was waiting to receive it. But owing to some obstruction it did not reach their House until Tuesday, 14 December. It may have been held off by agreement with the whigs to allow them more time to build their majority against the bill in the Lords. (There were eighty-seven peers present in the Lords on 8 December and 100 on the 14th.) More likely, Harley used his powers as Speaker to hold the bill off until the money bill was passed, as Godolphin suggested, for the result of the delay was that both the bills were sent to the Lords on the same day.[6]

As Godolphin had remarked, the whig lords had been busy gathering votes and proxies to oppose the bill. Hoping to force a direct vote on the bill itself, rather than resort to the subterfuge they had used the previous session to defeat it, they carefully calculated their strength for such a division. The earl of Sunderland made these computations for his party. Fortunately for the historian they have survived among his papers in the muniments at Blenheim Palace.[7] In the previous session, the whigs had won the key

[1] William Lowndes, secretary to the treasury, M.P., Seaford.

[2] John Howe, M.P., Glos., paymaster-general of the guards and garrisons, vice-admiral of Gloucester.

[3] John Brewer, M.P., New Romney, receiver general (treasurer) for prizes.

[4] Tuesday 9th of November at 6 [1703], P.M.V., fos. 209–10.

[5] Wednesday 8 December [1703], *ibid.*, fos. 151–2.

[6] See Oldmixon's account of the delay, p. 323.

[7] See below where they are printed with explanatory comments. I am grateful to the duke of Marlborough for permitting me to consult the Blenheim archives, and allowing me to print material from them.

division on 16 January 1703 by only two votes. When Sunderland made his first computations some time after parliament was up he credited the whigs with a net gain of two, although listing a number of peers as doubtful on both sides. Sunderland made a second set of calculations as the date of the introduction of the bill in the Lords approached. In this list he showed more optimism than he had earlier. He gave the whigs a majority of five votes counting doubtfuls (71 to 66). With this margin the managers now felt strong enough to risk the division.[1] The bill was read for the first time in the Lords on 14 December. 'After several hours debating, the question was putt, whither it should be read a 2d time, and carried in the negative by 12: yeas 59, (17 of them proxy's,) noes 71 (12 of them proxyes); ... the prince nor his proxy present.'[2] Sunderland underestimated the whig total by only two. His error in the tory column was greater. The decision of the queen's consort to absent himself may have encouraged the five peers that Sunderland had reckoned on to vote for the tories to absent themselves from the division.

Marlborough and Godolphin were both present and voted for the bill, even signing a protest upon its rejection. They could not risk an open rupture with the tories by voting against the bill,[3] but their refusal to canvass for it gave further encouragement to the opponents of this measure. Their inaction also served to widen the breach growing between them and the tory leaders. The defeat of this bill was, in fact, a principal factor in the rupture that occurred in the following April, when the remaining tory chiefs left the ministry. At the end of March, the earl of Nottingham, in his capacity of secretary of state, had inserted an advertisement for a

[1] 'A majority of their Lordships, who had made an Estimate of their Strength before the Bill came to them, oppos'd it in such a vigorous Manner, that it was hardly allow'd a Second Reading'. Pittis, p. 33.

[2] Luttrell, v. 369.

[3] Cf. Marlborough's letter to his wife in W. Coxe, *Memoirs of John, Duke of Marlborough* (1818–19), i. 220. 'I must be careful not to do the thing in the world which my Lord Rochester would most desire to have me do, which is to give my vote against this bill.'

The difficulties of the duumvirs and the attitude of the tory leaders were neatly set forth by Sir William Simpson in a letter to his friend John Methuen, the English ambassador to Portugal, on 7 Dec. 1703.

'The ministers are generally believed to have been ag[ain]st the conformity bill att first. but since they are not able to hinder it from being carryed by so great a majority they must comply with the party they cannot govern after the great example of mahomets conduct towards the mountain . . . The party proceed with great precipitation in dispatching this bill that they may have the more time to resent it if the ministers doe not deserve better of them by contributing what they can towards the passing the bill in the house off Lords. where ev[e]ry one makes prognosticks of its fate if they are inclined.

They say my L[or]d Tr[easure]r told S[i]r Ed[ward] S[eymou]r it was an ill time to presse this bill and if it did pass the commons it would not pass in the Lords house upon w[hi]ch he replyed my L[or]d doe but change Staves with me for a fortnight and I will undertake it shall passe both houses.' (University of Kansas, Kenneth Spencer Research Library, MS. C 163, X.)

printed edition of the bill in the official *Gazette* without notifying the treasurer beforehand, much to Godolphin's annoyance.[1] Shortly after Marlborough's departure for the continent in April, Nottingham delivered an ultimatum to the queen and the treasurer. Either they must entrust themselves entirely to the tories and adopt their policies or they must suffer the consequences. The secretary was convinced that Marlborough and Godolphin planned to 'putt all the business [of the government] into the hands of the Wiggs'[2] and feared for the safety of the Church. 'His aim seemed to bee to gett the Duke of Somersett and the Archbishop [of Canterbury] out at the Cabinet Councill. . . . He was very positive that the Queen could not govern but by one party or the other.'[3] Contrary to his expectations the queen accepted Nottingham's offer of resignation and took the opportunity to rid herself of two other high church leaders, the earl of Jersey and Sir Edward Seymour. To fill the place vacated by Nottingham, Godolphin persuaded the Speaker, Robert Harley, his closest collaborator and confidant, to take the seals of office. An astute politician, Harley had an unrivalled knowledge of the Commons and its management. His value to the government was never more apparent than in the following session, when the tories made a final effort to pass the occasional conformity bill and break the ministry.

When parliament sat again in October the situation for the government was precarious. Both parties were bent on forcing it out or bringing it to terms. The tories were alienated by the dismissal of their leaders from office. The whigs were unhappy because they had not been invited to fill the vacancies created. Only Marlborough's great prestige, buttressed by the celebrated victory at Blenheim, the political skill of Godolphin and Harley, and the firm support of the queen, stood between the duumvirs and disaster. The session began calmly enough with Harley's re-election as Speaker without opposition.[4] The normal legislative pattern commenced. But everyone recognized that a dénouement must come soon.

The tories had threatened a tack of the occasional bill to the land tax ever since its defeat in the Lords the previous February.[5] On Wednesday,

---

[1] Godolphin to the duchess of Marlborough, Munday 12 at night [27 March 1704], Blenheim MSS., E-20. 'I had seen the bill of Conformity in print before, but I did not know it was notified in the Gazette; nor doe I think that should have been without acquainting the Queen.' Coxe (i. 218) wrongly ascribes this letter and therefore this event to the beginning of the session rather than the end. The notice appeared in the *London Gazette* of 23 to 27 March 1704, no. 4004.

[2] Marlborough to Godolphin, 8 Apr. 1704, in Coxe, i. 229.

[3] Godolphin to the duchess, Tuesday night at 11 [18 Apr. 1704], Blenheim MSS., E-20. Coxe misquoted this letter (i. 229) and thus has misled subsequent students of the period as to Nottingham's demands.

[4] The tories had considered putting up William Bromley in opposition to Harley, but had given up the idea for lack of sufficient support. *Letters Illustrative of the Reign of William III*, ed. G. P. R. James (1841), iii. 269–71; Hist. MSS. Comm., *12th Rept.*, app. iii, *Cowper MSS.*, iii. 50.

[5] The Lords did not have the power to alter a money bill, only to reject it. Through this expedient the tories hoped to force the bill through the upper house without

8 November, Godolphin reported to Harley: 'I was told yesterday that there had been a meeting Monday night at the Fountain Tavern, of 150 members where it was resolved that the money bill should lie upon the Table till the bill of Occasional Conformity be passed'.[1] Harley must have sent a reassuring note, for Godolphin wrote again the same evening:

amendment, because the passage of the land tax was essential to support government expenditures. Certain contemporary writers suggest that the tack was attempted at the instigation of Harley, who hoped thereby to 'decoy them [the tories] into a snare'. However, this charge lacks substantiation from any ministerial source. Pittis, p. 57; [David Jones], *The Works and Life of Charles, Late Earl of Halifax* (1715), p. 110; [A. Boyer], *History of the Reign of Queen Anne, Digested into Annals* (1703–13), iii. 156; *Letters of Daniel Defoe*, ed. G. H. Healey (Oxford, 1955), p. 69.

[1] Hist. MSS. Comm., *Bath MSS.*, i. 64. This meeting had been set up at the end of the previous session. Hist. MSS. Comm., *10th Rept.*, app. iv, p. 338. Godolphin's information is corroborated by Mrs. Burnet in a letter to the duchess of Marlborough with some intriguing new details. 'I was told the Torys had a meeting of 61. Sir G[eorge] R[ooke] was one. The debate was about the Occationall Bill. Mr Bromly sayed he had brought it in twice so he desiered some other might do it now. They asked him if they might wish him joy of the Green Cloth and put him in mind that he had sayed if he lived to three score he would never come up to Parlement without that Bill in his pocket. The meeting broke up without coming to any resolution, that is, if my information be good. I hear Sir E[dward] Seymor is this night come to town. If so it will sone apper if they most incline to peace or contention.' 10 Nov., Blenheim MSS., E–30. The ambivalence of Bromley and some of the tories is also attested to by Simpson. 'They say Mr Bromly has accepted a place att the green cloth in the room of Tony Roe who is dead ... Wee are in expectation of the conformity bill being brought in and the party threaten to tack it to the mony bill. It is not believed they will be strong enough to carry the tacking in the house of commons, but it is thought the bill will passe that house. Sr Ed[ward] Seymor is not yet come to town w[hi]ch is the reason that nothing of moment is resolved on as yet.' 7 Nov., Kenneth Spencer Research Library, MS. C 163, XLII. Even the tory leaders in the Lords believed that pressing the bill at this time was imprudent, according to Simpson. 'My L[or]d R[ocheste]r and [Lord] Not[tingha]m tryed theyr credit with the university of Oxford to perswade them that in prudence the conformity bill shoud not be brought in this session, but they would not be perswaded, so it will be brought in.' 17 Oct., *ibid.*, XLV.

It is obvious that the party was not nearly so unanimous in its support for the re-introduction of the bill and the tack as historians have hitherto presumed. All the evidence points to Seymour and those who took his part as that segment of the party which forced the tories to adopt their uncompromising stand. The attempt to wean Bromley away from the diehards of his party is also noteworthy. The first vacancy at the green cloth had been promised to Sir John Bland, but Marlborough also wanted to provide for his brother-in-law Godfrey at the same board. He had planned to give Godfrey the place of the ailing Scarborough who awkwardly refused to die. Bland, therefore, was compensated with the place of Francis Robartes, a commissioner of the revenue in Ireland, Robartes in turn receiving the tellership of the exchequer made vacant by the death of Sir Christopher Musgrave. But though Rowe died in August and Bland received his place in September, the clerkship at the green cloth was not given to Godfrey until the end of November, after the introduction of the bill in the Commons, which lends credence to the rumours that it was first offered to Bromley in order to weaken the opposition. See Marlborough to Godolphin, 4 June, 6 July, 25 Aug., 29 Sept. 1704, Blenheim MSS., A1-14.

'I am glad you are so sanguine as to think the madness loses ground. I must own to you it frights me the more to see they [the tories] can have a strength in a matter which is not really supportable by one argument'.[1] The tory commoners awaited only the arrival of their leader, Seymour, to spur them into action.[2] Seymour was suffering from diabetes and other ailments; only his tough, unyielding spirit allowed him to attend at all. Godolphin was aware of the breathing spell allowed him, for he wrote to Harley on Sunday, 12 November: 'Sir E[dward] S[eymou]r being at last come to town, I hear Tuesday next is designed for the day of battel'.[3] Fortunately for posterity, Harley was confined to his house by illness for the next two weeks, except for his appearances in the House. Godolphin also fell ill, so they were obliged to make their plans for the defeat of the tack by letter. Through their missives the strategy they developed is revealed.

On 15 November, the day Seymour made his first appearance in the Commons, leave was asked to bring in the bill. Even then he could not stay until the question was put.

Leve was asked to bring it in by Mr Bromly and seconded by Sir Humphrey Mackworth. It was debated long and as you say all the strenth of argument ran against it ten to one. Speakers for it were, Bromly, Sir Humphrey Mackworth, Hungerford, Ceaser, &c; against it Lord Hartenton, Boyle, Smith, Stanhope, Holles, Dormer &c. The Devesion was 152 for it, amongest whom was How, and St Johns [secretary at war], if there was no mistake; against 126 Noes, amongst these was the secretary and controler [Thomas Mansell], the last the only persone of note that my informer observed to be a new vote. . . . I cannot [repeat] the arguements, but I hear, Boyle, and Stanhope with others spoak to admiration: and Bromly better then he used to do.[4]

The bill was carried by only twenty-six votes as against forty-three votes the previous session. The forces for moderation were gaining, but the treasurer was still annoyed.

I find plainly it was in the power of the Queen's servants to have kept out the Occasional bill. She has not much reason to thank them for it, not that I apprehend they can carry a tack or put a stop to the money, but when the bill is thrown out in the House of Lords, they will make use of that handle to throw dirt and stones at whom they have a mind to bespatter. This is what I chiefly expect from the event of this bill, and which might have been prevented if these gentlemen had thought fit.[5]

[1] Wednesday night at 11, Hist. MSS. Comm., *15th Rept.*, app. iv, *Portland MSS.*, iv. 363. The editor has dated this letter incorrectly as Nov. 1706.

[2] 'It is said Sir Edward Seymour is not like to be here the first day, and without him no angry point will be much maintained.' *Letters illustrative of the reign of William III*, iii. 271.

[3] Sunday at 4 12 November, British Museum, Loan 29/64/4. I must acknowledge my thanks to the duke of Portland for permission to quote from the Harley papers which he has placed on deposit in the British Museum.

[4] Mrs. Burnet to the duchess of Marlborough, *c.* 14 Nov., Blenheim MSS., E-30.

[5] Hist. MSS. Comm., *Bath MSS.*, i. 64–5.

Godolphin's main concern was the effect of this and other party disputes upon the course of legislation to finance the government and the war for the coming year. On 17 November he remarked to Harley:

The Comittee of Supply being now closed I hope the Land Tax will bee voted Monday, and hastned as much as is possible. I mean, that no time should bee spent upon any other part of the supply when the formes will allow the house to proceed upon that bill [the land tax], the speedy passing of which is of the last consequence both as to the quick raising of our next year's preparations and keeping down the Interest of money.[1]

On 18 November the Commons spent the day in a fruitless debate, which was little more than a party dispute. That the debate ended in a victory for the whigs was a source of comfort to the court, however. Mrs. Burnet described the contest to the duchess of Marlborough the next day.

I find wee [had] on yesterdays Victory a very good sign of the wekness or Disunion of the high [church] party; for the mater of the debate had the advantage of being a pretended previlidg of the House of Commons, which is a dear thing, and against Lord Halifax, a man who has there very many who hate him hartely, and yet the Majority was very considerable. Some high words past between Sir Edward Seymour and the solecitor [general, Sir Simon Harcourt]. Most of the Court went right and very harty; some rong, but that Mr Mansill should be in the last number I much wonder at. Sure it was some personal thing for the right was very visable.[2]

Harley had gone to the House that day only with effort, coming from a sick bed. On 19 November he was confined by the doctor to his home. The treasurer sent him a note commenting on the virulence of the tories against the whigs and their chiefs.

I wish both Mr. Sollicitor and Mr. St. Johns had been sensible a little sooner, that they must not expect any quarter from their old friends unless they goe along with them in everything, but I hope yesterday's battel secured us from the small shott of the party.[3]

Still another issue threatened to be raised at this time, the controversy between the two houses of parliament over the jurisdiction of the Lords in matters affecting elections to the Commons, the famous case of Ashby v. White. On 21 November Godolphin advised the Speaker:

[1] Fryday at 3 [17 Nov. 1704], P.M.V., fos. 191–2.
[2] Mrs. Burnet to the duchess, Sunday night [19 Nov. 1704], Blenheim MSS., E-30. Cf. her letter of 18 Nov., *ibid.*
[3] Sunday 19 [Nov.] at 2, P.M.V., fos. 199–200. Harcourt was indeed unnerved by the enmity displayed by the tories towards him. 'Universal madness reigns. The more inquiry I make concerning the Occasional Bill, the more I am confirmed in my opinion, that if much more care than has been, be not taken, the Bill will be consolidated [i.e., tacked]. I find the utmost endevours have been used on one side, and little or none on the other. . . . 'Tis not in my power to contribute much to your Service. The interest I had with my old friends I have entirely lost by endeavoring to serve them.' Harcourt to Harley, Saturday night [18 Nov. ?], Brit. Mus., Loan 29/138/7/2.

I am very much concerned for the matter you gave mee an Account of in your letter, and when you are apprehensive, I am sure there is but too much cause for it. I find Mr. Boyle[1] also much alarmed, and have agreed with him to meet tomorrow in the Evening about 7 at Mr. Secretary Hedges', with those Gentlemen of the House of Commons, to consider if anything can be proposed to deferr it in that house, and at the same time to think what course can bee taken to stop it in the other, but of that one must not speak to them, and therfore, I should wish you would speak to Mr. Secretary Hedges to appoint the meeting at 8 and lett me come at 7 either to your office, or your house which you like best.[2]

For reasons unexplained Harley suggested a postponement of the government managers' meeting until later in the week. Godolphin accepted the new date but added a caveat to the Speaker.

I think the meeting will bee best on Fryday morning for the reasons you give and I will bee ready hard by to attend you upon call. In the meantime I beg you to watch if any[thing] that passes in the House of Commons tomorrow should require a meeting of those Gentlemen and cause it to bee appointed, for unless those meetings bee kept up constantly and those who are called come willingly to them, and with a desire to agree, I can not think 'tis possible to succeed.[3]

On Friday, 24 November, the Commons agreed to postpone the debate on Ashby v. White for a week. The bill to prevent occasional conformity was read the first time that day and the House agreed by 192 to 138 to set a second reading.

The ministry was also under fire in the Lords. On 23 November, the same day that the bill was introduced in the Commons, Lord Haversham, a disgruntled whig peer, delivered his 'annual bomb', a speech criticizing the government. This opened a far-ranging series of debates covering the whole scope of administration activities. Godolphin's discomfiture at the attacks his ministry was undergoing was increased by physical suffering, for he had 'gotten so great a cold, that I can hardly hold up my head, or doe anything but cough, and grone'.[4] For the next week, however, all attention was devoted to the tack and the measures taken to defeat it. Even the major debates in the Lords took second place in the attention of the ministers and the interest of the public. At the meeting on Friday the government managers apparently laid out a programme to collect the necessary votes to defeat the tack, although some of the leaders were not very optimistic. Though suffering from his cold, Godolphin took an important share in the canvass by putting pressure on the place-holders susceptible to his influence. He wrote to Harley on Saturday, 25 November:

I take the occasion of your servants coming to enquire after mee to thank you for yours of last night, and I have sent to the Queen that she may pleas to speak

---

[1] Henry Boyle, M.P., Cambridge University, chancellor of the exchequer.
[2] Tuesday 10 at night 21 [Nov.], P.M.V., fos. 126–7.
[3] Wednesday night at 10 [22 Nov. ?], Brit. Mus., Loan 29/64/5.
[4] Sunday 19 [Nov.] at 2, P.M.V., fos. 199–200.

to the Prince to make his servants attend. I have likewise spoken to Mr. Churchill[1] to speak to him. He answers for Mr. Nicholas,[2] but not G[eorge] Clark[3] nor Tom: Conyers.[4] The last you are to answer for. He has promised mee also to speak to Hibson,[5] to St. Lo'[6] and to William Gifford.[7] I have also spoken to Mr. Lowndes to speak to Mr. Anslis[8] and Mr. Manley,[9] and to Mr. Bruer,[10] Mr. Whitfield[11] and Mr. Knatchbull,[12] and to all the Commissioners of the prizes.[13] Mr. Secretary Hedges may speak, if he pleases, to the 2 Bruce's[14] from mee, but I can't easily think either of them will fail us. I can at present think of nothing more, but that Mr. Secretary Hedges and you would please to summon for tomorrow night after the Cabinet Councill the Gentlemen of the House of Commons who usually meet at his house, and Mr. Churchill particularly should bee there, where they may concert who should more be spoken to and by whom, and what is there resolved may bee putt in practice the next day.[15]

Godolphin relayed his request to the queen through the duchess of Marlborough. The duchess, an ardent whig and inveterate meddler in politics, could not resist the opportunity to upbraid Anne for her partiality to the tories.

I rather choose to enter into things that I have been so unlucky in, than to give him the Trouble, who is not well, to write another Letter. And at the same time I can't resist saying that I think it a most wonderful extravagant thing that it

[1] George Churchill, M.P., St. Albans, admiral of the blue, member of the prince's council, gentleman of the bedchamber and chief adviser to Prince George; brother of the duke of Marlborough.

[2] Edward Nicholas, M.P., Shaftesbury, commissioner for managing the revenues of the prince, paymaster of the queen's private pensions and charities.

[3] George Clarke, M.P., Winchelsea, secretary to Prince George.

[4] Thomas Conyers, M.P., Durham, equerry to the prince.

[5] Sir Thomas Hopson(n), M.P., Newtown, vice-admiral of the red in 1703, commissioner of the navy, governor of Greenwich hospital.

[6] George St. Lo(e), M.P., Melcombe Regis, commissioner of the navy at Chatham.

[7] William Gifford, M.P., Portsmouth, commissioner of the navy.

[8] John Anstis, M.P., St. Germans. Anstis had been a commissioner of the prizes but was removed on 15 Aug. 1704. He appears to have had several minor places. On 27 May 1703 he was appointed general deputy to the two auditors of the imprests. On 17 Jan. 1704 he was granted a royal manor in Cornwall. He also acted as receiver-general of moneys arising by the sale of tin (a Crown monopoly). He voted for the tack in spite of the solicitations of the treasurer.

[9] John Manley, M.P., Bossiney, sub-commissioner of the prizes at Plymouth.

[10] John Brewer, M.P., New Romney, receiver-general (treasurer) for prizes.

[11] Walter Whitfield, M.P., New Romney, paymaster of marines.

[12] Edward Knatchbull, M.P., Rochester, commissary general of the musters for the marines and sub-commissioner of the prizes at Dover.

[13] Emanuel Scroop Howe, M.P., Morpeth; Edward Brereton, M.P., Denbigh; George Morley, M.P., Hindon; Robert Yard, M.P., Bristol; Anthony Duncombe, M.P., Heydon; and Alexander Pendarves, M.P., Penryn. Anthony Burnaby, the secretary of the prizes, was also an M.P., for Stockbridge.

[14] James Bruce, M.P., Great Bedwyn, and Robert Bruce, M.P., Marlborough, both brothers of Thomas, 2nd earl of Ailesbury, an exiled Jacobite peer. Neither were place-holders at the time and both voted against the tack. The two Bruces represented boroughs in Wiltshire where Hedges' country seat was located.

[15] Saturday at noon [25 Nov.], P.M.V., fos. 196–7.

should be necessary to take Pains with your own Servants and the Prince's to save Europe and the Crown upon your head.[1]

The queen, ignoring the duchess's remonstrances, promised her full support.

I am very sorry my Lord Treasurer's cold is so bad, and I will be sure to speak to the Prince to command all his servants to do their duty; if they should not obey him, I am sure they do not deserve to be any longer so; and I shall use my endeavours that they may not.[2]

The next day the treasurer continued his efforts, though by proxy, for his cold had incapacitated him. His first letter was to Harley.

I am very sorry to find you have stil need of medicines, and that so unreasonable a thing as this tack should need so much sollicitation and industry to prevent it. However, I shall omitt nothing in my power. I have sent abundance of letters and messages about. If I had been able to stirr I designed this evening to have spoke to my Lord Keeper, but now I must gett Mr. Secretary to doe it, my head is soe full of a cold, that I can scarce see.[3]

The duchess of Marlborough apparently doubted the success of the ministry's efforts, for Godolphin took time out to reassure her of his progress towards defeating the threatened tack.

I beleive you may bee very sure of Mr. Chetwynd[4] for the reasons you have given. He is very desirous of a place, and his friends too knowing to mistake the road to it. Neither are Wee so unactive as you think, for as much Care and pains has been taken as can bee taken, and I don't doubt but it will have a good Effect, and that Wee shall have a good majority, tho perhaps not all who are in the Queen's Service and the prince's; but in that Case, there must bee no present resentment showne nor soe much as threatened, tho I assure you when the session is over, I shall never think any man fitt to continue in his employment, who gives his Vote for this tack. The matter being of so great Consequence, it is good to bee sure, or else there are some that I could bee very well content might give that handle against them. I am told Mr. Guy[5] will bee in town today, and also Mr.

---

[1] Saturday [25 Nov.], Spencer MSS., Althorp. I am grateful to Lord Spencer for allowing me to reproduce letters in his archives.

[2] Spencer MSS., Althorp. The letter bears no heading but the date is evident from the duchess's letter and Godolphin's of the same date. It is printed in *Letters of Queen Anne*, ed. Beatrice C. Brown (1935), p. 255 but without the correct date being assigned.

[3] Sunday past 2 [26 Nov.], P.M.V., fo. 138.

[4] Walter Chetwynd, M.P., Stafford. His wife was the daughter of Viscount Fitzharding, a teller of the exchequer and a cousin of Godolphin's. Chetwynd followed the dictates of the court and was rewarded with the place of master of the queen's buck hounds in Oct. 1705.

[5] Henry Guy, M.P., Heydon. A former secretary to the treasury and a political agent for Robert Harley.

Pulteney,[1] but if not might not they yett bee sent to? I hear Sir Thomas Hales[2] will bee right.

Our people had a great meeting last night at Mr. Secretary Hedge's and are all very firm and confident.[3]

Godolphin, though still sanguine, was not quite so optimistic when he wrote to Harley on the same subject an hour later.[4]

Mr. Secretary Hedges has given mee an Account of the meeting last night, which looks very promising, and Mr. Lowndes tells mee he has done miracles, and will by noe means doubt the success; but while I see such an inveteracy as appears upon this occasion, I cannot bee without my apprehensions that it looks farther than wee are at present aware of, and these people would not bee so mad either to run all into confusion, or to run their own heads against a wall in this matter, but that, in case the latter happens, as I hope it will, they flatter themselves, that at least, they shall lay the foundation of a considerable opposition during the whole course of the Queen's reign, which they will still endeavour to cultivate and improve as time and opportunity gives them any encouragement.

This I believe is a measure settled among the heads of them in our house [the Lords], or else so many of the herd would not run blindfold into it at this time, which the successes of this year could naturally make men think pretty discouraging, but that seems to have had a turn quite contrary to what was expected, and the word seems to have been given out among them, *that they must struggle now, or else it will bee too late*, and that another year's prosperity will crush them forever; which in truth I take to bee the case, and hope it will prove soe, but nothing can bee done, I find, without so much labour and pain as makes one very often of opinion that the play is scarce worth the Candles. . . .

Mr. Lowndes promises to gett Manley. You must answer for Thomas Conyers and George Granvile.[5]

Godolphin communicated with Harley still once more on Monday to remind him that he was available for any last minute discussion on measures to defeat the tack.

I am glad to hear you have gone through the report of the bill today. Pray lett mee have the satisfaction of hearing how your cold is, and if you think of coming to Mr. Secretary Hedges's tonight. In case you do, I will stay at home to expect a summons, though otherways I don't see much occasion of my being there.[6]

[1] John Pulteney, M.P., Hastings. Pulteney had lost his place in the ordnance the previous year due to some indiscreet remarks about a peer. In 1707 he was restored to office as a commissioner of trade. Henry Guy had been a close friend of Pulteney's father, Sir William. Guy looked after the family's interests following the elder Pulteney's death. The principal recipient of his largesse was William, John's nephew, later to become famous as the antagonist of Sir Robert Walpole. Guy settled his estate on him. Daniel, John's son, was appointed envoy to Denmark in 1706. Another son (?), Thomas, was a page of honour to Queen Anne.

[2] Sir Thomas Hales, 2nd Bt., M.P., Kent. Though a teller for the bill in 1703 and 1704 he voted against the tack.

[3] Munday near one [27 Nov.], Blenheim MSS., E-20.

[4] Monday at 2 [27 Nov.], Brit. Mus., Loan 29/64/12.

[5] George Granville, M.P., Fowey. A follower of Harley's, he was governor of Pendennis Castle and his brother, Sir Beville, was governor of Barbadoes.

[6] Monday at 6 [27 Nov.], Brit. Mus., Loan 29/64/12.

The efforts of the ministry were crowned with success. In the words of Bishop Nicholson:

The Commons sat this Evening till Eight o'clock, from one, warmly debateing whether the Occasional Bill should be committed to the same Committe with the Land Tax—which Question, being at last put, was carry'd in the Negative. Yeas, 134. Noes, 251. This Defeat sat very uneasy upon many of our High-flyers; who were ventureing the Parliament and Nation's falling into any sort of Confusion, rather than not carry their point. When the Coaches began to move, I sent out my servant to enquire how matters went: And he presently return'd with a lamentable story that *The Church has lost it*. This, he said, he had from several Clergymen; as well as others. With Submission, I am of a contrary Opinion.[1]

Harley rushed the news of their success to Godolphin as soon as the tellers reported the count. Godolphin returned in kind. 'I heartily return your con-gratulations and hope this day, if rightly managed may prove the best for the Queen's service that Wee have seen a long time.'[2] The bill, standing alone, subsequently passed in the Commons but was defeated in the Lords on a motion for a second reading, 51 to 33. The trials of the ministry during this session were hardly over, but this show of strength in the most crucial issue demonstrated its capacity to survive. That the vote on the tack was regarded as a test of strength by the tories, was apparent to all observers. Mrs. Burnet commented to the duchess on its significance.

I am told by a half Torry their zeal is turned to rage, and they resolve to leve nothing undon to bring back their party to a Majority. . . . In one of their meetings they resolved if they carryed the tack, to have gon on to vote out the speaker, and chuse Mr. Bromly and then to atack Lord Treasurer, and then address the Queen to restore Lord R[ochester] to the chefe ministrie, to gett the solicetor turned out and Mr. Polly put in his place; and I suppose to have everything don by their direction.[3]

The day after the tack was defeated, the treasurer remarked to Harley: 'I was in hopes the victory upon the division last night, would have secured the future quiett of this sessions, and I think, if carefully managed, with the assistance of the Duke of Marlborough's coming over, it may doe soe still'.[4] Two days later he added, 'Some measure should bee speedily concerted to continue our present majority to the end of this parliament which might also lay a foundation of having one of the same kind in the next'.[5] As Godolphin had suggested to the duchess, no immediate reprisal was made against those place-holders who had voted for the tack, but the treasurer could hardly afford to allow this challenge to go unnoticed. On the day after the defeat of the tack he wrote to Harley: 'You can't bee

---

[1] A portion of this extract is printed in F. G. James, *North Country Bishop* (New Haven, 1956), p. 178.
[2] Tuesday night near 9 [28 Nov.], Brit. Mus., Loan 29/64/2.
[3] Mrs. Burnet to the duchess, [Dec. 1704], Blenheim MSS., E-30.
[4] Wednesday night at 10 [29 Nov.], P.M.V., fo. 136.
[5] Fryday night at 8 [1 Dec.], P.M.V., fos. 132–3.

possibly more in the right than to encourage those who were against the tack. I hope you will bid everybody doe it. I shall not fail of it myself, but I am sorry the humour continues in the others'.[1] On 1 December he gave evidence of his real intentions. 'It will bee fitt to consider when I see you next, what men shall bee pitched upon to bee made examples'.[2] Once parliament was up in March, Godolphin proceeded to remove some of the tackers from their offices, although he could not afford to dismiss them all.[3] But the treasurer did serve notice to those in place that loyalty to the court was expected from them in parliament.

In the following May, new elections were held for parliament. A list of the tackers was printed and widely circulated, the government and the whigs combining in an effort to defeat them. Much to Godolphin's chagrin, he had little success in purging the offending members. Ninety out of the 134 tackers were returned again, although four of these were subsequently unseated during the hearings on controverted elections.[4]

The importance of the ministry's victory in defeating the tack in the Commons went far beyond its immediate effect upon domestic politics. Besides demonstrating the staying power of the ministry, it was of major importance for the great coalition against Louis XIV. Marlborough summed up its significance in a letter to his wife.

I see the pains that has been taken to carry the tack. If they had succeeded it is what must have disturbed everything, for not onely in England but here [Holland] also they would have been so out of heart, that they would have advanced no monys, so that all our preparations must have stod stile. I hope 17 [Nottingham] and 18 [Rochester] did not know these fatal consequences when thay were so earnest for itt for it is most certaine no greater services could be done for France.[5]

But for the student of English parliamentary history the vicissitudes of this bill are of prime interest because of the way in which they illumine his knowledge of parliamentary management in the early stages of party development.

[1] Wednesday at 8 [29 Nov.], P.M.V., fo. 140.
[2] [1 Dec.], P.M.V., fos. 132–3.
[3] Among those tackers who lost their places were John Manley (removed 25 Apr. 1705); Alexander Pendarves (July 1705); Peter Shackerly, governor of Chester (20 March 1705); Charles Seymour, gentleman of the bedchamber to the prince (6 Aug. 1706); Charles Bertie, treasurer of the ordnance (3 May 1705); the earl of Dysert, lord lieutenant of Suffolk (Apr. 1705); and Charles Fox, paymaster of the forces abroad (Apr. 1705).
[4] Sir Willoughby Hickman, Bt. and William Levinz, for East Retford; Thomas Gery and Sir Christopher Hales, Bt., for Coventry.
[5] 8/19 Dec., Blenheim MSS., E-2. Cf. Daniel Williams to Harley, 29 Nov., Hist. MSS. Comm., *15th Rept.*, app. iv, *Portland MSS.*, iv. 152, and Burnet, v. 180.

APPENDIX

Sunderland's first list is in Blenheim MSS., D2–10. Drawn up *c.* November 1703 (before the death of the bishop of Bath and Wells on 26 November) it reproduces a division of 16 January 1703 with additional comments. The Lords divided five times that day on amendments to the bill. This list corresponds with the figures recorded for the first and second divisions in the *Lords Journal*: contents, 65; not contents, 63. The third division passed in the negative, 64 to 64, and the fourth and fifth amendments were retained, 55 to 49. Sunderland's list must refer to the vote on the penalties clause (the money clause), because it includes the bishop of Oxford for the amendment, and Nicholson noted his switch on that division. It is impossible, however, to reconcile the accounts of Nicholson, Burnet and the *Journal* completely. Nicholson states that the vote on the corporation clause, which was equal, came before that on the penalties clause. The *Journal* shows it coming afterwards. From the manner in which the proxies were recorded in the MS. worksheets by the clerks, by individual tallies after each division, one assumes that the divisions were recorded in the order in which they were taken in the House. The total of five set down in the *Journal* must be correct, although Nicholson mentions only two divisions and Burnet three. One is also intrigued by the latter's comment that a different person cast the deciding vote on each division, for Nicholson only mentions the switch of the bishop of Oxford.[1]

Four peers are listed in the *Lords Journal* as being present that day but are not found on the division list.[2] Apparently they chose to leave the House rather than declare themselves. The *Journal* is not completely accurate, however. According to the manuscript minutes there were 10 proxies for the amendments and 14 against them on the division recorded in this list.[3] A check of Sunderland's

---

[1] MS. Minutes and MS. Journals of the Lords, House of Lords Library; *Lords Journals*, xvii. 244; Luttrell, v. 258; *House of Lords MSS.*, new ser., v. 158–9; Burnet's and Nicholson's accounts, above, pp. 112-13.

A clue to the trimmers who switched or abstained, thus making the defeat of the bill possible, may be derived from another list, drawn up by the earl of Nottingham. Nottingham was a manager for the bill in the Lords. His estimate of the strength of the supporters and opponents of the measure is preserved among the Finch-Hatton Papers in the Northamptonshire Record Office. (No. 2900. I am grateful to the Record Office for permission to consult and cite this document.) Nottingham reckoned on 68 peers for the bill (that is, against the amendments) and 58 against it. It is a tribute to the efforts of the whigs that they succeeded so well in obtaining the necessary votes to carry the crucial divisions against the tories. A comparison of Nottingham's calculations with the actual division list suggests which peers were won over by the whigs to accomplish this victory. Three lords that Nottingham had expected to vote with the whigs were absent (St. Albans, Derby and Leicester) but they were compensated for by 3 peers who deserted the tory ranks to vote whig, contrary to Nottingham's expectations (Lucas, Ferrers, and the bishop of Bath and Wells). In addition to those he had listed under the headings 'pro' and 'con', Nottingham listed an additional 8 peers as uncertain or 'qre'. Of these one was absent (Grantham) and all the rest voted with the whigs (Southampton, Scarborough, Suffolk, Lovelace, Eure, and the bishops of Bangor and Hereford).

[2] The earls of Bridgewater, Leicester, Derby and Feversham.

[3] *House of Lords MSS.*, new ser., v. 158–9.

division list against the *Journal* reveals the names of 14 persons for the amendments[1] and 14 persons against them[2] who were not present but whose vote was recorded. The discrepancy in the former figure is explained in part by reference to the manuscript minutes, for Viscount Saye and Sele and the bishop of Bath and Wells are both listed there as being present. (Nicholson explains in his diary under this date that the bishop came in late when he found that he could not change the holder of his proxy.) This still leaves 2 to account for. Of the remaining 12 who would appear to have voted by proxy only 4 attended both before and after this date in the month of January. Of these 4 (Berkeley, Lovelace, Vaughan, and the bishop of Lincoln), Lovelace and Vaughan were the most regular attenders, appearing eleven and eight times respectively in January. It is not unreasonable to assume then that they were present and voted for the amendments though the clerk did not record their attendance.

*   *   *   *   *   *

Blenheim MSS., D2–10

G[ood]	B[ad]
Duke of Devonshire	The Prince
D. of Somersett	Ld. God[olphin] Treasurer
Q. D. of Southampton	Ld. Pemb[roke] President [of the Council]
D. of Bolton	
D. of Newcastle	D. of Normanby Priv[y] Seal
Ld. Carlisle E[arl] M[arshall]	D. of Richmond
Ld. Oxford	D. of Ormond
Ld. Huntington	D. of Northumb[erland]
Ld. Suffolk	D. of Schonberg
Ld. Dorsett	D. of Leeds
Ld. Manchester	D. of Bedford
Ld. Rivers	D. of Marlborough
Ld. Peterborough	Ld. Lindsey Gr[eat] Ch[amberlain]
Ld. Stamford	Ld. Jersey Ch[amberlain]
Ld. Kingston	Q. Ld. Kent
Ld. Sunderland	Ld. Northampton
Ld. Essex	Ld. Denbigh
Ld. Burlington	Ld. Carnarvon
Ld. Shaftesbury	Ld. Thanett
Ld. Radnor	Ld. Scarsdale
Ld. Berkeley	Ld. Sandwich
Ld. Portland	Ld. Anglesey
Ld. Mountague	Ld. Sussex
Ld. Torrington	Ld. Nottingham
Ld. Scarborough	Ld. Rochester
Ld. Bradford	Ld. Abingdon

[1] Suffolk, Dorset, Burlington, Shaftesbury, Berkeley, Coventry, Saye and Sele, Ferrers, Fitzwalter, Eure, Lovelace, Vaughan, and the bishops of Bath and Wells and Lincoln.

[2] Godolphin, Thanet, Willoughby of Brooke, Maynard, Leigh, Jermyn, Craven, Stawell, Guildford, Lempster, Weston, the archbishop of York, and the bishops of Winchester and Llandaff.

G[ood]	B[ad]
Ld. Romney	Q. Ld. Holderness
Ld. Coventury	Ld. Plimouth
Ld. Orford	Ld. Warrington
V. Say & Seale	V. Hereford
V. Townsend	V. Weymouth
Ld. Abergavenny	V. Longville
Ld. Ferrers	Ld. Delaware
Ld. Fitzwalter	Ld. Willoughby of Brook
Ld. Eure	Ld. North & Gray
Ld. Wharton	Ld. Chandos
Ld. Gray of Wark	Ld. Brook
Ld. Lovelace	Q. Ld. Pawlett
Ld. Mohun	Ld. Maynard
Ld. Vaughan	Ld. Howard of Escrick
Ld. Colpeper	Ld. Raby
Q. Ld. Lucas	Ld. Leigh
Ld. Rockingham	Ld. Jermin
Ld. Berkeley of Stratton	Ld. Byron
Ld. Cornwallis	Ld. Lexington
Ld. Ossulston	Ld. Craven
Ld. Herbert	Ld. Osborn
Ld. Haversham	Ld. Dartmouth
Ld. Sommers	Ld. Stawell
Ld. Hallifax	Ld. Guildford
Archb. of Canterbury	Ld. Chomley
B. of Worcester	Ld. Ashburnham
B. of Salisbury	Ld. Lempster
B. of Hereford	Ld. Weston alias Arran
B. of Ely	Ld. Barnard
B. of Litchfield	Arch. of York
B. of Norwich	B. of London
B. of Peterborough	B. of Durham
B. of Gloucester	B. of Winchester
B. of Bath and Wells	B. of Landaff
B. of Bristoll	B. of Carlisle
B. of Lincoln	B. of Rochester
B. of Chichester	B. of Exeter
B. of Oxford	B. of St. Asaph
B. of Bangor	
in all 65	in all 63

G[ood] to be depended upon this year that were absent	B[ad] to be depended upon this year that were absent
Ld. Derby	Ld. Guernsey
Ld. Leicester	Ld. Granville
Ld. Bolingbrook	Ld. Gore
Ld. Pagett	Ld. Conway
Ld. Effingham	B. of Chester

G[ood]	B[ad]
Ld. Harvey	
Ld. Willoughby of Parham	
in all 7[1]	in all 5[2]

G[ood] dead or absent	B[ad] dead or absent
Ld. Oxford	Ld. Jermine
Ld. Huntington	D. of Ormond
Possibly for some time Ld. Shaftesbury	D. of Schomberg[3]
in all 3	in all 3

Ld. Bridgewater uncertain last year chose to be absent	Ld. Exeter uncertain whither he will come up, but bad
Ld. Yarmouth uncertain Probably won't come up	Ld. Feversham chose to be absent
Ld. Rochford, uncertain whither he will come over but if he does certainly good	Ld. Albermale Probably will come, uncertain what he will be, more likely bad
D. of St Albans chose to be absent & probably will be so	Ld. Grantham probably absent as he was
	Ld. Trerice Probably not come if come's bad

*   *   *   *   *   *

The second list, in Blenheim MSS. VIII (23), was made up by Sunderland sometime between 26 November (when the bishop of Bath and Wells died) and 14 December, the day the bill was defeated in the Lords. It probably dates from before 8 December, judging from Godolphin's comment to Harley on that date.[4] As this list is a modification of the division list printed above it is only necessary to note the manner in which it differs. From the 65 lords who had voted for the amendments the previous session, he subtracted 4: Oxford (died 12 March 1703); Huntington (with the army in Flanders); Shaftesbury (living abroad in Holland); and the bishop of Bath and Wells (died 26 November 1703). To this net total of 61 he added 7 names: Derby, Leicester, Bolingbroke, Willoughby of Parham, Paget (a diplomat, on the continent the last year), Effingham (just come of age), and Hervey (created a peer in March). With the addition of 3 doubtfuls, St. Albans, Bridgewater and Feversham, the total estimate for the whigs was 71. From the previous tory sum of 63 he deducted 5: Ormonde

[1] Sunderland had originally written 6, then added Lord Willoughby and changed the total to 7.

[2] In a like manner, Sunderland had computed 4, then added the bishop of Chester, amending the total to read 5.

[3] Schomberg had been appointed captain-general and commander-in-chief of the forces in Portugal on 16 Aug. 1703 and Sunderland expected he would be leaving shortly with his troops. He did not actually depart from England until the following January.

[4] See above, p. 114.

(away in Ireland); Raby (envoy in Berlin); Jermyn (died in April and succeeded by his brother, Lord Dover, a catholic), and 2 whom Sunderland reckoned as doubtfuls, Richmond and Cholmondeley. To this net total of 58 he added 6 peers: Winchelsea (absent on a mission to Hanover the previous session); the bishop of Chester; and 4 new peers, created in March, Guernsey, Gower, Granville and Conway. With the 2 doubtfuls, Sunderland estimated the tory strength at 66.

Sunderland's calculations were vindicated when the bill arrived in the Lords on 14 December. The division list has been printed elsewhere,[1] so that it only remains necessary to reconcile it with Sunderland's reckoning. His estimate of 71 for the whigs was exactly right. He erred only slightly in the names. The whigs gained Richmond (who voted with the tories in January)[2] and lost Bridgewater. The tories did not show up as well as he expected. Instead of the 66 he postulated, they only polled 59. They gained Exeter and Bridgewater (husband of Marlborough's third daughter, Elizabeth), but lost the prince, Holdernesse (who left the House before the division), Warrington, North and Grey, Howard of Escrick, Lexington, Cholmondeley, and the bishop of Carlisle (who did not attend this session).

There are some discrepancies in the printed lists that have to be adjusted to reconcile Sunderland's estimate with the actual division. Pittis and Boyer both list 59 for the bill and 69 against it. Torbuck lists 57 for and 69 against it but prints the figures 59 and 71. Most of the contemporary authorities say that the bill was defeated by a majority of 12, and they are confirmed by the manuscript minutes of the Lords, which record 71 against the bill (with 12 proxies) and 59 for it (with 17 proxies). Torbuck lists 15 of the proxies[3] plus the 42 lords present, for a total of 59. A comparison with Pittis and Boyer proves that he omitted Lords Hereford and Brook. As they were not present, according to the *Journal*, they must have voted by proxy, thus bringing the total to the proper number of 17.

The discrepancies in the columns of those who voted against the bill may also be accounted for. Torbuck lists the 12 peers who voted by proxy,[4] but all the lists show only 57 additional peers for a total of 69 names, two short of the 71 who composed the majority. The missing names can be supplied from a manuscript version of the division which adds the names of the earl of Kingston and Lord Hervey to the 69 found in the printed lists.[5]

---

[1] Pittis, pp. 53–5; Boyer, *History of the Reign of Queen Anne*, ii, app., pp. 27–9; [John Torbuck], *Collection of the Parliamentary Debates in England* (1739–42), iv. 412–14.

[2] If he thought to ingratiate himself with the court by switching, he was to be disappointed. Five years later he wrote to Sunderland asking for his help in obtaining a place. 'I have received so many Rebukes from the Court that I am a little shy of being refused againe, . . . being the only man of our party that yet has never been countenanced'. Blenheim MSS., D1-32, Goodwood 15 Sept. 1708.

[3] Northumberland, Schomberg, Lindsey, Exeter, Sandwich, Willoughby of Brook, Maynard, Leigh, Craven, Lempster, Gower, Conway and the bishops of Durham, Llandaff, and Exeter.

[4] Suffolk, Carlisle, Dorset, Burlington, Montague, Coventry, Fitzwalter, Eure, Willoughby of Parham, and the bishops of Hereford, Gloucester, and Bristol.

[5] Cambridge University Library, MS. Mm. 6.42, cited in G. Holmes, *British Politics in the Age of Anne* (1967), 427n.

There is one final discrepancy. Sunderland also counted on Stamford and Scarborough for the whigs. All three lists include them as voting against the bill and Nicholson, in his diary, records Scarborough as speaking against it. As the 12 proxies are accounted for and the 2 lords were present in the House both the day before and on the following Monday, one can only assume that the clerks of the House failed to record their names among those present.

7

GODOLPHIN, THE WHIG JUNTO AND THE SCOTS: A NEW DIVISION LIST FROM 1709

CLYVE JONES

Division lists for the house of lords in the early eighteenth century are scarce.[1] Only seven are known for the reign of Anne.[2] Thus, the recent discovery of a list of a division in the Lords on 21 January 1709, on the disqualification of the duke of Queensberry from voting in the election of the Scottish representative peers, is of considerable importance,[3] even more so because of the subject of the division; little or nothing has been written on Anglo-Scottish relations in the post-Union British parliament since the appearance in 1964 of P. W. J. Riley's *The English Ministers and Scotland, 1707–1727*.

Ever since the Lords' debate on the ministry's Scottish policy in December 1705, when Lord Treasurer Godolphin had been saved by the Whigs from a Tory-inspired censure, the Whig Junto had been his main support in parliament. As their price for this, they had demanded office; firstly, the appointment of the earl of Sunderland as secretary of state and, once this was achieved in 1706, the advancement of Sunderland's Junto colleagues, Lords Somers, Orford and Wharton, as respectively lord president, lord high admiral and lord lieutenant of Ireland. In April 1707 a court Tory, Pembroke (already lord president since 1702), was made lord lieutenant in order to forestall Wharton's claim. Godolphin's refusal to recommend the promotion of others of the Junto lords, and the ministry's failure to secure bishoprics for Junto candidates, produced a serious rift between the Junto and the ministry. In November and December 1707 Whigs in the Commons combined with their Scottish allies to attack the court on the issue of the Scottish privy council. The fall of Robert Harley in February 1708, the consequent resignation of Harley's Tory followers who were replaced by Whigs, and the

1   For all known parliamentary lists for the English, Scottish and Irish parliaments, see *A Register of Parliamentary Lists, 1660–1761* (Leicester, 1979).
2   Tabulated in G. Holmes, *British Politics [in the Age of Anne]* (London, 1967), 421–35.
3   To be found in the 1st marquess of Annandale's papers in the Hope–Johnstone Papers (Black Japanned Box No. 12, bundle labelled 'Annandale Papers, 1708', but listed as 'Accounts, etc. 1709' in the National Register of Archives [Scotland] Report 393, p. 19). I am indebted to Major P. Hope-Johnstone for permission to publish it.

ministry's rescue by the Whigs from censure in the Commons on its
Spanish policy, all left Godolphin with little alternative but to
rely on the Junto. The queen, however, would not admit Somers
and Wharton to office; and a formidable crisis which would certainly
have broken upon the ministry on the opening of the new parliament
in November 1708 (for the Whigs had secured their first clear
majority in the Commons in Anne's reign at the general election in
May) was only defused by the death in October of Prince George
and the consequent collapse, through grief, of the queen's resistance.
Somers and Wharton entered the cabinet in November and
December shortly after parliament had opened. There had been a
month's delay between the prince's death and the appointment of
the Junto lords, caused by the problem of the Whigs' acceptance of
Pembroke as lord high admiral. The Junto wanted Orford as head
of the admiralty, but the queen was reluctant to remove such a
capable administrator as Pembroke, and Pembroke himself was
unwilling to act again as merely a stopgap to Whig pretensions.[1]
There is also evidence that Godolphin was prepared to call a halt
to his concessions to the Junto, and that he now aimed at a kind of
'moderating scheme'. According to Lord Coningsby, vice-treasurer
for Ireland and MP for Leominster in the British parliament,
Godolphin believed 'that he had devided those Lords [the Junto]
amonst themselves and consequently had broken their power'.[2]
Wharton's acceptance of office ahead of Orford had broken an
agreement among the Junto lords, and thus provoked a quarrel
between Orford and Wharton in which all five had become involved.[3]

In the light of this evidence of a divided Junto, which was opposed
by Godolphin who was considering some kind of middle way, the
new division list takes on a special importance; for it demonstrates in
some detail that hostility between the court and the Junto did indeed

1   For the crisis over the successor to Prince George at the admiralty see
H. L. Snyder, 'Queen Anne versus the Junto: the effort to place Orford at the
head of the Admiralty in 1709', *Huntington Library Quarterly*, xxxv (1971–2), 323–42.
The crisis continued through 1709, and Orford was not to become first lord of
the admiralty until November of that year.
2   See B[ritish] L[ibrary], Additional MS, 57862, fos. 47–50, 66–67:
[Coningsby] to [Marlborough], n.d. This undated draft can be placed in late
1709 or early 1710. Coningsby referred back to 'that right majority which we
had 9 months agoe'.
3   Coningsby's account states that Orford and Halifax, the two Junto lords
still out of office, thought 'that they were betrayed by lord wharton and my lord
Summers, which [forced?] my lord Summers to break intirely with my lord
wharton to justify himself to my lord orford soe that there was then noe Confidence
between any two of them but my Lord president and my Lord Sunderland'. While
Coningsby is not an especially reliable witness, his testimony is supported by
other evidence, concerning the relations between Somers and Wharton. This is
discussed in D. W. Hayton, 'Ireland and the English ministers, 1707–16' (Oxford
University D.Phil. thesis, 1975), 227–31.

persist into 1709, and that there was a court-led anti-Junto group in the Lords (centring on Lord Treasurer Godolphin). It also illustrates that the Junto may have been deliberately using Queensberry's conflict in Scotland with the Junto-supported 'Squadrone' party as a diversion from their internal squabbles and also as a means of rallying their supporters in the Lords in order to put pressure on the court for Orford's appointment.

In Scotland in 1708 there were basically three parties: the court party, led by Queensberry, but including the considerable interests of the earl of Seafield as a court manager and the duke of Argyll—supported by the ministry in England; the Tory or Jacobite party who had opposed the Union, nominally led by the duke of Hamilton, whose dominant motive in politics seems to have been his intense jealousy of Queensberry; and the 'New Party' or 'Squadrone Volante', which had kept out of any permanent alliance with any other party, but whose members' votes had been decisive in carrying the Union, led by the duke of Roxburghe and George Baillie of Jerviswood and supported by the Junto in England.[1]

The scare caused in the summer of 1708 by the pretender's invasion attempt had led the English government to arrest prominent Jacobite suspects. The transportation to London and the imprisonment there of the Jacobite leaders amongst the Scottish peers, headed by Hamilton, and his subsequent and successful approach to the Junto for release, with Queensberry having felt unable to support it for fear of being branded a Jacobite, led to an unholy alliance of Hamilton with the Squadrone and the Junto in an attempt to defeat Queensberry's court party at the election of sixteen representative peers on 17 June 1708.[2] Both the court and the Squadrone/Hamilton alliance fielded their own lists of sixteen peers: ten of the court list were elected,[3] while the opposition secured six places.[4]

At the election, twenty-four protests (nearly all of them by the Squadrone) were entered against the validity of the votes of several

1   For the state of Scottish politics at this time see P. W. J. Riley, *The English Ministers and Scotland, 1707–1727* (London, 1964), 17–23.
2   For the complex background to the election, the election itself and its political aftermath see ibid., 86–115.
3   Mar, Seafield, Loudoun, Leven, Wemyss, Rosebery, Northesk, Islay (the duke of Argyll's brother), Glasgow and Lothian.
4   Montrose, Roxburghe and Rothes (leading members of the Squadrone), together with Hamilton, Orkney (Hamilton's brother) and Crawford (a court peer who had deserted to the Squadrone in a calculated political manoeuvre, see Riley, *English Ministers*, 108). The last two peers were expected by Seafield and Mar to co-operate with the court's list of peers in the Lords (H[istorical] M[anuscripts] C[ommission], *Laing* MSS., ii, 147: Seafield to Godolphin, 20 June 1708; see also S[cottish] R[ecord] O[ffice], Mar and Kellie MSS, GD. 124/15/831/23, 25: Mar to Sir D. Nairne, 18, 21 June 1708). This forecast was to prove incorrect for the vote of 21 Jan. 1709.

Scottish peers.[1] Many of these protests were of a technical or legal nature (though most had the political aim of increasing the Squadrone's representation at Westminster). However, it is only with the first two protests, those of Hamilton and Marchmont (the latter a member of the Squadrone who had failed to be elected), that we need concern ourselves. Hamilton's protest was against Queensberry's voting for the representative peers while holding a *British* title which granted him the right to sit in the house of lords[2] (he had been created duke of Dover on 26 May 1708, the first creation in the new post-Union British peerage). Marchmont's protest was against Scottish peers with *English* titles voting in the election, a protest specifically aimed at Argyll, who as earl of Greenwich had sat in the Lords since 1705.[3] Though both protests, along with many of the others, were pressed as far as the house of lords, Marchmont's stood little chance of success, for the electoral rights of *English* peers with Scottish titles had been specifically guaranteed in an act passed by the British parliament in 1708.[4] Politically Marchmont's protest was also of far less significance. Though designed to disfranchise five peers whereas Hamilton's, if successful, would only disfranchise one,[5] those five peers were a fixed number: both the Scottish and English peerages had been 'frozen' at the Union, and no more could be created, whereas the granting of new British peerages to Scottish peers, as had happened to Queensberry, opened up the daunting prospect for the Junto of

---

1　　See W. Robertson, *Proceedings Relating to the Peerage of Scotland from . . . 1707 to . . . 1788* (Edinburgh, 1790), 33–36. One of the protests was by the marquess of Annandale, and this may account for the presence of this division list amongst his papers.

2　　For the protest see ibid., 33.

3　　Ibid., 33–34; Lambeth Palace MS, 1770, fo. 73v: Bishop Wake's diary, 21 Jan. 1709. Four other English peers besides Argyll held Scottish titles: Marlborough (Lord Churchill of Eymouth), Richmond (duke of Lennox), Ormond (Lord Dingwall), and Baron Osborne of Kiverton (Viscount Osborne of Dunblane), better known by his courtesy title of the marquess of Carmarthen, being the son of the duke of Leeds, who had resigned his Scottish title to his son in 1673. A sixth, the non-juror earl of Ailesbury (earl of Elgin), had been in exile since 1694. Riley (*English Ministers*, 115) confuses English and British peerages and thus is incorrect in stating that the voting of the other Scottish peers with British titles remained unchallenged: Queensberry was the only one.

4　　6 Anne, c. 78, clause v, where English peers were expressly enjoined to sign their proxies and lists by the title of their peerage in Scotland. As early as July 1708 Somers was warning Marchmont that legally his protest had little chance of success, though he urged its pressing nonetheless 'for he [Somers] had often known the sentiments of Private persons, and the house verie different. He [however] seems positive that the Duke of Dover can pretend to no vote' (SRO, Marchmont MSS, GD. 158/1097/6: R. Pringle to Marchmont, 20 July 1708).

5　　Technically, if Queensberry were to be disfranchised, so too for the 1708 election would have been the earl of Deloraine, whose proxy Queensberry had, for on 22 Jan. 1709 the house decided 'that a Peer of Scotland, who had not a right to vote at the election of the 16 Peers, had no right to give a vote as proxy' (HMC, *Manuscripts of the House of Lords*, new ser. viii, 3).

the crown's creating unlimited numbers of peers who would sit by right rather than by election, and who would in all probability form a bloc of government votes in the house and also in ensuingel ections of representative peers.[1]

The Junto campaign against Queensberry had also a more immediate political aim. By discrediting him and his followers, both in the Lords and Commons, the Whigs hoped sufficiently to weaken the court party in England as well as in Scotland, so that Lord Treasurer Godolphin could be forced to employ Squadrone candidates in government, and more particularly to appoint Montrose as secretary of state for Scotland.

The split in the ranks of the cabinet, with the Junto peers, Somers and Wharton, opposing the lord treasurer, was not lost on contemporaries: Peter Wentworth observed that

> The Torys rejoice that the Great Whigs begin allready to use the Lord Treasurer as they wou'd wish to oppose him publickly in the house, particularly Lord Summers, who upon the debate of the Duke of Queensburgh sett in the house in a double capacitty, differed very much in oppinion from Lord T[reasurer].[2]

Immediately after the election results were known in London in late June 1708, the Whig Junto began organising themselves and their Squadrone allies in Scotland[3] ready for the confrontation with the court in parliament. Sunderland, who had used his position as secretary of state to direct the Junto's Scottish allies in the election campaign,[4] appears also to have been the leading organiser of the

---

1   G. Burnet, *A History of His Own Times* (Oxford, 1833), v, 398. The more daunting prospect of the flood of new Scottish/British peers forming a pro-government bloc was effectively nullified by the Junto in Dec. 1711 when the Lords voted that Scottish peers who were given British titles had no right to sit in the house (see G. Holmes, 'The Hamilton Affair of 1711–12: a crisis in Anglo-Scottish relations', *Eng. Hist. Rev.*[1962]; see below, 151-76. That the Junto's fear of mass creations was not alarmist was demonstrated in 1712 when Anne created 12 peers at the behest of Harley to secure his position in the Lords. The Whigs, however, were not above using this device themselves: in Jan. and Mar. 1715 eight new peers were summoned to the Lords which, together with the removal of several Tories by impeachment or exile, tipped the balance in favour of the Whigs; in Ireland 12 new peerages (10 of them given to Irish MPs or ex-MPs) in Apr., May and Oct. 1715 secured a Whig majority in the Irish Lords (I owe this information to David Hayton); even as early as May 1709 Lord Lieutenant Wharton was considering a creation of new Irish peers 'unless some number of Temporal Lords that are in England, could bee gott over to balance the Bishops bench' (BL, Additional MS. 57861, fo. 113: Wharton to Coningsby, 31 May 1709).
2   *The Wentworth Papers, 1705–1739*, ed. J. J. Cartwright (London, 1883), 72.
3   Sunderland, Wharton, Somers, Halifax and Devonshire had been supplied by Marchmont with a detailed Squadrone analysis of the politics of both the 16 peers and the 45 MPs as early as 16 July 1708 (see SRO, Marchmont MSS, GD. 158/1097/6: R. Pringle to Marchmont, 20 July 1708).
4   See Riley, *English Ministers*, 105–9, for details of the campaign.

subsequent operations, Somers being gravely ill during the late summer. He wrote to Montrose for

> substantial proofs of the violence threats and promises used upon this occasion because that will effectually at one blow rid you, and us of that Subaltern Ministry. As for the Protestations you have entred we have looked them over and as far as we can judge enough will hold to throw out severall of the enemy and bring in several friends.

Further, he urged the Squadrone petitioners to hurry up to London:

> All our friends here are of opinion it would be much for the Common service, That as many of you both Lord and Commons, that are friends should be here early to concert measures before the Parliament meets . . .[1]

By October some of the Squadrone were in London and were over-confident in their expectations of a short session and a quick dispatch of their business.[2] The parliamentary session did not finally open until 16 November 1708. Two days later the four anti-Queensberry peers—Annandale, Sutherland, Marchmont and Ross—entered a petition, protesting that they should have been elected instead of the court peers—Lothian, Wemyss, Loudoun and Glasgow.[3] The house responded by ordering the clerks of the session who had been appointed by the lord register to attend at the election to come to London with all the relative papers, and later an order was given for witnesses to attend. The clerks were, however, involved in a coaching accident at Newcastle and this further delayed deliberations by the house.[4] The delay led to despondency in some quarters, and a pro-Squadrone correspondent wrote to Scotland that the Scots peers were 'too much the toole of parties occasioned by theire differences about their contraverted elections'. He went on to forecast that 'the sitting peers will be continued, and that better Regulations will be made for the future'.[5]

The Junto, however, were determined to press the petitions and held a four-hour long meeting with the Squadrone and their Tory allies at the duke of Devonshire's house in the evening of 11 December to iron out strategy and tactics.[6]

1   SRO, Montrose MSS, GD. 220/5/1/412, 422a: Sunderland to [Montrose], 3 and 24 July 1708. For the response of some of the Squadrone peers, see BL, Blenheim MSS, CI–20a.
2   SRO, GD. 220/5/1/443: Rothes to Montrose, 25 Oct. 1708.
3   HMC, *Manuscripts of the House of Lords*, new ser. viii, 2.
4   Ibid.; SRO, Clerk of Penicuik MSS, GD. 18/3138: Mar to J. Clerk, 14 Dec. 1708. (I should like to thank Sir John Clerk for allowing me access to his papers.)
5   SRO, Ogilvy of Inverquharity MSS, GD. 205/34: J. Pringle to W. Bennet, 18 Dec. 1708.
6   N[ational] L[ibrary of] S[cotland], Yester Papers, 14415, fos. 168–9 [?Rothes] to Tweeddale, 14 Dec. 1708 (partly in cipher: key, in Yester's hand, in ibid., 14496, fo. 106). Present at the meeting were Somers, Newcastle, Devonshire, Sunderland, Orford, Wharton, Townshend and Bolton of the English Whigs and Hamilton, Montrose, Roxburghe, Rothes, Baillie and Cockburn of their Scots friends.

The clerks, Sir James Dalrymple and John Mackenzie, finally delivered their papers to the Lords on 23 December, but the Christmas recess meant that they were not read until 10 January 1709. On that day a select committee was appointed to consider both the petitions and the papers. On 13 January the committee met, chaired by the Junto supporter Lord Mohun, and reported to the house four days later. On 18 January the house considered the report along with the duke of Hamilton's protest against Queensberry's vote. Counsel were called for, to advise the house on the general questions involved, and on 21 January Serjeant Pratt and Sir Peter King were heard for the petitioners while Sir David Dalrymple and Sir Thomas Parker spoke for the sitting members. There then began a long debate which lasted to the unusually late hour of 6 p.m.[1] Both sides quoted the Union Act in defence of their respective cases. The sitting members contested that the representative peers had 'no restraint on them' and consequently 'enjoy their full rights of Peers'. The petitioners, on the other hand, argued that the disfranchiscment of Queensberry was 'Agreeably to the Scots Act which says that they shall be chosen by the peers *whom they Represent*: which we are assured [reported Bishop Wake] were put in purposely to Exclude All others'. The sitting members then urged that the right to vote 'was allowed by the last Winters Act'.[2] The resulting vote revealed a wide breaching of party lines. As a contemporary noted, 'a great many other Lords, who used not to vote together (I hear) were on the same side in this Division'.[3]

The earl of Mar, in a letter to his brother, Lord Grange, explained the importance that the previous day's proceedings in the Commons had had in the defeat of Queensberry's case in the Lords:

> After the Councills pleading there was a good dale of debate in the House, at 1st the question was put and the Duke's vote was lost by seven, for it 50, against it 57. The Juncto and all they could make of their folks were against him: The Treasurer and all who depended on him and the Court independent of the Juncto for him. I belive there were 11 bishops there whereof only 3 for him. The Tories were divided and non for him but those who were particulare acquaintances of him or his friends and even some of those against him. The

1   Lennoxlove MS, CI/8034: [Hamilton] to [Selkirk] 22 Jan. 1709 (I should like to thank the duke of Hamilton for allowing me to use his family papers); Berks[hire] R[ecord] O[ffice], Downshire MSS, Trumbull Add. MS. 132: J. Tucker to Sir W. Trumbull, 21 Jan. 1709 (used with the kind permission of the marquess of Downshire). Bishops Wake (Lambeth Palace MS; 1770, fo. 73v) and Burnet (*History*, v, 397) agree that the debate was long, and Burnet adds that it was also 'well debated'.
2   HMC, *House of Lords Manuscripts*, new ser. viii, 3; Lambeth Palace MS, 1770, fo. 73v. See also Burnet, *History*, v, 397-9. The act referred to was 6 Anne, c. 78.
3   Berks RO, Downshire MSS, Trumbull Add. MSS, 132: J. Tucker to Sir W. Trumbull, 21 Jan. 1709.

occasion of this was his and most of our friends in the house of comons the day before going against Sir Simon Harcourt in his election. Had it not been for this, the vote had probablie gone the other way, for the whole Tories would have been for him, but our friends going thus in the house of Comons made severalls of them angrie with us. This we forsaw but could not help it, for had our friends been for Sir Simon in the House of Comons, the Treasurer and his friends would have been against us in the house of Peers and this affair could not be carried without a conjunction of the Treasurer and his friends with the Tories. Thus unluckily were we circumstantsiat, but there was no help for it.[1]

The vote by the Commons to declare void Sir Simon Harcourt's election for Abingdon was certainly a notorious case of a party majority being blatantly used to unseat an MP of the opposite party.[2] The 'titanic struggle' over Harcourt's case had begun on the afternoon of the 20 January and continued until 3 a.m. on the following morning.[3] Walpole reported that the battle had been 'the hardest service I ever saw in Parliament . . . It was much the fullest house that has been this Parliament, and the whole affair carried on with greater heat and warmth on both sides than usual', while another Whig member complained of being 'laid up of the gout, brought upon me by attending the House to turn out Sir Simon Harcourt longer than I was able, so you'll say I have suffered in a good cause'.[4]

Given that the Harcourt case caused a great deal of ill-feeling amongst the Tories (and even that staunch Whig, Bishop Burnet of Salisbury, was disturbed by it),[5] does Mar's account of the Queensberry vote stand up to analysis now that we have the division list? Firstly, we have to clear away a technical problem.[6] Because only the fifty 'contents' (pro-Queensberry) votes were marked off on a complete list of all those present in the House on 21 January 1709, we are left with sixty-two unmarked names of whom only fifty-seven can actually have voted against Queensberry. Of the five lords extra to the 'not-content' vote, we can with certainty eliminate one—the duke of Queensberry himself. He is listed as present but not voting with the 'contents', the explanation being that in a case

1   SRO, Mar and Kellie MSS, GD. 124/15/946/3: 22 Jan. 1708/9.
2   One contemporary observer thought the Whigs were indulging in revenge and intended to expel the same 'number that the Torys in their days of peace turned out in the session, I think 13, in which Sir Simon was particularly eminent' (BL. Add. MS, 33225, fo. 17: Francis Hare to Henry Watkins, 28 Jan. 1709).
3   For the case see Holmes, *British Politics*, 43, 319, 465 n
4   Cambridge University Library, Cholmondeley (Houghton) MSS, 65/6: Walpole to Marlborough, 21 Jan. 1709; Shropshire RO, Forester MSS, 1224/21/30: Sir William Forester to George Weld, 28 Jan. 1709. I am indebted to David Hayton for both these references.
5   Burnet, *History*, v, 396.
6   For a fuller discussion see below p. 147.

which directly concerned himself a peer abstained.[1] The identification of the remaining four supernumerary lords to the vote is
problematical. The only evidence we have is Mar's letter, where he
states his belief that there were only eleven bishops in the house at
the time of the vote, of which three (as he states correctly) voted
'content'. Thus only eight bishops voted 'not content', whereas we
have twelve unmarked bishops on the list. In the absence of any
stronger evidence we must assume that four of these twelve bishops
either left the house before the vote was taken or abstained. We
only have positive evidence for the presence of two 'not content'
bishops—Wake and Burnet who have both left accounts of the
debate.[2] We can therefore only speculate as to the identity of the
four extra bishops in the list. We may perhaps conjecture that both
Bishop Crew of Durham, a diehard Tory, and Bishop Dawes of
Chester, a moderate Tory but a protégé of Archbishop Sharp of
York who voted for Queensberry, absented themselves from the
vote. As for the other two, one can only suggest that they may be
Williams of Chichester and Cumberland of Peterborough. Williams
was to die barely three months later and may already have been
too ill to sustain a long debate, while Cumberland (though he did
not die until 1718) was old and infirm.[3]

Mar's first comment on the voting was that the Junto had pres-
surised their followers into voting against Queensberry and, knowing
the Junto's powers of organisation, one can accept this; yet the
division list shows that eight Whigs and twelve court Whigs supported the duke. The Junto had thirty-two Whigs and three court
Whigs on their side. The twelve court Whigs (six of whom held
pensions and four of the rest held office, one of them in the cabinet)[4]

---

1   The duke of Norfolk did not vote in a division on his own divorce bill on
2 Jan. 1693 nor did the earls of Bath and Montagu in a vote on their legal case
on 17 Feb. 1694 (E. Cruickshanks, D. Hayton and C. Jones, 'Divisions in the
House of Lords on the transfer of the Crown and other issues, 1689–94: ten new
lists', B[*ulletin of the*] I[*nstitute of*] H[*istorical*] R[*esearch*], liii (1980); above, 79-110.
2   It is unfortunate that the best observer of the House, Bishop Nicolson of
Carlisle, whose pro-Scottish inclinations and usual practice of noting the voting
patterns of his colleagues on the bishops' bench, would probably have led him
to comment on the division, did not arrive in London for the session until 5 Feb.
1709. He recorded on 6 Feb. that his 'First Visit [was] to Archbishop of York,
who kind and pleasant on the Junto and Flying Squadron' (Tullie House,
Carlisle: Nicolson's Diary, 5–6 Feb. 1709). See *The London Diaries of William Nicolson, Bishop of Carlisle, 1702-1718*, ed. C. Jones and G. Holmes (Oxford, 1985), p. 475.
3   The party affiliations of peers used in this analysis are based upon the records
of their voting during Anne's reign as printed in Holmes, *British Politics*, 425–35.
4   The pensioners were St Albans, Schomberg, Lincoln, Bridgewater, Manchester and Grantham; the office-holders were Somerset (master of the horse
and cabinet member), Kent (lord chamberlain of the household), Dorset (lord
warden of the Cinque Ports) and Cholmondeley (treasurer of the household).
The two who had no financial obligations to the Court were Radnor and Howard
of Effingham. The former was apparently an 'assiduous courtier', while the latter
was a 'poor lord' (ibid., 226, 391–2).

probably supported Queensberry because of their natural inclinations to support the court. Indeed it was reported that the most
important court Whig, the duke of Somerset, was 'not so well with
the junto as usual'.[1] The three court Whigs who voted with the
Junto were Richmond, Grafton and Westmorland. It is much more
difficult to decide why the eight other Whigs supported Queensberry.[2]
Cowper, the lord chancellor and a member of the cabinet, was of an
independent cast of mind, as befitted the crown's chief legal officer,
and he had opposed some of the actions of the Junto against
Godolphin in the past as being factious.[3] As early as July 1708 he
had made known to the earl of Seafield his thoughts concerning the
Squadrone's petitions: he wished

> that disputes about elections would meet with a more impartial
> determination in the Upper, then they have Sometimes had in the
> Lower house

and further hoped that

> the great inconvenience which must attend such disputes and the
> newness of 'em in the house of Lords, the great pleasure it will be to
> the enemys of the Union to observe them, the disparagement that
> it will bring on that good work, are all arguments, that make one
> wish to God, if possible, they might wholly or in some measure be
> prevented or lessened.

He feared, however, that there was 'very troublesome weather
gathering' and consequently resolved

> to follow in every particular the dictates of right reason (to the best
> of ones power), to pursue steadily the interest of the Kingdom, and
> not be very Sollicitous who is pleased or displeased with an action
> that is well intended.[4]

Cowper may in addition have thought that the legal position
favoured Queensberry. It is probably significant that, out of office,
he was to support Hamilton in his case before the Lords in 1711
against the line taken by his own Whig colleagues.[5]

Lord Rivers and the duke of Shrewsbury, though at this time
nominally Whigs, were in the following year to go over to Harley,
and Peterborough would also become a close ally of the new
Harleian regime. Though the latter was in 1709 antipathetic towards
Godolphin and Marlborough—he was to be a member of Harley's
court conspiracy against the lord treasurer in 1710—he was even

1   *Wentworth Papers*, 78: P. Wentworth to Raby, 25 Jan. 1709.
2   Cowper, Leicester, Rivers, Peterborough, Berkeley, Greenwich (Argyll),
Mohun and Shrewsbury.
3   See Holmes, *British Politics*, 111, 242.
4   SRO, Seafield MSS, GD. 248/572/7/32: Cowper to [Seafield], 1 July 1708.
5   Holmes, *British Politics*, 242.

more antipathetic towards Sunderland, the Junto manager of the Squadrone victory in Scotland.[1] The vote, against the line taken by his party, of Lord Mohun, who has been described as 'one of the Junto's loyallest if least reputable henchmen',[2] may be attributed to his personal detestation of Hamilton. Both were involved in a long-standing legal dispute over the estate of the 2nd earl of Macclesfield, and their feud was to lead to their deaths at each other's hands in a duel in 1712.[3]

These eight Whigs (along with the twelve court Whigs) may also have been in some cases swayed by the legal arguments, putting the law above party interest. It is worth noting that of the twenty Whigs and court Whigs who voted for Queensberry, eleven were to vote in the Hamilton case in 1711, seven (Cowper, Kent, Dorset, Manchester, Rivers, Shrewsbury and Cholmondeley) supporting Hamilton against the Junto and one (Schomberg) deliberately abstaining.

Mar's second observation—that all the court independent of the Junto voted for Queensberry—is more or less borne out by the division list. Hamilton noted that 'the Treasurer and all the Courtiers exerted themselves to the utmost',[4] and virtually all the court and court Tory peers voted 'content'. The only exceptions were Northumberland and Berkely of Stratton. The former, an office holder as constable of Windsor Castle and a pensioner, has been described as lending general support to the Godolphin ministry even when it was dominated by the Junto, because of his acknowledged obligation to the Churchills and his deference to the queen. Yet on the Queensberry vote, he went against the court.[5] He may well have been influenced by the other court Tory among the 'not contents', Berkely of Stratton, who in his turn may have been influenced by Dartmouth as he had been on previous occasions. Both Dartmouth and Berkely were moderate middle-of-the-road Tories who normally eschewed faction. Yet both supported the factious Junto/Squadrone attack on the court.[6] In this they were joined by thirteen other Tories.[7] Mar's explanation is that the Tories were divided among themselves. The hard-line, non office-holding Tories were

1   Ibid., 202, 226.
2   Ibid., 22.
3   For details see H. T. Dickinson, 'The Mohun–Hamilton duel: personal feud or Whig plot?', *Durham University Journal*, lvii (June 1965), 159–65. Both Hamilton and Mohun had married nieces of Lord Macclesfield.
4   Lennoxlove MS, CI/7953: Hamilton to one of his brothers, 27 Jan. 1709.
5   He also voted against the ministry in the Sacheverell vote (Holmes, *British Politics*, 255, 389.)
6   Ibid., 254–5. Dartmouth, however, commonly voted against the court during the years of Whig dominance (ibid., 389).
7   Northampton, Denbigh, Berkshire, Thanet, Abingdon, Plymouth, Jersey, Weymouth, Howard of Escrick, Guilford, Leominster, Bernard and Guernsey.

generally in opposition to the ministry, so only those Tories who were his particular friends, and not even some of those, voted for Queensberry, the reason being that the duke's clients and friends in the Commons had opposed the former Tory attorney-general, Sir Simon Harcourt, in his election case on the previous day. Although there is no known division list for the Commons' vote, Mar's evidence for a massive split in the Tory ranks carries conviction. Of the forty-five Scottish MPs, thirty-four had court connections[1] and their voting against Harcourt could well have made a crucial difference to the outcome. A possible but subsidiary reason why so many Tories in the Lords voted against the court may be that many of them entertained decidely anti-Scottish feelings. It is noticeable that of those who also voted in the Hamilton case two years later half, including Dartmouth, also voted against Hamilton despite the fact that the Tory ministry supported the duke.[2]

Although the political alignments of 1711 were different—a strongly Tory-supported court was opposed by a Whig party whose previous fissures had been healed by defeat, whereas in 1709 the court had been largely dependent upon Junto support—the two votes on Scottish questions in the reign of Anne for which we now have division lists show a pronounced degree of consistency in the pattern of voting.[3] Of the 107 lords who voted on the issue of the Queensberry peerage, only 67 (62 per cent) voted in the Hamilton case. Of those who voted on both occasions, 51 (76 per cent) voted for the same side each time. Of the seven lords who supported Queensberry but opposed Hamilton (i.e. switched from a court stance to a Junto/Tory one) two were Whigs (Leicester and Mohun), two were court Whigs (Lincoln and Bridgewater) and one (Pembroke) was a court Tory. The other two were Tories: the bishop of Winchester (like Pembroke, middle-of-the-road politically) and Scarsdale. Six Whigs or court Whigs, on the other hand, supported both Queensberry and Hamilton, adopting a pro-court stance in each case.[4]

There were nine lords who opposed Queensberry but supported Hamilton (i.e. switched from Junto/Tory to court). Of these six were Tories or court Tories (Northumberland, Denbigh, Berkshire, Abingdon, Howard of Escrick and Guilford), while only two were Whigs or court Whigs (Grafton and Ossulston). The remaining lord, Orkney, the brother of Hamilton, obviously switched on

1 Riley, *English Ministers*, 87.
2 Ten of the fourteen anti-Queensberry lords voted on 20 Dec. 1711 and five opposed Hamilton: Northampton, Thanet, Plymouth, Guernsey and Dartmouth.
3 The following analysis is based on the premise that to vote for Queensberry and Hamilton was a court position, while to vote against was a Junto one.
4 Cowper, Kent, Dorset, Manchester, Rivers and Cholmondeley.

personal grounds, and reflected the change in political allegiance of both brothers from Junto to court in the intervening years.[1]

It is clear from the figures that though there was some movement between the two divisions (24 per cent switched their vote) and these largely represented a conforming to party lines, there was still a significant number of lords in both votes (16 per cent) who defied their parties, out of a personal antipathy to Scottish peers or from obligations to the court.

The voting pattern among the Scottish peers in 1711 shows a distinct change from that of 1709. Only nine peers were present and voted in 1711, but all of them supported Hamilton. The Scottish peers had more to lose in 1711 (many of them coveted British peerages); the court had carried the whole of its list at the 1710 representative peers' election; and, no doubt, the Scots resented the anti-Scottish feeling which had increased since 1709 amongst English politicians.

The immediate aftermath of the disqualification of Queensberry in 1709 was that the Junto/Squadrone alliance went on to carry ten of their petitions against the votes in the representative election of the court's peers.[2] Yet even though this resulted in the quashing of nine votes, only Lothian was unseated—in favour of Annandale. This was somewhat short of the three or four changes Hamilton had forecast in July 1708.[3] The court, after the initial loss of the vote on 21 January, fought for 'every Inch of Ground. . . . but if Wharton had not taken the advantage of the unfrequency of the house . . . Lothian had still continued a sitting member'.[4] Sunderland, as might be expected, took a lead in organising the Junto campaign, and apparently spent 'so much of his time . . . in caballing and Parliament meetings' that Godolphin complained of the neglect of important foreign business.[5] According to an observer 'the Whigs and Squadrone has outvoted the other parties, and so runs them all out'.[6] The parliamentary success of the Junto and their allies failed, however, to prevent Queensberry's appointment to the Scottish secretaryship at the expense of their candidate, Montrose, though the latter was compensated by being made keeper of the Scottish privy seal. Roxburghe, the other leading Squadrone peer, became

1   See Riley, *English Ministers*, 153–4.
2   Of the original 16 petitions, 11 had been entered by the Squadrone.
3   See Riley, *English Ministers*, 109, 115. For the disqualified voters see Robertson, *Proceedings*, 44. Queensberry's vote and the proxy he held were two of those disqualified.
4   SRO, Ogilvy of Inverquharity MSS, GD. 205/34: J. Scott to W. Bennet, 8 Feb. 1709.
5   H. L. Snyder (ed.), *The Marlborough–Godolphin Correspondence* (Oxford, 1975), iii, 1211: Godolphin to Marlborough, [28 Jan. 1709].
6   SRO, Breadalbane MSS, GD. 112/40/6/2: [?] to [Breadalbane], 2 Feb. 1709.

a member of the privy council of Great Britain.[1] Hamilton, whose cynical alliance with the Squadrone in the 1708 election had enabled them to secure six representative seats in the Lords, was left out in the cold. Within two weeks of the Queensberry vote, one of Hamilton's brothers was reporting the duke's disgust at this slight and saying that he was proposing to alter the elections of representative peers 'to a rotation upon the foot of making som of the heads, British peers to make it go down [with the Scots]'. Lord Archibald Hamilton quite rightly saw such a scheme as a precedent 'of ill consequence and other violations of the Union eaven of greater consequence [might be] proposed next'.[2] The pushing by leading Scottish families for British peerages (and there was no decline in the demand after Queensberry's disfranchisement[3]) may have appealed to the Scots, but it revived fears in English peers of being swamped by pliant Scottish members in the Lords. Consequently, when Hamilton finally in September 1711 achieved his ambition of a British title, as duke of Brandon, the Lords voted in December of the same year

> that no Patent of Honour granted to any Peer of Great Britain, who was a Peer of Scotland at the Time of the Union, can entitle such [a] Peer to sit and vote in Parliament, or to sitt upon the Trial of Peers.[4]

This, together with the 1709 decision, barred both Hamilton and Queensberry[5] from an active part in Scottish national politics, other than in the rôle of campaigners in the election of representative peers.[6]

APPENDIX

'Lords present in the house of Peers, 21 January 1708 [/9]'
The original division list which has survived in the Hope–Johnstone Papers is unlike most lists for the Lords in layout and composition. It does not comprise two lists of lords, one for each side of the vote,[7] but is

1   Riley, *English Ministers*, 117–18.
2   Lennoxlove MS, CI/5572: Lord A. Hamilton to the duchess of Hamilton, 5 Feb. 1709.
3   E.g. Lord Yester's soliciting the queen for a British title for his father, Tweeddale (NLS, Yester Papers 7021, fo. 193: Yester to Tweeddale, 17 Nov. 1709). According to George Lockhart many of the Scottish peers before the Union 'had been bubled with the hopes of being themselves created British Peers' (A. Anfrere (ed.), *The Lockhart Papers* [London, 1817], i, 298).
4   *Lords' Journals*, xix, 346: 20 Dec. 1711.
5   That is, the third duke, the Queensberry of 1709 having died in July 1711. As a minor, he could not have taken his seat in the Lords in any case. He did attempt to sit in 1719 as duke of Dover, but failed because of the 1711 ruling over Hamilton.
6   Hamilton's son, who succeeded in 1712, was to play a leading rôle as an organiser in the 1722 election.
7   See Cruickshanks, Hayton and Jones, 'Divisions in the House of Lords', *BIHR*, liii (1980) ; see above, 79-110.

headed 'Lords present in the house of Peers 21 January 1708 [/9]' and is set out in the form of a list of lords present that day arranged in order of precedence (exactly as printed in the *Lords' Journals*, xviii, 608–9) with the exception of the bishop of Ely and the earl of Bindon who are incorrectly placed; the 'contents' in the vote are indicated by crosses.

Because of what we know of the method by which the Lords' presence lists were drawn up, we can be sure that this division list cannot be the original record of the division, but must be a later version. The original list of those present on a particular day, recorded in the house's manuscript minutes by the clerk assistant, was not set out in order of precedence but from the seated order of the lords, and the listing was subsequently rearranged in order of precedence when the minutes were written up as the draft journal.[1]

Why is the list in this format rather than set out neatly in two columns headed 'contents' and 'not contents'? Perhaps the compiler could record with certainty only the 'contents', but nevertheless wanted some indication of the 'not contents' and chose to take a list of all lords present with only the 'contents' marked? One of the lords involved in the division is most likely to have been the compiler (unless it was one of the clerks), possibly one of the tellers. As the list was found among some Annandale papers, one of his friends on the 'not contents' side is a likely contender; perhaps Annandale himself, sitting in the gallery of the house, recorded the division. In the list the following abbreviations are used to denote parties— C = court; CW = court Whig; CT = court Tory; SC = Scottish court party; Sq = Squadrone; Sq ally = an ally of the Squadrone in the 1708 election; T = Tory; W = Whig.

Division list on vote in House of Lords, 21 January 1709, on whether a peer of Scotland, who has a seat in the Lords by virtue of a patent passed under the Great Seal of Great Britain after the Union, has a right to vote in the election of the representative peers.

	Other present that day—57 noted
Contents	*Not Content*
L A B York [Sharp] (T)	L A B Cant[erbury] [Tenison] (W)
L B Wint[on: Winchester] [Trelawney] (T)	L B Durham [Crew] (T)
	L B Sarum [Salisbury][Burnet](W)
L B Rochester [Sprat] (T)	L B Cov[entry] & Litch[field] [Hough] (W)
L Chancelour [Cowper] (W)	
L Treasurer [Godolphin] (CT)	L B Peterburgh [Cumberland] (W)
L H Admarall [Pembroke] (CT)	L B Chichester [Williams] (W)
D Somerseat (CW)	L B Bangor [Evans] (W)
D Ormond (T)	L B Lincoln [Wake] (W)
D Beaufort (T)	L B Landaff [Tyler] (W)
D St Albans (CW)	L B Ely [Moore] (W)
D Shomberg (CW)	L B Chester [Dawes] (T)
D Shrewsberry (W)	L B Northwich [Trimmell] (W)

1   See C. Jones, 'Seating problems in the House of Lords in the early eighteenth century: the evidence of the manuscript minutes', *BIHR*, li (1978), 132–45.

Contents

Other present that day—57 noted

Not Content

D Buck[ingham] & Norm[anby] (T)
L Chamberlain [Kent] (CW)
M Loathian (SC)
E Lincolne (CW)
E Dorset & Midlesex (CW)
E Bridgwater (CW)
E Lycester (W)
E Manchester (CW)
E Rivers (W)
E Peterborough (W)
E Scarsdale (T)
E Feversham (CT)
E Radnor (CW)
E Berklay (W)
E Rochester (T)
E Rochford (C)[1]
E Grantham (CW)
E Greenwich [Argyll] (W)
E Pawlet (T)
E Chomondaly (CW)
E Mar (SC)
E Loudune (SC)
E Weemess (SC)
E Leven (SC)
E Northesque (SC)
E Seafei[l]d (SC)
E Roseberry (SC)
E Glasgow (SC)
E Islay (SC)
L Delavare (CT)
L Howard [of] Effing[ham] (CW)
L Hunsdone (CT)
L Mohune [Teller] (W)
L Byron (CT)
L Lexington (T)
L Osburne (T)
L Weston (T)
L Haversham (T)

L President [Somers] (W)
L Privy Seal [Newcastle] (W)
E Bindon (W)
L Steward [Devonshire] (W)
D Richmond (CW)
D Grafton (CW)
D Northumberland (CT)
D Bolton (W)
D Bedford (W)
D Montague (W)
D Hamilton (Sq ally)
D Montross (Sq)
D Roxbrugh (Sq)
D Dover [Queensberry] (SC)
L great Chamb[erlain]
　　[Lindsey] (W)
M Dorchester (W)
D Darby (W)
E Northampton (T)
E Danbigh (T)
E Westmorland (CW)
E Berkshyre (T)
E Stamford (W)
E Thanet (T)
E Sunderland (W)
E Essex (W)
E Abington (T)
E Plymouth (T)
E Scarsbrugh (W)
E Orford (W)
E Jarsay (T)
E Wharton (W)
E Crawford (Sq ally)
E Rothes (Sq)
E Orkney (Sq ally)
L V Say & Sale (W)
L V Townsend (W)
L V Weymouth (T)
L Howard [of] Esc[rick] (T)
L Rockingham (W)
L Berkley [of] Str[atton] (CT)
L Cornwallis (W)
L Osselston (W)

1　　William, 2nd earl of Rochford (1708–1710), appears in no other known division list, and is consequently difficult to classify. He was a professional soldier, however, and possibly a political follower of Marlborough; as an Irish MP he was classed as supporting the court in 1706 (BL, Additional MS, 9715, fos. 150–1).

Other present that day—57 noted
Not Content

L Dartmouth (T)
L Guilford (T)
L Lempster (T)
L Bernard (T)
L Halyfax [Teller] (W)
L Guarnsay (T)
L Harvey (W)
L Pelham (W)

8

THE HAMILTON AFFAIR OF 1711-1712:
A CRISIS IN ANGLO-SCOTTISH RELATIONS

GEOFFREY HOLMES

IN two and a half centuries of tolerably healthy life the Union of Scotland and England has acquired every appearance of permanence and and a distinct air of ' inevitability '. The hazards which attended its birth and infancy may seem, in contrast, remote and even a little unreal. Yet the fact remains that the partnership concluded in 1707 was essentially experimental, and that more than once during its first, uncertain, years preceding the '15 rebellion the experiment came perilously close to failure. This was palpably so during the Malt Tax storm in 1713, when the Union survived a hostile division in the house of lords by a mere four votes;[1] and it is scarcely less true of the crisis which arose some eighteen months earlier over the question of the duke of Hamilton's patent. But the Hamilton affair has, for some reason, been so sketchily treated by even the best secondary authorities that its full significance is not generally appreciated.[2] In particular, the conspicuous part it played in the party politics of the day has virtually escaped notice, although it was this which, more than anything, accounted for the excitement the affair aroused and for the serious blow it dealt to the stability of the Union.

[1] This crucial division on 1 June 1713 followed a long debate on a motion of the earl of Findlater for leave to bring in Repeal, though it was not a vote on the motion itself. See G. M. Trevelyan, *England under Queen Anne*, iii. 242 n. The political manoeuvres leading up to the debate of 1 June are described in detail by the Jacobite M.P., George Lockhart of Carnwath in [*The*] *Lockhart Papers* (2 vols., London, 1817), i. 418–34. The fullest printed account of the debate itself is in *The Parliamentary History of England*, vi. 1216–20, drawing largely on the contemporary histories of Boyer and Oldmixon. There is a brief, but quite sound, summary of the issues involved in the crisis in P. Hume Brown, *History of Scotland* (1909), iii. 150–3.

[2] For instance, two such standard works of reference as Sir George Clark's *The Later Stuarts* (Oxford History of England, 2nd edn., 1955) and Sir Lindsay Keir's *The Constitutional History of Modern Britain* (5th edn., 1953) surprisingly make no mention whatever of the Hamilton affair, while on the Scottish side the often admirable work of W. L. Mathieson, *Scotland and the Union . . . 1695 to 1747* (Glasgow, 1905), dismisses it in half a page. Where the case is discussed at all it is cited usually as a demonstration of the mutual antipathy which still existed between the former peers of Scotland and England, sometimes as a question of constitutional interest, very occasionally, *e.g.* in A. S. Turberville, *The House of Lords in the 18th Century* (1927), pp. 150–5, as both. Michael Foot, *The Pen and the Sword* (1957), pp. 332–3, 337–8, is almost alone in conveying some idea of its importance in the party war and in giving a brief account of the debate of 20 Dec. 1711 in the Lords.

Among the sixteen representative peers elected by the Scottish nobility on 10 November 1710 to sit in the third parliament of Great Britain was James Douglas, fourth duke of Hamilton. Earlier that year Hamilton had abandoned his alliance with the Godolphin ministry in London—an uneasy and incongruous alliance for one who was the champion of the Scottish Jacobites—and had hitched his wagon to the rising star of Robert Harley. When Harley began to construct a new ministry in August the duke had given him the support of his powerful northern interest, and at the subsequent general election, as well as in the election of Scots peers, had worked actively on his behalf.[1] In return he had come to regard as his due some special mark of the queen's favour.[2] He had watched fellow-countrymen like Queensberry, Montrose and, recently, Argyll prosper since the Union and expected for himself a reward commensurate with his royal lineage and extensive estates, for he recognized no superior north of the Border.

To begin with his pretensions did not meet with much encouragement. Harley found it inconsistent with his own essentially moderate objectives to give high office to men with patent Jacobite connections; so that for a while Hamilton had to rest content with such meagre crumbs as the lord lieutenancy of Lancashire and a seat in the privy council. But it was not political rewards alone he hankered after. For some time past he had set his heart on adding a British dukedom to his Scottish title. On the face of it, it seemed a perfectly reasonable ambition to cherish, since the only two Scotsmen of similar stature, Argyll and Queensberry, had already received comparable honours[3] and sat in the house of lords on the strength of them. Yet even here Hamilton met with initial disappointment. His first approaches in the summer of 1710 led to nothing, and it was only when he renewed his request to the queen in the following spring that he found the climate more favourable.[4] His own credit at Court was by this time good; Anne herself saw no objection to granting such a peerage; while Harley (now earl of Oxford and lord treasurer)[5] was probably relieved to find this seemingly innocuous way of satisfying the duke's ambition.

However, the proposal to confer a British title on Hamilton soon ran into unexpected difficulties. It was opposed in the Cabinet by secretary Dartmouth, who challenged its constitutional

---

[1] H[istorical] M[anuscripts] C[omission], *Portland MSS*. x. 342: Sir James Erskine to [earl of Mar?], 19 Sept. 1710; *ibid*. pp. 349–50: Mar to Harley, 7, 9 Nov. 1710.

[2] *Ibid*. pp. 330–1, 333: Mar to Harley, 20, 21, 25 Aug. 1710.

[3] In Argyll's case, the *English* earldom of Greenwich (1705); in Queensberry's the *British* dukedom of Dover (1708). The peerage of England, like that of Scotland, was 'frozen' at the Union and all fresh creations thereafter were in the new peerage of Great Britain.

[4] H.M.C. *Portland MSS*. x. 333; *ibid*. v. 5.

[5] He was raised to the peerage on 23 May 1711, at roughly the same time as Hamilton applied for his British title.

validity in the light of the terms of the Act of Union; [1] and according to Lockhart of Carnwath the news ' was no sooner publick than the greatest part of the English Peers (Whigs and Tories) exclaimd against it '—not on rational grounds, he implies, but as a sort of conditioned reflex induced by anti-Scottish prejudice. [2]   Lockhart's diagnosis of the cause of this reaction was superficial, [3] and his picture of Tory hostility was certainly exaggerated.   But the existence of *some* opposition on the Tory side was indisputable; and this, from Hamilton's point of view, seemed the most ominous feature of the situation.   His British peerage, even if granted, could still be challenged in the house of lords, and with an evenly-balanced Upper House it needed relatively few tory dissidents to cause the ministry embarrassment.   The serious alarm with which the Scots viewed the reaction of the English peers is demonstrated by the warning which Lord Mar gave to Oxford as early as 10 June. Hamilton was by no means alone in his aspiration for a British title, [4] and Mar left the treasurer in no doubt whatever how he and his colleagues regarded the duke's case: as a precedent of such importance to their entire order that the whole future of Anglo-Scottish relations might depend on its outcome.   '. . . should that hardship of the peerage be putt upon us, so contrair to all sense, reason and fair dealing, . . . how is it possible', asked Mar, ' that flesh and blood can bear it? and what Scotsman will not be wearie of the Union, and do all he can to get quitt?' [5]   Faced with the certainty of Scottish hostility if the peerage were *not* granted and the threat of English hostility if it were, the treasurer preferred to risk the latter.   But he allowed more than three months to elapse after the queen had consented to the grant before issuing Hamilton's patent, by which time most of the potential trouble-makers had dispersed to their country houses for the parliamentary recess and

[1] Mainly, it seems, on the ground that if Hamilton took his seat in the Lords in virtue of a British title it would contravene article xxii of the Treaty of Union—the article which fixed the representation of the Scottish peers in the united parliament. ' now they are like to interpret the 22. art. of Union as perversely as they did interpret soundly the act agt. intruding ', wrote Lord Balmerino to Harry Maule of Kellie on 9 June (S[cottish] R[ecord] O[ffice], Dalhousie MS. 14/352).

[2] See *A Letter from a Scots Gentleman residing in England to his Freind at Edinburgh* (London, 12 June 1711), reprinted in *Lockhart Papers*, i. 529-48.

[3] See p. 162 below.

[4] *E.g.* Mar himself pressed the treasurer for such a title at the same time as Hamilton on the strength of a former promise from the queen, and there were other Scottish peers who, even as early as May 1711, were ' talked of ' as likely candidates: H.M.C. *Portland MSS*. x. 355, 409; S.R.O., Dalhousie MS. 14/352: Balmerino to Maule, 19 May.

[5] H.M.C. *Mar and Kellie MSS*. p. 490: Mar to Oxford, 10 June 1711. *Cf.* a letter from Sir David Dalrymple to Oxford, written five days earlier: ' It is yet but the Skeatch of an Union (pardon the Expression). Real advantages are necessary to make an incorporating Union . . . if slavery or discontent prevail upon us here, the Gangrene must needs spread hastyly all over . . .' Brit[ish] Mus[eum]. Portland Loan (Harley MSS.), 133. I am much indebted to the duke of Portland for permission to use these papers.

he could hope for a more amenable House by the next session.[1] Not until 10 September 1711, then, did the patent creating Hamilton Baron Dutton and duke of Brandon in the peerage of Great Britain finally pass the Great Seal.

For a few weeks thereafter it seemed that Oxford's caution would pay dividends. Despite all Dartmouth's qualms and Mar's solemn warnings the patent had a quiet reception. Indeed it is just possible that little more would have been heard of the matter [2] but for the sudden change in the political situation in the late autumn of 1711. The signing of preliminaries of peace with France on 27 September so angered Britain's allies that the whigs were encouraged to plan a all-out attack on the ministry, to be launched as soon as parliament reassembled. Although the government's majority was impregnable in the house of commons its control of the house of lords was precarious, disturbingly dependent on a dozen or more Court whigs—' Trimmers ' who normally supported the administration, whatever its complexion, but were now under tremendous opposition pressure to vote against a Tory peace. It was this crisis which gave to the duke of Hamilton's patent a new and wholly unlooked-for significance in the eyes of both the English parties. To the tories, anxiously calculating each single vote in the Upper House, the sixteen Scottish votes became a potentially decisive factor, and for two to three weeks before parliament met on 7 December Oxford was urging his Scottish supporters to be at Westminster without fail by the first day of the new session. To the whigs too the conduct of the representative peers was a matter of the utmost concern. It was not that they had any serious hopes of their support, for they were well aware that the relative poverty of the Scots coupled with their lack of interest in English affairs normally bound them firmly to the government which had nominated them. What really perturbed the whigs was the prospect of having *more* than sixteen dependent Scots ranged against them in a finely-balanced House. For they suspected that Hamilton's new honour was not to be an isolated award, but the first of a series of such creations designed to enlarge the Scottish representation in

[1] *Cf. A Letter from a Scots Gentleman* . . . in *Lockhart Papers*, i. 545. Although the delay was mainly tactical there were other factors. A caveat was entered against the patent by a group of opposition peers and there was also some difficulty in persuading Lord Dartmouth to sign the necessary warrant. According to Peter Wentworth the warrant was actually in Dartmouth's hands as early as the first week in June. See A. Boyer, *Quadriennium Annae Postremum* (2nd edn., 1718), ii. 449; Dartmouth's note to G. Burnet, *A History of my own Time* (2nd edn., Oxford, 1833), vi. 89 (hereafter referred to as Burnet); [*The*] *Wentworth Papers*, (ed. J. J. Cartwright, 1883), p. 204.

[2] Kinnoull's memo. to Oxford, 19 Sept. 1711: ' . . . To send down my Ld. Mar to take care of the election of a new Peer ' (Brit. Mus. Portland Loan [Harley MSS.] 146) suggests that at this stage the introduction into the Lords of the new duke of Brandon was taken for granted. Even at the beginning of November the earl of Seafield was busy furthering his own campaign to fill the expected vacancy: H.M.C. *Portland MSS*. x. 201.

the Lords.[1] Though their fears may have been unnecessary they were quite genuine,[2] and together with the parlous situation of Oxford's ministry—its very existence hanging at this point on the votes of the Upper House—they explain the fervour with which the Junto lords in December 1711 contested the duke of Hamilton's patent.

They had made their intention evident enough from early November. By the middle of that month the duke had begun to feel most uneasy about his prospects; and Oxford seems to have shared his pessimism, for he seriously thought of sending Hamilton on a diplomatic mission to Vienna and so evading the issue of the patent until the ministry had weathered its other storms.[3] As for the rest of the Scottish peers, they now experienced afresh all the anxiety they had felt earlier in the summer and resumed their warnings to the government.[4] Alarm was not confined to one party in Scotland, or even to those whose immediate prospects were affected. Baillie of Jerviswood, for instance, though an opposition member, was by no means at one with his English allies at Westminster in their hostility to the patent: ' If he [Hamilton] lose it ', he wrote to Lord Polwarth on 13 November, ' the Union must break. What will be the consequences God knows, and therefore I cannot understand the meaning of the Whigs; for one would think that this will force Scotland to espouse the Pretender's right '.[5] It is not altogether surprising in the circumstances that when the second session of parliament opened on 7 December the new duke of Brandon did not take his seat in accordance with his recent title. Not until the ministers could guarantee his position would he expose himself to the indignity of a possible challenge; and so on this day of all days, when it was threatened with the repudiation of its whole peace policy, the government was deprived not only of Hamilton's own vote but also of those of several of his colleagues whose proxies the duke carried with him.[6] In the event only five Scottish peers out of sixteen attended, and though the ministry had

[1] *I.e.* creations leaving vacancies which would, in turn, be automatically filled by government nominees. Brit. Mus. Add. MS. 17677 EEE, fo. 395.

[2] At the beginning of December, when the queen was canvassing Lord Cowper's support both for the peace preliminaries and for the Hamilton grant, she made a point of denying any intention of making fresh Scottish creations: ' . . . In speaking on this subject was pleas'd to say to me, " That the House of Lords was already full enough. I'll warrant you, I shall take care not to make them more in hast ", etc.' *The Private Diary of Earl Cowper* (Roxburgh Club, 1833), p. 53. Cowper, formerly Godolphin's lord chancellor, was a moderate whig.

[3] H.M.C. *Portland MSS.* v. 107: Hamilton to Oxford, 9, 13 Nov. 1711; Brit. Mus. Lansdowne MS. 1236, fo. 262: The Queen to Oxford, 16 Nov. 1711.

[4] H.M.C. *Portland MSS.* x. 230: [Seafield] to Oxford, 1711 [probably November].

[5] H.M.C. *Polwarth MSS.* i. 2.

[6] *Wentworth Papers*, p. 224: Peter Wentworth to earl of Strafford, 14 Dec. 1711. ' As many proxies as could be got ready ' were despatched by Lord Kinnoull by ' the flying packet ' from Edinburgh on 3 Dec.: H.M.C. *Portland MSS.* v. 121.

the support of all five it was defeated in two vital divisions on the question of 'No Peace without Spain' by majorities of one and eight.[1]

The poor response of the Scots to the treasurer's recent appeals was a significant reflection of growing tension in the relations of the two countries. Oxford may have preferred to explain it away as an accident caused by flooded roads in the north;[2] but, as with the continued truculence of the Scottish peers throughout the next three months, it had its roots in personal frustrations and disappointments which had been building up for the best part of a year. In the first place, few of 'the sixteen' felt that the ministry had done anything like enough to reward their own services, with either offices or gratuities. The refusal to appoint a Scottish secretary of state after the death of Queensberry was a prime source of discontent, especially with Mar and Islay, the two leading aspirants to the post. It is true that the establishment of a new trade commission for Scotland in November 1711 had stayed some of the criticism, but though it gave employment ultimately to five of the sixteen only Eglinton and Balmerino were genuinely gratified by their new offices (Annandale, in fact, regarded his appointment as beneath his notice and at first declined it). Another grievance, not unconnected with the first, was the government's failure to purge public employments in Scotland of the members or allies of the hated 'Squadrone', in particular its reluctance to dismiss Montrose and Glasgow.[3] Indeed, since the end of the previous session Oxford had been receiving a steady stream of solicitations, exhortations and complaints of every kind from beyond the Border, and a plan for holding weekly meetings with Lord Mar to iron out Anglo-Scottish problems had produced little appreciable improvement.[4] On top of all this had now come the peerage dispute, which threatened to close, perhaps indefinitely, one of the most attractive avenues opened up to the Scottish peerage by the Treaty of Union. The cumulative effect was to subject the Union to its most serious period of stress since the attempted invasion of 1708 at the very time when the Oxford ministry most needed a quiescent Scotland, represented in the house of lords by a pliant contingent of peers.

Only a direct challenge to Hamilton's patent in parliament was needed to precipitate a genuine crisis out of these discontents, and this was not long delayed. Flushed with their triumph of 7 December, the whigs saw in the duke's affair an ideal opportunity to cause the government yet more acute embarrassment: not least because, by treating it as a *constitutional* rather than a political issue, they could

---

[1] H.M.C. *Polwarth MSS.* i. 3: George Baillie to Lord Polwarth, 8 Dec. 1711.
[2] *Letters and Correspondence of . . . Viscount Bolingbroke* (ed. G. Parke, 4 vols, 1798), ii. 49.
[3] Brit. Mus. Portland Loan (Harley MSS.) 146: Kinnoull to [Dupplin], 27 Oct. 1711.
[4] H.M.C. *Portland MSS.* x. 409.

hope for the sympathy and even support of a number of otherwise
loyal tories.   Despite ministerial protests that any discussion of the
patent would infringe the prerogative, the Lords rejected, by a
majority of three, a government motion for an adjournment on the
12th and ordered a full debate on Thursday, 20 December.[1]   ' I
designe to get into the house to hear the debate ', wrote Peter
Wentworth on the 14th, ' for there's a great deal to be said of both
sides, and if ever any cause was debated without party this will be
so'.[2]   And when the Lords assembled six days later the crowded
benches and galleries plainly testified to the uncommon interest
which the case had aroused.   There were 114 peers present—only
two fewer than on the momentous opening day of the session—and
four recent arrivals from the north had brought the Scottish representation up to nine,[3] even though Hamilton himself still held aloof.
The Court had left no doubt that it intended to fight the case with
the utmost energy, even persuading the queen to attend *incognito* in
the hope that her presence would influence wavering peers on a
question affecting her own prerogative.   In fact, with the house
of lords so clearly holding the balance of political power in the
existing crisis,[4] here were all the ingredients of a great parliamentary
occasion.

Since legal issues were involved the debate was preceded by the
hearing of counsel on Hamilton's behalf.   The duke had instructed
two of the most eminent lawyers of the day, Sir Thomas Powys and
Serjeant Pratt, and Powys's opening speech was a masterly piece of
legal exposition that did full justice to the occasion.[5]   He began by
asserting that the queen's prerogative with regard to the conferring
of honours and dignities was clear and unchallengeable and that *all*
the subjects of the new United Kingdom of Great Britain were
equally entitled to receive such honours at the queen's hands.   No
one would question the right of the commons of Scotland to such a
privilege.   How then was it possible to make a single exception in
the case of the Scottish peers?   To debar them from receiving
honours was to make a quite invidious distinction in one particular

---

[1] [*House of*] L[*ords*] J[*ournals*], xix. 342; Boyer, ii. 689–90.

[2] *Wentworth Papers*, p. 225.

[3] *Viz.* earls of Mar, Home, Loudon, Rosebery, Orkney and Islay; Viscount
Kilsyth; Lords Balmerino and Blantyre.   Six were still in Scotland: H.M.C. *Polwarth
MSS.* i. 3; *L.J.* xix. 345.

[4] *Cf.* Earl Poulet's remark to Strafford in a letter written on the same day as the
Hamilton debate: ' . . . the House of Lords prevailes over the Queens management with
us and the strongest House of Commons that ever meet.'   Brit. Mus. Add. MS. 22222,
fo. 188.

[5] Speaker Onslow, who heard the debate as a young man, later remarked that
Powys's speech ' was deemed a great performance ' (note to Burnet, vi. 86).   Peter
Wentworth, however, dissented from this view.   To his mind ' they both [*i.e.* Powys
and Pratt] seem'd as if they lay under difficulty, that they had no lawyers to answere,
but was to suppose what objections were to be made ' (to Strafford, 21 Dec. 1711.
Wentworth Papers. pp. 226–7).

case: indeed to reduce the Scots nobility to criminal status. Furthermore, Powys argued, to challenge Hamilton's patent was to claim that the royal prerogative of creating peers was restricted. Yet it was an accepted maxim of the constitution that the Crown could lose no prerogative that it had not already given up by the express words of an act of parliament. The Act of Union of 1707 contained no such specific limitation. It merely stated that the peers of Scotland were *by virtue of this treaty* to be represented in parliament by sixteen of their number, and the very use of these words, he suggested, seemed to intimate that other Scottish lords might sit by virtue of other rights, namely creation or succession. By the time Sir Thomas had concluded his case there was little left of a purely legal and constitutional nature for his second-string, Pratt, to say. The latter was content mainly to expatiate further on the prerogative and to insist that if the patent itself were acknowledged to be legal it entitled his Grace of Hamilton not merely to call himself duke of Brandon but to take his seat in the House in that capacity.[1]

Though the debate which followed lasted until eight o'clock, a very lengthy sitting by the standards of the day, the queen is said to have stayed in the House from start to finish.[2] To begin with their lordships clearly felt inhibited by Anne's presence—the departure of the two lawyers was followed by a long, embarrassed silence —but once the tory peer Lord Guernsey[3] had broken the ice, opposing Hamilton's right to sit as duke of Brandon, the leading partisans were soon warmly engaged. Throughout the debate the argument centred on two essential questions: one a question of legal interpretation (in this case, interpretation of the 22nd article of the Union, dealing with Scottish representation in the united parliament), the other a question of precedent (created by the elevation of the duke of Queensberry to a British peerage in May 1708 and the fact that he had sat and voted unchallenged, as duke of Dover, in two successive parliaments up to his death in July 1711). Opposition spokesmen naturally preferred to avoid the second question as far as possible. About Queensberry Lord Sunderland, for the Junto, could only argue that while the matter had been passed over

---

[1] Burnet, vi. 87; H.M.C. *House of Lords MSS.* N.S. ix. 173.

[2] *Wentworth Papers*, p. 226; Boyer, ii. 691. The Dutch agent, L'Hermitage, gave a different version: ' La reine alla a la chambre un peu devant 2 heures et S.M. y resta jusqu'a pres de 5 heures pour entendre les debats ': Brit. Mus. Add. MS. 17677 FFF, fo. 11. Altogether the proceedings lasted eight hours, having begun at noon: *L.J.* xix. 345.

[3] Formerly Heneage Finch, the celebrated lawyer. He was a man who normally commanded the respect and attention of the House, and the sophistry to which he appears to have resorted on this occasion illustrates the flimsiness of the opposition case: S.R.O. Dalhousie MS. 14/352: Balmerino to Maule, 24 Jan. 1712, reporting the debate of 20 Dec. Guernsey was the brother of Lord Nottingham who had deserted the tories earlier in the month over the issue of ' No Peace without Spain '.

in silence this did not necessarily validate his claim; nor was Hamilton's case thereby prejudged.[1]   With the first question, however, the whigs felt on safer ground.   They took up Powys's maxim that the prerogative could only be limited by act of parliament, and Halifax bent his considerable oratorical gifts to seek to show that such a limitation was imposed by the Act of 1707.   He urged that the Act of Union had made *all* peers of Scotland peers of Great Britain in every respect except two: namely, voting in the house of lords (a power vested only in their sixteen representatives) and sitting in judgment on their peers.[2]   Opponents of the patent had long since claimed that to increase Scottish representation beyond sixteen by any means would be to give the Scots a greater share of the legislative power than was designed at the time of the Union,[3] and Halifax reiterated this argument.[4]   In short, the Opposition did not dispute the queen's right to bestow what titles she pleased upon the Scots; but although conceding that she was free to create Hamilton duke of Brandon they argued that she could not give him the right to sit and vote in that capacity.[5]

From the government benches it was urged, especially by Lord Abingdon, that Hamilton's case was in every way identical with Queensberry's and that by its failure to take any action in 1708 the House had already prejudged the matter.   The only right of Queensberry's which had been challenged, insisted Abingdon, was his right of voting in elections of ' the sixteen ', and the very fact that this right was denied him by the House in January 1709 was itself clear proof that his status as a peer of Great Britain was accepted.[6]   The most impassioned speeches from the Tory side, as was to be expected, came from the Scots themselves, with Islay, Loudoun, Balmerino and Mar their chief spokesmen.   Their answer to the argument that the number of Scottish peers in parliament, as Scotsmen, must be confined to sixteen precisely in order to maintain the ' legislative balance ' was simple and categorical: since the proportion of Scots to English in both Houses had been carefully assessed in 1707 on the basis of comparative revenue, the ' freezing ' of the former could not in justice be accompanied by the

[1] Burnet, vi. 88; *Wentworth Papers*, p. 227.   The fact that the Books of the House, recording Queensberry's introduction in 1708, referred to his ' claiming ' his place was used by Sunderland as evidence that the case was never decided.

[2] Halifax based this argument on the 23rd article of Union.

[3] *Lockhart Papers*, i. 342; Boyer, ii. 689.

[4] As reported in *Wentworth Papers*, p. 229: Peter Wentworth to Strafford, 21 Dec. 1711.   See also Burnet, vi. 88.

[5] This was a distinction on which tory dissidents, notably Guernsey, laid particular stress as being perfectly consistent (so they claimed) with solicitude for the prerogative: *Wentworth Papers*, p. 227.

[6] *Ibid.* p. 227.   See also Hume Brown, *op. cit.* iii. 142.   Dr. W. Ferguson has pointed out to me that it was Hamilton himself who first pressed for Queensberry's disfranchisement after the 1708 election.   See Wm. Robertson, *Proceedings relating to the Peerage of Scotland from . . . 1707 to . . . 1788* (Edinburgh, 1790).

elevation of any Englishman to the new peerage.[1] Like Powys, the Scots made great play in the debate with the words *by virtue of this treaty* in the 22nd article of the Union, and those who had helped to negotiate the treaty reinforced his interpretation by insisting (unanswered by the opposition) that these words were put in for the very purpose of leaving the door open for peers other than the sixteen to sit by creation or succession.[2] Well before the end of the debate neither the House nor the ministers could have been in any doubt of the genuinely bitter feelings the whole affair had aroused in Scotland, and the bishop of Salisbury noted that the speeches of the Scottish peers were interspersed with ' intimations of the dismal effects that might follow, if it should go in the negative'.[3]

As he listened to these prognostications Oxford could no longer evade the unpalatable truth that something more than the existence of his own ministry was in danger. Now that the Hamilton case had become inextricably involved with the other elements in the general political crisis Mar's former prophecy that the Union itself might founder over this sorry affair seemed dangerously near to realization. In his own speech the treasurer had tried desperately to outmanoeuvre the whigs by proposing that the House should seek the opinion of the judges, as the question was primarily one of law; but though supported by two other Cabinet ministers, Poulet

[1] *Cf. Lockhart Papers*, i. 343; S.R.O. Dalhousie MS. 14/352, Balmerino's report of the debate. On the ratio of representatives to wealth and population see *The Treaty of Union of Scotland and England* (ed. G. Pryde, 1950), pp. 43–44.

[2] This, without doubt, was the most unanswerable part of Hamilton's whole case and the one which cast most discredit on the whigs, especially those Junto lords who had themselves been active in the Union negotiations. It also explains the singular bitterness with which the Scots reacted to the attack on the patent. ' . . . it is too certain ', writes Lockhart, ' that severall of the Scots Peers were cajoled and amused [in 1706] with the hopes nay assurances (as is well known to severall English lords) of being created hereditary Peers . . .': *Lockhart Papers*, i. 343. Again, in the memorial which was presented by twenty Scottish peers to Anne on 1 Jan. 1712 [see p. 163 below] this particular grievance is emphasized more than any other: ' the Commissioners for Scotland . . . did condescend to this Declaration, That they did not insist for greater Numbers (by virtue of this Treaty) of Representatives in the House of Peers, than Sixteen. Having been assured at that Time, by several of the Commissioners for England, that Your Majesty's Prerogative could never be thereby construed to be restrained from granting new Patents of Honour to the Peers of Scotland, with all the Priviledges depending thereupon; the Commissioners for Scotland thought it more reasonable, that the Peers of that Kingdom should, by their Zeal for Your Majesty's Service, endeavour to merit Your future Favour, as the Sole Fountain of Honour, than to interrupt the Progress of the Union . . . with any further Demands upon Your Majesty's Prerogative by Vertue of the Treaty. Upon the Faith of these Assurances, and the sacred inviolable Force of Publick Treaties, the Commissioners concluded the Treaty, and the Parliament of Scotland did ratify the Union.' *A Representation of the Scotch Peers 1711/12 on Duke Hamilton's Case* (London (?), 1712): the printed version of the Memorial, in pamphlet form.

[3] Burnet, vi. 88. The chief prophet of doom was Islay who, in the course of what Wentworth found ' a very moving speech ', said that ' he trembled to think of the consequence . . . for he was sure 'twould be deem'd a breach of the Union ': *Wentworth Papers*, p. 229.

and Harcourt, his proposal was opposed by Sunderland and Wharton on the specious ground that the matter was one of privilege rather than law, and was rejected on a vote by a majority of fourteen.[1] The flat refusal of the Junto lords to consult the judges on a matter so wholly within their province as the interpretation of the words of an act of parliament showed quite clearly that, for all their avowed solicitude for the constitution, they regarded the Hamilton affair primarily as a matter of political advantage. Nor were they interested in reaching any compromise on the main question. When an independent tory peer, Lord Pembroke, suggested towards the end of the debate that Hamilton's patent should be admitted only for the duration of his own life the idea was soon brushed aside. But despite the ruthlessness with which the whig leaders pressed their point and assailed the prerogative—a ruthlessness which disturbed some of their closest supporters and allies [2]—they were still strong enough to carry the final division by 57 votes to 52 on the resolution ' that no Patent of Honour granted to any Peer of Great Britain who was a Peer of Scotland at the time of the Union can entitle such Peer to sit and vote in Parliament or to sit upon the Trial of Peers '.[3] And not even Anne's presence was sufficient, in the event, to deter a number of non-ministerial tories or even two members of the government itself (Dartmouth and Berkeley of Stratton) from voting with the Opposition.[4]

Why did the house of lords reach this historic decision? Party motives, we can be sure, governed the hard core of uncompromising whigs; but this was not so with the Court whigs and tory rebels whose votes were the decisive factor. Were their judgments really swayed by the kind of legalistic or constitutional argument which had dominated the debate, or were there less obvious undercurrents at work? These are questions to which it is hard to give

[1] *Wentworth Papers*, p. 229; Brit. Mus. Add. MS. 17677 FFF, fo. 11: L'Hermitage to the States-General, 21 Dec. [O.S.], 1711. The voting was 63 to 49: H.M.C. *House of Lords MSS*. N.S. ix. 174. A Protest subsequently entered in the Journals of the House in the name of the Scots and ten other peers stressed the illogicality of this decision. To allow the hearing of counsel but refuse to hear the judges on the self-same question seemed singularly wrong-headed, especially as the judges had been specifically ordered to attend on the 20th and the opposition had acquiesced in this order: *L.J.* xix. 345,347.

[2] According to L'Hermitage ' un fort grand nombre ' of whig peers either absented themselves or executed a tactical withdrawal before the final division, and while he exaggerated the scale of the abstentions their existence is worth noting: Brit. Mus. Add. MS. 17677 FFF, fo. 11. Marlborough and Godolphin were among those sufficiently embarrassed to leave the Chamber before the second vote : *Wentworth Papers*, p. 229. Speaker Onslow later wrote: ' I was then a very young man, in all the warmth of party on the Whig side, yet I was much scandalised, I remember, at this behaviour of those I wished best to [*i.e.* the Junto] . . .' (note to Burnet, vi. 87).

[3] H.M.C. *House of Lords MSS*. N.S. ix. 174.

[4] See Dartmouth's note to Burnet, vi. 89. Other tories voting against Hamilton included Nottingham, Guernsey and Scarsdale: H.M.C. *House of Lords MSS*. N.S. ix. 174.

a clear-cut answer.   To any peer approaching the debate with an open mind the case which the lawyers, the government and the Scots together put forward on the duke's behalf must have seemed convincing.   But it is unlikely that very many of the ' marginal ' voters in the House came prepared to assess the matter purely judicially.   Lockhart, as we have seen, presupposed the existence of a widespread, almost instinctive, anti-Scottish prejudice in the light of which he normally interpreted most English behaviour. The Hamilton affair, to him, was certainly no exception, and his verdict has too readily found support among both Scottish and English historians.[1]   In reality the motives of the tory and moderate whig lords who voted against the patent on 20 December were at once more complex and more subtle.   Some doubtless shared Dartmouth's genuine constitutional scruples and so were predisposed in favour of the arguments advanced by the Junto. But the attitude of the majority was more probably determined by two considerations of a different nature.   One was the jealous concern many English peers felt for their own order and their apprehensions lest it should be swamped by a flood of Scottish creations:[2]   this was prejudice, no doubt, but not of the crude variety which Lockhart depicts.   The other, and more powerful, factor was the general aversion which both whig and tory peers had developed for the whole system of choosing sixteen Scottish representatives to sit in the Upper House.   The most recent example of this system in action, the proceedings at Edinburgh in 1710, had conclusively confirmed that the so-called ' election ' was a ludicrous formality, with success a virtual certainty for anyone on the official ministerial list of recommended peers; and the effect, as at least one Scotsman admitted, had been to make the English nobility as a whole ' weary of our elections '.   Some weeks after the debate of 20 December the earl of Mar wrote pessimistically to his brother that ' as long as they [the elections] last they have such an apprehension of the acquisition of strength the Crown gets by us, and as it were in opposition to both their parties, that they will ever treat us as enimies, Whige and Torie being alike affraid of the power of the Crown '.[3]   This ' apprehension ', unuttered though it was (for obvious reasons) in the debate itself, may well provide the most important key to the alarm and *furor* created in the Lords by the grant of Hamilton's patent, a grant which focussed new attention on the iniquities of the elective system by the threat of frequent ' by-elections ' which it seemed to carry.

[1] *E.g.* James Mackinnon, *The Union of England and Scotland* (1896), p. 423 ; Turberville, *op. cit.* p. 151.

[2] H.M.C. *House of Lords MSS.* N.S. ix., intro., p. xxii; *Lockhart Papers*, i. 341; Brit. Mus. Add. MS. 17677 FFF, fo. 11.

[3] H.M.C. *Mar and Kellie MSS.*, pp. 492, 495: Mar to Sir James Erskine, 27 Dec. 1711, 17 Jan. 1712.

The full consequences of the events of 20 December were not immediately apparent. It is true that the Scots, both at Westminster and north of the Border, reacted with considerable anger to the Lords' decision. Quite clearly they regarded it as a national rebuff, not merely as a personal one, and as early as the 21st ' some hot head fellows ' were already proposing, according to Wentworth, ' that neither Commoners nor Lords of that Nation ought to come into the house any more '.[1] But these extreme counsels did not at once prevail. Burnet tells how a meeting of the Scottish representative peers in London [2] resulted instead in a decision to make a formal representation to the queen, complaining of the Lords' vote as ' a breach of the union, and a mark of disgrace put on the whole peers of Scotland '. This memorial, drafted jointly by Mar, Islay and Hamilton, was submitted for the approval of the Scottish commoners at a further meeting on Sunday the 30th, before being signed by the peers on the 31st and presented to Anne on New Year's Day. The version subsequently printed [3] makes it plain that this was something more than a statement of grievances preceding a request for redress. It was intended to serve as a further reminder to the Court that failure to provide redress might well lead to the dissolution of the Union. True, the threat was decently veiled by fulsome professions of loyalty to the queen; but that it was meant to be implicit there can be no doubt.[4] What is not so certain is how this threat was interpreted by the signatories themselves. There were those who honestly saw in a formal dissolution of the Union the only honourable satisfaction for their grievances and who believed, like Rosebery, ' that the Whigs, Tories and Scots all desyre it . . . and that nothing stops it but the Court '; [5] but there seem to have been just as many who regarded it as a useful instrument of political bargaining, the likeliest way of bringing pressure on the ministry, rather than as a practicable expedient. ' As to dissolveing the Union in a Parliamentary way, I despair of it ', wrote the earl of Mar on 27 December, ' or if it were possible in doing of it, they would fix the succession, and in that case Scotland wou'd lose any aw it could have over England '; [6] and developing this theme in a later report to his brother in Edinburgh he explained that ' Tho' both

---

[1] *Wentworth Papers*, p. 229: Peter Wentworth to Strafford, 21 Dec. 1711. See also H.M.C. *Mar and Kellie MSS.* p. 491.

[2] Probably on 28 Dec. See H.M.C. *Mar and Kellie MSS.* p. 492.

[3] See note 2, p. 160.

[4] The crux of the matter was contained in this paragraph from the *Representation*: ' We beg leave to assure Your Majesty, That whatever may be Our Fate, we shall always be ready *either in a united or separate State* [my italics] to sacrifice every Thing that is dear to us, for the Defence of the Prerogative of the Crown, and for the Honour of Your Majesty and Your Successors.' See also Burnet, vi. 90–91; H.M.C. *Polwarth MSS.* i. 5: Geo. Baillie to Lord Marchmont, 1 Jan. 1712; *Wentworth Papers*, p. 236.

[5] H.M.C. *Mar and Kellie MSS.* p. 492: earl of Mar to Sir James Erskine, 27 Dec. 1711; S.R.O. Dalhousie MS. 14/352; Balmerino to Maule, 15 Jan. 1712.

[6] H.M.C. *Mar and Kellie MSS.* p. 492.

parties be wearie of the Union, they will upon no tearmes that I can yett see quitt with the Union in a legall way. . . . With you [in Scotland] I have no doubt but the dissolveing of the Union is thought to be possible and pritty easie in a Parliamentary way; but that I cannot conceave, and I fear it will be found so, and I wish our countrymen could be made to understand this.' [1]

That Mar and his sympathizers succeeded for a while in impressing caution on their colleagues is proved not only by the generally restrained tone of the memorial but by the attitude of the peers to a more extravagant representation made by Hamilton personally. The duke was satisfied neither with the memorial nor with the queens' encouraging reply, and in a personal audience with Anne he demanded 'in the name of the whole nation' that she should dismiss her secretary of state, Lord Dartmouth, from the government for voting against the patent, ' for they could never believe her majesty was ine arnest, whilst a man that had her seals in his pocket voted against them, and received no mark of her displeasure '. We have Dartmouth's own account of what took place at this interview:

> The queen said, she had done all she could to persuade me to comply: but I understood it to be against law, and she believed I acted sincerely, with affection to her service, and zeal for my country; therefore had deceived nobody; . . . [she] did not think it for her own service to comply with them in that particular: for she believed it would give great offence to the English lords, and do the Scotch more harm than good. Then duke Hamilton proposed, that an act of parliament might be brought in to confirm his and the duke of Queensbury's patents; to which the queen gave him no answer.[2]

If Dartmouth's story is accurate the duke was inviting a snub, and the fact that it was duly administered does not seem to have caused his colleagues much distress. They thought his action ill-advised and did not hesitate to say so. Indeed, the duke of Atholl called on Dartmouth the day after Hamilton's audience to disassociate both himself and the rest of the Scottish peers from what had been said and to ask him to convey their views to the queen.[3]

But while they were not prepared as yet to commit themselves publicly to extreme demands, in their private talks with ministers the peers made little secret of their growing exasperation. The treasurer, at least, was aware by the end of December that even if the Union itself managed to survive the immediate shock dealt it by the Hamilton affair the whole Scottish contingent was likely to prove most unreliable for weeks, possibly months, to come. Its leaders

---

[1] H.M.C. *Mar and Kellie MSS*. pp. 494–5: Mar to Erskine, 17 Jan. 1712.

[2] Dartmouth's note to Burnet, vi. 89. For several days after the vote of 20 Dec. there was a strong belief at Court that Dartmouth would be dismissed. See *Wentworth Papers*, p. 233: Peter Wentworth to Strafford, 28 Dec. 1711.

[3] Burnet, vi. 89 n.

had already taken care to warn the ministry unofficially that unless prompt satisfaction was forthcoming from the government side they would ' all join with the other partie ', and Oxford believed this to be a threat more capable of swift realization than the more spectacular official warnings about the fate of the Union.[1] In fact this situation may well have had more to do than is generally realized with the remarkable and highly controversial step which he took at the close of the Christmas recess, when twelve new peers were created *en bloc* to ensure the safety of his government and the passage of the peace preliminaries through parliament. Certainly, when Dartmouth subsequently asked him the reason for such a desperate measure Oxford's reply was that ' the Scotch lords were grown so extravagant in their demands, that it was high time to let them see they were not so much wanted as they imagined; for they were now come to expect a reward for every vote they gave '.[2]

When the house of lords reassembled on 2 January 1712 the first division, on a Court motion for adjournment, demonstrated to all but the most obtuse political observers that the treasurer's gamble had succeeded, at least in its immediate objective. Barring unforeseen developments the government could now expect to survive the current crisis; and this meant automatically that the problem of appeasing the duke of Hamilton in particular, and the Scots in general, lost something of its pressing urgency in ministerial eyes. ' Lord Treasurer's dozen ' had made ' the sixteen ' less indispensable. Nevertheless the problem had still to be resolved and it continued to exercise both the Cabinet and the queen a great deal during the first weeks of the new year. The crux of the problem was now this: since the events of 20 December it had been pretty clear that nothing short of an act of parliament reversing the decision of the Lords and restoring the *status quo* of 1707 would appease Scottish opinion at large;[3] yet the ministry, for all its recent accession of strength, could not guarantee the success of any such bill. Some Scottish peers, Mar for instance, might privately have accepted the justice of alternative schemes of compensation, but with feeling running so high and ' the bent of the country . . . so much for the dissolution of the Union ' they could scarcely afford publicly to accept any compromise.[4] On the other hand, as

---

[1] H.M.C. *Mar and Kellie MSS.* p. 493. Whether the Scottish leaders could have persuaded their more rabid tory colleagues, Eglinton and Balmerino for instance, to pursue such a policy is by no means certain. Eglinton avowed two weeks later that ' if we please he shall absent but if he be present by God he will never let the Whigs gain a vote of the tories if he cane help it ' : S.R.O. Dalhousie MS. 14/352: Balmerino to Maule, 15 Jan. 1712.

[2] Dartmouth's note to Burnet, vi. 95.

[3] This was what the duke had insisted on in his audience with Anne, and though his colleagues had not supported him then many of them believed in the necessity of such a measure.

[4] H.M.C. *Mar and Kellie MSS.* pp. 492, 495.

long as the peerage question continued to cut across normal party divisions [1] any expedient (like the proposed bill) which preserved the existing system of electing Scottish peers was sure to arouse sufficient tory opposition to jeopardize its success.

Such was the government's dilemma; and however sincere it was in its desire to accommodate the Scottish aristocracy [2] it could not be optimistic about its chances of reaching an acceptable settlement. Still, there was one circumstance in its favour. In the continued absence of any firm offer of terms from the whig opposition the Scots stood to gain little, at this juncture, by an immediate and open breach with the Court; they could hardly refuse to negotiate. In fact on Sunday, 13 January, their leaders [3] accepted a ministerial invitation to a joint meeting at the Cockpit in Whitehall with a group of Cabinet ministers. Its purpose was strictly limited—to discuss the preliminary steps to be taken after the adjournment [4]— but within this context it was successful. It was agreed that the representative peers should continue for the time being to support the ministry, pending an address to the queen to ' lay proposals ' before the House, and that if the address were carried these proposals were to be discussed beforehand with the Scots. [5]

The ministry's first objective, that of persuading the house of lords formally to reopen the peerage question, was successfully attained. In the course of her message to the House on 17 January Anne once again made her own views patently clear: she referred to the extreme concern felt in Scotland at the fact that the royal prerogative had been ' strictly barred ' against the Scottish peers alone, reminded the lords that this was ' a matter which sensibly affects her ' and requested ' their advice and concurrence in finding out the best method of settling this affair to the satisfaction of the whole Kingdom '. [6] After Oxford, in the brief debate that followed, had reiterated the absolute necessity of doing something ' to satisfie so great a part of the Nation ' the House agreed to a suggestion of Godolphin's that it should go into committee on this question the following day. [7] No doubt the fresh rumours that had

[1] In a letter to his brother, dated 17 Jan, Mar wrote: ' . . . As to this affair of ours, there is nothing so like a Whige as a Torie and nothing so like a Torie as a Whig—a cat out of a hole and a cate in a hole ' : H.M.C. *Mar and Kellie MSS.* p. 495.

[2] Even Balmerino, reluctant as he was to concede the existence of any good will on the part of the English, was forced to admit that ' certainly the queen is most heartie in our affair, so is the Treasurer, Shrewsbury, Paulett & Lord Keeper & some others ': S.R.O. Dalhousie MS. 14/352: to Maule, 15 Jan. 1712.

[3] They included Mar and Islay, but not Hamilton.

[4] Following the sitting on 2 Jan. parliament had been adjourned for a fortnight.

[5] H.M.C. *Portland MSS.* v. 138; *Mar and Kellie MSS.* p. 494. At the same time the Scots ' endeavoured to show the impractibility [*sic*] of any [expedient] succeeding ': *ibid.* 495.

[6] *L.J.* xix. 358; H.M.C. *Polwarth MSS.* i. 6: George Baillie to earl of Marchmont, 19 Jan. 1712.

[7] *Wentworth Papers,* pp. 253–4: Peter Wentworth to Strafford, 18 Jan. 1712.

begun to circulate of an intended parliamentary boycott by the Scots [1] helped to make the Lords more responsive to the promptings of the Court. In any event, a Committee of the Whole House, meeting on 18 January under Lord Ferrers's chairmanship, began an exhaustive discussion which was subsequently prolonged over three further sittings—on 21 and 25 January and on 4 February.[2]

Ironically the speed with which the Lords acted appears to have caught the ministry unprepared. Its own proposals were not ready by the 18th and government spokesmen on that day were forced to confine themselves mainly to generalities and the expression of pious hopes.[3] Nothing concrete was forthcoming from the government benches until the 21st and the suggestion made then was one that had already been privately canvassed for some weeks.[4] The House was invited to consider ' whether it would not be to make the Union more complete if a number of the Lords of the North part of Great Britain sat here by inheritance and not by election ', provided the rest of the Scottish peers consented to the change.[5] Discussion of this proposal occupied the rest of the sitting on the 21st and was then adjourned to the 25th without a vote being taken, but even on the first day it was clear that, as it stood, the plan would not command general support, so much so that Oxford had already begun to devise new expedients by the 24th.[6] For one thing, there was the practical difficulty of deciding how many Scottish peers should be given hereditary seats if the representative principle were abandoned. If opposition to the idea in Scotland was to be overcome the number would have to be high, and thirty-two seems to have been the minimum asked for by the Scots. To Lord Wharton, on the other hand, ' a number of hereditary peers meant only 16, not half a peer more '; and this was probably the view of most Junto whigs and not a few tories.[7] There was also the more basic problem of whether the representative

---

[1] Rumours that were not entirely without foundation. The idea had been seriously discussed by ' the sixteen ' at a private meeting on 15 Jan. but only Annandale was in favour of giving immediate effect to it: S.R.O. Dalhousie MS. 14/352: Balmerino to Maule, 15 Jan.

[2] H.M.C. *House of Lords MSS.* N.S. ix. 174–5.

[3] *Ibid.* 174. The treasurer, who had probably expected the House to rest content at first with an address to the queen to lay proposals before it, does not seem to have begun to formulate his own ideas until the following day. His draft notes, endorsed ' Scotland ' and dated 19 January 1711/12, are in Brit. Mus. Portland Loan (Harley MSS.) 29/218.

[4] Mar had told his brother on 27 Dec. of a proposal ' to offer us a considerable number of our families to be chose and made by the Queen peers, with all the priviledges of sitting, etc., as they are here to the number of perhaps thertie or some more; that the incapacity should be taken off the rest of us; that our titles and precedencies should continue, and that we should be capable of being elected in the House of Commons ': H.M.C. *Mar and Kellie MSS.* p. 492.

[5] H.M.C. *House of Lords MSS.* N.S. ix. 174; Burnet, vi. 99.

[6] Brit. Mus. Portland Loan (Harley MSS.) 29/218.

[7] S.R.O. Dalhousie MS. 14/352 : Balmerino to Maule, 24 Jan. 1712.

principle *could* legally be abandoned without dissolving the Union. The debate[1] mainly hinged, in fact, on which of the articles of the Union were ' fundamental ', and therefore unalterable by parliament, and which were not; and more especially on whether the article providing for an elective representation of Scottish peers should be considered ' fundamental '. At length, after a great deal of wrangling, the committee did manage to agree on the 25th that this article *was* alterable by parliament without any violation of the Union, provided it was done ' at the request of the Peers of Great Britain who were Peers of Scotland before the Union '. But the very use of the phrase ' at the request of ' in the resolution represented a defeat for the Court. The ministers had favoured a different formula, one which stipulated only the ' consent ' of the Scottish peers, not their ' request ', but the opposition objected that this word implied a retention of some legislative power by the Scots and sustained their objection in a division by 60 votes to 52; [2] so that the government was forced to accept an alternative which it well knew to be impracticable—for there was little or no chance of a full muster of the Scottish peers in Edinburgh agreeing to make the proposal which the resolution envisaged.[3]

Oxford had not quite shot his bolt, however. Between the third meeting of the committee on 25 January and its next appointed meeting on 4 February he made a new offer privately to the Scots. As Mar reported it, this was

> that the Queen should be enabled by an Act of Parliament to call the peers of Scotland togither to lay this matter before them, in order to their laying before her Majestie what they wou'd propose in this affair, and then betwixt and [*sic*] that meeting the Queen's servants wou'd concert with the Scots here a reasonable scheme to be laid before them. . . .[4]

The plan was open to two technical objections: that the peers of Scotland had no power to act alone, that is without the other two estates, least of all in effecting any modification of the treaty of

---

[1] The debates in the committee are nowhere well reported. Visitors were being fairly regularly excluded from the House at the time: see *Wentworth Papers*, p. 260.

[2] *Ibid.* p. 260; H.M.C. *Mar and Kellie MSS.* p. 496; *House of Lords MSS.* N.S. ix. 174.

[3] See H.M.C. *Mar and Kellie MSS.* p. 496: Mar to Sir James Erskine, 14 Feb. 1712. The Scots were being required, in effect, to propose the abolition of the existing system of election before being assured of any satisfactory substitute.

[4] *Ibid. Cf.* Oxford's memorandum of 24 Jan. in H.M.C. *Portland MSS.* x. 167; also the rather different scheme envisaged in his note of 19 Jan.: ' An Act to enable her ma^tie to convene all the Peers of Great Britain who were Peers of Scotland at the time of the Union or the successors to their honors to meet & elect out of such Peers a limited number to be commissioned by her ma^tie to treat with the like number of her Peers of Great Brittain in the like manner commissioned to consider of proper methods of rendring the Union more compleat with respect to the Peers of Scotland sitting in the Parliamt. of Great Britt. And that the Proceedings of the sd. Comrs. to be laid before her ma^tie & the Parlmt. of Great Brittain in their next Session ': Brit. Mus. Portland Loan 29/218.

1706; and that a meeting of all three estates could be construed as an *ipso facto* dissolution of the Union.[1] But neither was really responsible for the chilly reception given to the treasurer's offer when it was put before a meeting of Scottish peers and M.P.s at Westminster. The main complaint was that it was merely a delaying tactic on Oxford's part and, for this reason alone, should be emphatically rejected. If it were proposed in the House, the ministers were told, the Scots would vote against it. In consequence, when the committee met on 4 February there was no move at all from the government side for a fresh approach to the problem. The Scots, for their part, remained frankly unco-operative. Lord Mar announced bluntly to the committee that 'they had nothing to propose', while Islay 'declared for himself and his country Lords that he wished rather than hoped anything can come from it'.[2]

Thus the government's attempt to solve the problem in parliament ended disappointingly, if not surprisingly, in total deadlock. As the Dutch agent in London remarked, no party had shown any genuine willingness to compromise;[3] and in the last fortnight, at least, only the ministry had demonstrated any real enthusiasm for a settlement or any conviction that a solution was possible. More serious, it seemed that the only result of reopening the matter in parliament had been still further to aggravate the grievances already present, for the Scottish peers now proceeded to carry out their long-rumoured threat of boycotting the house of lords. They had already shown their hand on 31 January when they staged a 'walkout' just before an important vote was due on a Bill to repeal the Naturalization Act,[4] and the decision to carry out the full-scale boycott was taken at the same meeting as rejected Oxford's final proposal—that is, before the Committee of the Whole House held its final session. A cautious minority appear to have had private doubts of the wisdom of such a step (the failure of the token walkout on the 31st to embarrass the ministry in any way had been only too apparent),[5] but they were swept along by their more militant colleagues who saw it as the best way left of bringing pressure both on the Court and on the tory peers as a whole. 'We did not resolve to abandon the House entirely', explained Mar subsequently, 'but to neglect attending it, or when any of us should be

---

[1] S.R.O. Dalhousie MS. 14/352: Balmerino to Maule, 15 and 26 Jan. 1712.

[2] H.M.C. *Mar and Kellie MSS.* p. 496; *House of Lords MSS.* N.S. ix. 175.

[3] Brit. Mus. Add. MS. 17677 FFF, fo. 38: L'Hermitage to the States-General, 29 Jan./9 Feb. 1712.

[4] Even before this two of the sixteen, Annandale and Balmerino, had been making their own private protest by deliberately absenting themselves for several days: S.R.O. Dalhousie MS. 14/352: Balmerino to Maule, 24 and 26 Jan. 1712. See also Balmerino's letter to Oxford, 29 Jan. 1712, in H.M.C. *Portland MSS.* v. 141.

[5] A tory victory by 18 votes in the division on the repeal of the Naturalization Act had suggested that, on party issues anyway, Scottish support was certainly not indispensable: *Wentworth Papers*, p. 261.

there on a summons or by accident, we should not act til it was by the consent of the major parte of the sixteen present here '.[1] To the English tories, however, it was plain desertion; and to everyone the action seemed all the graver in view of fresh storms in Anglo-Scottish relations that were rapidly blowing up from the house of commons. Here the high tories, much to Oxford's embarrassment, were giving enthusiastic backing to a measure which had long been dear to the hearts of episcopalian members like George Lockhart and Sir Alexander Erskine: a Bill for according greater toleration to the episcopal church in Scotland. The alarm which presbyterians felt at the progress of the Toleration Bill was intensified by the prospect that it would be followed by a still more offensive measure, the restoration of rights of patronage in Scotland.[2] All in all, the outlook for the Union could not have seemed much bleaker than at the beginning of February 1712.

Then, quite suddenly and to the apparent astonishment of all observers, came a relaxation of tension. After only two days' absence from the House, on 7 and 8 February, the Scottish peers returned; and Burnet tells us that from then on they continued to take part in parliamentary business, without further protest, for the remainder of the session. As we shall see, Burnet rather exaggerates the suddenness with which the crisis was resolved. But it is fairly plain that from the time the Scots resumed their seats on 9 February the atmosphere began to improve, so that by the end of the month only the habitual Jeremiahs were prophesying the imminent demise of the Union. The causes of this transformation were naturally the subject of a good deal of speculation. The ministers vaguely explained that ' an expedient would be found that would be to the satisfaction of the peers of Scotland ', but when no such expedient was forthcoming the politicians were left to draw their own conclusions. The whigs clearly assumed, with the bishop of Salisbury, that such satisfaction as had been given the Scottish peers must have taken an essentially ' private and personal ' form. Indeed, Burnet's dark hints about the inroads made into the civil list at this time by Oxford probably reflect a supposition that was fairly

---

[1] H.M.C. *Mar and Kellie MSS.* p. 496. The original intention was for the Scottish commoners to join the peers in their stand, but this idea was eventually dropped: S.R.O. Dalhousie MS. 14/352: Balmerino to Maule, 24 Jan. 1712. John Anderson, in his *Historical and Genealogical Memoirs of the House of Hamilton* (Edinburgh, 1825), gives a brief and thoroughly unsatisfactory account of the Patent dispute in which he states that the boycott began after the adverse vote of 20 December and *ended* after the vote of the Committee on 25 January—a sorry confusion of the facts. Anderson believed, quite mistakenly, that the second vote went far towards appeasing the Scottish peers.

[2] See *Lockhart Papers*, i. 339–40, 378–9. The resentment aroused by the encroachment of a ' Prelatic Parliament ' on Scottish religious preserves can only be fully understood in the light of earlier presbyterian reactions to the Greenshields case (1709–11). See Trevelyan, *op. cit.* iii. 236–8.

general among both parties. The venality of the Scottish aristocracy was, after all, already a by-word among politicians; the
assumption that the treasurer could only have extricated his
government from the Hamilton crisis by scattering its *largesse* even
more generously than before was, in the circumstances, perfectly
logical.

Whether the assumption was correct is not so certain. It is a
point on which Oxford's own voluminous papers do not fully
enlighten us, but there is strong evidence to the contrary. In particular, it is possible to say with some confidence that the collapse
of the boycott was not primarily brought about by material inducements. The best the peers appear to have got from the ministry at
this juncture was vague promises of what would be done for them
as soon as the signing of peace made parliament less dangerous,[1]
and months later their expectations were as far from being fulfi ed as
in February.[2] Nor, as far as is known, was Hamilton himself bought
off. At the time it was confidently predicted that he would be
made master of the horse, a coveted Court appointment left vacant
in mid-January by the dismissal of the duke of Somerset, but expectation was disappointed ; similarly ungratified were the supposed
ambitions of the duchess of Hamilton to be groom of the stole, for
all the coffee-house gossip that she ' hath made her stays of late with
loops for the gold key '.[3] But in any case it is possible to find a
perfectly adequate motive behind the Scots' decision to resume
their attendance in the Lords without searching for examples of
bribery and corruption. The truth is that the experiment of the
boycott, brief though it was, had not been a happy one. Hamilton
had suffered more than anyone, since as a direct result of his colleagues' absence he was defeated in an important vote on 8 February
during the hearing of his law-suit over the Gerrard estate.[4] But
the main trouble was that the boycott coincided with the arrival in
the Upper House of the Toleration Bill (officially the Episcopal
Communion [Scotland] Bill), which passed the Commons on 7
February by 152 votes to 17, was given its first reading in the Lords

---

[1] H.M.C. *Portland MSS.* x. 266, 272: Mar to Oxford, 21 May, 4 June 1712.

[2] ' People will be so soured with delays ', wrote Mar in May 1712, ' . . . that most
of that country will not attend next sessions ' (*ibid.* x. 267). The light thrown by the
Harley papers on certain individual cases suggests that in the lifetime of this parliament
(*i.e.* up to the summer of 1713) the Scots were fed mainly on promises and but little on
hard cash. *E.g.* Eglinton in the early part of 1712 was given every reason to expect a
payment of £500, euphemistically described as a sum ' due to me before the Union ' ;
but he was still waiting ruefully for the money in Aug. 1713: *ibid.* x. 196, 203, 300.
Northesk, another who was promised the Queen's ' allowance ' during the 1712
session, had no satisfaction until the end of 1713 and even then had to be content with
reappointment to the Scottish trade commission: *ibid.* x. 204-5.

[3] *Wentworth Papers*, p. 258: Lord Berkeley of Stratton to Strafford, 25 Jan. 1712.

[4] H.M.C. *House of Lords MSS.* N.S. ix. 189; *Mar and Kellie MSS.* p. 497; *Wentworth
Papers*, p. 248. Hamilton's opponent in this law-suit was Lord Mohun, with whom he
fought his celebrated fatal duel in Nov. 1712.

on the 8th and was due for its second reading three days later.[1] So angry were the tories at losing Scottish support for their other business that a number of them decided to withhold their support from this Bill unless the Scots returned; some even resolved to vote with the whigs against it.

> This [Mar tells us] made severall of us think again, and tho' some of us would not have been for bringing in the bill at this time had they been consulted, yet since it was past one House we thought it being lost in the House of Lords would be of worse effects; . . . if the bill should chance to miscairie by our not attending we should get little thanks from our constituents at home.[2]

Accordingly a meeting of the representative peers was called at Hamilton's house, either on the evening of the 8th or on the morning of the 9th, to discuss the new turn of events. Of the twelve who attended five were opposed to returning to the house of lords, including Islay and Hamilton (the latter being openly antagonistic to the Bill itself); the other seven, including Mar and Home, favoured a return on the grounds that since the Bill ' only or principally concerned Scotland and not [*sic*] a bussiness of the parties here, it was not breaking our resolution to go to the House on this occation, espetially since our resolution was not to abandon the House but only to neglect attending it . . . '. Hamilton was reported ' exceeding angrie ' at the majority decision and tried to reverse it at a new meeting the following day, but without success.[3]

On 9 February, therefore, ten Scottish peers took their seats;[4] and while the proceedings on the Episcopal Communion Bill continued (*i.e.* on the 11th, 13th, and 15th) there were never fewer than this number in the House, all of them firmly supporting the measure. Again on the 23rd and 26th, after the amended Bill had been sent up again by the Commons for final consideration, the Scots were duly represented.[5] What many contemporary observers do not tell us,[6] though the fact is plain enough in the *Lords' Journals*, is that the boycott continued to operate on every parliamentary day between the 9th and 26th on which the House was not directly concerned with the Toleration Bill.[7] It was only when the Scots appeared in strength on 27 February—the day after the Lords had completed their work on the Bill—that they formally abandoned their policy

---

[1] *House of Commons' Journals*, xvii. 73; *L.J.* xix. 373, 375.

[2] H.M.C. *Mar and Kellie MSS.* p. 497.

[3] *Ibid.* The names of the peers attending these meetings are given in cipher but some can be identified from a similar cipher in H.M.C. *Portland MSS.* x. 342.

[4] The queen came to the House on this day, a Saturday, to give her assent to a number of bills and the Scots tried to pass off their reappearance by announcing ' they went purely out of respect to the Queen ': *Wentworth Papers*, p. 248.

[5] *L.J.* xix. 374–9, 383–5; Brit. Mus. Add. MS. 17677 FFF, fo. 56.

[6] This is true not only of Burnet but of L'Hermitage and Peter Wentworth.

[7] *L.J.* xix. 377 380–2.

of harassing the tories into revoking the decisions of 20 December and 25 January. But though the final capitulation was delayed, and was even now qualified by the continued resistance of two of the rebels,[1] it was none the less inevitable. The inconsistency of their recent conduct had further reduced the effectiveness of a stand which even at the start had been of questionable value. ' Our Scots Peers ' secession from the House of Lords makes much noise ', as a minister of the Kirk had written, ' but they doe not hold by it. They somtimes come and somtimes goe, and they render themselves base in the eyes of the English.' [2]

With the end of the boycott the whole peerage question receded for some time into the background. From March 1712 until the malt tax precipitated a new crisis in the following year Anglo-Scottish relations subsided into a relative, if still uneasy, calm. Hamilton himself made his peace with the ministry in the summer of 1712, although he characteristically maintained his personal protest against the Lords' proceedings by still refusing to enter the House.[3] In November a fatal duel with Lord Mohun ended his own interest in the case; but his death did not remove the lingering resentment of his countrymen. A fresh petition to the queen from the peers of Scotland in January 1713, though it failed to stimulate the government to fresh action, demonstrated how much the events of twelve months earlier still rankled.[4] It was no surprise, therefore, that the vote of 20 December 1711 provided a major grievance of ' the sixteen ' when they joined with the whigs in the great attack on the Union on 1 June 1713; [5] nor that it remained a firm barrier

[1] ' The Scots Peers are all boughted [enclosed in the fold] again, except the Duke of Hamiltoun and another [the marquess of Annandale] ', notes Wodrow in March 1712: Rev. R. Wodrow, *Analecta* (Maitland Club, 1842), ii. 30.

[2] *Ibid.* ii. 8 (20 Feb. 1712). One must recognize, however, that the dilemma created by the Toleration Bill was a genuine one. There is little specific evidence to support Mackinnon's charge that the stand of the Scottish peers collapsed mainly because of ' the self-seeking spirit of the Earls of Mar and Kinnoull, who, consulting their private interests rather than the honour of their order and their country, broke away from their colleagues in the course of the quarrel ': *The Union of England and Scotland*, p. 423.

[3] It is clear from the *Lords' Journals* that neither he nor the truculent Annandale took any part in the remainder of the session. Sir Herbert Maxwell, *A History of the House of Douglas* (2 vols, 1902), ii. 213, was wrong in thinking that the duke returned to the House along with his colleagues, *i.e.* at the end of February. Hamilton's reconciliation to the ministry came with his appointment as ambassador in Paris in Aug. 1712, and he was later confirmed in favour by the grant of the lucrative office of master general of the ordnance in September and the award of the Garter in October.

[4] This petition is printed in H.M.C. *Portland MSS*. x. 167–8. See also a petition of the Scottish peers [1712] concerning the creation of a hereditary parliamentary peerage: *ibid.* 474.

[5] Brit. Mus. Add. MS. 17677 GGG, fo. 202: L'Hermitage to the States-General, London, 9 June [N.S.] 1713. *Cf.* also [earl of Mar] to Oxford, 12 June 1713: ' If you do not now contrive some relief as to the Malt Tax in Scotland and some redress for that of the peerage, it will not be in the power of man to prevent addresses from all in Scotland against the Union by the meeting of the next Parliament ': H.M.C. *Portland MSS*. x. 296.

against reconciliation in the remaining troubled months of the reign, when the bulk of the Scottish contingent in both Houses was in semi-opposition.

Nothing could prevail, however, against the stubborn determination of the Lords to preclude any possibility of a Scottish ' invasion ' of their House. The apprehensions which lay at the root of this determination, as we have seen, defy any superficial analysis; but whether they sprang from plain anti-Scottish prejudice, or from a jealous solicitude among peers of English birth for the privileges of their own order, or from a purely political objection to strengthening the hand of the ministry of the day, they had this much in common: they persisted long after the purely party motives affecting the decision of December 1711 had lost all validity. They were still strong enough by 1720, for instance, to defeat an attempt by the second duke of Queensberry to claim the seat which his father had filled, as duke of Dover, up to the time of his death in July 1711.[1] In fact, a further sixty years and more were to elapse before the issues raised by Hamilton's patent were formally and conclusively settled. In the interim not only the dukes of Hamilton but every Scottish peer with a British title [2] remained technically subject to the disqualification imposed in 1711, in addition to the disfranchisement effected by the Queensberry decision of 17 January 1709.[3] Moreover the very combination of these two disabilities aggravated the injury done in the former case, as well as creating an injury out of the latter. The 1709 decision had remained a just one ' only so long as what was implicit in it remained true, namely, that such Scottish peers were allowed to sit as members in their own right '.[4] But, as Vicary Gibbs has pointed out, ' First to tell a man that because he is Duke of Brandon, he cannot vote as Duke of Hamilton . . . and to follow that up 2 years later by telling him that because he is Duke of Hamilton, he cannot sit and vote as Duke of Brandon . . . seems the height of injustice '.[5]

Yet despite the obvious unfairness of these two votes and the illogicalities which they involved [6] the resentment they caused in Scotland gradually died down, and by the seventeen-twenties, at any rate, it would be stretching the evidence to claim that they still imposed a violent strain on Anglo-Scottish relations. The fact

[1] W. S. Holdsworth, *History of English Law*, xi. 7. G. E. C., *Complete Peerage* (ed. Vicary Gibbs), iv. 447 n.

[2] Though not, ironically, those with a pre-Union English title, like Argyll.

[3] That is, the decision to deny a vote in the election of ' the sixteen ' to peers awarded a peerage of England before the Union, or of Great Britain after it. See p. 159 above.

[4] *Treaty of Union*, ed. Pryde, p. 53.

[5] G.E.C., *Complete Peerage*, iv. 447 n.

[6] See also Sir James Fergusson, *The Sixteen Peers of Scotland* (Oxford, 1960), p. 39. Not the least inane feature of the whole situation was the fact that English peers with Scottish titles were entitled to both the privileges denied to Scottish peers with British titles.

that for the greater part of the eighteenth century this double incapacity never affected more than a tiny proportion of the whole body of Scottish peers obviously played its part in assuaging the feelings of Scotsmen as a whole. But it was Walpole's government which, together with the house of Lords, provided the most effective balm. Acting on a precedent which, curiously enough, had been established by Oxford himself in December 1711, the whig ministry secured British earldoms in 1722 for the *eldest sons* of both Montrose and Roxburghe. Ten years before, at the very height of the Hamilton crisis, the heir of the earl of Kinnoull had been summoned to the house of lords as one of Oxford's ' dozen ' and had taken his seat unchallenged in his British dignity of Lord Hay. When in 1719 he succeeded to the earldom on his father's death the Lords decided that this did not invalidate his right to sit in virtue of his British title.[1] Presumably George I's ministers assumed in 1722 that these precedents would still hold good, though the fact that they chose to elevate two minors who could not take their seats for some years suggests a conscious effort to avoid any appearance of political sharp-practice. In any event, once Earls Graham and Ker had been accepted as members of the Upper House—as they were in 1727 and 1730, still during the lifetime of their fathers—they could hardly be ejected if and when they succeeded to their Scottish dukedoms of Montrose and Roxburghe.[2] By a simple yet ingenious device a way was thus found of evading, in certain individual cases, the consequences of the Hamilton vote. Had it ever been abused the dying embers of the Hamilton affair would probably have been stirred up afresh; but in fact it was an expedient employed very sparingly indeed.[3]

Not until 1782, however, did it finally become unnecessary. It was then that the eighth duke of Hamilton resurrected the seventy-year-old claim to a seat in the house of lords as duke of Brandon. This time the judges were consulted, and their opinion was unanimous that the royal prerogative was not curtailed by the Act of Union and that the duke was fully entitled to *all* the privileges of a

[1] Turberville, *op. cit.* p. 152.

[2] The 1st Earl Graham did not, as it happened, outlive his father; but his brother William succeeded to the British earldom in 1731 and then, without prejudice to his hereditary seat, to the Scottish dukedom in 1742. The 1st Earl Ker eventually succeeded his father as 2nd duke of Roxburghe in Feb. 1741.

[3] In 1766 Argyll's eldest son was created Lord Sundridge; but as the vote of Dec. 1711 had never affected the dukes of Argyll this was not a comparable case. In 1776 the heirs of the earls of Marchmont and Bute also received British peerages with the titles of Lord Hume of Berwick and Lord Cardiff (G.E.C., *Complete Peerage*, iv. 448 n.), but the former died during his father's lifetime (the earldom of Marchmont became extinct in 1794) and by the time Lord Cardiff succeeded to the earldom of Bute in 1794 this particular road to a hereditary seat at Westminster was no longer necessary. Professor Mark Thomson's statement that ' frequent advantage was taken of this way of giving the Scottish nobility hereditary seats in the House of Lords ', *A Constitutional History of England, 1642-1801* (1938), p. 185, is, I think, a little misleading.

peer of Great Britain.   When it decided to endorse this verdict on 6 June 1782 [1] the House not only remedied a personal and national injustice; it supplied an ending long overdue to a chapter of much importance in the early history of the Union.

[1] *L.J.* xxxvi. 517.

9

HANOVER, PENSIONS AND THE 'POOR LORDS',
1712-13

EDWARD GREGG, CLYVE JONES

Foreign diplomats in London during the War of the Spanish Succession regarded political inconsistency as a peculiarly English sin: it was generally assumed that such inconstancy was the product of venality. Memories of Louis XIV's successful bribery of Members of Parliament during the reign of Charles II were still strong; yet by the accession of Queen Anne, foreign rulers had become reluctant to subsidize British politicians. Furthermore Anne's last political manager, Robert Harley, Earl of Oxford and Lord Treasurer, raised the use of promises of places and pensions, or the non-payment of past arrears, to a fine art. During his ministry, 1710–14, the Whig opposition and their dissident Tory allies had little to offer as inducements for 'voting right', other than the hope of future preferment under the heir presumptive to the throne, Georg Ludwig, Elector of Hanover (later George I), an avowed opponent of Oxford's schemes for a separate Anglo-French peace.

Two documents preserved in the Niedersächsisches Staatsarchiv at Hanover list some of the 'poor lords' — a collection of impoverished peers — and possible pensioners during the last years of Anne's reign. In both 1712 and 1713, Marlborough and his friends in the Whig party pressed the Elector to pension some impoverished peers in order to try and ensure a Whig majority in the House of Lords. The first list (Appendix 1) mentions 15 names, the second (Appendix 2) 13. Seven names (Lincoln, Radnor, Colepeper, Fitzwalter, Stamford, Sussex, Yarmouth) appear on both lists, while the two Lords Willoughby of Parham were uncle and nephew. The first Whig proposal, made in 1712, called for pensions amounting to £10,600; a year later, the requested sum was reduced to £7,900, although an additional four or five thousand pounds was asked to influence elections to the common council of the City of London.

The two crises in December 1711 in which the Oxford ministry had been defeated, on 'No Peace without Spain' (7 and 8 December)[1] and on the attempt of the Scottish Duke of Hamilton to take his seat in the Lords by right of his British dukedom of Brandon,[2] had convinced the Whigs that their position in the upper House was the place from which they could defend the Protestant Succession, particularly if the Elector of Hanover could be persuaded to support their party openly. The Whig party, and, as the Whigs claimed, Hanover's prospects of succession were

---

[1] See C. Jones, 'The Division that Never Was: New Evidence on the Aborted Vote in the Lords on 8 December 1711 on "No Peace Without Spain"', *Parliamentary History* (forthcoming).

[2] See G.S. Holmes, 'The Hamilton Affair of 1711–12: A Crisis in Anglo-Scottish Relations', *E.H.R.*, LXXVII (1962), 257–82 ; see above, 151-76.

endangered when the Queen, hoping to ensure parliamentary ratification of the Tory peace schemes, created a dozen new peers on 30 December 1711–1 January 1712 (o.s.). The Duke of Marlborough, who was simultaneously dismissed from all his offices, immediately proposed to the Hanoverian envoy in London, Bothmer, that the Emperor Charles VI, the most ardent opponent of the Anglo-French agreements, should award annual pensions amounting to £10,600 to 15 lords for the duration of the war (Appendix 1).[3] This proposal, which envisaged financial support for several suspected Jacobites (Yarmouth, Winchilsea, Denbigh, Plymouth, Stawell, Saye and Sele) was rejected out of hand by the Emperor's special envoy to London, Prince Eugene.[4]

The second proposal was made after the 1713 session of Parliament, in which Oxford had barely weathered a second major Anglo-Scottish crisis over the malt tax and the possible repeal of the Union, and also the defeat of the French Commerce Bill.[5] The overwhelming Tory victory in the 1713 elections for the House of Commons had rendered the House of Lords, in the opinion of the Whigs, the only arena where they had any hope of sustaining Hanover's rights. In the autumn of 1713, Baron von Schütz was sent to London by the Elector with instructions to canvass all supporters of the Protestant Succession; only after he had established his liaisons with the opposition was he formally to notify the government of his appointment as envoy.[6] Schütz, reared in England where his father had for a long time been Hanoverian envoy, wrote an unsigned, undated memorandum (Appendix 2) concerning possible pensioners sometime between his arrival in London in September and Christmas of 1713. This list was probably compiled in October by Lieutenant-General William Cadogan, Marlborough's closest associate, and Charles, Earl of Sunderland, the Duke's son-in-law.[7] Indeed, although Schütz's list of suggested pensioners is written in the first person, it seems likely to have been Sunderland's composition, rather than that of the Hanoverian envoy.

Although the Whigs consistently represented the plight of the 'poor lords' as the one article which Hanover should not fail to neglect, and while Marlborough promised a loan of £20,000 (at interest) to the Elector for such subsidies,[8] Georg Ludwig rejected these proposals both in 1712 and 1713. Generally reputed to be the richest of the minor princes of

3   Niedersächsisches Staatsarchiv [hereafter N.S.A.], Hanover, Cal. Br. 24, England 109, ff. 98–101, Bothmer to the Elector, 1/12 Jan. 1712.
4   *Ibid*, ff. 115–23, Bothmer to Elector, 15/26 Jan. 1712; *Feldzüge des Prinzen Eugen von Savoyen* (21 vols., Vienna, 1876–92), 2nd ser. V, supp., pp. 20–21. Cf. Sir Winston Churchill, *Marlborough: His Life and Times* (4 vols., 1933–8), IV, 500, n.1.
5   For a discussion of this major crisis for the Oxford ministry, see G. Holmes and C. Jones, 'Trade, the Scots, and the Parliamentary Crisis of 1713', *supra*, pp. 47–77.
6   N.S.A., Hanover 91, Schütz 1, ff. 34–9, 'Premier Mémoire de S.A.E. Monseigneur l' Electeur, pour le Baron de Schutz', 28 Aug. 1713.
7   J. Macpherson, *Original Papers; Containing the Secret History of Great Britain, from the Restoration to the Accession of the House of Hanover* (2 vols., 1775), II, 506, 507. On 10 Nov. 1713, n.s. Schütz wrote to Robethon that the Whigs feared a loss of six or so 'poor lords' by their accepting Court expenses or by being absent from the Lords (B.L., Stowe MS. 225, ff. 264–5). For the roles of Cadogan and Sunderland, see E. Gregg, 'Marlborough in Exile, 1712–14', *Historical Journal*, XV (1972), 596–8.
8   Macpherson, *Original Papers*, II, 519–30.

Europe, Georg Ludwig was not only parsimonious but also exceedingly cautious politically. After the passage of the Act of Settlement in 1701, he attempted to appear publicly as a neutral in British party politics. Not only was he poorly equipped to enter into financial competition with Oxford, who controlled the vast patronage resources of the British government, but also any open support for the Whig party would have alienated the Tories and thereby rendered Hanover's prospects even less certain. Cautiously refraining from handing the ministry any excuse for breaking publicly with Hanover, the Elector declined to contribute to Whig causes beyond a few small *douceurs* to those who rendered special services (the Whig journalist George Ridpath, the Dutch resident L'Hermitage). While declining both the embarrassment and the burden of paying such pensions, the Elector sought to strengthen Whig pecuniary interest in Hanover's succession by encouraging Whig potentates to finance such pensions themselves, promising them prompt repayment with adequate interest as soon as he came to the throne.[9] As a mark of his good faith, the Elector reimbursed Sunderland for £300 which the latter had loaned to Lord Fitzwalter, while paying a further £300 direct to the indigent peer.[10]

Not all the peers on these two lists can strictly be called 'poor lords'. All of them were far from wealthy, but peers such as Chandos, Grantham, Stamford and St Albans were not in the same class as the two Lords Willoughby of Parham who feature in these lists. Members of a cadet branch of the family, they were small-scale farmers from Lancashire who unexpectedly succeeded to the title in 1680 and who had been granted a pension of £200 a year by the Crown to enable them to maintain the dignity of their peerage.[11] Peers were expected to have a sufficiently large income to keep up a standard of living corresponding to their rank in the peerage. Marlborough's wife had wanted to refuse the dukedom bestowed in 1702 because her husband lacked the financial resources to go with it. The problem was solved with a state pension of £5,000 a year.[12] The Duke of St Albans had a pension of £1,000 and his salary from several offices, but his wife considered that the total, especially when fitfully paid, was inadequate to support the dignity of a duke who was, as a bastard of Charles II, a member of the royal family.[13] The majority of the peers on these lists, however, were under severe financial embarrassment, particularly when expected to attend Parliament regularly, which was often a substantial drain on their resources.[14]

[9]   *Ibid.,* 580.
[10] *Ibid.,* 471.
[11] For details see P.J. Higson, 'A Neglected Revolution Family' (Liverpool Ph.D. thesis, 1970), especially pp. 333–50.
[12] *The Marlborough-Godolphin Correspondence,* ed. H.L. Snyder (3 vols., Oxford, 1975), I, 142.
[13] See her letters to Oxford in B.L., Loan 29/307–8. For a discussion of the problems of inadequate finance and the social standing of a peerage see J.V. Beckett and C. Jones, 'Financial Improvidence and Political Independence in the Early Eighteenth Century: George Booth, 2nd Earl of Warrington', *Bulletin of the John Rylands University Library* LXV, No. 1 (1982).
[14] See e.g. Lords Denbigh and Home, in G. Holmes, *British Politics in the Age of Anne* (1967), pp. 391, 394.

The Elector's rejection of the proposed subsidies could have affected the overall party balance in the Lords in 1712–14. This assumes, however, that those peers receiving pensions from Hanover would have turned up regularly and voted with the Whigs. Oxford's experience was that many of the government's pensioners were unreliable.[15] Moreover, of the 15 men mentioned in Appendix 1, Winchilsea and Willoughby of Parham (who had never attended the Lords after 1703) were to die by early 1713, while five were strong Whig supporters in any case. Therefore only eight votes could have been captured by Hanoverian pensions. Many of these were committed Tories. If a few could have been bribed to desert their principles, the Whigs would still have made no impression on the Peace votes of late May and early June 1712 when Oxford's majorities were 28 and 45 respectively, but might have been able to defeat the ministry in June 1713 over the malt tax and Union crisis, when Oxford had majorities of only two, four and eight. Of the 13 peers mentioned in Appendix 2, nine were committed Whigs who voted against the ministry, leaving only four pro-ministry votes to capture. Even this could have made some difference in the 1714 session when Oxford's ministry on some occasions scraped home by small majorities of one and two (13 and 17 April, and 30 June).

Pensioners (of whom the 'poor lords' formed an important group) were an important element in the management of the House of Lords. Along with other groups, most notably the Scots and those employed by the Crown — the Queen's servants — they formed 'the party of the Crown' in the upper House.[16] While he commanded the resources of government, Oxford was able to outbid any counter-offer that the Whigs might make for the loyalty of that small group of non-party peers whose financial circumstances laid them open to pressure. The Whigs, under the Hanoverians, were to extend his system of office and pension and many of those on the two lists printed here did in fact later receive government money to support the ministry of George I.[17]

---

[15] See notes on individual peers, below, Appendices 1–2.

[16] For a discussion of Oxford's attempt to create a 'party of the Crown' see C. Jones, '"The Scheme Lords, the Neccessitous Lords, and the Scots Lords": The Earl of Oxford's Management and 'the Party of the Crown' in the House of Lords, 1711 to 1714', *Party and Management in Parliament 1660–1784*, ed. C. Jones (forthcoming).

[17] The sources from which the information has been derived on pensions and voting behaviour, given below in the notes to the two Appendices, will be published in detail in Jones, 'The Scheme Lords'.

APPENDIX 1: *N.S.A., Cal. Br. 24, England 109, f. 119: Bothmer to the Elector, 15/26 Jan. 1712.*

[All cypher:] Mylord Radnor[18] mille livres Sterling. Mylord Stamfort[19] mille livres Sterling. Lincoln[20] six cent. Culpeper[21] quatre cent. Ces susnommez sont desja bons mais pauvres et ont besoin d'assistance pour estre conservez.

Mylord Winchelsea[22] mille livres Sterling. Dambigh[23] mille. Mylord Pleymouth[24] mille. Stanwel[25] six cent. Willoughby-Pasham[26] trois cent. Mylord Yarmouth[27] six cent. Candos[28] six cent. Sussez[29] cinq cent. Say-and-Seal[30] quatre

---

[18] The second Earl of Radnor was a Court Whig, whom Oxford had regarded as a doubtful supporter in October 1710. Despite frequent approaches by Oxford and a bounty of £1,200 granted in 1710 (of which only £500 was paid in 1711) he usually voted against the ministry, though he did support the Court on 7 June 1712 over an address to the Queen on the Peace. He was to be granted a pension of £1,000 a year in 1718 (*Calendar of Treasury Books*, XXXII, 548).

[19] The second Earl of Stamford was a Whig, whom Oxford regarded as a possible opponent in October 1710, but who in fact consistently opposed the ministry.

[20] The seventh Earl of Lincoln was a Court Whig, regarded as doubtful by Oxford in October 1710 but who consistently opposed the ministry. In January 1711 Kreienberg, the Hanoverian resident in London, reported that Lincoln was one of the peers unable to survive without their pensions, and in December that Lincoln had risked his pension by opposing the Court over 'No Peace without Spain'. Granted a pension of £600 in 1711, he received £250 in 1711, £600 in 1712 and £300 in 1713.

[21] The third Lord Colepeper, a Whig, regarded as a doubtful supporter by Oxford in October 1710, voted against the ministry. He was granted a pension of £600 in 1718 (*Cal. Treas. Bks.*, XXXII, 545).

[22] The fourth Earl of Winchilsea (*d.* Aug. 1712) was a Tory who supported Oxford despite his cousin Nottingham's joining the Whigs over the Peace proposals in December 1711. Seriously embarrassed financially by attending the Lords, he had informed Oxford in January 1711 that without aid he would be forced to retire to the country. In 1712 he claimed that his subsequent appointment to the Board of Trade was not enough to 'mend [his] circumstances' (Holmes, *British Politics*, pp. 393, 516).

[23] The fourth Earl of Denbigh, a Tory who consistently supported Oxford, received a £500 pension from the ministry in 1711. From 1712 to 1714 he failed to gain the arrears due to him. He also found attending Parliament a heavy burden (Holmes, *British Politics*, p. 391). He was appointed a teller of the Exchequer in 1713. His successor was granted a pension of £600 in 1718 (*Cal. Treas. Bks.*, XXXII, 230).

[24] The third Earl of Plymouth was a Tory whose only vote against the ministry was in the Hamilton peerage case in December 1711.

[25] The third Lord Stawell was a Tory whose only vote against the ministry was also in the Hamilton peerage case. He received a bounty of £1,000 in November 1712 to enable him to attend Parliament.

[26] The twelfth Lord Willoughby of Parham (*d.* Aug. 1712).

[27] The second Earl of Yarmouth was a Tory who consistently supported Oxford. He was given a bounty of £400 in 1713.

[28] The eighth Lord Chandos was a Tory who voted consistently with the ministry. Having married a merchant's daughter, he had been closely involved in both the Levant and the Old East India Companies. He had had as much as £9,500 invested in the latter company in 1689, though this slumped to £102 by 1699: B.L., Add. MS. 22185, ff. 12–13; India Office Library, Home Misc. 2 (unfol.).

[29] The first Earl of Sussex, a Tory, whose only vote against the ministry appears to have been on the questionable unparliamentary attempt of Oxford on 8 Dec. 1711 to reverse the ministry's defeat on the Peace proposals of the previous day. A pension of £1,200 was granted in 1712, but only £500 was paid. Sussex claimed the arrears in 1713 and 1714, and received £200 out of Oxford's own pocket in September 1713.

[30] The fifth Viscount Say and Sele consistently supported Oxford's ministry and was granted a bounty of £250 in 1712.

cent. Hundson[31] quatre cent. Fitzwater[32] douze cent Livres [i.e. £1,200] Sterling. [Robethon's notation:] Summa 10,600 livres Sterling.

APPENDIX 2: *N.S.A. Hanover 91, Schütz I, ff. 101–2: [Schütz's hand, undated]*

Lords who allways will be right out of Principle, butt are in the lowest Condition & therefore ought to be Consider'd both in Justice to them, & to encourage others.

Duke of St. Albans,[33] turn'd out of every thing, for his voting. 1000 *lib* a year.

Earle of Lincoln nott paid a farthing of his Pension, as one of ye Prince's Servants[34] & has hardly bread. 1000 a year.

Earle of Radnor turn'd out of his teller's Place, for voting right.[35] 1000 a year.

Earle of Grantham,[36] 1000 a year.

Lord Colepeper has nott in the World above 200 a year, & that incumbered; 4 or 500 a year.

Lord Haversham[37] perfectly honest, & very poor 500 a year.

Lord Willoughby of Parkam. The Poor man who was a Carpenter, & upon The title falling to him, last year, was offer'd by The Treasurer, under his own hand 1000 a year, which he refus'd, & came up to town & voted right, & allways will do

---

[31]   The eighth Lord Hunsdon was a Court Tory who consistently supported Oxford. In January 1711 Kreienberg reported that Hunsdon was unable to survive without a pension; in July he was granted a bounty of £200, and later the same year he used the crisis over the Peace votes on 7 and 8 Dec. to force a bounty of £1,000 out of the ministry for his support (Holmes, *British Politics,* pp. 385, 515, n. 8). He was granted a pension of £600 in 1718 (*Cal. Treas. Bks.,* XXXII, 546).

[32]   The fifteenth Lord Fitzwalter was a Whig whom Oxford had regarded as a supporter in October 1710 but who had usually voted against the ministry. He was listed as a supporter in the Hamilton peerage forecast made by Oxford, but abstained on the actual vote on 20 Dec. 1711. He did, however, vote for the Court on 2 Jan. 1712, despite the Junto's opposition to an extension of the adjournment sought by Oxford. He received £300 both from Hanover and Lord Sunderland in the winter of 1712–13. He was also granted a pension of £600 in 1718 (*Cal. Treas. Bks.,* XXXII, 545).

[33]   The first Duke of St. Albans, a Court Whig, considered doubtful by Oxford in October 1710, voted against the ministry. His annual pension of £1,000, granted him as a bastard of Charles II, was irregularly paid under Oxford (£750 in 1710 and 1711, nothing in 1712, his arrears of £2,500 in 1713, and £2,500 again in 1714). He was dismissed from his post of captain of the Gentlemen Pensioners in January 1712, but retained his hereditary post of Master Falconer, and the post of Master of the Register Office. In 1713 he was paid £3,400 arrears on two and a half year's allowances as Master Falconer.

[34]   Lincoln had been a Lord of the Bedchamber to Prince George of Denmark in 1708, the year of the Prince's death. For the complaints of a fellow servant of the Prince over non-payment of salary see Delawarr's letters to Oxford: B.L., Loan 29/307.

[35]   Radnor himself was never a teller of the Exchequer. His uncle Francis Robartes (*d.* 1718) held a tellership from 1704 to October 1710, and was succeeded in this lucrative post by Russell Robartes, Radnor's younger brother, who, despite his strong support of the Whigs until 1710, thereafter strongly supported the ministry. Russell Robartes confessed to Oxford in September 1713 that despite Radnor's previous support of the ministry and his financial obligation to Oxford, he 'had not answer'd, what I think in honor he ought to have done both to the Queene and your Lordship' (Holmes, *British Politics,* pp. 49, 402).

[36]   The first Earl of Grantham was a Court Whig whose pension had been unpaid since December 1711. Apart from his support of the Court in the Hamilton peerage case on 20 Dec. 1711, he voted with the Whigs.

[37]   The Whig second Lord Haversham had succeeded his Tory father in November 1710. Despite being canvassed by Oxford, he opposed the ministry.

so,[38] he has nott above 150 a year, last year Monsieur Kreimberg[39] promis'd him 300 a year & the expences of his journey which has nott been yett paid, butt upon all accounts ought.

Lord Fitswalter had a Pension from the Court of 600 a year, which for his voting was taken from him;[40] Monsieur Bothmar promis'd he should have the like sum continued to him, which he had last year [i.e. 1712], at Christmas next there will be a year due. As I was a kind of guarantee that this should be Continued, I must entreat, it may be paid & without it, there might be very ill consequences.

Lord Herbert never fail'd butt one vote, is Poor, & may be thoroughly fixed for 500 a year.[41]

Earle of Stamford I have been told, has something from Hannover, if not he should.

2.   The following lords are such as vote with the Court, but may be had for money.

Lord Howard of Escrick,[42] 500 a year.

Earle of Sussex, 500 a year.

Earle of Yarmouth, 500 a year.

Severall others might be nam'd, if the ministry of the Elector were empower'd to do, what he should judge necessary. Severall of the Scotch Lords without doubt, might be had.[43]

---

[38]   The fourteenth Lord Willoughby of Parham succeeded his brother in April 1713. The thirteenth Lord Willoughby had been awarded a pension of £400 by Oxford in March 1713, only £100 of which had been paid before he died. The fourteenth Lord, described by L'Hermitage, the Dutch envoy in London, as a weaver (B.L., Add. MS. 17677 GGG, ff. 229–30, despatch 19 June 1713), was a client of the Junto and accepted the patronage of Wharton and Sunderland (Holmes, *British Politics*, p. 402). The fifteenth Lord (*b.* 1714, *suc.* 1715) was granted a pension of £200 in 1718 (*Cal. Treas. Bks.*, XXXII, 550).

[39]   Kreienberg, Hanoverian resident in London November 1710 – July 1714.

[40]   The Elector of Hanover had reimbursed Sunderland for the £300 he had lent Fitzwalter in the winter of 1712–13 (see above, p. 179). There is no evidence that he had a pension from the Oxford ministry.

[41]   The second Lord Herbert of Chirbury was a Junto Whig, who because of his parlous financial circumstances was to support the Court in 1713–14, and received £500 from Oxford's own pocket between March and May 1714 (Holmes, *British Politics*, pp. 393, 516, n. 36–8). The vote he had failed on was probably his support of the Court on 7 June 1712 over an address to the Queen on the Peace. He also supported the Court on 8 June 1713 on the Malt Bill and was regarded by Oxford in the same month as a possible supporter of the French Commerce Bill. He was granted a pension of £600 in 1718 (*Cal. Treas. Bks.*, XXXII, 546).

[42]   The fourth Lord Howard of Escrick, a staunch supporter of Oxford, gave only one recorded vote against the ministry on 8 Dec. 1711. This listing of Escrick may be a mistake for the sixth Lord Howard of Effingham, who was a Court Whig 'poor lord' in receipt of a pension from Oxford (£600 in 1711, 1712, 1714, and £300 in 1713), and who had been regarded as 'doubtful' in October 1710. However, he usually voted against the ministry, though he did support Oxford on 7 June 1712. It was he, rather than Escrick, who was awarded a pension of £800 in 1718 (*Cal. Treas. Bks.*, XXXII, 546).

[43]   Stories concerning the venality of the Scottish peers were widespread and exaggerated. While on average they were less well off than their English counterparts (see Holmes, *British Politics*, pp. 393–4), and a few were downright poor, none the less only nine of the 23 representative peers to sit in the Lords 1710–14 received pensions or annuities. They were an important constituent of 'the party of the Crown' in the upper House, especially after the election of 1710, when for the first time the Crown's full list of peers was returned. Their not infrequent opposition to the Court was usually over strictly Scottish matters and when they received satisfaction or realized their cause was hopeless they returned to the Court. Only Lord Ilay followed his brother Argyll into permanent

The first Part of this Paper, would secure the numbers we allready have and encourage others. The latter if prudently manag'd would give a majority in spight of the Court.

The whole Summ here propos'd comes butt to between 8 or 9000 a year.

As for the Election of the Common Council for this year, 4 or 5000 would do, & That would nott be wanted a second time.

opposition in 1713, for which he lost his seat at the 1713 election. His case proved the ultimate dependency of the Scots on the Court. In 1714 only Loudoun (a Hanoverian Tory) showed any sustained opposition.

10

THE IMPEACHMENT OF THE EARL OF OXFORD
AND THE WHIG SCHISM OF 1717: FOUR NEW LISTS [1]

CLYVE JONES

ON 1 JULY 1717, Robert Harley, earl of Oxford and lord treasurer at the end of Queen Anne's reign, was formally acquitted from the charges of high treason and of high crimes and misdemeanours, for which the house of commons had sent him to the Tower two years earlier on 9 July 1715. He had been impeached by the whig government for his part in the Peace of Utrecht, which both the whigs and King George I had strongly opposed. Though most of the momentum of the impeachment had been lost by 1716, the king and the whig ministry were unwilling to let Oxford escape without punishment. Lord Townshend, who in 1717 was to be one of the main instruments in Oxford's release, even as late as November 1716, though he had become convinced 'that the charge of High Treason should be dropped, it being certain that there is not sufficient evidence to convict him of that crime', pressed vigorously for the continuation of the prosecution of the misdemeanour charges.[2] The reason why Townshend, along with Walpole and their followers, were within six months defending Oxford from those charges was that the whig party had split and Townshend and Walpole were out of the ministry, and were using Oxford's case to embarrass the government in the house of lords. Oxford, on his part, skilfully exploited the whig schism to obtain his freedom. Both parties to the temporary union of the tories and the Walpole/Townshend whig faction in the summer of 1717 were using each other to gain specific ends.

A recent analysis of the whig schism has shown that its origins can be clearly found in the jockeying for position by the whig leaders at the accession of George I.[3] Townshend's early triumph over the duke of Marlborough (the latter was fobbed off with the offices of captain general and master general of the ordnance instead of that of the groom of the stole which he coveted) was to be the basis for the future fissure of the whig party. Sunderland, Marlborough's son-in-law, was likewise outmanœuvred into the post of lord lieutenant of Ireland. He had wanted to be Secretary of State, the post occupied by Townshend. The latter also carried his brother-in-law, Robert Walpole, with

[1] I am indebted to Her Majesty the Queen for her gracious permission to refer to manuscripts in the Royal Archives at Windsor; to Lady Anne Bentinck for allowing me to print the list from the Portland Loan in the British Library; and to Mr. Christopher Harley for permission to print the list from the manuscripts in his possession at Brampton Bryan Hall, Bucknell, Shropshire. I should like to thank Professor Edward Gregg, Dr. David Hayton and Dr. Christopher Wright, who located several manuscripts referred to in this article, and to the former County Archivist at Hereford, Miss E. M. Jancey, and her staff. My thanks are also due to Dr. Eveline Cruickshanks and Dr. Hayton, of the History of Parliament Trust, who read an early draft of this article and who put their extensive knowledge of the early 18th-century parliament at my disposal. Finally Professor W. A. Speck was kind enough to lend me his transcripts of the Carnarvon/Harcourt correspondence from the Huntington Library, Stowe MS. 57, vols. xiii–xv, for which I am extremely grateful.

[2] W. Coxe, *Memoirs of the Life and Administration of Sir Robert Walpole* (3 vols., 1798), ii. 123: Townshend to Stanhope, 16 Nov. 1716.

[3] W. A. Speck, 'The whig schism under George I', *Huntington Libr. Quart.*, xl (1976–7), 171–9. For previous accounts see Coxe, i. 93–112; B. Williams, *Stanhope* (1932), pp. 230–52; J. H. Plumb, *Sir Robert Walpole: the Making of a Statesman* (1956), pp. 222–42; J. J. Murray, *George I, the Baltic and the Whig Split of 1717* (1969); R. Hatton, *George I: Elector and King* (1978), pp. 193–206.

him into the ministry, as paymaster of the forces and subsequently in 1715 as chancellor of the exchequer.

Sunderland's chance of splitting Townshend and Walpole away from the king came upon George's departure for Hanover in the summer of 1716. The prince of Wales was to be left as regent with, as the king wished, circumscribed powers. The friction between the various whig factions over the issue of the prince's executive role in his father's absence led to the dismissal of the duke of Argyll, a friend of the prince and an enemy of the Marlborough interest. Later in the summer Sunderland followed the king to Hanover to consolidate his position.

It was a difference of opinion over the conduct of foreign policy in the north between the king and Townshend which led to the latter's dismissal as Secretary of State in December 1716. He was replaced by Stanhope. The king, however, well aware of the value to the ministry of the brothers-in-law, tried to retain them. Both felt betrayed, however, by Sunderland and Stanhope, and the former had not forgiven his relegation to Ireland in 1714. Therefore the suggestion that Townshend be offered the lord lieutenancy may have emanated from Sunderland, though Stanhope claimed credit for the offer.[4] Townshend, on being assured by the king personally that he need not go to Ireland, and upon Walpole's being told that Townshend's acceptance would be a prelude to a better post, accepted the offer on 13 February 1717.[5] But the reconciliation between the two factions in the ministry was unable to surmount the mutual hatred that the brothers-in-law and Sunderland had for each other. By early March the government had finally split into two irreconcilable groups.

Still the king tried to keep the ministry united in some form. The prince of Wales's opposition to his father, which had been clandestine at first, now became more open. He absented himself from parliament and from the cabinet, while encouraging his supporters in both Houses to oppose the ministry. Townshend began openly to work against the king in the Lords, while in the Commons Walpole chose not to exercise his managerial skills, though he continued to vote with the Court. George I's anti-Swedish foreign policy was put at risk in early April in the Commons when the debates on supply were barely carried by the ministry against the opposition of Walpole's followers (though Walpole again voted with the Court) and those of the prince.

In the Lords, Townshend voted on 25 March against the mutiny bill.[6] He was dismissed from the lord lieutenancy on 9 April,[7] and on the following day Walpole resigned as chancellor of the exchequer, taking with him from the Commons Paul Methuen, Secretary of State for the South, William Pulteney, Secretary-at-War, his own brother Horace Walpole, Sir William St. Quintin and Richard Edgcumbe. Orford resigned from the admiralty, and the duke of Devonshire returned from Newmarket to resign the lord stewardship on 16 April. Devonshire was to assume the nominal leadership of the breakaway faction in the Lords, though the real leader was Townshend. Walpole remained unchallenged in the Commons. The policy of the two brothers-in-law was now to show the Court that they were indispensable by going into outright uncompromising opposition. The logic of the situation demanded some sort of understanding with the tories.

[4] Williams, p. 252.

[5] Hatton, pp. 192–6.

[6] There were two votes on 25 March on the mutiny bill (in the committee of the whole house, when the vote was 19–65, and on the third reading, when the figures were 32–9), and it is likely that Townshend opposed the Court on the first. Williams, p. 250 and Plumb, p. 241 state Townshend joined in a protest on this vote. There is no evidence of this (see *Lords Journals*, xx. 430–1).

[7] Coxe, ii. 168–9.

A prorogation of the parliament until 6 May soon followed,[8] and most members left town. Rumours abounded that the Court was having difficulty filling the vacant places: would Manchester or Pembroke (a Court tory in the previous reign) replace Devonshire? There was even talk that Lord Chancellor Cowper would resign.[9] By 23 April both sides were reported as mustering their forces, and Duncan Forbes, deputy-advocate in Scotland, concluded that all would depend on the part the tories played.[10] They seemed to be acting the role that Erasmus Lewis, a friend of Oxford, hoped that they would when he reported in January 1717 that both factions of the whigs had begun to make 'their Court to the Tory's, who I hope will be a body by themselves, & not serve as recruits to either of the other two'.[11] The stage was set for the intervention of Lord Oxford.

By early May a printed version of a letter supposed to have been written by Baron Bothmer, one of the king's closest Hanoverian advisers at the British Court, to Schütz, a former Hanoverian envoy to England, was being 'handed about with Great Secrecy'. Dated 21 April, it looked forward to the meeting of parliament on 6 May.

What Effect the late Changes may produce, will be best seen at the next Meeting of the Parliament. If the rigid TORIES, from whom we have little Reason to expect a tolerable Usage, should be able to draw W[alpole] and his Party over to them, we may easily divine where the Storm will fall. Upon which, Sir, we determin, if we should not be strong enough to prevent their Uniting, to exert, at once, the Power of the Crown, and by a useful Majority in the Upper House, render their Designs ineffectual.[12]

The letter goes on to indicate that the Court had considered the earl of Oxford as a possible subject over which the government's strength in parliament might be tested. The Court might have hoped to use the issue to split the Walpole whigs from the tories before they cemented their union. A postscript indicated that a list of 'sure Lords' had been drawn up by the Court, on whom it thought it could rely.[13] Within the month, Lord Oxford was making similar calculations of support and opposition should he demand a reopening of the impeachment proceedings.[14] The whig schism gave Oxford the first chance he had had in two years to organize his acquittal if he and his tory supporters in the house of lords could play their hand with sufficient skill.

•It has been known for some time that the detailed tactics which Lord Harcourt pursued in the Lords were conceived by Oxford himself in consultation with

---

[8] *Lords Journals*, xx. 445.

[9] Though Cowper was to vote against Oxford on 24 June and absent himself from the vote on 1 July, he was reported as looking upon the exclusion of Oxford and Harcourt from the act of grace in July 1717 as 'a very great hardship and was the last man of the council who consented to it' (Huntington Library, Stowe MS. 57, vol. xiv: Carnarvon to Harcourt, 12 July 1717). In Apr. 1718 he resigned from the ministry.

[10] National Library of Scotland, MS. 6415 (Halkett of Pitfirrane Papers), items 17, 18, 20: Forbes to John Macfarlane, 16, 18, 23 Apr. 1717.

[11] *The Correspondence of Jonathan Swift*, ed. H. Williams (5 vols., Oxford, 1963–5), ii. 246: Lewis to Swift, 12 Jan. 1717.

[12] Entitled *A True Translation of Baron Bothmar's Letter to Monsieur Schutz. April 12, 1717* (1717), it was sent by Forbes to Macfarlane on 4 May (Nat. Libr. Scot., MS. 6415, items 23, 23a).

[13] This list has not been found, and the postscript names only Lords Carteret and Colepeper. The first, as it turned out, supported Oxford. Professor Hatton has shown that the Court as early as 12 Feb. 1717 had drawn up a list of peers and M.P.s who were for the king (Bolton, Kingston, Kent, Roxburghe, Sunderland, Marlborough and Stanhope), and for the prince (Orford, Devonshire, Townshend, Parker, Walpole and Methuen). The latter group could be expected to oppose the Court in parliament (Hatton, pp. 202, 352 n. 68).

[14] Brit. Libr., Loan 29/1/2 (see below, table, column 1).

Lords Trevor and Harcourt and the duke of Shrewsbury.[15] Thus Harcourt persuaded the House to insist that the charges of high treason be prosecuted first by the Commons before those of misdemeanour, against the wishes and inclinations of the Commons. This led to a breach between the two Houses through which Oxford's acquittal was pushed by the Lords. What the first new list tabulated below shows is that Oxford also had access to sufficient up-to-date political information to be able to calculate with a high degree of accuracy the probable voting pattern of the whole house of lords.[16] Though the forecast is not in Oxford's hand, it does have emendations, corrections and additions in his hand, which proved to be more accurate on the whole than the original listing. This list may well have been supplied by Harcourt, who was in constant contact with Oxford in the Tower.

Oxford's correspondence reveals that other lords and M.P.s were visitors to the Tower during his imprisonment. These included the former High Church M.P., Lord Cheyne, William Bromley, M.P. for Oxford University, and Bishops Smalridge of Bristol and Gastrell of Chester. Many old friends and colleagues also wrote to him, such as Lords Dartmouth, Carnarvon, Carleton and Shrewsbury.[17] All could have kept him informed of political developments. Oxford's correspondence in the Tower in May and June 1717 (though not extensive) reveals precisely who in the Lords were organizing the campaign for the reopening of the trial. The central group, as we have seen from Oxford's memorandum,[18] were Harcourt (former lord keeper and chancellor in Oxford's ministry), Trevor (former lord chief justice of the common pleas who was one of Oxford's dozen peers created in 1712) and Shrewsbury (former lord chamberlain in Oxford's ministry). Added to these was Lord Poulett (former lord steward under Oxford) whom the forecast list reveals as the chief agent used by Oxford for persuading the peers on the list to vote as required.[19] Lord Dupplin

---

[15] See C. Roberts, *The Growth of Responsible Government in Stuart England* (Cambridge, 1966), p. 418, based on a memorandum entitled 'Querys to Consult Lord Trevor, Lord Harcourt, and the Duke of Shrewsbury' (Brit. Libr., Loan 29/34/4). It is undated and not in Oxford's hand. A similar document, endorsed in Oxford's hand, 'June 6. 1717' is to be found at Longleat House, Warminster (Portland Miscellaneous MSS., Bundle of Anonymous letters addressed to Harley, item 13). I should like to thank the marquess of Bath for allowing me access to his papers.

[16] For an analysis of how accurate Oxford's forecast proved, see below, The Lists, section A.

[17] Brit. Libr., Loan 29/204: Oxford to Lord Harley, 7 Aug., 27 Dec. 1716; Oxford to Auditor Edward Harley, 23 March, 18 Apr., 5 May 1716; Carleton to [Oxford], 25 May 1717; Shrewsbury to [Oxford], [16 May 1717]; Bishop Smalridge to [Oxford], 30 Sept. 1717; Loan 29/310: Bromley to [Oxford], 'Sunday night. 9 of the clocke'. See also *ibid.*, Loan 29/70/10: Oxford to [Auditor Harley], 3 Jan., 9 June, 8 July 1716.

[18] See n. 15 above.

[19] Lord Poulett was the only such agent (written by Oxford on the list against the name of the peer he was to contact) who had the job of persuading an opponent (Westmorland) and a doubtful opponent (Rockingham). With the first he failed, but the second abstained. His other charge, in which he was more successful, was Townshend, a doubtful supporter. The other agents of persuasion employed by Oxford were Bishop Bisse of Hereford (who was to tackle Bishop Tyler of Llandaff); someone called 'Grahme', who is probably James Grahme, M.P. for Westmorland (written by Oxford against Annandale's name), though Oxford's brother in his memoir states that Grahme was negotiating at the time of the petition in late May to prevent its presentation (Hist. MSS. Comm., *Portland MSS.*, v. 668); the dowager duchess of Grafton, married to Sir Thomas Hanmer (she was to persuade her son, the 2nd duke of Grafton); Lord Abingdon (the duke of Ancaster); someone called 'Hutchsonn', who was probably Archibald Hutcheson, M.P. for Hastings, man of business to the duke of Ormond before his flight (Lord Carlisle); Lord Carleton (his relation, Lord Burlington); a 'Mr Miller', probably Thomas Miller, M.P. for Chichester (Lords Scarbrough and Bristol); 'Mr Bromley', who was William Bromley, M.P. for Oxford University (Lord Leigh); and finally 'Mr Lewis', who was probably Erasmus Lewis, former M.P. for Lostwithiel, and steward to Oxford after 1714 (Lord Lexington), and who being 'wholly taken up with the men of the Law' was able to keep Swift in touch with the progress of the impeachment (*Correspondence of Swift*, ii. 270–4: 15, 18 June, 2 July 1717).

(Oxford's son-in-law and another of his dozen peers) must also be added to this central group. He conferred with them on tactics,[20] but his special talent (developed while an M.P.[21] and a member of the Lords during Oxford's ministry) for 'whipping' members to the House was put to good use, as a letter from Lord Carleton testifies:

I was informed by my Lord Dupplin of the time when your Lordships Petition would be presented, and as I gave my attendance that day, so I will not fail to be in the House as often as anything relating to that matter, which so nearly concerns your Lordship comes before the Lords.[22]

The other main member of Oxford's defence team was Bishop Atterbury, who was informed by Oxford through his son, Lord Harley (who also was used to whip in support) 'that I leave my self to his and my friends direction; and to judge for me as they find the Temper of the House'.[23] This group was obviously capable of feeding accurate information into the Tower. The duke of Shrewsbury, for example, informed Oxford on 16 May that he was confident that there were some peers in the House 'who had voted for committing you to the Tower, and were now willing to offer your Petition'.[24]

Consequently by mid May 1717 Oxford was confident enough of the probable support of the breakaway faction of the whigs in the Lords under Townshend and Devonshire to prepare his detailed forecast. He must certainly have completed his list of supporters and opponents by 22 May when he formally petitioned the house of lords for a reopening of proceedings against him.[25] This petition coincided with the opening of hostilities against the government by Walpole in the Commons. The parliament had reassembled on 6 May, and Duncan Forbes reported in three letters over the first week of its sitting that 'things go thus smoothly' noting that on 7 May the Court carried a division by 188 to 80, the tories being unsupported by Walpole's faction.[26] On 20 May Walpole opened his campaign in earnest.

Yesterday things came to a flat Contradiction between Stanhope and Walpole [reported Forbes], wherin W[alpo]le upraided the other with treachery in betraying friendship, and talked in the house of some foreigners offering offices to sale . . .

Four days later, on 25 May, Forbes wrote that

in ane Election Contraverted wherin the Court Exposued the sitting Members, with all their Might, These Members upon a division were thrown out by a Majority 189, to 120, which Mortified certain people very Much.
      Yesterday the Sence of the house haveing by the former Days arguing appeared against

[20] Brit. Libr., Loan 29/204: Shrewsbury to [Oxford], Thursday mor[ning], [16 May 1717], printed in *Portland MSS.*, v. 526.

[21] See G. Holmes, *British Politics in the Age of Anne* (1967), p. 310n.

[22] Brit. Libr., Loan 29/204: Carleton to [Oxford], 25 May 1717, printed in *Portland MSS.*, v. 526.

[23] Brit. Libr., Loan 29/204: Oxford to Lord Harley, 11 June 1717. Cf. draft letter by Oxford of the same date (below, n. 32).

[24] *Ibid.*: Shrewsbury to [Oxford], [16 May 1717]. Oxford tried, through Lord Gower, to get the whig duke of Rutland to present his petition. Rutland refused because of 'an invincible diffidence' which made 'him incapable of speaking in publick assemblyes', but promised to support Oxford, a promise he kept (Longleat House, Portland Misc. MSS., Bundle of Anonymous letters, item 16: Gower to [Oxford], 'Monday night' (?20 May 1717]).

[25] *Lords Journals*, xx. 466. The forecast list (Brit. Libr., Loan 29/1/2) is to be found inside a manuscript copy of Oxford's petition to the Lords.

[26] Nat. Libr. Scot., MS. 6415, items 24–6: Forbes to Macfarlane, 7, 9, 11 May 1717.

Mr A[islabie']s scheme for Bargaining with the Bank that Minister was Constrained to abandon his own project and to bring in Resolutions agreeable to Mr W[alpo]lles.[27]

Though there is no evidence of a formal agreement between Walpole and the tories, William Bromley reported to Lord Oxford on 29 May that

the Court and some of the Secret Comittee I beleive design to charge Walpole with undertaking what he cannot perform; he is aware of it; and to ward of that Blow, he will probably be as bold an Asserter as ever, and appear as forward to go on with the Trial, for he has said to me *if I bluster you must take no notice of it, for I shall mean nothing.*[28]

More significantly, a letter in the Harley Papers reveals that not more than two days before his petition was presented by Lord Trevor to the Lords, Oxford had sent a document to the Speaker of the Commons, Spencer Compton. This could only have been a copy of the petition, perhaps with an outline of his intended strategy. Compton was a close associate of Walpole, and the Speaker's brother, the earl of Northampton, who had been Oxford's channel of communication, reported back to Oxford on 21 May that

I received the honour of your Lordship's Letter and according to your directions have shewn the enclosed to the Speaker, who approves of it and thinks you are much in the right in what you design to do and I hope it will have the desired effect.[29]

This probably was the confirmation of Walpole's support that Oxford had been hoping for. The following day his petition was presented.

Walpole, however, must have had an ambivalent attitude towards the reopening of Oxford's impeachment. Having been imprisoned in the Tower himself by the tories in 1712, he could fully appreciate Oxford's feelings. Politically, however, Oxford had been an anathema to him and outright support for his enemy must have been out of the question. Yet he could not afford to alienate the tories by opposing Oxford, and the political logic of his position demanded he side with them. This is probably why Spencer Compton was used to sanction Oxford's plan. Walpole's former colleagues in the ministry could not be unaware of his difficult situation, and his inclusion on a list of M.P.s invited by Secretary Addison to meet in his office on 14 June 'to consult upon certain Matters relating to the Impeachment of the Earl of Oxford'[30] probably represents their attempt to squeeze the greatest possible embarrassment for Walpole out of his position. His solution was to stay away from the committee responsible for the impeachment, re-established by the Commons, and whose chairman he had previously been.

Townshend, on the other hand, threw himself unequivocally into Oxford's defence. The Court party in the Lords attempted to delay the reopening of the trial, but Townshend advocated the earliest possible date and with tory support won the division on 27 May by 85 to 44 for setting 13 June for the trial. Two days

[27] *Ibid.*, items 28–9: 21, 25 May 1717. The election was for Minehead (*Commons Journals*, xviii. 565, 566).

[28] Brit. Libr., Loan 29/204: Bromley to [Oxford], 29 May 1717.

[29] *Ibid.*, Loan 29/308: Northampton to [Oxford], 21 May 1717.

[30] Public Record Office, SP 35/9/19: Charles Delafaye to ?, 13 June 1717. The attached list of M.P.s is in Sunderland's hand. Besides Walpole, Sunderland named Sir Joseph Jekyll, Nicholas Lechmere, Spencer Cowper, Lawrence Carter (chairman of the committee set up on 30 May by the Commons to consider the impeachment), George Baillie of Jerviswood, Thomas Pengelly, James Reynolds, James Craggs, John Aislabie and Addison himself. The word 'Comptroller' is written next to Walpole's name. This may be a reference to Hugh Boscawen, comptroller of the household, and a strong supporter of the new ministry.

earlier 'the Court Party were but 47 against 85, a vast majority for the trial'. So confident were the tories that on this vote they helped defeat the tory Lord North and Grey's motion that the late prorogation had ended the impeachment. It was reported that 'all the Tory Lords in England are either come or coming up for the Earl of Oxford's trial'.[31] There is no doubt that the tories were organizing their forces, and there is some evidence that Oxford himself was writing letters from the Tower urging forth his supporters.[32] Certainly the first two votes on his impeachment on 25 and 27 May registered the highest attendance at any division in the Lords (132 and 129 respectively) since the opening of Oxford's impeachment on 9 July 1715.[33] Lord Nottingham was encouragingly reported as saying that on the vote on 25 May (to determine whether prorogation had terminated proceedings on the impeachment) 'some of the Whigs and Court wish they had voted with him'.[34]

The Commons, despite much opposition,[35] now asked the Lords to delay the trial so as to be able to inspect the papers and records concerning the impeachment. The Lords acquiesced and postponed the date to 24 June. Bromley wrote to Oxford that 'the Lords have now appointed the same Day for your Lordships Trial as they did for Lord Somers's, to see it end as that did will be the greatest Satisfaction'.[36]

On that day

Ther was a prodigious croud of Ladies & Gentlemen in Westminster hall, the King cam yr and the P[rince] & princes. The house of Lds was very full ther was about 150 peers and Bishops in ther robs, . . . the Impeachment and the anser were read, which took up five hours.[37]

Thereafter, according to the account left by Bishop Smalridge, Richard Hampden opened the case for the prosecution

and read not without frequent sticking and blundering, a long Speech extracted mostly out of the Severall Articles of Impeachment and consisting of the warmest and most aggravaiting parts of those Articles. Then Sir Joseph Jekyl began, and said his Province was to make good the 1st Article of the Impeachment, and to Vindicate it against the Exceptions made to it by the Lord at the Barr. Lord Harcourt immediately stood up, and moved for an Adjournment to the House. When We were setled there He opened the Reasons for his Motion to Adjourn; in an handsom and Learned Speech shewed the difference of proceeding in the Triall of a Lord for High Crimes, and for High Treason; . . . He then shewed there was no Precedent of a Lord impeached for Treason, and for Misdemeanors, where Anything was tried, by the Treason. He represented the Mischiefs to

[31] Hist. MSS. Comm., *Stuart Papers*, iv. 355: Hugh Thomas to ?, 3 June 1717.

[32] Brit. Libr. Loan 29/10/25: fragment, dated 11 June 1717. A fuller draft of this letter is extant (Longleat House, Portland Misc. MSS., Bundle of Anonymous letters, item 2) in which Oxford ends by urging the recipient to 'act as you shal judge best when you talk with our friends at the meeting of the House'.

[33] Hist. MSS. Comm., *House of Lords MSS.* (new ser.), xii. 195, 198.

[34] Brit. Libr., Loan 29/204: Bromley to [Oxford], 29 May 1717, printed in *Portland MSS.*, v. 526–7. They may well have become apprenhensive over the possible consequence of proceeding with the prosecution.

[35] See Roberts, p. 417.

[36] Brit. Libr., Loan 29/204: 29 May 1717. Lords Somers and Orford were acquitted in 1701 after impeachment for their part in the Partition Treaties. Oxford by this stage had become convinced his salvation lay in the Lords as it was 'vane to do anything in the Commons' (*ibid.*, Loan 29/70/10: Oxford to [Auditor Harley], 9 June 1717).

[37] *More Culloden Papers*, ed. D. Warrand (5 vols., Inverness, 1923–30), ii. 175–6: [Lord Lovat] to Duncan Forbes, 25 June 1717. See also brief description in Royal Archives, Windsor, Stuart Papers 21/43.

the Peers, if Way should be given to such a procedure, because then the Commons would, whenever they accused a Lord of Misdemeanors, add some Articles of Treason, which they would never have Occasion to prove, or go about to prove, having their End in the Imprisonment of the Lord, and the treating Him as accused of Treason. He ended with a Motion, that the Commons should not be admitted to proceed in giving Evidence upon the Articles of High Crimes and Misdemeanors, till the Lords had first given Judgment upon the Articles of High-Treason. This Motion Seconded with a Short Speech by Lord North. Opposed by Lord Sunderland who did not answer what had been said by Lord H[arcourt] but urged the danger of a breach with the House of Commons whose Right it was to proceed in what Method they pleased. A long Debate for Several Hour° For the Question, which Lord Harcourt had put, spoke Lord Trevor, Bishop of Rochester, Bishop of Chester (each very short) Duke of Bucks, Lord Townshend, Earl of Abingdon, Lord Ferrers, Earl of Anglesea, Lord Ilay, Duke of Argyle (these 2 very long, and very Sharp upon the Lord Sunderland) and Lord Parker and Lord Cowper, the only Persons that Spoke on the Other Side. Earl of N[ottingham] observed there were difficulties, which He could not Answer on both sides, when He had represented these his Motion was, that the Commons should begin with the Articles of Treason, but that it should be Signified to them that if Any of the Facts laid in the other Articles had a tendency to prove the Treason, they should be [at] Liberty to prove those Facts, tho' they were contain [ed in] the Articles of Misdemeanors. Urged by Lord Harcourt that there was no need of telling the Commons this; that to be sure they were at Liberty to bring whatever proofs they could of the Treasons. The Question at last put, whether the Question as first proposed, should be now put. Contents 88. Not-Contents 56. The Question [it] self put. No Division upon it. Bishops Absent 6, viz. Durham, Worcester, Peterborough, Norwich, Ely, Chichester. Went out before the Question, who had all declared they would be for it 3, viz. Canterbury, Winchester, Carlisle. Contents 9, York, London, St. Davids, Bath and Wells, Rochester, Hereford, Bristol, Chester, St. Asaph. Not-contents 8, Litchfield, Lincoln, Landaff, Salisbury, Gloucester, Oxford, Bangor, Exeter.[38]

It is with this vote that three of the new Lords' lists are concerned.[39]

Though it has previously been known who the principal whigs were who voted with the tories on 24 June,[40] not until now has it been possible to delineate in detail how the whig schism was reflected in the membership of the house of lords. Twenty-nine peers and one bishop, formerly Court supporters, voted for Oxford.[41] Of these, the whiggism of the bishop (Wynne of St. Asaph) and of three peers (Castleton, Clarendon and Hunsdon) is not certain, but as Oxford had forecast the opposition of three of them and changed his forecast of Castleton's vote from 'doubtful pro' to 'doubtful pro query', the Court probably regarded them as deserters. Besides these thirty who openly supported Oxford, another six peers and three bishops who were whigs and formerly Court supporters left the chamber before the vote.[42] We can only surmise at the motives which led to their abstention, though in the case of the three bishops we can get close to their reasons. Though all three were whiggish in their politics, two (Nicolson of Carlisle and Trelawney of Winchester) were what may be termed

[38] Bodleian Library, MS. Ballard 7 fos. 62–3: [Bishop Smalridge] to Arthur Charlett, 25 June 1717. Cf. Lovat's account in *More Culloden Papers*, ii. 175–6.

[39] Brampton Bryan Hall, Harley MS. C.64, bundle 117 (photocopy in Hereford Record Office); Brit. Libr., Egerton MS. 2543 fos. 398–9; Royal Archives, Windsor, Stuart Papers 21/44 (see below, table, column 2).

[40] Roberts, p. 418 lists 9 peers.

[41] Abergavenny, Ancaster, Belhaven, Bridgwater, Bristol, Burlington, Carleton, Carteret, Castleton, Clarendon, Cornwallis, Delorain, Derby, Devonshire, Dorset, Grafton, Greenwich (Argyll), Halifax, Howard of Effingham, Hunsdon, Islay, Longueville, Lumley, Orford, Richmond, Rutland, Tadcaster, Townshend, Willoughby de Eresby and Bishop Wynne of St. Asaph.

[42] Cleveland, Montagu, Onslow, Rockingham, Romney, Scarbrough, Archbishop Wake of Canterbury, Bishop Nicolson of Carlisle and Bishop Trelawney of Winchester.

'state whigs', that is they followed a moderate whig line in secular politics while holding a 'tory' line on church affairs by, for example, supporting the Occasional Conformity and Schism Acts. Both had previously been tory in their political leanings, though Nicolson had abandoned his position much earlier than Trelawney.[43] Archbishop Wake was of a more orthodox 'church whig' stand, having opposed both the above-mentioned acts, though he was to oppose their repeal in 1718, having been alienated by Sunderland and Stanhope's anti-clerical policies. Both Nicolson and Wake had close associations with the household of the prince of Wales; in fact Wake was later to be banned from the Court, because of his association with the princess. The political stance of the prince may have affected the bishops' actions.[44] However, two other reasons can be found for their abstention. Nicolson had long been a friend of Oxford, despite their political differences. Their mutual interest in matters antiquarian had brought them together in Anne's reign, and Nicolson spent a good deal of time in Oxford's library. It is certain that their friendship prevented Nicolson voting against Oxford, and Nicolson undoubtedly shared Wake's objections to the impeachment on grounds of conscience.[45] Nicolson was in constant contact with the archbishop in late June and early July 1717.[46]

The lists for the vote on 24 June certainly emphasize the strength of whig support for Oxford. What they do not show, however, is how many of the thirty-nine former Court supporters who voted for Oxford or abstained were genuine followers of Walpole and Townshend in their split from the ministry, or were supporting Oxford (as Nicolson and Wake did) out of a sense of justice. Shrewsbury had informed Oxford that there were some peers in the House who had helped in committing him in 1715, but who now wished to support him.[47] How many of these were acting from conscience? A possible answer to this question may lie in a list of those thought to be government supporters in the Lords drawn up in November 1717.[48] This list of 'Lords to be summoned to a meeting against the sitting of the Parliament 1717' was probably instigated by Sunderland, who as Secretary of State appears to have taken on the role as leader of the Lords.[49] Eight of the whig peers who voted for Oxford or abstained are on this list. A further two are listed as queried government supporters.[50] That these ten peers should be regarded five months after Oxford's acquittal as government supporters was a result of the policy pursued by the king in the summer of 1717. Realizing the vulnerability of his ministry after the Oxford vote, he deliberately cultivated his opponents, both in the Lords and the Commons (with the exception of Walpole and Townshend, whom he snubbed). While at Newmarket in October 1717, he invited all those attending the races to dine with him

[43] For an analysis of Nicolson's political record see *The London Diaries of Bishop Nicolson of Carlisle, 1702–18*, ed. Clyve Jones and Geoffrey Holmes (Oxford, 1985), pp. 24-7. Nicolson abandoned his tory position between 1705 and 1707, whereas Trelawney continued occasionally to vote tory till 1713 at least. Though in 1711 he considered himself a friend to the late whig ministry (*ibid.*, 2 Apr. 1711), he evinced a 'great respect' for Oxford by 1713 (Brit. Libr., Loan 29/138/5: Harcourt to Oxford, 6 Aug. 1713).

[44] Nicolson was to be translated to Derry in 1718 for his opposition to the government over the proposed repeal of the Occasional Conformity and Schism Acts, and his attitude to Oxford's impeachment may also have contributed to this Irish banishment.

[45] See Wake's journal of the impeachment proceedings, 10 July–3 Sept. 1715, Christ Church, Oxford, Wake MS. 19 fos. 1–6.

[46] See Wake's diary, Lambeth Palace MS. 1770 fo. 192.

[47] Brit. Libr., Loan 29/204: [16 May 1717].

[48] P.R.O., SP 35/10 fo. 174 (below, table, column 6).

[49] See J. C. Sainty, 'The origin of the leadership of the house of lords' ; below, 211, 221.

[50] The 8 government supporters were Carteret, Cornwallis, Derby, Halifax, Longueville, Onslow, Rockingham and Romney. The two queried supporters were Castleton and Howard of Effingham.

(including Devonshire, Rutland, Orford and Methuen), and he even stayed a night with Orford at his house at nearby Chippenham.[51]

Moving to the other side of the vote, we find that the lists reveal that there were fifty-five whig Court supporters in the House on 24 June, including eight bishops.[52] Many of these, of course, held government offices or were drawing government pensions. Office- or pension-holders were not, however, only to be found on the Court side. Of the thirty-nine former Court supporters who voted for Oxford or abstained, we find that eleven were holding government places of some kind in England, Scotland or Ireland at the time of their vote. Of these, Montagu's was hereditary and for life, while his wife, a daughter of Marlborough (one of Oxford's strongest opponents) held a post in the prince of Wales's household. Three of the whigs who supported Oxford also held posts in the prince's household. A further five peers had recently resigned or been dismissed from government places. Scarbrough, who abstained, had been dismissed as chancellor of the duchy of Lancaster in May 1717, but had been appointed to a lucrative Irish sinecure instead; thus he remained one of the eleven office-holders. In addition to these there was one Court supporter (Clarendon)[53] who held an Irish pension and who voted for Oxford and a tory (Pembroke) who likewise held a pension and supported Oxford. They retained their pensions despite their vote. In fact there were two whigs who voted for Oxford, Abergavenny and Rochford, who were nonetheless granted pensions shortly afterwards, on 26 July 1717. Lord Teynham was also granted one at the same time:[54] though of tory leanings and considered a supporter by Oxford, he had voted against him on 24 June. Thus office-holding or having a pension appeared not to play a significant role in deciding how a peer voted. Only one place-holder, Delawarr, was dismissed following the vote,[55] and this may have been unconnected with the Oxford impeachment. Lord Lonsdale (who incidently was not a supporter of Oxford), in a letter of acceptance of the offer of the post of lord of the bedchamber in late July 1717, gives confirmation of the impression that political opposition in the Lords to the Court, if based on conscience, was no bar to preferment.[56]

After the vote in the Lords on 24 June, the House filed back into Westminster Hall and informed the Commons that they must first proceed with the charges of treason. The Commons vainly protested, and then left the Hall. In the following days the rift between the two Houses widened, as Oxford and Harcourt had hoped and forecast. After refusing to meet the Commons in a free conference, the Lords resolved that the trial should resume on 1 July. This followed two

[51] *Annals and Correspondence of the Viscount and the first and second Earls of Stair*, ed. J. M. Graham (2 vols., Edinburgh, 1875), ii. 25, 28; P.R.O., SP 35/10/5: Tilson to Delafaye, 5 Oct. 1717.

[52] Annandale, Berkeley, Bolton, Bradford, Buchan, Byron, Cadogan, Carlisle, Cholmondeley, Cobham, Colepeper, Coningsby, Cowper, Fitzwalter, Godolphin, Haddington, Harborough, Haversham, Herbert of Chirbury, Kent, Kingston, Lincoln, Lonsdale, Loudoun, Manchester, Marlborough, Montrose, Newburgh, Newcastle, Orkney, Parker, Pawlet of Basing, Portland, Radnor, Richmond, Ross, Rothes, Roxburghe, St. Albans, Somerset, Stamford, Sunderland, Sutherland, Tankerville, Torrington, Warrington, Westmorland, and Bishops Hoadley of Bangor, Hough of Coventry and Lichfield, Blackburn of Exeter, Willis of Gloucester, Gibson of London, Tyler of Llandaff, Potter of Oxford and Talbot of Salisbury.

[53] Clarendon probably held this pension, worth £2,000 a year, in payment for his role as chairman of committees in the Lords. See J. C. Sainty, *The Origin of the Office of Chairman of Committees in the House of Lords* (House of Lords Record Office Memorandum no. 52, 1974), p. 3.

[54] *Calendar of Treasury Books, 1717*, pt. ii, p. 466.

[55] On 17 July 1717 (*ibid.*, pp. 30, 435).

[56] Hist. MSS. Comm., *Lonsdale MSS.*, p. 122: Lonsdale to [James Lowther], 21 July 1717.

divisions on 27 June, both with narrow majorities of 7 and 3 in a very full house.[57]

On 1 July the Commons did not appear. Consequently the Lords withdrew to their own House, where Harcourt (having before prayers that day held a conference with Poulett, Lord Chancellor Cowper and Buckingham)[58] moved that they discharge Oxford from his treason charges, the Commons having failed to appear to prosecute him. Sunderland, no doubt realizing that all was lost and wishing to clear the decks, proposed instead that the House discharge Oxford from misdemeanours as well as treasons.[59] The House adopted Sunderland's proposal without a vote, and when the House returned to Westminster Hall the 107 lords present all solemnly voted to discharge Lord Oxford. The two lists tabulated below which record this vote, taken in conjunction with the vote on 24 June, show that many of the ministerial whigs who had opposed Oxford on the 24th voted for his acquittal on 1 July.[60] They, like Sunderland who absented himself from this final vote, must have wearied of the whole affair and wished to see an end.

At the close of the formal voting, the lord steward, the duke of Kent, who had conducted the proceedings in Westminster Hall, declared

My Lords Upon Revising the Paper I made use of I find that Robert Earl of Oxford . . . is Acquitted of the Articles of High Treason . . . and He is by the whole House so Acquitted.

Oxford was brought to the bar and acquainted with the decision. The prisoner was then discharged and the lord steward dissolved the commission by breaking his staff, 'Upon which, ensued Hussas and Claps etc.'[61]

On 3 July Oxford took his seat again in the house of lords. The king, however, was not so generous and Oxford was forbidden the Court[62] and was shortly after excluded, along with Harcourt, from the act of grace promulgated by the king.

Though the Walpole/Townshend faction of the whigs had found a ready ally in the tory party over the acquittal of Lord Oxford, the two groups proved to be uneasy bedfellows. The tories were determined to gain the maximum advantage out of the whig schism and were thus unwilling to ally themselves permanently with either the ministry or the new whig opposition. 'The three parties subsist separately without any sort of understanding with one another,' wrote an observer in July, 'so that hitherto all projects for drawing any of the Tories into either of these parties notwithstanding all offers, have been entirely defeated'.[63] Walpole had learned in the Commons that any attempt to use the tories was dangerous for the opposition whigs. Fortunately for him the breach between the king and his son widened into a complete rupture with a dramatic quarrel in November 1717. Walpole and Townshend could now rely for their parliamen-

[57] Brit. Libr., Lansdowne MS. 885 fo. 58: 'An Account of the Earl of Oxford by his brother'. This information is omitted from the printed version in *Portland MSS.*, v. 668–9.

[58] *Portland MSS.*, v. 669.

[59] Brit. Libr., Loan 29/266/2; W. Harlwick, *The History of the Third Session of the Present Parliament: with what pass'd most Remarkable at the Tryal of the Earl of Oxford* (1717), pp. 101–2 (see below, table, column 3). The latter list is also printed in *A Complete Collection of State Trials*, comp. T. B. Howell (33 vols., 1816–26), xv. 1173.

[60] Roberts, p. 419, not having the lists for the vote on 24 June, is thus wrong in stating that 30 ministerial peers who opposed Oxford's acquittal had withdrawn before the formal vote in Westminster Hall. Of the 55 ministerial lords who had voted against Oxford on 24 June, 34 withdrew while 21 voted for his acquittal.

[61] Brit. Libr., Loan 29/266/2.

[62] *Ibid.*, Loan 29/153/3: Newcastle to [Oxford], 2 July 1717.

[63] *Stuart Papers*, iv. 453: [James Murray] to [Mar], 3 [/14] July 1717.

tary opposition upon the support of the prince of Wales and his personal following in the Commons.

With the loss of the prince's party to Walpole, the ministry felt obliged to approach some members of the tory party for support. Carnarvon was apparently offered the post of first lord of the treasury which he refused.[64] Trevor was introduced to the king by Sunderland and he assured his Majesty 'of the steadiness of His zeal and allegiance; that he had neither friendship with those His Majesty had displac'd, nor animosityes to those He thought fit to employ, on the contrary He had an Honour and value for them, and wou'd readily concur with them in carrying on his Majesty's service . . .'.[65]

In the period May to July 1717, Oxford and his friends in the house of lords had exploited with consummate parliamentary skill a temporary coming together of the tories with one of the whig factions, which was prepared for reasons of expediency to assist Oxford in obtaining his release from the Tower. The events of the summer and autumn of 1717 rendered this alliance void.

THE LISTS

A. *Oxford's Forecast of Support and Opposition*

1) British Library, Loan 29/1/2. This list, the bulk of which is not in Oxford's hand, consists of four loose-leaved folios, folios 2 and 3 being inserted into 1 and 4. There are four lists. First on the left side of folio 1 recto there is a list of four peers (headed by the prince of Wales) and seven bishops (three of the latter have been crossed out). Beside three of these names Oxford has written three other names ('Grahme' next to Lord Annandale, 'E. Poulet' next to Rockingham, and 'B. Hereford' next to the bishop of Llandaff, whose name Oxford has crossed out). These names inserted by Oxford appear to be the agents used by him to persuade the peers by whose name they are placed to support Oxford (see above, note 19). This first list has been taken to be Oxford's calculations of doubtful opponents.

Secondly on the right side of folio 1 recto is the beginning of the second list of forty-four peers. It starts with the Lord Chancellor Cowper and ends with Viscount St. John (arranged, as are all the lists, in order of precedence). Three other peers, Clarendon, Warrington and Jersey, have been inserted at their appropriate place in the order of precedence after the original compilation of the list. Oxford has written only one name of an agent of persuasion on this list (Poulett against Lord Westmorland). This second list continues on the folio 1 verso with a list of barons and bishops. Oxford has written 'New des[er]ter' in front of Lord St. John of Bletso's name and 'q' after it (see below, table, note 95). At the end of this list Oxford has written the names of the three bishops he crossed off the first list: St. Asaph, Llandaff and Exeter. This second list appears to be Oxford's opponents.

The other half of Oxford's forecast is laid out in the same manner. Two lists start on folio 3 recto (folio 2 being left blank): one on the left side starting with the duke of Somerset and ending with Lord Carleton (doubtful supporters). The fourth list on the right side of folio 3 recto begins with the duke of Shrewsbury and continues on to folio 3 verso, ending with eight bishops (supporters). Several of the names on these two lists have been marked by Oxford (for details see below, table, notes). Also several peers have the

---

[64] Speck, pp. 178–9.

[65] Huntington Library, Stowe MS. 57 vol. xiii: Carnarvon to Harcourt, 3 Nov. 1717. This meeting between Trevor and the king was arranged by Sunderland shortly before he drew up his list of government supporters prior to the opening of parliament. Even if no tories came into office, their support in the Lords would be important to the ministry. This approach by Sunderland in the autumn of 1717 helps place his negotiations with the tories in 1721 in a better perspective. See G. V. Bennett, *The Tory Crisis in Church and State, 1688–1730* (Oxford, 1975), pp. 226–30.

names of agents of persuasion written in by Oxford next to them. The fourth folio has been left blank.

It is now possible, because we have a division list for one of the votes on Oxford's reopened impeachment proceedings in 1717, to assess the accuracy of the forecast made by Oxford and his friends. If one arranges the forecast from left to right, from opponents (cons) to supporters (pros) through the varying degrees of opposition and support (d = doubtful, q = query), one arrives at the following tabulation.

Cons Total	cons	cons q	d cons q	d cons	d pros	d pros q	pros q	pros	Pros Total
89	79	1	0	9	17	4	1	64	86

An analysis of the actual voting pattern on 24 June 1717 gives the following results.

Vote	*Forecast* cons	cons q	d cons q	d cons	d pros	d pros q	pros q	pros
con	48	—	—	3	2	—	—	1
went out	7	—	—	2	1	—	—	—
absent	12	—	—	3	1	—	1	7
pro	12	1	—	1	13	4	—	56

By converting the ratio between the forecast and the vote into percentages the high degree of accuracy of the forecast is clearly seen. The following percentages only express positive voting as a percentage of the forecast, i.e. 48 cons as a percentage of 79 cons forecast.

cons	cons q	d cons q	d cons	d pros	d pros q	pros q	pros
60·7%	—	—	33·3%	76·4%	100%	—	87·5%

57·3%   84·8%

This analysis points to Oxford's highly tuned political instincts and talent which appear to have remained intact despite two years in prison away from active politics. Even if the original listing of the forecast was not Oxford's work, he revised the list from his own pre-1715 experience and from the information fed to him in the Tower by friends and former colleagues.

Oxford made seven alterations to the forecast in his own hand, while three others were made in a hand not Oxford's. The following table shows how accurate the alterations proved:

Names	Original forecast	Oxford's alteration	Vote
Castleton	d pro	d pro q	pro
Orford	d pro	d pro q	pro
Rochford	d pro	d pro q	pro
St. John of Bletso	con	con q	pro
Bishop of Exeter	d con	con	con
Bishop of Llandaff	d con	con	con
Bishop of St. Asaph	d con	con	pro
		Other alteration	
Clarendon	d pro	con	pro
Jersey	d pro	con	went out
Warrington	d pro	con	con

Although the numbers are small, it can be seen that Oxford tended to err on the side of caution. This is understandable as his life was at stake. Also his amended forecast indicated there were only eighty-six supporters or possible supporters and eighty-nine opponents or possible opponents, thus there was little margin for error. Even so he got only two altered forecasts wrong, and they turned out to be in his favour. Of the other three alterations, only one turned out to be accurate.

Only a handful of pre-1761 forecast lists are known to have survived for the house of lords,[66] and Oxford's of 1717 appears to be one of only two which were not prepared with

[66] See *A Register of Parliamentary Lists, 1660–1761*, ed. D. Hayton and C. Jones (Leicester, 1979), pp. 5–6, 31–58.

a specific division in mind.[67] Thus it is important in representing the art of parliamentary forecasting in the Lords in two ways: first, no other act of forecasting the voting behaviour of the House was conducted under such disadvantageous circumstances where the main participant in the forecast had been out of active politics for two years and was relying upon information fed to him by others, a system which illustrates a high degree of political sophistication; secondly, no other forecast attempted to analyse the probable voting behaviour of the whole House, including those who were known to be unlikely to attend.

B. *The Division on 24 June on Oxford's Impeachment*

There are three versions of this division list.

1) Brampton Bryan Hall, Harley MS. C.64, bundle 117. This is the list tabulated below (table, column 2), and the differences between it and the other two versions are recorded in the notes to the table.

This list is on a single sheet of paper folded to form two folios. Folio 1 is blank, except for the following legend at the head of folio 1 verso: 'A List of the Lords that voted June 24 1717 in Ld O-- Case. Copyed'. The list itself occupies both sides of folio 2, and is headed on folio 2 recto by the following: 'June 24 1717. A List of the Lords that voted in the Tryall of the Earl of Oxford, wether the Commons should begin with the Treason Articles first or proceed in order; with the names of those that were absent, those marked thus * were at the Question but went out'. The division list follows in four columns, two headed 'Against the Question', and two 'For the Question'. The names are arranged in order of precedence. There are fifty-six names against the question and eighty-eight for. The names of those for the question runs over into the first column on the left side of folio 2 verso. The other column on folio 2 verso is headed 'Absent', and contains thirty-two names.

2) Royal Archives, Windsor, Stuart Papers 21/44. This list, on a single sheet of paper, is endorsed on the back, 'List of the Lords who voted in the first vote concerning Lord Oxfords being to be tryed on the Article of Treason. 1717'. The list is in four columns, two headed 'For treason, consequently for him', and two headed 'Against'. There are eighty-eight names, arranged by precedence, in the first two columns, and fifty-six in the second two.

3) British Library, Egerton MS. 2543 folios 398-9. This list is headed on folio 398 recto: 'For the Message June 1717 at the E[arl] of Ox[ford] and E[arl] M[ortimer's] Tryall not to admit the Commons to proceed on the Misdeameanor first'. Its layout, occupying folio 398 recto and verso, and 399 recto, is more extensive than the other two lists. The lords are arranged in seven columns headed, from left to right across the folios, 'Pro', 'Contra', 'Withdrew', 'Absent', 'Beyond Sea', 'Minors', and 'R[oman] C[atholic]'. The totals given for each column are 88, 56, 10, 27, 7, 17, and 13 respectively. The rest of folio 399 recto is occupied with a table setting out the numbers in each column but subdivided by rank in the peerage, with the bishops added. Folio 399 verso is blank except for the endorsement 'List of Peers June 1717'.

---

[67] Cf., for example, the forecast of the vote of 2 Jan. 1693 on the duke of Norfolk's divorce bill which was based on a division list compiled only two days earlier. See E. Cruickshanks, D. Hayton and C. Jones, 'Divisions in the house of lords on the transfer of the crown and other issues, 1689-94: ten new lists', above, ch. 5, 101-2. The other forecast not made with a specific division in mind is on the East India Company bill of 1700 (P.R.O., C 113/37).

TABLE

Column (1) British Library, Loan 29/1/2, forecast by Oxford of supporters, opponents and doubtfuls, should his impeachment be reopened, dated c. 22 May 1717 (pro = supporter, con = opponent, d = doubtful, q = q(uery) on list).

Column (2) Brampton Bryan Hall, Harley MS. C.64, bundle 117 (with differences noted from British Library, Egerton MS. 2543 fos. 398-9 and Royal Archives, Windsor, Stuart Papers 21/44), division list on those for and against the Commons beginning with the treason articles or proceeding in order (pro = for the question, a supporter of Oxford; con = against the question, an opponent of Oxford; a = absent from the House that day; went out = abstained from the vote).

Column (3) British Library, Loan 29/266/2 (with differences noted from W. Harlwick, *The History of the Third Session of the Present Parliament; with what pass'd most Remarkable at the Tryal of the Earl of Oxford* (1717), pp. 101-2), list of those who voted for the acquittal of Oxford in Westminster Hall. All the lords present voted 'content' (pro); those marked 'a' were listed as present in the House that day (*Lords Journals*, xx. 522), but were absent from the vote in Westminster Hall.

Column (4) Office-holders (g = held government office or in the king's household, pw = held office in the prince of Wales's household, I = held Irish office, S = held Scottish office, (g) = dismissed from office in 1717).

Column (5) Party affiliation based on previous voting record in Lords or as M.P. in Commons (W = whig, T = tory). See G. Holmes, *British Politics in the Age of Anne* (1967), especially pp. 421-35.

Column (6) Public Record Office, SP 35/10 fo. 174, list of lords summoned to the ministry's pre-sessional meeting, November 1717 (+ = present on list).

Name	(1) Forecast	(2) Vote 24 June	(3) Vote 1 July	(4) Office-holder	(5) Party affiliation	(6) Nov. 1717 Government supporter	Remarks
Abergavenny, 13th baron	con	pro	pro		W		Pension granted 26 July 1717
Abingdon, 2nd earl	pro	pro	pro		T		
Ancaster, 1st duke	d pro	pro	pro	g	W		Hereditary lord great chamberlain
Anglesey, 5th earl	pro	pro	pro		T		
Annandale, 1st marquess	d con	con	a		W		Pension
Ashburnham, 3rd baron	pro	pro	pro		T		
Aylesford, 1st earl	d pro	a			T		Brother of Nottingham
Barnard, 1st baron	pro	a			T		
Bathurst, 1st baron	pro	pro	pro		T		Cr. 1712, one of Oxford's 'dozen'
Belhaven, 3rd baron	con	pro	pro	pw	W		Lord of bedchamber to prince 1714
Berkeley, 3rd earl	con	con	a	g	W		Lord of admiralty May 1717
Berkeley of Stratton, 4th baron	pro	pro	pro		T		
Berkshire, 4th earl	pro	a			T		Pension granted 26 July 1717
Bingley, 1st baron	pro	pro	pro		T		Cr. 1713

Name							Notes
Bolton, 2nd duke	con[68]	con	a	I		W	Lord lieutenant of Ireland Apr. 1717
Boyle of Marston, 1st baron	pro	pro	pro			T	Supported Oxford 1710–13; 4th earl of Orrery (I)
Bradford, 2nd earl	con	con	a			W	
Bridgwater, 4th earl	con	pro	a	pw		W	Lord chamberlain to princess 1714
Bristol, 1st earl	d pro	pro	pro			W	
Brooke, 7th baron	pro	a				T	
Bruce, baron	pro	pro	pro			T	Cr. 1711 (in father's barony), one of Oxford's 'dozen'
Buchan, 9th earl	con	con	pro			W	Pension
Buckinghamshire, 1st duke	pro	pro	pro			T	
Burlington, 3rd earl	d pro	pro	pro	I		W	Lord treasurer (I) 1715 (for life)
Bute, 2nd earl	con	a[69]				W	1st earl of Arran (I)
Butler of Weston, 1st baron	pro[70]	pro	pro?[71]			W	Pension
Byron, 4th baron	d pro q[72]	con	pro?			T	Master of the robes
Cadogan, 1st baron	con	a	a	g		W	
Cardigan, 3rd earl	pro	pro	pro			T	
Carleton, 1st baron	d pro	pro	pro			W	
Carlisle, 3rd earl	d pro	con	pro			W	
Carnarvon, 1st earl	pro	pro	pro		+[73]	T	Lord of bedchamber
Carteret, 2nd baron	con	pro	pro	g	+	W	
Castleton, 1st viscount	d pro q[74]	pro	pro		+ q[75]	W?	
Chesterfield, 4th earl	—	a					
Cholmondeley, 1st earl	con	con	pro	g		W	Treasurer of household
Clarendon, 3rd earl	con[76]	pro	pro		+	W?	Chairman of committees in Lords, with pension (I)
Cleveland, 2nd duke	con	went out	pro			W	Pension
Cobham, 1st baron	con	con	pro			W	
Colepeper, 3rd baron	con	con	a			W	
Compton, baron	pro	pro	pro			T	Cr. 1711 (in father's [Northampton] barony), one of Oxford's 'dozen'
Coningsby, 1st baron	con	con	a			W	
Conway, 1st baron	pro	pro	a		+	T	
Cornwallis, 4th baron	con	pro	pro	g	+	W	Postmaster-general
Coventry, 4th earl	pro	a				W	
Cowper, 1st baron	con	con	a	g	+	W	Lord chancellor
Dartmouth, 1st earl	pro	con	pro	g		T	
Delawarr, 15th baron	con	pro	pro			T	Treasurer of excise 1715, dismissed July 1717

TABLE—*continued*

Name	(1) Forecast	(2) Vote 24 June	(3) Vote 1 July	(4) Office-holder	(5) Party affiliation	(6) Nov. 1717 Government supporter	Remarks
Delorain, 1st earl	con	pro	pro		W		Chancellor of duchy of Lancaster 1714
Derby, 10th earl	con	pro	pro		W		Lord president, dismissed March 1717
Devonshire, 2nd duke	d con	pro	pro	(g)	W	+	Groom of stole, dismissed 1717
Dorset, 7th earl	pro	pro	pro	(g)	W		
Exeter, 6th earl	pro	a			T		
Ferrers, 1st earl	pro	pro	pro		T		
Fitzwalter, 15th baron	con	con[77]	pro		W		Cr. 1712, one of Oxford's 'dozen'
Foley, 1st baron	pro	pro	a		T		Cofferer of household 1714; pension
Godolphin, 2nd earl	con	con		g	W		
Gower, 2nd baron	pro	pro	pro		T		Lord of bedchamber, dismissed 1717
Grafton, 2nd duke	d pro	pro	pro	(g)	W	+	Chamberlain to princess 1716;
Grantham, 1st earl	con	a		pw	W	+	pension (I)
Greenwich, 1st earl	d pro	pro	pro		W		2nd duke of Argyll (S); friend of prince Pension
Guildford, 2nd baron	pro	pro	pro		T		Auditor of exchequer for life
Haddington, 6th earl	con	con	a		W		3rd baron Sherard (I)
Halifax, 1st earl	con	pro		g	W	+	Cr. 1711
Harborough, 1st baron	con[78]	con	a		W	+	
Harcourt, 1st baron	pro	con	pro		T		
Hatton, 2nd viscount	pro q[79]	'Beyond the Sea'					
Haversham, 2nd baron	con	con	pro	g	W		Treasurer of excise 1717
Hay, 1st baron	pro[80]	pro	pro		T	+	Cr. 1711, one of Oxford's 'dozen'; son-in-law of Oxford; imprisoned in Tower as Jacobite 1715–24 June 1717; known by father's courtesy title as Viscount Dupplin
Herbert of Chirbury, 2nd baron	con	con	pro[81]		W		Pension
Hereford, 9th viscount	pro	pro	pro		T		
Holderness, 3rd earl	con	a[82]	a		W		
Howard of Effingham, 6th baron	con	pro	a		W		
Hunsdon, 8th baron	con	pro[83]	pro		W?	+q	

Name							Notes
Islay, 1st earl	d pro	pro	pro	S	W		Lord justice general 1710 for life; brother of Argyll
Jersey, 2nd earl	con[84]	went out[85]			T	+	Imprisoned 1715 as Jacobite
Kent, 1st duke	con	con	pro	g	W	+	Lord steward 1716
Kingston, 1st duke	pro	con	pro	g	W	+	Lord privy seal 1716
Lansdown, 1st baron	pro	pro[86]	pro		T		Cr. 1712, one of Oxford's 'dozen'; imprisoned in Tower as Jacobite 1715–8 Feb. 1717
Leicester, 6th earl	con	a	pro	g	W	+	Lord of bedchamber Feb. 1717
Leigh, 3rd baron	pro	pro	pro		T		
Lexington, 2nd baron	pro	a	pro		T		
Lichfield, 2nd earl	pro	con	a		T		
Lincoln, 7th earl	con	pro	pro	g	W	+	Joint paymaster-general 1715
Longueville, 2nd viscount	d pro	con	pro		W	+	Cr. earl of Sussex Sept. 1717
Lonsdale, 3rd viscount	con	a	pro		W		
Lothian, 2nd marquess	d con	con	pro		W		Pension
Loudoun, 3rd earl	con	pro	pro		W		Master of horse to prince 1714; cr. 1715 (in father's [Scarbrough] barony)
Lumley, baron	d pro	pro	pro	pw	W	+	Lord of bedchamber 1714.
Manchester, 4th earl	con	con	pro	g	W		Cr. 1712, one of Oxford's 'dozen'
Mansell, 1st baron	pro	pro	pro		T		
Marlborough, 1st duke	con	con	a		W		Cr. 1712, one of Oxford' dozen'
Masham, 1st baron	pro	pro	pro		T		
Maynard, 3rd baron	con	a	a		T		Cr. 1712, one of Oxford's 'dozen'
Middleton, 1st baron	pro	pro	pro		T		Hereditary master of great wardrobe; wife was lady of bedchamber to princess
Montagu, 2nd duke	con	went out	a	g	W		Keeper of great seal (S) 1716
Montrose, 1st duke	con	a	a	S	W		Cr. 1712, one of Oxford's 'dozen'; 1st Viscount Windsor (I)
Mounjoy, 1st baron	pro[87]	pro	pro		T		Brother of Cholmondeley
Newburgh, 1st baron	con	con[88]	pro		W		Lord chamberlain of household 1717
Newcastle, 1st duke	con	con	a	g	W	+	
Northampton, 4th earl	pro	pro	pro		T		
North and Grey, 6th baron	pro	pro	pro		T		
Nottingham, 2nd earl	d pro	pro			T		
Onslow, 1st baron	con	went out	a	g	W	+	Teller of exchequer 1715

TABLE—*continued*

Name	(1) Forecast	(2) Vote 24 June	(3) Vote 1 July	(4) Office-holder (g)	(5) Party affiliation	(6) Nov. 1717 Government supporter	Remarks
Orford, 1st earl	d pro q[89]	pro	a		W		1st commissioner of admiralty 1714–Apr. 1717
Orkney, 1st earl	con	con	pro		W		Lord of bedchamber 1716
Osborne, baron	pro	pro[90]	pro	g	T	+	Cr. 1713 (in father's [Leeds] barony;; son-in-law of Oxford
Parker, 1st baron	con	con	pro		W		Lord chief justice Queen's Bench 1710
Pawlet of Basing, baron	—	con[91]	a		W		Cr. 1716 (in father's [Bolton] barony)
Pembroke, 8th earl	pro	pro	pro		T		Pension
Plymouth, 2nd earl	pro	con	pro		T		
Portland, 1st duke	pro	con	pro		W		
Poulett, 1st earl	pro	con	pro		T		
Radnor, 2nd earl	con	con	a	g	W		Treasurer of chamber 1714
Richmond, 1st duke	con	con	a	g	W		Lord of bedchamber 1714
Rochester, 2nd earl	pro	pro	pro		T		
Rochford, 3rd earl	d pro q[92]	pro	pro		W	++	Pension granted 26 July 1717
Rockingham, 1st earl	d con	went out[93]	a		W		
Romney, 1st baron	con	went out	a		W		
Ross, 12th baron	con	con[94]	a		W		
Rothes, 9th earl	con	con	a	g	W	+	Secretary of State Scotland 1716
Roxburghe, 1st duke	pro	pro	pro	g	W		Captain of band of gentlemen pensioners 1714
Rutland, 2nd duke	con	pro	pro		W		
St. Albans, 1st duke	con	con	pro		W		
St. John of Bletso, 9th baron	con q[95]	pro	pro		T?		
St. John, 1st viscount	con	a	a		W		Bolingbroke's father
Salisbury, 5th earl	pro	pro	pro		T		
Sandwich, 3rd earl	—	a	pro		T		
Say and Sele, 5th viscount	pro[96]	pro	pro		T		
Scarbrough, 1st earl	d pro	went out	a	(g)I	W		Chancellor of duchy of Lancaster 1716–May 1717; vice-treasurer (I) May 1717
Scarsdale, 4th earl	pro	pro	pro		T		Committed to Tower 1715–16 as Jacobite

Name				g		+	Notes
Schomberg, 3rd duke	con		a		W		
Shrewsbury, 1st duke	pro	pro	pro		T		
Somerset, 6th duke	d pro	con	pro		W		Lord of bedchamber 1714; ambassador to France 1715
Stair, 2nd earl	con	'Beyond the Sea'[97]		g	W	+	Pension 1715
Stamford, 2nd earl	con	con	a	g	W		
Stawell, 3rd baron	pro	pro	pro		T		
Strafford, 1st earl	pro	pro	pro		T		Impeached 1715, no further action after 1716
Suffolk, 6th earl	con		a		W		Deputy earl marshal 1706, 1st lord of trade 1715
Sunderland, 3rd earl	con	con	a	g	W		Secretary of State North Apr. 1717
Sutherland, 16th earl	con	con	a		W		Pension
Tadcaster, 1st viscount	d pro[98]	pro	pro		W		8th Earl Thomond (I)
Tankerville, 1st earl	con	con	a		W		
Teynham, 8th baron	pro	con	pro		T?		Pension 26 July 1717
Thanet, 6th earl	pro	pro			T		
Torrington, 1st baron	pro	con	a		W	+	A lord of treasury 1715
Townshend, 2nd viscount	d pro	pro	pro	(g)	W		Lord lieutenant of Ireland Feb.–Apr. 1717
Trevor, 1st baron	pro	pro	pro		T		Cr. 1712, one of Oxford's 'dozen'
Uxbridge, 1st earl	pro	pro	pro		T		Cr. Baron Burton 1712, one of Oxford's 'dozen'
Wales, prince of	d con	con	a				
Warrington, 2nd earl	con[99]	con	a	g	W	+	Pension
Westmorland, 6th earl	con	con	a		W		Lord of bedchamber 1715
Willoughby de Eresby, baron	d pro	pro	pro		W	+q	Cr. 1715 (in father's [Ancaster] barony) 1715
Willoughby of Broke, 12th baron	pro	pro	pro		T		
Yarmouth, 2nd earl	con	con	a		T		
Bishops							
Bangor (Hoadley)	con	con	a		W		Friend and spiritual adviser to the princess of Wales
Bath and Wells (Hooper)	pro	pro	pro		T		Intimate of the prince of Wales's household; lord almoner 1716
Bristol (Smalridge)	pro	pro	pro		T		
Canterbury (Wake)	d con	went out	pro		W		
Carlisle (Nicolson)	con	went out	pro	g	W		

TABLE—*continued*

Name	(1) Forecast	(2) Vote 24 June	(3) Vote 1 July	(4) Office-holder	(5) Party affiliation	(6) Nov. 1717 Government supporter	Remarks
Chester (Gastrell)	pro	pro	pro?[100]		T		
Chichester (Manningham)	d con	a			T		
Coventry and Lichfield (Hough)	con	con	pro		W		
Durham (Lord Crew)	pro[101]	a			T		
Ely (Fleetwood)	con				W		
Exeter (Blackburn)	con[102]	con	a		W		
Gloucester (Willis)	con	con	a		W		
Hereford (Bisse)	pro	pro	pro		T		
Lincoln (Gibson)	d con	con	pro		W		
Llandaff (Tyler)	con[102]	con	a		W		
London (Robinson)	pro	pro	pro		T		
Norwich (Trimnell)	con	a			W		
Oxford (Potter)	d con	a[103]	a		W		
Peterborough (Cumberland)	con	pro	pro		T		Former tutor to Sunderland
Rochester (Atterbury)	con[102]	pro	pro		W?		
St. Asaph (Wynne)	pro	pro	pro		T		
St. Davids (Ottley)	con	con	a		W		
Salisbury (Talbot)	con	went out	pro		W		
Winchester (Trelawney)		a	pro		W		Died 30 Aug. 1717
Worcester (Lloyd)	—	a			W		
York (Dawes)	pro	pro	pro		T		

[68] Listed as Lord Orrery.

[69] Omitted from Harley MS. C.64/117 and Stuart Papers 21/44, but listed as absent in Egerton MS. 2543.

[70] Listed as Lord Arran.

[71] Listed as voting in Loan 29/266/2, but omitted from Harlwick.

[72] 'q' inserted in Oxford's hand.

[73] Sunderland and Stanhope approached Carnarvon in the autumn of 1717 with the offer of the post of first lord of the treasury (Speck, pp. 175–8).

[74] 'q' inserted in Oxford's hand.

[75] Listed as 'Lord Sanderson'.

[76] Originally 'pro', but crossed out and inserted in 'con' list.

[77] Omitted from Stuart Papers 21/44.

[78] Listed as Lord 'Sherrard'.

[79] 'q if in England' inserted in Oxford's hand. He is omitted from Harley MS. C.64/117 and Stuart Papers 21/44, and described as 'Beyond the Sea' in Egerton MS. 2543.

[80] Listed as Viscount Dupplin in Loan 29/1/2 and Harley MS. C.64/117.

[81] Listed in Harlwick, but not in Loan 29/266/2.

[82] Omitted from Harley MS. C.64/117, originally listed as absent in Egerton MS. 2543 but crossed out and listed as 'Withdrew', listed as 'Against' (con) in Stuart Papers 21/44.

[83] Listed as 'pro' in Harley MS. C.64/117 and Stuart Papers 21/44, but as 'pro q' in Egerton MS. 2543.

[84] Originally listed as 'pro', but crossed out and inserted in cons.

[85] Listed as absent in Harley MS. C.64/117, omitted from Stuart Papers 21/44, but listed as 'Withdrew' in Egerton MS. 2543.

[86] Wrongly listed as 'Lonsdale' in Harlwick.

[87] Listed in Loan 29/1/2 and in Harley MS. C.64/117 as Lord Windsor.

[88] Listed in Harley MS. C.64/117 as 'Newbury'.

[89] 'q' inserted in Oxford's hand.

[90] Listed in Harley MS. C.64/117 by his father's courtesy title of marquess of Carmarthen.

[91] Listed in Harley MS. C.64/117 by his father's courtesy title of marquess of Winchester, listed in Egerton MS. 2543 as 'St. John of Basing', and omitted from Stuart Papers 21/44.

[92] 'q iff in England' inserted in Oxford's hand.

[93] Listed as 'went out' in Harley MS. C.64/117, as absent in Egerton MS. 2543, and omitted from Stuart Papers 21/44.

[94] Listed as con in Harley MS. C.64/117 and Stuart Papers 21/44, but omitted from Egerton MS. 2543.

[95] 'q' and 'New des[er]ter' inserted in Oxford's hand.

[96] 'if in Towne' added in Oxford's hand.

[97] Omitted from Harley MS. C.64/117 and Stuart Papers 21/44, but listed as 'Beyond the Sea' in Egerton MS. 2543.

[98] Listed as Lord Thomond.

[99] Originally listed as pro, but crossed out and inserted in cons.

[100] Listed in Harlwick, but not in Loan 29/266/2.

[101] Listed with the barons as Lord Crew.

[102] Originally listed as doubtful con, but crossed out and inserted in cons in Oxford's hand.

[103] Omitted from Harley MS. C.64/117 and Stuart Papers 21/44, listed as absent in Egerton MS. 2543.

11

THE ORIGIN OF THE LEADERSHIP OF THE HOUSE OF LORDS

J.C. SAINTY

THE DESIGNATION 'leader of the House' as applied to the house of lords only acquired general currency in the nineteenth century. However, the position itself began to evolve towards the beginning of the previous century. It is the purpose of this article to examine its origin and early history and to identify, so far as possible, the predecessors of the later leaders.[1]

Fundamentally the circumstances which gave rise to the evolution of a government leader were the same in each House. As a result of the Revolution Settlement of 1688 parliament became an essential element in the constitutional framework of the country. Thereafter annual sessions were inevitable and parliament could no longer be regarded as a more or less temporary institution to be dispensed with as soon as the financial requirements of the Crown had been met. This new situation imposed upon the king's ministers the necessity of reassessing their relationship with parliament. The process of reassessment, which embraced a wide range of matters including such questions as the nature of ministerial responsibility and the relations between the administration and the parties, took time to fulfil itself. It is not until after the accession of George I that the government can be clearly seen to have at its disposal the means of securing a stable parliamentary basis. The two preceding reigns were periods of adjustment and experimentation. This was particularly so in the field of parliamentary management.

The importance of organizing a parliamentary following had, of course, long been recognized by ministers. Danby, in particular, had appreciated the need to build up support for the government in the two Houses.[2] Before the Revolution, however, there had in the last analysis been no compelling reason to raise parliamentary management above the level of a series of improvised responses to problems as they arose. Two new factors now made the evolution of a continuous strategy essential. In the first place the necessity of securing an annual supply resulted in ministers being much more dependent on parliamentary support than had been the case before. Secondly the fact that the country was almost continuously at war during the quarter century that followed the accession of William III made it highly desirable to reduce to a minimum the occasions when government and parliament were in open conflict. Foreign powers, recognizing the enhanced standing of parliament, naturally tended to see such conflict as

[1] I am most grateful to Professor I. R. Christie for commenting on a draft of this article.

[2] A. Browning, *Thomas Osborne Earl of Danby* (Glasgow, 1944–51), iii. 33–217.

evidence that the avowed policies of the government would not be pursued effectively and to modify their attitudes accordingly. A clear-sighted observer like Sunderland was fully aware of the problem thus posed and stressed the importance of systematic parliamentary management as an element in its solution.[1] To Sunderland there was 'nothing more necessary than to observe a good method during the holding of a Parliament, and to foresee events, so as not to be surprized, and to be in a condition to remedy them'.[2] Yet it took time for his ideas to become fully accepted and for successive ministries to devise effective means of gaining the initiative in the two Houses and of adapting parliamentary procedures to their own ends. Both Godolphin and Harley attached great importance to parliamentary management but the evidence of their activities in this direction suggests that the whole question was still at a formative, experimental stage during Anne's reign.[3] Indeed, until ministries themselves acquired more stability and cohesion than they had yet displayed it was obviously difficult for it to progress far beyond this point.

Ultimately the solution to the problem was to be found in the practice of entrusting the function of managing the government's business to a senior minister in each House rather than to a group of leading politicians of relatively ill-defined status as had been the case earlier. The responsibilities of the ministers concerned came to include the tasks of keeping lists of members and of ensuring maximum attendances at important divisions as well as the duty of acting as the channel through which the details of the latest developments in government policies were conveyed to selected supporters in order that they might be properly equipped to defend those policies in parliament. The process by which these various functions were transmuted into a programme of systematic parliamentary management was a gradual one, the details of which remain in many respects obscure.

The evidence suggests that an important factor in this process may have been the development of the procedural device of the address in reply to the king's speech from the throne. In its modern form the address in reply seems to have had its origin in the parliamentary response to the king's speech made on 24 February 1696 immediately after the discovery of the assassination plot, an occasion which the government skilfully exploited to capitalize its support in the two Houses.[4] Thereafter there was a general

---

[1] J. P. Kenyon, 'The earl of Sunderland and the king's administration 1693–1695', *Eng. Hist. Rev.*, lxxi (1956), 576–602; Kenyon, *Robert Spencer, Earl of Sunderland* (1958), pp. 256–300.

[2] *Miscellaneous State Papers*, ed. P. Yorke, 2nd earl of Hardwicke (1778), ii. 458.

[3] G. S. Holmes, *British Politics in the Age of Anne* (1967), pp. 309–11, 345–403; H. L. Snyder, 'Godolphin and Harley: a study of their partnership in politics', *Huntington Library Quarterly*, xxx (1966–7), 246–52.

[4] *Lords Journals*, xv. 679, 680, 682; *Commons Journals*, xi. 465, 466; *House of Lords MSS.* (*New Series*), ii. 202–3, 204–13. For the general political implications of the plot, see D. A. Rubini, *Court and Country 1688–1702* (1968), pp. 64–7. Sunderland particularly remarked on the 'good success' achieved in the field of parliamentary management in 1696 (*Miscellaneous State Papers*, ii. 458). In 1740, however,

awareness in government circles of the desirability of securing rapid and favourable addresses in reply to royal speeches. During Anne's reign the address in reply became a regular feature of the proceedings in both Houses. The addresses themselves were printed and published by the Lords and Commons and, so long as they were favourable, served as valuable propaganda which strengthened the government's position both at home and abroad.[1] However, careful and detailed planning was necessary in order to ensure that the proceedings turned out to the advantage of the government. Ultimately this came to include private meetings of members of both Houses on the eve of the session to hear the speech read prior to its delivery from the throne on the following day as well as the selection and briefing of movers and seconders of the address in advance of the debate. It is doubtful whether all the rituals associated with the speech and the address had crystallized before Anne's death. Certainly peers were being selected in advance of the debate to move the address as early as November 1707[2] and in April 1713 there appeared to be nothing particularly remarkable about drafting the terms of the Lords' address in reply at the same time as the speech from the throne itself.[3] On the other hand there is no evidence to show that the system of regular pre-sessional meetings for the Lords was established before the accession of George I.[4]

While, therefore, at least some of the familiar procedures associated with the address in reply were available to Anne's ministers, there is considerable evidence, particularly for the Lords, that they were not always successfully exploited. In 1707, for example, the peer selected to move the address was unable to make any progress against opposition spokesmen who successfully insisted that the House should first consider the state of the nation.[5] In 1711 the government failed to defeat a hostile amendment to the address with serious consequences for its prestige.[6] It was, no doubt, incidents like these which brought home to ministers the importance of a co-ordinated system of parliamentary management which would ensure, at the least, that

Hardwicke expressed the view that 'the alteration in the mode of addressing begun about 35 or 36 years ago, when as honest and able men were ministers as in any time, duke of Marlborough, lord Godolphin, &c.' (*Cobbett's Parliamentary History*, xi, col. 616 n.; *Lords Journals*, xxv. 537). See also Snyder, *ubi supra*, pp. 247–8.

[1] In the Lords addresses in reply were regularly printed from 1696. In the Commons it was customary to print an especially large number of the *Votes* which contained the texts of the addresses (S. Lambert, 'Printing for the house of commons in the 18th century', *The Library*, xxiii (1968), 30).

[2] *Cobbett's Parl. Hist.*, vi, col. 597.

[3] *Ibid.*, col. 1171 n. For a similar case of concurrent drafting in Nov. 1777, see British Library (formerly British Museum), Additional MS. (hereafter cited as Add. MS.) 34414 fos. 337–44.

[4] In the Commons such meetings were described as customary in 1720 (W. Coxe, *Memoirs of Sir Robert Walpole* (1798), ii. 201). For their probable origin see Holmes, pp. 365–6; Snyder, *ubi supra*, p. 248. For the procedure observed, see P. D. G. Thomas, *The House of Commons in the 18th Century* (Oxford, 1971), pp. 39–44.

[5] *Cobbett's Parl. Hist.*, vi, col. 597; *Lords Journals*, xviii. 338.

[6] *Cobbett's Parl. Hist.*, vi, cols. 1035–42.

the government's position was not weakened as a result of a failure to maximize its potential following in the two Houses. Of course the need for such a system did not arise only in connection with the address; constant vigilance was required throughout the session if success was to be assured. Nevertheless, the arrangements made in preparation for the address assumed a special significance in this context for a variety of reasons. In the first place the very fact that the speech was a recurrent feature of each session undoubtedly encouraged the growth of regular procedures, which came in time to have a kind of prescriptive sanction. Responsibility for these procedures was, perhaps, the most distinctive characteristic of the ministers charged with the management of the two Houses.[1] Secondly, the summoning of members to the eve of session meeting had a purely practical aspect in that it provided a mechanism for bringing government supporters to London in time for the opening of parliament. Finally, these arrangements had a special importance for the Lords since the evidence relating to the pre-sessional meetings for that House provide almost the only indication of the identity of the ministers who undertook its management before the accession of George III.

Before considering this evidence something must be said about the differing evolution of the position of manager or leader in each House. The significance of the position of government leader in the house of commons has long been recognized and the succession of individuals who occupied it is clearly established from 1714.[2] Its special character arose principally from the central importance which control of the Commons assumed in the stability of any ministry. It was, however, given a particular definition by the conventions which governed the distribution of the principal offices between the two Houses during the eighteenth century. After 1714 a pattern soon established itself whereby, of the effective cabinet members, the lord chancellor, the lord president, the lord privy seal and the two Secretaries of State were selected from the Lords while only the first lord of the treasury was drawn from the Commons. During the relatively infrequent periods when the first lord of the treasury was in the Lords, one of the Secretaries sat in the Commons.[3] In either event there was usually only one senior minister in the Commons who undertook, in addition to his departmental duties, the task of management in the sense of organizing a following

[1] L. B. Namier, 'The circular letters; an 18th-century whip to members of parliament', *Eng. Hist. Rev.*, xliv (1929), 588–611.

[2] Leaders of the house of commons from 1714 to 1801 are listed in R. Sedgwick, *The House of Commons 1715–54* (1970), i. 135 and L. B. Namier and J. Brooke, *The House of Commons 1754–90* (1964), i. 538–9. See also Thomas, pp. 232–5.

[3] L. B. Namier, *Collected Essays*, vol. 2, *Crossroads of Power* (1962), pp. 114–17. Between 1714 and 1807 the leadership of the Commons was undertaken by a minister other than the first lord of the treasury or a Secretary of State only in the following cases: Walpole as paymaster general Sept. 1714–Dec. 1716; Feb.–Apr. 1721, Pelham as paymaster general Feb. 1742–Aug. 1743, Grenville as treasurer of the navy Oct. 1761–May 1762, Fox as paymaster general Oct. 1762–Apr. 1763 and North as chancellor of the exchequer Jan. 1768–Jan. 1770.

for the government in that House. But his role was enhanced and made more positive by his unique position. Simply because he seldom had a colleague of comparable standing he was bound to undertake much the greater part of the burden of presenting and defending government policies.[1]

In the Lords the situation was different. While the political vitality of the House and the strength of the opposition groups within it have perhaps been underestimated, it remained the case that any ministry to which the king gave his willing support had the means to ensure numerical superiority in the Lords during the eighteenth century.[2] Consequently less skill was required to manage a following for the government there than was the case in the Commons. On the other hand, the fact that five of the six senior ministers were customarily members of the Lords meant that responsibility for defending the government's position was inevitably diffused amongst them. Indeed in so far as there were rivalries amongst these ministers themselves, this factor actively militated against the emergence of a single government leader on the model of the Commons. Nevertheless the need to organize a following still remained. Even the advantages in terms of places and pensions which the government enjoyed in relation to the house of lords did not, of themselves, produce the necessary voting strength when it was required. The government could only be certain of a majority on all occasions if a system of careful planning and preparation was maintained and operated by a single minister on a continuing basis.

The earliest evidence that systematic attention was being given to this question is a list of 'Lords to be summoned to a meeting against the sitting of the Parliament 1717'.[3] The fact that this list survives amongst the state papers suggests that it was drawn up in preparation for the session which began on 21 November 1717 on the instructions of Sunderland, the northern Secretary of State.[4] It should be read in conjunction with another similar list, drawn up for Stanhope, Sunderland's successor as northern Secretary, in connection with the opening of the following session. In this case the peers were 'desired to meet as usual, at Earl Stanhope's Great Room in the Cockpit to morrow being Monday the 10th of November 1718 at Six of the Clock in the Evening'.[5] This formula was to be repeated with insignifi-

[1] Before 1794 the only instances of a Secretary of State other than the leader of the House sitting in the Commons are those of Germain 1775–82, Ellis 1782, North 1783 and Grenville 1789–90.

[2] Holmes, pp. 382–403; D. Large, 'The decline of the "party of the Crown" and the rise of parties in the house of lords, 1783–1837', *Eng. Hist. Rev.*, lxxviii (1963), 669–77; below, 233-41.

[3] P.R.O., S.P. (hereafter cited as S.P.) 35/10 fo. 174.

[4] The only other Secretary of State in the Lords at the time was Roxburghe, the Scottish Secretary. Before 1801 there seems never to have been any question of the holder of the office of third Secretary of State being involved in the management of the Lords.

[5] S.P. 45/1; S.P. 35/48 fo. 100. As a rule these meetings took place at the minister's private house. However, during the period when Grenville managed the House as Foreign Secretary (1791–1801) they were held at his office (*The Times*, 29 Dec. 1794, 29 Oct. 1795, 6 Oct. 1796, 20 Nov. 1798).

cant variations in all the later summonses. The purpose of the meetings is made explicit in a letter, which is undated but which can be definitely attributed to the years 1724–9. It was written by the Hon. Thomas Townshend, under secretary to his father, the 2nd Viscount Townshend, to an unnamed person who was presumably one of the officials in the Secretary of State's office. In it Townshend tells his correspondent that 'My father desires you will be so good as to draw the usual Summons for all the Whig Lords to meet at his house to morrow night, in order to consider of the King's Speech'.[1] Plainly these meetings, which continued to be held until the end of the eighteenth century, are to be seen as the counterpart of the pre-sessional Cockpit meetings held for members of the house of commons.[2]

In the light of subsequent evidence it is clear that the peer who summoned these meetings was the minister with the general responsibility for managing the house of lords in the government interest. Meetings are documented with a fair degree of regularity from 1717 to 1736.[3] There is a serious gap between the latter date and 1754 after which information is again available. Such as they are, the facts support the conclusion that from 1717 to 1754 the management of the Lords was one of the functions of the Secretary of State for the northern department.[4] As already suggested, Sunderland (1717–18) probably undertook the responsibility of summoning the peers. There is evidence that his successors, Stanhope (1718–21), Townshend (1721–30) and Harrington (1730–42) did so and this may have been the case with Carteret (1742–4) as well. There is no indication that the

---

[1] S.P. 36/68 fo. 428. The letter is signed 'T.T.'. Townshend was under secretary from Apr. 1724 to Sept. 1729. Many of the surviving lists of those summoned are to be found amongst the state papers at the Public Record Office which suggests that the work of preparing them was undertaken by clerks in the Secretaries' offices. From 1790 when Grenville began to manage the House until 1812 when Liverpool became first lord of the treasury regular payments of £100 a session were made out of the contingent funds of the Home, Foreign and Colonial Offices to clerks in those offices for a service that was variously described as 'summoning the Peers' and 'sending Notices of Proceedings in the House of Lords' (P.R.O., H.O. 82/3; F.O. 366/1292; C.O. 701/1). See also *Reports from Committees of the House of Commons* (1803), xii. 318–19. Between 1812 and 1832 this business was carried on, under successive 'leaders of the house' by a clerk in the Home Office, John Henry Capper, who received from the treasury remuneration for himself and for the messengers whom he employed (P.R.O., T 38/743 pp. 38, 100; T 38/552 pp. 257, 248; T 38/18 p. 339; T 28/20 p. 336).

[2] The last peers' meeting for which definite evidence exists was held on 19 Nov. 1798 (*The Times*, 20 Nov. 1798). The practice of holding such meetings was probably discontinued in 1800 at the same time that the Cockpit meetings were dispensed with (*ibid.*, 28 Oct. 1801 and 23 Nov. 1802; E. Hughes, 'The discontinuance of the eve-of-the-session meetings at the Cockpit', *Eng. Hist. Rev.*, lii (1937), 296–7; *The Later Correspondence of George III*, ed. A. Aspinall (1962–70), iii. 476 n. 1, hereafter cited as Aspinall). They were replaced by pre-sessional dinners. Pelham gave such a dinner for the Lords on the eve of the session of 1802–3 (*The Times*, 29 Oct. 1802).

[3] References for these meetings will be found in the list following.

[4] M. A. Thomson first drew attention to the likelihood of this arrangement (*The Secretaries of State 1681–1782* (1932), p. 26 n. 1).

two following northern Secretaries, Harrington (1744–6) and Chesterfield (1746–8), undertook the duties, but, equally, there is nothing to show the contrary. There are two pieces of evidence that indicate that Newcastle managed the Lords as northern Secretary between 1748 and 1754. The first is his report to the king of the debate on the address on 29 November 1748.[1] As will be seen these reports were later the responsibility of the minister in charge of the business in the Lords. The second is the duke of Northumberland's letter of 10 January 1751 accepting Newcastle's invitation to move the address in reply to the speech at the beginning of the forthcoming session.[2] Reference has already been made to the fact that the pre-selection of the mover and seconder of the address had been part of the 'stage management' of the opening of the session since the reign of Anne. It seems likely that this task had from an early date fallen to the minister responsible for managing the Lords. Northumberland's letter on this occasion seems, however, to be the first positive indication of the fact.[3]

When, in March 1754, Newcastle was transferred from the northern secretaryship to the office of first lord of the treasury he took the management of the Lords with him. The evidence of the eve of session meetings shows that he retained it until his departure from office in May 1762 except for the period between November 1756 and July 1757 when Devonshire undertook it, also as first lord of the treasury. The substantial amount of material relating to divisions, potential government supporters and proxies that survives amongst Newcastle's papers bears witness to his concern with the problems of parliamentary management in the Lords.[4]

From the accession of George III in 1760 the collected correspondence of the king[5] throws important light on the duties associated with the management of the Lords and the identity of those who exercised it. In the correspondence are to be found many letters from the king to the minister in question on Lords' business and also the reports by the minister to the king on the proceedings of the House. In the absence of any significant collection of royal correspondence of earlier date it is impossible to say when the practice of making these reports began. Newcastle's report to the king of 29 November 1748 has already been mentioned; there is nothing to suggest that it was unusual at that date. Only a portion of the reports made to George III survives but their fullness shows that the king attached considerable importance to them. The reports themselves contain lists of those speaking for and against the question under discussion, a summary of the arguments

---

[1] Add. MS. 32717 fo. 361.

[2] Add. MS. 32724 fo. 63. See also Halifax's letter to Newcastle 21 Nov. 1758 (Add. MS. 32885 fo. 469).

[3] The drafts of letters to be sent by Stormont to prospective movers and seconders of the address in 1779 and 1780 are to be found in S.P. 37/13 fos. 236–40; S.P. 37/14 fos. 329–44.

[4] This material is to be found principally in Add. MSS. 32994–32999.

[5] *The Correspondence of George III*, ed. Sir J. Fortescue (6 vols., 1927–8), hereafter cited as Fortescue; Aspinall.

and, where relevant, the numbers who voted in the divisions. An examination of the reports shows that the person making them was also the minister with the management of the House. George III attached particular importance to receiving an account of the eve of session meeting and was careful to instruct Grafton in 1766 on his duty to supply him with a list of those who had attended it.[1]

Given the relative paucity of information from other sources the correspondence of George III provides important evidence for the identity of those responsible for managing the Lords. As already indicated Newcastle continued to undertake the necessary business as first lord of the treasury until his removal in May 1762. What happened then is not entirely clear. Bute became first lord of the treasury and head of the ministry but there is no evidence to connect him with the management of the House. What evidence there is indicates that it was undertaken not by Bute but by Egremont at whose house the eve of session meeting on 24 November 1762 was arranged to take place.[2] When Bute's ministry was formed in May 1762 Egremont was Secretary for the southern department and the only Secretary of State in the Lords, the northern Secretary, George Grenville, being selected from the Commons. In October 1762 Grenville was replaced by Halifax, a member of the Lords. However, there is nothing to indicate that Egremont was displaced from the management of the House by Halifax as might have been expected if the old convention which had associated this function with the northern secretaryship had still been operative. The earliest evidence that Halifax was acting in this capacity is of November 1763 after Egremont's death.[3] While, therefore, the facts are not conclusive it would appear that Bute did not undertake the management of the Lords and that this resulted in the task being entrusted to the only other suitable minister, Egremont, the southern Secretary, who acted until his death. The old connection between the northern secretaryship and the management of the House was thus broken and a new convention came into operation whereby the function was associated with the senior of the two Secretaries in point of service, whatever his department happened to be.[4] Apart from the years 1765–70 when the

[1] Fortescue, no. 414. The detailed lists which survive for the meetings held on 16 Dec. 1765 and 13 Jan. 1766 also contain the names of 'Notable Absentees' (*ibid.*, nos. 160, 189–90). Between 1765 and 1782 the numbers present varied between 60 and 70 (*ibid.*, nos. 160, 189–90, 417, 4008). In connection with the meeting in Dec. 1765 Rockingham wrote to Newcastle 'I imagine that no Circular Letters are sent to the *Lords* but only a List of *those* who it is desired should attend and which is carried with a Compliment by a Messenger' (Add. MS. 32972 fos. 176–7). It was a matter of comment that 'Duke of Newcastle, Duke of Devonshire, Ld. Rockingham & some others of the Wig Party are not summoned with the rest of the Peers' to the meeting on 24 Nov. 1762 (*Notes and Queries*, ccv (1960), 394).

[2] *Notes and Queries*, ccv (1960), 394.

[3] Fortescue, no. 29; correctly dated 15 Nov. 1763 by L. B. Namier, *Additions and Corrections to Fortescue's Edition of the Correspondence of George III (Vol. I)* (Manchester, 1937), p. 18.

[4] The office of third Secretary of State with responsibility for the colonies, created in 1768 and abolished in 1782, was held by peers until 1775. There is no

management was undertaken by Rockingham and Grafton, successive first lords of the treasury, this convention appears to have been strictly observed until 1782. The principle involved was explicitly stated by Stormont in a letter to the king in September 1780.[1]

After the reorganization of the secretariat in March 1782 the management of the Lords continued to be associated with the Secretaries of State when it was not undertaken by the first lord of the treasury. In June 1803 Liverpool stated that 'The Home Secretary of State has properly the Management of the House of Lords, if he is a Member of that Body'.[2] However, this was not often the case in practice. Shelburne had the management as Home Secretary for a brief period in 1782 as did Sydney between 1783 and 1789. In the latter year the Home Secretary was selected from the Commons and Leeds, the Foreign Secretary, took over as the only Secretary of State in the Lords. He was displaced in the following year by the Home Secretary, Grenville, who retained the management after his transfer to the Foreign Office in 1791 until his resignation in 1801. There seems to have been no question of his displacement in 1794 when, with the appointment of Portland, the Home Secretary once again sat in the Lords.[3] Apart from the cases of Pelham (1801–3) and Hawkesbury (Liverpool) (1804–6 and 1807–9) no Home Secretary managed the House thereafter.[4] However, the convention that the management should be exercised either by the first lord of the treasury or by one of the Secretaries of State was strictly observed until 1841 when the function was entrusted to the duke of Wellington as a member of the ministry without office.

Allusion has already been made to the factors which caused a distinct evolution of the post of government manager in each of the two Houses. Nevertheless, while it is right to stress the negative role of the minister charged with the management of the Lords compared with that of his counterpart in the Commons, some weight should be given to the more positive aspects of his functions. For much of the eighteenth century little prestige seems to have been attached to the business of parliamentary management in the Lords. If the minister who happened for the time being to undertake it took a leading part in the proceedings of the House in comparison with his cabinet colleagues this was likely to be because of his skill as a debater rather than as a result of any special position accorded to him in virtue of his management function. However, in the course of time the situation altered. The first indication of this is to be found in September

evidence that they had any claim to be entrusted with the management of the House. See also p. 211, n. 4.

[1] Fortescue, no. 3148.

[2] Add. MS. 38236 fo. 261. See also Hobart's remarks quoted below.

[3] Portland was not given the management even after Grenville's resignation in Feb. 1801. This was probably because his departure from the Home Office was already in contemplation. In the event he did not actually resign until July.

[4] With the exception of a very brief time in July–Aug. 1827 (when parliament was prorogued), the only occasions when the Home Secretary sat in the Lords after 1809 coincided with periods when the prime minister was also a peer and led the House.

1780 when a dispute occurred over the nominations to fill a vacancy amongst the Scottish representative peers. Stormont, the northern Secretary and manager of the Lords at the time, objected to having his nomination interfered with by North. This was partly because Stormont felt that this was a matter which fell properly within his province as northern Secretary but also because he considered that any diminution of his rights would injure his prestige as the peer entrusted with the management of government business in the Lords. Describing his conversation with North to the king in a letter of 23 September Stormont said that he had

added that if the Secretary of State for the Northern Department and who when he happens to be Senior as is my Case has what is called the official Lead in the House of Lords, was to have no Voice in Matters of this kind it was impossible for Him so circumstanced to appear there with credit to himself or to be of the least use to the Service.[1]

Clearly the concept of a leader as opposed to a mere manager was already in the process of evolution.

Further light is thrown on this process during the younger Pitt's first administration. By 1790 serious difficulties had arisen in the Lords where there was a dearth of competent ministerial spokesmen. The Foreign Secretary, Leeds, who had the lead at the time 'never took a very active Part in Debates'.[2] Only Thurlow, the lord chancellor, possessed significant debating talents and he had been alienated from the government to such an extent that he required tactful treatment if he was not to be actively hostile to his colleagues in the House. The government was, therefore, dangerously exposed to attack from the opposition. In these circumstances Pitt wrote to the king on 20 November drawing attention to 'the inconveniences which have for some time been felt from the want of a regular conduct of the detail of business in the House of Lords'. As a solution to this difficulty he recommended the placing of

some proper person in the House of Lords in a situation to attend constantly to the conduct of of (sic) all domestick business, and who may at the same time keep up a constant communication and avoid accidental misunderstandings with the Chancellor.[3]

Pitt proposed that Grenville, the Home Secretary, should be selected for this task. In a letter of 21 November the king agreed that Grenville should be created a peer for the purpose.[4] Leeds remained Foreign Secretary but was obliged to surrender the management of the House to him.

This was clearly a turning point in the evolution of the position. For the first time the lead was recognized as a distinct function and not merely an

[1] Fortescue, no. 3148.

[2] P.R.O., 30/8/171 fos. 157-63, Richmond to Pitt, printed in A. G. Olson, *The Radical Duke* (Oxford, 1961), p. 216.

[3] Aspinall, no. 635. See also Pitt's letter to Hawkesbury 23 Nov. 1790 (Add. MS. 38192 fo. 75).

[4] P. H. Stanhope, 5th Earl, *Life of William Pitt* (1861-2), ii, app., pp. xii-xiii.

adjunct to the office of the minister who happened to be undertaking it. Futhermore, it was evident that in future the person selected to fill the position would, in addition to his duty of managing the House in the old sense, be required to assume a special responsibility for expounding and defending government policies beyond what would be expected of him as a cabinet minister who happened to sit in the Lords—to act, in fact, as a leader in the modern sense. An examination of the Lords' debates shows that Grenville undertook the exposition and defence of government policies in a way which has no earlier parallel. During the ten years that he had the lead there was scarcely any debate of importance in which he did not take a prominent part. This set the pattern for the future. As a natural consequence the disposition of the lead was thereafter a factor in ministerial arrangements which required special consideration. At the same time the growing prestige attached to the post made it an object of ambition and contention. This is illustrated by the long letter which Richmond, master general of the ordnance, wrote to Pitt at the time of Grenville's elevation. While containing a good deal of special pleading the letter probably reflects reactions which were fairly widespread in the House at the time. In Richmond's view, 'To call up a younger Brother to the House of Peers for the evident Purpose of giving him the Lead there is a Degree of Reflexion upon the whole House of Lords, that there is no one there fit for such a Situation'.[1] On a more personal note Richmond complained that after having

defended your Measures as a Minister under Lord Sidney (sic) and the Duke of Leeds...to continue to act a second part under every change and particularly under one which is avowedly made for the sole purpose of giving the House of Lords another Leader would be depriving myself of every sort of Consideration which I may hope to have in that House and rendering myself totally useless there.[2]

The leadership of the House next became an issue on the resignation of Pitt's ministry in February 1801. Addington, the incoming prime minister, originally intended to associate the lead with the office of Secretary of State for war and to give it to Pelham who was to be made a peer in order to undertake it. In the event Hobart successfully laid claim to the office and was given the lead while Pelham remained in the Commons.[3] In June, however, Pelham was called up to the Lords in his father's barony with a view to his succeeding Portland as Home Secretary, an event which occurred

---

[1] Olson, p. 215. It is interesting to note in this connection that, of Grenville's three successors, Hobart had only been two years in the Lords before he was given the lead while neither Pelham nor Hawkesbury had had any experience of the House before they undertook it.

[2] Olson, p. 217.

[3] Aspinall, iii. 505 n. 1, 563 n. 3 and no. 2794; *Diaries of Sylvester Douglas*, ed. F. Bickley (1928), i. 164–5, 172; *Diaries and Correspondence of 1st Earl of Malmesbury*, ed. J. H. Harris, 3rd earl of Malmesbury (1844), iv. 5–12; Add. MS. 33108 fos. 114–17.

at the end of the following month.[1] As the opening of the new session drew
near Hobart realized that this development might create problems over the
leadership. Accordingly he approached Addington early in October and
'had a full conversation...upon the House of Lords Management and
stated all I felt on the subject with perfect candour'. Addington's opinion
was 'that I should continue to execute the functions which I had performed
in the last session'.[2] Hobart thereupon wrote to Pelham, who, as Home
Secretary, was responsible for Irish matters, to inform him that he was, at
Addington's suggestion, arranging for letters to be written to the Irish peers
desiring their attendance at the opening of the new session.[3] Pelham was
thus alerted to the fact that the lead was to remain in Hobart's hands and
he at once wrote to Addington to enquire 'if any new arrangements had
taken place as he had understood that the motions in the House of Lords on
the part of the Government were to be made by him'.[4] This placed Addington in a position of some embarrassment as he explained to Hobart in an
interview on 7 October. Hobart described this interview in a letter to
Auckland on the following day:

Mr. Addington then said he was under considerable difficulty, for altho' it was
certainly true that Lord Pelham's being called up to the House of Lords had
originated with a view to such an arrangement, yet it was equally so that *his
hesitation* had placed it in my hands, and that, however he might feel that, if the
subject was to start de novo, the Secretary of State for the Home Department
from many causes was the Person on whom it would naturally fall, my Possession
renders it a matter of great embarrassment to him to know what to do and the
more especially as he was convinced that the withholding it from Lord Pelham
would be productive of disagreeable consequences both as it affected Lord Pelham
and the Duke of Portland.[5]

Hobart told Addington that he 'could never understand any reason for
giving way in any point to Lord Pelham'.[6] Nevertheless, he agreed to
stand down provided that Addington undertook to show Pelham a strongly
worded letter in which he stated that his 'acquiescence in the arrangement
proceeds from no other motive than that of an anxiety to relieve you from
Embarrassment'.[7]

[1]Aspinall, nos. 2456, 2487; *Lords Journals*, xliii. 380.
[2]This statement occurs in a letter from Hobart to Auckland which is printed in
Journal and Correspondence of William, Lord Auckland, ed. R. J. Eden, 3rd Baron
Auckland (1861–2), iv. 141. The letter, which is dated simply 'Tuesday night' has
been misplaced by the editor. It clearly precedes the letter of 8 Oct. quoted below
and can be securely attributed to 6 Oct.
[3]Add. MS. 33108 fos. 104–5, 6 Oct. 1801.
[4]Add. MS. 34455 fos. 434–5.
[5]*Ibid.* fo. 435.
[6]*Ibid.* fos. 435–6.
[7]This letter, dated 7 Oct. 1801, and Addington's covering note, dated the following day, are to be found in Add. MS. 33108 fos. 114–17. I am indebted to Mr.
Michael McCahill for this reference.

Summarizing his attitude to the dispute Hobart told Auckland that his 'real feeling' was

that Lord Pelham's conduct manifests considerable presumption and on that account I do not like to see him carry his point; but as for my own inclination, independent of any desire to get Mr. Addington out of a Difficulty would influence my decision, it would be rather in favour of my relinquishing a Duty to which in the manner I was likely to execute it no great credit would have attached, altho' some expense and considerable trouble attend it, so that upon the whole, to tell you the truth, I am by no means dissatisfied.[1]

Hobart returned to the matter once again in a letter to Auckland of 14 October:

I must fairly acknowledge, that having gratified my own feelings by writing the letter which you have seen, and of which Mr. Addington enclosed a copy to Lord Pelham, I am by no means sorry that the drudgery of the House of Lords is placed in Lord Pelham's hands, and more especially, as in point of strict official propriety and practice (except in the case of the Duke of Portland, and perhaps other exceptions that I know nothing of) it would seem to belong to the Home Department.

Since the Union the communication with and patronage of Ireland furnish an additional argument. I cannot, however, help adding that in Lord Pelham's situation I would not have made the claim.[2]

Obviously Pelham attached importance to securing the lead and Hobart, despite his protestations to the contrary, was evidently ruffled by the whole affair. The incident, like that of 1790, showed clearly that the leadership of the Lords had emerged as a position of significance in its own right and that, because of the prestige that now attached to it, the susceptibilities of those aspiring to it would have to be taken into account if disruption in the harmonious relations between ministers was to be avoided.

Pelham's successor was Lord Hawkesbury who assumed the lead on being summoned to the House in November 1803. He evidently found his position in the Lords sufficiently attractive to compensate him for the apparent setbacks that his career had suffered—first his premature removal from the Commons and then, in May 1804, his transfer from the Foreign to the Home Office. Writing to the earl of Bristol on 26 December 1804, Hawkesbury's father, the earl of Liverpool, thus characterized his mood:

Hawkesbury is perfectly well and appears to be in high Spirits. He likes the Business of the Foreign Office better than that of the office he now holds; and yet I suspect that in the present Moment, he likes better the Department he is in, because it connects him more with the Royal Family, with whom he is on the best Terms, and is rather more fit for the Management of the House of Lords, which he must necessarily have, and which I take to be his Ruling Passion.[3]

[1] Add. MS. 34455 fos. 436–7.
[2] *Journal of Lord Auckland*, iv. 139 where the editor has misread 'payment' for 'argument' (Add. MS. 34455 fo. 441).
[3] Hervey papers, Bury St. Edmunds and West Suffolk Record Office Acc. 941/ 56/8. I am much indebted to Mr. Michael Collinge for drawing my attention to this

The position of leader was finally consolidated under Hawkesbury, who succeeded his father as earl of Liverpool in 1808 and who, except for the brief period of the Grenville ministry in 1806–7, led the House continuously from 1803 to 1827.[1] However, the adoption of the term 'leader of the House' passed only gradually into current usage. This was, no doubt, due in large measure to the fact that the leadership was undertaken by the prime minister from 1812 to 1841 with only two brief intermissions in 1827 and 1834–5.[2] There was thus little necessity for the use of a distinct term to describe the situation.[3] Even after 1841 when the prime minister was increasingly drawn from the Commons there was at first no consistent usage. The duke of Wellington, who led the House under Peel between 1841 and 1846, was on occasion referred to in the House as 'the noble Duke who represents Her Majesty's Government in that House'.[4] Another term which was frequently used by ministers was 'Organ of the Government in the House of Lords'. Wellington was so described by Peel in a letter to the queen of August 1842 and the term was the one which occurred most naturally to those involved in the negotiations at the time of the formation of Palmerston's ministry in February 1855 when Lansdowne felt it necessary to allude to 'what is called the leadership of the House of Lords'.[5] However, there is little doubt that he and his colleagues were guilty of a certain pedantry and archaism. Greville, in giving evidence to a select committee of the house of commons in 1848, had seen no need to apologize for describing Lansdowne as 'leader of the House of Lords'[6] and, as the nineteenth century progressed, the term came to be universally accepted as the description of the peer responsible for conducting the business of the government in the house of lords.

letter and to Mr. K. Hall for locating it. According to Lord Harrowby, Hawkesbury declined the office of first lord of the admiralty in 1805 on the ground that 'it was impossible to keep his situation as Minister of the House of Lords together with the Admiralty, and he neither liked giving up the former, nor was it easy to replace him in it' (Aspinall, iv. 315 n.).

[1] For a list of leaders of the House after 1803, see J. C. Sainty, *Leaders and Whips in the House of Lords, 1783–1964* (House of Lords Record Office Memorandum no. 31, 1964), pp. 2–6.

[2] See also Large, below, ch. 12, pp. 257-8 where the significance of the position is, perhaps, somewhat underestimated.

[3] In Apr. 1827 Colchester stated that the negotiations between Canning and Lansdowne had broken down because the latter 'requires to be the leading minister in the Lords, and Canning insists upon its being Mr. Robinson' (*Diary and Correspondence of Lord Colchester*, ed. C. Abbot, 2nd Baron Colchester (1861), iii. 486).

[4] Hansard, *Parliamentary Debates*, 3rd ser., lxix, col. 11, 9 May 1843.

[5] *The Letters of Queen Victoria 1837–61*, ed. A. C. Benson and R. B. Brett, 2nd Viscount Esher (1908), i. 421; iii. 102–3; Lord E. Fitzmaurice, *Life of 2nd Earl Granville* (1905), pp. 95–6.

[6] *Report of Select Committee on Miscellaneous Expenditure*. H. C. 543 (1), p. 237 (1847-8). XVIII (1), 301.

APPENDIX

LIST OF PEERS RESPONSIBLE FOR THE MANAGEMENT OF THE HOUSE OF LORDS
1717–1803[1]

Sunderland, Charles (Spencer) 3rd earl of   Apr. 1717–March 1718

As Secretary of State (North) in Sunderland ministry.

The only evidence that Sunderland undertook the management of the Lords is the existence of a list of peers to be summoned 'to a meeting against the sitting of the Parliament 1717' (S.P. 35/10 fo. 174). Although there is nothing to indicate for whom the list was drawn up, its survival amongst the state papers suggests that it was prepared for a Secretary of State in connection with the session which began on 21 Nov. 1717. Apart from Roxburghe, the Scottish Secretary, the only Secretary of State in the Lords at the time was Sunderland who had been appointed to the northern department in Apr. 1717. It is conceivable that he assumed the responsibility for managing the House at the same time and continued to exercise it until his removal to the office of first lord of the treasury in March 1718.

Stanhope, James (Stanhope) 1st Viscount (cr.   March 1718–Feb. 1721
Earl Stanhope 14 Apr. 1718)

As Secretary of State (North) in Sunderland ministry.

The only evidence that Stanhope was responsible for the management of the Lords is the fact that the eve of session meeting on 10 Nov. 1718 was held in his room (S.P. 45/1; S.P. 35/48 fo. 100). It seems likely that he took over in March 1718 on succeeding Sunderland as Secretary of State for the northern department and continued to act until his death in office on 5 Feb. 1721.

Townshend, Charles (Townshend) 2nd Viscount   Feb. 1721–May 1730

As Secretary of State (North) in Sunderland-Walpole-Townshend and Townshend-Walpole ministries.

A meeting of peers was held at Townshend's house on 14 March 1723 (S.P. 35/42 fo. 200). Eve of session meetings at his house are documented for 7 Jan. 1724 (S.P. 35/48 fos. 14–16), 19 Jan. 1726 (S.P. 45/7 p. 41), 26 June 1727 (*ibid.* p. 39) and 12 Jan. 1730 (S.P. 45/1). It seems likely, therefore, that he took over the management of the Lords on succeeding Stanhope as Secretary of State for the northern department in Feb. 1721 and continued to be responsible for it until his departure from office in May 1730.

Harrington, William (Stanhope) 1st Lord (cr.   May 1730–Feb. 1742
earl of Harrington 9 Feb. 1742)

As Secretary of State (North) in Walpole ministry.

Eve of session meetings at Harrington's house are documented for 20 Jan. 1731 (S.P. 45/1), 12 Jan. 1732 (*ibid.*), 15 Jan. 1733 (*ibid.*), 16 Jan. 1734 (Add. MS.

---

[1] In this list the description of successive ministries has been taken from R. Sedgwick, *The House of Commons 1715–54* (1970), i. 135 and L. B. Namier and J. Brooke, *The House of Commons 1754–90* (1964), i. 539.

32993 fos. 36–7) and 14 Jan. 1736 (S.P. 36/13 fos. 62–4). It seems clear that he took over the management of the Lords in May 1730 on succeeding Townshend as Secretary of State for the northern department and exercised it until his appointment as lord president of the council in Feb. 1742. Newcastle's enquiry as to where the eve of session meeting should be held in Nov. 1742 appears to have been directed to him as the person who had previously had the management of the House (Add. MS. 32699 fo. 517).

Carteret, John (Carteret) 2nd Lord (succ. as   Feb. 1742–Nov. 1744
2nd Earl Granville 18 Oct. 1744)

As Secretary of State (North) in Carteret ministry.

The only direct evidence that Carteret undertook the management of the Lords is Harrington's opinion that Carteret's house was 'the proper place' for the eve of session meeting in Nov. 1742 (Add. MS. 32699 fo. 517). As Secretary of State for the northern department and as the active head of the ministry it would seem reasonable to suppose that he did so, taking over from Harrington in Feb. 1742 and acting until his departure from office in Nov. 1744.

Harrington, William (Stanhope) 1st earl of   Nov. 1744–Oct. 1746

As Secretary of State (North) in Pelham ministry.

There is no direct evidence that Harrington had the management of the Lords during these years. However, in the absence of any indication to the contrary, it seems probable that he took over from Granville on succeeding him as Secretary of State for the northern department in Nov. 1744 and acted until his appointment as lord lieutenant of Ireland in Oct. 1746.

Chesterfield, Philip Dormer (Stanhope)   Oct. 1746–Feb. 1748
4th earl of

As Secretary of State (North) in Pelham ministry.

There is no direct evidence that Chesterfield had the management of the Lords. However, it seems likely that he took over from Harrington on succeeding him as Secretary of State for the northern department in Oct. 1746 and acted until his departure from office in Feb. 1748.

Newcastle, Thomas (Pelham Holles) 1st duke of   Feb. 1748–Nov. 1756

As Secretary of State (North) (Feb. 1748–March 1754) and first lord of treasury (March 1754–Nov. 1756) in Pelham and Newcastle ministries.

The earliest indication that Newcastle was responsible for the management of the Lords is his report to the king of the debate on the address on 29 Nov. 1748 (Add. MS. 32717 fo. 361). On 10 Jan. 1751 Northumberland accepted his invitation to move the address (Add. MS. 32724 fo. 63). Eve of session meetings at Newcastle's house are documented for 31 May 1754 (Add. MS. 32995 fos. 242–5), 13 Nov. 1754 (*ibid.* fos. 344–7) and 12 Nov. 1755 (Add. MS. 32996 fos. 275–9). It seems, therefore, that Newcastle took over the management in Feb. 1748 on his transfer from the southern department to succeed Chesterfield as

Secretary of State for the northern department and that he continued to exercise it following his transfer to the office of first lord of the treasury in March 1754, acting until his departure from office in Nov. 1756.

Devonshire, William (Cavendish) 4th duke of   Nov. 1756–July 1757

As first lord of treasury in Pitt-Devonshire ministry.

The eve of session meeting on 1 Dec. 1756 was held at Devonshire's house (Add. MS. 32869 fos. 189, 211). It seems, therefore, that he took over the management of the Lords on succeeding Newcastle as first lord of the treasury in Nov. 1756 and retained it until his departure from office in July 1757.

Newcastle, Thomas (Pelham Holles) 1st duke of   July 1757–May 1762

As first lord of treasury in Pitt-Newcastle and Bute-Newcastle ministries.

Eve of session meetings at Newcastle's house are documented for 29 Nov. 1757 (Add. MS. 32997 fos. 300–3), 22 Nov. 1758 (Add. MS. 32998 fos. 187–94), 12 Nov. 1759 (*ibid*. fos. 327–33), 17 Nov. 1760 (Add. MS. 32999 fos. 80–6) and 5 Nov. 1761 (*ibid*. fos. 341–7). It is clear, therefore, that Newcastle took over the management of the Lords on succeeding Devonshire as first lord of the treasury in July 1757 and retained it until his departure from office in May 1762.

Egremont, Charles (Wyndham) 2nd earl of   May 1762–Aug. 1763

As Secretary of State (South) in Bute and Grenville ministries.

Although Bute became head of the ministry and first lord of the treasury in May 1762 he appears not to have assumed the management of the Lords. This function seems to have been undertaken by Egremont, then the only Secretary of State in the House. The only direct evidence of this is the fact that the eve of session meeting on 24 Nov. 1762 was arranged to take place at his house (*Notes and Queries*, ccv (1960), 394). When the ministry was reconstructed after Bute's departure from office in April 1763 Egremont became the senior of the two Secretaries of State in the House and presumably continued to undertake its management until his death in office on 21 Aug. 1763.

Halifax, George (Montagu Dunk) 2nd earl of   Aug. 1763–July 1765

As Secretary of State (South) in Grenville ministry.

Halifax's reports to the king of Lords' proceedings extend from 15 Nov. 1763 (Fortescue, no. 29; correctly dated by Namier, *Additions and Corrections*, p. 18) to 22 May 1765 (Fortescue, no. 80). The eve of session meeting on 9 Jan. 1765 took place at his house (*Grenville Papers*, ed. W. J. Smith (1852–3), iii. 114). It seems, therefore, that Halifax took over the management of the Lords on succeeding Egremont as senior Secretary of State in Aug. 1763 and continued to act until his departure from office in July 1765.

Rockingham, Charles (Watson Wentworth)   July 1765–Aug. 1766
2nd marquess of

As first lord of treasury in Rockingham ministry.

Rockingham's reports to the king of Lords' proceedings extend from 16 Dec. 1765, when the eve of session meeting was held at his house, to 3 June 1766 (Fortescue, nos. 160, 332). On occasion his reports were amplified by Grafton (*ibid.*, nos. 228, 230, 265). Rockingham evidently took over the management of the Lords from Halifax on his appointment as first lord of the treasury in July 1765 and retained it until his departure from office in Aug. 1766.

Grafton, Augustus Henry (Fitzroy) 3rd duke of   Aug. 1766–Jan. 1770

As first lord of treasury in Chatham and Grafton ministries.

Grafton took over the management of the Lords in Aug. 1766 on succeeding Rockingham as first lord of the treasury. His duties in respect of eve of session meetings were made clear to him in a letter from the king of 10 Nov. 1766 (Fortescue, no. 414). His first report to the king of Lords' proceedings contains an account of the meeting held at his house on that date (*ibid.*, no. 417). His last report is dated 27 Apr. 1769 (*ibid.*, no. 714). He relinquished the management of the Lords on his resignation in Jan. 1770.

Weymouth, Thomas (Thynne) 3rd Viscount   Jan.–Dec. 1770

As Secretary of State (South) in North ministry.

On Grafton's resignation in Jan. 1770 his office of first lord of the treasury was given to North, a member of the Commons. In these circumstances the management of the Lords fell to be undertaken by one of the Secretaries of State. While there is no direct evidence of Weymouth having undertaken this task, it would have been in accordance with current convention for him to have done so in his capacity of senior Secretary. He would presumably have continued to act until his resignation in Dec. 1770.

Rochford, William (Nassau de Zuylestein) 4th   Dec. 1770–Nov. 1775
earl of

As Secretary of State (South) in North ministry.

The earliest evidence that Rochford was managing the Lords is the fact that the eve of session meeting on 20 Jan. 1772 took place at his house (*Cal. Home Office Papers 1770–2*, p. 418; S.P. 37/9 fos. 9–12). His reports to the king of Lords' proceedings extend from 20 Feb. 1772 to 15 March 1775 (Fortescue, nos. 1021, 1617). He issued the earliest known parliamentary 'whip' to government supporters in the Lords on 2 Dec. 1774 (*Cal. Home Office Papers 1773–5*, p. 261; S.P. 37/10 fos. 353–4). For some reason the eve of session meeting on 25 Nov. 1772 took place, not at his house, but at that of his colleague, Suffolk (*Cal. Home Office Papers 1770–2*, p. 577; S.P. 37/9 fo. 313). Rochford evidently assumed the management of the Lords in Dec. 1770, on succeeding Weymouth as senior Secretary, and acted until his resignation in Nov. 1775.

Suffolk, Henry (Howard) 12th earl of   Nov. 1775–March 1779

As Secretary of State (North) in North ministry.

That Suffolk undertook the management of the Lords is indicated by the facts that his under secretary, William Eden, drafted the Lords' address in reply to the speech in Nov. 1777 (Add. MS. 34414 fos. 337–44) and that he issued a parliamentary 'whip' to government supporters on 6 Dec. 1778 (S.P. 37/27 fos. 50–1). It would appear that he took over in Nov. 1775 on becoming senior Secretary in succession to Rochford and acted until his death in office on 6 March 1779.

Weymouth, Thomas (Thynne) 3rd Viscount   March–Nov. 1779

As sole Secretary of State (March–Oct. 1779) and Secretary of State (South) (Oct.–Nov. 1779) in North ministry.

That Weymouth undertook the management of the Lords is clear from the king's letter to him of 5 Nov. 1779 asking him to send out the usual letters to the peers seeking their attendance at the opening of the session (Fortescue, no. 2820). It would seem, therefore, that he took over the responsibility in March 1779 on becoming sole Secretary on Suffolk's death. Although Weymouth did not actually resign the seals until 25 Nov. 1779 he had in fact ceased to act by 7 Nov. 1779 when it was arranged that the necessary duties in connection with the forthcoming session should be undertaken by Stormont, his successor as senior Secretary (*ibid.*, nos. 2822, 2846).

Stormont, David (Murray) 7th Viscount   Nov. 1779–March 1782

As Secretary of State (North) in North ministry.

Although still junior Secretary, Stormont was entrusted with the management of the Lords early in Nov. 1779 in view of Weymouth's impending resignation (Fortescue, no. 2822). The eve of session meeting on 24 Nov. 1779 was arranged to take place at Stormont's house (*ibid.*, no. 2846). Drafts of letters from him to prospective movers and seconders of the address in reply at the opening of the session exist for Nov. 1779 (S.P. 37/13 fos. 236–40) and Oct. 1780 (S.P. 37/14 fos. 329–34). Stormont's reports to the king of Lords' proceedings extend from 6 June 1780 to 19 Dec. 1781 (Fortescue, nos. 3047, 3473). In a letter to the king of 23 Sept. 1780 he described himself as having 'what is called the official Lead in the House of Lords' in his capacity of senior Secretary of State (*ibid.*, no. 3148). He relinquished this function on his departure from office in March 1782.

Shelburne, William (Petty) 2nd earl of   March 1782–Apr. 1783

As Home Secretary (March–July 1782) and first lord of treasury (July 1782–Apr. 1783) in Rockingham and Shelburne ministries.

On the formation of the Rockingham ministry in March 1782 the management of the Lords was assigned to the Home Secretary, Shelburne, rather than to the first lord of the treasury, Rockingham. Shelburne continued to undertake it on succeeding Rockingham as first lord in July. His reports to the king of Lords' proceedings extend from 13 May 1782 to 18 Feb. 1783 (Fortescue, nos. 3735, 4121). His position is illustrated by Thurlow's letter to the king of 27 May 1782 (*ibid.*, no. 3779). The eve of session meeting on 4 Dec. 1782 took place at Shelburne's house (*ibid.*, no. 4008). Shelburne ceased to have the management of the Lords on his departure from office in Apr. 1783.

Portland, William Henry (Cavendish Bentinck)   Apr.–Dec. 1783
    3rd duke of

As first lord of treasury in Fox-North ministry.

Portland's reports to the king of Lords' proceedings extend from 14 Apr. to 17 Dec. 1783 (Fortescue, nos. 4306, 4543). It is clear, therefore, that he had the management of the Lords as first lord of the treasury throughout the Fox-North ministry.

Temple, George (Nugent Temple Grenville) 3rd Earl   Dec. 1783

As sole Secretary of State in Pitt ministry.

As the only Secretary of State between 19 and 23 Dec. 1783 the task of managing the Lords fell to Temple (Aspinall, i. 6 n. 2).

Sydney, Thomas (Townshend) 1st Lord   Dec. 1783–June 1789

As Home Secretary in Pitt ministry.

Sydney managed the Lords throughout his period of office as Home Secretary from Dec. 1783 to June 1789 (Olson, p. 217). His reports to the king of Lords' proceedings extend from 3 Feb. 1784 to 23 May 1789 (Aspinall, nos. 29, 516).

Leeds, Francis Godolphin (Osborne) 5th duke of   June 1789–Nov. 1790

As Foreign Secretary in Pitt ministry.

Leeds took over the management of the House when he became the only Secretary of State in the Lords on Sydney's resignation. Although he remained Foreign Secretary until June 1791 the lead was taken from him and given to Grenville in Nov. 1790 (Olson, pp. 216–17).

Grenville, William Wyndham (Grenville)   Nov. 1790–Feb. 1801
    1st Lord

As Home Secretary (Nov. 1790–June 1791) and Foreign Secretary (June 1791–Feb. 1801) in Pitt ministry.

Grenville was created a peer in Nov. 1790 for the specific purpose of undertaking the lead in the Lords (Aspinall, no. 635; Stanhope, ii, app., pp. xii–xiii; Olson, pp. 214–18; R. P. Grenville, 2nd duke of Buckingham, *Memoirs of the Court and Cabinets of George III* (2nd edn., 1853–5), ii. 179–81). He continued to act until his resignation in Feb. 1801, having been transferred from the Home to the Foreign Office in June 1791.

Hobart, Robert (Hobart) Lord   Feb.–Oct. 1801

As Secretary of State for war in Addington ministry.

Hobart was given the lead on the formation of the Addington ministry in Feb. 1801. He was obliged to relinquish it to Pelham in Oct. of the same year (Add. MS. 33108 fos. 114–17; Add. MS. 34455 fos. 434–7, 444–5; *Journal of Lord Auckland*, iv. 138, 139, 141).

Pelham, Thomas (Pelham) Lord   Oct. 1801–Aug. 1803

As Home Secretary in Addington ministry.

Pelham was summoned to the Lords in his father's barony in June 1801 and was appointed Home Secretary in the following month. In Oct. he successfully laid claim to the lead on the basis of a promise made to him by Addington on the formation of the ministry (Add. MS. 33108 fos. 114–15; Aspinall, no. 2794). Pelham ceased to lead the House on leaving the Home Office in Aug. 1803.

THE AGE OF REVOLUTION AND REFORM
1750 – 1850

BIBLIOGRAPHICAL NOTE

THE AGE OF REVOLUTION AND REFORM (1750-1850)

[The numbers in brackets refer to items in the bibliography, above pp xvii-xxix. Chapter numbers refer to the essays printed below.]

The historiography of Parliament during the second half of the eighteenth century has been dominated by the House of Commons, especially in the massive volumes of *The History of Parliament: the House of Commons, 1754-90* edited by Sir Lewis Namier and John Brooke (3 vols. London, 1964). As William Lowe has observed, the Lords 'has been largely ignored by historians' (chapter 13); ignored that is except by the pioneering work of David Large whose article of 1963 on the decline of the 'party of the Crown' and the rise of parties can truly be described as seminal (chapter 12). His analysis of the constituent parts of the Crown's party — Scottish and (after 1801) Irish representative peers, bishops and officers of the royal household — which, he claims, sustained the ministerial leaders in the Lords in the late eighteenth century, shows that it disintegrated in the early nineteenth century and that by the 1830s all peers appear to have accepted party alignments.

Large's work encouraged others to look at two of the major constituents of the party of the Crown in greater detail: the Scots and the bishops. Both William Lowe for the Scots and the bishops (chapter 13 and no. 128) and McCahill for the Scots (chapter 14) showed that these sections of the Lords conducted themselves at times in a much less uniform manner than Large and the older orthodox view stated for the late eighteenth century. For the older view, see Turberville (141-42). G. M. Ditchfield has also shown that the Scots were particularly independent of ministerial control when their own especial interests were under threat (chapter 15). The norm, however, for both the Scots and the bishops was to provide support of the King's administration.

Parliamentary reform, of course, loomed large in the politics of this period and the work of Ditchfield (chapter 16, and to some extent 135 and chapter 15) has shown that the Lords were involved in this question. Public opinion, indeed, was not an unknown factor in the daily functioning of the upper house as Lowe (127) has shown, although he is incorrect in stating that the 1760s saw the first development of the protest as a form of organised public propaganda. This can be pre-dated to the age of Walpole in the early 1720s. Other views of reform and revolution can be found in Turberville (138, 147, 151) and Davis (148).

Sack discusses the often fraught relationship between the Lords and the Commons in the early nineteenth century when patronage was important (chapter 17). Most MPs followed the dictates of their aristocratic patrons though there were many examples of independence from the wishes of peers.

A new factor in the political consideration of the Lords after 1801 was the advent of the Irish representative peers and bishops. Apart from the early work of Turberville (141), this aspect has only been tackled in print by Large who looks at the attitude of the House towards legislation affecting Ireland and analyses those peers with Irish land interests (chapter 18).

The century covered by this section was one not only of momentous political change, but also one of social and economic upheaval associated with the Industrial Revolution. The work of McCahill is pre-eminent in this area of the study of the Lords (chapters 19-20). The character of the peerage did change significantly between 1750 and 1830. Several Crown servants – many of whom lacked property extensive enough to support a peerage – were rewarded with peerages, pensions and estates. They entered a House of Lords which had been the preserve of the great landowners, and their entry prompted a scramble for promotions within the older peerage. (See also the work of Turberville and Richards, 143-44.) The economic influence of the peerage was increased in the Industrial Revolution by the willingness of the Lords to support legislation which encouraged manufacturing, often on behalf of those unrepresented in Parliament (chapter 20).

In contrast to the previous section of this volume, only Ditchfield has relied extensively on the use of parliamentary lists (chapters 15-16). This may well reflect a decline in the number of lists that were made or in the rate of their survival.

No modern work of analysis covers the whole of this period and, again, the work of Turberville provides a starting point with a detailed narrative of politics in the Lords although it is a little dated (112 and 131). Michael McCahill's *Order and Equipoise* (132) is the only modern monograph on the late eighteenth century House and it is a recommended point of departure.

5. The House of Lords in 1741-42.

Engraving by John Pine, by courtesy of the House of Lords Record Office.

King George II enthroned in the old House of Lords at the end of the session, 1742. The peers are in their parliamentary robes, with the bishops sitting on the left, while Speaker Onslow and the Commons are in attendance.

12

THE DECLINE OF THE 'PARTY OF THE CROWN' AND THE RISE OF PARTIES IN THE HOUSE OF LORDS, 1783-1837[1]

DAVID LARGE

'IT is, I believe, the first time,' wrote Greville in 1839, 'that there is no party in the House of Lords supporting the crown . . . but all are either Whigs or Tories arrayed against each other and battling for power.'[2] Such a situation would have surprised and perhaps gratified Edmund Burke, who, in 1770, in his *Thoughts on the Cause of the Present Discontents*, had lamented that 'the generality of peers, far from supporting themselves in a state of independent greatness, are but too apt to fall into oblivion of their proper dignity and run headlong into an abject servitude to the court'. To him it seemed regrettable that those ' so jealous of aristocracy, make no complaints of the power of those peers (neither few nor inconsiderable) who are always in the train of a court, and whose whole weight must be considered as a portion of the settled influence of the Crown '.[3] Of course to accept Burke *au pied de la lettre* is to invite criticism but investigation shows that his remarks have substance, if taken simply as an indication of the strength of the party of the Crown in the house of lords in the late eighteenth century.

To demonstrate this in detail, however, is not quite so simple as might be thought. Contemporaries, of course, do refer to various constituents of the party, such as members of the royal household, the bishops and the Scottish representative peers, and how they behaved on particularly crucial occasions such as the Lords' rejection of Fox's India Bill in 1783, or their deliberations on Lord Rawdon's motion on the regency Bill in December 1788,[4] but it is difficult to ascertain what happened in the more ordinary course of events, such as, for instance, in the period between these two crises. Their lordships' ' conversations ' were much less fully reported

[1] I wish to thank my colleague Mr. P. V. McGrath and Mr. M. G. Brock of Corpus Christi College, Oxford, for most valuable assistance and the duke of Wellington, Earl Fortescue and Lord Hatherton for their kindness in allowing me to use material from their family papers.

[2] G. L. Strachey and R. Fulford, eds., *The Greville Memoirs* (7 vols., London, 1938), iii. 92.   [3] E. Burke, *Works* (1852 edn.), iii. 125–6.

[4] See, for example, the references in R. Pares, *King George III and the Politicians* (Oxford, 1953), p. 41.

than the debates of the Commons, and except on occasions of the order of those just mentioned, there is, I believe, no certain way of telling how the peers voted save for the totals of 'contents' and 'not contents' recorded in *The Parliamentary History* or *The Parliamentary Register*.[1] The *Journals* provide the names of those present each time the House met, but it was not until 1857 [2] that the names and total number of peers declaring their opinions were recorded there, although, from about 1830 onwards, *Hansard* and *The Mirror of Parliament* nearly always provide such information.

The figures of voting totals show that between 1783 and 1788 Pitt's ministry had a comfortable lead over the peers of the Fox-North persuasion. For instance, on seven divisions on various major topics, such as the Irish propositions in 1785, the Anglo-French treaty of 1787, and the ministry's Indian policy, which may fairly be taken as indicating the respective voting strengths when any serious business was in hand, the peers averaged seventy-one for Government and thirty-one against. The figures, it may be noted were remarkably steady. What was the composition of the Government majority and to what extent was it made up of peers who were part of 'the settled influence of the court?' If division lists could be found the matter could be decided at once, but prolonged search has not produced any such lists.[3]

In their absence, however, a crude test can be devised to give some idea of the composition of the Government majority. Approximate division lists can be constructed by taking lists in the *Journals* of those present on the day of the division, singling out the names of the Opposition peers, and counting the rest as Government supporters. The names of the Opposition peers can be ascertained with a fair degree of accuracy and certainly more easily than the more numerous Government supporters. The signed protests of Opposition peers preserved in the *Journals* provide considerable evidence, so do speeches made in opposition in the House; there

---

[1] The lists for these occasions are in *An Authentic Account of the Debates in the House of Lords on Monday Dec. 9th . . . 1783* (J. Debrett, London, 1783), *Parliamentary History*, xxvii, 890–1 and *Parliamentary Register*, xxvi. 72–74. From about 1800 the printed debates usually supply on major occasions the names of peers voting with the minority but not those in the majority.

[2] *Lords Journals*, lxxxix. 535–6, 548–9. A select committee inquired into the question of 'putting upon record both the numbers and names of the Lords who take part in divisions' and its recommendation that this should be done in the *Journals* was carried into effect.

[3] The leading London newspapers and periodicals do not give such lists and I have not come across any in the correspondence of the period. The French chargé d'affaires in London provided précis reports of proceedings in the house of lords for his government in which occasional reference is made to the party situation there, particularly to the ministry's comfortable majority and the behaviour of the royal princes and cabinet ministers (Archives des Affaires Étrangères ser. 1 Angleterre, vol. 553, fos. 349, 351, 364–5, vol. 559, fos. 194–7, 207 ,213, 220, vol. 560, fo. 99 and vol. 564, fos. 291–8, 379–89). These reports, however, contain no division lists.

are fairly numerous scattered references in contemporary sources as to who were the Opposition peers;[1] and a few clues can be gained from the extant raw material from which the *Journals* were ultimately prepared.[2] By contrast it would be much more difficult to compile a list of Government supporters for they did not ' protest ' and, except on particularly contentious occasions, the silent voters, for the ministry quite naturally did not attract the notice of contemporary writers. In default of division lists this admittedly crude method of reconstructing them [3] does produce a picture of the Government forces in the Lords that carries conviction in that it is in substantial agreement with contemporary observations as to the political behaviour of the various kinds of peers who contributed to form ministerial majorities in the Upper House. This picture is most simply revealed in tabular form.

Table I assembles the figures of those peers present at seven debates on major issues between 1783 and 1788 and shows the number of those who voted with the Opposition and of those who cast a vote for the Government. The number of those who abstained from voting is obtained by adding the figures of those who voted for the Government and those who cast a vote against it and subtracting the result from the total of those present; the result appears in the fourth column as abstainers. As explained hitherto it is one of the imperfections of this proceeding that these abstainers have to be treated as Government supporters which therefore brings the total Government strength to the figures given in the fifth column.

Taking the total strength of the Government supporters as given in column 5 of Table I, it is possible to break this down into its constituent parts. Table II shows the number of Scottish representative peers, bishops, household officers, new recruits and newly

[1] The proxy books in the house of lords record office provide some guidance to the affiliations of the less prominent peers by giving both the names of peers holding proxies and those whose proxy has been given together with the dates when given and when cancelled.

[2] Two series of papers in the house of lords record office provide a little help without, however, giving full division lists; the clerk assistant's sheets record the way some peers voted, particularly on amendments to the Irish propositions in 1785, while the manuscript minute books provide total figures of contents and not contents with the names of the respective tellers which are not given elsewhere. For these series, see *House of Lords Record Office Memorandum*, no. 13, pp. 7–9.

[3] Among the imperfections are that those who attended but did not vote have to be treated as government supporters. However this is not a serious matter in view of their small numbers. Furthermore a considerable consistency in voting habits among Opposition peers has to be assumed. This, I think, is justifiable, in view of the contemporary references to ' the mere party men ' who made up most of their strength. Occasionally a glimpse is vouchsafed of independently minded peers supporting the Opposition, but it is plain that when this happened it was rare enough to be commented upon and the names of such peers noted, see, for example, *H.M.C. Rutland MSS.* iii. 229. Highly independent peers such as Lansdowne and Bishop Watson have left sufficient evidence for their voting practice to be deduced with reasonable certainty.

honoured peers who figure among the Government supporters on each division. Their number is totalled in the fifth column.

TABLE I

DIVISION LISTS, 1785–88

Date of Division		Col. 1 Number[1] present	Col. 2 Opposition[2]	Col. 2 Government	Col. 3 Abstainers	Col. 5 Total of Government and Abstainers
1 March	1785	110	24	73	13	86
8 July	1785	93	27	58	8	66
1 March	1787	124	35	85	4	89
19 April	1787	102	29	70	3	73
18 May	1787	99	35	51	13	64
21 February	1788	136	33	88	15	103
17 March	1788	120	32	75	13	88

TABLE II

GOVERNMENT SUPPORTERS AND ABSTAINERS [3]

Col. 1 Scottish representative peers	Col. 2 Bishops	Col. 3 Household officers	Col. 4 Peers created, promoted or honoured by the king with ribbands on Pitt's recommendation [4]	Col. 5 Total
8	13	13	10	44
6	5	13	6	30
9	15	14	12	51
8	14	9	12	43
9	8	6	7	30
6	17	15	13	51
8	14	11	10	43

If the party of the Crown in the Lords is defined simply as ' the thanes, high priests and household cavalry '[5] together with the new recruits and newly honoured, and column 5 of Table II is compared

[1] L. J. xxxvii. 196–7, 346, 606, 655, 705, xxxviii. 84, 119–20.

[2] The figures of contents and not contents given in *Parliamentary History*, which agree with those in *Parliamentary Register*, have been checked with the MSS. minutes preserved in the house of lords record office. In general there is agreement, but for 1 Mar. 1787 the minutes give the number of government supporters as 85, instead of 81, and this figure has been preferred.

[3] Care has been taken not to count a peer more than once so that, for example, the duke of Queensberry, who was a Scottish representative peer on the government list, a member of the royal household, and in 1786 received a barony in the peerage of Great Britain, is recorded in only one of these categories.

[4] Promotions and awards are only taken into account if given before the division in question and during Pitt's ministry.

[5] This phraseology was commonly used, see, for example, H. Walpole, *Letters* (ed. P. Toynbee), xii. 215, Lord John Russell, ed., *Memorials and Correspondence of Charles James Fox*, ii. 220 &c.

with column 5 of Table I it is quite plain that the ministry had a group of supporters without which their numbers would have been far more equally matched with those of the Opposition.

The rest of the Government supporters on these divisions averaged thirty-nine against an average Opposition muster of thirty-one. Among the remainder of the Government voters one category stands out, the office holders: the lord chancellor, lord president, lord privy seal, the two secretaries of state, the joint postmasters-general, the master of the mint, the master general of the ordnance, the first lord of the admiralty, the chancellor of the duchy of lancaster and the president of the board of trade were all peers at this time and almost always they were present to support the ministry with their votes. There also may be noted among Government supporters military men, such as Cornwallis, Amherst and Harrington, whose future careers or possession of regiments depended upon royal and ministerial approval; a few peers, such as Walsingham, who owed a useful sinecure appointment to the ministry [1]; a few personal friends of Pitt, such as the young earl of Westmorland; and a relative or two of the prime minister. But there were comparatively few of those whom Wellington, in 1821, described as 'the independent peers ',[2] who came up and delivered a regular vote for Pitt's ministry, or even registered a proxy opinion, for proxy voting was little in evidence at this time. In short, 'the settled influence of the Crown' in producing votes for the ministry in the Upper House and ensuring the Lords subservience to the executive, was a major factor. This is, of course, what might have been expected, but there is a difference between anticipating and knowing.

Furthermore, if the attendance of the peers is analysed, it becomes plain that the value of the party of the Crown in the Lords was not confined to swelling votes when important business was on hand. If twenty attendances or more in a session be taken as an admittedly arbitrary test of good attendance, the result may be tabulated as shown on the next page.

Of the ' other peers who attended on twenty or more occasions ' (col. 7 *supra*) Government supporters outnumbered those of the Opposition in the proportion of about three to two. Thanks to the party of the Crown, the ministry's forces were always ready at hand, those of the Opposition generally were much less in evidence and special exertions were needed before a good turn-out could be obtained.

While the situation just analysed endured, there was little reason to apprehend that ministers should suffer the numerous frustrations

---

[1] He became vice-treasurer of Ireland in 1784.

[2] F. Bamford and duke of Wellington, eds., *The Journal of Mrs. Arbuthnot, 1820–1832* (2 vols., London, 1950), i. 98.

and defeats later experienced by Grey or Melbourne. Even the
regency crisis of 1788 did not really disrupt the party of the Crown
for the rats were very few and of Pitt's ninety-eight supporters
voting 'not content' to Lord Rawdon's motion, no less than fifty-
two were bishops, officers of the household, Scottish representative
peers or men created peers, promoted in rank or honoured with
ribbands on his recommendation.[1]   In the seventeen-nineties the
Government majority and executive influence in the Lords increased.

ALL PEERS ATTENDING ON 20 + OCCASIONS

Session	(1) Scottish representative peers	(2) Bishops	(3) Household officers	(4) Peers created promoted or honoured with ribbands on Pitt's recommendation	(5) Office holders	(6) Total of columns 1–5	(7) Other peers attending more than 20 times
1785	7	6	5	4	9	31	34
1787	8	8	3	3	9	31	21
1787–8	8	15	11	14	10	58	83

Not only was the Opposition more than halved by the Portland
faction coming over to Pitt, but there was a brisk translation of
country gentlemen from the Commons to the Upper House and a
relatively lavish distribution of British titles to Irish and Scottish
peers.   Addington enjoyed the same comfortable majority in the
Lords as Pitt had done as may be seen from Fox's estimate in June
1803 that among the peers there were eighteen Pittites, fourteen
Grenvillites and ten of his own following, the rest being ministerialists.[2]   Admittedly, when the Opposition groups coalesced, the
Government's majority dwindled sharply in April 1804, but, although
Addington's personal following in the Lords was minute—it was
estimated at five in September of this year—and his popularity
almost zero at this time, the various calculations by Government
and Opposition put the latter's strength at between 72 and 111 and
the ministry's at between 111 and 115.   Addington himself thought
at the time probably correctly, that his majority on Lord Stafford's
motion, if he had faced it, would have been ten.[3]   When Pitt

[1] See above, p. 234, n. 1, for division lists.
[2] *Memorials C. J. Fox*, ii. 222–6; Fox was, no doubt, basing his figures on the
divisions forced by each group at this time.   On the peace of Amiens issue the Grenvillites had numbered 10 and 16, Fox's friends numbered 10 when they divided on the
king's message relating to discussions with France on 23 May 1803, Pitt's followers
were 18 when they divided the House on 2 June, without the support of the Fox-
Grenville forces, and on 6 June, the latter, without the support of the Pittites, numbered
17.   See *Parliamentary History*, xxxvi. 191, 738, 1514 and 1573, which lists the names of
the minorities in each case except the last.
[3] Duke of Buckingham, ed., *Memoirs of the Court and Cabinets of George III* (4 vols.,
London, 1855), iii. 351; Lord Colchester, ed., *Diary and Correspondence of Charles Abbot*,

formed his ministry in 1804, although he could only get eighteen peers to support him in Opposition, an analysis of the House made for him in September 1804 set down 203 peers supporting the ministry against fifty for Fox and Grenville, five for Addington, twenty-one for the Prince of Wales, forty-two doubtful and twenty-two minors and Roman Catholic peers.[1]   Over half of Pitt's supporters consisted of traditional constituents of the party of the Crown [2] and his feeble ministry had in fact a two to one majority at the least on all major divisions in the Upper House.   Similarly, Grenville and Fox, although mustering fifty supporters only according to the treasury list of 1804, were supported in office by 100 peers even on the slave trade issue and their military policy was approved in the Lords by majorities of fifty to sixty.[3]   Likewise on 4 January 1811 when ministers were narrowly defeated in the Lords on the regency question, of their 102 votes, forty-three came from the bishops, the representative peers and the household officers.[4]

In brief, then, in the first decade of the nineteenth century, it would appear that the support of the party of the Crown in the Upper House was of considerable importance in giving a party leader the upper hand there at least on major issues, however small his personal following was among the peers, although on matters not vital to a ministry's survival such support was a more uncertain quantity.[5]   It was still also the practice when a minister was in difficulties in the Lords for him to turn to these forces for help, the bishops, for instance, being mustered by Addington in April 1804,[6] while his opponents tried to seduce them.   Pitt, for instance,

Lord Colchester (3 vols., London, 1861), i. 499; the Prince of Wales's group also joined the Opposition at this point, see third earl of Malmesbury, ed., *Diaries and Correspondence of 1st Earl of Malmesbury* (4 vols., London, 1844), iv. 298; *H.M.C. Fortescue, MSS.*, vii. 219; Lady Minto, ed., *Life and Letters of Sir Gilbert Elliot, 1st Earl of Minto* (3 vols., London, 1874), iii. 319, 321-2.

   [1] *Chatham Papers*, P[ublic] R[ecord] O[ffice] 30/8, vol. 234, a general abstract of the state of the house of lords with the peers ranged under the headings P(itt), F(ox), and G(renville), A(ddington), Pr(ince of Wales), D(oubtful) and minors and catholics.   I have to thank Professor Aspinall for kindly drawing my attention to this.

   [2] Of the 203 supporters of Pitt, 76 were bishops, members of the royal household, Scottish or Irish representative peers, while another 24 owed their creations or promotions to Pitt and 10 were colonels of regiments or employed in the royal service in various parts of his dominions.

   [3] A. S. Turberville, *The House of Lords in the Age of Reform, 1784-1837*, pp. 141-3; but there were indications that the party of the Crown was not supporting the Talents as effectively as earlier ministeries, see, for example, A. Aspinall and A. E. Smith, eds., *E[nglish] H[istorical] D[ocuments]*, xi, no. 234, p. 288.

   [4] *Parl. Deb.*, 1st ser., xviii. 747-8; *cf.* when three weeks later the government mustered 98 in trying to defeat Lansdowne's motion 42 votes came from the same sources.

   [5] See, for example, *E.H.D.* xi, no. 236, p. 289.

   [6] Malmesbury, *Diaries*, iv. 294; Bishop of Bath and Wells, *The Journals and Correspondence of William, Lord Auckland*, iv. 193 and *cf.* Hawkesbury summoning similar help in 1808 (*E.H.D.* xi, no. 235, pp. 288-9).

at this time tried his hand with the household cavalry and succeeded at least in one case, advising Amherst, a lord of the bedchamber, to remain neutral and not to vote for Addington. Amherst did so and was dismissed by the king for his offence.[1] Indeed at this time the party of the Crown was also still assumed to respond to royal wishes if these happened to run counter to those of his ministers as was indicated during the crisis over the Grenville ministry's Bill relating to Roman Catholics and dissenters in the armed forces. The Grenvilles testified to this when they concluded that although it might be possible to carry their Bill through the Commons against the opposition of the king, the Pittites and Sidmouth's followers, it could not be done in the Lords. The king had told Lord Grenville that, ' he regretted having given any consent upon the subject (of the Bill) and should certainly think it right to make it known that his sentiments were against the measure '. ' This ', wrote Thomas Grenville, ' seems to Lord Grenville to make the success of the bill in the House of Lords quite impracticable.'[2] The Grenvilles made no reference to George III's action in December 1783 but the clear inference is that the king's opinion plainly manifested would be sufficient to deprive his ministers of the support of the party of the Crown and ensure their defeat. Moreover Perceval, in discussing with Sidmouth what the king's tactics should be in handling his ministers on this question, referred to the possibility of his being driven ' to the utmost [*sic*] extremity of disposing of the measure by his Friends in your House' (*i.e.* the house of lords) ' or by his own negative '.[3] Also Portland's highly irregular offer to help George III turn out his minister at this time was in part based on the belief that the Bill could be ' ultimately defeated, though not sooner, I fear, than in . . . the Lords ', if the king's wishes were ' distinctly intimated '. Admittedly, Portland went on to urge the use of the royal veto if necessary, but it is plain that he regarded such a step as being a very last resort and was almost certain that the manoeuvre of 1783 could be repeated.[4] Speaker Abbot's laconic remark in April 1807, when Portland had become minister, ' in the Lords division for Lord Grenville's side, proxies

---

[1] Minto, *Life*, iii. 316; 5th Earl Stanhope, *Life of Rt. Hon. William Pitt* (4 vols., London, 1861–2), iv. 148–51 ; L. V. Harcourt, ed., *The Diaries and Correspondence of Rt. Hon. George Rose* (2 vols., London, 1860), ii. 139–42 ; *E.H.D.* xi, no. 231, p. 287; the point that excited contemporaries was that Amherst's dismissal came *after* Pitt had replaced Addington and the Opposition interpreted this as showing that George III's confidence in Pitt was limited, but the king's action can also be read as showing his determination that his family should behave correctly in politics acknowledging him and not the politicians as their master.

[2] Buckingham, *Court and Cabinet*, iv. 135.

[3] Perceval Papers, Brit. Mus., Add. MS. 49, 185 (uncatalogued), Perceval to Lord Sidmouth, 11 Mar. 1807. This letter is incompletely printed and misleadingly abbreviated in S. Walpole, *Life of Rt. Hon. Spencer Perceval, i.* 229–30.

[4] M. Roberts, ' The Fall of the Talents, March 1807 '; *E.H.R.*, l, p. 72, n. 3.

included: 90, for the ministers, *or rather for the King*, 181 ', seems much to the point.[1] Indeed Blackstone's description of the position of the Lords in the eighteenth-century constitution surely is less true than Archdeacon Paley's remark that one of the ' proper uses of the Lords ' was, ' to fortify the power and secure the stability of regal government by an order of men naturally allied to its interests ', or Thomas Gisborne's observation in 1794, that the nobility were inclined ' to give every decree of preponderance to the monarchial branch of the constitution '.[2]

How and when, then, did the change come about which resulted by the eighteen-thirties in all the peers being ' either Whigs or Tories ' so that the support that ministers could count upon in the Upper House depended entirely upon the party alignments there? The question can be answered, in part, by observing what happened to the particular constituents of the party of the Crown, for the waning of the influence of the Crown in the Lords, as in other spheres was a gradual, piecemeal process. We may begin with the Scottish representative peers.

In effect, as is well known, the ministry controlled the election of most of the sixteen peers, twelve of them in 1784, nine of the thirteen elected outright in 1790 and eleven when the disputes about the eligibility of votes were settled in 1793 and thirteen in 1796. However, when a henchman was entrusted with this business—and, of course, with much other government business and patronage in Scotland as well—for many years, he was able to build up a great interest, as Dundas did in Pitt's time, and the possibility emerged that if he ceased to be a minister he might use his influence on his own account, independently of the ministry. This is in fact what Dundas, now Lord Melville, did, particularly in 1806, and again in 1807, when he sent out his own lists in competition with those of the ministry and secured the return of seven and then fifteen of his friends. At this point it appeared as if the Scottish representatives peers were becoming a Melville faction in the Lords rather than a constituent of the Crown's phalanx. But the power of ' Henry the ninth ', although on the wane since 1796, was still too significant to be neglected by ministers. Portland bought the attachment of the family to his ministry in 1807 by appointing Henry's son, Robert, president of the board of control, and, as Lord Henry Petty remarked at the end of the year 'Melville was more than ever minister *de facto* in Scotland '. In 1809 Perceval offered the father an earldom and the son, office and a seat in the Cabinet, in order to retain their support.[3] From 1807 until 1830

[1] Colchester, *Diary*, ii. 120.

[2] *The Works of William Paley* (5 vols., Oxford, 1838), ii. 381. T. Gisborne, *An Inquiry into the Duties of Men in the Higher and Middle Classes of Society* (London, 1794), p. 96.

[3] H. Furber, *Henry Dundas, 1st Viscount Melville*, pp. 175–279; H.M.C. Laing, *MSS.* ii. 681–2; H. E. Maxwell, ed., *Correspondence and Diaries of T. Creevey* (London,

Robert Dundas, who succeeded as Second Viscount Melville in
1811, was a minister of the Crown, except for the brief period of
April 1827 until January 1828. He took over from his father the
management of the Scottish peers on behalf of the government.
There continued to be government lists so that, for instance, in
1820 we find Melville submitting one to Liverpool for approval
and the prime minister's papers contain a copy of a letter ' enclosing
a list of the sixteen Scottish peers who have the good wishes of
government at the approaching election ' which was despatched
to the electoral body: fourteen of the names on the list were duly
returned.[1] Plainly, too, most of the Scottish representative peers
were still counted as virtually automatic supporters of the ministry
in the Lords for in 1821, Creevey, a close observer of the proceedings
there on the Queen Caroline case, disgustedly commented, ' it was
the two sets of Union peers (Irish and Scotch) and those villains
of the church, that nearly destroyed for ever the character of the
House of Lords by supporting the government '.[2]

But gradually the majority of the Scottish peers seem to have
become so accustomed to supporting the Liverpool government,
and particularly that section of it ranged under Wellington, which
included Melville himself,[3] that they ceased to be merely part of a
Crown garrison in the Lords. This was fairly clearly revealed in
1827 when they refused to support Canning's ministry, ten of the
sixteen voting against it on the corn question, three abstaining
and only three supporting in the time honoured manner. Canning,
quite correctly, described their behaviour as ' unprecedented '.
Aberdeen was convinced that, if there had been a dissolution in
the summer of that year, the Scottish peers would ' have stood firm
(*i.e.* for the tory opposition to Canning), possibly paying the
government the compliment of returning the three who adhere
to it ', and Melville reported to Wellington's adjutant, Arbuthnot,
that in Scotland ' almost all the great leading interests are on our
side '.[4] In short the Scottish representative peers were becoming
members of a party in the Lords—that section of the tories led by
Wellington.[5] But the duke's accession to office in 1828 masked

1905), p. 85; Colchester, ed., *Diary*, ii. 218. Lists of the Scottish and Irish representative peers are to be found in the *38th Report of the Deputy Keeper of the Public
Records* in Parliamentary Papers, 1877, xlvi, C, 1747.

[1] Liverpool Papers, Brit. Mus., Add. MS. 38, 283, fos. 125, 145, 168–70, 189, 191–
4, 214.

[2] *Creevey*, pp. 338–61; 32 of the government's 123 votes on the second reading of the
Bill of Pains and Penalties came from Creevey's source: the Opposition had 95 supporters.

[3] Melville, although 'a catholic' resigned simply out of loyalty to Wellington, in 1827.

[4] A. Aspinall, ed., *The Letters of George IV*, no. 1361. H.M.C. *Bathurst*, *MSS.*, p.
641; A. Aspinall, ed., *The Formation of Canning's Ministry*, Camden Society, 3rd ser.
(1937), lix, no. 349.

[5] A. Wellesley, ed., *Despatches, Correspondence and Memoranda of 1st Duke of Wellington*
(8 vols., London, 1856–80), iv. 174, for Wellington, Melville and Lauderdale ' whipping ' Scotch peers.

this development for it meant that the sixteen simply returned to their accustomed role of supporting the government.

The advent of Grey's ministry and its sponsorship of a parliamentary reform bill removed the mask. By January 1831 it was reported that Wellington 'thinks he has all the Scotch peers'[1] and at the election of that year the government's apologists declared that in keeping with reform principles it was giving up the practice of 'sending down to Edinburgh, as heretofore, a signed list of representative peers'.[2] In fact, though, an effort was made by the government to draw up a list and secure the election of peers likely to support it, but the effort came to very little. There were two difficulties as Lord Holland observed: there was a disposition not to disturb those once elected and to convert Scottish 'representation in the House of Lords *de facto* as they could not *de iure* into what the Irish is by Law'; and secondly there was the determination of what the election showed to have been a considerable body of the Scottish peers, not to vote for anyone who supported the ministry or its reform bill whether they were already one of the sixteen or not. Ministers discussed the possibility of creating vacancies in the sixteen and weaning the Scottish peers from their opposition by grants of United Kingdom peerages, but in the light of whig calculations Grey concluded that 'the account is undoubtedly a very unpromising one, so unpromising that I am afraid no addition, that would be *possible* to the peerage if the Scotch election proves unfavourable, would correct it'. The election did prove unfavourable. Of the peers patronized by the group of whig noblemen who sought to manage it, Falkland scraped home with the smallest number of votes of any successful candidate;[3] Napier, a known sympathizer with the ministry, just retained his place among the sixteen, being second from the bottom of the poll and only two further ministerial supporters, Belhaven and Queensberry, were elected on a respectable number of votes. Both had been representative peers throughout the reign of George IV. On the other hand, Kinnaird, Reay, Elphinstone, and Errol all of whom had been regarded as suitable candidates by the Government management committee, failed to secure election, the last named being compensated by being made a United Kingdom peer immediately after the election.[4] Hence when the division was taken on the

---

[1] A. Aspinall, ed., *Three Early Nineteenth Century Diaries* (London, 1952), p. 43 (Ellenborough, 27 Jan. 1831).

[2] *The Times*, 16 May 1831, quoting *The Edinburgh Courant*.

[3] Possibly Falkland owed something to being a son-in law of William IV, though Errol who was in the same position collected only 14 votes. This last may have been because some of the Scottish peers knew that the king and Grey had already settled that he should be created a United Kingdom peer (Grey MSS., University of Durham, Grey to Holland, 29(?) April 1831).

[4] Grey MSS., Holland to Grey, 21, 24, 25 April, Grey to Holland, 2 June; Rosebery to Grey 7 June 1831. Like the whigs among the Irish peers those among the

second reform bill in the Lords on 7 October 1831 twelve of the sixteen Scottish peers were to be found voting against the ministry and in the 1832 election the whole business was managed by Melville on behalf of the conservative opposition in the Lords. Queensberry and Napier of the previous sixteen were excluded from the conservative list since they had supported Grey, two vacancies were created by the grant of United Kingdon peerages to Falkland and Belhaven, who also supported the ministry, and these were filled by conservatives and the final result was, as Melville reported to Wellington, fifteen of the sixteen were committed to support him in the Lords. The sixteenth, Lord Elphinstone, only managed to creep in, as Melville explained by ' a small piece of vanity on the part of our friends, who tried to get more numbers than the other candidates (although quite safe), and for that purpose exchanged votes with some of the enemy, who in return took special care not to vote for any of our friends whom they suspected to be weak '. He was confident that, ' if every one of the 16 candidates on our side pledges himself to vote for our list exclusively, including himself, the whole 16 will be ours '.[1] In fact in the eighteen-thirties the sixteen representative peers became part of the Conservative Party in the Upper House voting with that party and not for the ministry of the day, and the conservative leaders made arrangements for the management of the elections and of Scottish business in the House as part of their party organization. For example Buccleuch took over from Melville ' charge of the parliamentary and other concerns of the party in Scotland ', as Wellington described the business, and then in 1838, Aberdeen was asked by the duke to take over from Buccleuch who was going abroad. Wellington outlined the duties involved as being the management of the election of the Scottish representative peers, ' which will not be difficult as we have returned the whole 16 ', attention to Scottish legislation in the Lords, but not the attendance of Scottish peers which was looked after by ' Lord Redesdale, Arbuthnot and myself '.[2]

At this point it is convenient to consider the Irish representative peers whose destiny was the same as that of their Scottish counterparts. It seems clear that originally an Irish representative peerage was looked upon simply as a piece of patronage at the disposal of the government of the day, rather like an extra, if inferior, rank

Scottish nobility expressed their dissatisfaction with the electoral system, proposing that the 16 should be life members of the Upper House while the disqualification on eldest sons of Scottish peers from sitting in the Commons for burghs and counties should be removed, Rosebery to Grey, 8 June 1831 (*ibid.*).

[1] Melville to Wellington, 15 Jan. 1833 (Wellington MSS.).

[2] Aberdeen to Peel, 14, 25 Nov. 1838 in Peel Papers, Brit. Mus., Add. MSS. 40, 312, and Wellington to Peel, 30 Oct., 26 Nov. 1838 in Aberdeen Papers, Brit. Mus., Add. MSS. 43,060.

in the table of honours.[1]   Candidates did not so much canvass the electorate as seek the backing of the minister in office.   Lord Mountcashell, for instance, approached Perceval in this way in 1809 receiving the reply that similar applications for the next vacancy had been made to Portland and that he stood by his predecessor's pledge to Lord Gosford.[2]   Such support was apparently tantamount to election—certainly in this case Gosford was duly returned—and contemporaries referred, as Lord Kirkwall did in 1820, to his cousin, the Marquis of Thomond, 'being appointed to be one of the representative peers of Ireland'.[3]   Naturally, receiving their seats at Westminster in this way Irish representative peers were under some obligation to support the ministry, or at least not to come out in open opposition, which very few of them did.   For example, between the union and the formation of Liverpool's ministry in 1812, of thirty-six who were Irish representative peers during these years, only seven can be traced as having voted against ministers.   It is not surprising to find that when Pitt's ministry took stock of its parliamentary position in September 1804, twenty of the Irish representative peers were set down as favouring the ministry, only one the Fox-Grenville combination, and three were in the Prince of Wales train, the remaining few being listed as doubtful.[4]   Yet, of course, the sanction which bound the Scottish representative peers to the Crown—exclusion from the government list at the next general election, if they did not behave—was lacking in the Irish case since Irish peers sat for life.   The attendance records show that they did not attend very assiduously and they cannot be regarded as such useful constituents of the party of the Crown in the Lords as the Scottish peers.

[1] See C. Ross, ed., *Correspondence of 1st Marquess Cornwallis* (3 vols., London, 1859), iii. 244, 273–9, 286.   Government procedure in the matter was modelled on that used in managing the Scottish peers: Portland recommended Castlereagh to avoid the appearance of government intervention by getting 'their principal friends' to manage the first election as Melville did in Scotland (Marquess of Londonderry, ed., *Memoirs and Correspondence of Viscount Castlereagh* (12 vols., London, 1848–53), iii. 368–70.

[2] Liverpool Papers, Brit. Mus., Add. MSS. 38, 244, fos. 126–9; *cf.* Charleville's application for government support in 1801 for the vacancy created by the death of Rossmore, one of the original 28 representative peers, and Hardwicke and Addington's favourable reply on the grounds that Charleville had both supported the union 'without any engagements for himself and his friends and had recently provided the government with a seat in parliament for the borough of Carlow'.   Trouble arose in this instance because the king, Portland and Cornwallis had given a prior promise of government support on the first vacancy to the marquess of Thomond.   He was, however, compensated by being created a peer of the United Kingdom.   (Sidmouth Papers, Devon C.R.O., Hardwicke to the king, 25 Aug. Addington to the king, 31 Aug., and king to Addington 1 Sept. 1801.)

[3] Liverpool Papers, Brit. Mus., Add. MSS. 38, 284, Kirkwall to the king, Wellington in 1828 took the line that the king's consent was needed before pledging government support for a candidate, and instances exist of George IV both approving and disapproving of candidates (Wellington, *Despatches*, iv. 613–14, v. 91–92, vi. 262–3), 13 Apr. 1820.

[4] Chatham Papers, P.R.O. 30/8, vol. 234, a general abstract of the state of the house of lords.

Nevertheless, ministeries did find some support from them, so that, for instance, when Liverpool was looking for every vote to get the second reading of the Bill of Pains and Penalties through the Lords in 1820, he was supported by eleven of the seventeen representative Irish peers who cast a vote on that occasion. Even in 1827 the majority of those who bothered to vote did not desert Canning for Wellington as the Scots did.[1] The change came with Grey's ministry: when the Reform Bill eventually reached the Lords in 1831, the Irish representative peers came out against the ministry, only four supporting it and nineteen voting against it, and from that time onwards down to 1841 almost all of them voted with the tory opposition in the Lords, the elections being controlled by Wellington and Peel with a view to preventing either the whigs or the ultra tories from filling up vacancies. The change in this last respect can be pinpointed with some accuracy: when a vacancy occurred with the death of the earl of Bandon on 26 November 1830, the government appear to have continued to control elections and Westmeath was returned who supported the ministry over the Reform Bill and generally voted with it in the thirties, but when Conyngham's death in 1832 created another vacancy, Lord Downes, early in 1833, ran as Wellington's candidate, reported in detail the progress of his canvass to the duke and was returned by a handsome majority to join the tory opposition.[2] From then onwards the choice of Irish representative peers was virtually made by the leader of the Conservative Party in the Upper House, or as one disgruntled Irish liberal peer put it a generation later, they were made in Lord Derby's drawing room, and Irish liberal peers had no hope of election.[3]

The bishops did not become simply appendages of the Conservative Party in the Lords as was the case with the Scottish and Irish peers, although William IV plainly thought they had when in 1833 he severely rebuked them for voting with that party against his ministers' foreign policy.[4] Nevertheless there was a considerable change in their political behaviour during this period. In the eighteen-thirties, to the fury of radicals, far more often than not, a majority of the bench was to be found ' in direct and angry

[1] On Wellington's notorious amendment on the corn question, which may be regarded as a political trial of strength in the Upper House between the ministry and its opponents, 9 supported the former and 5 the latter.

[2] See my ' The House of Lords and Ireland in the Age of Peel, 1832–50 ' in *Irish Historical Studies*, ix ; below, 376-7 for the Irish representative peers in the thirties.

[3] The complaints of the Irish liberal peers form a recondite branch of literature, see, for example, Lord Langford, *A Letter to Viscount Melbourne on the Peerage* (1837) and a useful collection of protests, proposals for reform and correspondence on the matter between 1866 and 1880 made by Lord Gort (*National Library of Ireland, Dublin,* MS. 2076).

[4] *The Greville Memoirs*, ii. 385; *Lord Brougham, Life and Times, written by himself* (1871), iii. 275.

collision with the king's prime minister on political questions ', as Greville once put it.   On the other hand, in George III's reign, the critic's cry had been that the bishops were simply the slaves of whatever minister was in office and ultimately of the king.   Fox, for instance, had blamed the subservience of the bishops to George III's wishes, for the defeat of his India bill.   But to present the change as starkly as this is to oversimplify and no single generalization really fits the whole bench in regard to its political behaviour.

At any time in the eighteenth century the bench was a mixture of prelates: some, such as Bishop Hurd, were king's friends in every sense of the term, a minority were party men, and occasionally there existed prelates of an independent cast of mind and behaviour such as Bishop Watson.   The point is well illustrated by the bishops' behaviour in December 1783.   Nineteen of the twenty-six prelates voted on Fox's Indian proposals on 17 December and one more recorded his opinion on the preceding and analogous division on the 15th.   Of the twenty, twelve voted against the ministers, *i.e.* for the king, while eight remained loyal to Fox and North.   Of the twelve, six owed obligations either over their appointment or promotion to the king personally and two more had as patrons men who were plainly favoured by the king.   While of the eight supporting the Bill at least five had close connections with or owed obligations to Lord North.   In this case the majority of bishops voting had personal obligations one way or the other.   But even bishops who had no such obligations, unless they were exceptionally independent or the most inveterate party supporter tended to vote with the king or government from self interest, especially in the form of the hope of preferment from the Crown to a richer see, or natural propensity to support the established order.   Hence, as our previous figures have shown, the bench provided useful reinforcement for the party of the Crown and adverse votes from bishops were rare.   For instance, in all the twists and turns of party alignments between the formation of Addington's ministry in 1801 and that of Liverpool in 1812, of fifty-four bishops occupying English sees only ten recorded a vote hostile to ministers, together with one Irish bishop.   Also, it appears that by the latter date bishops were still solicited on occasions by ministers to case votes to ensure that unwanted Bills did not pass the Lords.[1]

Nevertheless there were always a few bishops, usually close friends of their patrons, who were true party men, standing by their party leader whether in or out of office.   Bishops Tomline, Huntingford and, in a lesser degree, Shipley, answer this description, being virtually chaplains to their party as others acted the

[1] *Memoirs of the Life of Sir Samuel Romilly written by himself* (1840), ii. 325 referring to the loss of a criminal law reform Bill in the Lords in 1810.

part of men of business.   George III was well aware of this for in setting aside Pitt's desire for the elevation of Tomline to Canterbury in 1805 he is reported to have observed ' if a private secretary of a first minister is to be put at the head of the church I shall have all my bishops party men and politicians '.[1]   Gradually, however, things changed.   The king's share in the making and translation of bishops dwindled until George IV found himself, for instance, unable to fulfil his promise to secure the translation of Bishop Pelham from Exeter to Winchester in 1820 in face of Liverpool's opposition.[2]   Yet it should be noted that the king appears to have been able to get his own way with a weak minister like Goderich,[3] and Queen Victoria later found means of exercising influence in these matters.   Nevertheless the dwindling of the sovereign's share in making and translating bishops did not lead to the bishops all becoming ' party men and politicians '.   Liverpool took less and less note of political considerations in making recommendations and laid stress on ' the selection of meritorious individuals ', though it should be observed that merit included being a sound ' protestant ', a criterion which, of course, had significant political implications in that it was bound to exclude many whig clerics from consideration.[4]   Certainly Liverpool's emphasis on learning, talent and a high moral character as prime qualifications was not consistently followed, it being possible to quote a number of examples in which the politics of a candidate for preferment was inquired into, nevertheless, it is probably fair to say that the emphasis gradually shifted to an inspection of their non-political qualities.[5] The upshot was that bishops gradually felt more free to express their own views on questions of the day rather than feeling obliged to support the king's ministers or the particular party leader who had recommended their elevation.   Of course this did not happen all at once: Bishop Blomfield, for instance, felt it necessary in 1829 to apologize for having voted against the ministry and in particular against Wellington to whom he owed his translation from Chester to London.[6]   Even in the eighteen-thirties the process was not quite complete: the urgings of William IV and Grey that

[1] Malmesbury, *Diaries*, iv. 383.

[2] A. Aspinall, ed., *The Diary of Harry Hobhouse*, pp. 32–33.

[3] *The Greville Memoirs*, ii. 191; *E.H.D.* xi, no. 140, p. 185; *The Journal of Mrs. Arbuthnot*, ii. 151.

[4] See Liverpool and Goderich's correspondence with the king over Copleston's appointment (Liverpool Papers, Brit. Mus., Add. MS. 38, 302, fos., 200–2; A. Aspinall, ed., *The letters of George IV*, nos. 1403–4, 1420, 1427–30).

[5] Whig magnates were slow to follow Liverpool's lead; for instance, Earl Spencer discussing in 1837 the exclusion of bishops from the Lords, admitted that their presence ' does complicate choosing bishops ' as their votes have to be considered.   (Spencer to Ebrington, 25 Feb. 1837, Fortescue Papers at Castle Hill, Devon.)   For later examples and Queen Victoria's position see Sir Ivor Jennings, *Cabinet Government* (3rd edn. 1959), pp. 451–9.   [6] *Hansard's Parliamentary Debates*, new series, xxi. c. 122–3.

the bishops should reconsider their opposition to the Reform Bill and return to their traditional role were not without effect as was shown by the fact that a dozen of them voted for the third Reform Bill and helped materially to secure its second reading in the Lords.[1] But broadly speaking it seems fair to characterize the opposition of many bishops to numerous items of the reforming legislation of the Grey and Melbourne ministeries as an expression of their personal conservatism rather than of loyalty to party or to the supposed principles of Lord Liverpool who had recommended many of them for the bench. The bishops, for the most part, had become independents as far as politics were concerned and an excellent example that demonstrates this is surely the case of Earl Grey's younger brother. Grey, just as many an eighteenth-century politician had done, had secured a bishopric for him, but as was not the case with a Brownlow North, for example, the new bishop's subsequent political behaviour shows that he felt little obligation to support his brother: he acted in an independent manner. The change in episcopal political behaviour, then, contributed to the decline of the party of the Crown, though not to the growth of party in the Lords except in so far as the former promoted the latter.

In regard to officers of the royal households sitting in the Lords, three questions arise, first, their number, secondly, by whom were they appointed to their posts, and thirdly, what was their political behaviour. The number of these peers was reduced both absolutely and relatively during this period: in 1782 on the eve of Burke's famous act, in a house numbering about 230 members, there were twenty-four peers holding posts in the king's household, three in the queen's establishment and another three in that of the Prince of Wales, but when George IV died, in a house of over 400, the number had fallen to eighteen.[2] As for the question of appointment, closely connected with that of political behaviour, broadly speaking in the eighteenth century under pressure from party leaders the trend was for household posts to become 'political'

[1] A. S. Turberville, *The House of Lords in the Age of Reform*, 1784–1837, p. 314. It should be added that Harrowby, the leading Waverer, also played a big part in bringing about this conversion.

[2] The Civil List Act of 1782 abolished the Jewel Office, the Great Wardrobe, the Foxhounds and the Staghounds, the heads of which departments had generally been members of the Upper House, see G. Rose, *Observations Respecting the Public Expenditure and the Influence of the Crown* (London, 1810), p. 40. The master of the robes, an office which plainly was reserved for the king, ceased to be usually held by a peer after the death of Selsey in 1808. The Prince of Wales's household, when established in 1781, was chosen by the king, North being invited 'as a friend, not a minister' to comment on the choice (see Sir John Fortescue, ed., *The Correspondence of King George III* (6 vols., London, 1927–8), no. 3201), but, of course, it soon ceased to be a constituent of the party of the Crown in the Upper House, becoming the nucleus of an independent squadron there. Likewise, of course, the absence of a queen's household in George IV's reign helps to explain the fall in numbers.

in the sense that appointments to them came to be included in the political arrangements made on the change of an administration, rather than being simply reserved entirely for the king himself. The practice, although resisted by both George III and IV, who were apt to claim the right to appoint whom they pleased when crossed in this matter, appears to have gradually increased in scope, particularly from the fall of North onwards.[1] On this occasion George III complained bitterly of ' a more general removal (from office) of other persons, than I believe ever was known before ': ' all my ministers except the Chancellor, and most of my Court except yourself (the Duke of Montagu, Master of the Horse), Lord Ashburnham (Groom of the Stole) and my bedchamber in its different branches are . . . swepped [*sic*] '.[2] This was not mere petulence on the king's part for it is plain that more of the household offices held by peers were removed on changes of ministry from this time onwards, or, in other words, that party factions gradually reduced the number of these king's friends in the Lords by converting part of the household, and eventually almost all of it, into a set of offices for rewarding their supporters.[3]

To take some examples: from 1761 to 1782 Lord Talbot had remained lord steward year after year as ministeries came and went, but from 1782 onwards the office became ' political ', the politicians generally securing their nominees and occasionally, as when Rutland held the post in the Shelburne administration, a seat in the Cabinet was attached to it.[4] In the same year, 1782, the master of the buckhounds also ceased to be an appointment reserved for the king in the manner of the groom of the stole which remained so throughout our period,[5] Jersey taking over ' Lord Bateman's hounds ' which

[1] The sharpest assertion of royal claims was George IV's in 1821, see A. Aspinall, ed., *The Letters of King George IV, 1812–1830*, no. 946. Ministerial claims, it is sometimes said (*e.g.* Pares, *op. cit.* pp. 145–6) reached a climax in 1812 in Grey and Grenville's rejected demand that all household offices should be considered ' political '. I think, however, that Ponsonby's statement (*Parl. Deb.*, xxiii. 432) that the whigs were asking nothing new is the correct interpretation, for according to him they were asking for changes in *some* but not all the offices and, in any case, Moira admitted the right of the whigs to make such a demand; he rested his rejection of it not on the novelty of the claim but on its inexpediency at this particular time, as Professor Roberts has pointed out (see M. Roberts, The ministerial crisis of May–June 1812, *E.H.R.*, li, 474-5).

[2] *Correspondence of George III*, nos. 3592, 3596.

[3] One of the court offices invariably held by a peer was already ' political ' by 1783, *i.e.* the lord chamberlain for whom see North's reference to the variety of peers who held it during the first twenty years of the reign (*Correspondence of George III*, no. 3622), *cf.* Pitt's removal of Salisbury as chamberlain in 1804 because he was an Addingtonian. Liverpool was following tradition in 1812 in refusing the royal nominee for the post, Conyngham, although, of course, other factors entered into his refusal to bow to the regent's desire.

[4] Lord E. Fitzmaurice, *Life of Shelburne* (3 vols., London, 1876), iii. 359.

[5] The groom of the stole was successfully reserved for himself by the king in 1782, as we have seen, Ashburnham throwing it up during the second Rockingham administration simply out of a pique in not getting a garter (see *Correspondence of George III*, no. 3665) and thereafter, as Ponsonby admitted in 1812, it was not one of the offices which

he had looked after since 1757.   He was the removed unwillingly by the coalition in May 1783, his place being taken by Lord Hinchinbrook who held the post until 1806 when Albemarle was accepted by George III at Fox's desire only to lose the job to Cornwallis in 1807, appointed on the recommendation of Portland.   On the death of Cornwallis in 1823 Liverpool successfully claimed against George IV that the office was not one reserved for the king, and secured the appointment of Maryborough.[1]   Similarly the captain of the gentlemen pensioners became more decidedly a political office in 1782 when Mount Edgecumbe was turned out most unceremoniously after holding the post for the past ten years, having succeeded on Lichfield's death who had enjoyed it also for ten years. Thereafter appointments to the post were included in the political arrangements made on changes of ministry.[2]

On the other hand the majority of offices in the royal household held by peers still remained in the king's hand after 1782; even Portland, in the following year, declared that he had no intention of meddling with ' the charge of the horse or the bedchamber '.[3] Nevertheless the tendency was gradually for more and more offices to become political.   The master of the horse, for instance, was formerly in royal hands when in 1781 the king appointed his particular intimate, Montagu, to the position which he kept until his death in 1790 in spite of intervening political upheavals.[4]   In 1790 Montrose took over, who was also a close friend of George III, but in 1795 Pitt's friend Westmorland was appointed and thereafter the office gradually moved into the political orbit; in 1806, for instance, Hertford was removed by the Talents in favour of Carnarvon, who in turn lost the post to Montrose when Portland formed his ministry.   By 1812 the whigs could justly claim that it was usual for it to be included in the political arrangements made

changed with administrations.   Weymouth held it after Ashburnham until his death in 1796, Roxburgh until his death in 1804 and Winchelsea until the regency was established.   From then until the accession of Queen Victoria it was held by the Marquess of Winchester.   On the other hand, before 1782, the Gold key does appear to have figured on occasion as a ' political ' office, for instance, Weymouth, pre-eminently a politician in the seventeen-seventies rather than the courtier he later became, held it from March to November 1775 while waiting ' till another office more to his mind became vacant ' and in the latter month the king offered it with a seat in the ' effective cabinet ' to Dartmouth (see *Correspondence of George III*, nos. 1621, 1623, 1740-6).

[1] *Correspondence of George III*, nos. 3605, 4336, 4340-1, 4349-50; *Letters of George IV*, no. 1079; *H.M.C. Carlisle MSS.*, p. 621.

[2] *H.M.C. Carlisle MSS.*, p. 620;   De Farrers held it until the Fox-North coalition came in when he was replaced by Jersey, who did not continue to hold it until 1790, as *G.E.C.* says, but was replaced, when Pitt came in, by De Ferrars, shortly afterwards created earl of Leicester and in 1790 promoted to be master of the mint.   The next holder, Falmouth, kept it until 1806, but St. John was installed by the Talents, only to be removed in the following year in favour of Falmouth again who held it until his death in 1808.

[3] Fitzmaurice, *Shelburne*, iii. 380.

[4] For Montagu see J. Wake, *The Brudenells of Deane*, pp. 311-28.

on the change of an administration.[1] The captain of the yeoman
of the guard almost suffered this fate in 1783 in that Dorset, who
had obtained the post on the intercession of North just before his
fall, following the death of the previous occupant who had held it
since 1747, was removed when the Fox-North coalition came in,
and, then a new peer was brought in when Pitt took office for the
first time. But thereafter it was held continuously until 1804 by
Aylesford who only relinquished it for promotion to lord steward
and his successor, Macclesfield, remained in office down to 1830.
But in William IV's reign appointments to it became purely a
matter for the politicians.[2]

As for the lords of the bedchamber, generally speaking in
George III's reign they remained in office as ministeries came and
went until they died,[3] unless they voted the wrong way and were
dismissed by the king as Queensberry was in 1788. Nevertheless
occasionally the king was prepared to listen to recommendations
from the politicians in making new appointments, rather surprisingly permitting Rockingham this favour in his second ministry.[4] This thin end of the wedge appears to have led ministers
eventually to count more and more on the complaisance of the
king in the making of household appointments and to assume that
it was only right and proper that their adherents should get such
posts. Complaints began to be heard in the first decade of the
nineteenth century that the king appointed and dismissed lords of
the bedchamber without consulting his ministers[5] although, as
George IV showed, the sovereign could and did ignore such
complaints. At least one lord of the bedchamber was appointed
by him while Prince Regent, who was well connected with the
whig opposition and apparently Liverpool was not consulted over
an appointment in 1821.[6] Nevertheless it is clear that in William
IV's reign a considerable proportion of the bedchamber had certainly become political and reshuffles took place each time a new
minister took office. For example, when Grey formed his ministry,

[1] *H.M.C. Dropmore, MSS.*, vii. 218; Lord Holland, *Memoirs of the Whig Party*
(London, 2 vols., 1852), ii. 72–73; *Parl. Deb.*, xxiii. 432 where Ponsonby claimed the
mastership of the horse to be a ' political ' office on a par with the lord chamberlain,
lord steward and captain of the gentlemen pensioners, all being ' almost always changed
on every administration '.
[2] *Correspondence of George III*, nos. 3515, 4308 which last shows the removal of
Dorset and the accommodation of Cholmondeley in the household as captain of the
yeoman of the guard. In William IV's reign Macclesfield was removed in favour of
a supporter of Grey's ministry, Clanricarde, and when Peel came in, his supporter
Courtown was given the post, only to be turned out when Melbourne formed his
ministry in April 1835.
[3] Typical examples are Boston, a lord of bedchamber from 1782 to 1825, Denbigh
from 1763 to 1800 and Onslow who spent most of his life in courtly office from 1776
to 1814.   [4] *Correspondence of George III*, nos. 3665–6, 3687.
[5] G. Rose, *Diaries*, ii. 139–42.
[6] *Letters of George IV*, no. 16; Liverpool Papers, Brit Mus., Add. MS. 38, 289,
fo. 123.

four of the twelve lords appointed by the new king in July 1830 were replaced, while the introduction of the Reform Bill led to a further three resignations in 1831 by tories who then discovered how difficult it was to reconcile their political views with the old fashioned notion that an officer of the household should support ministers in whom the king had confidence. In the same year, too, Grey succeeded in an unprecedented manner in removing Lord Howe from office as lord chamberlain to the queen for having given a tory vote against ministers. Before this, noble members of the queen's household had held office virtually for life.[1] Grey did not, though, immediately succeed in making appointments in the queen's household political for the queen stubbornly refused to have a new chamberlain. Nevertheless when the matter was reopened in 1832 in negotiations for the return of Lord Howe, that nobleman's attempt in concert with Wellington to reverse Grey's victory by making his return conditional on having the liberty to vote as he pleased came to nothing. The king on Grey's advice stood firm on the doctrine that officers of the queen's household should not be free to vote in such a manner as to give the impression that the royal household was divided against itself, and eventually early in 1833 the earl of Denbigh was appointed to the vacant post apparently against the queen's wishes since Howe remained in attendance upon her without title or salary, until the coincidence of his political views with those of the new tory ministers allowed of his return on 16 December 1834.[2] Likewise at the same time seven lords of the bedchamber in office under Melbourne made way for seven tories who duly retired with Peel in April 1835, presumably because they were unwilling to accept Melbourne's invitation to stay on provided they would support his ministry. In this, since the king's hostility to his new ministers was plain, the invitation amounted to asking the Lords to become whigs or retire. Peel's claim in 1839 in the bedchamber ' crisis ' rested on past practice and the emergence early in Victoria's reign of the seventh Lord Byron with the epithet ' non-political ' attached to his post of lord of the bedchamber, the first of his kind, I believe,

[1] For instance the post of master of horse to the Queen Consort was held by the third earl Waldegrave from 1770 until his death in 1784 and by the fourth earl from 1784 until his death in 1789 and by Harcourt from then until his death in 1809 and by his son from then until the Queen's Consort's own death in 1818. *Cf.* Effingham's tenure of the post of secretary and comptroller from 1784 until 1814 and then treasurer until his death in 1816; *E.H.D.* xi. 27 and nos. 246–8, 293–6.

[2] *E.H.D.* xi. 27 and nos. 246–8, pp. 293–6; *The Journal of Mrs. Arbuthnot*, ii. 424–5, 430–1; *The Greville Memoirs*, ii. 319, 337, 339–41; A. D. Greenwood, *Lives of the Hanoverian Queens of England* (1911), ii. 387–8; L. J. Jennings, ed., *The Correspondence and Diaries of J. W. Croker* (1884), ii. 118–19; *Three Early Nineteenth Century Diaries*, p. 151, Ellenborough (15 Oct. 1831) reports that *The Times* announced the appointment of the fifth marquess of Queensberry to succeed Lord Howe, but the report was without foundation, the earl of Denbigh not being appointed until eighteen months later.

merely emphasizes by contrast what had happened to most of his companions.[1]

Finally we have to consider briefly the political behaviour of the household peers. One point is plain: they were expected to support a ministry in which the king had full confidence on questions deemed grave enough to affect the stability of that government. Whatever their private opinions it was considered that they should support the king and his ministers and as late as 1827 it was reported that the lords of the bedchamber had been ordered to vote for Canning or be turned out,[2] although it may be noted in 1828 Wellington said he would not have minded Montrose, the lord chamberlain, voting against his ministry if he had done it quietly and decently by proxy. As it was Montrose called attention to his offence and hence was sharply rebuked.[3] What, however, was the position when the king and his ministers were not in harmony? If the household peers were dilatory in supporting ministers this was widely interpreted as meaning that the king was not fully behind his ministry and in an age when loyalty and attachment to the sovereign was still a considerable political force this meant a strengthening of the Opposition's position in the Lords. In cases where a real conflict between the king and his ministers existed the household peers followed their royal master's wishes as they did in December 1783,[4] or as it was generally assumed they would do in 1807. But gradually, as party leaders exerted control over appointments, the household officers were expected to support them rather than the king, should conflict exist between the king and his ministers. Wellington, for instance, in 1829 forced a reluctant king to instruct his family to support, or at least not to vote against a measure which the king had accepted only by the exercise of *force majeure*.[5] In brief 'the family' became more and more in effect part of the party structure of the Lords. Its members resigned from their posts when the king changed his minister in 1827 in order to follow party leaders with whose views they sympathized and party leaders 'whipped' them as they did any other kind of peer.[6]

---

[1] G.E.C., *Complete Peerage*, ii 458.

[2] *The Journal of Mrs. Arbuthnot*, ii. 123-4.

[3] Wellington, *Despatches*, iv. 410-12.

[4] Only 10 peers holding office in the royal household cast a vote in opposition to the king's known wishes in either of the two critical divisions on the India Bill in December 1783. Two of these, however, transferred their proxy votes from the Fox-North coalition to its opponents on the second division, while of the other 8, 4 held posts in the household which had become ' political ' *i.e.* lord steward, lord chamberlain and the captains of the yeoman of the guard and gentlemen pensioners; another, the treasurer to the Queen Consort, was Lord North's father, which leaves, in effect, only 3 peers in the household who went against the royal wishes.

[5] Wellington, *Despatches*, v. 550-1.

[6] *E.g.* Wellington did so in 1830 (*Despatches*, vi. 531).

But we need linger no longer over the fate of the various kinds of peers of the party of the Crown, except to note the evolution during this period of the lord chancellor from king's chancellor to party politician which was complete by 1832.[1] Although it must be added that, by contrast, peers in the diplomatic service, generally though not invariably, remained bound by the convention that they should support (by proxy) the ministry by whom they were employed, whether their political opinions coincided with the ministry or not, and hence must be considered as still part of the household troops.[2] Nor is it necessary to dwell on the waning of the Crown's capacity to influence members of the Upper House by the use of money, patronage and ' imperceptible influence ', for this has already been amply demonstrated.[3] But some comment is required on the manner on which the use of honours affected the Upper House. Some contemporaries professed to believe that Pitt's lavish creations, particularly of lawyers, soldiers and sailors, weakened the Lords by making more of its members dependent on the Crown.[4] But a better case can be made out for the view of Lord Camden in 1811 that the increased size of the Lords would eventually prove embarassing to future ministers,[5] for one of the conditions which made it possible for the party of the Crown to be an effective force in the eighteenth-century House was simply the chamber's relatively small membership.[6] Lord North, during the regency debates in 1789, was in effect calling attention to this when he pointed out that the eighteen peers belonging to the king's household ' voting on one side made the difference of 36 on a division; and was that nothing? '[7] It was not especially if one counts in most of the Scottish peers and some of the bishops as well—in a House of not much over 200 members as in the seventeen-eighties, but it was far less significant in one of double the size as was the case by the eighteen-thirties. In brief, lavish creations had the effect of swamping the party of the Crown in the long run, although in the short run a minister could, no doubt, count on strengthening his position in the Lords by judicious creations, promotions or ribband distributions, as Lord North did, for instance, in 1776 when ten new peers were made simultaneously.[8] In fact, however, without going into the much discussed question of the motives which prompted the expansion of the peerage between 1776 (the true starting point) and 1830, swelling ministerial majorities in

[1] A. Aspinall, ' The Cabinet Council, 1783–1835 ' in *Proc. British Academy,* xxxviii (1952), 231–5.

[2] S. T. Bindoff, ' The unreformed diplomatic service, ' *Trans. Roy. Hist. Soc.* 4th ser., xviii. 143–72.

[3] A. S. Foord, The waning of the influence of the Crown, *E.H.R.,* lxii. 484-507.

[4] *E.g. E.H.D.* xi, no. 145, 204–5.   [5] *E.H.D.* xi, no. 146, 205.

[6] In 1714 the total membership was 213 and in 1780, 220.

[7] *Parliamentary Register,* xxv. 410.

[8] A. S. Turberville, *The House of Lords in the Eighteenth Century,* p. 363.

the Lords was always a minor consideration in peer-making and appears to have become entirely lost sight of in the days of Lord Liverpool. Even in the eighteen-thirties the Grey and Melbourne ministeries did not seriously try to weaken the Opposition forces in the Lords by using the engine of honour. True, between 1833 and 1841 they were responsible for advising fifty-one creations, but it is plain that a variety of motives not really connected with the state of parties in the Upper House explain these creations. Six, for instance, were consolation prizes for whig M.P.'s of long standing defeated at the polls, two were similar rewards for shelved ministers, and a considerable number must be looked on in the same light such as the peerages given to Coke of Norfolk, Stanley of Alderly or Parnell who had been a whig M.P. for thirty-nine years. Reward for past services rather than building party strength in the Lords seems to have been the chief motive for the bulk of whig creations and in fact the voting strength of whigs in the Lords in the eighteen-forties was rather less than greater after their years in office which surely indicates plainly enough the ineffectiveness of Crown influence in the Lords.[1]

The crumbling of the party of the Crown and the waning of other forms of Crown influence meant in effect the opening of the door for the further development of parties in the Lords and of contests between them, far more frequent and intense than had been the case between 1783 and the late eighteen-twenties to which time W. S. Gilbert justly applied his well known lines. The relative violence of political life in the Lords between 1827 and 1841 was not only the result of a stream of reforming measures reaching the Upper House, but also of a minor revolution within the House which left Canning, Grey or Melbourne in a much weaker position than a North, a Pitt, or even a Grenville had been. The former could rely virtually only on their own *party* supporters, whom it was worth trying to organize.

Evidence as to the growth of party organization is, however, not easy to come by, although it is plain that by the early eighteen-thirties the Opposition peers disposed of a tolerably efficient if simple machinery for summoning peers to meetings or to attend the House, collecting promises and so forth. The duke of Wellington was assisted by 'a whipper in' who did this donkey work. Down to his death early in 1837 Lord Rosslyn filled the post, being succeeded by Lord Redesdale until he broke with the ministry

---

[1] I estimate that the maximum strength of the whigs in the thirties, excluding bishops, was just over 130, 80 to 90 represented a good division for them and 30 to 40 was not unknown on tolerably important occasions. In the forties the whig peers rarely, if ever, mustered over 100, and even when trying to make a good showing 80 to 90 seems to have represented the very best they could do and lesser numbers were the general rule.

over the Maynooth question in 1845.[1] Thereafter Dalhousie and St. Germains tried to fill the gap but apparently not with much success for Peel complained in 1846 that he could not find out from them the important fact of what strength the minister was likely to muster in committee on the Corn Bill in the Lords.[2] To assist them with the clerical work of whipping the English and Irish peers —a separate system was used for the Scottish peers as we have seen— a small office staff was established in Duke Street. It was maintained by subscription from the politically active tory peers paid into a special bank account in the whipper in's name. The subscribers themselves formed the main body of those peers whom the duke invited each year to dine with him at Apsley House on the eve of a new session and their contributions allowed the keeping of two clerks and a messenger boy.[3]

When machinery of this kind was first established by Opposition remains obscure. Pre-sessional meetings of Opposition peers were a long established tradition,[4] but although references can be found, particularly to the third Lord Holland and second Earl Fortescue, as having acted as managers of the whig peers in the Upper House before 1830,[5] no precise evidence as to the nature of their activities has been found.[6] On the government's part the need for an officer and whipper in was plainly less than for the Opposition groups. Official channels and clerical help were available: the lord lieutenant of Ireland, for instance, could be and was approached to contact Irish peers.[7] Nevertheless someone had to be made responsible for co-ordinating such activity, holding pre-sessional meetings and steering government business through the Lords and to this end there emerged a quite unofficial office, that of government leader of the house of lords.[8] It appears to

[1] Wellington Papers, *e.g.* Rosslyn to Wellington, 12 Jan. 1836, indicates his work; Peel Papers, Brit. Mus., Add. MS. 40, 461, Redesdale to Wellington, 4, 7 April 1845, referring to his post; *Annual Reg.* sub. deaths 4 Jan. 1837 refers to Rosslyn as ' " whipper in " of the tories in the House of Peers ' and Lord Redesdale, *Memories* (1915), i. 23 refers to his father's job. *Cf.* Lady R. Weigall, *Correspondence of Lady Burghersh with the Duke of Wellington* (1903), p. 88. Wellington refers here to his death ' as a terrible loss ' and the difficulty of replacing him.

[2] Peel Papers, Brit. Mus., Add. MS. 40, 484, Peel to Arbuthnot, 2 May 1846.

[3] Wellington Papers, Rosslyn to Wellington, 14 Dec. 1836, with list of subscribers, financial statement for 1836 and references to previous subscriptions for the same purpose in 1835.

[4] Malmesbury, *Diaries*, ii. 475 for an example in 1792.

[5] *E.g.* T. H. S. Escott, *Society in the Country House*, pp. 306–7 records being told this when visiting Castle Hill. *Cf.* from an earlier period, the duke of Richmond's activities in 1771 in having dinners for his friends in the Upper House every day after a debate there, and his soothing and managing of ' that great being (*i.e.* Chatham) who never dines ' (L. Sutherland, *The Correspondence of Edmund Burke*, ii. 197).

[6] There is no trace of such activities in the Fortescue Papers at Castle Hill.

[7] *E.H.D.* xi. no. 163, p. 213 for an example of this in 1809.

[8] As late as 1827, *The Times*, 25 April could describe leading ' in the House of Lords ' as ' a phrase most unconstitutional . . . which has sprung up of late years ', and in discussing whether Landsowne or Goderich should lead during Canning's ministry

have been the accepted practice during the eighteenth century that this role should be undertaken by one of the secretaries of state, possibly always that for the northern department, and from 1782 onwards by the home secretary, if he sat in the Lords. For there are indications that Sydney acted as such in the late seventeen-eighties,[1] while Pitt's elevation of William Grenville to the peerage and the home secretaryship in 1790 appears to have been designed, in part, to permit him to take the lead for the ministry in the Lords and neutralize any damage the unruly Thurlow might perpetrate.[2] Certainly in 1801 Portland took it for granted that Pelham, the new home secretary, should handle government affairs in the Lords, and Hawkesbury, home secretary in Pitt's second administration was likewise treated as leader for the government in the Upper House.[3] Not unnaturally, however, the simple fact that the prime minister so often sat in the Lords during the first four decades of the nineteenth century[4] and hence was automatically leader, meant that the office did not really develop as a distinct institution until later in the century; it might be claimed that the third marquess of Landsowne, between 1846 and 1850 was really the first recognizable modern leader for the government in the Lords in the sense that he carried the main burden of speaking there, over-shadowing both his other colleagues and Lord Chancellor Cottenham in a manner virtually unprecedented. At some stage, as yet impossible to be precise about, the government leader acquired the help of a whipper in to marshall his forces. Wellington, when prime minister and leading in the Lords, had one, and the same was true of Grey and Melbourne.[5]

The scattered and fragmentary evidence cited above is, however, sufficient to show that *pari passu* with the decline and virtual disappearance of the party of the Crown in the Upper House there

the paper's dictum was, 'he would in any case lead who possessed most personal weight and dignity, the formal duty also would no doubt be conceded to Lord Lansdowne '.

[1] M. A. Thomson, *The Secretaries of State, 1681–1782*, pp. 25–26. G. Browning, ed., *The Political Memoranda of the 5th Duke of Leeds*, Camden Society, new ser., xxxv. 128, 131.

[2] Liverpool Papers, Brit. Mus., Add. MS. 38, 192, Pitt to Hawkesbury, 23 Nov. 1790.

[3] H. Twiss, *Life of Lord Chancellor Eldon* (3 vols., London, 1844), i. 396, 509.

[4] That the lead in the Lords was not clearly attached to any particular office in the absence of the prime minister is shown by Ellenborough's remark on a debate there on 30 Sept. 1831, 'Lord Lansdowne (Lord President) was not there. Some think he is annoyed at the lead being given to Goderich (Secretary for War and Colonies) in Lord Grey's absence' (*Three Early Nineteenth Century Diaries*, p. 138).

[5] *The Greville Memoirs*, ii. 276 (1 Apr. 1832) refers to Lord Dover 'who makes lists manages proxies and does all the little jobbing, whipping in, busy work of the party...'; Lord Broughton, *Recollections of a Long Life* (6 vols., London, 1909–11.), v. 219, 27 July 1839) refers to Viscount Falkland playing this part. Inquiries into the whereabouts of his private papers, if any, have drawn a blank; Lord Hatherton's Diary (Staffs. R. O. Hatherton MSS.), 20 July 1835, refers to whipping arrangements in

was emerging a primitive form of party organization suitable enough for the conditions of political life prevailing among their lordships. One reason why this remained primitive is well indicated by the recently ennobled Lord Hatherton's observation in 1835, 'the unintelligible thing to me, who am used to the whipping in the House of Commons, is the squeamishness that exists about asking peers to stay in town and attend this committee. Who shall make such a request to such august persons as the Dukes of Devonshire and Sutherland?'[1] Only the premier or a cabinet minister might succeed. However by 1846 the test of whether a peer was setting about becoming a party leader in the Lords would be not only that he should separate himself from others on a matter of principle but also that he should take steps to organize a following. Indeed until he did this, it was not quite plain that he was a party leader.[2]

the Lords and says ' the List is put into the hands of Lord Strafford (the late Sir John Byng) who is a perfect old woman, totally devoid of the address and tact for the task. The Post Master General has usually kept the List. But neither he nor anyone else would now undertake it '; for Shaftesbury's role as ' whip ' under Wellington, see A. Aspinall, English Party Organization in the Early Nineteenth Century ', *ante*, xli. 397. It is not quite accurate to say these ' whips ' were unofficial personages. This is true of Shaftesbury, Dover (whose brief career in Grey's ministry took place before he became a peer) and Strafford, but Falkland held office as a lord in waiting while, if Hatherton is correct about the post master general keeping a list and presumably being a kind of ' whip ', the holder of the office from 1830 to June 1834, the duke of Richmond, was actually a cabinet minister.

[1] Hatherton's Diary, 20 July 1835.
[2] Peel Papers, Brit. Mus., Add. MS. 40, 481, Lincoln to Peel, 1 Jan. 1847.

13

BISHOPS AND SCOTTISH REPRESENTATIVE PEERS IN THE HOUSE OF LORDS, 1760-1775* *WILLIAM CURTIS LOWE*

Despite all the attention lavished on the mid-eighteenth-century parliament, the House of Lords has been largely ignored by historians. The Whig historians of the nineteenth century were concerned with tracing the development of the House of Commons as the principal vehicle of constitutional progress, and in this century Namierites and neo-Whigs have alternately challenged and defended the Whig position, basing their arguments almost entirely on their views of proceedings in the lower chamber.[1] The House of Lords was easy to neglect, one suspects, because most historians assumed that the upper House could be conveniently explained away as an appendage of the crown where an institutionalized majority of bishops, Scottish representative peers, place-holders, and newly-created peers could easily maintain a ministry.[2] This, in turn, has led to a tendency to explain events in the House of Lords at any point in the century in terms of a static political structure, largely without regard to current issues or changes in the "structure of politics" at the national level.[3]

The two most conspicuous segments of the "Party of the Crown"

---

* I would like to thank Professor Robert A. Smith of Emory University for his comments on an earlier draft of this article; as well as to express my appreciation to Earl Fitzwilliam and his Trustees for permission to consult and quote from material in the Wentworth Woodhouse Muniments, and to His Grace, the Duke of Newcastle for permission to consult and microfilm items in the Newcastle (Clumber) Manuscripts.

1. Perhaps the best example of this preoccupation with the House of Commons is the series somewhat misleadingly called *The History of Parliament*. This impressive scholarly achievement confines itself almost exclusively to the Commons, and even its biographical sketches treat cursorily or completely neglect the subsequent careers of most M.P.s who became peers. See, for example, the entries for William Henry Cavendish Bentinck, third Duke of Portland, and William Bouverie, first Earl of Radnor: Sir Lewis Namier and John Brooke, *The History of Parliament: The House of Commons, 1754-90*, 3 vols. (London, 1964), II, 84-85, 106.

2. This view generally prevails in A. S. Turberville, *The House of Lords in the XVIIIth Century* (Oxford, 1927), still the only scholarly survey of the subject. For more recent statements of this viewpoint, see Richard Pares, *King George III and the Politicians* (Oxford, 1953), pp. 41-42 and E. N. Williams, *The Eighteenth Century Constitution* (Cambridge, 1965), p. 136. David Large, "The Decline of the 'Party of the Crown' and the Rise of Parties in the House of Lords, 1783-1837," *English Historical Review* (hereafter *EHR*), 58 (1963); above, 233-59, accepts this picture of the House's political structure as his point of departure.

3. Thus John Cannon in his important work, *The Fox-North Coalition: Crisis of the Constitution, 1782-4* (Cambridge, 1967), prefaces his treatment of the India Bill's consideration in the Lords with the statement that "It was, in fact, unknown for the government to be defeated in the House of Lords. . . . In practice, it was an adjunct of the crown, and the Scottish representative peers, the bishops and the household peers, augmented by the ministers and their friends, constituted an automatic majority for the government of the day" (p. 125).

in the Lords (and the two most abused for their alleged political servility) were the bishops and representative Scottish peers. The second
Earl of Effingham expressed the conventional political wisdom of the
eighteenth century when he told the House in 1780 that "those two
descriptions threw a great weight into the scale of the Crown,"[4] and
historians have generally echoed this view. In the past two decades
scholarship has begun to modify this picture for both ends of the century,[5] though the old clichés still hold sway for the decades from Walpole
to North.

To be sure, the bishops and Scottish representative peers were
numerically significant: they numbered forty-two in a House whose total
membership seldom rose above two hundred until the 1780s.[6] Though
each was unique in its character and composition, the two groups had in
common a non-hereditary basis that set them apart from the other members of the House, and the circumstances of their recruitment were
commonly believed to subject the two groups to a high degree of government influence. The purpose of this article is to test the view that
the political structure of the House of Lords was dominated by an institutionalized majority by examining in some detail the parliamentary
participation of its two most conspicuous constituents during the fifteen
sessions from the accession of George III to the outbreak of the American Revolution. We will suggest that, as far as this important period is
concerned, the traditional characterization of the bishops and Scottish
representative peers as voting blocs on which inevitable ministerial
majorities were built is badly in need of qualification and redefinition.

I.

Since the eighteenth century, both the bishops of the Church of
England and the representative peers of Scotland have suffered from
a bad press, though the inherent conflict between the spiritual and
political offices of bishop has perhaps subjected the right reverend bench

---

4. *Parliamentary History*, XXI, 229; partially quoted in Williams, *Eighteenth
Century Constitution*, p. 138.
5. Geoffrey Holmes, *British Politics in the Age of Anne* (London, 1967) contains
an excellent chapter on the House of Lords, and includes a number of instances of both
episcopal and Scottish opposition to ministers. Large's article, mentioned above, shows
the changing character of the House's politics in the late eighteenth and early nineteenth
centuries. Michael W. McCahill, "The Scottish Peerage and the House of Lords in the
Late Eighteenth Century," *Scot. Hist. Rev.*, LI (1972); below, pp. 283-307, shows that this
segment of the House's membership was much less uniform in its parliamentary conduct
in the 1780s and 1790s than many (including Large) have thought.
6. Turberville's widely-quoted estimate of 220 as the average pre-1783 membership
of the House of Lords (*House of Lords in the XVIIIth Century*, p. 5) is rather too high
and was apparently reached by adding the 42 bishops and representative peers to the
total number of English and British peers (including minors and Roman Catholic peers).
There were 157 adult conforming English and British peers in 1760 and one duke of
the blood royal. In 1775 these categories numbered 159 and 2 respectively.

to greater ridicule for their alleged subservience to ministers. General episcopal support of the ministry of the day in the House of Lords has long been noted, and usually ascribed to desire for secular emolument and clerical advancement, material motivations that dovetailed nicely with the Erastian tradition of the Anglican Church. The bishops have often been seen as essential to the maintenance of ministerial majorities in the upper House.[7] In support of this view, the spectacular example of the Excise crisis of 1733-34 is often cited, when a rout of Walpole's forces in the Lords was only prevented by the adherence of twenty-four of twenty-five voting prelates.[8] No less an authority than Richard Pares has declared the bishops "almost a laughing-stock for their subservience,"[9] and most historians have assumed that episcopal support can explain ministerial survival in almost any close divisions in the Lords. Thus the author of one of the more important recent works on the politics of George III's reign looks at Grafton's narrow three-vote victories of 26 May 1767 and concludes that "the great experiment in non-party government had saved itself in the House of Lords by a handful of bishops" — this in divisions where the majority of bishops present had voted *against* the ministry.[10]

That this view of episcopal conduct in the Lords is so widespread is due largely to the work of the late Norman Sykes, who was especially interested in tracing the Whig transformation of the Church in the early eighteenth century, and the maintenance of this position under Walpole and the Pelhams. It is ironic that the examples of massive episcopal support drawn from Sykes's work on this period should have served to establish a picture of episcopal subservience for the century as a whole, for a careful reading of Sykes includes clear instances of episcopal non-support, especially in the 1760s.[11]

Indeed such instances suggest the dangers of applying long-term generalizations too literally to any particular part of the century. Considered on the basis of the objective evidence of attendance, verbal participation, and voting records, the bench of bishops during the first decade and a half of George III's reign emerges as something less than a strong and solid ministerial phalanx.

The basic measure of political participation is attendance. Though the House of Lords did have the unique option of proctorial representation, proxies were hedged with certain limitations, not the least of which

---

7.   Turberville, *House of Lords in the XVIIIth Century*, pp. 422-23; Norman Sykes, *Church and State in England in the XVIIIth Century* (Cambridge, 1934), pp. 61-67.
8.   Sykes, *Church and State*, pp. 50-51.
9.   Pares, *George III and the Politicians*, p. 41.
10.   Frank O'Gorman, *The Rise of Party in England. The Rockingham Whigs, 1760-1782* (London, 1975), p. 205. For episcopal voting in these divisions, see Table I below.
11.   Sykes, *Church and State*, Ch. 2.

was a prohibition against their use in committees.[12] As ministers usually held a majority of proxies, a skillful opposition would wait and pitch its attacks in committee. It was no accident that the closest divisions (and ministerial defeats in 1765 and 1766) occurred at this stage of the House's proceedings.[13] This put a premium on attendance, and one should expect any group on whom ministerial control of the House depended to have attended regularly, especially on days of important political business.

The bishops were overall the most regular in attendance of the groups composing the House's membership, though this statement requires qualification. Individual patterns of attendance varied widely: Archbishop Cornwallis was among the House's most attentive members, attending between one-half and two-thirds of meetings most sessions; while Bishop Beauclerk of Hereford was quite the opposite, attending on average less than 3 times a session and not attending at all 7 of the 15 sessions between 1760 and 1775. In fact, individual prelates missed entire sessions on 31 occasions during this period, and 16 sessions saw individual bishops come but once.[14]

The best method of gauging the political impact of episcopal attendance is to look at it on days of divisions. There were 84 days during these 15 sessions when the House of Lords divided on issues of significant political content.[15] On 42 of these — exactly one-half — episcopal attendance represented more than thirteen per cent of those present

12. Proxies were governed by the House's Standing Orders 79-85 and by customary usage. The written proxies were entered with the House's clerks and recorded in a book that could be consulted by any member of the House. Proxies remained valid until the reappearance of the donor or the end of the session. The maximum number of proxies any peer could hold was two; only a bishop could hold an episcopal proxy and only a lay lord a secular proxy. The use of proxies was to some extent limited by the practice of pairing, a device used on a modest scale during this period. See, for example, Nottingham University Library, the Duke of Manchester to the Duke of Portland, [received 2 July 1767], and Lord Walpole to Portland, 24 June [1767], Portland Papers, PwF 6918, 8924.

13. For example, of the 100 divisions of greatest political content between 1760 and 1775, proxies were called for in 29. In none of these did they reverse the decision reached by the peers present.

14. This information is based on compilations from the daily lists of those present in the *Journals of the House of Lords* (hereafter *JHL*), XXX-XXXIV. It might be noted that the lists in the *JHL* are not absolutely accurate, and it is sometimes possible to prove the presence of a peer not included in the published lists. The frequency of such omissions, however, is not great and does not invalidate the use of the lists as records of general attendance habits of individual peers. For a table of sessional attendance totals for members of the House during this period, see my 1975 Emory University Ph.D. thesis, "Politics in the House of Lords, 1760-1775," pp. 945-53.

15. The determination of what was or was not a division of "significant political content" is inevitably subjective as some divisions were obviously more overtly "political" than others. In this category I have included divisions in which the question at issue was itself of political importance, questions less inherently political but which precipitated partisan positions by government and/or opposition, and procedural questions masking clearly partisan differences of opinion. The 84 days used here as a standard for testing attendance witnessed 100 divisions.

(the proportion of the House's total membership composed by the bench), while for the same number of days episcopal attendance was less.[16] This performance is not particularly impressive and it is small wonder that contemporaries sometimes commented on the lack of episcopal attendance.[17]

Proxies were only partially effective in mitigating the effects of episcopal absences. Quite apart from the practical limitations on their employment, they were not always used when they might have been. Of the 31 sessions completely missed by individual bishops between 1760 and 1775, only 11 were even partially covered by proxies. Some bishops simply never gave proxies: Bishop Pearce of Rochester attended the House but six times during the last six years of his life, but never once attempted to cover his absence with a proxy.[18]

Those bishops who did attend seldom made an impression in debate.[19] Bishops generally spoke only on matters touching the Church, such as the Dissenters' Relief Bills of 1772 and 1773, and only occasionally did a prelate venture forth on more overtly political topics.[20] It was by their silent votes that the bench most affected the political structure of the House, and it is by this test that their reputation as regular ministerial supporters must ultimately be judged.

An examination of extant division, majority, and minority lists from the 1760s reveals that a surprising number of bishops voted, at least occasionally, with the opposition. Of 31 individual bishops who sat in the House between the formation of the Old Whig opposition in the winter of 1762-63 and the session of 1768-69, no fewer than 21 can be shown to have voted against the government on at least one occasion, and many did so in numerous divisions.[21]

---

16. This statement is based on the daily lists in the *JHL*. Taking all 84 days together, the bishops made up 13.4% of those present.

17. For example, see Bodleian Library, Brownlow North, Bishop of Worcester, to the Earl of Guilford, 11 November [1775], North MSS, d. 26, f. 24. It might be pointed out that age was an important factor inhibiting episcopal attendance. The average age at elevation of the 42 men who held episcopal office between 1760 and 1775 was 49, while the average age of the bench as a whole in 1765 was 60. The bishops were notoriously subject to physical infirmities, and ill-health was a frequently cited excuse for parliamentary absence.

18. House of Lords Record Office (hereafter HLRO), Proxy Books, 1760-61 to 1774-75. It might be noted, as a rough gauge of the bishops' use of proxies, that of 921 proxies entered in these 15 sessions, 99 (or 10.8%) were from bishops.

19. On the bishops' reputation for silence, see Bishop Newton's autobiography in *The Works of the Right Reverend Thomas Newton, D.D., Late Lord Bishop of Bristol and Dean of St. Paul's* (London, 1787), I, 137; and Bishop Warburton, "Thoughts on Various Subjects," *A Selection from Unpublished Papers of the Right Reverend William Warburton, D.D., Late Lord Bishop of Gloucester*, ed. Rev. Francis Kilvert (London, 1841), pp. 341-42.

20. For example, Hinchliffe of Peterborough and Archbishop Cornwallis both spoke on American affairs in 1775: *Parliamentary History*, XVIII, 269-91, 655-76.

21. Ashburnham, Beauclerk, Cornwallis, Egerton, Ewer, Green, Hume, Johnson, Keene, Keppel, Lowth, Lyttelton, Mawson, Newcome, Newton, Pearce, Squire, Terrick,

Episcopal opposition was manifest in the first parliamentary sallies undertaken by the Old Whig opposition in the Lords. On 28 March 1763, 9 of 20 voting bishops opposed Bute's cider tax.[22] Less numerous were the 3 bishops (out of 22 present) who in November of the same year voted against the resolution that parliamentary privilege did not extend to cases of seditious libel.[23]

It was, however, in the three sessions from 1765 to 1767 that episcopal opposition became strongest, as three different administrations wrestled with the problem of putting together a dependable majority in the House of Lords. In 1765, the bishops played a pivotal role in the rejection of the non-political Ecclesiastical Estates Bill (which carried the tacit approval of the Grenville ministry), and several continued to oppose.[24] Eight prelates opposed the ministers' attempt to change the poor law in at least one of three divisions on Gilbert's Poor Bill (one of which was lost by the ministers).[25] Five (out of 14 bishops present) voted against the Regency Bill later in the same session.[26]

Even more pronounced was episcopal opposition to the first Rockingham administration's American measures in 1766. The government lost two embarrassing divisions on resolutions designed to pave the way for the repeal of the Stamp Act, and each time a majority of bishops voted with the opposition.[27] On the Stamp Act repeal itself, Rocking-

---

Trevor, Warburton, and Yonge each voted with the opposition at least once in this period. For the extant voting records of members of the House during the period 1760-1775, see my Ph.D. thesis, pp. 966-74.

22. British Library, Newcastle Papers, Add. MS 32947, f. 337. It is likely that at least 8 bishops (out of 17 present) voted against the same bill two days later. See *Parliamentary History*, XVI, 1316, and BL, Add. MS 32948, ff. 9-10. At lea t one bi hop, Beauclerk of Hereford, appears to have voted against the Cider Tax because of the threat it was thought to represent to the economic interests of his diocese, and received a hero's welcome on his return to Hereford: *Gentleman's Magazine*, XXXIII(1763), 255.

23. BL, Newcastle Papers, Add. MS 32953, f. 109. Wilkes, to whose case this resolution related, was originally brought to the attention of the House of Lords on a complaint of breach of privilege against Bishop Warburton (in connection with the *Essay on Woman*) and his cause was not popular with the bench. See Sykes, *Church and State*, pp. 55-56.

24. BL, Bishops Yonge and Hume to Newcastle, 26 March 1765, Newcastle Papers, Add. MS 32966, ff. 105, 107. The bill was defeated by 56 votes to 23 with all bishops present against it.

25. Sheffield Central Library, Wentworth Woodhouse Muniments (hereafter WWM), Rockingham Papers, R53-22, R53-9. BL, Newcastle Papers, Add. MS 32966, ff. 149, 156, 158-59. Archbishop Drummond, at least, had a very negative opinion of the bill, terming it "the most pernicious sketch of democratical intention that has been in this country, tho' I have seen the Militia established & the revenues of the crown altered" (Ibid., letter to Newcastle, 2 Apr. 1765, ff. 146-47). On the confused political situation surrounding the ultimate defeat of Gilbert's Poor Bill and the role it played in the demise of the Grenville administration, see Derek Jarrett, "The Regency Crisis of 1765," *EHR*, LXXXV(1970), 282-315.

26. BL, Newcastle Papers, Add. MS 33035, ff. 134-35.

27. On 4 Feb. 1766 the bishops divided 9 to 8 against the government (with one abstention) in a division lost to 63 votes to 60: BL, Newca tle Papers, Add. MS 33035, ff. 276-77. Two days later as many as 11 of the 16 bishops present may have voted against the government in a division it lost by 55 votes to 59: Sheffield Central Library,

ham's 12-vote majority among those present was only marginally enhanced by the 10 bishops (of 17 present) who voted for the bill's
commitment.[28]

For sustained episcopal opposition in large numbers, pride of place
must go to the session of 1766-67. In a two-month opposition campaign
that came close to winning control of the House of Lords, the Grafton-
led Chatham administration was hard-pressed. Division lists survive for
seven divisions during May and June 1767, and as the following Table
shows, the ministry was able to win a majority among the bishops present on only one occasion:[29]

TABLE I
EPISCOPAL VOTES, MAY-JUNE, 1767

Date	6 May	22 May	26 May	26 May	2 June	17 June	25 June
Bishops supporting Government	6	8	8	8	9	9	5
Bishops in Opposition	9	8	9	9	9	7	7

Even in the much more settled atmosphere of 1768, episcopal opposition
continued, and 7 of 17 bishops present voted against the second East
India Company Dividend Bill.[30]

The participation of bishops in the oppositions of the turbulent
mid-1760s was underlined by the appearance of episcopal signatures
on the written protests of these years. The right to dissent in writing
from an action of the House was one of the Lords' singularities, and
to join in a protest was viewed as a strong and public statement of

---

WWM, R53-56. It should be noted that the list of 60 peers voting with the government on 4 Feb. 1766 printed in O'Gorman, *Rise of Party*, p. 538, contains numerous
inaccuracies and is, in fact, a list of peers (less Rockingham) who attended the eve-of-
session meeting at the Marquess's house on 16 Dec. 1765: cf. *The Correspondence of
King George the Third*, ed. Sir John Fortescue, 6 vols. (London, 1927-28), I, 200-01.
The partial list of the opposition given by O'Gorman is correct as far as it goes, though
the full majority was recorded by Newcastle in the list cited above.

28. BL, Newcastle Papers, Add. MS 33035, ff. 389-91. Episcopal proxies in this
division were eight to one for repeal. Bishops also voted against the government in at
least two other divisions in the session of 1765-66. On 17 Dec. 1765, two bishops voted
for an amendment to the address of thanks, fifteen supported the address, and one abstained: Sheffield Central Library, WWM, R53-12. A partial division for 28 May 1766
reveals two bishops opposing the government on the window tax and five supporting it:
Correspondence of George III, I, 344.

29. The divisions of 6 May (BL, Newcastle Papers, Add. MS 33036, ff. 451-54),
22 May (Ibid., Add. MS 33037, ff. 17-19), and the two divisions of 26 May (Ibid.,
ff. 51-54) each concerned the Massachusetts Bay Indemnity Act; that of 2 June related to
consideration of papers on Quebec (Ibid., ff. 73-74, 77-78); while those of 17 June
(Ibid., ff. 111-12, 115-16, 119) and 25 June (Ibid., ff. 151-52, 155) were relative to
the East India Company Dividend Bill. Proxies were voted only in the first and sixth
of these divisions, and both times episcopal proxies went against the government: two to
one on 6 May and three to one on 17 June. Thus if proxies are counted, the government lost its single episcopal majority. For the political background to these divisions,
see John Brooke, *The Chatham Administration, 1766-1768* (London, 1956), pp. 142-57.

30. BL, Newcastle Papers, Add. MS 33036, f. 285.

opposition.[31] Protests by bishops were not common, and prior to 1763 the last one had occurred in 1742.[32] During the 1760s, however, such protests became commonplace: no fewer than 12 episcopal signatures adorned the 7 protests registered between 29 November 1763 and 4 February 1768.[33]

On the basis of this evidence, it is clear that during the 1760s the bishops fell far short of upholding their reputation as a ministerial voting bloc. One factor affecting the conduct of the bench was the continuing connection of a number of bishops with the Duke of Newcastle after the latter embarked on an opposition career in 1762-63 (with a brief interval in office during the first Rockingham administration). The Duke's fondness for ecclesiastical patronage is well known, and the bench in 1762 was largely his composition.[34] Contemporaries (and some historians) have stressed the desertion of the Duke by the bishops he had preferred.[35] Yet what is remarkable, in view of the bench's reputation for ministerial servility, is not the failure of the bishops to follow Newcastle *en masse* into opposition, but the fact that a significant minority remained loyal to the Duke until his death in 1768. This influence was, quite fortuitously, bolstered by the quirks of episcopal mortality, which left subsequent ministers few opportunities before the late 1760s to alter the composition of the bench.[36]

The presence of Newcastle in the opposition presented many bishops with a dilemma. Some, such as Archbishops Secker and Drummond, responded by staying away from parliament or abstaining from voting.[37] Even this, however, had the effect of reducing the bench's strength as a Court block. As Newcastle's papers abundantly show, the Duke con-

---

31. Despite the House's occasional attempts at punishment, protests (unlike votes and speeches) were usually published.

32. *JHL*, XXVI, 131-32; J. E. Thorold Rogers, *A Complete Collection of the Protests of the House of Lords with Historical Introductions*, 3 vols. (Oxford, 1875), II, 24-28.

33. *Ibid.*, pp. 63-98 prints six of the protests. The seventh was Lord Temple's lone dissent from the King's Brothers' Annuity Bill on 7 April 1767 (*JHL*, XXXI, 559). This protest, like others to which no reasons were appended, was omitted by Thorold Rogers.

34. Norman Sykes, "The Duke of Newcastle as Ecclesiastical Minister," *EHR*, LVII(1942), 59-84. As Sykes shows, Newcastle was surprisingly successful in preferring his own candidates in the interval between George III's accession and his own resignation.

35. Horace Walpole, *Memoirs of the Reign of King George the Third*, ed. G. F. Russell Barker (London, 1894), I, 134; W. E. H. Lecky, *A History of England in the Eighteenth Century* (New York, 1903), III, 206.

36. There was but one vacancy during the Bute administration, one under Grenville, one during the first Rockingham administration (when Newcastle was back in office), and one during the Chatham administration before the summer of 1768.

37. BL, Newcastle to the Duke of Devonshire, 16 Nov. 1762 (copy), Newcastle Papers, Add. MS 32945, f. 53. Neither Secker nor Drummond can be shown to have voted in opposition with Newcastle, though both recorded numerous absences and abstentions on days of divisions and both loyally supported the Duke when he returned to office in 1765-66.

tinually tried to influence episcopal conduct, and in every important division until his death, Newcastle acted as a parliamentary whip to varying numbers of bishops.[38]

Yet, as the strong episcopal opposition to the Rockingham administration shows, Newcastle's friends were not the only bishops willing to vote against ministers, and the Duke's influence was but the most obvious example of a general process affecting the bench's parliamentary conduct in the 1760s: bishops were to an increasing extent following the fortunes of relatives or patrons among the more politically active of the House's hereditary members. During the unstable political climate of the 1760s, when today's ministers might very well be tomorrow's opposition, many bishops found past ties to important politicians a more promising course than blind allegiance to the ministry of the day, even if it meant a period in opposition. Well might Bishop Egerton of Bangor take the occasion of Bedford's resignation in 1765 to assure the Duke of his "respectful and most sincere attachment."[39] Two sessions in opposition rebounded to the good bishop's credit, and soon after the Bedfords returned to office in 1768, Egerton was translated to Lichfield and Coventry, following this three years later with a further translation to the prized See of Durham.[40]

Nor was such loyalty always purchased at the price of future expectations. Despite the eighteenth-century Church's reputation for venality, it did contain men capable of acting out of so simple a motive as gratitude, as the conduct of the bishops who stuck with Newcastle after his second resignation in 1766 attests. When in 1767 Bishop Hume of Salisbury chose to follow the Duke's directions (to leave his proxy with another bishop in opposition) over those of the Earl of Lincoln (that he abstain entirely), Hume replied to Lincoln's indignation:

> Let me entreat you . . . to consider that the present Question is not about private Offices of Friendship and Feelings of the Heart . . . but — Who as a publick Minister has conferred most upon me, & has the first Right to demand my following him in publick Affairs.[41]

---

38. Newcastle remained influential with Green, Hume, Johnson, Mawson, and Yonge until his death. Ashburnham and Cornwallis were loyal to the Duke during his first period in opposition (1762-65), but were alienated by the Duke's machinations over the See of Salisbury in 1766 (as were their noble relations) and refused to follow the Duke into opposition in 1767. On the Salisbury episode, see Sykes, "Newcastle as Ecclesiastical Minister," *EHR*, LVII(1942), 77-83.

39. Bedford Estate Office, London, Egerton to Bedford, 13 July 1765, Woburn MSS, LII, f. 54. Bishop Egerton was a cousin of the Duke of Bridgewater and an in-law of Bedford and Lord Gower.

40. Bury St. Edmunds and West Suffolk Record Office, Egerton to Grafton, 13 Aug. 1768, Grafton MSS, 423/345.

41. Nottingham University Library, 9 June 1767, Newcastle (Clumber) MSS, NeC 2961. Lincoln was Newcastle's nephew and principal heir and Hume had been his tutor.

From the mid-1760s, each of the political groups active in the House of Lords could look for support from its "own" bishop or bishops. The Old Corps Whigs, now identified with the Marquess of Rockingham, enjoyed the support of Newcastle's following, Lord Albermarle's brother (Keppel of Exeter), and Newcome of St. Asaph (from a connection with the Cavendish family). The Bedfords, as we have seen, numbered Bishop Egerton among their followers. The Grenvilles were able to call on Lord Lyttelton's brother (the Bishop of Carlisle), Lord Trevor's uncle (the Bishop of Durham), and Newton of Bristol; until the deaths of the first two (in 1768 and 1771 respectively) and until the last was won away by Grafton in 1768 with the lucrative *commendam* of the Deanery of St. Paul's.[42] Other prelates followed the fortunes of individual patrons less definitely aligned.[43] Horace Walpole was not far from the truth when he blamed the large number of bishops voting with the opposition in 1767 on "the Crown permitting great lords to nominate to bishoprics: the reverend fathers sometimes having at least gratitude of further expectations, if they have no patriotism."[44]

After Grafton enticed the Bedfords into the ministry in early 1768, the opposition in the Lords was dealt a numerically decisive blow, and under the more stable administrations of Grafton and North the bishops returned to general support of the government. Grafton himself was a fairly able dispenser of episcopal patronage, and from 1768 increased episcopal mortality created more opportunities for him (and later North) to alter the bench's composition.[45] By 1769 most of Newcastle's former episcopal supporters were either dead, supporting the Court, or abstaining.[46] In the well-attended and Wilkes-dominated session of 1770, the

---

When Lincoln broke with Newcastle and followed Pitt, Hume remained loyal to the Duke. For Lincoln's role in Hume's translation to Salisbury, see Sykes, "Newcastle as Ecclesiastical Minister," *EHR*, LVII(1942), 80-81, and the draft of Lincoln's letter to Pitt, [27 July 1766], Newcastle (Clumber) MSS, NeC 2960. Hume was unmoved by Lincoln's stinging reply (NeC 2962), and prior to the next session sent Newcastle a blank proxy, "which can be filled up by whomsoever you please should represent me." BL, Hume to Newcastle, 19 Nov. 1767, Newcastle Papers, Add. MS 32987, f. 51.

42. Newton, *Works*, I, 115; Bury St. Edmunds and West Suffolk Record Office, Newton to Grafton, 3 and 22 Aug. 1768, Grafton MSS, 423/344, 423/346. In the first of these letters Newton wrote: "I would also scorn to solicit a favor, if I did not mean to be grateful for it."

43. E.g., Bishop Hinchliffe was a loyal follower of the Duke of Grafton, going into opposition with him in the autumn of 1775 (Bodleian Library, Bishop North to Lord Guilford, [27 Oct. 1775], North MSS, d. ff. 47-49); while Bishop Ewer followed the Marquess of Granby (his former pupil) and the Duke of Rutland, voting with the opposition on several occasions in the mid-1760s and early 1770s.

44. Walpole, *Memoirs of George III*, III, 45-46.

45. Between August 1768 and May 1775, ten bishops died, resulting in the same number of elevations and eight translations.

46. For example, in the division of 2 Mar. 1769, relative to the Civil List, only one bishop (Keppel) voted with the opposition, while six voted with the Court and four

fledgling North ministry was able to count on overwhelming episcopal support.[47]

It appeared as though normality was returning. Yet the extent to which the bishops represented ministerial props in the 1770s can easily be exaggerated. There remained a small minority of bishops who continued to vote with the opposition: Keppel kept up his family's tie with the Rockinghams, Ewer was in opposition in 1770 and 1771, Lowth voted with the opposition in 1770 and again on the Royal Marriage Bill in 1772, while from the early 1770s Shipley of St. Asaph acted with the Chathamites.[48] While this was a far cry from the opposition episcopal majorities of 1767, it did mean that the bench's support of Grafton and North was never absolute.

Inconsistent attendance also did much to damage the bench's traditional characterization as a ministerial voting bloc. After the session of 1770, the numbers attending divisions in support of the North ministry were seldom impressive, save on the defeats of the Dissenters' Relief Bills.[49] Otherwise numerical support by the bench during the early 1770s was mediocre at best. Compare in the following Table, the average attendance of bishops on days of political divisions during the middle and later 1760s (when bishops were frequently in opposition) with that for the first half of the 1770s:[50]

---

abstained: Sheffield Central Library, WWM, R1-1258. Of those who had voted with Newcastle in 1767, one (Hume) voted with the government and two others (Green and Johnson) abstained.

47. Only Keppel and Ewer voted regularly with the opposition in 1770, while Bishop Lowth did so once (Sheffield Central Library, WWM, R5).

48. On Shipley, see Peter Brown, *The Chathamites* (London, 1967), pp. 325-38. On Lowth, see Horace Walpole, *Journal of the Reign of King George the Third from the Year 1771 to 1783*, ed. J. Doran (London, 1859), I, 36-37, 94-95.

49. Twenty-one bishops attended the second reading of the initial Dissenters' Relief Bill on 19 May 1772 (*JHL*, XXXIII, 416) and seventeen the second on 2 April 1773 (*ibid.*, 597-98). Both bills were supported by the Rockinghamite and Chathamite oppositions and were defeated by large margins. A division list for the 1772 bill shows all bishops present voting against the bill (Public Record Office, State Papers Domestic, 37/10, f. 219), while a minority list for the 1773 division includes only Green of Lincoln among the bishops present (*Parliamentary History*, XVII, 790-91). The King and North relied on the bishops to follow their own inclinations in throwing out these bills, and let them pass through the Commons. Rochford, the government leader in the Lords, orchestrated their defeat behind the scenes. See George III to North and reply, 2 April 1772, *Correspondence of George III*, II, 334-35; and Rochford to various bishops and peers, 27 March [1773], *Calendar of Home Office Papers of the Reign of George III, 1770-1772*, ed. R. A. Roberts (London, 1881), p. 64.

50. These figures have been arrived at by averaging the daily episcopal attendance recorded in the *JHL* on days of political divisions. The number of days of such divisions in each session were: 1765, six; 1765-66, seven; 1766-67, nine; 1767-68, one; 1768-69, three; 1770, fourteen; 1770-71, eleven; 1772, six; 1772-73, eight; 1774, five; 1774-75, ten. When the two Dissenters' Relief Bills are eliminated, the average episcopal attendance on days of divisions in 1772 and 1772-73 is reduced to 14.8 and 5.0 respectively.

TABLE II

AVERAGE EPISCOPAL ATTENDANCE ON DAYS OF POLITICAL
DIVISIONS (BY SESSION), 1765-1775

Session	1765	1765-6	1766-7	1767-8	1768-9
Average	15.3	15.4	15.7	17	11.3
Session	1770	1770-1	1772	1772-3	1774	1774-5
Average	16.2	11.3	15.8	6.5	6.2	11.6

In only one session after 1770 were even half the bishops likely to attend on days of political divisions, and when the possibility is considered that one or two of those may have voted with the opposition and others may have abstained, the bench's potential as a ministerial bloc is further reduced.[51] North's bishops were a far cry from Walpole's "well-drilled cohorts."

It is thus easy to overrate the bishops' importance as a prominsterial force. During much of the 1760s many bishops — at times a majority — were sympathetic to the various combinations of politicians who composed the opposition, while during the later 1760s and 1770s, when the majority of bishops could once again be reckoned among the Court's supporters, the bench's attendance was such as to deprive the ministers of a significant proportion of its numerical strength.

II.

As with the bishops, the Scottish representative peers have usually been seen as the willing props of a permanent ministerial majority, this position being the result of non-hereditary recruitment which, it was felt, made them peculiarly liable to manipulation by the government. The parliamentary status of the Scottish peerage was defined by the Act of Union of 1707: Scottish peers were granted all the rights and privileges of the peers of England (and subsequent peers of Great Britain) save those of sitting and voting in the House of Lords and sitting upon the trial of peers. Instead the Scottish peerage was to be represented at Westminster by sixteen of their number, elected by the body of adult, Protestant Scottish peers. Elections for all sixteen places were to be held at each general election, with any interim vacancies supplied at by-elections. Further limitations on the Scottish peers eligible to vote or be chosen were effected by the House of Lords in 1709 and 1711.[52]

---

51. Though systematic reckoning of abstentions is impossible, the superficial impression left by surviving voting lists is that bishops were more likely to abstain than were other categories of the House's membership. Of 47 abstentions specifically noted on voting lists that relate to the whole House during our period, 11 (or just over 23%) were by bishops. See the voting records in my Ph.D. thesis, pp. 968-74.

52. 6 Anne. c. 11. c. 78; Sir James Fergusson, *The Sixteen Peers of Scotland* (Oxford, 1960), pp. 13-19. In 1709 the House of Lords decided that no peer sitting in the House

The partisan struggles of Anne's reign placed a premium on sixteen additional votes in the upper House, and almost on the morrow of the Union, ministers began the practice of exerting government influence to secure a slate of friendly representative peers. The process became institutionalized in the form of the "Queen's List" (or "King's List" after 1714), inclusion on which was tantamount to nomination to the House of Lords.[53] The regularity with which this list was returned during the first eight decades of the eighteenth century has led historians to assume that the peers who composed it followed obediently along in the wake of the ministry of the day, with their loyalty further ensured by the need to maintain access to government patronage.

Little of the traditional view of the Scottish representative peers is the product of actual examination of their parliamentary record. A recent study of the Scottish peerage during the 1780s and 1790s, by Dr. Michael W. McCahill, has shown less consistency in the politics of the representative peers than might be thought. Viewing their activities as part of an assertive trend towards equality and integration with the British peerage, McCahill shows that even in the days of Dundas's power, peers' elections were not always conducted according to the wishes of government and that individual representative peers often associated themselves with the parliamentary opposition.[54]

Though the parliamentary activities of the Scottish representative peers in the 1760s and 1770s were not always affected by the same influences as later in the century, the available evidence (and voting records are much more abundant for the 1760s and 1770s than later) shows that the representative peers' contribution to the upper House's politics was neither consistent nor uniform, though often because of different reasons than those described in McCahill's article.[55]

Any inquiry into the parliamentary role played by the Scottish representative peers must begin with consideration of their attendance. As with the bishops, it is not unreasonable to expect regular habits of

by virtue of a British peerage could vote in peers' elections, while in 1711 the House decreed that no British peerage granted to one who was a peer of Scotland at the time of the Union could entitle that peer to sit in the upper House: *JHL*, XVIII, 609, XIX, 346-47; Geoffrey S. Holmes, "The Hamilton Affair of 1711-12, A Crisis in Anglo-Scottish Relations," *EHR*, 77 (1962); above, 151-76. The House reversed the first decision in 1793 and the second in 1782.

53.   Holmes, *Politics in the Age of Anne*, p. 395.

54.   McCahill, "Scottish Peerage and the House of Lords," *Scottish Historical Review*, LI(1972), 177-96; below, 288-307.

55.   One of the most important differences in the influences on the parliamentary conduct of the Scottish peers in the 1760s and 1770s and the last two decades of the century is that during the earlier period the assertion of equality with the English peerage, stressed in McCahill's article, is not nearly as noticeable. A related difference is that in the 1780s and 1790s most of the greater Scottish peers who did not already possess British peerages received them, while before 1782 all but a handful of Scottish peers had perforce to center their parliamentary ambitions on peers' elections. On this, see note 79 below.

attendance, especially since the Scots, alone among the House's members, were chosen for the sole purpose of sitting in parliament. A few Scots, such as the Earls of Marchmont and Abercorn, were among the House's best attenders, though others, such as Lord Irvine and the fourth Marquess of Lothian, were regular only in their absences.[56] Most fell somewhere in between, and many were very erratic in their habits of attendance.

Regarding the Scots as a group during the period 1760-75, it is difficult to come to any conclusion save that they were disappointing attenders. The sixteen certainly never attended *en bloc*: the quiet session of 1761-62 was the only one of the entire period to witness the personal attendance of all representative peers. In general, Scottish attendance was better in the first few sessions of the reign, in 1768-69, and in 1774-75. During the early 1770s Scottish attendance fell off markedly. The beginning of each session brought letters from representative peers informing ministers of their impending absence,[57] and increasing numbers of Scots missed entire sessions. Six did not attend at all in the session of 1770, and the next 3 sessions were completely missed by 7, 9, and 7 representative peers respectively. Though the attendance of the Scots picked up in 1774-75 and was good in later years,[58] their performance in the early 1770s does little to justify their traditional reputation.

The political importance of the Scots' habits of attendance can be further clarified by looking at their participation on days of political divisions. The following table shows the sessional average of attendance by representative peers on these •days from the mid-1760s to the mid-1770s:[59]

---

56. Marchmont and Abercorn each attended the House more than fifty times a session in all of the fifteen sessions from 1760 to 1775. Lothian attended the House in only two of the six sessions he was a representative peer (1768-74), while Irvine attended the House but thirty-one times in eight sessions following his election in 1768.

57. For example, Scottish Record Office, the Earl of Stair to Lord [Suffolk or Rochford], 17 Nov. 1772 (copy), Stair MSS, GD 135/167; the Earl of Breadalbane to Suffolk, 1 Dec. 1774, *Calendar of Home Office Papers of the Reign of George III, 1773-1775*, ed. R. A. Roberts (London, 1889), p. 261. On behalf of the representative peers, it might be pointed out that they seem to have left proxies more frequently than did the bishops. Of 921 proxies entered in the Proxy Books between November 1760 and May 1775, 101 (or almost 11%) were from representative peers (who composed approximately 8% of the House's membership).

58. McCahill has studied Scottish attendance in detail for several sessions in the 1780s and 1790s and concluded that "a significant proportion of representative peers were very active members of the House" ("Scottish Peerage and the House of Lords," *Scottish Historical Review*, LI (below, 298). See also his table on "Levels of Participation" on p. 297. As far as the 1760s and 1770s are concerned, it is open to question how far participation on select committees can be equated with involvement in parliamentary politics. Most of the important (and partisan) legislation of this period was submitted to a committee of the whole House. Select committees usually dealt with public bills of less than national importance as well as private bills. Their primary political importance was probably in providing a means whereby peers could influence legislation affecting the localities in which they had interests.

59. These averages have been arrived at by the same process (changing bishops for Scots) described in note 50 above.

TABLE III

AVERAGE ATTENDANCE BY SCOTTISH REPRESENTATIVE
PEERS ON DAYS OF POLITICAL DIVISIONS (BY SESSION)
1765-1775

Session	1765	1765-6	1766-7	1767-8	1768-9
Average	9.7	7.7	6.9	10	8
Session	1770	1770-1	1772	1772-3	1774	1774-5
Average	5.4	6.1	5.5	4.9	6.5	8.5

On the 84 days of this period that witnessed political divisions, the attendance of Scottish representative peers amounted to less than eight percent (the proportion of the House's membership made up by the 16) on 57 of the days. Thus the Scots failed to distinguish themselves from the rest of the House by virtue of their attendance on precisely those days when their voting support was most required.

Indeed contemporaries were aware of the frequent absences of Scottish peers, and George III commended on it on more than one occasion. In 1770 he gave as one of his reasons for approving the candidacy of Lord Dysart, an Englishman with a Scottish peerage, the prospect that "he will undoubtedly prove a constant attender," and four years later the King talked Lord Abercorn out of retiring by telling him that he was "one of the few of the Sixteen that had regularly attended and one of the still fewer peers that attended private Bills."[60]

Those Scottish peers who did attend usually kept a low profile, and only about 5 or 6 of the 33 individuals who sat as representative peers during this period played a conspicuous role in the House's political or legislative affairs. Lord Bute was of course a central figure in the early and middle 1760s.[61] Less well-known, though more consistent, was the constant political support and parliamentary advice given each ministry of the period by the third Earl of Marchmont.[62] A few Scots aided the operation of the House by chairing committees, often on mundane pieces of legislation.[63] Apart from an occasional speech, how-

---

60. George III to North, 9 Nov. 1770 and 5 Oct. 1774, *Correspondence of George III*, II, 166; III, 141.

61. John Brewer, "The Earl of Bute," in *The Prime Ministers*, ed. Herbert Van Thal (New York, 1975), pp. 105-13. Despite the fact that Bute exercised an important influence throughout the early and middle 1760s, his personal impact on the House of Lords was surprisingly slight. After his less than spectacular ministerial leadership of the House, Bute seldom attended (though he remained a representative peer until 1780), and his post-ministerial parliamentary career was highlighted only by his "private" opposition to the Rockingham administration's American policy in 1766.

62. See, for example, Marchmont to Rockingham, 1 Feb. [1766], Sheffield Central Library, WWM, R1-569; National Library of Scotland, William Fraser to Marchmont and draft reply, 9 Oct. 1774, Marchmont-Rose Correspondence, MS 3523, ff. 58-59.

63. Marchmont, Abercorn, and Cathcart all chaired various select committees and occasional committees of the whole House during this period: HLRO, Manuscript Minutes, Minute Books, 1760-61 to 1774-75, Committee Books, 1760-61 to 1774-75.

ever, few of the other Scots made much of an impression in parliamentary affairs.

Despite erratic attendance and general lack of parliamentary prominence, something of the representative peers' reputation could be salvaged if it were demonstrable that when present, the Scots invariably supported the ministry of the day. This, however, was not the case, especially in the mid-1760s when ministers were weakest and such bloc support was most needed. While it may be argued that the six Scots present (with two proxies) who voted against the repeal of the Stamp Act in March 1766 represented an exceptional instance, owing to the King's unwillingness to punish those voting against that measure from conviction, five of the six had opposed earlier that session, as had two other Scots.[64] Indeed the first Rockingham administration had a very difficult time with the representative peers: in three of the four largest divisions of the 1765-66 session, more representative peers voted against the government than with it.[65]

Rockingham was not the only minister to face opposition from Scottish representative peers. Lord Dunmore crossed Bute in February 1762 by voting (in the first division of the reign) for a premature resolution against the war in Germany.[66] Three or four Scots (out of nine who attended it) voted against Gilbert's Poor Bill in 1765.[67] In 1767, three Scottish peers were once again to be found in opposition during the parliamentary crisis of that session.[68] In short, ten different representative peers voted in person against the ministry of the day in at least one division between 1762 and 1767, and two more did so by proxy. Six Scottish signatures appear on the protests of the same period.[69]

---

64. Abercorn, Bute, Cathcart, Eglinton, Loudon, and March all opposed the repeal in person, Rothes and Sutherland did so by proxy: BL, Newcastle Papers, Add. MS 33035, ff. 389-91. All of these but Cathcart and the proctorial votes had opposed in the divisions lost by administration on 4 and 6 Feb. (Ibid., ff. 276-77; Sheffield Central Library, WWM, R53-6), as had the Duke of Argyll. Lord Morton also voted against the government on 4 Feb. Abercorn had opposed at the opening of the session (BL, Newcastle Papers, Add. MS 33035, f. 206). Three representative peers (Argyll, Dunmore, and Marchmont) voted for the repeal of the Stamp Act in person and three more (Breadalbane, Hyndford, and Stormont) did so by proxy.

65. These were those of 4 and 6 Feb. and 11 March 1766. No Scots were in the minority of five (against 125) that opposed the "Declaratory" resolution of 3 Feb. 1766. Another Scottish opposition vote in the session was recorded by Eglinton on the Window Tax Bill in May 1766: *Correspondence of George III*, I, 344.

66. BL, Newcastle Papers, Add. MS 33035, ff. 69-70.

67. Sheffield Central Library, WWM, R53-22, R53-9; BL, Newcastle Papers, Add. MS 32966, ff. 149, 156, 158-59. Abercorn and Breadalbane voted with the opposition in all three divisions, and Morton did so in the first two. Eglinton may also have opposed in the second: Rockingham, author of the list for this division, was unsure of the exact composition of the majority and included Eglinton as a possible opposition vote.

68. Abercorn, Breadalbane, and Eglinton all appeared in the opposition at various points in the session: BL, Newcastle Papers, Add. MS 33036, ff. 451-54; Add. MS 33037, ff. 17-19, 51-54, 73-74, 77-78, 111-12, 115-16, 119, 151-52, 155.

69. Thorold Rogers, *Complete Protests*, II, 63-98.

After 1768 the representative peers, like the bishops, returned to a more consistent support of the Grafton and North ministries, though this support was neither numerically impressive nor unqualified. The early 1770s, as we have seen, witnessed a decline in the Scots' parliamentary attendance, and there continued to be occasional defectors. In 1768 the tenth Earl of Eglinton voted against the second East India Company Dividend Bill, while in 1773 the Duke of Atholl swam against the ministerial tide in supporting the second Dissenters' Relief Bill.[70] More conspicuous, and embarrassing to the administration, was Lord Stair's outspoken advocacy of the American colonists in 1774, for which he received the thanks of the Council of Massachusetts Bay.[71] It was, in fact, only after the sixteen peers elected in November 1774 took their seats that the Scottish representative peers began to combine fairly regular attendance with unstinting support for the ministry of the day.[72]

Lack of consistent attendance did much to reduce the effectiveness of the representative peers as a ministerial bloc, especially their habit of missing entire sessions. One obvious barrier to frequent attendance was distance. With a few exceptions, the representative peers were still residents of Scotland, and the journey to the capital required sustained absence from their estates. The Dukes of Atholl and Gordon, active estate improvers (as were increasing numbers of Scottish peers), alternated winters in London with year-round residence in Scotland from the session of 1768-69 to that of 1774.[73] The readiness of other peers to attend the House was reduced by the pursuit of careers in state service. Four representative peers of our period held government posts that required extended residence outside the country and thus necessitated extended absence from the House of Lords.[74]

Another important factor affecting both the attendance and parliamentary conduct of the Scots was their perception of the role of representative peer. To most Scottish peers parliamentary status was conceived of primarily as an honor, rather than as a call to political battle,

---

70. BL, Newcastle Papers, Add. MS 33036, f. 285; *Parliamentary History*, XVII, 790-91.

71. Scottish Record Office, William Bollan (Massachusetts Agent) to Stair, 29 Sept. 1774, Stair MSS, GD 135/167, f. 131. Stair also wrote two pamphlets on American affairs.

72. For example, in 1774-75 eleven of the representative peers attended the House twenty times or better, and as Table III shows, on average slightly over half attended on days of important business. There is no record of any representative peer voting with the opposition during the session.

73. Atholl attended the House in 1768-69, 1770-71, and 1772-73; Gordon in 1770, 1772, and 1774. From 1770-71 to 1772-73 the one attending held the other's proxy: HLRO, Proxy Books, 1770-71 to 1772-73.

74. Lord Stormont was envoy to Warsaw (1756-61) and ambassador to Austria (1763-72) and France (1772-78). Cathcart was ambassador to Russia (1768-71). Dunmore was resident governor of New York (1770-71) and Virginia (1771-75). Rothes was commander-in-chief of the forces in Ireland (1758-67).

and it was often mentioned in the same breath as the Order of the Thistle.[75] Lord Breadalbane's reaction was typical, when he reported to his son-in-law that he had been returned to the "King's List" after a six-year absence:

> Being in tolerable good health, I hope to be able to bear the fatigue of a few sessions with the assistance of a Proxy. & it is a feather in the Cap of my family, which in this part of the Kingdom is look'd upon in a higher light than it really deserves.[76]

That English contemporaries (and later historians) failed to understand the Scottish view of representative status is due largely to their interpretation of the "King's List." It has traditionally been seen as the means by which the needy Scottish peerage sold its political soul, providing English ministers with sixteen reliable votes in return for access to the largesse of the state.[77] It is obvious that government influence was employed with considerable success in the election of representative peers and many Scots did show their gratitude by loyally supporting the King's ministers. Yet this is not a rounded picture of the "King's List," nor is it valid for all periods of the century. The manipulation of peers' elections originated in the partisan struggles of Anne's reign, and received its definitive form under Archibald Campbell, first Earl of Islay and (from 1743) third Duke of Argyll.[78] Under Walpole and the Pelhams the loyalty of the northern kingdom was a very real concern. The "King's List" was more than a simple exchange designed to net sixteen government votes, and early on began to show itself as part of the complex fabric of Scottish patronage. This in effect limited the possible choice to the great families of Scotland, and their titles and family names are constantly repeated among the sixteen over the course of the century.[79] Bute and his brother (James Stuart MacKenzie) controlled

75. See, for example, National Library of Scotland, Atholl to John Mackenzie of Delvine, 13 July 1767, Delvine MS 1405, f. 161.
76. BL, Breadalbane to Hardwicke, 11 Oct. 1774, Hardwicke Papers, Add. MS 35421, f. 216.
77. For example, see the Duke of Richmond's comments to the House on 10 March 1780, in a debate on a motion for a list of places and pensions held by peers: *Parliamentary History*, XXI, 231-32.
78. John M. Simpson, "Who Steered the Gravy Train, 1707-1766?" *Scotland in the Age of Improvement*, eds. N. T. Phillipson and Rosalind Mitchison (Edinburgh, 1970), pp. 47-72.
79. One of the reasons for this was the lack of alternate ways, apart from the Order of the Thistle, with which the greater Scottish families could mark their importance. The decision of the House of Lords in 1711 (mentioned in note 52 above) effectively forbade the creation of existing Scottish peers as British peers until reversed in 1782. This ban could only be circumvented by the grant of a British peerage to the heir of a Scottish peer who, when succeeding to the Scottish title, combined the two titles and continued to sit in the House of Lords by virtue of the British title. (McCahill's contention, below, ch. 14, p. 287, n. 2, that such peers had to be returned among the sixteen representative peers after succeeding to the Scottish peerage is incorrect.) The relative rarity of creations of eldest sons is witnessed by the fact that in 1775 only four Scottish

Scottish patronage from Argyll's death in 1761 until 1765, but were offered only one opportunity of choosing a representative peer. In the latter 1760s, English ministers began to cast their nets wider and provoked the first seriously contested peers' elections since 1734, with the government being compelled to drop their original nominee in 1771.[80]

The tendency of Scottish peers to see their parliamentary status primarily as an honor helps to explain one of the most noticeable aspects of the Scots' parliamentary performance: their general lack of integration into the partisan politics of the upper House. Though most representative peers seemed willing to follow Bute in the early 1760s, few later affiliated with the parties of the great English politicos. Even Lord Stair, in open opposition in 1774, described himself as an individual looking to "disinterested principles" rather than as a follower of Rockingham or Chatham.[81] Nor did those who generally supported the ministry of the day do so with much enthusiasm. Lord Marchmont, perhaps the only representative peer of this period to establish a record combining regular attendance with support for each successive government, held a low opinion of those he served.[82] The Duke of Atholl, who normally supported the ministers during his alternate sessions in London, disliked politics in general, commenting in 1770 that "Ther's faults on all sides & Evry days experience Convinces me that Planting Trees is a more agreeable & more honest business than either supporting or opposing Ministers."[83]

In fact, to judge from a sampling of their correspondence, it would appear that many representative peers simply lacked interest in the partisan politics that increasingly marked the upper House's conduct of affairs.[84] They were much more interested in such Scottish affairs as

peers sat in the House of Lords by virtue of British peerages granted after 1711: the Dukes of Argyll (as Lord Sundridge), Roxburghe (as Earl Ker), and Montrose (as Earl Graham) and the Earl of Kinnoull (as Lord Hay). A fifth, the Duke of Buccleuch, sat as Earl of Doncaster by virtue of an English peerage granted to a seventeenth-century ancestor.

80. Lord Irvine, an Englishman with a Scottish peerage, was elected in 1768. The ministers' nomination of Lord Dysart, another Englishman, in 1771 provoked an opposition among the Scottish peers that continued (unsuccessfully) after the ministers threw over Dysart for Stair. The General Election of 1774 was also contested. See Fergusson, *Sixteen Peers*, pp. 81-84; and McCahill, "Scottish Peerage and the House of Lords," *Scottish Historical Review*, LI(1972), 178-83; below, 289-94.

81. Scottish Record Office, Stair to William Bollan, 4 Oct. 1774 (copy), Stair MSS, GD 135/167, f. 131.

82. See, for example, National Library of Scotland, Marchmont to George Rose, 25 Dec. 1774 and 8 Jan. 1775, Marchmont-Rose Correspondence, MS 3523, ff. 85, 87. In the first letter Marchmont wrote: "The whole of this reign looks to me like a stone going down hill that never rests till it come to the lowest point of all."

83. National Library of Scotland, Atholl to John Mackenzie of Delvine, 10 Dec. 1770, Delvine MS 1406, ff. 117-18. The previous day Atholl had described the House's proceedings as "only helping one another to do nothing," paraphrasing Gay: "Its all a Farce & all things show it I thought so once but now I know it" (Ibid., f. 115).

84. It is interesting to note in this regard that only six of the thirty-three Scots who

came before the House. It is instructive in this regard to compare the attendance of representative peers in the two sessions of 1768-69 and 1772. The first was the session in which the celebrated Douglas peerage case reached the House of Lords (on appeal from the Court of Session), a case arousing great interest in Scotland.[85] The second was the session dominated by the Royal Marriage Bill, a measure in which the King took a greater personal interest than in any other of the period.[86] The session of 1768-69 was one of those best attended by Scots, and nine representative peers were present on twenty or more occasions. In 1772, nine of the representative peers did not attend the House at all, and only four came as often as twenty times.[87] If the Scots were really the integral part of the "Party of the Crown" that they have traditionally been pictured, this disparity is difficult to explain. Rather, many appear to have been essentially non-political aristocrats who may normally (but not invariably) have supported the government when in the House, but who regarded their parliamentary status primarily as an honor.

III.

Available evidence about the bishops and Scottish representative peers during the first fifteen years of George III's reign makes it clear that the degree and regularity of support manifested by these essential constituents of the "Party of the Crown" were not of the order to justify their usual characterization as significant means of ministerial control in the House of Lords. In order to be institutionalized, a voting bloc must be dependable, especially during times of sustained political activity and crisis, and it was during the three critical sessions from 1765 to 1768 that the Scots and (especially) the bishops signally failed to perform in a uniform manner. There was, to be sure, some importance in enhancing already established ministerial majorities, as bishops and representative peers did to varying degrees after 1768. This, however, is not the same as acting as a means by which control of the House is established in the first instance.

From the activities of the Scots and bishops may be drawn a larger lesson. The true character of the upper House's political structure in these years is to be found less in "automatic" majorities than in the

---

sat as representative peers during this period had previous parliamentary experience in the Commons. By contrast, the 250 British and English peers who sat in the House from 1760 to 1775 numbered 127 former M.P.s.

85. BL, Breadalbane to Hardwicke, 25 Aug. 1767, Hardwicke Papers, Add. MS 35451, f. 172. On the Douglas case, see A. Frances Steuart (ed.), *The Douglas Cause* (Glasgow and Edinburgh, 1909).

86. For example, see his letters to North of 4 and 26 Feb. 1772, *Correspondence of George III*, II, 310, 325.

87. Though seven of the Scots left proxies, three of the five divisions on the bill took place in commiteee: HLRO, Manuscript Minutes, Minute Book 1772.

mainstream of national politics. The issues and alignments of the 1760s and 1770s that led first to ministerial instability and then to more than a decade of stable government with a permanent opposition determined as much the parliamentary politics of the Lords as they did those of the Commons. Indeed the dominating colonial issue of 1774 and 1775 did much to restore a semblance of the conduct traditionally expected of bishops and representative peers in the last sessions before the war.[88] The eighteenth-century House of Lords was not a static institution, and anyone seeking the character of its proceedings at any particular point in the century should look first at the content of its politics rather than the recruitment of its members.

---

88. For example, Bishop Ewer and Lord Breadalbane, both of whom had voted in the opposition earlier in the period, both supported punitive measures against the colonies. Many bishops were alienated by opposition to an American episcopate, and Ewer termed the colonists "infidels and barbarians . . . living without remembrance or knowledge of God" on this score. *A Sermon Preached before the Incorporated Society for the Propagation of the Gospel in Foreign Parts at their Anniversary Meeting . . . February 20, 1767* (London, 1767). Breadalbane felt American resistance was "as much a Rebellion as those of 1715 & 1745" and that "all the Sophistry of Opposition" could not prove it otherwise. BL, letter to Hardwicke, 11 Dec. 1775, Hardwicke Papers, Add. MS 35451, f. 220.

14

THE SCOTTISH PEERAGE AND THE HOUSE OF LORDS
IN THE LATE EIGHTEENTH CENTURY

MICHAEL W. McCAHILL

The whigs of the late eighteenth century, who gloried in the balance and precision of the British constitution and strove to preserve its purity intact, did not attempt to hide their horror and distaste when they looked upon the sixteen representative peers of Scotland who sat in parliament by virtue of the act of union. Instead of being independent spokesmen of their order those noblemen were the docile satellites of the crown. Worse still, their abject adherence resulted neither from principle nor from an appreciation of ministerial talents but from the government's control of peerage elections and its liberal distribution of patronage into Scottish pockets.[1]

Modern historians, despite their normally sceptical attitude towards whig complaints, have accepted the Foxite indictment of the Scots peers and consigned them to membership of the 'party of the crown'.[2] In so doing, these scholars obscure the role played by the Scottish members of the house of lords. Like the whigs, modern historians have assumed that the government did dominate Scottish politics between 1770 and 1800. In fact, the system of management was in a state of considerable flux in the last decades of the eighteenth century, and even Henry Dundas could not consolidate his power until the late 1790s. Equally, historians have

---

1   In a debate on Scottish pensions Fox complained that it cost as much to keep the Scots in good humour as it had to crush the rebellion (P[arliamentary] H[istory], xxi, 21 Feb. 1780, 94). *The Rolliad: Probationary Odes and Political Miscellanies* (London, 1795), 167, summarised the whig distaste for Scottish peers with unusual venom:

> Alike in loyalty, alike in worth,
> Behold the sixteen nobles of the north:
> Fast friends to monarchy, yet sprung from those
> Who basely sold their monarch to his foes:
> Since which, atoning for their father's crime,
> The sons, as basely, sell themselves to him:
> With ev'ry change prepar'd to change their note,
> With ev'ry Government prepar'd to vote,
> Save when, perhaps, on some important bill,
> They know by second sight, the royal will.

2   Richard Pares, *George III and the Politicians* (Oxford, 1953), 41–42; A. S. Turberville, *The House of Lords in the Age of Reform, 1784–1837*, ed. R. J. White (London, 1958), 107–11; David Large, 'The decline of the "Party of the Crown" and the rise of parties in the House of Lords, 1783–1837', *Eng. Hist. Rev.*, lxxviii (1963), 677–8 ; above, 241-2.

often failed to take into account the changes which occurred in
Scotland in these years, changes which had a momentous effect
upon the Scottish peers and which served to cement the bonds
between England and Scotland.

The basis for political order in Scotland in the second half of the
eighteenth century was laid by Archibald, third Duke of Argyll.
The duke possessed enormous personal influence in the west highlands and was also an adroit political manoeuvrer. But his unquestioned supremacy derived from the confidence which the government reposed in him. Without this support his position would have
been an empty one, since only London could provide the jobs and
pensions a manager needed to control Scotland.[1] Thus, when the
Rockinghams withdrew their support from the next manager,
James Stuart Mackenzie, he ceased to exercise any significant
influence in Scottish politics.

Stuart Mackenzie's fall in 1765 marks the beginning of a political
interregnum in Scotland which lasted until Henry Dundas began
to consolidate his position in the 1780s. During the intervening
years ministers, plagued by political instability, were unable to
secure the services of men of Argyll's calibre. Instead they were
forced to undertake the burden of management themselves.[2] Given
the leading politicians' ignorance of Scotland and the rapacity
of their Scottish advisers, the results of the new system were bound
to be unsatisfactory. In fact by 1770 even peerage elections, usually
the most decorous of events, were proving difficult to manage.

In restoring order to Scottish politics Dundas, like Argyll, relied
primarily upon the support of the London government. Pitt gave his
colleague full authority in Scotland and, armed with vast stores of
jobs and pensions, Dundas created an impressive political empire.
Yet the traditional inducements were insufficient to eliminate
opposition. The whig party continued to grow until the time of the
French Revolution, and at the election of 1790 Dundas even had to
surrender six representative peers to his opponents.[3] In short,
conditions within Scotland had changed to the extent that the
factors which had permitted Argyll to exercise virtually unquestioned
leadership were insufficient to guarantee Dundas a similar hegemony.

1   J. M. Simpson, 'Who steered the gravy train, 1707–1766?' in *Scotland in the
Age of Improvement*, ed. N. T. Phillipson and Rosalind Mitchison (Edinburgh,
1970), 60–69.
2   Stuart Mackenzie correctly assumed that the direction of Scotland would
pass to the responsible government departments on his retirement (*Selections from
the Family Papers Preserved at Caldwell*, ed. William Mure [Glasgow, 1854], ii, 34–
35; Rosalind Mitchison, *A History of Scotland* [London, 1970], 343).
3   *The Correspondence of George, Prince of Wales, 1770–1812*, ed. Arthur Aspinall
(London, 1963), ii, no. 517, Portland to Capt. Payne, 27 July 1790.

Between 1760 and 1790 Scotland was awakened and in many respects transformed by the stimulus of its own 'renaissance' and by a period of prolonged economic growth. The Scottish Enlightenment at once enhanced the pride and self-consciousness of the Scots and awakened them to a more appreciative understanding of the positive influence England had had upon its northern partner. Such men as Alexander Carlyle and David Hume welcomed the introduction of English ideas and institutions. At the same time they hoped to redefine the Union in such a manner that Scotland would be elevated from her subordinate position to a full and equal partnership with England.[1]

While the Enlightenment forced Scots to re-examine their attitudes towards England, economic growth led to a rise in incomes which permitted more of them to mingle extensively in English society. Between 1750 and 1815 there was an estimated eightfold increase in rents.[2] Enriched by this development, lesser peers and country gentlemen began to join the great magnates on their annual trek to London. More and more of their children were sent to English schools and universities to complete their education. Within Scotland itself the improvements at Inveraray Castle and the construction of Hopetoun House are splendid monuments to the determination of the Scottish peers to live in surroundings as magnificent as those of any English noble family.[3]

Such momentous changes were bound to have repercussions on Scottish political life. Many lawyers and landlords recognized that Scotland had been fundamentally altered by its dependence on its southern neighbour. They welcomed the prospect of further change, but they were aware that it was first necessary to free themselves from the cultural and political practices of the past. In their attempts to adapt their country's political structure to changing realities, some were drawn into the new Scottish whig party, whose members took the lead in a variety of Scottish reform movements. They sought to expand the political nation by reforming the burghs and enlarging the county suffrage; they encouraged the introduction of English judicial principles by advocating a system based on civil

---

1   [A. Carlyle], *The Question Relating to a Scots Militia Considered* . . . (Edinburgh, 1760), 25–26; Janet Adam Smith, 'Some eighteenth-century ideas of Scotland', *Scotland in the Age of Improvement*, 108–13.
2   R. H. Campbell, *Scotland since 1707* (Oxford, 1965), 153. Between 1774 and 1815 the annual income of the Breadalbane properties increased from £4,914 to £23,000 (Malcolm Gray, *The Highland Economy, 1750–1850* [Edinburgh, 1957], 147).
3   One consequence of anglicization was that landlords found themselves cut off from their neighbours. John Ramsay doubted if a neighbouring peer, whose wealth permitted him to spend much time in England, would ever be a true Angus man. See *Letters of John Ramsay of Ochertyre, 1799–1812*, ed. B. L. H. Horn (S[cottish] H[istory] S[ociety], 1966), 58.

jury trials; and they attempted to restore Scottish control of peerage elections.[1]

As important as these new goals was the persistence with which they were upheld. In 1760 parliament refused to extend the militia to Scotland. Some Scots responded by organising the Poker Club, whose members endeavoured over the next twenty years to rectify what they considered a denial of Scotland's just rights. The pride induced by their own achievements had made some Scots less willing to acquiesce on all occasions in the wishes of England. At the same time, increased rent rolls permitted men who had formerly been dependent upon the largesse of government to oppose its wishes.[2]

Obviously, if Dundas wished to consolidate his power he had to deal with the awakening aspirations in a manner acceptable to a proud and increasingly independent people. Though he under-took to secure such legislation as his important allies favoured,[3] the range of demands for change was so diverse that he could not satisfy everyone. Moreover, some of the proposed reforms, including the expansion of the suffrage and the elimination of government in-fluence at peerage elections, worked directly against his own political interests. So long as those causes attracted significant sup-port the whigs were able to prevent Dundas from absolutely con-trolling Scotland. Only when the hysteria created by the French Revolution submerged these essentially local issues was he finally able to rout his opponents and consolidate his power.

The Scottish peers, while eager to integrate themselves more closely into England, were not blind to the existence of English prejudice and of practices which hindered the possibility of their being accepted as equal partners of the English peerage. As more Scots began to move south, demands inevitably arose for the elimination of those obstacles which tended to render the peers inferior in the eyes of their English colleagues.

Perhaps the clearest indication of the nobility's desire to gain equality with the English peerage was a sudden sharp rise in Scottish applications for British peerages. Between 1707 and 1782 few Scots received such honours. Most were unable, in any case, to support the dignity of a British peerage, but the primary cause of the limited

1   N. T. Phillipson, 'The Scottish Whigs and the Reform of the Court of Session, 1785–1830', unpublished Ph.D. dissertation, Cambridge University, 74–84; 'Scottish public opinion in the age of association', *Scotland in the Age of Improvement*, 140–3.
2   Sir Lewis Namier and John Brooke, *History of Parliament: The House of Commons, 1754–1790* (London, 1964), i, 171–2.
3   The duke of Argyll accepted Dundas's leadership because he believed that his extraordinary influence with Pitt made him most capable of aiding Scotland (*Letters of George Dempster to Sir Adam Ferguson, 1756–1813*, ed. J. Fergusson [London, 1934], 169).

number of creations was a standing order adopted by the house of lords in 1711. That order prohibited any Scottish peer who received a British peerage from taking his seat in the upper house.[1] Though the government was partially able to circumvent this restriction, the lords' action prevented most Scots peers from sitting in the house unless they were elected to the sixteen.[2] As long as most nobles were poor, this system was acceptable, but it was bound to be challenged when their wealth and confidence increased.[3]

Between 1782 and 1806 government policy with regard to the bestowal of peerages changed radically. In 1782 there were six Scots who were eligible to sit in the house of lords by right of their British peerages[4]: by 1806 twelve more had been added.[5] Equally significant was the change in the qualifications needed by Scots in order to obtain British peerages. Before 1782 only leading political figures and great magnates were eligible.[6] Although the twelve new creations after 1782 included three dukes and seven earls who stood near the top of the roll of Scottish peers, by no means all were immensely rich.[7] And only two, Stormont and Lauderdale, were of any political importance in this period.

The more frequent bestowal of British peerages after 1782 resulted from the government's own political exigencies and the changing attitudes of the Scottish nobility. In 1784, when Dundas forwarded to Pitt the applications of three dukes, Atholl, Gordon and Queensberry, he asked him to consider

> what their feelings now are, when by the acquisition of immense independent fortunes, enabling them to hold compleat intercourse in society with the peerage of this part of the kingdom, still in point of parliamentary situation the highest in rank in Scotland feel themselves inferior to the lowest of rank of peerage in England.

No longer did these men regard government support at peerage elections as an important favour. Indeed some refused to stand for

1   *Lords' Journals*, xix, 346, 20 Dec. 1711.
2   Peerages were bestowed upon the eldest sons of magnates, who then sat in the house until they inherited their fathers' Scottish peerages. Thereafter they had to be returned among the sixteen.
3   In 1782 the standing order of 1711 was successfully challenged by the duke of Hamilton (*Lords' Journals*, xxxvi, 517, 6 June 1782).
4   Argyll, Buccleuch, Hamilton, Montrose, Kinnoul and Roxburghe.
5   Abercorn, Atholl, Breadalbane, Cassillis, Eglinton, Galloway, Gordon, Lauderdale, Moray, Morton, Queensberry and Stormont.
6   The two commoners elevated in this period, Murray and Wedderburn, were judges. The dukes of Argyll, Hamilton and Queensberry were given peerages before 1711. Between 1711 and 1782 the eldest sons of the dukes of Argyll, Montrose and Roxburghe as well as those of the earls of Bute, Kinnoul and Marchmont were honoured.
7   Lord Galloway, for example, had to petition Pitt for an office on the grounds that he was unable to support his enormous family (P[ublic] R[ecord] O[ffice], Pitt Papers, PRO 30/8/138, fo. 34, Galloway to Pitt, 21 July 1788).

the sixteen, 'not from any objection to parliamentary attendance, but from a feeling that they suffer in reputation without gaining in consequence by it'.[1] By 1800 the demand for peerages had increased,[2] and many of the new applicants shared the misgivings of their predecessors in 1784.[3]

Peers who were not wealthy appear to have been as conscious of rank and status, and as eager to prove their equality with the British nobility, as their richer colleagues. Some pressed their claims on the ground that peers of inferior rank or even commoners had already attained hereditary seats. Lord Galloway believed that, as a man closely related to several great English families, he should be immediately honoured, while Lord Somerville argued that since everything about him but his peerage was English he should not be forced to endure the 'pain' of Scottish peerage elections any longer.[4]

The large numbers of creations and applications for peerages demonstrate that by the turn of the century the Scots were extremely conscious of rank. There had always been some resentment at the low status accorded to the Scottish nobility under the Union settlement,[5] but by the end of the century distinctive treatment of the peerages of England and Scotland seemed completely unjustifiable to many Scots noblemen. In pressing for British peerages, however, they were not trying to erase all traces of their national background. Scottish dukes, for example, did not apply for the same rank in the British peerage. Most were content to sit in the house as barons or earls. They simply felt that, given their wealth and power, it was unsuitable for men of their position to be made to feel inferior to the lowest English baron.

Although Dundas appreciated the sentiments of his noble supporters, the government's disposal of peerages was nonetheless determined primarily by political considerations. Indeed, in the increasingly partisan atmosphere of the late eighteenth century, the ability to create peers was a vital party resource. New ministries, particularly those formed in December 1783 and in 1806, quickly and extensively exercised this power, not only as a means of rewarding allies but also to demonstrate to waverers the king's confidence in those cabinets and the prospects which might attend a transfer

1   PRO, Pitt Papers, PRO 30/8/157, fos. 351–4, Dundas to Pitt, 25 Jan. [1784].
2   In 1800 Dundas reported that one marquess and twelve earls had applied for British peerages (S[cottish] R[ecord] O[ffice], Melville Castle MSS, GD. 51/1/55/2, Dundas to Aboyne, 29 May 1800 [copy]).
3   E.g. Aboyne to Dundas, 31 May 1800. Ibid., 51/1/55/3.
4   Ibid., 51/1a/26, Lady Stafford to Dundas, 9 Aug. 1794; PRO, Pitt Papers, PRO 30/8/138, fo. 42, Galloway to Pitt, 30 June 1793; *The Later Correspondence of George III, 1783–1810*, ed. Arthur Aspinall (Cambridge, 1966–70), iv, no. 3442, Somerville to George III, 14 Apr. 1807.
5   SRO, Melville Castle MSS, GD. 51/1a/15, Lady Glasgow to Dundas, 13 Aug. 1791; Henry Meikle, *Scotland and the French Revolution* (Glasgow, 1912), 12.

of support to them.[1] Atholl, Gordon and Queensberry were rewarded because they had always used their political influence on the government's behalf.[2] Dundas occasionally used British peerages to cement electoral agreements.[3] Lavish creations were made in 1794 and 1795 to conclude the agreement between the ministry and the Portland whigs.[4]

Political factors help to explain why British peerages were granted to specific individuals; they do not account for the government's frequent use of a favour so sparingly awarded in the past. In fact administrations in the later eighteenth century possessed few other rewards to recompense great landlords for their services. At a time when partisan tensions had begun to mount, the increasing wealth of these men made them less dependent upon the pecuniary favours which governments could offer. Thus Dundas found that, apart from a few particularly lucrative offices and membership of the Order of the Thistle, peerages were the only adequate reward for a lord's consistent and valuable loyalty.[5]

The demand for British peerages was but one manifestation of the Scots' self-conscious determination to assert their dignity. Between 1770 and 1790 an increasing number of peers challenged the right of the government to interfere in peerage elections. It was widely believed that ministers controlled the outcome of those contests and were therefore able to reduce the victors to the status of puppets. Such subservience on the part of its representatives naturally diminished the prestige of the nobility as a whole. The reformers hoped that by restoring the control of elections to Scotsmen they would improve the calibre of the sixteen and render them more honourable and effective participants in British political life.

In theory the process of selection of the sixteen peers was simple and inexpensive. Candidates were expected to stand as individuals and canvass on their own behalves. The voters demonstrated their preferences by appearing at the Register House on election day, by sending a signed list of their choices or by giving a proxy to an ally or friend.[6] In fact the government had the strongest voice in determining the outcome of elections. Before each contest the cabinet

1   *The Historical and Posthumous Memoirs of Sir Nathaniel Wraxall*, ed. H. B. Wheatley (London, 1884), iii, 254–5.
2   PRO, Pitt Papers, PRO 30/8/157, fos. 351–4, Dundas to Pitt, 25 Jan. [1784].
3   Ibid., fos. 53–57, 63–64, Dundas to [?], 2 Sept. 1788; Dundas to Pitt, 29 Sept. [1788]; N[ational] L[ibrary of] S[cotland], Melville Papers, Box 1053, fos. 23–24, John Bushby to Dundas, 14 Sept. 1793.
4   North Riding Record Office, Zetland Papers, ZNK X2, Lord Fitzwilliam to Sir Thomas Dundas, 7 July 1794.
5   PRO, Pitt Papers, PRO 30/8/157, fos. 351–4, Dundas to Pitt, 25 Jan. [1784].
6   James Fergusson, *Sixteen Peers of Scotland* (Oxford, 1960), 75–107.

consulted its Scottish advisers and the king and then compiled a list of the peers it wished to support.[1] A variety of tactics was used to secure the return of these men. Lacking a powerful Scottish manager between 1768 and 1780, ministers relied heavily on an official letter despatched by the appropriate secretary of state to each Scottish peer.[2] Because this device was unpopular, however, Dundas used more discreet modes of persuasion. Supporters were informed of his wishes by post and the letters were often supplemented by direct interviews with him or one of his lieutenants.[3] Implicit in these appeals was a threat: failure to support government nominees would prevent a recalcitrant peer from securing future patronage.[4] Thus the ministers invariably secured the return of a majority of their nominees. Since most of the victors owed their election entirely to government influence, they were generally bound to its support in the house of lords.[5]

A rebellion of the Scottish peers against ministerial intervention broke out in 1770 after the nomination of Lord Dysart to a vacancy. Many objected to Dysart because he possessed no Scottish estates but opposition was aimed primarily at the government which had attempted to impose him. Even after ministers had transferred their support to the earl of Stair, who had vast Scottish estates, opposition persisted. Its candidate, Breadalbane, was unsuccessful but made a creditable showing and received the votes of eighteen peers— Aboyne, Breadalbane, Buccleuch, Buchan, Crawford, Eglinton, Elgin, Elibank, Elphinstone, Glencairn, Haddington, Home, Hopetoun, Hyndford, Kellie, Moray, Selkirk and Tweeddale.[6]

Who were the independent peers and what brought them together? Men from all levels of the Scottish peerage had rallied to

1 SRO, Melville Castle MSS, GD. 51/1a/197/8 (copy), Dundas to Cassillis, 23 May 1796; *Political Memoranda of Francis, Fifth Duke of Leeds*, ed. Oscar Browning (London, 1884), 99–100; NLS, Melville Papers, Box 1053, fos. 69–71, Buccleuch to Dundas, 3 Mar. 1796.
2 SRO, Dalhousie Papers, GD. 45/14/484, Suffolk to Dalhousie, 1 Oct. 1774; SRO, Morton Papers, GD. 150/113, Sydney to Morton, 19 Nov. 1787.
3 SRO, Breadalbane Papers, GD. 112/45/1, Dundas to Breadalbane, 13 Apr. 1803. In 1790 Dundas proceeded to Edinburgh to organise the election while William Grenville secured what votes he could in England (*H[istorical] M[anuscripts] C[ommission], 13th R[eport]*, iii, *Fortescue*, i, 591–603).
4 In 1787 Dundas informed Buccleuch that a peer who failed to support government nominees could not expect to receive future patronage. SRO, Buccleuch Papers, GD. 224/30/10, Dundas to Buccleuch, 22 Nov. 1787.
5 The government was not free to put any peer it wished on its list. It was bound by tradition to support the candidature of great magnates, representatives who had previously sat among the sixteen and the candidates of particularly important supporters. NLS, Melville Papers, Box 1053, fos. 69–71, Buccleuch to Dundas, 6 Mar. 1796; *Memoirs and Correspondence of Viscount Castlereagh*, ed. Marquess of Londonderry (London, 1848–51), iii, 368–70, Portland to Castlereagh, 28 July 1800; *HMC, 13th R.*, iii, *Fortescue*, i, 602–3, Dundas to Grenville, 4 Aug. 1790.
6 *Scots Magazine*, xxxii (1770), 638.

Breadalbane, but the majority were drawn from its middle ranks.[1] Young men like Buccleuch worked closely with the elderly Lord Elibank. The group gained cohesion from its association with Edinburgh at a time when that city was the centre of Scottish intellectual life. Seven peers were members of either the Poker Club or the Select Society,[2] while three others, Buchan, Moray and Kellie, were active in the city's intellectual life and played leading roles in other 'improving' societies.[3]

The independents' links with the Poker Club are of particular importance. Although the Club never officially supported electoral freedom and some of its members strongly opposed the campaign,[4] it supplied two of the peers' most effective spokesmen, Buccleuch and Elibank, and several members who were not peers contributed polemical and historical material during the next twenty years.[5] In addition, the champions of electoral freedom drew heavily upon the ideas originally put forward by the advocates of a Scottish militia. Both movements shared a common sense of national grievance. Both claimed that their particular problems, if unresolved, would weaken the Union and perhaps undermine the principles of the British constitution. The peers lamented the servility of their colleagues, advocates of a militia condemned the weakness of Scottish members of parliament; each group recognised that if significant advances were to be made the Scottish people as a whole had to be awakened from their lethargy and indifference.[6]

In the eyes of the government's critics, its control of peerage elections was a new phenomenon. They did not deny that ministries had possessed some influence in the past, but until recently, it was argued, the elections had been managed by a great peer

> well acquainted with the inclinations, pretensions, and merits of all
> the peers; who treated them with respect and delicacy; and, though

1   Buccleuch, Breadalbane, Eglinton and Hopetoun were wealthy magnates. Elphinstone and, still more, Glencairn and Kellie were impoverished.

2   Aboyne, Elgin and Selkirk belonged to the Select Society; Buccleuch, Glencairn and Haddington were members of the Poker Club; Elibank belonged to both: D. D. McElroy, *Scotland's Age of Improvement: A Survey of Eighteenth Century Literary Clubs and Societies* (Washington State University, 1969), 48–59; Charles Rogers, *Social Life in Scotland from Early to Recent Times* (Edinburgh, 1886), ii, 370; *Memoirs of the Life and Writings of the Honourable Henry Home of Kames*, ed. A. F. Tytler (Edinburgh, 1814), iii, Appendix, 78–80.

3   Kellie was a leading musician, Buchan was the founder of the Society of Antiquaries of Scotland and Moray was a member of the Agricultural and Highland Societies.

4   Henry Dundas naturally opposed this movement, as did Baron Mure, an older political manager (*Caldwell Papers*, i, pt. ii 266).

5   [Robert Cullen], *Address to the P--rs of Scotland* (Edinburgh, 1771); William Robertson, *Proceedings Relating to the Peerage of Scotland* (Edinburgh, 1790).

6   [A. Carlyle], *The Question Relating to a Scots Militia*, 25 ff.; [Adam Fergusson], *The History of the Proceedings in the Case of Margaret, Commonly Called Peg* . . . (Edinburgh, 1761), 85–89, 101–2, 183–7.

in close connection with the ministry, instead of receiving instructions or mandates from them, gave directions to them, for whom it would be proper to exert their influence.[1]

In contrast, the present government, by sending out letters nominating Lord Dysart, appeared to assume that the electors would obediently acquiesce in its choice. Not only was this seen as a threat by peers who depended on ministerial favours, it was an unconstitutional intrusion by the executive in another branch of the constitution. Indeed, government intervention was the most insidious type of innovation. It denied the Scots nobility freedom in elections[2] and reduced each representative peer to the level of

an instrument singled out, and posted in the house of lords, by appointment of the minister at the time, for the end of supporting his measures, whatever they are or may be; and who in case of failure must expect to be turned out at the expiration of his term of seven years; . . . he is supposed to be of such pliant materials, that in the event of change of administration, the next minister makes no doubt of finding him equally obsequious, and ready to renounce his former connections.[3]

The reformers were aware that much of the blame for the lamentable status of the representative peers rested upon the Scottish nobility themselves. Lord Elibank explained his colleagues' obsequiousness on the grounds that their poverty made them dependent on ministerial largesse.[4] A later observer, the earl of Selkirk, reversed the blame: for him the great magnates, needing steady sources of patronage to maintain their interests, were the cause of the degradation.[5] The most sophisticated analysis, however, was made by the earl of Buchan. He contended that the Union deprived the peerage of the means of preserving their identity. Without a forum in which they could define their standpoints on major issues and protect their collective dignity, peers had become isolated individuals—ripe prey for the blandishments of ambitious ministers.[6]

The supporters of 'free elections' tried to demonstrate to their weaker colleagues that the elimination of ministerial influence would enhance the dignity of the Scottish peerage and benefit not only Scotland but the whole of Great Britain. If a Scottish representative were actually chosen by the free vote of his colleagues, his prestige in the lords would surpass that of the greatest English magnate. To the dignity of his title and family he would add the approbation of

1   Scots Magazine, xxxii (1770), 638.
2   Ibid., 639, 697; Robertson, Proceedings Relating to the Peerage, 383.
3   Lord Elibank, Considerations on the Present State of the Peerage of Scotland . . .
(London, 1771), 14–15.   4   Ibid., 18–19.
5   SRO, Morton Papers, GD. 150/113, Selkirk to Morton, 7 Aug. 1786.
6   Earl of Buchan, A Plan for the Better Regulation of the Peerage of Scotland
(Edinburgh, 1780), 20–21.

his order, which had singled him out as a person worthy of the highest of trusts. Such prestige would reflect upon the Scottish peerage as a whole and would stimulate a spirit of self-improvement among younger peers. The Scottish nobility, indeed all Scots, could logically expect a more positive defence of their own just claims from such men than from ministerial pawns. Finally, the king's government would be more ably served by independent representatives than by weaklings who docilely accepted the dictation of a minister. The independent peer would support those policies which he felt were beneficial for the nation as a whole and would not permit the political convenience of the minister to colour his judgment.[1]

Though they renewed their efforts at the general election of 1774, the independents were not able to secure the election of more than a few of their number to the representative peerage.[2] Interference by the government continued unchecked and at the election of 1780 all its candidates were returned unopposed. The placidity of that election should not, however, be interpreted as a sign of the movement's collapse. Rather it marks the beginning of a new phase of its history during which its supporters were transformed from a diverse coalition of individuals into a disciplined body under the leadership of the whig party. This development within the movement for 'free elections' is entirely logical and understandable. Opposition to government interference at peerage elections almost coincided with the rise to power of Henry Dundas, who naturally viewed the problem raised by the independent peers in political terms. Since those peers voted against some of his candidates, he regarded them as unshakeable members of the opposition.[3]

A preoccupation with political considerations was not unique to Dundas; it also characterised the ministry's response to several questions about the Scottish peerage which came before the house of lords in the late 1780s. In 1787 Stormont and Hopetoun introduced motions which would have prevented British peers from sitting as representatives of the Scottish nobility and from voting at elections. In both cases ministers opposed these resolutions because they feared their impact on the government's electoral position.[4] A year later the lord chancellor failed to get the house to rescind a resolution

1   Elibank, *Considerations on the Scottish Peerage*, 1–12, 16–27.
2   Breadalbane was returned to parliament in 1774 and in 1776 he was joined by the earl of Eglinton. Both were elected with the support of the government which hoped by that means to weaken the independent movement (J. Fergusson, *Sixteen Peers*, 86–87).
3   SRO, Buccleuch Papers, GD. 224/30/10, Dundas to Buccleuch, 22 Nov. 1787.
4   *Annual Register*, xxix (1787), 93–98, 145–7; *PH*, xxvi, 18 May 1787, 1158–67. William Grenville complained in 1790 that the Hopetoun motion cost the government two supporters at the election (*HMC, 13th R.*, iii, *Fortescue*, i, 596–7, Grenville to Dundas, 29 July 1790).

which barred the so-called Lord Rutherfurd from the honours and
privileges of the Scottish peerage. In this instance the government
required the vote of the fraudulent peer in order to carry the election
of its candidate, Lord Cathcart.[1]

In contrast to the government the Scottish peers demonstrated that
they were unwilling to permit political considerations to infringe
the dignity of their order. Apart from the duke of Queensberry,
who as a new British peer had an obvious interest in defeating the
Stormont and Hopetoun motions, the only other peer to speak for
the ministerial position was the earl of Morton.[2] On the question
relating to Cathcart's election, only Morton and Cathcart supported
the government. Eight others, four of whom normally stood by
Pitt's administration, voted with the opposition.[3]

By the late 1780s it had become impossible for peers to support
Pitt's administration and at the same time to be vigorous opponents
of government interference at peerage elections. The rigidity of
Dundas's position forced them to make a choice.[4] His rise to power
also confirmed the major lesson of the 1770s—that an unorganised
group of individuals was incapable of standing successfully against
the government. The opposition needed cohesion in order to utilize
its resources to the full. It is entirely understandable that the
whigs should have been called upon to lead and draw together the
movement. Their crusade against the growing influence of the
crown fitted perfectly with a campaign to eliminate ministerial
influence from peerage elections. For their part the whig leaders
welcomed an accession of strength in their contests against the
government. In 1784 Fox and his colleagues were eager, for example,
to give their blessing to a 'proper constitutional list' of peers, but
they were equally anxious to purge those lords who had deserted them
over the India Bill.[5]

1   *Scots Magazine*, l (1788), 68–71; *Times*, 7 Feb. 1788. Cathcart carried the
election of 1788 by one vote. The whigs immediately challenged Rutherfurd's
vote in the hope of securing the return of their candidate, Lord Dumfries (SRO,
Minutes of the Election of Sixteen Peers for Scotland, PE/8, fos. 118–20;
Times, 12 Feb., 22–28 Apr. 1788).
2   *Annual Register*, xxix (1787), 93–98, 145–7; *PH*, xxvi, 18 May 1787, 1158–67.
Morton wished to obtain a British peerage for himself, but he also appears to have
been convinced by the government's case (SRO, Morton Papers, GD. 150/113,
Morton to Selkirk, 25 Sept. 1786 [copy]).
3   The eight were Breadalbane, Kinnaird, Stormont, Selkirk, Balcarres,
Elphinstone, Galloway and Hopetoun. The last four normally supported the
government (*Scots Magazine*, l [1788], 201).
4   In 1790 the government opposed the return of the earls of Strathmore and
Hopetoun, generally its allies, because they gave their support to those peers who
sought to eliminate ministerial intervention (Hopetoun House Papers, uncatalogued, Strathmore to Hopetoun, 5 Sept. 1789; PRO, Pitt Papers, PRO 30/8/181,
fo. 71, Strathmore to Pitt, 24 July 1790; ibid., 30/8/157, fo. 116, Dundas to Pitt,
8 Aug. 1790).
5   A. Fergusson, *The Honourable Henry Erskine, Lord Advocate for Scotland* (London
and Edinburgh, 1882), 250–3.

Whig support undoubtedly increased the number of peers who opposed government interference at peerage elections.[1] Yet five of the peers who cast their votes for whig candidates in 1790 had voted for 'free elections' in the seventies[2] and eight other opposition supporters in 1790 were the heirs of men who had opposed government interference in 1770 and 1774.[3] Moreover, the movement continued to draw the bulk of its adherents from the middle ranks of the peerage. Most significantly, the majority of supporters remained Scottish-orientated. Only six lived extensively in England or pursued careers which compelled them to be absent abroad.[4]

The whigs made their power felt in Scotland by transforming the diverse and unorganised group of independents into a disciplined bloc of support. Shortly after the collapse of the coalition in December 1783 Henry Erskine and Sir Thomas Dundas compiled a list of opposition candidates in concert with the whig leadership in London.[5] Lacking a powerful figure among these candidates to appeal to the peers, they never succeeded in gathering a disciplined following behind them.[6] Despite this failure, and aided by the willingness of the Prince of Wales to lend his name to the whig cause, the party's hold over its followers steadily increased.[7] Thus it was able to secure the return of two advocates of 'free elections', Lords Kinnaird and Selkirk, in the special election of 1787.[8] The next year in another contest the government directly committed itself to support Lord Cathcart, and although Cathcart did eventually carry the election, he did so by only one vote.[9] The crowning whig triumph, however, occurred in 1790. In that election the whigs had slightly fewer supporters than the government but their organisation rivalled that of Dundas. So effective was whig discipline in that highly partisan contest that fewer than half of the party's supporters disobeyed official instructions. Moreover, none of the deviant peers gave more

1   In 1770 eighteen peers had opposed the government nominee. In 1790 twenty-nine peers supported most of the whig candidates (SRO, Minutes of the Election of Sixteen Peers for Scotland, PE/8, 123–37).
2   Aboyne, Dumfries, Haddington, Kinnaird and Selkirk.
3   Breadalbane, Crawford, Dundonald, Elibank, Glencairn, Hopetoun, Strathmore and Tweeddale. Printed lists of the voting in the general election of 1774 can be found in Robertson, *Proceedings Relating to the Peerage*, 388.
4   Dysart, Lauderdale, Lothian, Stormont, Strathmore and the Prince of Wales. In contrast fifteen of the thirty-one government supporters lived exclusively in England, held offices which required long absences from Scotland or spent most of their time on their English estates.
5   A. Fergusson, *Henry Erskine*, 250–3.
6   D. E. Ginter, *Whig Organization in the General Election of 1790* (Berkeley and Los Angeles, 1967), 3–4, quoting a letter from Lord Elphinstone to William Adam, 15 Mar. 1784.
7   PRO, Pitt Papers, PRO 30/8/157, fos. 46–7, Dundas to Pitt, 11 Aug. 1788.
8   Ibid., 30/8/121, fos. 226–7, Cathcart to Pitt, 29 Mar. 1787.
9   SRO, Morton Papers, GD. 150/113, Sydney to Morton, 19 Nov. 1787. See above, p. 294, n. 1.

than three of his sixteen votes to opponents of the whigs.[1] As a result, the whig party was able to return five of its own nominees.[2]

The election of 1790 marked the zenith of the movement for 'free elections'. Those local questions which had dominated Scottish politics in the 1780s were soon to be submerged in the fears awakened by the French Revolution. Within three years the whig party began to break up and, as reform became more closely equated with upheaval, their former allies regarded Fox and his friends with increasing horror. With all but a few peers accepting Pitt's leadership, peerage elections ceased to be contests. In 1796 the sole Foxite candidate, the cranky earl of Lauderdale, was overwhelmingly rejected by his colleagues, who realised, even without Dundas's prompting, that Lauderdale's views were antithetic to order and stability.[3]

The reaction of the Scottish peerage against the French Revolution worked immensely to Dundas's advantage, and by 1796 he had reached the pinnacle of his power. It is vital to remember, however, that his power was secured not only by his own cleverness, nor even by his ability to negotiate and dispense patronage, but by his rôle as the local spokesman for a government and a cause whose principles and policies embodied the fears and hopes of the Scottish nobility and gentry. Moreover, he could never completely control peers' elections. At a special election in 1803, for example, three candidates offered themselves: Lauderdale, Elphinstone, who was a friend of the Prince of Wales, and Dundas's candidate, Lord Kellie. What is remarkable about this contest is the extent to which peers ignored Dundas's commands. Morton considered that it made no difference who was elected, so long as Lauderdale was kept out.[4] Most of his colleagues evidently agreed; while some committed themselves to Kellie as a means of pleasing Dundas, a larger number explained that they had to vote for Elphinstone either because he was a friend or because of a prior agreement.[5] A year later, at another special election, Somerville expressed his outrage at the tone of Dundas's appeal for support; he wrote that the letter contained 'some passages the most insolent and biting, according to my feeble judgement, that ever were addressed to any peer of these realms'.[6]

1   SRO, Minutes of the Election of Sixteen Peers for Scotland, PE/8, 123–37.
2   See above, p. 295, n. 2. In fact six whig supporters were returned at the election of 1790, but Lord Eglinton, one of them, was nominated by the government and received its support at the election.
3   SRO, Minutes of the Election of Sixteen Peers for Scotland, PE/8, fos. 151–6; Melville Castle MSS, GD. 51/1c /197/17, Galloway to Dundas, 21 June 1796.   4   J. Fergusson, *Sixteen Peers*, 90.
5   SRO, Breadalbane Papers, GD. 112/45/1, Dundas to Breadalbane, 15 Apr. 1803; NLS, Melville Papers, Box 3, fos. 4–32.
6   *Later Correspondence of George III*, iv, no. 2965, Somerville to General Harcourt, 10 Nov. [1804].

Coming from a lord of the bedchamber, who wished only to serve the king's government, this shows how unwilling the Scots peers might be to give continuous obedience to Dundas.

Just as the whig critics overstated the degree of the government's control over the outcome of peerage elections, they also exaggerated the representatives' servility in the house of lords. An examination of the parliamentary conduct of the sixteen between 1784 and 1801 reveals that those men were diverse in their interests, constructive in their activities and surprisingly adventurous in their politics. In contrast, the Scottish peers with British titles, men whom the whigs expected to be independent because they were not obliged to the government for their seats, were uniformly regular in their support of the administration.[1]

The following table compares the respective levels of activity of representative peers and those Scottish peers who had British peerages. It embodies the results of attendances compiled over two periods of two sessions each, 1785–6 and 1794–5, together with an examination of the *Lords' Journals* and the records of parliamentary debates.[2] These sources demonstrate that the peers can conveniently be differentiated into three groups. In the first are those members who rarely, if ever, appeared in the house and hence played no role in business. The second contains men who attended more than five

LEVELS OF PARTICIPATION IN THE HOUSE OF LORDS

| | *1785* | | *1786* | |
	Rep. Peers %	Br. Peers %	Rep. Peers %	Br. Peers %
Group I (inactive)	12·5	71·4	31·25	71·4
Group II (passive)	25·0	28·6	31·25	14·3
Group III (active)	62·5	0	37·5	14·3

| | *1794* | | *1795* | |
	Rep. Peers %	Br. Peers %	Rep. Peers %	Br. Peers %
Group I (inactive)	37·5	41·7	66·7	41·7
Group II (passive)	12·5	25·0	13·3	33·3
Group III (active)	50·0	33·3	20·0	25·0

1   Some whigs who despaired of breaking government influence in peerage contests argued that the independence of the sixteen might be increased if they were not forced to stand for election. They advocated a variety of plans, including the rotation of seats among the whole peerage, the establishment of a system comparable to that eventually created for Irish representative peers, or lavish creations of British peers (Buchan, *Plan for the Regulation of the Scottish Peerage*, 23–27; *PH*, xxi, 3 June 1780, 686–8; Earl of Selkirk, *A Letter to the Peers of Scotland* [London, 1807], 11).
2   The house of lords sat 109 days in 1785, ninety-six in 1786, ninety-eight in 1794 and 107 in 1795.

times a session but who were purely passive participants save on those occasions when business touched directly on their interests. The third type of member not only attended frequently but also performed essential services in the house.

It is apparent from the table that a significant proportion of the representative peers were very active members of the house of lords. The nature of their participation, however, varied considerably. Several Scots nursed serious political ambitions. Inevitably their parliamentary conduct was determined by their broader goals. As leaders of the whig party in the lords, Stormont and Lauderdale, for example, carefully followed the course of important government legislation in order to seize a ripe opportunity for attack. They participated in all major debates and generally sought to advance the interests of their party not only because they believed in its principles but also because they wished to secure office.[1]

Most Scots, however, did not aspire to high office, and thus their energies were not focused exclusively on political aspects of parliamentary business. A careful examination of the *Lords' Journals* and the manuscript collections of Proceedings in Committees on Private Bills for the years 1783–1801 indicates that there was a small but coherent group, serving under the leadership of the lord chairman of committees, which was familiar enough with the intricacies of parliamentary procedure to perform the menial but necessary chores of the house of lords.[2] These men sponsored bills in which no other peer had interest; they presided over committees on both private and public legislation; and the more knowledgeable advised those who wished to bring in their own legislation. Between 1784 and 1796 an average of four representative peers performed such tasks,[3] and from 1789 to 1792 Lord Cathcart directed their labours as lord chairman.

For some, the willingness to undertake parliamentary duties was politically motivated. Lord Kellie appears to have enjoyed his labours, but he also wished to serve and please Dundas. Similarly, a diligent independent like Lord Hopetoun had to follow the course of most important legislation if he was to make good his claim that

1   Stormont's efforts were rewarded in 1794. Following the Portland whigs' alliance with the government, Stormont was made lord president. Lauderdale had to wait until the Foxites returned to power in 1806 before being made a commissioner to France and keeper of the great seal of Scotland.
2   The Proceedings in Committees on Private Bills are to be found in the H[ouse of] L[ords] R[ecord] O[ffice]. These manuscripts list the chairman of each committee on a private bill.
3   In the 1780s Abercorn, Cathcart, Dunmore, Elphinstone, Galloway, Hopetoun, Kinnaird, Moray and Morton participated in this business. In the 1790s Elphinstone, Glasgow, Kellie, Somerville and Stair were among the most active representative peers.

he judged measures according to their content.[1] Other peers simply enjoyed participating in parliamentary business. The young earl of Morton proudly informed his uncle, the earl of Selkirk:

> My conduct, since I have sat in parliament, has been such as I am not ashamed to avow to the world. I will venture to say that no peer who has a seat in the house has attended his duty in *publick business* (particularly those from Scotland) or private causes with more assiduity than I have done. I have spared neither pains nor time to get the best information on every question.[2]

Likewise, Lord Cathcart solicited government support for his candidature because his 'object in wishing to get into parliament was to endeavour to come forward in business, to be useful, and therefore to be employed'.[3] Several other peers seem to have undertaken their parliamentary duties in order to bolster their pretensions for some particular reward. Moreover, once his ambition had been realised, the nobleman's attention to business tended to falter.[4]

The sudden shift of the representatives' attention away from parliament in 1795 can also be explained in terms of individual responses to the circumstances of the time. Three Scots—Balcarres, Cathcart and Elgin—were serving in military or diplomatic posts abroad. Several others turned their attention in this period to the countryside. The potential danger of a French invasion or of a domestic insurrection induced many peers to raise and train regiments from their own estates. For a man like the earl of Breadalbane, who was never more than a passive participant in the house, such service seemed far more valuable in dangerous times than his continued, silent support of the government in the lords.[5]

In contrast to the representative peers the noblemen who had British titles in 1784 had little interest in parliamentary affairs. The second duke of Montrose and the ninth earl of Kinnoul were both too old and sick to attend, while the young duke of Hamilton could not be diverted from the pleasures of the bottle and the flesh to appear

---

1   SRO, Melville Castle MSS, GD. 51/1c/197/1, Kellie to Dundas, 27 July 1790. Hopetoun informed the house of lords on one occasion that he spoke as a country gentleman would in the other house (*PH*, xxvii, 19 Mar. 1788, 236–7).
2   SRO, Morton Papers, GD. 150/113, Morton to Selkirk, 25 Sept. 1786 (copy).
3   PRO, Pitt Papers, PRO 30/8/121, fos. 226–7, Cathcart to Pitt, 29 Mar. 1787. Cathcart's ambition was soon satisfied, for in 1789 he was made lord chairman of committees.
4   Lord Galloway not only wanted a British peerage but also an office to support his huge family (PRO, Pitt Papers, PRO 30/8/138, fos. 34, 36, 42, Galloway to Pitt, 21 July 1788, 7 May 1789, 30 June 1793). Morton and Abercorn, both of whom were extremely active in the 1780s, also secured British peerages.
5   SRO, Breadalbane Papers, GD. 112/40/11, Breadalbane to [?] no date, [draft]. Hopetoun and Eglinton undertook similar responsibilities and neglected their parliamentary duties in consequence.

very often.[1] The fifth duke of Argyll was the first of his family to forego a political career. Instead he concentrated his energies on the improved cultivation of his estates and the economic development of the highlands. The fourth duke of Gordon confessed to Dundas that he disliked coming to London because he was too poor to support himself in a style equal to his station. In any case he knew nothing of politics.[2] Only the dukes of Buccleuch and Roxburghe attended regularly, but they played no important rôle in parliamentary business.

Obviously the indifferent participation of these men is to be explained in terms of their own particular interests and personalities. This conclusion is reinforced if we examine the activity of the peers who entered the ranks of the British peerage between 1785 and 1801. Kinnoul and Montrose were replaced, in 1787 and 1790 respectively, by sons who harboured political ambitions.[3] More importantly, Pitt elevated five nobles to the British peerage—Abercorn, Galloway, Moray, Morton, and Stormont—all of whom had been active as representatives. Though their attendance was in some cases less frequent when they sat by right of their own peerage, the differences are in most instances very slight and can be accounted for by such factors as age, local duties or absence abroad.

The active attention many representative peers gave to the details of parliamentary business indicates that they were perhaps more than ministerial pawns. The key test for the validity of the traditional attacks on the representatives, however, rests on the political loyalties of these peers. Professor Holden Furber makes generally excellent estimates of the Scots' political affiliations after each general election in our period.[4] Unfortunately his calculations are

1   Dr Moore, the young duke's tutor, found him to be friendly, but also idle, extravagant and 'accustomed to have every desire, every little caprice indulged'. (*Intimate Society Letters of the Eighteenth Century*, ed. Duke of Argyll [London, 1910], ii, 346–9, 410). In later life he had a fondness for 'low company', and he permitted himself 'to be led astray by the spirit of dissipation' (*GEC*, *The Complete Peerage*, ed. Vicary Gibb *et al.* [London, 1910–40], vi, 272).

2   Eric Cregeen, 'The changing rôle of the house of Argyll in Scotland', *Scotland in the Age of Improvement*, 19–21; NLS, Melville Papers, Box 5, fos. 1–5, Gordon to Dundas, 6 Dec. 1783.

3   Montrose was master of the horse from 1790 to 1795 and joint paymaster general from 1791 to 1800. In Pitt's second administration he was president of the board of trade. Kinnoul was anxious to secure some post but had no pretensions to high political office (University of Nottingham Library, Portland Papers, Pwf. 4949, 4954, Kinnoul to Portland, 25 Aug. 1794, 30 Nov. 1794; PRO, Pitt Papers, PRO 30/8/149, fo. 208, Kinnoul to Pitt, 1 Aug. 1795).

4   Dr Furber concluded that twelve representatives in 1784 were friendly to Dundas and four were hostile. In 1790 eleven of the thirteen peers on the government list were eventually returned, and three of those chosen in 1796 were Dundas's enemies (Holden Furber, *Henry Dundas: First Viscount Melville, 1742–1811* [London, 1931], 204, 235–6, 264). Prof. David Large erroneously interprets these estimates by asserting that twelve Scots supported the government in 1784, eleven in 1790, and thirteen in 1796 ('Decline of the "Party of the Crown" ', *Eng. Hist.*

static and therefore misleading. Since he did not follow the representatives throughout the course of any of the three parliaments between 1783 and 1801, he did not discover that fluctuations of opinion were a recurrent part of the Scots' political character.

Any analysis of the political alignments of the late eighteenth century is bound to be somewhat impressionistic, owing to a lack of division lists. Despite this limitation the evidence is clear enough to reveal that within our period there were two significant shifts of opinion among the representative peerage. The first, in the late 1780s, is marked by a surprisingly general rejection of governmental leadership. The second, in the mid-1790s, takes place amidst the collapse of the whig party and the consolidation of support behind a government which strove to maintain the existing social and political framework.

At the outset of the parliament of 1784 government leaders could rest assured that most of the sixteen would support their policies. Thirteen of them backed its major legislation,[1] though several of these were independent enough to withdraw their allegiance when they felt government policies were ill-conceived or contrary to their own interests.[2] Only Lords Stormont and Cassillis remained permanently in opposition.[3]

Rev. 77; see above, 241). An enemy of Dundas was not necessarily an enemy of the government. Lord Elphinstone was elected without government support in 1784 but still supported Pitt (Ginter, *Whig Organization in the Election of 1790*, 3). Breadalbane, who opposed Dundas, still gave his proxy to Hopetoun, a government supporter, during the debates on the Irish trade propositions in 1785 (HLRO, Proxy Book, 1785). Only two of the four enemies of Dundas, Stormont and Cassillis, were firmly in opposition in 1784 (Frank Brady, *Boswell's Political Career* [New Haven and London, 1965], 113). In 1796 the three peers who were not allies of Dundas, Breadalbane, Cassillis and Tweeddale, did support the administration and were backed by it at the election (SRO, Melville Castle MSS, GD. 51/1c/197/6, Cassillis to Dundas, 25 Mar. 1795; SRO, Breadalbane Papers, GD. 112/40/11, Dundas to Breadalbane, 29 Apr. 1796). Finally, a peer on the government list did not necessarily have to support the government. Though he was returned with government support in 1790, Eglinton was claimed by Portland as a supporter of the whigs. See above, p. 300, n. 2.

1   Queensberry, Lothian, Morton, Moray, Abercorn, Galloway, Eglinton, Aberdeen, Breadalbane, Hopetoun, Dunmore, Balcarres and Elphinstone. Queensberry, Lothian, Aberdeen, Dunmore and Galloway opposed the Coalition's India Bill in 1783 (*Parliamentary Register*, xiv [1783-4], 107-8). Morton and Moray gave their proxies to government supporters in 1785 or 1786 (HLRO, Proxy Books, 1785-6). Eglinton concluded an alliance with Dundas in the spring of 1784 (Brady, *Boswell's Political Career*, 107-12). For Breadalbane and Elphinstone see above, p. 300, n. 4.

2   Lord Balcarres did not firmly commit himself to Pitt until 1793 (Lord Lindsay, *Lives of the Lindsays* [London, 1858], ii, 357). Though he claimed he was a government supporter at the election of 1790, Hopetoun opposed the government's Hawkers and Pedlars Bill in 1785 and in 1788 the Wool and Distillery Bills (*Times*, 30 July 1785, 12 June 1788; *Parliamentary Register*, iii [1788], 246-9).

3   See above, p. 300, n. 4. Since he did not attend the house, Lord Dalhousie is not included in these calculations.

Three factors undermined the tremendous advantage the government enjoyed in 1784. The by-election of 1787 produced two stalwart proponents of 'free elections', Lords Selkirk and Kinnaird. Together with Lord Breadalbane they normally opposed Pitt, though without ever formally joining the whig party.[1] The influence of the Prince of Wales and his brothers was a second important catalyst. Lord Lothian revelled in his close association with the princes, and Eglinton proved his devotion by going to some trouble to secure the parliamentary attendance of men who would support the proposals for an increased income for the Prince of Wales. Both these men backed his cause during the regency crisis and maintained their ties with the opposition for the duration of the parliament of 1784.[2] Thirdly, frustrated ambition may have induced Lord Aberdeen to transfer his allegiance. Having been refused a British peerage by Pitt, he appears to have had expectations of success if a new government came into power.[3]

The combined effect of these factors was highly detrimental to the government's hold on the Scots. By the late 1780s eight peers were either members of the opposition or associated with groups that worked with it.[4] The government could count on only seven peers, two of whom, Hopetoun and Balcarres, remained fairly independent.[5] The tide of political events in the succeeding decade, however, overwhelmed the whig opposition and enormously increased Pitt's following in the house of lords. The election of 1790 cost the opposition two supporters,[6] but the shock of the French Revolution and the outbreak of the continental war tore apart the loose bonds which had

---

1   Kinnaird and Breadalbane signed the petition for a third party (Essex Record Office, Braybrooke Papers, D/DBy C9/44, 'Third Party Circular'). All three were considered members of the 'Armed Neutrality' during the regency crisis (*Memoirs of the Courts and Cabinets of George the Third*, ed. Duke of Buckingham and Chandos [London, 1855], ii, 79–80, Bulkeley to Buckingham, 27 Dec. 1788).
2   *HMC, 14th R.*, i, *Rutland*, iii, 408, Lothian to Rutland, 26 Aug. 1787; *Times*, 5 May 1787; *PH*, xxvii, 26 Dec. 1788, 890–1.
3   B[ritish] M[useum], Liverpool Papers, Add. MS 38220, fo. 202, Aberdeen to Hawkesbury, 23 Oct. 1786.
4   Breadalbane, Cassillis, Eglinton, Kinnaird, Lothian, Selkirk and Stormont opposed the government on the regency question (*PH*, xxvii, 26 Dec. 1788, 890–1). All save Lothian and Eglinton were on the whigs' list of candidates in 1790, and Eglinton was later claimed as a supporter. See above, p. 300, n. 4. Lord Aberdeen did not attend divisions on the regency question. He did give his proxy to Lord Fitzwilliam later in the session of 1789 and he was on the opposition slate in 1790 (HLRO, Proxy Book, 1788–9).
5   Cathcart, Elphinstone, Galloway, Hopetoun, Moray and Morton supported the government on the regency question (*PH*, xxvii, 26 Dec. 1788, 890–1). In addition Lord Balcarres gave his proxy to a government supporter in 1789 and was on the government list at the general election of 1790 (HLRO, Proxy Book, 1788–9).
6   Aberdeen, Cassillis, Lothian and Kinnaird were not returned. Two new whigs, Lauderdale and Dumfries, were elected (SRO, Minutes of the Election of Sixteen Peers for Scotland, 137–8).

held the whigs together. By 1794 only Lord Lauderdale persisted in opposition and he was not returned in 1796. For the duration of Pitt's first ministry the representative peers as a body supported the government.

In contrast to the representative peers, the Scots who sat in the house of lords by right of a British peerage were remarkably loyal to the administration. Argyll, Buccleuch and Gordon were all ardent disciples and allies of Dundas, while Roxburghe was an intimate friend of George III.[1] The new creations of British peers only augmented the ranks of government adherents. Naturally the minister advanced men who were willing to follow his lead, and none of the eight Scots raised to the British peerage before 1801 found any difficulty in meeting this requirement. In fact, only one British peer, the tenth earl of Kinnoul, opposed the government for any length of time between 1784 and 1801.[2]

It should be readily apparent that the characterisation of the Scottish members of the house of lords as whigs bears very little relation to reality. Moreover, the continued use of whig stereotypes by modern historians is not only misleading but also supports the incorrect idea that there was a distinction between the two types of Scottish members of parliament. In fact, personal idiosyncracies and interest can explain the minor differences between the two. As their reaction to the French Revolution demonstrates, the Scottish peers were essentially united on fundamental questions of principle.

In supporting an administration which proclaimed its determination after 1793 to uphold the existing framework of society, the Scottish peers adopted the same course as the great majority of their English colleagues. Threats of upheaval undoubtedly awakened similarly alarming visions for members of both peerages because their essential interests had become virtually identical. In fact, the Scottish peerage ceased to be a distinct national nobility in the last quarter of the eighteenth century. Though prejudice and old institutional practices continued to set them apart, the peers' willingness to use emerging British political parties as the medium of expression for their own views indicates their willingness and ability to move out into a broader political arena.

1   See above, p. 300, n. 2; NLS, Melville Papers, Box 5, fos. 14–15, Gordon to Dundas, 24 Mar. 1786; BM, Paget Papers, Add. MS 48403 (provisional classification), Lord Uxbridge to A. Paget, 20 Mar. 1804.
2   Kinnoul was in the Portland wing of the party. He spoke against the limits put on the Prince of Wales's regency, against the government's Spanish policy in 1790 and its Russian policy in 1792 (*PH*, xxvii, 29 Dec. 1788, 891–3; *Annual Register*, xxxii [1790], 98; *PH*, xxxix, 20 Feb. 1792, 854–5). By 1794 Kinnoul had followed his friend Portland into the government camp. Thereafter he spoke in defence of Pitt's policies (e.g. *PH*, xxxi, 30 Dec. 1794, 969–70).

Despite the more intimate involvement of the Scots in English life, it was inevitable that they should remain to a certain extent a distinct, alien group within the house of lords. The act of union had done little more than add a small number of Scottish delegates to an assembly whose members were, almost without exception, ignorant of conditions in the north. Not surprisingly, the Scots soon found that leading politicians were incapable of dealing intelligently with Scottish questions unless guided by men like Argyll or Dundas. Even with such support, the Scots were aware that they had little chance of carrying their own points of view in the face of strong English opposition.[1]

In the years following the Union the Scots developed a system of securing legislation with a minimum of intervention from London. Ministers soon discovered that their northern subjects were extremely sensitive to change, especially if imposed by London. They were therefore prepared to permit the Scots themselves to write and approve locally much of their own legislation before it was sent to Westminster. Assembled together at head court meetings, Scottish freeholders not only instructed their members how to vote on government proposals; they also discussed the merits of proposed Scottish legislation. So well established was this practice that Dundas found it impossible to pursue his proposals for the reform of the court of session after they were criticised by the freeholders. The other traditional means by which Scottish interests were brought before the parliament was through associations of landlords. The plans to build roads in the highlands or to develop the potentialities of the fisheries were approved in London because they had widespread support from the landed interest.[2]

Given the wealth and power of the peers, it is hardly surprising to find that large numbers of them were involved at all levels of this legislative process. In some instances they rallied discontent against unpopular government acts.[3] In others they initiated new legislation and organized local support behind it.[4] In London the peers expedited the passage of local legislation by appearing in the house in fairly large numbers when a matter of national interest was under consideration.[5]

1   The proponents of a Scottish militia, for example, launched their campaign in 1759. They were unable to overcome English fears of an armed Scotland. Thus, it was not until after the outbreak of the French Revolution that the militia was finally established.
2   H. J. Hanham, *Scottish Nationalism* (Cambridge, Mass., 1969), 50–53; Phillipson, 'The Scottish Whigs and the Court of Session', 3–6, 136–56.
3   *Scots Magazine*, xlvi (1784), 551–2; ibid., xlviii (1786), 95–96.
4   SRO, Breadalbane Papers, GD. 112/40/11, Kinnoul to Breadalbane, 28 July 1796.
5   Nine peers attended the second reading of the Forfeited Estates Bill in 1784 and seventeen appeared to support the second reading of a bill designed to remove

While there was never a united Scottish national party, the peers did put aside their normal partisan affiliations when discussing purely local questions. Thus, when Lord Thurlow attempted to postpone the popular Forfeited Estates Bill he was strongly opposed by two government supporters, Lords Balcarres and Dunmore.[1] Similarly the proponents of the Highland Society Bill, most of them Pittites, waged a prolonged struggle against Thurlow's opposition and by their persistence eventually overcame his objections.[2] In other instances whigs as well as government adherents united behind a popular measure. Thus, when Lord Kellie brought in a bill to relieve Scottish episcopalians of old penalties, he was supported by government adherents like Lord Elgin and opposition spokesmen like Stormont.[3]

The Scots were able to secure their desired legislation when the specific proposals were of a purely local nature. On such occasions the rest of the house remained indifferent or did not choose to interfere. They fared less well, however, when the government introduced measures which discriminated against Scottish national interests. In 1788 an outcry arose over a bill restricting the right of Scottish distillers to take out licenses to sell their products in the south. Several peers took up the local complaints in the lords. Hopetoun and Stormont attacked the administration's measure for being contrary to an earlier act which had permitted all Scots who were properly licensed to sell their goods in England.[4] More seriously, Lord Kinnaird accused the government of violating the Act of Union. By establishing new restrictions, ministers were erecting new barriers to the free exchange of goods between Scotland and England. It was just this open market, Kinnaird argued, that had converted many Scots to the idea of union.[5] Though these peers earned the thanks of their countrymen for their efforts, they were unable to prevent the passage of the bill because of the numerical superiority of the supporters of the English interests.

The late eighteenth-century peerage maintained a strong sense of its territorial responsibilities. It is not unusual to find groups of peers putting aside their partisan differences and uniting to support some purely regional project. Such certainly was the case with the Scots. Because of the uniqueness of their national background and

penalties placed on Scottish episcopalians (*Lords' Journals*, xxxvii, 159; xxxix, 388). Scots interested in a particular measure under consideration took care to see that the representative peers attended. In 1787 each member of the sixteen was urged by a committee of peers to attend and support the Stormont and Hopetoun motions (SRO, Morton Papers, GD. 150/113, Selkirk to Morton, 5 Jan. 1787).

1   *PH*, xxiv, 16 Aug. 1784, 1263–71.
2   *Times*, 9, 16 June 1789.   3   *PH*, xxix, 2 May 1792, 1341–9.
4   *Parliamentary Register*, iii (1788), 246–50.   5   Ibid., 322–3.

the depth of English ignorance, they were compelled to stand
together fairly frequently. Yet the basis for their unified action was
the common support of a specific bill. As partisan tensions mounted
in the late eighteenth century the possibility of anything like a
Scottish national party diminished.

The union of England and Scotland was enormously reinforced
in the second half of the eighteenth century. By bolstering the Scots'
sense of accomplishment, the Scottish Enlightenment enabled them
to establish more confident relationships with England at the same
time as rising rents made more extensive intercourse possible.
The rise in agricultural income was but one consequence of a period
of prolonged economic growth which bound Scotland more closely
to the English economy and stimulated changes which, by breaking
down regional peculiarities, contributed to the common social
development of both countries.

The changing position of its peerage clearly reflects Scotland's
ability to achieve a closer, more cohesive relationship with England.
In the last decades of the eighteenth century the two distinct national
nobilities began to give way to a truly British peerage. Such a
transformation naturally required English acquiescence, and this
the government encouraged by bestowing British peerages on an
increasing number of Scots. Undoubtedly its motives were primarily
political. Yet the creations also demonstrate an implicit rejection
of the assumptions which underlay the standing order of 1711:
that there should be two distinct peerages of England and Scotland
and that the latter should be subordinate to the former. It was not
enough, however, for Englishmen to consent to this transformation;
many aspects of their political and social lives had to be altered before the Scots could play a significant role. Few Scots, for example,
actively involved themselves in the struggle of rival English factions
for power at Westminster as long as they received a steady flow of
patronage. Only when the range of political discussion was expanded
to encompass subjects pertinent to their interests were they likely
to become active participants.

The more congenial English climate is not sufficient to account for
the union of the peerages. The crucial element in this process was
the willingness of the Scots to take advantage of the new climate
and demonstrate by their conduct that the barriers which had divided
the two nobilities had diminishing validity. The Scots peers, in
short, found themselves more closely linked to their English colleagues by class interests. Naturally they sought to establish a more
equal partnership. That neither those peers who sought British
peerages nor their colleagues who attempted to eliminate government influence at peerage elections completely attained their

objectives does not mean that the Scots failed in their essential purpose. An examination of their parliamentary conduct is the clearest indication of the degree to which the two groups had merged. In the late eighteenth century Scottish peers did not form a distinct bloc in the house of lords. Instead of being loyal adherents of 'the party of the crown', they reflected in their conduct the whole range of parliamentary activity. More significantly, at a time when their political consciousness was increasing, it found expression not through uniquely Scottish institutions but through the medium of the emerging British political parties.

It would be misleading to argue that the developments within the Scottish peerage were typical of Scottish society as a whole. The nobility was obviously too small and privileged a group to serve as an effective national barometer. Their wealth and parliamentary duties permitted the peers to maintain much more extensive contacts with the south than the vast portion of the population. Yet, if the peers were more advanced in the process of assimilation, other political developments seem to indicate that their experiences were not unique. The Scottish whigs drew their support from landlords, lawyers and merchants who hoped to see the principles of the English constitution incorporated into the Scottish political fabric. The 1790s revealed the close relationships which existed between the English and Scottish radical groups of the lower middle and working classes. Though the degree of their integration was more complete than that of other Scots, the peers had embarked on a course which was to attract most of their countrymen in the nineteenth century.

15

THE SCOTTISH REPRESENTATIVE PEERS AND
PARLIAMENTARY POLITICS, 1787-1793[1]

G.M. DITCHFIELD

The 1780s witnessed the appearance or re-appearance of an extraordinary number of constitutional and broader political issues concerning the Scottish peers and their sixteen representatives in the house of lords. Fortunately the whole background to this question has been explored recently in a most illuminating exposition.[2] The present paper seeks to examine some of these issues in more detail and in particular to concentrate upon the crucial Lords' division of 13 February 1787 which helped to focus public attention on the relationship between the Scottish peerage and Westminster.

The sixteen peers of Scotland assumed major political importance both at the start and at the end of the eighteenth century. In between, moreover, they remained a constant source of discussion. There were not only regular disputes over individual votes in the peerage elections at Holyrood House but also serious schemes for reform of the entire system. They included Harley's vague and unrealised promise of change in 1712,[3] the plan to create twenty-five hereditary seats for the Scottish representative peers in the Peerage Bill of 1719,[4] the demand for ballot, together with the removal of improper influence and votes for unproven titles in 1734[5] and Richmond's bill of 1780.[6] At the same time there were suggestions that the Scottish representative peers, along with the bishops, should be excluded from the house of lords altogether because of their obvious vulnerability to government influence.[7] Finally from 1770 there

---

1 I wish to thank Kent County Council and the administrative trustees of the Chevening Estate for permission to consult and publish extracts from the Stanhope Papers at the Kent County Council Record Office, County Hall, Maidstone.

2 Michael W. McCahill, 'The Scottish peerage and the house of lords in the late eighteenth century,' above, 283-307.

3 G. S. Holmes, 'The Hamilton affair of 1711–1712: a crisis in Anglo-Scottish relations', *Eng[lish] Hist[orical] Rev[iew]*, lxxvii (1962), 274; above, 168.

4 A. S. Turberville, *The House of Lords in the Eighteenth Century* (Oxford, 1927), 158.

5 W. Cobbett, *Parl[iamentary] Hist[ory of England . . . to 1803]*, ix, 483–511.

6 The duke of Richmond's famous bill for annual parliaments and universal manhood suffrage, which was thrown out by the Lords on 3 June 1780, included provisions for 'giving an hereditary seat to the sixteen peers which shall be elected for Scotland, and for establishing more equitable regulations concerning the peerage of Scotland', *Parl. Hist.*, xxi, 686.

7 C. C. Weston, *English Constitutional Theory and the House of Lords 1556–1832* (London, 1965), 177.

arose a campaign by 'independent' peers to free peerage elections from the grip of administration and the 'tyranny' of the government list.[1] All these questions were revived in the 1780s, giving rise to a series of divisions in the house of lords, of which the most important is printed here. In the light of these decisions there were renewed proposals for reform, notably by the third Earl Stanhope, grandson of the author of the Peerage Bill of 1719. But the fundamental issue remained the same: Scottish representation in the house of lords and government influence in its composition.

The act of Union of 1707 had provided that the 154 members of the Scottish peerage should elect sixteen of their number to serve in the upper chamber of each parliament of Great Britain. But it was by no means clear whether these were to be the only Scottish members of the house of lords. The question soon arose as to whether a peer of Scotland with a British title conferred after the Union could take his seat in the house of lords on an hereditary basis, irrespective of election to the sixteen. Initially the answer seemed to be in the affirmative when the second duke of Queensberry in the Scottish peerage received the British dukedom of Dover in 1708.[2] There was no demur when he entered the Lords and his right to do so was implicitly recognised when he was forbidden, as a British peer, to vote in Scottish peerage elections.[3] But this was overturned on the elevation of the Scottish duke of Hamilton as duke of Brandon in 1711. At the climax of this *cause célèbre*, which infuriated the Scottish peers and even threatened the stability of the union itself, the house of lords resolved on 20 December 1711 'that no patent of honour granted to any Peer of Great Britain, who was a Peer of Scotland at the time of the Union, can entitle such Peer to sit and vote in Parliament, or to sit upon the trial of Peers'.[4] Anti-Scottish motives, the fear of government 'packing' of the upper house and the immediate considerations of party all contributed to the decision.[5] Nor did the first two easily subside. The second duke of Dover was not allowed to take his seat in 1720.[6] Not until 1782 were Scottish

1   McCahill, 'Scottish Peerage', 290ff.
2   G. E. C., *The Complete Peerage*, ed. Vicary Gibbs, et al. (13 vols., London, 1910–40), x, 694–6.
3   *Journals of the House of Lords* [*LJ*], xviii, 609 (resolution of 21 Jan. 1708/9); Turberville, *House of Lords in the eighteenth century*, 149. There is a detailed analysis of the Lords' voting on this resolution in C. Jones, 'Godolphin, the Whig Junto and the Scots: a new Lords division list from 1709', above, 133-49.
4   *LJ*, xix, 346–7, quoted (not quite accurately) in Turberville, *House of Lords*, 151. As the same author (ibid., 151) observes, 'It was not disputed that the Sovereign could raise any subject, Scottish or otherwise, to the dignity of a British peerage; the question was whether the Act of Union contained a limitation debarring a Scots peer, upon whom a British title had been conferred, from receiving a writ of summons to the house of lords.'
5   See above, 174.
6   R. S. Rait, *The Parliaments of Scotland* (Glasgow, 1924), 192. The first duke of

peers with post-Union British titles permitted this privilege, when the eighth duke of Hamilton was finally granted the writ of summons which had been denied to his great grandfather seventy-one years earlier.[1] This exclusion of Scottish peers other than the sixteen had to a very limited extent been circumvented by the practice of conferring British titles not upon Scottish peers themselves but upon their eldest sons, who were then not debarred from the house of lords on succeeding to the Scottish honour.[2] Only gradually did it become apparent that Scottish representation in the Lords was not necessarily confined to the sixteen, but the pretence that it was so restricted was not completely abandoned until 1782.

It was against this background that the peerage issues of the 1780s emerged. The resolution of the Hamilton case had made it possible for the crown to bestow the full status of a British peerage upon peers of Scotland at the very time when economic, cultural and social factors were encouraging many Scottish peers to aspire in that direction.[3] The increasing demand by Scots for British peerages coincided with an easing of the supply. In 1784 Dundas urged Pitt to exploit this possibility of rewarding supporters among the Scottish magnates, adding darkly 'there is no want of promises and expectations upon this precise subject, held out by the opposition to the present Government'.[4] Accordingly, peers of Scotland benefited from no fewer than thirteen creations to or promotions within the British peerage between 1784 and 1806.[5] As soon as members of the sixteen were included in these new creations, however, there was bound to be renewed inquiry into the representation of the Scottish peers in the house of lords, and such inquiry was not long delayed.

As early as 1786 two Scottish representative peers, the eighth earl of Abercorn and the fourth duke of Queensberry were raised to the British peerage as Viscount Hamilton and Baron Douglas

---

Dover had died in July 1711, before the Hamilton decision and unaffected by it. But his son and heir, who succeeded as second duke, came of age in 1719 and tried to take his seat in the Lords the following year.

1   *LJ*, xxxvi, 517 (6 June 1782); Holmes, 'Hamilton affair', above, 175-6.

2   G.E.C. iv, 447, for the six cases of this sort. See also the useful clarification of this point in W. C. Lowe, 'Bishops and Scottish representative peers in the house of lords, 1760–1775', *Journal of British Studies*, xviii; above, 278, n. 79. In the 1780s there were also four peers with pre-Union English titles who were also Scottish peers and who sat in the Lords as of right: the Prince of Wales, (duke of Rothesay), earl of Doncaster (duke of Buccleuch), duke of Richmond (duke of Lennox) and the duke of Leeds (Viscount Dunblane): A. Mackenzie, *A View of the Political State of Scotland at the late General Election* (Edinburgh, 1790), 8.

3   McCahill, 'Scottish peerage', above, 284-9.

4   P[ublic] R[ecord] O[ffice], Pitt Papers, 30/8/157, f. 354, Henry Dundas to Pitt, 26 Jan. 1784.

5   Details in Turberville, *The House of Lords in the Age of Reform* (London, 1958), 444–54.

respectively.[1] Their elevation to the status of hereditary peers,
entitled to a writ of summons to the house of lords, was not in doubt
after 1782. But could they now remain representative peers as well,
sitting in a dual capacity or, should vacancies among the sixteen
automatically arise, be concerned in consequent by-elections?
There were precedents of a sort. In 1711–12 the first duke of Brandon,
although barred from the Lords under his British title, had remained
a representative peer, as duke of Hamilton, until his death in
November 1712.[2] The duke of Atholl had been elected a representative peer in 1734 and had succeeded to the British barony of Strange
three years later, but was allowed to continue undisturbed as a
representative peer until the next general election in 1741.[3] But
there was something odd about each of these cases. Had he lived,
Hamilton would probably have found his status as a representative
peer under challenge; Scottish peers with post-Union British
titles had already been declared incapable of voting in peerage
elections, and exclusion from the sixteen might have been the next
step on the grounds that he who cannot vote cannot be elected.[4]
Atholl, moreover, had acquired his British title through inheritance,
not creation: he was thus not affected by the Hamilton precedent
and there could be no accusation in his case of seeking to 'pack' the
representative peerage with government supporters.

But it was precisely this threat which concerned the parliamentary
opposition of the 1780s. The 'independent' Scottish peers, with their
suspicion of Dundas and the government list, and the Portland
Whigs with their anxiety about the 'influence of the crown,' found
an identity of interest on the subject.[5] The whiggish *Caledonian
Mercury* suspected that the ministry was hoping to keep Abercorn
and Queensberry 'in the double capacity of representing Scotland
and England, until some matters are settled to get their friends
elected' and that this delay amounted to 'an infringement on the
constitution'.[6] The lead was taken by Viscount Stormont who, as
a Scottish representative peer of thirty-three years' standing and a
Northite member of opposition, was influenced by both these

1   The British honours of the Queensberry family, notably the dukedom of
Dover, had become extinct on the death of the third duke in 1778: G.E.C., x, 697–8.
2   William Robertson, *Proceedings relating to the Peerage of Scotland from January 16,
1707, to April 29, 1788* (Edinburgh, 1790), passim, makes it clear that there was no
by-election until Hamilton's death on 15 Nov. 1712, almost a year after the Lords
decided that he could not sit as duke of Brandon.
3   G. E. C. i, 318. Robertson (*Peerage of Scotland*, 181) thought it 'remarkable' that
'no proclamation was issued for electing a new Representative of the Peers of
Scotland in his Grace's room' and that Atholl 'continued to sit in the House of
Lords with a double character, as a Peer of Great Britain, and as one of the Sixteen
Representatives of the Peerage of Scotland'.
4   Rait, *Parliaments*, 191.
5   McCahill, 'Scottish peerage,' above, 295ff.
6   *Caledonian Mercury*, 8 Feb. 1787.

currents of thought. Early in 1787 he demanded a closer scrutiny of the promotions of Abercorn and Queensberry. On 5 February he persuaded the Lords to examine the matter in committee; on 8 February the British patents of the two were laid before the house;[1] on 13 February the whole affair was fully debated. On that day the house of lords resolved itself into a committee of privileges and Stormont argued convincingly that the status of these two representative peers had been fundamentally changed.[2]

Taking the two cases separately, Stormont first moved 'that the Earl of Abercorn, who was chosen to be of the number of the Sixteen peers who, by the treaty of union, are to represent the peerage of Scotland in parliament, having been created Viscount Hamilton by letters patent under the great seal of Great Britain, doth thereby cease to sit in this House as a representative of the peerage of Scotland'. He contended that the decision of 1782 had removed a serious injustice to the Scottish peerage but complained of the unfortunate consequences which might follow if undue advantage were taken of it. 'An hereditary seat and a temporary seat by election are not only different, but incompatible, for this obvious reason,' he declared, 'the hereditary seat takes away the whole effect of the relation that should subsist between the representative and those who chuse him.'[3] It was not simply that the hereditary peer was no longer answerable to his constituents. Most Scottish peers could not sit personally in the house of lords and once their representatives became hereditary peers the principle of 'virtual representation' broke down: 'the moment you are admitted to a personal share in the government, your right to share in it virtually by representation must cease.'[4] The reasonableness of his argument impressed his aristocratic audience as well as subsequent historians.[5]

There were only two speeches on the government side. Lord Chancellor Thurlow urged that no new elections were necessary and cited in support of his view the singularly inappropriate instance of the duke of Richmond 'who, as Duke of Lennox was entitled to and enjoyed all the privileges of a Scotch Duke'.[6] His claim that Abercorn and Queensberry, and others in their position, might continue to sit as representative peers was strongly challenged by

1   J. Debrett, *Parliamentary Register*, xxii (Lords), 7; *LJ*, xxxvii, 590.
2   The report of the debate of 13 Feb. 1787 which has been used here can be found in *Parl. Reg.*, xxii (Lords), 19–29. There are also reports in *Parl. Hist.*, xxvi, 597–607; *Scots Magazine*, xlix, 66–70; *Caledonian Mercury* 17 and 20 Feb. 1787; and *Edinburgh Evening Courant*, 17 Feb. 1787.
3   *Parl. Reg.* xxii (Lords), 20.
4   Ibid.
5   See for example Turberville, *The House of Lords in the Age of Reform*, 104–5.
6   *Parl. Reg.*, xxii (Lords), 27. This was not a valid parallel because Richmond (in his capacity as duke of Lennox) was not a representative peer and his English title dated from before the Union.

Loughborough for the opposition.[1] Stormont's resolution on Abercorn's patent was carried by 52 to 38 and the house immediately accepted without a vote an identically worded motion regarding Queensberry.[2] These resolutions were reported to, and accepted by, the house of lords on the next day, 14 February 1787.[3]

Earl Stanhope's almost complete list of the voting in this division quickly reveals the extent to which it took the form of a confrontation between government and opposition. Ministers sought to resist Stormont's motion, with its possible danger to their allies among the representative peers. Three members of the cabinet—Stafford, Thurlow and Sydney—voted against it. It was no coincidence that the latter two were also the staunchest opponents in the Lords of any type of parliamentary reform in this period. Those traditional supporters of administration in the Lords, who were often regarded as the 'party of the crown', provided at least twenty-three of the thirty-eight votes against Stormont. As the following table shows, most of the elements which constituted the 'party of the crown'[4] threw their weight against Stormont's motion of 13 February 1787:

	Pro.	Con.
Office-holders	3	6
Household (excluding representative peers)	6	7
Scottish representative peers	10	2
Newly created or promoted peers (excluding households and office-holders)	3	6
Bishops	4	2
	26	23

The voting of the Scottish representative peers was markedly discrepant from that of the remainder of the 'party of the crown'. Even the voting of the bishops can be explained by the omission of some of them from the 'Con' total.[5] Only two representative peers (Morton and Aberdeen) voted against the motion, while Abercorn

1   Ibid., 28.
2   See J. C. Sainty and D. Dewar, *Divisions in the House of Lords. An Analytical List 1685 to 1857* (London, 1976), card 5. The voting figures are incorrectly given as 52–28 in Turberville, *House of Lords in the Age of Reform*, 104.
3   *LJ*, xxxvii, 594–5. The debate of 13 Feb. took place in the committee of privileges and was thus not recorded in the *Journals*. The House of Lords Record Office holds the manuscript minutes, which do not record these proceedings, and the Clerk Assistant's Sheets which do. But because Stormont's motion was only reported to the Lords on 14 Feb. this date was at times referred to as the date of the motion itself.
4   This definition of the 'party of the crown' is indebted to D. Large, 'The decline of the "Party of the Crown" and the rise of parties in the house of lords, 1783–1837', above, 235ff.
5   See Appendix.

and Queensberry appear to have abstained. The vote clearly demonstrates that political independence among the Scottish representative peers of the later eighteenth century which recent historians have detected[1] but which still needs to be substantiated by division lists. This independence, moreover, can best be appreciated in the context of the continuing loyalty of the other customary adherents of government in the house of lords. Without the representative peers the 'party of the crown' would have provided a 21 to 16 'Con' vote instead of a 26 to 23 'Pro' vote.[2] Indeed four more names—those of Galloway, Moray, Dunmore and Balcarres—may now be added to Professor McCahill's list of seventeen Scottish representative peers who opposed government at some point between 1783 and 1806.[3] Usually their commitment to government was fairly reliable and their independence would not necessarily extend to other issues[4] but they were far from mere lobby-fodder. At the same time the supposedly more independent Scots with post-Union British titles voted by two (Strange and Norwich) to one (Cardiff) against the motion.[5]

The opposition element in the 'Pro' vote is equally easy to detect. All ten of the leading opposition peers named by McCahill[6] voted for the motion, as did their ally the Prince of Wales. An illuminating comparison, moreover, can be drawn between the division of 13 February 1787 and the voting of the peers on the regency question less than two years later. On 26 December 1788 those who had supported Stormont's motion voted 26 to 17 in favour of opposition on the regency while his opponents voted 25 to 0 for the government.[7] Evidence of a similar sort about extra-parliamentary attitudes can be derived from the Scottish press which, despite the

1   McCahill, 'Scottish peerage', passim, and W. C. Lowe, 'Bishops and Scottish representative peers', 272-80. This independence was also detected by the *Edinburgh Advertiser*, 16–20 Feb. 1787, which correctly informed its readers that 'all the Scots peers now in London voted for a new election . . . excepting the Earls of Morton and Aberdeen'.
2   This calculation takes no account of the five 'Con' voters not named in Stanhope's division list.
3   Michael W. McCahill, *Order and Equipoise. The Peerage and the House of Lords, 1783–1806* (London, 1978), 161, n. 2.
4   On four motions for parliamentary reform in the years 1783–8, the Scottish representative peers voted in almost exactly the same way as the other sections of the 'party of the crown'; See G. M. Ditchfield, 'The house of lords and parliamentary reform in the 1780s', below, 327-45.
5   The fourth duke of Atholl was created Earl Strange in the British peerage in 1786, having served as a representative peer from 1780–4 (not 1780–6, as is stated in *G.E.C.* i, 320–1). He was the great nephew of the second duke, but had not inherited the English barony of Strange. The fourth duke of Gordon was created earl of Norwich in 1784. John Stuart, eldest son of the third earl of Bulte, was created Baron Cardiff in 1766 and did not succeed to his father's Scottish title until 1792.
6   McCahill, *Order and Equipoise*, 123-4.
7   The division in the Lords of 26 Dec. 1788 occurred on an amendment by Rawdon to give the Prince of Wales an immediate regency with full powers. The

competing sensation of the Hastings trial, gave widespread coverage to the peerage debates. Several Scottish newspapers regarded support for Stormont's motion as a 'patriotic' defence of Scottish interests.[1] As the *Edinburgh Advertiser* commented approvingly after the debate:[2]

> The decision in the House of Lords, respecting the Scots Peerage, has given general satisfaction. How could it be otherwise? It was founded in justice and common sense, to set politics and the Union aside. The Scots Peerage is at best but scantily represented, but to permit English peers to represent them, would have been abridging the representation to a mere name, if not destroying it altogether.

Praise was heaped upon those peers who had spoken for Stormont's motion. The 'Pro' vote of 13 February 1787 was clearly seen as a combination of opposition and the more independent supporters of government, with the question of the Scottish peerage the kind of issue which could bring them together. Informed public opinion in Scotland seems to have responded in much the same way.

It remained to be seen whether this decision meant that a Scottish representative peer who acquired a British peerage by inheritance as distinct from direct creation had to forfeit his place among the sixteen. In the only previous case of this type, that of Atholl between 1737 and 1741, there had not been such an outcome. Referring to Atholl's peculiar position, Stormont declared on 13 February 1787, 'There was very little chance that a similar case, that of an old English honour devolving upon a Scotch peer, should happen again.'[3] But soon something very similar did happen. By an odd quirk of irony Stormont himself became a peer of Great Britain when on 20 March 1793 he succeeded his uncle, the celebrated lawyer, as earl of Mansfield. It was widely assumed that a vacancy thereby arose among the sixteen[4] and Lauderdale, a prominent opposition peer, invoked the resolutions of 13 February 1787, demanding that a writ be issued for a new peerage election. On 14 June 1793, however, his motion to this effect was lost by 32 to 26.[5] Times had changed since 1787, and so had opinion in the

---

division list is printed in *Parl. Hist.*, xxvii, 890–1. It is curious to reflect that Queensberry, newly elevated as Baron Douglas and one of the symbols of government influence, deserted the administration over the regency and was dismissed from his lordship of the bedchamber as a result: *G.E.C.* x, 701–2.

1   See for example *Caledonian Mercury*, 8 Feb. 1787.
2   *Edinburgh Advertiser*, 20–23 Feb. 1787. For a similar view see *Edinburgh Evening Courant*, 22 Feb. 1787.
3   *Parl. Reg.*, xxii (Lords), 23.
4   See, for example, *Caledonian Mercury*, 21 Mar. 1793.
5   *Parl. Reg.*, xxxvi, 261; Sainty and Dewar, *Divisions in the House of Lords*, card 5. Lauderdale was a representative peer from 1790 to 1796.

house of lords. Stormont was now a staunch supporter of a broadly-based government at war with revolutionary France; in 1794 he was to be appointed to high office in that government. There was accordingly no new writ or by-election and the second earl of Mansfield remained a representative peer until the dissolution of parliament in 1796.[1] His example was followed by the earl of Eglintoun who was created Baron Ardrossan in the United Kingdom peerage on 15 February 1806. He too defied Lords' protests, which insisted that his elevation was an attack on 'that Security for the Defence and Preservation of their Rights, which the Petitioners conceive cannot exist when the Representative has not an Identity of Situation and Interest with his Constituents, and no sufficient Motive to value their Suffrages'.[2] Eglintoun remained a representative peer until the next general election, in December 1806— precisely the practice which Morton had advocated when opposing Stormont's motion in 1787. As with so many eighteenth-century attacks on supposed government 'influence', the consequences of that vote were more symbolic than practical.

Nonetheless the consequences extended to other issues during the following six years. Because of Stormont's resolution, by-elections were necessary to fill the two vacancies caused by the removal of Abercorn and Queensberry from the sixteen. They were held in April 1787 and two opponents of government, Selkirk and Kinnaird, were elected.[3] Controversy arose, however, from the fact that votes were cast in this election by two holders of post-Union British peerages, Gordon and Queensberry; although their votes did not affect the result[4] there were complaints at the election meeting itself that the Lords' resolution of 21 January 1709 had been defied.[5] The protests mounted and were quickly taken up in the house of lords.

1   Stormont inherited the earldom of Mansfield by a special remainder (*G.E.C.* viii, 390) granted to him in 1792. It is important to note that he did not cease to be a representative peer in 1793 as is stated in D. E. Ginter, *Whig Organisation in the General Election of 1790* (Univ. of California Press, 1967), 4, n. 2. Ginter follows the error in the *Dictionary of National Biography* in describing Stormont as secretary of state for the southern (instead of northern) department in 1779–82. The version in *G.E.C.* viii, 391, n. (a), is correct, except that Stormont did not remain a representative peer until his death. He was not a candidate in the Scottish peerage elections in July 1796 and died on 1 Sept. of that year.

2   *LJ*, xlv, 695–6 (13 June 1806). The *Journals* print four petitions from Scottish peers sympathetic to the opposition against Eglintoun's continuing as one of the sixteen. Interestingly, however, they did not win the signature of any of the representative peers of the time.

3   The voting figures were Selkirk 41, Kinnaird 26, Cathcart 25, Dumfries 7: See Robertson, *Peerage of Scotland*, 434–5.

4   Ibid.; both voted for Selkirk and Cathcart.

5   For the protests of Selkirk and Kinnaird and the pained reply of the clerks that they were obliged to record all votes and all protests, see ibid., 436–8.

On 18 May 1787 Hopetoun, himself one of the supporters of opposition among the representative peers, opened the second Lords' debate on that subject in three months.[1] It was clear, he contended, that in 1709 the Lords had determined that a peer of Scotland who was created a peer of Great Britain after the Union was not entitled to vote in peerage elections. His claim that no such peer had ever so voted was not quite correct; in 1734 the dukes of Hamilton and Queensberry had both voted and had also been unsuccessful candidates.[2] The second duke of Atholl, moreover, voted regularly in peerage elections after inheriting the barony of Strange in 1737.[3] But these were the only cases of the sort, and the resolution of 1709 was also understood to apply to holders of those British peerages which had originally been bestowed on the eldest sons of Scottish peers.[4] In his insistence that the resolution of 1709 be confirmed, Hopetoun received warm support from Stormont, Stanhope, Kinnaird and Denbigh. Those who spoke against him included cabinet ministers (Thurlow and Sydney) and Scots with some personal interest in the question (Queensberry himself and the ambitious Morton).[5] By 51 votes to 35 the Lords adopted Hopetoun's motion to re-affirm the resolution of 1709 and to transmit a copy to the lord clerk register with an implicit rebuke for accepting the two improper votes of Gordon and Queensberry.[6] This was an apparent victory for those favouring 'free elections' to the representative peerage. Behind it, of course, lay the fear that peerage elections might be unduly influenced by the friends of government. In the strictly constitutional sense Hopetoun's case was watertight, although it was argued on the other side that the resolution of 1709 need be no

---

1   For the Lords debate of 18 May 1787, see *Parl. Reg.*, xxii (Lords) 156–70; *Parl. Hist.*, xxvi, 1158–67; *Scots Mag.*, xlix (1787), 373–6, and *Caledonian Mercury*, 24 and 26 May 1787.
2   Robertson, *Peerage of Scotland*, 154–60; Sir James Fergusson, *The Sixteen Peers of Scotland* (Oxford, 1960), 39–40; *Caledonian Mercury*, 26 May 1787.
3   Robertson, passim.
4   Mackenzie, *Political State of Scotland*, 7. lists nine 'Scotch Peers created Peers of Great Britain since the Union who do not vote at Elections'. They included Hamilton, Queensberry, Atholl, Gordon and Abercorn. The other four were either Scottish peers who inherited post-Union British peerages along with their Scottish titles (Montrose, Roxburgh, Kinnoul) or were still the eldest sons of Scottish peers when the British title was conferred upon them (Argyll, who was created Baron Sundridge (GB) in 1766 and succeeded as fifth duke of Argyll in 1770). According to Fergusson, *The Sixteen Peers*, 39–40, Montrose and Roxburgh had their votes accepted by the clerks at the election of 1734 despite being 'disqualified by British peerages conferred in 1722'. In fact their votes were accepted because they were entirely valid, since neither was a British peer at the time. The British peerages were conferred in 1722 not upon them but upon their eldest sons, neither of whom had succeeded to his father's title by 1734.
5   Morton's support for the government over this issue was at least partly motivated by his desire for a British peerage; see above, 294, n. 2.
6   *LJ*, xxxvii, 709.

more sacrosanct than the Hamilton precedent of December 1711, which had been swept away in 1782.[1]

It is difficult to avoid the conclusion that the two votes of 13 February and 18 May 1787 were very similar, even though no division list survives for the latter. The voting figures themselves were almost identical: Stormont's resolution was carried 52 to 38, Hopetoun's 51 to 35. The fundamental aim behind each was the same and it is likely that a supporter of one would also endorse the other. The *Lords Journals* show that 31 of the 52 'Pro' voters and 21 of the 33 known 'Con' voters of 13 February were present on 18 May.[2] Five of the six 'Pro' speakers on 18 May had also voted 'Pro' on 13 February.[3] Of the five 'Con' speakers on 18 May, three had voted 'Con' on 13 February; of the other two, one (Queensberry) had not voted at all and the other (Richmond) had voted 'Pro' on 13 February and only spoke against Hopetoun's resolution on technical grounds.[4] The Scottish representative peers had been urged to attend on both occasions and did so in high numbers.[5] The list of 13 February 1787 undoubtedly casts much light upon the division of 18 May.

But this 'victory' of May 1787 was short-lived. The intricate and much disputed peerage election of 1790 helped to convince Dundas that the exclusion of Scottish peers with post-Union British titles was an unnecessary handicap to government interests and he favoured either 'the opinion of the judges' or a 'short explanatory law' to admit them to the franchise.[6] Ultimately however this solution was not required. In the election of 1790 Abercorn and Queensberry defiantly voted. The clerks, obedient to the decision of May 1787, would not accept their votes and a series of protests followed.[7] The final outcome of the election was not clear until the summer of 1793 when the Lords resolved the outstanding issues. On 13 May 1793 Grenville secured the defeat of Kinnoul's motion to disqualify the two questionable votes and carried a motion of his

---

1   Morton's speech, 18 May 1787: *Parl. Reg.*, xxii (Lords), 168.
2   See appendix for their identification.
3   The exception was Kinnaird who had not been a representative peer in Feb. 1787.
4   *Parl. Reg.*, xxii (Lords), 168–9. Richmond made clear his agreement with the principle of Hopetoun's motion but complained of the lack of notice which had been given and the consequent absence of one of the peers concerned (Gordon). He also urged the desirability of proceeding legislatively rather than by Lord's resolution.
5   See McCahill, above, chapter 14, p. 304,\note 5. The *Lords Journals* show that fourteen of the sixteen were present on 13 Feb. 1787 (the exceptions being Dalhousie and Elphinstone) and twelve on 18 May.
6   Dundas to W. W. Grenville, 1 Aug. 1790; *Historical Manuscripts Commission 13th Report*, iii, Fortescue MSS, i, 596–7.
7   These proceedings are outlined in Mackenzie, *Political State of Scotland*, 15 ff.

own that the matter be referred to the judges.[1] But when the committee of privileges made this recommendation to the house of lords on 23 May it was rejected by 31 to 30 and the house immediately passed, 48 to 41, a motion that 'the votes of the Duke of Queensberry and the Earl of Abercorn, at the last election of the sixteen peers of Scotland, ought to have been counted, if duly tendered'.[2] These majorities were small but decisive. Although this resolution was never officially communicated to the lord clerk register,[3] its authority was thereafter accepted and there was no further obstacle to the participation in peerage elections of the growing number of Scottish peers with British titles.

This was by no means the only source of controversy over the representative peers in the 1780s. The death of Dalhousie necessitated a by-election among the sixteen in January 1788, the government candidate, Lord Cathcart, defeating his 'independent' opponent, Dumfries, by 28 to 27. Although no peer of Great Britain became involved, there was still a disputed return. Dumfries immediately challenged Cathcart's election, attacking the validity of one of his votes. The pretended 'Lord Rutherford' had voted, by signed list, for Cathcart, in defiance of a ruling by the house of lords in 1762 that neither of the two individuals who then laid claim to that honour should be entitled to vote in respect of it until a satisfactory claim had been established.[4] On 5 February 1788 Selkirk took up the matter in the Lords, asking that it be referred to the committee of privileges. His move to do so was lost 29 to 20 but this was not the end of the story.[5] On 13 February Dumfries petitioned against the 'Rutherford' vote and the return of Cathcart. His cause was championed by Kinnaird, Selkirk and other 'independent' peers, and the house of lords on 21 April 1788 passed three resolutions against the government: firstly, by 25 votes to 18, that Cathcart's election had been an 'undue return'; secondly, that the 'Rutherford' vote in favour of Cathcart should have been rejected; thirdly, that the lord clerk register and his deputies 'ought to conform to the Resolutions of this House'.[6] Voting figures and a

1   *Parl. Reg.*, xxxvi, 211–216. Because these debates took place in the committee of privileges they are not recorded in the *Lords Journals* or Sainty and Dewar, *Divisions in the House of Lords*.
2   *Parl. Reg.*, xxxvi, 226–9; *Scots Mag.*, lv (1793), 377–8; Sainty and Dewar, *Divisions in the House of Lords*, card 5. For details of the voting of individual peers in the contest of 1790 see PRO, Pitt Papers, 30/8/234, f. 260, 'Table of the Election of the Sixteen Peers of Scotland, 24 July 1790'.
3   Fergusson, *Sixteen Peers*, 42, 47.
4   Robertson, *Peerage of Scotland*, 447–9; *Scots Mag.*, l (1788), 48. The clerks defended their acceptance of this vote by pointing out that the Lords' resolution of 1762 excluded only two named claimants to the Rutherford title and that the 'Rutherford' vote in 1788 had been cast by a third: *Scots Mag.*, l, 200.
5   *Parl. Reg.*, xxiv, 253–63.
6   *LJ*, xxxviii, 150; Sainty and Dewar, *Divisions in the House of Lords*, card 5.

division list are only available for the first of these resolutions,[1] but they reveal another interesting clash between government and opposition. The division list bears comparison with that of 13 February 1787. Seventeen of the 'Pro' voters on the earlier occasion voted on 21 April 1788, and they divided 15 to 2 for the resolution—that is to say, against Cathcart and the government interest. Five 'Con' voters of 13 February all voted the other way. The supporters of 'free elections' in 1787 were thus prominent in opposing the government nominee in the following year. The representative peers voted 8 to 2 against Cathcart,[2] while the Scottish peers with post-union British titles divided equally, two on each side. As in the vote of 13 February 1787 the representative peers showed themselves more independent of government than their hereditary compatriots. Many supporters of Stormont's motion clearly were prepared to back the opposition case on 21 April 1788, a fact too easily obscured by the ultimate confirmation of Cathcart's election.[3]

Predictably the debates of the 1780s rekindled suggestions for improving the mode of election to the sixteen; and these ideas were aired even before the Irish act of Union had illuminated the relatively unfavourable position of the Scottish peerage by enacting that the twenty-eight Irish representative peers should be elected for life, with the remainder eligible for election to the Commons. In particular that perennial reformer, Earl Stanhope, was encouraged to take up the subject. His credentials for doing so were impeccable. He had interested himself in a variety of reforming causes, contributed impressively to the Scottish peerage debates of 1787-8 and preserved a division list for Stormont's motion. He had taken up the alleged injustice whereby the eldest sons of Scottish peers were incapacitated from representing or voting in Scottish constituencies,[4] championing the attempt of the radical young Lord Daer to enrol as a voter in the Stewartry of Kirkcudbright in 1789.[5] In the late 1780s Stanhope began to prepare a bill to

---

1   *Scots Mag.*, l (1788), 201, for the list; McCahill, 'Scottish Peerage', 294, no. 1.
2   McCahill, 'Scottish Peerage', above, 294.
3   Although the disqualification of the Rutherford vote temporarily deprived Cathcart of his majority, he successfully challenged one of Dumfries's votes (that of Lord Colville of Ochiltree). Each side accordingly lost one vote, and on 29 Apr. 1788 Cathcart was declared elected, as before, by a majority of one: *Parl. Reg.*, xxiv, 349–50. McCahill is thus incorrect in asserting ('Scottish peerage', 294) that the government 'required the vote of the fraudulent peer' to secure Cathcart's return.
4   Rait, *Parliaments*, 290–1. Under this rule Francis Charteris, MP for Haddington burghs, was obliged to relinquish his seat in May 1787 when the succession of his father to the earldom of Wemyss made him the eldest son of a Scottish peer. For this odd case see Sir Lewis Namier and John Brooke, *The History of Parliament: the House of Commons 1754–1790* (3 vols., London, 1964), ii, 209–10. There was no comparable restriction upon the eldest sons of English peers.
5   The attempt of Daer, the eldest son of the earl of Selkirk, to enrol was thwarted

clarify the procedures for choosing the sixteen and, for a time, it appeared that such a bill might be introduced. Thurlow and Kinnaird referred to it as a possibility on 18 May 1787[1] and so did Stanhope himself the next year. Addressing the Lords on the Rutherford case on 5 February 1788, he insisted on the need for a measure 'to rescue the Peerage (of Scotland) from the abuses to which they were liable'.[2]

The correspondence and drafts of the bill in the Stanhope papers reveal his intentions and priorities. With the aid of detailed research into previous cases and with the advice at the outset of the eminent Scottish judge Lord Hailes,[3] Stanhope drew up 'An Act for the further and better regulating the Election of the Peers to represent the Peers of Scotland in Parliament'. One of his concerns was to restrict government influence and his bill would accordingly have given statutory force to Stormont's resolution, extending it to Scottish representative peers who inherited British titles.[4] But his principal aims were to revise the methods laid down at the Union for choosing the sixteen and the removal of 'several inconveniences, difficulties and abuses' which had arisen in the conduct of peerage elections.[5] Stanhope sought to tidy the Union roll and purge it of dubious peerages; to prevent the acceptance of votes in respect of dormant peerages; and to ensure that Scottish peers inheriting titles other than by direct descent should have to prove their right of succession before admission to the roll. No further dispute such as that over Rutherford was to be allowed to arise. Stanhope envisaged specific procedural changes. His bill would have established a peerage court, composed of all Scottish peers who did not also have British titles, which would meet each July in Edinburgh to receive the report of a smaller 'peerage annual committee' charged with regulating the Union roll and ascertaining 'proofs

---

by the local freeholders, whose objections were sustained by the court of session in 1792. Daer appealed to the house of lords in the following year and lost again, although Stanhope spoke in his support: *Scots Mag.*, lv (1793), 278–9; *LJ*, xxxix, 582. The printed statements of the cases in the Lords of Daer and his opponents, together with extensive notes on the affair by Stanhope, may be found in the Stanhope Papers, C80/4.

1   *Parl. Reg.*, xxii (Lords), 159, 165.
2   Ibid., xxiv, 261.
3   There is a bundle of notes by Stanhope on previous decisions in Scottish peerage cases in Stanhope Papers C80/3; see also Stanhope to Lord Hailes (copy), 31 Mar. 1786, and Hailes to Stanhope, 6 Apr. 1786 in Stanhope Papers C80/2. For the background to Stanhope's interest in reform, see Aubrey Newman, *The Stanhopes of Chevening. A Family Biography* (London, 1969), chaps. 5 and 6.
4   MS draft of Scottish peerage bill: Stanhope Papers, C80/2, p. 16.
5   Ibid. The details of peerage elections were specified in the act of Union (5 Anne, c. 8), articles xxii and xxiii, and the 'Act to make further provision for electing and summoning sixteen peers of Scotland' (6 Anne, c. 23). These acts are printed in D. Pickering (ed.), *The Statutes at Large*, xi, 207–10 and 375–82 respectively.

relative to each & every fact' asserted about Scottish honours.[1] The peerage court was to be empowered to resolve (by ballot) complaints, incorrect entries and disputed enrolments. The new system was intended to take effect in 1788. On election day the Scottish peers would elect a 'praeses' and a group of five peers with the responsibility of supervising the elections and preparing minutes. An element of public scrutiny was to be built into the whole proceedings, with the minutes of election meetings to be sent to the clerk of the crown in chancery, where any Scottish peer or his agent could have access to them.[2] Above all, the system of resolving election disputes was to be reformed. In the eighteenth century the lord clerk register and his assistants were 'merely Ministerial officers'[3] with no judicial discretion, and the meeting of peers could not 'judge of the grounds of protest'.[4] The only possibility was the lodging of protests with the clerks and submitting them for determination to the house of lords, a procedure whose clumsiness became particularly apparent in the peerage election of 1790. Stanhope's bill would have given the 'praeses' a casting vote in the event of a tie and the peerage court the power to settle disputed votes.

Stanhope's bill never saw the light of day and was apparently not even printed. It was probably submerged under the welter of his other reforming activity and quietly abandoned in the French revolutionary period. But the changes which he favoured commanded much contemporary support and some of them slowly materialised in the course of the nineteenth century. In 1832 the eldest sons of Scottish peers became eligible to serve as MPs for Scottish seats. Acts of 1847 and 1851 regularised the procedures for electing the sixteen and provided for the elimination from the Union roll of doubtful or extinct peerages. Any peerage in respect of which no vote had been received for fifty years or more could now be deleted from the roll.[5] In 1869 there were abortive proposals that the number of Scottish representative peers be increased and that they be elected for life, like their Irish counterparts.[6] At the same time there were changes in the rôle of the lord clerk register. Lord Frederick Campbell, holder of this office from 1768 to 1816, never attended peerage elections and their conduct was by convention delegated to deputies. But after the act of 1879 had freed him

---

1   MS notes for Scottish peerage bill: Stanhope Papers C80/1.
2   MS draft of Scottish peerage bill: Stanhope Papers C80/2, p. 20.
3   *Gentleman's Magazine*, lx (1790) ii, 664.
4   Mackenzie, *Political State of Scotland*, 15, where the procedures as they applied in 1790 are outlined.
5   L. O. Pike, *Constitutional History of the House of Lords* (London, 1894), 286; Fergusson, *Sixteen Peers*, 20, 28–32.   6   Pike, *Constitutional History*, 367.

from the responsibility of supervising the archives,[1] the lord clerk register began to act as returning officer at peerage elections, exercising as a Scottish peer the powers of the 'praeses' envisaged in Stanhope's bill. Finally in 1963 the remaining peers of Scotland were all granted 'the same right to receive writs of summons to attend the House of Lords and to sit and vote in that House as the holder of a peerage of the United Kingdom',[2] —an outcome which at least some Scottish peers would have wished in 1707.

The determination by the Lords of these peerage questions in the late 1780s was not without broader political significance. Details of the voting have hitherto been comparatively limited, and division lists such as that of 13 February 1787 are almost unknown. The issues, moreover, formed part of a wider debate over the so-called 'influence of the crown', economical reform and the desire to restrict executive sway over the legislature. In that the purification of parliament and electorate was the common aim, the exclusion from the sixteen of Scottish peers with British titles bears comparison with the removal of government contractors from the Commons and the disfranchisement of revenue officers in 1782. Nor would it be fanciful to place the views expressed over the representative peerage in the context of a firmer assertion of Scottish interests within the Union. The campaigners for burgh reform, the petitioners of the Church of Scotland seeking relief from the Test Act, the opponents of the proposal to reduce the number of judges of the court of session, all were pressing, more or less consciously, in that direction. Although never publicly agitated in Scotland the peerage question was one factor which helped important elements among the Scottish nobility and gentry to see their nation as 'standing apart from England and, at the same time, moving into a closer relationship with it'.[3] The Scottish representative peers were not immune from this climate of opinion. The peerage controversies of the 1780s helped to draw forth their independent streak which is exemplified in the list of 13 February 1787, a document which serves to refute the more extreme charges of servility made against them and amply confirms what Professor McCahill diagnosed as their 'surprisingly high rejection of governmental leadership', at least before the French Revolution.[4] Less surprising, perhaps, is the fact that it was an independence most fully displayed over Scottish issues.

1   Fergusson, *Sixteen Peers*, 111. This function was now transferred to the deputy clerk register.
2   Peerage Act, 1963, clause 4 (11 & 12 Eliz. 2, c. 48).
3   N. T. Phillipson, 'Scottish public opinion and the Union in the age of the Association', in N. T. Phillipson and R. Mitchison (eds.), *Scotland in the Age of Improvement* (Edinburgh, 1970), 126.
4   Above, 301.

APPENDIX

EARL STANHOPE'S LIST OF THE LORDS' DIVISION ON STORMONT'S
MOTION, 13 FEBRUARY 1787

This division list is reproduced as it appears in the Stanhope papers, Kent
Archives Office, U1590, item C80/5. Stanhope named all 52 peers who
voted 'Pro' and 33 of the 38 who voted 'Con'. Probably the five missing
'Con' voters were bishops; Stanhope's last entry in the 'Con' column was
'Bps of Lincoln', implying that others should have been added.

One teller is included in the totals of those voting on each side; in this
division the tellers were Galloway (Pro) and Morton (Con).[1] Stanhope
lists Craven as an earl when he was in fact a baron. Craven and St John,
though named here, do not appear in the list of peers present on 13 February
1787 in *Lords Journals*, xxxvii, 593–4, but the *Journals* were not always
completely accurate in this respect.[2]

Square brackets have been used to provide necessary additions; rounded
brackets are Stanhope's own. Original spellings have been retained. An
asterisk indicates those peers who were also present on 18 May 1787.

'On the Question relative to the Peers of Scotland 13 Feby. 1787. Division
in House of Lords.'

	Pro.			*Con.*
*	Prince of Wales		* Dukes of	Chandos
*	Duke of Cumberland			Bridgewater
* Dukes of	Manchester			Montagu
*	Richmond		Marquis of	Stafford
*	Portland		*	Buckingham
*	Devonshire		* Earls of	Morton
* Marquis of	Carmarthen		*	Chatham
	Lothian			Effingham
* Earls	Hopetoun		*	Strange
*	Galloway			Norwich
*	Shaftesbury		*	Aberdeen
*	Stanhope		*	Abingdon
*	Stamford		*	Aylesford
*	Fitzwilliam		*	Aylesbury
*	Moray		V[iscount]	Weymouth
*	Cassilis		* Lords	Thurlow
*	Breadalbane		*	Sydney
	Uxbridge		*	Walsingham
	Dunmore		*	Hawkesbury
*	Eglintoun		*	Scarsdale
*	Denbigh		*	Sommers

1   Sainty and Dewar, *Divisions in the House of Lords*, card 5, for identification of
the tellers.
2   See C. Jones, 'Seating problems in the house of lords in the early eighteenth
century: the evidence of the manuscript minutes', *Bulletin of the Institute of Historical
Research*, li (1978), 132–45.

	Pro.		*Con.*
*	Craven	*	Harrowby
	Ferrers	*	Ducie
	Fauconberg	*	Delaval
	Rochford	*	Digby
*	Westmorland		Dacre
*	Scarborough	*	Southampton
*	Balcarres		Brudenall
*	Sandwich		Gage
	Winchelsea	*	Boston
*	Derby		Fortescue
*	Carlisle		Qy. Archp. of Canterbury [Moore]
	Leicester		Bps. of Lincoln [Thurlow]
* V[iscount]	Stormont		
	Mount-Edgecumbe		
*	Hampden		
	Falmouth		
*	Dudley & Ward		
Lords	Rodney		
*	Rawdon		
*	Ponsonby (i.e. E. of Bessborough)		
	Loughborough		
	Bulkeley		
*	Amhurst		
	Cardiff		
	Porchester		
	Vernon		
	St. John		

Arch. of York [Markham]
Bps of St. Asaph [Shipley]
      Norwich [Bagot]
      Llandaff [Watson]

D. of Queensberry   – did not vote
E. of Abercorn   – did not vote
      Cholmondeley – locked out (would have been *Pro*)
Qy. Abergavenny
      Camden   – went away
Qy. Dartmouth
Qy. Waldegrave
Qy. V. Wentworth
Ld. Grantley   – went away
      Brownlow   – did not vote
      Middleton   – did not vote
Qy. Teynam

16

THE HOUSE OF LORDS AND PARLIAMENTARY REFORM IN THE SEVENTEEN-EIGHTIES[1]

G.M. DITCHFIELD

THE PUBLICATION in 1976 of J. C. Sainty and D. Dewar's analytical list of divisions in the house of lords between 1685 and 1857[2] provides a welcome stimulus to further inquiries in this area. The compilers express the hope that their labours in the cause of division lists will 'encourage the search for such lists and facilitate their identification when found'.[3] They indicate 136 occasions in the parliaments of 1780–4 and 1784–90 when divisions in the house of lords took place, but the names of those voting on each side were hardly ever recorded. This article offers the addition of four lords' division lists from the seventeen-eighties to the total of those already known. Each concerns some aspect of parliamentary reform and each is located in the papers of Charles, 3rd Earl Stanhope, who drew them up. It is proposed here to examine these lists and to place them in the context of reform bills to which they belong. Stanhope was an incorrigible compiler of parliamentary lists and had excellent means of access to the necessary information.[4] Even before his succession to the title on 7 March 1786 he seems to have attended debates in the Lords. The lists of June 1783 and July 1785 both date from the period when, as Lord Mahon, he was M.P. for Chipping Wycombe. As a relative of Pitt, with his father in the upper Chamber and with a host of other connections, he had every opportunity of obtaining immediate and accurate knowledge about the voting of the peers. Lords' division lists for these years are rare and it was not until 1857 that such lists were officially published.[5] As a consequence historians of the late eighteenth century have been restricted in their studies of the house of lords at the very time when that body played an important and at times decisive role in parliamentary politics.[6]

These four lists help to reinforce the impression that no decade in the eighteenth century witnessed so detailed a concentration on electoral reform as did the seventeen-eighties. The issues themselves—fraudulent voters, disputed returns, expenses, bribery—were far from new, but parliamentary attention was focused upon them more intensely than ever before. This is most obvious in the disfranchisement measures associated with Economical Reform, in the reform of the borough of Cricklade and in Pitt's three motions for parliamentary reform.

---

[1] I wish to thank the Kent County Council and the Administrative Trustees of the Chevening Estate for permission to consult and publish extracts from the Stanhope Papers at the Kent County Council Record Office, County Hall, Maidstone.

[2] *Divisions in the House of Lords: an Analytical List, 1685–1857*, comp. J. C. Sainty and D. Dewar (House of Lords Record Office Occasional Pubns., ii, 1976).

[3] *Ibid.*, p. 5.

[4] Other parliamentary lists in the Stanhope Papers include undated surveys of the house of commons (U1590 C79/1), a division list of the house of lords (*ibid.*) which is undated but is clearly that on the India Bill of 15 Dec. 1783, differing only very slightly from the version published in the *Political Magazine*, v (1783), 404–5, and a Lords' division on the question of the Scottish peerage, 13 Feb. 1787 (U1590 C80/5).

[5] *Divisions, 1685–1857*, p. 5. For detailed comments on attendance and voting procedures in the Lords see *ibid.*, pp. 7–14 and C. Jones, 'Seating problems in the house of lords in the early 18th century: the evidence of the manuscript minutes', *B.I.H.R.*, li (1978), 132-45.

[6] See the understandable complaints made about the shortage of Lords' division lists by D. Large, 'The decline of "the Party of the Crown" and the rise of parties in the house of lords, 1783–1837', *Eng. Hist. Rev.*, lxxviii , above, 234 & n., and by M. W. McCahill, *Order and Equipoise: the Peerage and the House of Lords, 1783–1806* (1978), p. 145 n. 1.

Limited reform of this type was a continuing theme throughout this period. Three of its fruits were the 'Act to limit the duration of polls and scrutinies' (25 Geo. III, c. 84; 1785), the 'Act to prevent occasional inhabitants from voting in the election of members to serve in parliament for cities and boroughs' (26 Geo. III, c. 100; 1786) and W. W. Grenville's 'Act for the further regulation of the trials of controverted elections' (28 Geo. III, c. 52; 1788). Apart from these legislative enactments there was a cluster of measures which failed in the house of commons, such as Marsham's bill to disfranchise ordnance and navy personnel in 1786, Sawbridge's repeated motions to shorten the duration of parliament and Sheridan's proposals to reform the Scottish burghs. No doubt even those measures which were enacted lacked effectiveness; arguably too some became over-obsessed with minutiae. But they ensured that the regulation of elections was never far from the attention of either house of parliament.

In this current of reformist activity Stanhope was a prime mover. The three division lists of 1783–6 and the canvassing list of 1788 all reflect his interest in the principles and technicalities of electoral reform. A protégé of Shelburne and friend of Wyvill, he had thrown himself eagerly into the County Association movement from its inception, especially in Kent, and quickly established a reputation as an advocate of reform on his election to the house of commons in 1780.[7] He belonged to the Society for Constitutional Information and gave full support to motions for reform, including those of Pitt.[8] Thanks in part to his energy, parliamentary reform was not entirely abandoned with the defeat of Pitt's third motion on 18 April 1785: it persisted in narrower forms throughout the decade, bursting forth in its full colours once more with Flood's celebrated effort of March 1790. The succession of bills painstakingly prepared and introduced by Stanhope helped to maintain this process. They not only embodied the traditional 'country' concern to reduce the so-called 'influence of the Crown' and to free parliament from excessive dependence upon the executive but, in the issue of the 'rights of voters', reflected the more 'democratic' stirrings of the later eighteenth century as well. The latter element had already appeared before the Lords in the form of Richmond's fruitless bill for adult male suffrage and annual parliaments in 1780.[9] Stanhope represented both principal types of reformist motivation and formed a link between the two.

In particular his work reflected growing public concern over the conduct and cost of county elections. Some changes were indeed made. In 1780 the law governing the qualification for the county vote was amended: freeholders now had to present a certificate of land tax assessment made within six months before the election.[10] In 1785 the maximum duration of all polls was restricted to fifteen

---

[7] See A. Newman, *The Stanhopes of Chevening: a Family Biography* (1969), ch. v; P. L. Humphries, 'Public opinion and radicalism in Kentish politics, *c.* 1768–1784' (unpublished University of Kent at Canterbury M. A. thesis, 1979), chs. vii, viii.

[8] Mahon spoke in favour of Sir George Savile's motion for a committee to consider the petition of the delegated counties for a redress of grievances on 8 May 1781 (W. Cobbett, *Parliamentary History of England* (36 vols., 1806–20), xxii, col. 199); was a teller for Sawbridge's motion for shorter parliaments on 30 May 1781 (*ibid.*, xxii, col. 358); was a teller for Pitt's reform motion of 7 May 1783 (*ibid.*, xxiii, col. 875) and voted for Pitt's reform motion of 18 Apr. 1785 (*ibid.*, xxv, col. 477).

[9] Richmond's bill was rejected without a division by the peers on 3 June 1780 (*ibid.*, xxi, cols. 686–8; A. G. Olson, *The Radical Duke; the Career and Correspondence of Charles Lennox, 3rd duke of Richmond* (Oxford, 1961), pp. 48–9).

[10] 20 Geo. III, c. 17; E. and A. G. Porritt, *The Unreformed House of Commons* (2 vols., Cambridge, 1903; repr., New York, 1963), i. 24–5. The act was passed in 1780 and came into effect 1 Jan. 1781. Previously the time qualification had been 12 months. There is a survey of the changes in the legislation governing the qualification for the county franchise in Porritt, i, ch. ii.

days.[11] But Stanhope wanted to go further than this. He sought to establish a register of county voters and reduce the costs of county elections by allowing the poll to be held simultaneously in several places. He made careful studies of at least two previous bills which had tried to move in this direction—Fuller's bill of 1774[12] and the measure introduced by Thomas Powis and Sir Cecil Wray in 1778–9.[13] The latter proposal, despite Stanhope's reservations about it, particularly influenced him and helped to mould his own county register bills.[14] In conjunction with Wyvill, and soon also with Wilberforce, he began to formulate a series of county election bills and to take the lead in parliamentary discussions on the subject. He made characteristically meticulous preparations, pursued detailed antiquarian research into the history of the franchise and even contemplated the publication of a volume of electoral statutes in 1788.[15]

Each of the four bills covered by these lists—those of 1783, 1785, 1786 and 1788—was a product of this endeavour. That of 1783 was mainly concerned with bribery; the other three dealt with the registration of county voters. The house of lords was a vital arena for the stream of bills which Stanhope initiated in the seventeen-eighties. While, as might have been expected, some failed in the Commons, others (including three of the four under consideration here) were defeated in the Lords after a successful passage in the Commons, and the bill of 1788 was actually carried in both Houses to achieve a place, albeit briefly, in the statute book. These four efforts, then, form part of a pattern, of which a brief outline is necessary.

The first list printed here, that of 25 June 1783, came at the height of the young Mahon's parliamentary crusade against bribery. In 1782 he had introduced a bill 'to prevent Bribery and Expense in Elections of Members to serve in Parliament'. Its purpose was to suppress corruption and to reduce the travelling costs of voters and candidates by allowing the sheriff to move the poll to different places in the constituency. At an early stage Mahon separated the bribery and polling components of the bill and pushed ahead with the former.[16] Despite the eloquent support of Pitt and despite Mahon's concessions to his opponents[17] the bill encountered consistent criticism, notably from Fox. On 21 June 1782 the 'incapacitating' clause which would have imposed penalties on those found guilty of bribery[18] was lost in a Commons committee by 66 votes to 40,

---

[11] 25 Geo. III, c. 84. The 15 days did not include Sundays. See also L. B. Namier and J. Brooke, *The History of Parliament: the House of Commons, 1754–90* (3 vols., 1964), i. 4.

[12] *Commons Journals*, xxxiv. 771 (19 May 1774); *Parl. Hist.*, xviii, cols. 53–4 (12 Dec. 1774); J. Cannon, *Parliamentary Reform, 1640–1832* (Cambridge, 1972), p. 209 n. 3.

[13] *Commons Journals*, xxxvii. 263, 360, 417.

[14] See Mahon to Wyvill, 14 Feb. 1786, C. Wyvill, *Political papers, chiefly respecting the attempt of the county of York . . . to effect a reformation of the parliament of Great Britain* (6 vols., York, 1794–1806), iv. 534. There is a copy of the bill in Stanhope Papers, U1590 C79/7. It was a prelude to the 1780 act (which Powis and Wray also had a large part in introducing) and proposed that freeholders should give certificates of their identity and status upon oath; a summary or abstract of these certificates was to be entered in books for reference by candidates and other interested parties. This was a clear step in the direction of a register. Mahon's reservations about the bill derived from his fear of errors in land tax assessments.

[15] A draft of this projected volume can be found in Stanhope Papers, U1590 C79/3.

[16] I. R. Christie, *Wilkes, Wyvill and Reform* (1962), pp. 148–9. Mahon introduced the polling bill on 12 June 1782 but it was postponed for a month on 21 June and subsequently abandoned (*Commons Journals*, xxxviii. 1053, 1121).

[17] *Parl. Hist.*, xxiii, col. 107 (21 June 1782).

[18] The penalty for a candidate so convicted was to be disqualification from the current parliament and for a voter it was to be disfranchisement for life. There was criticism of the unequal nature of the penalty but of course an individual could be punished in both capacities.

whereupon Mahon in dudgeon withdrew the bill altogether.[19] During the following session, 1782–3, he was closely involved in the preparation of two polling measures, the 'Bill for the more easy and convenient attendance of freeholders at elections of Knights of Shires' and the 'Bill for the better preventing fraudulent votes in elections of Knights of Shires'. Both finally failed in the Commons on 19 June 1783.[20]

But Mahon's main hope lay in a revival of his attack on election costs, now divided into separate 'bribery' and 'expenses' bills. When they reappeared in the Commons in May 1783 Mahon enjoyed a much easier passage than a year earlier. True, the expenses bill was lost on 12 June when Fox and others secured a long postponement of the committee stage[21] but the bribery bill went through the Commons 'without opposition'.[22] For the first time one of Mahon's schemes had reached the house of lords and even there it came tantalizingly close to success. It received a formal first reading on 16 June 1783.[23] But on 25 June Sandwich carried a motion by the narrow margin of 18 votes to 16 to defer the committee stage for two months and the bill consequently failed.[24] The former 'incapacitating' clause for errant voters had been altered to a fine of £500—which Sandwich suggested was too high. The arguments used against the bill—that it threatened to deprive the poorest electors of travelling expenses and thus effectively disfranchise them, and that it would be costly and unworkable in practice—could not be dismissed lightly. But to Mahon the galling aspect of the defeat was that it was caused by those peers who voted by proxy: there were six proxies against the bill and only two in its favour.[25] He never forgot that it was 'carried by the Majority of Peers present'[26] or that two of the proxies against the bill were 'brought by the D. of P.[ortland]'.[27] His annoyance with Portland is significant. That two prominent Northites—Stormont and Sandwich—spoke and voted against the bill was predictable; that the nominal head of the government and of the whig party should actively work (as well as vote) against it helped to alienate Mahon and other reformers from the Fox–North coalition.[28]

---

[19] See Mahon's letter to Wyvill of 22 June, quoted in Christie, p. 149; *Parl. Hist.*, xxiii, col. 109; G. Stanhope and G. P. Gooch, *The Life of Charles, 3rd Earl Stanhope* (1914), pp. 50–1; Sir N. W. Wraxall, *Historical and Posthumous Memoirs*, ed. H. B. Wheatley (5 vols., 1884), ii. 341–2, where the voting figures are incorrectly given as 66—26 instead of 66—40.

[20] J. Debrett, *Parliamentary Register*, x. 195; *Commons Journals*, xxxix. 492–3. The texts of both bills can be found in Stanhope Papers, U1590 C79/1.

[21] *Parl. Hist.*, xxiii, col. 995; Stanhope and Gooch, p. 55.

[22] Mahon's MS. note on the printed text of the bill, Stanhope Papers, U1590 C79/1. The passage of the bribery bill of 1783 in the Commons is not well reported. It was read a third time and passed on 5 June (*Commons Journals*, xxxix. 466).

[23] *Lords Journals*, xxxvi. 693.

[24] See reports of the Lords' debate of 25 June 1783 in *Parl. Hist.*, xxiii, cols. 1049–50; *London Chronicle*, 24–26 June 1783; *Gazetteer and New Daily Advertiser*, 26 June 1783.

[25] See Appendix I.

[26] Mahon's MS. note on the text of the bill; Stanhope Papers, U1590 C79/1. The peers present divided 14—12 in favour of the bill. There is a note on proxy voting in *Divisions, 1685–1857*, pp. 11–13 and McCahill, pp. 16–18.

[27] Version of the division list in Stanhope Papers, U1590 C56. Mahon also complained 'The Division being very early, Lord Chatham and several Friends to the Bill came too late for the Division'.

[28] The Lords' division list of 25 June 1783 was printed in an almost complete state in the *York Chronicle* of 11 July 1783, together with a comment deploring the defeat of the bill. (I am indebted for this reference and for other information in this paragraph to Christie, pp. 191–2.) The Yorkshire reformers admired Mahon's efforts. On 20 June 1783 the *York Chronicle* had printed a summary of the bribery bill of 1783 with a warm commendation of its contents. In particular it argued that if

Mahon had already been irritated by Fox's resistance to his bribery and expenses bills; this completed his disenchantment with the Portland whigs.

In 1784 and 1785 Mahon introduced three further bills. A bribery bill which appeared in the unreal political atmosphere of March 1784, shortly before the general election, passed in the Commons without difficulty but lapsed with the dissolution of parliament before it could make much progress in the Lords.[29] Apart from an abortive attempt the following year to consolidate the existing bribery laws into one act[30] Mahon never revived it. His concern with elections henceforth was to be concentrated upon the registration of county voters. Accordingly his main parliamentary effort in 1785, which gave rise to the second list printed here, was to promote his 'Bill for the better securing the Rights of Voters at County Elections'. It would have replaced the 1780 act with a register of county electors. The spring of 1785 had seemed briefly to augur well for the reforming cause with Pitt's motion of 18 April and W. W. Grenville's first attempt to amend his father's Controverted Elections Act of 1770.[31] But after 18 April and the crushing of the reformers' hopes, Mahon's registration bill had a rather foredoomed appearance and in the circumstances it is perhaps surprising that it advanced as far as it did. After a false start in April, Mahon, in conjunction with Robert Smith and the two members for Yorkshire, Duncombe and Wilberforce, guided the bill through the Commons. On 20 June 1785 it received a third reading by 51 votes to 20 and was despatched to the Lords.[32] The next day the peers read it a first time and ordered it to be printed, but it was not until 22 July that it was read a second time and committed.[33] Five days later a motion that the order for the committee be discharged was carried by 14 votes to 4 and the bill was lost.[34] One reason for the defeat appears to have been the lateness of the session, which opponents of the bill used as an excuse for not proceeding further.[35] Probably the time of year was responsible for the low attendance: only twenty-two peers are listed in the *Journals* as present on that day.[36] But more serious was the hostility of Thurlow and Sydney who, according to one well-informed observer, had 'thrown out' the bill.[37] Although Sydney did not vote against the bill on 27 July Thurlow did and most reports of the debate print

Mahon's aim of reducing the cost of county elections were achieved 'the only material objection to the augmentation of the county representation would be removed' (*ibid.*).

[29] For the stages of Mahon's bill of 1784 'for preventing Bribery at Elections' see *Parl. Hist.*, xxiv, cols. 765–8. On 23 March 1784 it was read a first time in the Lords and ordered to be printed, but parliament was formally dissolved two days later.

[30] Mahon's 'Bill to explain, amend and reduce into one Act of Parliament all the laws now in being for preventing Bribery and Expence in Elections of Members to serve in Parliament' was introduced in the Commons 22 Apr. 1785 but was repeatedly postponed in committee and finally abandoned (*Commons Journals*, xl. 1059). There is a printed copy of the text of the bill in Stanhope Papers, U1590 C79/1.

[31] *Parl. Hist.*, xxv, cols. 432–78, 392–409.

[32] *Commons Journals*, xl. 1089.

[33] *Lords Journals*, xxxvii. 328, 371. Mahon sent a circular dated 22 July 1785 to members of the house of lords to urge their attendance for the second reading (Public Record Office, Kew, HO 42/7/311, cited in E. C. Black, *The Association: British extra-parliamentary political organization, 1769–93* (Cambridge, Mass., 1963), p. 129 n. 93).

[34] *Lords Journals*, xxxvii. 377 (27 July 1786). Technically the Lords ordered a committee on the bill 'this day three months'. On 2 Aug. this order, too, was discharged (*Lords Journals*, xxxvii. 381).

[35] See Wilberforce's letter to Stanhope, 12 March 1786, Stanhope Papers, U1590 C57/2.

[36] *Lords Journals*, xxxvii. 376.

[37] Thomas Orde to the duke of Rutland, 1 July 1786, Hist. MSS. Comm., *14th Rept.*, app. pt. i (Rutland MSS. vol. iii), p. 319.

two powerful and critical speeches by the Lord Chancellor.[38] Of Mahon's supporters only Richmond made any strenuous effort for the bill.

The bill of 1786, however, was much better prepared and supported. In the first place Wilberforce had planned a polling bill for Yorkshire alone. Mahon was dubious about this idea[39] and persuaded him first to turn it into a national measure[40] and then to take over its management in the Commons after his own succession to the peerage.[41] It was Wilberforce indeed who urged the newly-elevated Stanhope to speed up the bill's progress, adding 'Pitt has promised to meet your Lordship, Duncombe and myself, that we may settle any point which may be still doubtful, and also assures me of his *warm Support*'.[42] Pitt's assurances were genuine. He spoke in favour of the reformers on 15 May 1786 when the commons voted by 98 votes to 22 to commit the bill[43] and made clear his full moral approval.[44] The third reading was carried in the Commons by 38 votes to 16 on 23 June.[45] The following day Stanhope wrote to Pitt requesting aid for the bill in the house of lords.[46] Its passage was so widely expected that Sydney's sense of pique apparently led him to contemplate resignation.[47] The principles of the bill were very similar to those of 1785: freeholders were to be registered twelve months before the election in order to qualify for the vote; a register was to be established in each parish; the poll books were to be divided into parishes and to correspond to the registers and returning officers were, in Stanhope's words, to be 'official and ministerial' instead of exercising the judicial function of scrutinizing votes.[48]

At first the bill advanced rapidly in the Lords. On 26 June 1786 it was read a first time; on 29 June the second reading was carried and Sydney's motion for postponement of the committee stage was defeated by 11 votes to 4.[49] This was a

---

[38] See in particular *London Chronicle*, 26–28 July 1785. For Mahon's version of the 1785 defeat in the Lords and his attack on Thurlow see *Parl. Reg.*, xix. 99 (13 Feb. 1786). His 'flaming' and 'very disorderly' speech was reported by Daniel Pulteney in a letter to the duke of Rutland, 14 Feb. 1786, *Hist. MSS. Comm.*, *14th Rept.*, app. pt. i (Rutland MSS. vol. iii), p. 282, and is partly quoted in Stanhope and Gooch, pp. 64–5.

[39] Mahon to Wyvill, 14 Feb. 1786, *Wyvill Papers*, iv. 534–5.

[40] R. I. and S. Wilberforce, *Life of William Wilberforce* (5 vols., 1838), i. 113–14; J. Holland Rose, *William Pitt and National Revival* (1912), p. 206.

[41] R. Anstey, *The Atlantic Slave Trade and British Abolition, 1760–1810* (1975), p. 179; J. Pollock, *Wilberforce* (1977), p. 42. Mahon and Wilberforce had been granted leave to bring in the bill on 13 Feb. 1786 (*Parl. Reg.*, xix. 97–9).

[42] Wilberforce to Stanhope, 12 March 1786, Stanhope Papers, U1590 C57/2.

[43] *Parl. Hist.*, xxvi, col. 3.

[44] Holland Rose, p. 206; J. Ehrman, *The Younger Pitt: the Years of Acclaim* (1969), p. 228 and n. 2.

[45] *Parl. Reg.*, xx. 406-7.

[46] Stanhope to Pitt, 24 June 1786 (copy), Stanhope Papers, U1590 C57/2.

[47] Orde to Rutland, 1 July 1786, Hist. MSS. Comm., *14th Rept.*, app. pt. i (Rutland MSS. vol. iii), p. 319.

[48] Text of bill 'for the better securing the Rights of Voters at County Elections' in Stanhope Papers, U1590 C79/7; Stanhope and Gooch, pp. 70-2; *Parl. Hist.*, xxvi, cols. 178–86. If the legality of a voter's credentials could be established by the registration procedure, returning officers would no longer need to act judicially in scrutinizing votes, in deciding upon objections and hearing submissions from counsel. They would simply be officials who recorded the votes as they were cast and the expensive and time-consuming affair of scrutinizing votes at the poll would be eliminated.

[49] *Lords Journals*, xxxvii. 535, 544; *Divisions, 1685–1857*, microfiche card 5. A division list of 29 June 1786 in the *General Evening Post*, 29 June–1 July 1786 gives 'For the Bill' (i.e. against Sydney's motion for postponement) the following peers: Richmond, Carmarthen, Stanhope, Salisbury, Chatham, Hopetoun, Rodney, Hawke, Walsingham, Beaulieu, Dudley and Ward; and 'Against the Bill' Sydney and the bishops of Bristol (Christopher Wilson), Lincoln (Thomas Thurlow) and Bangor (John Warren). Lists of the minority only, giving the same 4 names, can be found in *Parl. Hist.*, xxvi, col. 184 and *Parl. Reg.*, xx (Lords), 144. The *Kentish Gazette* of 30 June–4 July 1786 prints a version of this

minor triumph but these four determined opponents were unyielding.[50] A series of amendments was debated on 4 July when an attempt by Bishop Warren to replace the freeholder's oath (and the attendant threat of prosecution for perjury) with a straightforward financial penalty failed by 10 votes to 8.[51] Other small amendments were reported on the same day.[52] The climax came on 7 July when a motion that the bill, with amendments, should pass was defeated by 38 votes to 15.[53] It is clear that with Thurlow ill the principal lead against the bill was taken by Sandwich, Sydney and Bishop Warren.[54] Thus was the Home Secretary 'tranquillized' and harmony restored to the cabinet.[55]

Wyvill's well-known attribution of the defeat in the Lords to 'a formidable coalition of the King's Friends and the Whig Aristocracy'[56] is at least partly borne out by the third list printed here.[57] Certainly the 'party of the Crown' contributed to the unfavourable result[58] and there was a high turnout of opposition peers against the bill.[59] But Wyvill saw the underlying cause of the bill's rejection in the probability that it 'really was not popular out of doors' and felt that because of the numerous types of property which qualified for the county franchise the proposed register would be 'too complicated and troublesome, as well as too remote from the present practice'.[60] To Stanhope the element of change was a virtue. In a characteristically trenchant letter he refuted Wyvill's objections and observed that the most serious deficiencies in the bill had been exposed by Bishop Warren. He proposed to meet the bishop's objections over the use of the land tax commissioners and the oath to be taken by voters, while preserving the essential principles of the bill.[61] His tactics henceforward were to make sufficient modifications to the 1786 bill to ensure the passage of a similar measure in a later session.

The next steps led to the act of 1788. There were some abortive preliminaries. Early in 1787 Wilberforce introduced a county election bill with a rather

division list identical to that in the *General Evening Post* except that it names Portland instead of Bishop Warren in the minority. The other versions, all naming Warren, are probably correct.

[50] All 4 (Sydney, together with Bishops Wilson, Thurlow and Warren) voted against the bill again when it was finally defeated on 7 July 1786.

[51] *Divisions, 1685–1857*, card 5. For Warren's speech, expressing the fear that a multiplication of oaths would lead to their being brought into contempt, see *General Evening Post*, 4–6 July 1786.

[52] *Lords Journals*, xxxvii. 563.

[53] Not 4 July, as stated in *Parl. Reg.*, xx (Lords), 155, or 5 July (*Parl. Hist.*, xxvi, col. 184). For the correct date of 7 July see *Lords Journals*, xxxvii. 568; *Divisions, 1685–1857*, card 5.

[54] *London Chronicle*, 6–8 July 1786. Stanhope noted later that, at various stages, Warren made 3 speeches against the bill (Stanhope to Wyvill, 14 Dec. 1786, *Wyvill Papers*, iv. 547). *Parl. Reg.*, xx (Lords), 155–7 indeed records that the decisive vote took place on a motion by Warren 'that the bill do not pass'. But *Divisions, 1685–1857*, card 5 makes clear that the question was 'that the bill do pass', with Contents 15 and Not Contents 38. This is corroborated by the report of the debate in *General Evening Post*, 6–8 July 1786.

[55] Orde to Rutland, 14 July 1786, Hist. MSS. Comm., *14th Rept.*, app. pt. i (Rutland MSS. vol. iii), p. 323.

[56] Wyvill to Stanhope, 17 Dec. 1786, *Wyvill Papers*, iv. 542.

[57] Appendix III.

[58] See table below. In particular no bishops voted for the bill and 6 voted against.

[59] Of the 10 leading opposition peers named by McCahill, pp. 123–4 no less than 8 voted, in person or by proxy, against Stanhope's bill of 1786.

[60] Wyvill to Stanhope, 17 Dec. 1786, *Wyvill Papers*, iv. 542. He also complained that freeholders might regard the register as a potential threat to their exercise of the franchise and that neglect to register might cause a 'diminution of good votes'. Stanhope had been warned of this objection to his bill of 1785 in a letter from a Kentish correspondent, J. Hinde (5 Apr. 1785, Stanhope Papers, U1590 C57/1).

[61] Stanhope to Wyvill, 24 Dec. 1786, *Wyvill Papers*, iv. 545–51. For a summary of Warren's objections to the bill see *Parl. Hist.*, xxvi, cols. 184–5.

different purpose from that of Stanhope: the local constables would compile lists of voters in each parish on the basis of jury lists. Stanhope, still wedded to his idea of voluntary registration, disliked this idea and it was quickly dropped.[62] In addition to his campaign against the slave trade Wilberforce became seriously ill early in 1788. Stanhope accordingly left the Commons management of his 1788 bill to the prominent laywer and member for Hindon, Edward Bearcroft. The new bill proposed an electoral register on the 1786 pattern, for which draft registers were prepared; freeholders were to be responsible for their own registration and could register in their own parishes, for which separate poll books were to be kept. The elaborate procedures which would make all this possible were to be complete by the summer of 1789 and a list of freeholders for each county was to be published by the king's printer. Stanhope had been careful to meet the points raised by Warren in two important particulars. Firstly the land tax commissioners were to be given a much smaller role; they were no longer to determine 'whether any particular District is or is not a separate and distinct Parish' according to the terms of the bill, or to make out 'a complete List of all the separate and distinct Parishes within the County', as had been stipulated in the 1786 bill.[63] They were to fulfil only the duties of register-keepers, but Stanhope would have been prepared to modify even this provision and entrust the task to the parish clerks.[64] Secondly the oath was greatly simplified and transformed into a general declaration by the freeholder that he was what he claimed to be. In this way Stanhope avoided the argument that oaths when used frequently served only, in Warren's words, 'to lessen that reverence for oaths which the Legislature ought by every possible way to keep up'.[65]

The bill passed the Commons on 22 May 1788.[66] Already Stanhope had sought sympathy in high places. He wrote to Thurlow with prospective drafts[67] and re-engaged the attention of Pitt, who not only repeated his previous warm support but helped to facilitate the bill's passage.[68] Other preparations went ahead rapidly. Stanhope compiled a comprehensive canvassing list of the house of lords and his findings, even allowing for over-optimism, offered hope for the bill's progress. The various gradations of 'Friends' to the bill outnumbered its known enemies by 103 to 18.[69] Even Bishop Warren was now 'Friendly'. Consequently success in the Lords was easily attained, though not well reported. The absence of any full account of proceedings on the bill renders Stanhope's list

---

[62] Wilberforce was given leave to bring in the bill on 26 Apr. 1787 (*Commons Journals*, xlii. 686) but it went no further. For the differences between his bill and Stanhope's see Pollock, p. 100. Stanhope expressed his unease in letters to Wyvill of 12 Dec. 1787 and 3 Jan. 1788 (copies, Stanhope Papers, U1590 C79/5, C55). He was worried about the possibility of fictitious freehold votes, about the way in which the absence of certificates for land tax assessments would leave the constable with nothing to guide his judgement in enrolling voters and about the inaccuracy of jury lists. For Wyvill's defence of Wilberforce's proposed bill see his letters to Stanhope of 23 Dec. 1787 and 25 Jan. 1788, Stanhope Papers, U1590 C55.

[63] Printed text of the 1786 bill, pp. 24–5; Stanhope Papers, U1590 C79/7.

[64] 'Objections to 28 G. 3 ch. 36' with 'Answers, or Remedy', Stanhope Papers, U1590 C79/3. Bishop Warren had complained that as the 1786 bill would involve the land tax commissioners—'plain country gentlemen'—in much trouble and expense, 'it was not to be expected that they would take much pains about it' (*Parl. Hist.*, xxvi, col. 184).

[65] *Ibid.*

[66] *Commons Journals*, xliii. 497.

[67] Stanhope to Thurlow, 10 May 1788 (draft); 'Copy of Bill as sent to the Lord Chancellor May 16, 1788', Stanhope Papers, U1590 C79/2, C79/7.

[68] Pitt to Sir Lloyd Kenyon, master of the rolls, 11 Apr. 1788, Hist. MSS. Comm., *14th Rept.*, app. pt. iv (Kenyon MSS.), p. 525. See also Stanhope to Kenyon, *ibid.*, pp. 525–6.

[69] See Appendix IV.

all the more valuable. The only recorded division on the bill (16 June 1788) was a procedural one on the timing of the report stage.[70] With most members of the government sympathetic and all but a hard core of opponents converted or at least acquiescent,[71] Stanhope enjoyed the rare pleasure of carrying one of his measures in the Lords. There was more support from all quarters than in 1786.[72] The bill, with amendments, was finally passed in the Lords on 17 June and two days later the Commons accepted the amendments. Royal assent followed on 25 June.[73] The full title was 'An Act for the better securing the Rights of Persons qualified to vote at County Elections' (28 Geo. III, c. 36).[74]

'I am astonished at your success', confessed Wyvill, 'and could not have thought that any personal canvas, but that of the Minister, could have brought down five and forty Lords to support a measure calculated to diminish the power of the Aristocracy'.[75] It was, as Veitch noted, a 'small but valuable change'.[76] Stanhope, moreover, had designed it as the prelude to further electoral reform. The provisions for district registration were to serve as the base upon which a bill to reduce costs by establishing several polling places in county constituencies might be founded.[77] 'District Polling is an object of still greater consequence than the Register we have now got', wrote Wyvill. 'It is indeed the final end for which that regulation has been so strenuously pressed'.[78] Others had hopes of a similar sort.[79] But these ambitions were soon cut short. Objections to the act, which hitherto had come from inside parliament, now flowed from outside. To some extent Stanhope in his paper 'Objections to 28 G. 3 ch. 36' with 'Answers, or Remedy'[80] had anticipated their form, if not their volume. The main complaint now concerned costs. In February 1789 a parliamentary estimate placed the printing costs alone at £55,000.[81] The act itself had made clear that the printing and other expenses would be met from the county rate.[82] This unleashed a series of petitions, twenty-four of which reached the house of commons between February and April 1789. They were presented by the freeholders,

---

[70] *Lords Journals*, xxxviii. 230; *Divisions, 1685–1857*, card 5. Here it is stated that a motion that the report be delayed for one day was defeated by 15—6. This is confirmed (though with slightly different voting figures) by the *St. James's Chronicle*, 14–17 June 1788 and by the *General Evening Post*, 14–17 June 1788, which print brief speeches by Thurlow advocating delay and by Stanhope opposing it.

[71] For the more sympathetic attitude of the various sections of the 'party of the Crown' in 1788 see the table below. But Home Secretary Sydney and Lord Chancellor Thurlow were still unconciliated. Sydney referred indignantly to 'that insufferable madman Stanhope's bill' in a choleric letter to Hawkesbury, 12 June 1788 (British Library, Liverpool Papers, Additional MS. 38223 fo. 87). Thurlow, according to Wyvill, engaged in 'insidious opposition' to the bill (Wyvill to Stanhope, 25 June 1788, Stanhope Papers, U1590 C55).

[72] Of the 10 leading opposition peers (see n. 59 above) 4 were now 'Friends' or 'Friendly,' 4 'Against' and 2 'Uncertain' but 'promised not to be Against'.

[73] *Lords Journals*, xxxviii. 233, 240, 248.

[74] The text of the bill may be found in *The Statutes at Large*, ed. D. Pickering (46 vols., Cambridge and London, 1762–1807), xxxvi. 386–415.

[75] Wyvill to Stanhope, 25 June 1788, Stanhope Papers, U1590 C55; see also Wilberforce's letter of congratulations to Stanhope, 9 July 1788, U1590 C57/2.

[76] G. S. Veitch, *The Genesis of Parliamentary Reform* (1913), p. 103.

[77] Stanhope to Wyvill, 24 Dec. 1786, *Wyvill Papers*, iv. 550.

[78] Wyvill to Stanhope, 25 June 1788, Stanhope Papers, U1590 C55.

[79] In 1788–9 Wilberforce and Duncombe planned a District Polling Bill for Yorkshire alone, but it was never introduced. See Wyvill to Stanhope, 21 Sept. 1788, Stanhope Papers, U1590 C55; Pollock, pp. 100–1.

[80] Stanhope Papers, U1590 C79/3.

[81] *Commons Journals*, xliv. 127–8. £38,000 had already been spent and the expenditure of a further £17,000 was anticipated.

[82] Clause xxix; *Statutes at Large*, xxxvi. 402.

justices or grand juries of eighteen English and four Welsh counties.[83] Apart
from the financial burden, the petitions complained of inconvenience, com-
plications and the possible loss of the franchise by inattentive freeholders. There
was another grievance. As the Kent petition observed, the expenses of the act

appear to be extremely oppressive and unequal, for, as they are directed to be paid out of
the County Rates, they will fall wholly upon the Occupiers of Lands and Tenements by
whom such Rates are paid, whereas the greater Part of such Occupiers are not
Freeholders, and have no Right to vote at County Elections.[84]

The Warwickshire petition made the same point—that copyholders, though still
unenfranchised, would be subsidizing the privilege of the electorate.[85] This, then,
was the background to the termination of the act. Significantly the first step was
taken by eight M.P.s for county constituencies who were given leave to introduce
a repeal bill on 12 March 1789.[86] Two weeks later ministers themselves brought
in a suspending measure, clearly in the hope of heading off permanent repeal,
which Pitt was anxious to prevent.[87] The county members, however, were
unrelenting. Both repeal and suspending bills proceeded rapidly with little
debate and both received the royal assent on 19 May 1789.[88] Stanhope's act had
lasted for less than one year, had never been tested in a general election and was
accorded only one sentence in Holdsworth.[89]

According to Veitch the argument of expense was merely an 'excuse' for the
abandonment of the act, implying that parliament 'repented hastily of its virtue'
because of a reversal of principle.[90] Porritt on the other hand suggested that the
repeal could be construed as a 'response to public agitation'.[91] The latter view is
surely nearer the truth, although the 'agitation' was hardly comparable to that
against Walpole's excise scheme or the Jewish Naturalization Act of 1753.[92] It
amounted to discreet and respectable pressure from the tax-paying classes at a
time when a general election was due within two years. The fatal weakness of
Stanhope's registration act lay in its apparent threat to increase the cost of county
elections at the very time when there were growing demands that such costs be

[83] *Commons Journals*, xliv, *passim*. There were 2 separate petitions from the grand jury and
magistrates of Oxfordshire, and one from the mayor, bailiffs and burgesses of Liverpool. An attempt
to move a petition against the act at a meeting of Yorkshire magistrates in March 1789 was defeated
(Wyvill to Stanhope, 20 March 1789, Stanhope Papers, U1590 C55).

[84] Petition from the magistrates for Kent, *Commons Journals*, xliv. 149. See also the Berkshire
petition, *ibid.*, p. 108.

[85] *Ibid.*, p. 280; Porritt, i. 27. For a note on copyholders see Cannon, p. 87 n. 3.

[86] *Commons Journals*, xliv. 169, where the 8 county members are named.

[87] *Ibid.*, p. 240. The suspending bill was introduced under the names of Sumner, Bearcroft, Arden
(master of the rolls) and Pitt. In 3 speeches on 27 March Pitt defended Stanhope's act, urging further
consideration, amendment or suspension to counter the hostility to it: 'it was going too far to talk of
a total repeal of the act' (*Parl. Reg.*, xxv. 535–6, 538). Although Pitt failed to save the act it can hardly
be said that he 'silently acquiesced in its repeal' (Black, p. 129).

[88] *Lords Journals*, xxxviii. 424. No division in the Lords on either bill appears in *Divisions,
1685–1857*. The texts of the suspending act (29 Geo. III, c. 13) and of the repeal measure (29 Geo. III,
c. 18) may be found in *Statutes at Large*, xxxvi. 593, 595–6. Significantly, the suspending act merely
stated that 'it is expedient to suspend' Stanhope's Register Act, while the repeal measure harshly
insisted that 'the carrying of the said act into effect would be attended with a great and continual
expence, and be productive of many hardships and inconveniences to freeholders and others and the
said act would prove inadequate to answer the purposes thereof'.

[89] W. Holdsworth, *A History of English Law* (17 vols., 1938–72), x. 556.

[90] Veitch, p. 103 and n. 4.

[91] Porritt, i. 28.

[92] *Ibid.*

curtailed. Nearly half of the English counties (eighteen of forty) petitioned against the act and the total of twenty-four petitions compares with a mere twelve in favour of parliamentary reform in 1785.[93] No doubt Stanhope's parliamentary opponents were delighted by this development and they certainly exploited it. But Wyvill's explanation—that the motive for repeal was fear that the act, by reducing election expenditure, would 'emancipate the Counties from the influence of Wealth and a few powerful Families'[94]—begs the question as to why it was passed at all.

'The same cannot be proposed again, nor any thing like it' wrote Stanhope in 1792.[95] The plans for a 'General District Polling Bill' were dropped.[96] Stanhope never initiated another measure of parliamentary reform, although he continued to intervene on the subject. Later in 1789 Captain G. C. Berkeley, member for Gloucestershire, steered through the Commons a bill which would have emphasized that, in county elections, 'A Mortgagor, in Possession, may continue to vote, notwithstanding the Interest of such Mortgage may be such as to reduce the clear yearly Value of the Estate for which he claims to vote below Forty Shillings'.[97] In the Lords Stanhope attacked it vehemently on the ground that 'it tended to introduce a dangerous system of fictitious votes' which could be exploited by an unscrupulous landowner.[98] His speech contributed to the bill's failure. Two episodes of 1790 were simply footnotes to what had gone before. In the spring a bill 'for the further prevention of delay in Elections of Members to serve in Parliament' passed the Commons but was frustrated by a long postponement in the Lords.[99] In the summer a modified version of Berkeley's bill finally became law.[100]

At the end of the decade Stanhope could at least look back upon a more favourable reception in the Lords than that accorded to Richmond's bill of 1780. But he had nothing solid by way of legislative enactment to show for his efforts: even the success of 1788 proved transitory. It is hardly surprising that Stanhope wrote ruefully to Wyvill, 'It is not in the House of Commons that we want strength, but in the House of Lords, and that for obvious reasons'.[101] This article has tried to show what some of those 'obvious reasons' were. The lists confirm the divisions in Pitt's cabinet: most of its titled members favoured Stanhope's work, but the bills of 1785 and 1786 foundered on the obstinacy of Thurlow and Sydney.[102] Pitt himself emerges as rather more consistent and less opportunistic

[93] Cannon, p. 92.

[94] *Wyvill Papers*, iv. 551 n. This sentiment is not reflected in the petitions against the act, which complained about increased, not diminished, expenditure.

[95] Stanhope to Wyvill, 16 Sept. 1792, *ibid.*, v. 81.

[96] *Ibid.*, iv. 551.

[97] *Commons Journals*, xliv. 399. There is a copy of the printed text of this bill, with critical annotations by Stanhope, in Stanhope Papers, U1590 C79/1. The full title was 'A Bill to explain and amend the several Acts, passed in the Seventh and Eighth Years of the Reign of King William the Third, the Eighteenth Year of King George the Second and Twentieth Year of King George the Third, touching the Election for Knights of the Shire to serve in Parliament for that part of Great Britain called England'. Although Namier and Brooke, ii. 85 state that there is no record of Berkeley having spoken in the Commons before 1790, *Parl. Reg.*, xxvi. 176, 263–4 prints speeches by him on this bill on 21 May and 16 June 1789.

[98] *Parl. Reg.*, xxvi (Lords), 262–3 (3 July 1789), when Berkeley's bill was rejected without a division.

[99] *Lords Journals*, xxxviii. 633 (12 May 1790); *Divisions, 1685–1857*, card 5.

[100] *Lords Journals*, xxxviii. 679–80, 684. This measure (30 Geo. III, c. 35) is printed in *Statutes at Large*, xxxvii. 56–8.

[101] Stanhope to Wyvill, 24 Dec. 1786, *Wyvill Papers*, iv. 547.

[102] Although Sydney had voted (and indeed spoken) for the bribery bill of 1783 this was 6 months before the formation of Pitt's ministry.

than, perhaps, has always been appreciated.[103] But he had to recognize that the various elements which constituted the 'party of the Crown', though genuinely divided on the issue of parliamentary reform, were usually hostile to it, as the accompanying table illustrates.

The 'party of the Crown' and parliamentary reform in the house of lords, 1783–8[104]

	1783		1785		1786		1788	
	For	Against	For	Against	For	Against	Friends/ Friendly/ Well disposed	Disinclined/ Against
Office-holders	0	2	2	3	4	1	8	2
Members of household	1	3	1	2	1	5	6	3
Bishops	1	2	0	3	0	6	8	1
Scottish representative peers	0	1(2)	1	1(2)	1	2(3)	7	1(2)
Peers created or promoted by Pitt	—	—	0	0	1	1	18	0
Total	2	8	4	9	7	15	47	7

It is a measure of Stanhope's energy that, excluding those 'uncertain', a majority of this vital group was prepared to accept his bill of 1788. The votes of bishops, for instance, had previously been hostile (though never solely responsible for a defeat) but the canvassing list named only one as unfriendly. Much the same is true of the Scottish representative peers, among whom Hopetoun was Stanhope's most consistent supporter, Galloway and Morton his most persistent antagonists. But the subject of parliamentary reform in the Lords was neither a clear-cut 'party' affair nor the occasion for a confrontation between government and opposition. Indeed some of the most prominent whig grandees, as well as many independent peers, joined Pitt's lord chancellor and Home Secretary in defence of the *status quo*. The majority against Stanhope before 1788 had not simply been a government one, nor was it simply a government majority in his favour in that year. The disaster from his point of view was that even when 'strength' in the house of lords was temporarily obtained, other pressures asserted themselves.

[103] Pitt's efforts on behalf of the bribery and expenses bills of 1782–3 have already been noted. He gave active support to Stanhope's bill of 1786 and it was not his fault that it was defeated. It is hardly the case that he 'was finally moved to exert himself', as it were for the first time, in 1788, as is claimed in Black, p. 129.

[104] This table is indebted to the definition of the 'party of the Crown', above,   pp. 233-37. Following his practice (table II, p. 672) no peer is counted in more than one group. Thus newly created or promoted peers who were also office-holders are included only in the latter category; in 1785 the only newly created or promoted peers who voted on the election bill were office-holders. Scottish representative peers who held office are treated in the same way, except that the actual number of those who voted in each division is added in brackets in the relevant column. The lists of office-holders and members of the royal household in McCahill, pp. 219–25 have been used for purposes of identification.

These episodes amply justify recent observations about the poor state of the reformist cause in the period immediately before the French Revolution.[105] Nor was there much prospect for Stanhope's other aspirations. In 1789 his move for religious liberalism came to grief and this was followed by his total isolation in the Lords in opposing the French war.[106] Yet there was a positive side to this activity. By raising important issues and giving them an airing he helped to ensure that they remained before the public attention. His perseverance in the seventeen-eighties helped to secure widespread acceptance of the principle of registration of voters. It became increasingly apparent that here was at least a partial solution to the perennial problem of confusion and malpractices in county constituencies—a solution which was ultimately adopted on a permanent basis. In the end Stanhope's act of 1788 was thwarted not by the peers but by outside objections to its practical difficulties. Admittedly there is no reason to suppose that the house of lords was any more receptive to suggestions of an enlargement of the franchise or a redistribution of seats at the end of the seventeen-eighties than previously. But the act of 1788 was nonetheless a harbinger of future electoral developments.[107] In promoting it Stanhope rendered some service to the cause of parliamentary reform. In preserving division lists on that subject he made a contribution to our knowledge of voting behaviour in the house of lords.

APPENDICES

The four lists of 1783–8

These lists are presented as they appear in the Stanhope Papers, Kent Archives Office, U1590. The list of 1783 belongs to item C79/2, the other three to C79/1. Each list of 'Contents' and 'Not Contents' in 1783, 1785 and 1786 contains one teller: unlike the practice in the Commons, tellers in the house of lords were included in the totals of those voting on each side. The tellers for each division are identified in Sainty and Dewar, *Divisions in the House of Lords*, and are named here. Square brackets have been used for editorial additions; the use of rounded brackets is Stanhope's own. Original spelling has been retained, although standard abbreviations have been expanded. Specific points about each list are dealt with in the accompanying notes.

APPENDIX I

The list of 25 June 1783: Stanhope Papers, U1590 C79/2

Note: The division took place on a motion that the House be put into a committee upon the bill 'on this Day Two Months'. This meant effectively that the bill should be abandoned. 'Contents' were therefore voting against the bill, 'Not Contents' for it. There is another version of this list in Stanhope Papers, U1590 C56. It is identical to that printed here except that none of the bishops is named; exactly the same is true of the version in the *York Chronicle*, 11 July 1783. In the list printed here, Bishops Watson and Thurlow are named by Mahon;

---

[105] Cannon, pp. 140–1.

[106] Newman, ch. vi; A. S. Turberville, *The House of Lords in the Age of Reform, 1784–1837* (1958), pp. 92 ff.; G. M. Ditchfield, 'Dissent and toleration: Lord Stanhope's bill of 1789', *Jour. Eccles. Hist.*, xxix (1978), 51–73.

[107] Cannon, p. 209 and n. 3 has a note on the later development of registration.

Warren's name is added in square brackets since Mahon merely wrote '——(Bishop of Bangor)'. None of these lists names the proxy voters.

Lord Grosvenor is named here but does not appear in the list of peers present on 25 June 1783 in *Lords Journals*, xxxvi. 706. The tellers were Radnor (Not Contents) and Sandwich (Contents).

House of Lords 25 June 1783
Division on Lord M. Bribery Bill.

For committing the Bill [i.e. Not Contents]	Against it [i.e. Contents]
Lord Ravensworth	Lord Mansfield
Earl Ferrers	Lord Sandwich
Lord Sidney	Lord Walsingham
Lord Grosvenor	Lord Stormond
Lord Coventry	Duke of Portland
Lord Radnor	Lord Galloway
Lord Abingdon	Lord Onslow
Lord Effingham	Lord Walpole
Lord Rodney	Lord Sandys
Lord Rawdon	Lord Mumford [Montfort]
Lord King	[Warren] (Bishop of Bangor)
Lord Saye and Sele	Thurlow (Bishop of Lincoln)
Lord Chedworth	
Watson (Bishop of Llandaff)	
14. 2 proxies	12. 6 proxies
In all 16	In all 18

APPENDIX II

The list of 27 July 1785: Stanhope Papers, U 1590 C79/1

Note: The vote took place on a motion that the order for a committee of the whole house on the bill should be discharged. The 'Contents' were thus voting against the bill, the 'Not Contents' for it. Lord Sandys is named here but not in the list of peers present on 27 July 1785 in *Lords Journals*, xxxvii. 376. The tellers were Galloway (Contents) and Effingham (Not Contents).

Division in House of Lords on my Registration Bill, 1785.

[Contents, i.e. against the bill]	[Not Contents, i.e. for the bill]
Lord Gower	Lord Eff[ingham]
Lord Hawke	Lord Carmarthen
Lord Amherst	Lord Hopetoun
Lord Sandys	Duke of Richmond
Lord Chancellor [Thurlow]	
Archbishop of Canterbury [Moore]	
Lord Morton	
Lord Galaway	
Lord Chedworth	
Bishop of Bristol [Wilson]	
Lord Mumford	
Bishop Thurlow [of Lincoln]	
Earl Ferrers	
Lord Wentworth	

APPENDIX III

The list of 7 July 1786: Stanhope Papers, U1590 C79/1

Note: The list is arranged here in two columns; in the original it appears in four columns. The proxy voters appear opposite those peers who presented their proxy votes. The figure 'against' the bill should be 38; one proxy voter is missing in Stanhope's list. The tellers were Stanhope (Contents) and Galloway (Not Contents).

7 July 1786. Division in House of Lords on the County Election Bill.

[Contents]

For the Bill		Proxies for
Marquess of Carmarthen		⎰ Duke of Leeds ⎱ Earl of Effingham
Earls	Camden (x)	
	Stanhope	
	Radnor	
	Hopetoun	
	Grosvenor	
	Spenser	
Viscounts	Howe (x)	
	Hampden	
Lords	Walsingham	Earl of Hilsborough
	Saye and Sele	
	Hawke	
	12	+ 3 Total 15

(x) (x) Lord Camden and Lord Howe had Proxies but went away before the Proxies were called.

Persons who voted *for* the Bill in other stages in 1786

Duke of Richmond
Lord Rawdon
Lord Rodney
Earl of Besborough
Lord King
Earl of Effingham
Earl of Chatham
Earl of Beaulieu

8
12 above
____
20 *For*, in different stages in 1786.

[Not Contents]

Against the Bill		Proxies Against
Duke of Portland		⎰ Lord Teynham ⎱ Lord Cardiff
Duke of Devonshire		Earl Fitzwilliam
Duke of Beauford		
Earls	Sandwich	Earl of Exeter
	Bathurst	⎰ Lord Middleton ⎱ Lord Brudenell

Galloway	{ Earl of Morton { Earl of Leicester
Carlisle	Viscount Stormond
Derby	
Viscount Wentworth	Earl of Chesterfield
Bishops Lincoln [Thurlow]	
Bangor [Warren]	{ Bishop of Ely [Yorke] { Bishop of Bath & Wells [Moss]
Bristol [Wilson]	Bishop of Winchester [North]
Lords Foley	Earl of Egremont
Loughborough	{ Lord Porchester { Earl of Buckinghamshire
Sidney	{ Lord Borringdon { Earl of Denbigh
Scarsdale	{ Earl of Balcarres { Viscount Mount Edgecumbe
Southampton	
17	+ 20 Total 37

APPENDIX IV

The canvassing list of 1788: Stanhope Papers, U1590 C79/1

Note: This list appears to have been compiled in May and June 1788. In the original the names are grouped in six columns, under the six headings devised by Stanhope. Here they are printed in two columns, the first comprising the 121 peers whom Stanhope classified, the second consisting of the 130 'Uncertain' on the registration bill. Those peers whose names are italicized (and were underlined by Stanhope) were either minors (marked M) or Catholics (marked R.C.). The order in which Stanhope listed the peers in each category was dukes, marquesses, earls, viscounts, barons, Scottish representative peers and bishops. In some cases Stanhope bracketed together two titles of the same peer, and this has been retained here. Lord Say and Sele, a 'Friend' to the bill, died on 1 July 1788, six days after it received the royal assent. Stanhope entered his name in the list but afterwards crossed it out.

House of Lords in 1788; as to my County Register Bill, brought up by Edward Bearcroft Esq.

Friends	*Uncertain* The + signifies has promised *not* to be *against*
Duke of Norfolk	Duke of Somerset
Leeds	Grafton
Marquess of Lansdown	Beauford
Earl of Huntingdon	St. Albans
of Suffolk	Bolton
of Exeter	Bedford
{ of Doncaster } { i.e. Duke of Buccleugh }	Marlborough
	Rutland M
of Shaftesbury	+ Chandos
of Coventry	Dorset
of Tankerville	Bridgewater
Stanhope	Newcastle
of Effingham	Montagu

[*Friends*, contd.]

of Powis
of Ilchester
Spencer
of Chatham
of Uxbridge
{ of Norwich }
{ Duke of Gordon }
Grosvenor
Beaulieu
Camden
Viscount Hampden
{ Lord Saye and Sele }
{ (since dead) }
{ Osborne }
{ i.e. Marquess of Carmarthen }
Teynam
{ Hay }
{ Earl of Kinnoul }
Fortescue
{ Ponsonby }
{ Earl of Bessborough }
Ducie
{ Cardiff }
{ Viscount Mount Stuart }
Hawke

Brownlow
Loughborough
Walsingham
Lord Rodney
Rawdon
Bulkeley
Heathfield
(Scotch Peers)
Earl of Selkirk
Earl of Breadalbane
Earl of Hopetoun
Lord Kinnaird
[Bishops]
St. Davids (Horsley)

Friendly
Duke of Richmond
{ Duke of Brandon }
{ Duke of Hamilton }
Ancaster
Manchester
Northumberland
Marquess Townshend
Earl of Scarborough
of Sussex
of Harrington
{ Brooke }
{ i.e. Earl of Warwick }
Harcourt
of Fauconberg

[*Uncertain*, contd.]

Marquess of Buckingham
+   Stafford
Earl of *Shrewsbury*   R.C.
of Pembroke
of Salisbury
of Northampton
of Peterborough
of Winchilsea
of *Thanet*   M
of Essex
+   of Carlisle
of Abingdon
of Gainsborough
of Plymouth
of Rochford
of *Albermarle*   M
of Jersey
of Oxford
of Strafford
of Dartmouth
of Bristol
Cowper
of Harborough
of *Pomfret*   M
{ Graham }
{ i.e. Duke of Montrose }
{ Ker }
{ i.e. Duke of Roxburgh }
of Ashburnham
of Orford
of Portsmouth
of Egremont
of Guildford
Cornwallis
of Hardwicke
of Darlington
of Hilsborough
of Aylesbury
of Clarendon
of Mansfield
{ Strange }
{ Duke of Athol }
Viscount Montagu
Weymouth
Bolingbroke
Falmouth
Torrington
{ Leinster }
{ i.e. Duke of Leinster }
Courtenay
Maynard
Mount Edgecumbe
Sackville   M
{ Hamilton }
{ Earl of Abercorn }
Lord *Clifford* (of Appleby)   M

[*Friendly*, contd.]

Delawar
of Radnor
of Leicester
Viscount Hereford
Lord Monson
Sondes
Scarsdale
Boston

{ Lovel and Holland [of Enmore] }
{ Earl of Egmont }

{ Sundridge }
{ Duke of Argyll }

Porchester

Lord Grantley
Suffield
[Scotch Peers]
Earl of Balcarres
Lord Elphinston
[Bishops]
Bangor (Warren)
Landaff (Watson)
Bristol (Wilson)
Lincoln (Pretyman)

Well Disposed

Earl of Berkeley
Poulett
Cholmondeley
Ferrers
of Aylesford
Waldegrave
of Buckinghamshire
of Hertford
Bathurst
of Abergavenny
of Lonsdale
Talbot
Viscount Dudley & Ward
Howe
Lord Dacre
St. John
Onslow
Romney
Milton
Southampton
Lovaine
Eliot
Somers
Berwick [of Attingham]
Delaval
[Scotch Peers]
Earl of Moray
[Bishops]
Archbishop Canterbury (Moore)
Winchester (North)

[*Uncertain*, contd.]

Audley
Stourton　R.C.
Willoughby de Broke
Lord Coniers [Conyers] (son
Marquess of Carmarthen)　M
Howard de Walden
Petre　R.C.
Arundel　R.C.
{ *Clifton* }　M
{ Earl of Darnley }
Dormer
Byron
Craven
Clifford of Chudleigh　R.C.
Boyle
Middleton
Cadogan
King
Mountford
Sandys
Stawell
Grantham　M
Pelham
Holland　M
Vernon
Digby
Amherst
Rivers
Harrowby
Foley
Gage
Brudenell
Bagot
Ashburton　M
Lord Camelford
Carteret
Grey de Wilton
Boringdon
Shireborne
{ Douglas }
{ Duke of Queensborough }
{ Tyrone }
{ Earl of Tyrone }
Carleton
+　Hawkesbury
{ Dorchester }
{ (Was Sir Guy Carleton) }
[Scotch Peers]
Marquess of Lothian
Earl of Eglinton
Earl of Cassilis
Earl of Dalhousie
Earl of Aberdeen
Earl of Dunmore
+ Viscount Stormont
[Bishops]

[*Friendly*, contd.]
St. Asaph (Shipley)

Disinclined
Duke of Devonshire
Earl of Denbigh
    of Macclesfield
Viscount Wentworth
Lord Sydney
[Scotch Peers]
Earl of Morton
⎧ Earl of Galloway ⎫
⎨ but he is [said?] ⎬
⎩ to have the Colic ⎭

Against

Duke of Portland
Earl of Derby
    of Westmorland
    of Stamford
    of Chesterfield
    of Sandwich
        Fitzwilliam
Lord Chedworth
        Walpole
        Thurlow
[Bishops]
Durham (Thurlow)

[*Uncertain*, contd.]
Archbishop York (Markham)
London [Porteus]
Chichester [Ashburnham]
Bath & Wells [Moss]
Salisbury (Barrington)
Peterborough (Hinchcliffe)
Ely [Yorke]
Rochester [Thomas]
Worcester [Hurd]
Oxford [Smallwell]
Exeter [Ross]
Lichfield & Coventry [Cornwallis]
Gloucester [Hallifax]
Norwich [Bagot]
Carlisle [Douglas]
Hereford [Butler]
Chester [Cleaver]

Friends and Friendly are 74. Well Dispos'd = 29. Absent, Papists, Minors, Uncertain = 130. Against and Disinclined 18. Total = 251.

Peers and Lords of Parliament—besides Prince of Wales, Duke of York, Duke of Gloucester and Duke of Cumberland; making in all 255.

6. External view of the House of Lords from Old Palace Yard, 1826-34.

Engraving by Samuel Russell, by courtesy of the House of Lords Library.

A. The House of Lords. Formerly the Court of Requests, it had been converted into the Lords in 1801 when the old House was found to be too small to accommodate the influx of Irish representative peers and bishops after the union with Ireland in 1800. Built in the twelfth century and known as the White Hall, it had been used as the meeting place for the Lords in the early fifteenth century. The building had ceased to be used as the Court of Requests before the Civil War and then became the central public meeting place for those interested in parlimanetary affairs and an unofficial adjunct to the courts of law situated in Westminster Hall. It largely survived the fire in 1834 which destroyed most of the old Palace of Westminster and was fitted out to form a temporary home for the House of Commons until their new chamber was completed in 1851. It was then demolished.

B. Westminster Hall.

C. The Law Courts. Built by Sir John Soane in 1823-4. Previously the Courts had been housed in Westminster Hall.

D. The Painted Chamber. Built in the thirteenth century it was used as the regular meeting place for the House of Lords in the reign of Henry VII. Later it became the regular venue for the joint conferences between the Lords and the Commons. After the fire of 1834 it was fitted up as the House of Lords, and served as such 1835-47.

E. The Lords' Library, with the Royal Entrance in front. Built by Sir John Soane in 1822-6.

F. The Royal Gallery. Built by Soane in 1823-4 on the site of the old House of Lords. Most of Soane's work escaped the fire of 1834 but was demolished in 1851 to make way for the present palace.

17

THE HOUSE OF LORDS AND PARLIAMENTARY PATRONAGE IN GREAT BRITAIN, 1802-32

JAMES J. SACK

Any discussion of the relationship between the two houses of parliament during the eighteenth and nineteenth centuries necessarily involves a consideration of the extent to which members of the House of Lords dominated the selection and the subsequent political behaviour of individual M.P.s. Yet, even when substantial evidence in the form of voting lists and electoral registers becomes available during the early nineteenth century, no modern attempt has been made to determine either how many constituencies were under the control of patronal peers or how cliental M.P.s behaved once ensconced in parliament. This is a study of these and related problems. For, if the number of constituencies controlled by the peerage can be determined, and sufficient division lists for the two houses survive – a condition first met in the early nineteenth century – a number of interesting questions can be asked regarding the nature of a supposedly deferential section of the House of Commons. What follows, then, is a quantitative analysis of the patronal relationship between both houses, based largely on the appendix to this communication, the sources and implications of which are discussed in turn, and the voting lists in the *Parliamentary debates*.

Few issues agitated parliamentary reformers more violently during the generation prior to the passage of the first (1832) Reform Bill than what was to them the obvious and indefensible influence exercised over the return of numerous members of the House of Commons by members of the House of Lords. Through hereditary ownership, outright purchase, and timely cultivation of constituencies by the peerage, the House of Commons, in the words of the radical editor of the anti-corruption *Black book*, 'originally intended to represent the property, intelligence, and population of the state, has become the mere organ of the Aristocracy; who, according to the constitution, ought not to have the least influence over its deliberation'.[1] And the furious parliamentary reformer, John Cartwright, wondered if the peerage sought 'to secure to itself two hereditary Houses of parliament instead of one'.[2] Ministerial whips of necessity took account of the power of this aristocratic control of members of the House of Commons when they came to calculate the strengths or weaknesses of their particular administration. Addressing himself to just this problem in 1827, J. W. Croker was merely uttering a truism when he told Canning 'how powerful the aristocracy is...and how necessary it is to have a fair proportion on the side of a Government'.[3]

---

[1] *Black book* (London, 1820), p. 389.

[2] John Cartwright, *Letter to Mr. Lambton* (London, 1820), p. 20.

[3] Louis J. Jennings, ed., *Correspondence and diaries of the late Right Honourable John Wilson Croker, 1809 to 1830* (London, 1885), I, 369.

This aspect of the unreformed political system did not lack defenders. When the reform of parliament was being discussed in 1831, the ultra-tory *Blackwood's Edinburgh Magazine*, while admitting that it was nominally irregular, saw aristocratic sway in the House of Commons as a means to allow property to achieve its natural level of influence in the state.[4] Then there was the old argument of rotten boroughs giving patrons the chance to return poor but promising men of business to the Commons. Despite obvious elements of self-service in such reasoning, both patrons and prospective M.P.s were fully sensible of the merits of such a system. In 1818, when the second marquess of Buckingham offered St Mawes borough, with its thoroughly cowed electorate of around twenty-five, to William Conyngham Plunket, the Irish statesman, he maintained that: 'the means of giving such men as [William] Windham, [Francis] Horner & yourself the opportunity of coming into Parliament from St. Mawes...in my mind furnishes perhaps the only apology'.[5] In 1806 Francis Horner, a reformer and co-founder of the *Edinburgh Review*, wanted to come into parliament not for an unstable Treasury seat but rather for a 'good close Whig borough, the property of a very staunch old Whig family'.[6] Despite these more than occasional apologia, however, by 1830 many whose fathers or grandfathers had decided that the power of the crown was increasing and ought to be diminished had reached the same conclusion in regard to the power of the great aristocratic borough-mongers.

The peers often paid enormous sums to achieve mastery over constituencies. The fifth Lord Monson purchased Gatton for £180,000 shortly before Lord Grey introduced a Reform Bill which abolished Gatton and, perhaps understandably, changed Monson from a whig to a tory overnight.[7] The second earl of Caledon purchased Old Sarum for £60,000 and the third earl of Darlington bought Camelford for £58,000.[8] Even once acquired, many patrons had to pay a continuing sum to cultivate the electors and keep out rivals. Over a period of time, the second Earl Grosvenor's interest at Chester borough allegedly cost him £370,000;[9] for every general election at Shaftesbury he paid 20 guineas to each of 300 voters; and at Stockbridge, £60 apiece to more than 100 voters.[10] Those who voted for the fourth duke of Newcastle's nominee at Newark received a half ton of coal at Christmas and around 30 per cent lower rents than the prevailing price.[11] At Cambridge borough, under the patronage of the fifth duke of Rutland, a 'Rutland Club' was formed for the purpose of treating 30 to 60 guests with a monthly supper or a bi-monthly dinner, paid for by the duke, with 'excellent [food]...excellent wines, and plenty of both'.[12]

Such immense expenditure of energy or money was sometimes required on the part of patrons that the end result was deemed more trouble than it was worth. Both

---

[4] 'The present cabinet in relation to the times', xxix (1831), 147.

[5] Buckingham to Plunket, 16 May 1818, Plunket papers, National Library of Ireland, Dublin, PC 920.

[6] Leonard Horner, ed., *Memoirs and correspondence of Francis Horner, M.P.* (Boston, 1853), I, 381.   [7] William Carpenter, *Peerage for the people* (London, 1841), p. 524.

[8] H. Stooks Smith, *Parliaments of England* (London, 1850), III, 100; *Key to both houses of parliament* (London, 1832), p. 307.

[9] William Carpenter, *People's book* (London, 1831), p. 244.

[10] *Key to parliament*, pp. 397-9, 403-4.

[11] John Golby, 'A great electioneer and his motives: the fourth duke of Newcastle', *Historical Journal*, viii (1965), 207.

[12] *Appendix to the first report of commissioners on the municipal corporations of England and Wales*, Part iv, Parl. Papers, xxvi (1835), v, 2205.

the twelfth duke of Norfolk at Arundel and the fourth duke of Newcastle at East Retford found themselves in that situation and gave up their interests – Newcastle having spent £60,000 to keep up his influence in a borough that necessitated constant bribery.[13] The first Lord De Dunstanville found himself so harassed by the corporation at Bodmin that J. W. Croker thought him more their 'agent than their master'.[14] The baron was fully expected to care for distressed corporators, repair the church and the streets, pay for election entertainment, contribute money for the enlargement of the Guildhall, and act as a general employment agency. He thus seemed quite content to discontinue his patronage over the borough in the interest of the third marquess of Hertford, who engaged to perform all those tasks which De Dunstanville found so distasteful.[15]

Some peers lost their interest in constituencies through neglect of the electors. The fourth duke of Marlborough had scant difficulty controlling the Spencer-Churchill pocket borough, New Woodstock. He also employed around 100 servants from New Woodstock at Blenheim Palace. When the fifth duke made other domestic arrangements, he not only occasioned the rise of an anti-Marlborough New Woodstock opposition but actually lost one seat at the general election of 1820.[16] The Leveson Gowers in the person of the second marquess of Stafford were important parliamentary patrons in both England and Scotland during the first decade of the nineteenth century. Yet, through bad management of a century-old interest, Stafford lost one seat for Staffordshire in 1820; through raising the rent on his properties, he lost two seats at Newcastle-under-Lyme between 1812 and 1815; and through the sale of his Lichfield property to Lord Anson, he lost one seat for Lichfield in 1831. Only Stafford's Scottish interests over Sutherland and the Tain Burghs, belonging more particularly to his wife, the countess of Sutherland, were intact at the time of the 1831 reform crisis.[17]

As Professor Gash has reminded us, any classification of constituencies in regard to their control by a member of the House of Lords is 'full of pitfalls' and certainly can be absolutely guaranteed only by the local historian.[18] One not only encounters problems in determining exactly which peer controlled which constituency over which length of time, but also the very word 'control' presents myriads of difficulties. As that indefatigable nineteenth-century classifier of constituencies T. H. B. Oldfield was quite aware, the line between a patron's absolute non-controvertible *nomination* rights over a constituency and the more subtle aspects of a patron's *influence* over a constituency is often difficult to ascertain, much less quantify. For the purposes of this article, concerned as it is more with events in the Commons than in the constituencies, I have normally used *nomination* and *influence* as indistinguishable terms if the interest resulted in an obvious nominee of a particular peer achieving a seat in the House of Commons.

The situation in regard to influence is most knotty in counties. Derbyshire, despite its 3,600 voters, resembled a close borough where the duke of Devonshire was always

[13] For Norfolk, see Carpenter, *People's book*, p. 130. He recovered his Arundel interest during Queen Victoria's reign. Charles R. Dod, *Electoral facts*, ed. by H. J. Hanham (Brighton, 1972), p. 8. For Newcastle, see *Key to parliament*, p. 297; Golby, 'A great electioneer', pp. 208–9.
[14] Jennings, ed., *Correspondence of Croker*, I, 165.
[15] *Report on municipal corporations*, Part I, Parl. Papers, XXIII (1835), II, 446.
[16] Ibid. II, 141.
[17] Ibid. part III, IV, 1959; Carpenter, *People's book*, p. 124.
[18] Norman Gash, *Politics in the age of Peel* (London, 1953), p. 438.

able to return one M.P. in his interest.[19] Such a county presents no difficulties on the Table of Patronage in the appendix to this article. Some English counties, however, do. The exact relationship between a prominent landowning peer and a knight of the shire to whom he gave his electoral interest remains sometimes indeterminate. For giving one's support to a county member at a general election did not always (or even usually) create a formal patronage tie. Several times during the early nineteenth century the third earl of Hardwicke did indeed accord his considerable Cambridgeshire electoral interest to Lord Francis Godolphin Osborne without creating anything remotely resembling a patronal–cliental relationship.[20] Yet the situation in a shire was obviously more complicated when a peer gave his electoral interest to his own son or a near relation. And viewing such circumstances, contemporaries were never quite sure whether they should regard certain English counties as under patronage or not.

Witness the elusive situation in early-nineteenth-century Northamptonshire, Devon and Buckinghamshire, where, respectively, the Earls Spencer and Fortescue and the duke of Buckingham returned their eldest sons, the Viscounts Althorp and Ebrington and the marquess of Chandos. Unlike Buckinghamshire, Northampton-shire and Devon are not generally listed by interested contemporaries as shires under any form of aristocratic patronage.[21] It is not immediately obvious why that is so. Spencer and Fortescue probably paid out as large sums of money to secure their family interests in their native shires as did Buckingham in his.[22] Perhaps the often radical political commentators felt that frequently held electoral contests as in Devon and the generally progressive stance of M.P.s such as Ebrington and Althorp made the two viscounts less susceptible to the cruder aspects of patronal (or paternal) pressure than the decidedly illiberal Chandos in Buckinghamshire. If so, this may be a whiggish view of politics as, in the final analysis, Chandos was far more prone than his cousin Ebrington or his neighbour Althorp to display significant and steady opposition to his father and patron's political views. Therefore, recognizing that (at least in English counties) the wider suffrage generally precluded exactly the type of definite patronal–cliental connexion which subsisted in boroughs, I have found it advisable to include on the Table of patronage in the appendix those interests for English counties, such as Spencer's in Northamptonshire and Fortescue's in Devon, where a close relation of a great landowning peer sat on that peer's interest for parliament.

Forgetting for a moment the distinction between nomination and influence, the patronage lines in English and Welsh boroughs are usually straightforward enough.

---

[19] *Key to parliament*, p. 317.

[20] D. C. Moore, *Politics of deference* (New York, 1976), pp. 45–6, 50.

[21] See, for example, Cartwright's register of patronage in a *Letter to Mr. Lambton*, pp. 25–30, where he lists, correctly, the second marquess of Buckingham and Lord Carrington as influencing the return of two Bucks M.P.s. Yet, rather inconsistently, he omits a reference to Spencer's return of Althorp for Northants.

[22] Chandos expected the duke of Buckingham to pay for his uncontested elections for the county – which at the general election of 1826 amounted to £2,500. Buckingham's private diary, 20 May 1827, Stowe–Grenville papers, Huntington Library, San Marino, California, ST 98. The Fortescue interest in Devon was always an on-again, off-again one and cost the first earl a considerable amount: over £10,000 at the successful general election of 1818 and almost £6,000 at the unsuccessful one in 1820, when Ebrington resigned the poll at the end of the third day. Devon county election bill of 1818, 1262 M/15; Robert Ballment to Ebrington, 2 April 1820, 1262 M/19: Fortescue papers, Devon Record Office, Exeter.

However, the Scottish electoral system, that 'one great rotten borough' of radical complaint,[23] also contains complexities in sorting out the correct relationship between patron and member. It is often difficult to determine just where individual aristocratic patronage starts and where Treasury influence leaves off. Then, the grouping of burghs increased the strength of individual town councils and left a residue of tangled relationships, often varying from general election to general election, between the councils and local aristocrats. Some Scottish counties present no problem. Argyllshire and Sutherland were almost pocket constituencies of the duke of Argyll and the marquess of Stafford.[24] However, Scottish counties were single-member constituencies which perforce denied to their leading aristocratic and gentry families that cosy division of seats which often prevailed in England's two-member shire constituencies. In Peeblesshire, for example, it is rather difficult to determine whether, in the final analysis, the Montgomery family or the dukes of Buccleuch and Queensbury, both interests having worked together harmoniously since the mid-eighteenth century, returned the one member.[25] As to burgh electoral politics, Professor Ferguson has wisely warned us not to confuse the type of patronage rife in closed corporations in England with that in the northern kingdom.[26] To further confuse matters, as compared to the southern kingdom much less work has been done on local Scottish electoral history. So the weakest section of the Table of patronage in the appendix is that pertaining to Scotland.

In determining the Table of patronage in the appendix, I have examined, correlated, and (in many instances) discarded material gained from numerous sources pertaining to the relationship between peers, constituencies and M.P.s. Most parliaments elected after 1802 yield one or more such minute examinations as contemporaries were becoming more and more curious as to the nature of local politics and the extent to which the House of Commons was truly dominated by the aristocracy. For the three parliaments elected between 1802 and 1812, there is Joshua Wilson's judicious and indispensable *Biographical index to the present House of Commons* with separate editions published in London in both 1806 and 1808. The 1812–18 parliament elicited the mistake-ridden 'Classification of the Commons' House in the year 1817' by John Cartwright.[27] That parliament, however, also saw the most important source for the entire early nineteenth century in the six-volume study published in London in 1816 by T. H. B. Oldfield, *The representative history of Great Britain and Ireland*. John Cartwright's account of the parliament of 1820, contained in a *letter to Mr. Lambton*, is much better organized and researched than his similar endeavour of three years earlier. If not as detailed as one might wish, still one of the most informative sources for patronal–constituency relationships in the parliament elected in 1826 are private letters of J. W. Croker to the prime minister, George Canning, written in 1827.[28] Two of the more accurate and knowledgeable accounts concerning constituency politics were published during the two parliaments elected

[23] John Wade, *Extraordinary black book* (London, 1831), p. 244.

[24] Sir Lewis Namier and John Brooke, *History of parliament: the House of Commons, 1754–1790* (London, 1964), 1, 470–1, 497. In the 1850s the eighth duke of Argyll still dominated the county. Dod, *Electoral facts*, p. 6.

[25] Namier and Brooke, *House of Commons*, III, 159.

[26] W. Ferguson, 'Dingwall Burgh politics and the parliamentary franchise in the eighteenth century', *Scottish Historical Review*, XXXVIII (October 1959), 108.

[27] This list is contained in Cartwright's *Abridgment of 'The English constitution produced and Illustrated'* (London, 1824).

[28] Jennings, ed., *Correspondence of Croker*, 1, 368–71.

in 1830 and 1831, in the compilations known as *The people's book* and *A key to both houses of parliament*:[29]

Outside the boundaries of the 1802–32 time period, yet none the less crucial for an accurate understanding of constituency politics as related to the aristocratic issue in the early nineteenth century, are the three-volume *History of parliament: the House of Commons, 1754–1790*, edited by Sir Lewis Namier and John Brooke, and, perhaps less well-researched than his 1816 continuation, T. H. B. Oldfield's 1792 work, published in London, *The entire and complete history, political and personal, of the boroughs of Great Britain*. On the far side of the 1832 divide, the first report of commissioners on the municipal corporations of England and Wales, for the 1835 session of parliament, and the various electoral guides of Charles R. Dod,[30] provide essential information.

Contemporaries frequently made lists, sometimes crude but often insightful, of the extent of aristocratic dominance of the House of Commons. In 1793, from a well-researched list compiled by the Society of the Friends of the People, *The Annual Register* reported that 71 peers were responsible for the return of 163 (out of 513) M.P.s in England and Wales.[31] Twenty-three years later, T. H. B. Oldfield thought that 85 peers in England and Wales and 18 other peers in Scotland returned respectively 214 and 29 M.P.s.[32] In 1820 the radical parliamentary reformer John Cartwright recorded 83 peers returning 183 English, Welsh or Scottish M.P.s.[33] Just before the introduction of the Reform Bill in 1831, in a highly inaccurate, out-of-date list, the *Gentleman's Magazine* maintained that 80 members of the House of Lords returned 179 English, Welsh, or Scottish M.P.s.[34]

In the present century, E. Porritt in his study of the pre-1832 House of Commons suggests that one-half of the M.P.s in the early nineteenth century owed their seats to patrons (not all, of course, peers).[35] A. S. Tuberville, the historian of the House of Lords, put the percentage of M.P.s returned by peers at about one-third of the total.[36] Table 1 presents my own assessment of the number of patronal peers and their cliental M.P.s during the course of the nine parliaments under discussion – the slight fall-off of cliental M.P.s at the general election of 1831 occurring because the great popular enthusiasm for 'the bill, the whole bill, and nothing but the bill' led to a few peers losing control over their constituencies.

---

[29] Throughout the period, the various *Black* and *Red books* put out by radicals to attack, among other victims, sinecure-holders, are interesting though not always soundly organized and collated. They include: P. F. McCallum, *Le livre rouge or a new and extraordinary red book* (London, 1810); *The extraordinary red book* (London, 1816); *Black book* (London, 1820); *The new parliament: an appendix to the black book* (London, 1826); Wade, *Extraordinary black book*. Likewise, there are several similarly inspired tracts such as: *Biographical list of the House of Commons, elected in October, 1812* (London, 1813); W. G. Lewis, *Peep at the Commons* (London, 1820); *Peep at the peers* (London, 1820); *Links of the lower house* (London, 1821).

[30] *Electoral facts*, ed. by Hanham, and *Who's who of British members of parliament*, ed. by Michael Stenton (Harvester Press, 1976).

[31] xxxv (1793), appendix pp. 94–7.

[32] T. H. B. Oldfield, *Representative history of Great Britain and Ireland* (London, 1816), VI, 285–95.

[33] Cartwright, *Letter to Mr. Lambton*, pp. 25–30. If the Irish peers and M.P.s are included the numbers become 97 peers and 200 commoners.

[34] CI (Feb. 1831), I, 172–3.

[35] E. Porritt, *Unreformed House of Commons* (London, 1903), I, 309.

[36] A. S. Tuberville, *House of Lords in the age of reform, 1784–1837* (London, 1958), p.247.

Table 1. *Number of patronal peers and cliental M.P.s in England, Scotland and Wales, 1802–1832*

Parliamentary election	Number of peers returning British M.P.s	Number of British M.P.s returned by peers
1802	98	224
1806	99	226
1807	101	234
1812	97	228
1818	95	215
1820	94	204
1826	92	205
1830	98	214
1831	90	195

Of course, what gave the peers great authority in political deliberations was not only their great electoral power in the constituencies *per se* but also their control over elected M.P.s. For as Tuberville remarked, 'the nominated member was commonly expected to carry out the wishes of his patron after his election and to conduct himself in Parliament in accordance with his patron's mandate'.[37] To the young Charles Grey it was 'the chicane and tyranny of corruption' that a member of the British House of Commons 'is to have no conscience, no liberty, no direction of his own, [but]...is sent here by my lord this, or the duke of that, and if he does not obey the instructions he receives, he is not to be considered as a man of honour and a gentleman'.[38] For it was seemingly part of the political model of the period that the M.P. who failed to follow the explicit dictates of his patron would resign his seat.[39]

The exact monetary expenses incurred by M.P.s who accepted seats from noble patrons varied of course from constituency to constituency, depending upon a variety of circumstances and personal relationships. Only when the relevant editions of the *History of parliament* for the early nineteenth century are published are we likely to get as exact an accounting as possible of the contractual terms for each member. However, it seems fairly safe to surmise that on the whole relatives of peers received their seats on more generous terms than most non-relatives. For example, the fourth duke of Newcastle appears to have paid the election expenses for his family while charging others one-half of their election costs.[40] The first duke of Buckingham and Chandos always paid the election expenses of his son, the marquess of Chandos, M.P. for Buckinghamshire, and frequently for his brother, Lord Nugent, M.P. for Aylesbury, even though both parliamentarians openly opposed his politics on critical

[37] Ibid.
[38] William Cobbett, ed., *Parliamentary history of England: from the earliest period to the year 1803*, XXXIII (1797–9), 128–9.
[39] Porritt, *Unreformed House of Commons*, I, 309.
[40] Golby, 'A great electioneer', p. 211.

matters of national interest.[41] On the other hand, even so relatively impecunious a figure as Francis Horner was expected to pay at least part of his own election expenses when Buckingham returned him for St Mawes borough in 1813.[42] It is rare to discover a peer offering a seat to a non-relative at no monetary expense – though the tradition was certainly present in instances of rich peers and up-and-coming young men of business in the Commons. Thus the sixth duke of Bedford in 1809 and the third marquess of Lansdowne in 1830 charged W. C. Plunket and T. B. Macaulay nothing for boroughs under their control.[43]

With many patronal–cliental relationships, the arrangement was a co-operative one. The seventh Viscount Bulkeley, the patron of Beaumaris, made it clear that Thomas Frankland Lewis need pay only £500 at a general election and he himself would pay the remainder including the dinners.[44] The first earl of Lonsdale charged James Law Lushington £2,000 at Carlisle though he himself paid two or three times that sum.[45] At other times the patron charged a flat rate that amounted to a purchase of the borough involved on the part of the M.P. Thus Sir Francis Burdett acquired Boroughbridge from the fourth duke of Newcastle (then a minor) in 1796 for £4,000. Such a flat purchase may often have involved a lessening of commitment to the patron's political line.[46] Yet, given the plethora of candidates for seats in the House of Commons and the desirability of such a career, one assumes that a patron normally looked carefully at the political views of a prospective cliental M.P. before selling him a seat.

The political terms under which cliental M.P.s sat for parliament also varied from constituency to constituency. It was certainly not always a totally slavish relationship. Macaulay, when offered Calne at no expense by Lord Lansdowne, stipulated that he must have freedom of action on the anti-slavery question.[47] When returning him for Downton for the first time in 1801, the second earl of Radnor encouraged his young son, Viscount Folkestone, to conduct himself in an 'independent and forthright' manner. Folkestone more than took him at his word, and while what his biographer terms 'cross words' sometimes passed between father and son, the

[41] Buckingham to East, 3 May 1828, Box 145; Tindal to Ledbrooke, 17 Nov. 1828, Box 228; Ledbrooke to Chandos, 4 March 1829, Box 225; Stowe–Grenville papers. The whiggish Nugent was given so much money for electoral expenses that the toryish Buckingham accused him of 'picking my pocket of the Key', and then leaving Aylesbury borough in the possession of Buckingham's enemies when he resigned in 1832. Buckingham to Thomas Grenville, 14 Nov. 1832, Grenville papers, Buckinghamshire Record Office, Aylesbury, M.F. 632:2. Both the second Earl Fitzwilliam and the third earl of Hardwicke paid election expenses for their close relations. Catalogue of the Fitzwilliam Manuscripts, Fitzwilliam papers, City Library, Sheffield, F 48d; Hardwicke to C. Yorke, 8 March 1810, Hardwicke papers, British Library, Add. MSS 35394.

[42] Morland to Buckingham, 14 May 1813, Stowe–Grenville papers, Box 284.

[43] Plunket, however, refused the offer. Bedford to Plunket, 19 Nov. 1809, Plunket papers, PC 921. For Macaulay, see John Clive, *Macaulay: the shaping of the historian* (New York, 1974), pp. 139–40.

[44] Lady Bulkeley to T. F. Lewis, 12 Dec. 1824, Harpton Court papers, National Library of Wales, Aberystwyth, C/377.

[45] J. R. McQuiston, 'The Lonsdale connection and its defender, William, Viscount Lowther, 1818–1830', *Northern History*, xi (1976 for 1975), 170–1, 175.

[46] Golby, 'A great electioneer', p. 205. Historians have indeed sometimes wondered whether the M.P. who purchased his seat felt obligated politically to the seller. J. B. Owen, 'Political patronage in eighteenth century England', in *Triumph of culture: eighteenth century perspectives*, ed. by Paul Fritz and David Williams (Toronto, 1972), p. 380.

[47] Clive, *Macaulay*, pp. 139–40.

viscount evidently felt justified in differing from the earl on nearly every important national issue over the following quarter century.[48] At times an exceedingly formal agreement was the result of negotiations between a prospective M.P. and a borough-monger. In April 1831, during the midst of the reform crisis, the first duke of Buckingham and Chandos and Sir Edward B. Sugden 'Agreed that' in regard to the duke's rotten borough of St Mawes 'so long as Sir E. B. Sugden shall continue to pursue the same line of political conduct he has followed during the last Session of Parliament, he cannot be called upon to vacate his seat, altho' the Duke of B should change his political opinions...'[49] At other times, however, the M.P. who accepted a borough from a noble patron came off less honourably in the transaction. The same duke of Buckingham who so clearly spelled out the rather generous terms offered to Sugden forced Sir Edward Hyde East, his prospective M.P. for Winchester, to swear 'allegiance to *me* exclusively' in order to obtain his seat and even to support Catholic emanicpation – an issue upon which East apparently had severe qualms.[50]

We know enough from both published and unpublished political correspondence that relations between patronal peers and their once-ensconced M.P.s were not always harmonious. At times M.P.s felt obliged to resign (or at least offer to do so) due to the changing political line of their patron. When the second marquess of Stafford appeared about to switch from Pittite to Grenvillite moorings in 1805, John Charles Villiers, his M.P. for the Tain Burghs, simply resigned his seat.[51] Such scruples, however, were not invariably felt by an M.P. When the toryish second marquess of Lansdowne in 1807 desired to remove the whiggish Joseph Jekyll, his M.P. for Calne, under the patronage of the Petty family since 1762, the corporation refused to co-operate and re-elected Jekyll free from all expenses.[52] The attachment of a borough to a sitting M.P. regardless of the desires of a nominal patron thus sometimes interrupted the influence of a noble family over a borough, as Davies Gilbert and the first Lord De Dunstanville discovered at Bodmin after 1820.[53]

Two issues during the early nineteenth century which particularly rankled patronal–cliental relationships were Catholic emancipation and the reform of parliament – the former more than the latter as it was in the forefront of the national political consciousness for well over a quarter of a century. At the general election of 1826 the anti-Catholic first earl of Falmouth refused to return his M.P. for Mitchell, George Thomas Staunton, because of his pro-Catholic views.[54] Two other anti-Catholic peers, the fourth duke of Newcastle and the first marquess of Aylesbury, both either forced or strongly encouraged two pro-Catholic M.P.s to resign in the middle of a parliament.[55] During the midst of the reform crisis of 1831,

[48] Ronald K. Huch, *The radical Lord Radnor* (Minneapolis, 1977), p. 7.

[49] Memo of a conversation between the duke of Buckingham and Sir E. B. Sugden, 22 April 1831, Fremantle (Cottesloe) papers, Buckinghamshire Record Office, Aylesbury, p. 39.

[50] Buckingham to W. Fremantle, 16 Sept. 1822, 18 Feb. 1823, Fremantle (Cottesloe) papers, p. 56.

[51] Villiers to Stafford, 16 May 1805, Sutherland papers, Staffordshire Record Office, Stafford, D 868/11/18.   [52] Oldfield, *Representative history*, v, 152.

[53] Jennings, ed., *Correspondence of Croker*, i, 167; *Key to parliament*, p. 841.

[54] George Thomas Staunton, *Memoirs* (London, 1856), p. 116.

[55] For Newcastle, H. G. Knight in 1815 and Sir William Clinton in 1829. William W. Bean, *Parliamentary representation of the six northern counties of England* (Hull, 1890), p. 733; G. I. T. Machin, *The Catholic question in English politics, 1820 to 1830* (Oxford, 1964), p. 151; Golby, 'A great electioneer', p. 212n. For Aylesbury, J. T. Brudenell and Lord Bruce in 1829, Machin, *Catholic question*, p. 151.

Sir James Scarlett, long a member of one borough or another controlled by the conservative whig Lord Fitzwilliam, for 'having spoken and voted against the reform bill' was 'called upon' to – and did – resign his seat.[56] And for similar reasons, the first marquess of Cleveland rid himself of his M.P. for Winchelsea, Henry Dundas, even before the short-lived parliament of 1830 had run its course.[57] M.P.s strongly motivated by ideological considerations, however, were not always so obliging, as the first earl of Harrowby discovered in 1827. This pro-Catholic peer attempted to dislodge his anti-Catholic brother, Richard Ryder, from the Ryder family borough of Tiverton, but the decidedly anti-Catholic electorate of 24 would have none of such tactics.[58]

Just because either a familial relationship was present among the practitioners of constituency politics or a patronal peer was responsible for returning his relatives to the Commons did not in itself guarantee the peace of a borough or more than ordinary compliance with the patron's wishes on the part of a cliental M.P. While kinship ties may indeed have been one of the chief props of the pre-1832 British political system, family loyalty should not be overstressed as a predictor of political behaviour or as a sign of *status quo* politics. Colonel Thomas Graham opposed the interest of his brother-in-law, the fourth duke of Atholl, in Perthshire in 1807 and 1812; as did Vere Paulet that of his brother, the fourth earl Poulett, at Bridgwater in 1806 and 1807.[59] The Spencer-Churchills, as family representatives of the fifth duke of Marlborough, quarrelled incessantly at New Woodstock after 1826, and at an election in 1838 the marquess of Blandford ran against his own brother, Lord John Spencer-Churchill.[60] The third earl of Portsmouth lost control of Andover to his own brother, Newton Fellowes, in 1818, after a clumsy attempt to deprive him of his seat.[61] The first Lord Carrington was so distraught when his eldest son Robert Smith, M.P. for Buckinghamshire, supported the Reform Bill that he urged him to avoid his home, 'as I might be tempted to use language which you would never forget...'.[62] And various and assorted sons or cousins of the first duke of Buckingham, the fourth duke of Newcastle, the first marquess of Aylesbury, and the second marquess of Stafford learned the danger of too blatant an opposition to the wishes of their noble patrons.[63]

Still, if the evidence is clear that some patronal–cliental conflict was indeed present in the political arrangements of pre-1832 parliaments, is there any way of determining how much? In any absolute sense, no. Many sensitive issues, having originated and

[56] Carpenter, *People's book*, p. 355.

[57] Ibid. pp. 241–2.

[58] Machin, *Catholic question*, pp. 150–1.

[59] Oldfield, *Representative history*, IV, 446; Smith, *Parliaments of England*, III, 162; *Dictionary of national biography* under 'Graham, Thomas'.

[60] Gash, *Politics in the age of Peel*, p. 226.

[61] *Key to parliament*, p. 292.

[62] Michael Brock, *The Great Reform Act* (London, 1973), p. 181.

[63] For Buckingham, see James J. Sack, 'Decline of the Grenvillite faction under the first duke of Buckingham and Chandos, 1817–1829', *Journal of British Studies*, XV, 1 (1975), 126–8. For Newcastle and Aylesbury, see footnote 55 above. For Stafford, see Horner to Grey, 27 Oct. 1815 (copy), Horner papers, London School of Economics, VI. J. T. Ward, although he emphasizes the importance of family attachments in the attitudes of West Riding landowners towards the corn laws, makes it clear that peers and their heirs were sometimes in fundamental disagreement, for example the thirteenth duke of Norfolk and Lord Arundel and the third marquess of Londonderry and Lord Castlereagh: 'West Riding landowners and the Corn Laws', *English History Review*, LXXXI, 319 (1966), 262, 268.

been defeated in a rambunctious House of Commons, never reached the more sedate House of Lords. There is no readily available yardstick to determine exactly how many M.P.s rejected or ignored the instructions of their noble patrons on such issues. Only when M.P.s and their patronal peers voted on the same (or very similar) questions in their respective houses of parliament can some degree of certainty enter the equation and allow us to ask certain questions which go to the heart of the entire model of politics which the patronal–cliental relationship presupposes (assuming that we know which peers returned which M.P.s).

The 'Aye' and 'Nay' division lists of the *Parliamentary debates* for the pre-1832 parliaments do not begin to approach the abundance of those after the passage of the first Reform Bill. Still, when the available lists are co-ordinated with the Table of patronage in the appendix to this article, especially on such important national issues as the 1811 Regency crisis, Catholic emancipation, and parliamentary reform, enough survives to draw more than tentative conclusions on questions involving the discipline of M.P.s. Did M.P.s indeed toe the mark on crucial national issues by voting in a manner similar to their noble patrons? If they failed to do so, were they removed from parliament as soon as possible? Exactly how many patronal peers experienced such problems during the last years of the British *ancien régime*? Was Porritt correct in his assumption that the peers were most exacting in demanding obedience from their own relatives who sat for parliament on their interests?[64]

I have examined the available division lists in the *Parliamentary debates* between 1802 and 1831, for the only ten issues[65] where both the positive and negative votes of both peers and commoners have been recorded. Some of the division lists correlate between Commons and Lords more perfectly than others. When the question at issue in 1828 was the outright repeal of the Test and Corporation Acts, one receives a

---

[64] Porritt, *Unreformed House of Commons*, I, 323.

[65] The following are found in Thomas Curson Hansard, ed., *Parliamentary debates*. (1) Gower's amendment to the fifth resolution on the Regency, xviii (1 Jan. 1811), 598–601; Lansdowne's amendment on the first resolution on the Regency, xviii (4 Jan. 1811), 747–8; Lansdowne's amendment on the household, xviii (25 Jan. 1811), 1027–9. (2) Wellesley's motion on Roman Catholics, xxiii (1 July 1812), 868–71; Grattan's motion for a committee on Roman Catholic claims, xxiv (2 March 1813), 1074–8; on the Catholic relief bill, xxvi (24 May 1813), 361–5. (3) Grattan's motion on the Roman Catholic question, xxxiv (21 May 1816), 676–8; Grattan's motion on the Roman Catholics, xxxvi (9 May 1817), 438–42; Donoughmore's motion on the Roman Catholics, xxxvi (16 May 1817), 678–80. (4) Plunket's motion for a committee on Roman Catholic claims, 2nd ser. iv (28 Feb. 1821), 1030–4; on the Roman Catholic disability removal bill, 2nd ser. v (17 April 1821), 356–9. (5) Burdett's motion for a committee on Roman Catholic claims, 2nd ser. xii (28 Feb. 1825), 840–4; 3rd reading of Roman Catholic relief bill, 2nd ser. xiii (10 May 1825), 558–62; 2nd reading of Roman Catholic relief bill, 2nd ser. xiii (17 May 1825), 766–8. (6) Russell's motion for repeal of test and corporation acts, 2nd ser. xviii (26 Feb. 1828), 781–4; repeal of test and corporation acts in Lords, 2nd ser. xix (23 April 1828), 236–7. (7) Burdett's motion on Roman Catholic relief, 2nd ser. xix (12 May 1828), 675–80; motion on Roman Catholic relief bill in Lords, 2nd ser. xix (10 June 1828), 1294–7. (8) 2nd reading of Catholic bill in Commons, 2nd ser. xx (6 March 1829), 892–6; 3rd reading of Catholic bill in Commons, 2nd ser. xx (30 March 1829), 1633–8; 2nd reading of Catholic bill in Lords, 2nd ser. xxi (4 April 1829), 394–7; 3rd reading of Catholic bill in Lords, 2nd ser. xxi (10 April 1829), 694–7. (9) 2nd reading of reform bill, 3rd ser. iii (22 March 1831), 805–16; Gascoyne's motion for preserving the present number of English M.P.s, 3rd ser. iii (19 April 1831), 1689–1700; 2nd reading of reform bill in Lords, 3rd ser. ix (7 Oct. 1831), 907–18. (10) 2nd reading of reform bill in Commons, 3rd ser. vii (6 July 1831), 465–76; 3rd reading of reform bill in Commons, 3rd ser. viii (21 Sept. 1831), 339–44; 2nd reading of reform bill in Lords, 3rd ser. ix (7 Oct. 1831), 907–18.

Table 2. *Number of recorded conflicts between patronal peers and cliental M.P.s,*
1811–31

Peerage	Number of individual peers experiencing conflicts	Number of conflicts
Buckingham	1	7
Carrington	1	7
Harrowby	1	7
Mount Edgcumbe	1	6
Falmouth	1	5
Hopetoun	1	5
Lonsdale	1	5
Marlborough	1	5
Radnor	2	5
Stafford	1	5
Bute	1	4
Foley	1	4
St Germans	2	4
Anglesey	1	3
Camden	1	3
Cholmondeley	1	3
Grantley	2	3
Lauderdale	1	3
Leeds	1	3
Warwick	2	3
Aylesbury	1	2
Buccleuch	2	2
Delawarr	1	2
Hardwicke	1	2
Hertford	2	2
Mulgrave	1	2
Poulett	1	2
Queensbury	1	2
Rutland	1	2
Seaford	1	2
Abercromby	1	1
Arbuthnot	1	1
Argyll	1	1
Bulkeley	1	1
Caledon	1	1
Calthorpe	1	1
Clarendon	1	1
Cleveland	1	1
Clinton	1	1
De Dunstanville	1	1
Dynevor	1	1
Eglintoun	1	1
Fife	1	1
Forester	1	1
Galloway	1	1
Gordon	1	1
Grafton	1	1
Grosvenor	1	1
Harewood	1	1
Heytesbury	1	1

Table 2 (*cont.*)

Peerage	Number of individual peers experiencing conflicts	Number of conflicts
Home	1	1
Manchester	1	1
Norfolk	1	1
Northumberland	1	1
Northwick	1	1
Onslow	1	1
Orford	1	1
Portsmouth	1	1
Salisbury	1	1
Townshend	1	1
Westmoreland	1	1

definite correspondence between peers and the M.P.s sitting under their patronage. On other occasions, the issue is not nearly so clear cut. For example, in January 1811, during the Regency crisis, the surviving division lists on the various opposition amendments to Perceval's original Regency Bill are not taken from the same resolutions in both houses of parliament. In the Commons, Gower's successful amendment to the fifth resolution of the bill had to do with the size and control of George III's household; in the Lords, Lansdowne's equally successful amendment to the first resolution involved a less stringent interpretation than the government's of the restrictions on the future Regent's powers. The division in the Lords in late January on another amendment of Lansdowne's also related to the size of the king's household, but the issue was by no means an exact replica of Gower's previous amendment. Yet, since the proponents and opponents of the entire bill fell into a rough governmental-oppositionist line, one should still be able to draw certain conclusions – though not nearly as absolute ones as on the 1828 example.

Problems may also arise on division lists regarding the Catholic question in both 1812–13 and 1816–17. The marquess of Wellesley's motion in July 1812, that the House of Lords 'early in the next session of parliament' take up the Catholic question with a view to its settlement, was followed by two somewhat dissimilar votes in the Commons in 1813; Grattan's motion for a committee of the whole house to consider the Catholic claims in March; and the vote on the Roman Catholic Relief Bill itself in May. Then in May 1816 Grattan made a motion on the Catholic question similar to that of Wellesley's four years earlier. It failed, though the division was recorded in the *Parliamentary debates*. A year later the Catholic question was again discussed, voted on, negated, and recorded in both houses of parliament. In order to obtain the largest possible sampling, on both the 1812–13 lists and the 1816–17 lists, I have combined and compared the two Commons' votes with the single Lords' vote. The 1816–17 example probably presents no major disqualification for inclusion on the following tables save for a certain awkwardness created by the passage of twelve months between one of the Commons' votes and the Lords' deliberations. However, it is possible that some of the peers who supported Wellesley in 1812 might have changed their minds – and hence their instructions to client M.P.s – because of the absence of a secure veto (by the king on the papal appointment of Irish bishops) in the 1813 bill.

Much more questionable would have been the inclusion on the following tables of the proceedings involving Queen Caroline's divorce case. There is no question that the meagre ministerial 'victories' in the Lords in November 1820, on the second and third readings of the bill of pains and penalties,[66] demoralized the king, his ministers, and their supporters, and led political observers to foresee a new government in the offing. Such did not occur. Tavistock's motion in the Commons two and a half months later scolding ministers for their overall conduct of the queen's case received an impressive vote – for an opposition measure – but was still soundly defeated.[67] The Commons had no intention of destroying the Liverpool ministry. The fact that the queen's case saw a seemingly larger than normal number of M.P.s in conflict with their patronal peers[68] might well reflect a desire by conservative peers to appease the lower orders by keeping the queen while, with Tavistock openly calling for a new ministry and parliamentary reform,[69] instructing cliental M.P.s to keep the government too. During the debate on Tavistock's motion Horace Twiss, an independent tory, avowed that 'Upon any question which had been personal to the queen, he should have been unwilling to take an active part against her; but, when the motion was not against the queen but against the government...an opinion might be expressed without any thing invidious to that illustrious person.'[70] Hence the division lists from Queen Caroline's case are probably not illustrative of any trends involving patronal–cliental relations.

Other extant Lords–Commons division lists of dubious quality for current purposes would be the series running from the second reading of the Reform Bill in the Commons in December 1831, through Lyndhurst's motion in the Lords to postpone the disenfranchising clauses in the Reform Bill in May 1832.[71] The political situation during those five months were extremely volatile, as proposals for a modification of the whigs' Reform Bill were canvassed for and discussed. Thus a cliental M.P. was likely to receive such extremely confusing and varying instructions from a patronal peer that no straightforward Lords–Commons correspondence emerges in voting patterns.

Bearing in mind that at any one time from 1802 to 1832 between 90 and 101 peers returned British M.P.s to parliament, on the ten recorded issues under discussion, 67 individual peers (or the holders of 61 peerages) experienced conflicts with the M.P.s whom they returned. As can be seen from Table 2, 31 peers had only one

[66] Hansard, ed., *Parliamentary debates*: 2nd reading of bill of pains and penalties, 2nd ser. III (6 Nov. 1820), 1698–1700; 3rd reading of bill of pains and penalties, 2nd ser. III (10 Nov. 1820), 1744–6.

[67] Ibid. Tavistock's motion on the conduct of ministers with regard to the proceedings against the queen, 2nd ser. IV (6 Feb. 1821), 507–11.

[68] For purposes of comparison with Table 4, 27 cliental M.P.s were in seeming conflict with their patronal peers on this issue. Yet only 6 M.P.s may have been removed from their constituency for this vote – a far lower percentage (22·2) than normal for the period.

[69] Hansard, ed., *Parliamentary debates*: Tavistock's motion on the conduct of ministers with regard to the proceedings against the queen, 2nd ser. IV (6 Feb. 1821), 363.

[70] Ibid. 418.

[71] Ibid. 2nd reading of reform bill in Commons, 3rd ser. IX (17 Dec. 1831), 547–56; 3rd reading of reform bill in Commons, 3rd ser. XI (22 March 1832), 780–5; 2nd reading of reform bill in Lords, 3rd ser. III (13 April 1832), 453–60; Lyndhurst's motion to postpone the disenfranchising clauses, 3rd ser. XII (7 May 1832), 723–8.

Table 3. *Percentage of patronal peers in conflict with cliental M.P.s, 1811–31*

Issue	Overall percentage of patronal peers in conflict with their M.P.s	Percentage of *voting* patronal peers in conflict with their M.P.s
Regency question,[a] 1811	10·8	16·4
Catholic question,[b] 1812–13	13	18·5
Catholic question,[b] 1816–17	15·4	23·3
Catholic question, 1821	12·5	18·7
Catholic question,[b] 1825	17·4	22·7
Test and Corporation Acts, 1828	14·4	33·3
Catholic question, 1828	20·2	24
Catholic question,[c] 1829	21·3	26·4
Reform Bill,[b] March–October 1831	21·7	24·4
Reform Bill,[b] July–October 1831	10·7	12·3

[a] Two lists in the Lords; one in the Commons.
[b] Two lists in the Commons; one in the Lords.
[c] Two lists in the Commons; two in the Lords.

recorded conflict with a member of parliament on one issue; 12 peers, on two issues; 9 peers, on three issues; 4 peers, on four issues; 7 peers, on five issues; 1 peer, on six issues; and 3 peers, on seven issues.

As can be seen from Table 3, the percentage of peers having conflicts with their M.P.s seems to have grown as the nineteenth century advanced – at least until the house-cleaning of constituencies which accompanied the general election of 1831.

A. D. Harvey may indeed be correct in suggesting recently that the power of the aristocracy over constituency politics was actually growing stronger,[72] but this point may be slightly mitigated by a growing tendency within the House of Commons to oppose the interests of those same patronal peers. This may herald a growth in issue-orientation in the House of Commons in the place of more traditional and automatically functioning kinship and patronage groups.

And the peers may in a way have responded in kind to a changing political atmosphere. In the parliament elected in 1818, 60·3% of all the members from

[72] A. D. Harvey, *Britain in the early nineteenth century* (London, 1978), p. 4.

Table 4. *The fate of dissident cliental M.P.s*

Issue	Number of cliental M.P.s in conflict with patronal peers	Number of dissident cliental M.P.s who *might* have lost their seats	Percentage of dissident cliental M.P.s who *might* have lost their seats
Regency question, 1811	11	5	45·5
Catholic question, 1812–13	16	6	37·5
Catholic question, 1816–17	20	8	40
Catholic question, 1821	12	6	50
Catholic question, 1825	17	7	41·2
Test and Corporation Acts, 1828	18	7	38·9
Catholic question, 1828	25	4	16
Catholic question, 1829	23	6	26·1
Reform Bill, March–October 1831	25	10	40
	167	59	

England, Wales and Scotland were returned for the same constituency they had represented in the old 1812–18 parliament. However, of those M.P.s who had voted against their noble patrons on the Catholic emancipation question in 1812–13 and 1816–17, only 44% and 45% respectively were returned for the same constituency in 1818. The message to a potential dissident is obvious. In the parliament elected in 1830, there was a 64·6% return of members for the same constituency that they had represented in the 1826–30 parliament. Of those M.P.s who voted against their noble patrons on the Catholic emancipation question in 1828 and 1829, 72% and 62·5% respectively were returned from the same constituency in 1830. Thus, those M.P.s who opposed their patronal peers on the most divisive national issue of 1828 actually had a far higher return rate to the House of Commons for the same constituency than the average M.P.; and on the crucial Catholic vote in 1829, only slightly lower. Where this apparently growing tendency toward independency on the part of some peers and their M.P.s quite obviously breaks down is on the issue of the Reform Bill itself. At the general election of 1831, 67·7% of the British M.P.s were returned for the same constituency they had occupied during the short parliament of 1830–1. However, of those who voted in March 1831 on the second reading of the Reform Bill against the interest of the peers who had returned them (and who in turn recorded their vote on the Reform Bill in October 1831), only 36% were returned for the same constituency. Evidently, some of the tolerance of the 1820s had evaporated in the full glare of schedules A and B, which abolished some boroughs entirely and reduced others to single-member constituencies. Or perhaps when all was said and done, and despite all the talk of civil conflict in Ireland during the late 1820s, religious issues failed to rouse a generally secularized aristocracy with quite the gusto or passion which a possible loss of some of their political influence did.

Table 4 examines nine relevant[73] issues between 1811 and 1831 and presents the percentage of cliental M.P.s who for independence of their patronal peers *might* have lost their seats in parliament. Yet the actual number of M.P.s forced from the House of Commons by an irate patronal peer is undoubtedly much lower than the percentages in Table 4 suggest. These represent the maximum possible even when one has omitted M.P.s who died or who for obvious and easily ascertainable reasons – to accept a peerage or a colonial office for example – left the House of Commons or whose patronal peer lost his constituency. Some M.P.s after all may have voluntarily retired.

On the same nine issues, Table 4 shows that 167 M.P.s were in conflict at one time or another with the peers who returned them. Of the 167 M.P.s, 59 (or only 35·3%) *might* have been cast from parliament by their patronal peers. Of the 167 M.P.s, 84 (or 50·3%) were relatives of the patronal peer and 83 (or 49·7%) were non-relatives. Of the 59 M.P.s who *might* have been forced from parliament, only 17 (28·8%) were relatives of the patronal peer and 42 (71·2%) were non-relatives. Thus, contrary to the accepted wisdom, a relative of a peer had a far smaller chance than non-familial connexions of being cast from parliament for an act of disobedience.

One need not exaggerate the above conclusions. At any given time the majority of individual M.P.s followed the dictates of their patrons; which, after all, were most probably their own views as well. The overwhelming tendency of, for example, whig (or 'Catholic') peers would be to return dependable whig (or 'Catholic'), not tory (or 'Protestant'), members to the House of Commons. Yet, looking at the situation from the viewpoint of the individual M.P., one can still observe a definite fissure in the patronal–cliental relationship. This is especially true if one considers the numbers of abstentions. Members could have abstained on any number of grounds involving physical indisposition or travel and not necessarily connected with opposition to their patronal peer's political line. However, as in modern parliamentary practice, the act of abstention from voting was often an expression of dissatisfaction short of outright rebellion. Table 5 examines only those division lists on which there was a fairly exact correspondence in time and in context (hence eliminating the division lists for the 1811 Regency crisis and the 1812–13 Catholic question) between the terms of the proceedings in the Commons and in the Lords.

---

[73] Obviously, issue 10 on Table 3 – the votes on the Reform Bill during the summer and autumn of 1831 – would not qualify for inclusion on this table because the subsequent general election took place under the reformed franchise.

Table 5. *Percentage of cliental M.P.s not in support of voting patronal peers*

Issue	Percentage of cliental M.Ps voting in opposition to patronal peers	Percentage of cliental M.P.s voting in opposition to patronal peers or abstaining
Catholic question, 1817	11·9	38·1
Catholic question, 1821	7·1	33·1
Catholic question, May 1825	9	27·5
Test and Corporation Acts, 1828	16·5	44
Catholic question, 1828	13·7	25·1
Catholic question,[a] 1829	10·8	37·6
Reform Bill, 1831[b]	12·2	16·5
Reform Bill, 1831[c]	6·4	12·7

[a] There are several division lists recorded in the *Parliamentary debates*. The best comparisons for this purpose would be the third reading of the Catholic Bill in the Commons on 30 March and the second reading in the Lords five days later.

[b] Comparing the second reading of the Reform Bill in the Commons on 22 March with the second reading in the Lords on 7 October.

[c] Comparing the third reading of the Reform Bill in the Commons on 21 September with the second reading of the Reform Bill in the Lords on 7 October.

Thus, at least on contentious religious issues anywhere from 25% to 44% of the cliental M.P.s were not supporting the stated and public positions of their patronal peers.

The cliental members of the unreformed parliament, for all of Lord Grey's fears, did not slavishly follow the dictates of 'my lord this, or the duke of that'. On just the ten occasions discussed above and recorded in the *Parliamentary debates*, over 60% of the patronal peers at one time or another (and often more than once) had to face the question of the defection of a cliental M.P. There was some ideological imperative working within the seemingly most deferential section of the pre-1832 House of Commons. Hence, despite the increasing power of peers over constituencies, the early nineteenth century saw perhaps as numerous examples of the independency of parliamentarians as did the more discussed 1740s or 1970s.[74]

[74] See Owen, 'Political patronage', pp. 374–9; Philip Norton, *Dissension in the House of Commons* (London, 1975), pp. 609–13.

Appendix. *Table of patronage, 1802–1832*

Peer	Constituency	Number of seats and length of patronage
Abercromby[a]	Clackmannanshire	(1) 1821–6; (1) 1830–1
Anglesey (Uxbridge)	Anglesey	(1) 1802–32
	Caernarvon Boroughs	(1) 1802–30; (1) 1831–2
	Milborne Port	(2) 1802–32
Anson (Lichfield)	Lichfield	(1) 1802–32
	Great Yarmouth	(1) 1818–32
Arbuthnot	Kincardineshire	(1) 1826–32
Argyll (Sundridge)	Argyllshire	(1) 1802–32
	Ayr Burghs	(1) 1802–32
Athol (Strange)	Perthshire	(1) 1807–32
Aylesbury	Great Bedwyn	(2) 1802–32
	Marlborough	(2) 1802–32
Balcarras (Wigan)[b]	Wigan	(1) 1820–5; (1) 1826–31
Bath	Bath	(1) 1802–32
	Weobley	(2) 1802–32
Bathurst	Cirencester	(1) 1802–12; (2) 1812–18; (1) 1818–32
Beauchamp	Worcestershire	(1) 1802–31
Beaufort	Gloucestershire	(1) 1802–31
	Monmouth	(1) 1802–32
	Monmouthshire	(1) 1802–32
Bedford	Bedford	(1) 1802–30
	Bedfordshire	(1) 1802–32
	Camelford	(2) 1802–12
	Tavistock	(2) 1802–32
Berkeley	Gloucestershire	(1) 1802–10
Beverley	Bere Alston	(2) 1802–32
Bolingbroke	Wootton Bassett	(1) 1802–7; (1) 1811–12
Bradford	Wenlock	(1) 1802–26
Braybrooke	Berkshire	(1) 1812–25
Bridgewater	Brackley	(2) 1802–3; (1) 1803–29
Bristol	Bury St Edmunds	(1) 1802–32
Brownlow	Clitheroe	(1) 1802–32
	Grantham	(1) 1802–6; (1) 1807–12; (1) 1818–26
Buccleuch and	Edinburgh	(1) 1802–32
Queensbury	Edinburghshire	(1) 1802–32
(Doncaster)[c]	Peeblesshire	(1) 1802–32

[a] This peerage was held by Mary Anne, Baroness Abercromby in her own right, until 1821.

[b] Between the death, in 1825, of the sixth earl, a Scottish representative peer, and the creation of the seventh earl as Baron Wigan (U.K.) in 1826, the seventh earl was not in the House of Lords.

[c] The fifth duke was a minor from 1819 to 1827.

Appendix (*cont.*)

Peer	Constituency	Number of seats and length of patronage
	Roxburghshire	(1) 1814–32
	Selkirk Burghs	(1) 1802–7; (1) 1812–31
	Selkirkshire	(1) 1802–32
Buckingham	Aylesbury	(1) 1806–32
	Buckingham	(2) 1802–32
	Buckinghamshire	(1) 1802–32
	St Mawes	(2) 1802–32
	Saltash	(2) 1807–7
	Winchester	(1) 1818–32
Buckinghamshire	Lincoln (City)	(1) 1802–14
Bulkeley	Beaumaris	(1) 1802–22
	Caernarvonshire	(1) 1802–22
Bute	Banbury	(1) 1830–2
	Buteshire	(1) 1806–7; (1) 1812–18; (1) 1820–6; (1) 1830–1
	Cardiff Boroughs	(1) 1802–32
Caledon	Old Sarum	(2) 1802–32
Calthorpe	Bramber	(1) 1802–31
	Hindon	(1) 1806–32
Camden	Bath	(1) 1826–30
	Breconshire	(1) 1806–32
Camelford	Bodmin	(1) 1802–4
Carlisle	Cumberland	(1) 1806–20
	Morpeth	(1) 1802–32
	Yorkshire	(1) 1830–2
Carnarvon	Cricklade	(1) 1802–12
Carrington	Buckinghamshire	(1) 1820–32
	Chipping Wycombe	(1) 1831–2
	Leicester	(1) 1802–18
	Midhurst	(2) 1802–18
	Nottingham	(1) 1806–18
	Wendover	(2) 1802–32
Carysfort	Huntingdonshire	(1) 1806–7; (1) 1814–18
Cawdor	Carmarthen	(1) 1806–21
	Carmarthenshire	(1) 1806–7
	Nairnshire	(1) 1806–7; (1) 1812–18; (1) 1820–6; (1) 1830–1
Cholmondeley	Castle Rising	(1) 1802–32
Clarendon	Wootton Bassett	(1) 1802–7; (1) 1820–31
Clinton[d]	Ashburton	(1) 1802–32
	Callington	(2) 1802–20
Cornwallis	Eye	(2) 1802–23

[d] The tenth baron was a minor until 1808.

Appendix (*cont.*)

Peer	Constituency	Number of seats and length of patronage
Curzon (Howe)	Clitheroe	(1) 1802–32
Darlington	Camelford	(2) 1818–19; (1) 1820–32
(Cleveland)	Durham	(1) 1802–31
	Ilchester	(1) 1820–6; (2) 1826–7; (2) 1830–2
	Tregony	(2) 1806–12; (2) 1818–30
	Winchelsea	(2) 1802–32
De Dunstanville	Bodmin	(2) 1804–26
	Penryn	(1) 1802–6; (1) 1807–7 (1) 1812–18
Delawarr	East Grinstead	(2) 1827–32
Derby	Lancashire	(1) 1802–32
	Preston	(1) 1802–30
Devonshire	Derby	(1) 1802–32
	Derbyshire	(1) 1802–32
	Knaresborough	(2) 1802–32
Dorset[e]	East Grinstead	(2) 1802–15
Dundas	Berkshire	(1) 1802–32
	Orkney and Shetland	(1) 1807–12; (1) 1818–20; (1) 1826–32
Dynevor	Carmarthenshire	(1) 1802–6; (1) 1807–31
Eglintoun	Ayrshire	(1) 1807–11; (1) 1818–29
(Ardrossan)[f]		
Egremont	New Shoreham	(1) 1802–32
	Sussex	(1) 1807–31
Exeter[g]	Rutland	(1) 1802–12
	Stamford	(2) 1802–31; (1) 1831–2
Falmouth	Mitchell	(1) 1806–26; (1) 1830–2
	Truro	(2) 1802–20; (2) 1826–32
Fife	Banff District	(1) 1806–7; (1) 1827–31
	Banffshire	(1) 1827–32
Fitzwilliam	Higham Ferrers	(1) 1802–32
	Malton	(2) 1802–32
	Northamptonshire	(1) 1831–2
	Peterborough	(2) 1802–32
	Yorkshire	(1) 1807–32
Foley	Droitwich	(2) 1802–31; (1) 1831–2
	Herefordshire	(1) 1807–18
	Worcestershire	(1) 1802–3; (1) 1806–32
Forester	Wenlock	(1) 1821–32

[e] The fourth duke was a minor until 1814.
[f] The thirteenth earl was a minor after 1819.
[g] The second marquess was a minor between 1804 and 1816.

Appendix (*cont.*)

Peer	Constituency	Number of seats and length of patronage
Fortescue	Devon	(1) 1818–20; (1) 1830–2
Galloway (Stewart)	Kirkcudbright Stewartry	(1) 1803–26
	Stranraer Burghs	(1) 1802–32
	Wigtownshire	(1) 1812–16
Gordon	Aberdeenshire	(1) 1802–32
Grafton	Bury St Edmunds	(1) 1802–32
	Thetford	(1) 1802–32
Grantley	Guildford	(1) 1802–6; (1) 1807–12; (1) 1826–30; (1) 1831–2
Grey	Northumberland	(1) 1831–2
Grimston (Verulam)	St Albans	(1) 1802–8; (1) 1830–1
Grosvenor (Westminster)	Chester	(2) 1802–7; (1) 1807–18; (2) 1818–30; (1) 1830–2
	Cheshire	(1) 1830–2
	Hindon	(1) 1826–32
	Shaftesbury	(2) 1821–32
	Stockbridge	(1) 1822–6; (1) 1831–2
Guildford	Banbury	(1) 1802–30
Hamilton	Lanarkshire	(1) 1802–27
	Selkirk Burghs	(1) 1807–12
Hardwicke	Cambridgeshire	(1) 1802–10
	Reigate	(1) 1802–32
Harewood	Northallerton	(1) 1802–32
	Yorkshire	(1) 1802–6; (1) 1812–18
Harrowby	Tiverton	(2) 1802–32
Hertford	Aldeburgh	(1) 1826–9; (2) 1829–32
	Bodmin	(1) 1826–32
	Orford	(2) 1802–32
Heytesbury	Heytesbury	(2) 1828–32
Home	Berwickshire	(1) 1807–32
Hopetoun[h]	Dumfriesshire	(1) 1809–32
	Haddingtonshire	(1) 1809–26
	Linlithgowshire	(1) 1809–32
	Stirling Burghs	(1) 1809–19; (1) 1820–30
Lansdowne	Calne	(2) 1802–32
	Chipping Wycombe	(1) 1802–6
Lauderdale	Berwickshire	(1) 1826–32
	Haddington Burghs	(1) 1806–7; (1) 1812–32
	Haddingtonshire	(1) 1826–32
Leeds	Helston	(2) 1802–32
Londonderry (Stewart) (Vane)	Durham (City)	(1) 1820–31; (1) 1831–2

[h] The fifth earl was a minor from 1823 to 1824.

Appendix (*cont.*)

Peer	Constituency	Number of seats and length of patronage
Lonsdale	Appleby	(1) 1802–32
	Carlisle	(1) 1802–31
	Cockermouth	(2) 1802–32
	Cumberland	(1) 1802–31
	Haslemere	(2) 1802–32
	Westmorland	(2) 1802–31; (1) 1831–2
Lyttelton	Bewdley	(1) 1802–18
Manchester	Huntingdonshire	(1) 1802–6; (1) 1818–20; (1) 1826–32
Manvers	East Retford	(1) 1830–2
	Nottinghamshire	(1) 1802–16
Marlborough	Heytesbury	(1) 1802–12
	New Woodstock	(2) 1802–20; (1) 1820–6; (2) 1826–32
	Oxford (City)	(1) 1802–12; (1) 1818–20
	Oxfordshire	(1) 1802–15
Middleton	Newark	(1) 1805–32
Middleton	Whitchurch	(1) 1802–18
Minto	Roxburghshire	(1) 1806–14
Monson[i]	Gatton	(2) 1830–2
	Lincoln (City)	(1) 1806–18
Montrose (Graham)	Dumbartonshire	(1) 1806–10; (1) 1830–2
	Stirlingshire	(1) 1802–21
Mount Edgcumbe	Bossiney	(1) 1802–26
	Fowey	(1) 1802–26
	Lostwithiel	(2) 1802–32
	Plympton Erle	(1) 1802–32
Mulgrave	Scarborough	(1) 1802–32
Newcastle[j]	Aldborough	(2) 1802–32
	Basset Law	(1) 1830–1
	Boroughbridge	(2) 1802–18; (1) 1818–20; (2) 1824–32
	East Retford	(2) 1802–7; (1) 1807–12
	Newark	(1) 1802–32
Norfolk[k]	Arundel	(1) 1802–6; (2) 1806–19; (1) 1819–20
	Carlisle	(1) 1802–20
	Gloucester (City)	(1) 1802–18
	Hereford (City)	(2) 1802–18
	Horsham	(2) 1806–8; (2) 1812–32

[i] The fifth baron was a minor between 1809 and 1830
[j] The fourth duke was a minor until 1806.
[k] As a Roman Catholic, the twelfth duke was not in parliament between 1815 and 1829.

Appendix (*cont.*)

Peer	Constituency	Number of seats and length of patronage
	New Shoreham	(1) 1802–32
	Steyning	(2) 1802–32
Northampton	Northampton (City)	(1) 1802–20
Northumberland	Launceston	(2) 1802–32
	Newport (Cornw.)	(2) 1802–32
	Northumberland	(1) 1807–12
Northwick	Evesham	(1) 1819–32
Onslow	Guildford	(1) 1802–12; (2) 1812–26; (1) 1826–31
Orford	King's Lynn	(1) 1802–31
Pelham	Lewes	(1) 1802–6
Pembroke	Wilton	(2) 1802–32
Petre[1]	Thetford	(1) 1802–26
Portland	Buckinghamshire	(1) 1802–9
	King's Lynn	(1) 1822–32
	Nottinghamshire	(1) 1812–14; (1) 1816–26
Portsmouth	Andover	(1) 1802–18
Poulett	Bridgwater	(2) 1802–6; (2) 1807–20
Powis	Bishop's Castle	(2) 1802–19; (1) 1819–20; (2) 1820–32
	Ludlow	(2) 1802–32
	Montgomery	(1) 1802–32
Queensbury (Douglas of Amesbury)	Dumfries Burghs	(1) 1802–10; (1) 1818–32
	Dumfriesshire	(1) 1802–4
Radnor	Downton	(2) 1802–32
	Salisbury	(1) 1802–32
Richmond	Chichester	(1) 1802–32
	Sussex	(1) 1802–6; (1) 1831–2
Rosebery	Stirling Burghs	(1) 1819–20
Rosslyn	Dysart Burghs	(1) 1802–5; (1) 1830–1
Rutland	Bramber	(1) 1802–32
	Cambridge	(2) 1802–32
	Cambridgeshire	(1) 1802–30
	Grantham	(1) 1802–12
	Leicestershire	(1) 1802–31
	Newark	(1) 1802–5
	Scarborough	(1) 1802–32
St Germans	Liskeard	(2) 1802–32
	St Germans	(2) 1802–32
Salisbury	Hertford	(1) 1817–31
Sandwich[m]	Huntingdon	(2) 1802–32

[1] As Roman Catholics, the tenth and eleventh barons were not in parliament.
[m] The seventh earl was a minor after 1818.

Appendix (*cont.*)

Peer	Constituency	Number of seats and length of patronage
	Huntingdonshire	(1) 1802–14
Seaford	Seaford	(1) 1826–31
Shaftesbury	Dorchester	(1) 1802–32
	Dorset	(1) 1831–2
Somers	Hereford (City)	(1) 1818–32
	Reigate	(1) 1802–32
Spencer	Northamptonshire	(1) 1806–32
	St Albans	(1) 1802–7
Stafford	Brackley	(1) 1803–25
	Lichfield	(1) 1802–31
	Newcastle-under-Lyme	(2) 1802–12
	Staffordshire	(1) 1802–20
	Sutherland	(1) 1802–32
	Tain Burghs	(1) 1802–32
Sydney	Whitchurch	(1) 1802–32
Thanet	Appleby	(1) 1802–32
Townshend	Great Yarmouth	(1) 1802–18
	Tamworth	(1) 1802–18; (1) 1820–32
Warwick	Warwick	(1) 1802–31
Waterford (Tyrone)[n]	Berwick-upon-Tweed	(1) 1823–32
Westmoreland	Lyme Regis	(2) 1802–32
Wharncliffe	Bossiney	(1) 1826–32
Yarborough	Great Grimsby	(2) 1802–7; (2) 1812–18
	Lincolnshire	(1) 1807–23; (1) 1831–2
	Newton (Hants)	(1) 1802–32

[n] The third marquess was a minor after 1826.

7. Passing the Reform Bill, 1832.

A portrait by S. W. Reynolds, by courtesy of the House of Lords Record Office.

The House of Lords sat in the former Court of Requests between 1801 and 1834. Before the throne sit the six Commissioners, being from the left: the Marquess Wellesley, the Marquess of Lansdowne, the Lord Chancellor (Lord Brougham), Lord Holland, the Earl of Durham, and the Prime Minister (Earl Grey). The Clerk of the Crown has just read the title of the Reform Bill prior to the declaration of royal assent. The date is 7 June 1832. The benches holding supporters of the Whig government are full while the Tory opposition stayed away as did King William IV.

18

THE HOUSE OF LORDS AND IRELAND
IN THE AGE OF PEEL,
1832-50

DAVID LARGE

I

Before considering the manner in which the house of lords handled Irish questions in the age of Peel[1] a brief examination of the ties between the United Kingdom upper house and Ireland is necessary. A striking fact that requires emphasis is the growth between 1783 and 1832 of the 'Irish interest' in the lords. In the eighteenth century, when the British house of lords was a relatively small body of little over 200 members, the number of peers with a stake in Irish land was only about one eighth of the whole body. Several of these, too, owned wide lands in England and their main interests lay there. But by the time the first reformed parliament was opened on 29 January 1833 the 'Irish interest' in the lords had become a formidable body. In a house that had doubled in numbers since 1783 virtually one peer out of every four had a stake in Ireland through the ownership of land, and the majority of these were men whose economic interests were exclusively centred on their Irish estates. Moreover this 'Irish interest' maintained its strength in the lords right down to the formation of Gladstone's first ministry as the table below makes clear.

[1] I have to thank his grace the duke of Wellington for kind permission to examine and quote from the Wellington MSS at Apsley house.

	1783	1801	1815	1833	1847	1867
Total number of members of the house of lords - -	230	334	357	423	450	464 [2]
Number of members possessing land in Ireland, or Irish mortgages - - -	31	83	77	105	125	116
Number of members who may have possessed land in Ireland	8	18	21	22	15	22

This growth in the size of the 'Irish interest' in the lords was certainly one of the roots of the intransigent attitude adopted by the upper house on Irish questions in the age of Peel and later.

The increased 'Irish interest' in the lords was due in part to the fact that under the act of union 28 representative Irish peers sat in the house; but equally important was the fact that the abolition of the Irish house of lords created an incentive for Irish peers who failed to secure election as representative peers to acquire United Kingdom titles in order to become once more members of a legislature. Moreover, prime ministers between 1800 and 1832, although anxious to avoid profuse creations, were not unsympathetic to Irish peers soliciting such titles. Liverpool, for instance, in rejecting an application for a peerage from a country gentleman in 1814, observed that some of the Irish and Scottish peers 'say with a good deal of reason that, if we were commoners of old family and large property, we

---

[2] This table has been compiled by using the works listed below for references to peers owning estates in Ireland :—T. Campbell, *A philosophical survey of the south of Ireland* (Dublin, 1778); A. Young, *A tour in Ireland* (Dublin, 1780); W. Wilson, *The post chaise companion* (Dublin, 1784; 3rd ed., Dublin, 1805); *Annual Reg., 1797*, p. 31; the *Statistical surveys* prepared for the Royal Dublin Society for counties Antrim, Armagh, Cavan, Clare, Cork, Donegal, Down, Dublin, Galway, Kildare, Kilkenny, Leitrim, Londonderry, Mayo, Meath, Monaghan, Roscommon, Sligo, Tyrone, Wicklow, and Wexford, and King's County and Queen's County; E. Wakefield, *An account of Ireland, statistical and political* (London, 1812); W. S. Mason, *A statistical account or parochial survey of Ireland* (Dublin, 1814–19); Lewis, *Topog. dict. Ire.; The parliamentary gazetteer of Ireland* (Dublin, 1844); *A list of petitions filed in the incumbered estates court in Ireland, 1849–53* (Dublin, 1854); *Owners of land (Ireland)*, (C 1097) H.L. & H.C., 1874, lxxii; *Owners of land (Ireland)*, H.C. 1876, (422), lxxx; J. Bateman, *The great landowners of Great Britain and Ireland* (London, 1878 and 1883).

might doubt whether it was in our interest to be created peers, but the anomalous situation of a Scotch or Irish peer, with half the privileges of the peerage, places us in an ambiguous . . . situation, and makes us anxious to be invested with all the privileges which are considered belonging to our rank'. As a consequence, Liverpool regarded elevations of those 'who were actually already Scotch or Irish peers' as being in a special category separate from the normal applicants for peerages.[3] Hence there was a steady trickle of Irish peers acquiring United Kingdom titles and thus entering the house of lords.[4]

The 'Irish interest' in the lords, however, was not an organized group. It had no eve-of-session dinner parties in a leader's house, and no small office to manage the business of whipping up peers as the duke of Wellington and his friends had. Nor was any one peer in either of the main parties detailed off to look after Irish business in the lords and to secure attendance of Irish peers, as was the case with Scottish affairs.[5] The 'Irish interest' in fact emerged sporadically from among the ranks of the parties in the lords on particular issues directly concerning it, notably on land and poor law questions. Increased Irish representation in the upper house really reinforced the conservatism of that body. For not only were the 28 elected peers chosen from an Irish peerage that had been swollen to unheard-of proportions by Pittite creations, but Earl Grey's whig connection was the only political group that had not played a part in manipulating these elections, or in recommending grants of United Kingdom titles for Irish peers, between the union and 1830. Hence it is not surprising that of the 'Irish interest' of 105 in January 1833 only 34 could be classed as whigs, although it should be noted that among them

[3] B.M., Add. MS 38260, ff. 95–8.
[4] The total from 13 Jan. 1801 to 29 Jan. 1833 was 34. In addition, of course, there were some United Kingdom titles conferred during this period on commoners whose principal estates were in Ireland (e.g. W. B. Ponsonby who was created a baron in 1806), which helped to swell the 'Irish interest' in the lords.
[5] Rosslyn to Wellington, 14 Dec. 1836, gives evidence of party organization in the lords, and Melville to Wellington, 15 Jan. 1836, shows the rôle of Melville in Scottish business (Wellington MSS); cf. Aberdeen to Peel, 14, 25 Nov. 1838 (B.M., Add. MS 40312), and Wellington to Aberdeen, 30 Oct., 26 Nov. 1838 (B.M., Add. MS 43060).

were some of the greatest landowners in Ireland such as
Lansdowne, Fitzwilliam, Devonshire, Leinster and Sligo. The
representative peers were a particular stronghold of the tories
for 24 of the 27 in January 1833 were tories, and the election
of Lord Downes to fill the vacancy created by the death of the
marquis of Conyngham raised the figure to 25. No wonder
the liberal Lord Langford—who had no seat in the lords—
complained in 1837 that such was the tory majority in the Irish
peerage that 'no liberal can hope to be elected'.[6] The balance
of forces in the Irish peerage can be guaged effectively from
the circumstances of Lord Downes' election in 1833. He sent
frequent reports to Wellington of his candidature which cast
much light on these curious elections. To bring the 'electorate'
to the 'poll' was not easy, for Lord Downes sent the duke a
list of 67 peers who had not qualified themselves to vote, adding
that this was 'a troublesome and expensive business'. Later
he sent a remarkable map of the route that an Irish magistrate
would travel to collect subscriptions of oaths and so forth
from Irish peers living in the English countryside, so that they
would be legally qualified to vote. Finally he enclosed a full
statement of the poll : Downes, who was Wellington's candidate,
76; Lismore, the government candidate, 31; and 25 who did
not vote. Downes claimed, and probably correctly, that his
votes were the highest ever obtained in such an election, hence
the contest may be taken as indicating very clearly the tory
predominance in the Irish peerage.[7]

The only problem that faced the tories in these elections was
succinctly stated by the earl of Belmore in 1833 when he wrote,
'the government cannot return an Irish peer unless the
conservatives are divided'.[8] They were frequently divided,
and, like it or not, Peel and Wellington were forced to intervene
in the elections to prevent either a whig, or just as bad, an
ultra tory from being returned. Peel and Wellington were
accustomed to consult each other, decide who was to be the

[6] Lord Langford, *A letter to Viscount Melbourne on the peerage*
(1837), p. 7.

[7] Lord Downes to Wellington, 7, 18, 22, 23, 29 Jan., 7, 23, 27 Feb.,
30 Mar. 1833 (Wellington MSS).

[8] Belmore to Wellington, 9 Jan. 1833 (Wellington MSS).

party candidate and use their influence on his behalf. They took into consideration the peer's political influence, the extent of his property in Ireland, whether he resided for long or short periods, whether he was popular among the chief resident peers, and whether he had promises of a substantial number of votes.[9] The whole business from the party leaders' point of view was troublesome and annoying, so much so that Peel was anxious to be rid of it. In 1836 he suggested leaving the Irish peers 'to fight each his own battle', although ruefully he added, 'the risk is, if there is no controlling power, the conservatives might be divided and a whig get in'.[10] Wellington replied in a highly characteristic letter which deserves quotation. ' I'd like ', he wrote, 'to leave the vacancies alone. I have all the trouble, and all the odium, attending the preference of the claim of one to those of others. But the influence we have in this matter is the same as we have upon others in the house of lords—many peers come to me asking how they are to vote for representative peers, just as they make the same enquiry upon any other question in the house of lords. I ask nobody to vote, there is no canvass, not a single peer has been asked by me for his vote. But if we let things go, then the whig-radical party in the Irish peerage will get in, . . . it would be an evil at present to let government each year add one or two of their men to the house of lords.' The duke added significantly, 'Roden would use the influence you don't want to use, to keep men like Lords Miltown and Rossmore out of the house—surely it is better to have our nominees than those of Roden, Farnham and the duke of Cumberland'.[11] Peel confessed that the duke was right. The conservative leaders went on making sure their nominees were returned as Irish representative peers.

II

Turning now to the manner in which the lords handled Irish questions, we may divide the topic into three phases : the lords' attitude to Irish legislation and the Irish executive between

[9] Wellington to Peel, 5 Mar. 1842 (B.M., Add. MS 40459); Peel to Wellington, 20, 22 May 1845, 2 May 1846 (B.M., Add. MS 40461); Peel to Wellington, 17 Aug. 1836 (Wellington MSS).

[10] Peel to Wellington, 31 Aug. 1836 (Wellington MSS).

[11] Wellington to Peel, 2 Sept. 1836 (Wellington MSS).

1832 and the fall of Melbourne in 1841, their reception of
Peel's Irish policy between 1841 and 1846, and, as a revealing
tailpiece, their handling of the famine question.

In the first phase one overriding factor has to be constantly
remembered: the tory peers could command a majority in the
lords, as the reform bill struggle revealed with crystal clarity.
Hence if the Grey and Melbourne ministries were to pass
their Irish measures through the upper house unscathed they
would have to rely either on the co-operation of the tory peers
or on coercing them successfully. The key to co-operation lay
in the willingness and ability of Peel and Wellington to carry
their noble followers with them should they decide to support
ministerial measures. The key to coercion lay in the ministries'
own hands: they could create more whig peers, or threaten to
do so, to swamp the tory majority; they could secure
overwhelming majorities in the commons for their measures and
depend on this to overawe the lords, or they could rely on
extra-parliamentary agitation to play the same rôle.

If coercion was not applied, and if Peel would not co-
operate, then a measure was almost certainly doomed to
rejection or remodelling in the lords. For example in 1835
and 1836 the ministerial attempts to settle the tithe question
and to reorganize the church of Ireland, involving a recognition
of the appropriation of surplus revenues for secular purposes,
were objected to by Peel. Both were amended drastically in
the lords to suit his views and abandoned by the ministry.[12] In
1836 the ministry tried to pass a measure to reform the Irish
municipal corporations. On this occasion, since the corporations
had been damned so effectually by a preceding investigation, a
plant for a counter-proposal on conservative lines was worked
out by the leading conservatives in the commons, and Wellington
was carefully wooed into accepting it. It was this plan that the
tory majority in the lords, led by Lyndhurst, but guided by the
duke, wrote into the government's measure and thus destroyed
it.[13] Peel could rely on the tory majority in the lords to reject

[12] *Parl. deb.*, xxx, cols 715–45, 872–934; xxxv, cols 435–43, 446–515;
G. Kitson Clark, *Peel and the conservative party*, p. 284; *The correspondence and diaries of J. W. Croker*, ed. L. J. Jennings, ii. 282–3.
[13] W. F. Moneypenny and G. E. Buckle, *Life of Disraeli*, i. 328 for
Disraeli's account of the conservative plan, in which he exaggerates

or remodel any ministerial measure for Ireland of which he disapproved, since his disapproval was bound to be shared by the tory peers in full measure. It was this factor which enabled him to propose in the commons the compromise plan of 1837 by which, in return for a church and tithe bill which should omit the obnoxious appropriation clause, and an Irish poor law bill that should provide a satisfactorily high basis for an electoral qualification in town elections, a bill permitting the establishment of new corporations in the larger towns in Ireland would be allowed to pass the lords and commons.[14] It was the tory majority in the lords, too, that ensured that in the long run the ministry would tacitly be forced to accept the compromise. The Melbourne cabinet tried to wriggle out over the corporations bill. In 1838 the ministerial bill retained the £5 electoral qualification. Hence the tory peers went into action and wrote in the higher qualification of £10 on the basis of the poor law rating; this they hoped, in concert with Peel, would prevent a mass of lower middle class catholics seizing control of the new corporations. The same thing happened in 1839. In 1840 the bill finally satisfied Peel and it passed the lords.[15] Peel himself in 1836 had described his party's happy position: with ' 300 conservatives in the commons to back the lords in rejecting bad measures ' the party combined 'power with *irresponsibility* '.[16]

Clearly the first hurdle to be surmounted if a ministerial bill for Ireland was to be accepted in the lords was the securing of Peel's co-operation. But it was only the first hurdle. Much then depended on Peel's influence with Wellington. Then, if the duke was prepared to agree with Peel, the question was:

Lyndhurst's part. Peel's anxiety to win over Wellington, and his loyalty to him, once the duke was committed, in spite of pressure from Stanley for the lords to adopt less drastic amendments to the corporation bill, is shown in Peel to Wellington, 10 Jan., 12 Feb., 11, 12 Mar. 1836, and Rosslyn to Wellington, 9, 10 Feb. 1836 (Wellington MSS); *Parl. deb.*, xxxii, cols 1119–66; xxxiii, cols 233–306, 704–37, 1043–62.

[14] For the negotiations leading to the compromise plan see G. Kitson Clark, *Peel and the conservative party*, pp. 332–59.

[15] *Parl. deb.*, xliv, cols 150–67, 276–83, 702–16; xlix, cols 597–620, 747–63, 1143–5; liii, cols 1160–80; lv, cols 438–51.

[16] Hardinge to Wellington, 9 Nov. 1836, indicating Peel's opinion (Wellington MSS).

would Wellington be able to carry with him enough of the heterogeneous body of tory peers in support of a ministerial measure, or would the ultra tories reject his leadership altogether and muster so strongly as to overwhelm the whig peers and Wellington's own followers. In short, while Peel's position was crucial in regard to the passage of Irish legislation through the lords, so was Wellington's.

Wellington was not always willing to follow Peel and understandably so. His instincts were ultra tory, but more important, he had to try to keep his party together in the lords. Lurking behind him was always the spectre of the violent, diehard, ultra tory peers such as Cumberland, Londonderry and Roden, or rather irresponsible figures such as Lyndhurst, willing to lead the ultras in wild courses. Yet Peel's advice, and his own reasoning, told the duke that it might well be disastrous if the tory peers used their majority to do what the ultra tories wanted to do : reject the ministeries' measures wholesale and turn them out. For what haunted Wellington—and Peel himself often enough—was the fear that if the evil necessity of a Grey or Melbourne ministry was not kept in power, revolution would follow. Such was Wellington's dilemma. It did not arise when Irish legislation was confined to coercion bills. Wellington and the ultra tory peers were then committed to comparatively mild squabbles as to whether the coercion bill was stern enough or not. The bill of 1833 had a sufficiently quiet passage through the lords, and it was possible for one tory peer to write to Wellington that he thought ' it too good to be true that you and Peel were committed by the government to re-establish peace in Ireland '.[17] But almost without exception every measure concerning Ireland, outside coercion bills, meant that Wellington was subjected to the advice of Peel, counselling moderation, on the one hand, and on the other to the hue and cry of the ultra tories in full chase hunting down a ministerial proposal which they were convinced would be utterly disastrous to Ireland. It was an unenviable position and it was not surprising that on occasions the duke jibbed and refused to heed the wisdom of Peel. When he did so there was no hope for a ministerial measure in the lords unless

[17] Northumberland to Wellington, 25 Jan. 1833 (Wellington MSS); *Parl. deb.*, xv, cols 719–58.

coercive action was resorted to. The clearest case was the tithe bill of 1834.

In that year the duke was estranged from Peel. It had nearly broken his heart to allow the 'church robbery' bill, as he called it, of the previous year to pass the lords, and the ultra tory peers were pressing him hard to lead a vigorous opposition to the ministry in the lords.[18] The ultras were determined to kill the tithe bill, the ministry's chief Irish measure of the session. Peel, on the other hand, favoured it. It had no appropriation clause and it seemed to offer an excellent opportunity both to save something for the church of Ireland and to set at rest a very vexing problem. But Wellington cast in his lot with the ultra tories and the bill was rejected in the lords. Afterwards Wellington explained to Aberdeen his reasons. 'In the first place the bill itself was abominable and', he continued, 'I could not have commanded a majority in the lords if I had allowed the second reading unopposed'.[19] Undoubtedly the second reason was more potent than the first: Wellington helped to pass plenty of bills which he had described as 'abominable' both before and after 1834.

But generally Wellington, and it is much to his credit given the man he was, ended by co-operating with Peel, even though time and time again he seemed on the verge of not doing so. The cost of accepting Peel's advice, however, was high for the duke. In critical situations it led to a complete breach with the ultra tory peers. The classical example occurred in 1833 over the Irish church temporalities bill. On this question the duke was subjected to intense pressure from the ultra tory peers headed by the duke of Cumberland. Long before the bill reached the lords, Cumberland had been rallying his forces.[20] Most of the English bishops came up to his expectations, particularly the

[18]Charles Arbuthnot to his son, 20 Aug. 1833 (*The correspondence of Charles Arbuthnot,* ed. A. Aspinall, Camden third series, lxv. 175); for the duke's estrangement from Peel see Aberdeen to Peel, 5 May 1834, Peel's memo. of 10 May 1834 and Arbuthnot to Aberdeen, 2 May 1834 (B.M., Add. MS 40312); cf. Wellington to Aberdeen, 23 May 1834 (B.M., Add. MS 43060); Duke of Buckingham and Chandos, *Memoirs of the courts and cabinets of William IV and Victoria,* ii. 94–9.

[19] Wellington to Aberdeen, 4 Sept. 1834 (B.M., Add. MS 43060).

[20] H. Twiss, *Life of Eldon,* iii. 195; *The Standard,* 13, 14 Feb., 12, 14, 16, 23 Mar. 1833; *Blackwood's Magazine,* xxxiii, no. 205 (Mar.

chaplain of the ultra tories, Phillpotts of Exeter, who declared his ' unalterable resistance to the wicked views of his majesty's ministry '.[21] On the other hand, to the royal duke's dismay, the Irish primate let him down. Archbishop Whately was quite right when he said afterwards that the primate had given his assent to the bill in the main, and then kept quiet about this, being content to be applauded as a fearless opponent.[22] Cumberland's letters, corroborated by those of Viscount Beresford, show clearly that Archbishop Beresford had indeed acquiesced.[23] The ministry in fact had seduced the Irish bench by dealing directly with it without consulting the English bishops, as van Mildert of Durham bitterly complained to his high tory friends.[24] Cumberland was not deterred: he tried hard to enlist Peel's and Wellington's support for an outright rejection of the Irish church bill in the lords.[25] Peel refused and his advice to Wellington was that the bill should be accepted.

What was Wellington to do? His faithful man of business, Earl Rosslyn, advised him that to follow Peel would mean a ' decided split ' among the tory peers.[26] And indeed there was just such a split long before the bill reached the lords. Cumberland virtually usurped Wellington's place as leader of the tory peers, trying to enlist them ' in a constant attendance and in active opposition ' as one of them told Wellington.[27] After much fluctuation of mood the duke appeared to have made

1833), p. 366; *Fraser's Magazine*, viii, no. 60, pp. 419–20; *Parl. deb.*, xvi, cols 778–88, 995–7, 1323–5; xvii, cols 380–4; xix, cols 302, 718; Lord Brougham, *Life and times by himself*, iii. 273–4.

[21] Phillpotts to Wellington, 8, 13 Feb. 1833 (Wellington MSS).

[22] E. J. Whately, *Life of Archbishop Whately*, i. 195, 237–41.

[23] H. van Thal, *Ernest Augustus, duke of Cumberland and king of Hanover*, appendix iv, pp. 277–89; Viscount Beresford to Wellington, 22 Feb. 1833, enclosing a letter from the archbishop of Armagh (Wellington MSS).

[24] E. Hughes, ' The bishops and reform, 1831–33, some fresh correspondence ', in *E.H.R.*, lvi (July 1941). 479; Rosslyn to Wellington, 12 Mar. 1833 (Wellington MSS).

[25] Cumberland to Wellington, 5 Mar. 1833, also enclosing his correspondence with the archbishop of Armagh (Wellington MSS).

[26] Rosslyn to Wellington, 12 Mar. 1833 (Wellington MSS).

[27] Camden to Wellington, 28 Mar. 1833 (Wellington MSS); Ellenborough's diary, 10 Mar. 1833, in *Three early nineteenth century diaries*, ed. A. Aspinall, p. 315.

up his mind to restore his prestige by accepting the ultra tory position, for when the bill finally made its appearance in the upper house he attacked it in angry and passionate terms. It appeared as if the main concilatory measure towards Ireland proposed by the ministry in 1833 was doomed to rejection by a reunited and triumphant tory peerage. Three days later, however, Wellington executed a tactical withdrawal by deciding not to oppose the second reading of the bill after all. Peel and Aberdeen seem to have been the instruments behind the duke's withdrawal, for Aberdeen appears to have impressed upon the duke how very angry Peel had been when he had heard of Wellington's speech against the bill, and to have persuaded the duke that it was much too dangerous to risk a fight with the ministry in the lords.[28]

The cost of Wellington's retreat was a complete schism with the ultra tory peers. They were outraged at Wellington's defection, and a general meeting attended only by ultra tory peers was held at Cumberland's house at which the royal duke pledged himself to fight the bill to the bitter end. The ulterior object was to dethrone Grey and form a ministry of their own, without Peel if need be.[29] It was a wild, impracticable scheme, but it was taken very seriously at the time both by its sponsors and opponents. In the lords itself, on the second reading, the ultras raged for two nights against the Irish church bill. On the third night Wellington evidently felt that he must somehow try to mollify them and yet remain loyal to Peel. Hence his speech accepted the principle of the bill but subjected it to so much criticism that he raised the hope that it would be possible to alter it substantially in committee. The division was instructive: the ultra tories, to the surprise of Wellington's whipper-in, divided 'much stronger' than expected. The ministry in fact only carried the day by intensely active lobbying

---

[28] Ellenborough's diary, 13 July 1833, in *Three early nineteenth century diaries,* pp. 347–8.

[29] Buckingham to Wellington, 13 July 1833, in which he asserted that the ultras 'neither can or will retreat' and, 'should Sir Robert Peel . . . decline to co-operate in government in the house of commons, there are many who feel their duty calls upon them to rescue the country out of the hands in which it is placed with the least possible delay, although he may shrink from that duty' (Wellington MSS).

among their own supporters, more of whom voted in this
division than on any other occasion between 1833 and 1841, as
well as by the fact that Wellington and some of his associates
abstained from voting.[30]

Significant amendments might easily be carried against the
ministry in committee as Peel realised. Hence he intervened
with a powerful warning letter to Wellington. His main theme
was the impossibility at present of forming an alternative
government that could command a majority in the commons,
and be able to 'pass those bills which are essential for the
maintenance of the church in Ireland'. He meant, as he
explained, bills to provide a substitute for church cess—one of
the objects of the ministry's measure now being discussed—and,
'the infinitely more important question of the provision of a
substitute for tithe', since, argued Peel, 'unless this is found
immediately there is an end of tithe or any equivalent for it'.[31]
Peel's letter took effect, although not as completely as he
evidently hoped. The ministerial press was soon reporting a
diminution of opposition to the Irish church bill in the lords.
On the other hand Wellington tried to amend it in such a
fashion as to reconcile the ultra tory peers without driving the
ministry to desperation. His most important attempt was a
proposal to circumvent the proposed reduction in the number of
Irish bishoprics by leaving the consequent union of sees to be
carried out by governmental action rather than by act of
parliament. Should a conservative ministry come into office the
union of bishoprics might be avoided or undone without recourse
to parliament. But Brougham and Grey, to Wellington's
dismay, saw through this, and insisted that the whole principle
of the bill was imperilled. The duke then tried to withdraw
his amendment, plainly agreeing with Peel that the ministry
must not be defeated. The fury of the high tory peers was
unbounded. One report says that as the duke was trying to
withdraw his motion, 'there was a terrible crash of " no " from
the seats behind and the high-flying tory lords went out before

---

[30] *Parl. deb.,* xix, cols 725–82, 807–82, 918–1018; the division figures
were ministerialists 157; ultra tories 98; Rosslyn to Mrs Arbuthnot,
20 July 1833 (*The correspondence of Charles Arbuthnot,* as above, lxv.
171).
[31] Peel to Wellington, 20 July 1833 (Wellington MSS).

the division '.[32]   The ministerialists carried their point narrowly, and thereafter, apart from a minor defeat that caused a further flurry, the bill went through the lords without incident.

But even when open breaches with the ultra tory peers were avoided Wellington had to endure almost constant grumbling from them, and was compelled to take a good deal of evasive action.   This was particularly the case in regard to the ultra tory crusade against the Irish executive during Melbourne's second ministry.   From the very beginning in 1835 they maintained that the Irish executive was simply the tool of the arch-agitator O'Connell, and this remained until 1841 their leading war cry.   Every scrap of evidence to support the thesis that a secret, organised conspiracy existed, aiming at repeal of the union and the destruction of protestantism, was collected and paraded before the upper house in wearisome detail by the ultra tory peers.   Their charges were often unwarranted, their outlook was intensely sectarian, but it would be unjust to question their sincerity.[33]

The effect of such displays was not great.   The Irish executive did not alter its course, although Drummond was frequently called upon to arm the lord lieutenant with batteries of facts and figures for replies in the lords, and himself had to submit to an unpleasant cross-questioning by a select committee obtained by the orange peers in 1839.[34]   The orange campaign in the lords embarrassed the conservative leaders more than it did the Irish executive, for it revealed the schisms in the party more clearly even than the debates on Irish legislation.   It justified the observation in *Fraser's Magazine* for January 1837 that, ' the great question on which, we fear, the conservative party is not yet fully agreed is what policy shall be pursued

[32] *The Globe,* 24 July 1833; E. J. Littleton's diary, 23 July 1833, in *Three early nineteenth century diaries,* ed. A. Aspinall, pp. 350–1; *Parl. deb.* xix, cols 1084–1103.

[33] The chief members of the group of Irish ultra tory peers were Roden, Londonderry, Glengall, Lorton, Downshire, Westmeath, Farnham, Enniskillen and Thomond.   *Parl. deb.,* xxvii, cols 1118–25; xxviii, cols 340–65; xxxix, cols 212–24, 339–54; xlii, cols 33–9, 264–9; xliii, cols 746–57, 989–1043; xlv, cols 601–8, 907–16; xlvi, cols 10–25.

[34] R. B. O'Brien, *Life and letters of Thomas Drummond,* pp. 327–33, 339–53.

towards the papists of the empire? '.[35] The orange peers had no doubts : they traced all the trouble to the granting of catholic emancipation and in doing so, in effect, passed judgment on Peel and Wellington. There were even definite proposals before the lords to repeal the emancipation act. No wonder Brougham exclaimed ' Ye gods '.[36]

There is no need to expatiate on Peel's distaste for all this : he did not want to emerge eventually as head of a ministry committed to maintaining the cause of orangeism in Ireland in its most uncompromising form. Hence Wellington had to tread delicately. He had to restrain the orange peers as much as possible in order to avoid a breach with Peel, and yet go far enough with them to maintain party unity in the upper house. In the main he succeeded. The orange peers' only success was their obtaining a select committee in 1839 to inquire into the state of Ireland since 1835 ' with respect to the commission of crime ', which provoked a brief political crisis indicative of the kind of damage that could result when the duke's control over his orange followers faltered. What had happened was simply that Wellington was under the mistaken impression that Peel approved the motion for a select committee.[37] For the main part the duke pursued a steady policy of dissociating himself from orange extremism, which was to be seen at its clearest in his attitude to the question of the condemnation of the orange society in 1836.

Peel was most anxious that the party should give no support to Cumberland and his friends in the society, for, as he intimated privately to Wellington, it was the only impediment now to a cordial understanding with Stanley and Graham for which he had been working so busily. The duke agreed. The ultra tory peers tried to shift him. Winchilsea prepared to move an address in the lords to save the society and sent it to Wellington, pathetically hoping that Winchilsea ' will not be separating himself from the duke or the party ', and arguing that non-resistance would lead to ' the end of the legislative independence of our house '. The iron duke replied with a bombardment shattering the idea and stressing that ' the house

[35] *Fraser's Magazine,* xv, no. 85 (Jan. 1837), p. 94.
[36] *Parl. deb.,* xxxix, cols 339–54.
[37] G. Kitson Clark, *Peel and the conservative party,* pp. 412–5.

of lords must be cautious and must not provoke a collision with the commons'. For a few days there were rumours that the orange peers were going to stage a major demonstration, and almost daily reports of their doings were sent from the house of lords to where the duke was staying down at Stratfield Saye —avoiding trouble. Winchilsea was the first to capitulate, admitting to the duke that as a clash between the lords and commons was inevitable—on the rest of the ministry's programme for Ireland—it should be ' on a question on which we can elicit the strongest public feeling in our favour '. Even an ultra tory could recognise the dependence of the upper house upon public opinion. But fiercer spirits led by Londonderry were not so easily suppressed. He tried to get Rosslyn to put a whip on for a debate on the orange society in the lords. But Rosslyn was the duke's confidential friend and he refused point blank, and Cumberland himself was not ready for a demonstration either. When it came to the point he spoke on the subject in the lords ' in prudent and measured tones ', as Rosslyn reported to Wellington. Londonderry and Wynford could not be entirely restrained but in essence, as the debate in the lords showed, the iron duke had won. The conservative party was not to be tarred with the orange brush.[38]

One last example of Wellington's careful avoidance of commitments to extreme tory crusades is worth a mention. All through the 'thirties, Bishop Phillpotts of Exeter, with immense eloquence and with the approval of the ultra tories, subjected the Irish education commission to severe criticism in the lords. Individual case after case was cited to prove that ' the system of national education would never be adapted to the feelings, the principles, and the wants of the protestant popualtion of Ireland '. There was no limit to the bishop's polemical fervour : to him the national schools were ' the theatres of the coarsest and fiercest Roman catholic agitation by O'Connell and the arch-agitator of the west, the so-called archbishop of Tuam, Dr MacHale '. The effects of this campaign on the education system were negligible—as usual the

[38] Winchilsea to Wellington, 29 Feb., 3 Mar. 1836, Wellington to Winchilsea, 2 Mar. 1836, and Rosslyn to Wellington, 1, 3, 4, 7, 9 Mar. 1836 (Wellington MSS); *Parl. deb.*, xxxi, cols 861–3, 930–9, 1173–5, 1258–1300.

real sufferers were Peel and Wellington—for debates on the subject merely kept alive schisms in the conservative party. Peel had declared in favour of the national education scheme in his brief ministry of 1834–5 and Wellington was loyal to this commitment. He made it clear in private to Phillpotts that he did not want the question raised in the lords, and in 1836 the archbishop of Canterbury came to his help, by declaring his opposition to a scheme of Phillpotts to secure an inquisitorial select committee of the lords on the subject. Phillpotts, who was not famous for his obedience to primates, bowed on this occasion. Wellington prevented the agitation becoming serious enough to bring about a vote in the upper house adverse to the government and very embarrassing to Peel but, of course, he could not make the bishop of Exeter keep quiet. No one could.[39]

What was then the upshot of the lords' handling of Irish questions between 1833 and 1841? First it would be true to say that the legislation affecting Ireland in these years was almost as much the work of Peel and Wellington as of the ministries concerned. The tory majority in the lords was a valuable, though by no means easily controlled, weapon in the hands of the conservative leaders by which the whigs were forced to be content with what the conservatives would grant them. The timing of nearly all their legislative measures was dictated by their opponents. On the other hand the executive in Ireland was much more free to pursue its own policy. This need not have been the upshot if the ministries had brought themselves to coerce the lords. Grey showed that firmness could be very helpful over the Irish church temporalities bill in 1833 but Melbourne lacked Grey's streak of hard determination. Nor was he an effective debater and in fact ministerial measures from 1835 onwards were poorly defended in the lords. In addition Melbourne's alliance with O'Connell, and the tendency of his cabinet's measures to disturb ascendancy interests in Ireland, discouraged whig peers. Their attendance in the lords fell off markedly from 1835 onwards. Overriding all this was the reluctance of the elderly whigs in the cabinet to

---

[39] Phillpotts to Wellington, 15, 17 Feb., 14 Mar. 1836 (Wellington MSS); *Parl. deb.*, xxviii. cols 129–50, 1206–29; xxix, cols 172, 603–16, 725–9; xxxi, cols 246–71; xxxii, cols 274–308, and passim.

contemplate coercion or reform of the lords.   Melbourne
believed in the 'independence of the lords' no less staunchly
than did Peel in any of his declarations, but he did far less than
Peel in practice to curb the lords' use of that independence to
veto or amend legislation.   In 1834 when Grey maintained that
he would have resigned rather than be dictated to by the lords
over the tithe bill Melbourne's cabinet did nothing.[40]   In 1835
when the whole of the ministry's programme for Ireland was
emasculated in the lords this was treated merely as a setback
subsidiary to the victory won after much fierce struggle over the
English municipal corporations bill.   Melbourne believed it best
to let passions cool and try again next year.[41]   The prime
minister was very angry indeed when in 1836 the lords rewrote
the Irish corporations bill.   Yet he refused to even contemplate
Lord John Russell's mild suggestion that the creation of a few
whig peers, holding out the threat of further creations, should
be carried out in order to bring the tory peers to heel.[42]   The
truth of the matter was that Melbourne's views were very close
to Peel's on many of the issues involved and the attraction of
a quiet life was overwhelming.   He was far more willing to
give up the appropriation clause than Russell; and he told the
latter that 'he rather acceded to poor laws in Ireland than
approved them'.[43]   Two excuses, and it must be admitted that
they were weighty ones, existed for the failure of Melbourne's
cabinets to apply pressure on the lords.   Lacking a strong
majority in the commons from 1835 onwards, and in the absence
of any vigorous demonstration of public feeling in England on
Irish questions, it was much more difficult for Melbourne to
apply coercion or firmness to the lords than it had been in Grey's
time.

[40] *Correspondence of the Princess Lieven and Earl Grey*, ed.
G. Le Strange, iii. 3–5; J. C. Hobhouse, *Recollections of a long life*,
ed. Lady Dorchester, iv. 362.

[41] Only Russell seems to have been uneasy and all that this led to was
a proposal for the creations of a small number of new peers (Spencer
Walpole, *Life of Lord John Russell*, i. 250).

[42] Ibid., i. 266–7; J. C. Hobhouse, *Recollections*, v. 57; *Parl. deb.*,
xxxiv, cols 874–85, 960–3.

[43] Melbourne to Russell, 4 Sept. 1837 (Russell papers, P.R.O.,
30/22/2).

But it was not the whigs who suffered most from the lords' handling of Irish affairs but O'Connell, and, from a diametrically opposite point of view, the ultra tories. O'Connell realised this himself and characteristically sought in 1835 and 1836 to remove the obstacle of the lords by rallying public opinion in northern England and Scotland to demand a reform of the upper house on moderately radical lines. He boasted in 1835 that he had succeeded in arousing such a demand.[44] In fact it already existed but was confined to radical circles in England. During his tours of these years O'Connell's audiences appear to have been chiefly those already converted to the need for reforming the lords. In reality he had failed, as was not surprising. The controlling action the tory peers had exercised over Irish legislation, combined with whig reluctance to coerce the lords, was an important element in causing O'Connell to abandon his experiment of co-operating with the whigs and to fall back, with much depleted support, on a policy whose prospects of success were not very bright.

As for the ultra tory peers, they had been forced step by step to accept Peel's decisions on the attitude to be adopted towards whig legislation for Ireland. They had grumbled constantly, they had staged rebellions, they had declaimed furiously in the lords for they were the permanent opposition in the 'thirties. They remained so in the years of Peel's ministry.

III

Indeed from the very beginning Peel's cabinet, by its cautious moderation in handling Irish affairs, created disappointment among the Irish tory peers. In the lords there were complaints in 1842, for example, that the Maynooth grant had not been stopped, that the national education scheme had been continued, that the church of Ireland's request for a state grant for its education society had not been complied with, that the minor drainage bill of 1842 infringed the rights of private property and that the government was not active enough in putting down

[44] *The Pilot*, 21, 31 Aug., 14, 18, 21, 25, 30 Sept. 1835; *The correspondence of D. O'Connell*, ed. W. J. Fitzpatrick, ii. 33–4, 48, 57–9, 70.

outrages.[45]   By the middle of 1842 the monster repeal meetings began to attract their lordships' attention and provide a more urgent grievance among the tail of Peel's following in the upper house.   Strong dissatisfaction with the ' do nothing government' was voiced there throughout the summer, and one ultra tory even warned the house that, as Peel had been ' loud in the past against Roman Catholic emancipation, so was he now against repeal . . .'   But, as Brougham pointed out in his best sarcastic manner, the orangemen were in the same boat as they had been in in the 'thirties : if they turned out Peel they could not possibly find an alternative leader and form a government.   They had to be content with growling for the yeomanry of Ulster to be called out and with fruitless demands for permission to hold orange processions.[46]   The revised arms bill of 1843 did nothing to mollify them for they believed the chief secretary had made too many concessions to the opposition during its passage through the commons.[47]   Only the proclamation of the Clontarf meeting and the prosecution of O'Connell really pleased them.   A delighted Roden thanked the government in the lords, but there was a sting in his remark that ' it was better to be late than never '.   Moreover the verdict of the law lords on O'Connell's appeal disgusted them.   Wharncliffe, acting as leader for the ministry at this time (1844), was hard put to it to prevent tory peers outvoting the majority of whig law lords and upholding, as they believed, the majesty of the law.[48]   But all told this ultra tory grumbling, largely the work of Irish tory peers, was a muted opposition.   The house of lords in the first four years of Peel's ministry was, as Stanley said in 1844, ' in a state of inanition '.   In recent years, *The Times* noted in 1845, ' twenty was a good house and were it not for the fact that walls have ears the arguments of our noble legislators would stand as little

[45] *Parl. deb.,* lxi, cols 411–3; lxii, cols 458–9; lxiii, cols 964–73; lxiv, cols 272, 547–50; lxv, cols 171–4; lxvi, cols 317–22.

[46] *Parl. deb.,* lxix, cols 1–12, 319–30, 922–38, 1224–6; lxx, cols 470–2, 1099–1189.

[47] Lord Malmesbury, *Memoirs of an ex-minister,* i. 145.

[48] *Parl. deb.,* lxxii, cols 602–80; *The Greville memoirs,* ed. G. L. Strachey and R. Fulford, v. 188; *The correspondence and diaries of J. W. Croker,* ed. L. J. Jennings, iii. 21–3; *Blackwood's Magazine,* lvi, no. 344 (Nov. 1844), pp. 539–69; *The letters of C. C. F. Greville and H. Reeve, 1836–55,* ed. A. H. Johnson, pp. 92–4.

chance of notoriety as the conversations after dinner yesterday in Grosvenor Square'.[49]   The reasons for this state of affairs do not concern us here.

However, the corn law question and the maturing of Peel's Irish policy certainly prodded the lords into life in 1845.   The prime minister, whose objectives in regard to Ireland are well known, had no illusions as to the reception which his policy of attracting moderate catholic support for the executive government in Ireland would meet from among the Irish ultra tory peers.   'Their cry was', he wrote, 'rely on the protestants, they are loyal; the *juste milieu* is wholly unsuited to Ireland!'[50] He was right in the main, although it is only fair to say that the ultra tories did not contest the only part of Peel's programme that reached the lords in 1844, namely the charitable bequests bill.   On the other hand, in the recess of 1844–5 the already existing breach between Peel and the ultra tory peers was widened considerably by Roden and his friends, who chose to take a prominent part in a renewed campaign aganist the national education scheme.   In February 1845 the prime minister marked his displeasure by informing the lord lieutenant that no honours were to given to 'any peer that has taken part in demonstrations of this kind'.[51]   But what really made the breach open and notorious once more was the announcement of the ministry's further measures of liberal-conservative reform for Ireland, and especially the Maynooth bill.

Peel and his entourage expected opposition in the upper house, but they were confident and contemptuous of the orangemen.   'How foolish they are', wrote Graham in January 1845; 'we labour night and day to save them in spite of themselves'.[52] The Irish ultra tories thought they knew better.   Instead they prepared for a crusade against the Maynooth bill by closer association with the church of Ireland.   Much was hoped from the archbishop of Cashel, whose turn it was to sit in the lords in 1845, and who was expected to lead an onslaught both on

[49] C. S. Parker, *Sir Robert Peel from his private correspondence,* iii. 154–6; *The Times,* 7 June 1845.

[50] C. S. Parker, *Peel,* iii. 116–7.

[51] Peel to Heytesbury, 4 Feb. 1845, and Heytesbury to Peel, 6 Feb. 1845 (B.M., Add. MS 40479).

[52] Graham to Peel, 11 Jan. 1845 (B.M., Add. MS 40451).

the Maynooth bill and the national education scheme. But, as the lord lieutenant informed Peel, there was really little to fear from him, for he was ' a coarse, vulgar man with a considerable impediment in his speech . . . very little calculated to produce a favourable impression in the upper house '.[53] More dangerous from Peel's point of view, was the fact that the Maynooth bill stung the high protestants among the English peers into activity in mobilizing opinion in the country against the bill. Winchilsea and Kenyon, for example, were responsible for circulating the established clergy of each parish asking them to find signatures for a subjoined petition form denouncing a bill ' which encourages, endows, aggrandizes, and perpetuates the unconstitutional and dangerous domination of a foreign, hostile, spiritual power '.[54] A considerable section of the tory press responded to the call and so did some of the conservative peers in conflict with the government over its treatment of the agricultural interest.

But, as *The Times* put it, ' the lords had become too much the humble servant of a rather imperious leader ' to reject the bill.[55] Moreover not all the conservative peers were habitués of Exeter Hall. Even among the Irish tory lords Peel and Wellington could count on a few supporters such as Wicklow, Clare, Clanwilliam and Rosse. But the most valuable support the ministers received in the upper house on the Maynooth question came not from their own supporters but from the whig peers. The Irish contingent among them were plainly not very willing to help the bill pass. Stanley thought it necessary during the debates to make a strong plea to their leader, the duke of Leinster, to speak in support of the measure, but when the division was taken it was found that the ministry's majority was composed of a solid bloc of nearly 100 whig peers. The rest consisted of government placemen and a relatively small band of loyal conservative peers. Without the whig peers the 73 ultra tories and the bishops who divided against the second reading would have outnumbered the ministerial supporters. The lords debates on the Maynooth bill showed with great clarity what

[53] Heytesbury to Peel, 14 Feb. 1845 (B.M., Add. MS 40479).

[54] Captain Edward Henry A' Court to Peel enclosing the circular and petition form (B.M., Add. MS 40566 f. 47).

[55] *The Times,* 7 June 1845.

a wide gap existed between the conservative leaders and many of their followers in the upper house.[56]

Nevertheless the bill had passed and further nasty medicine awaited the discontented tory peers. The prime minister shortly afterwards rejected a personal appeal by the Irish primate for funds for the church of Ireland's education society, and Wellington with all his famous brusqueness refused to heed the grumbles in the lords of the Irish tory peers about this.[57] The next dose was more alarming. It was the tenants' compensation bill, brought to birth, as *The Times* inelegantly put it, ' by the obstetrical aid of Lord Stanley from Lord Devon's huge blue mountain '.[58] After a quiet introduction this produced a revolt in the upper house, a revolt that cut across party lines and involved the ' Irish interest '. Both whig and tory peers with estates in Ireland rallied to the standard of Lord Londonderry, who was convinced that the bill would establish a commissioner in Dublin to dictate what arrangements should take place between a landlord and a tenant. He collected, so he said, the signatures of 36 peers protesting at being put under this junto and launched an impassioned assault in the lords on the second reading. Curiously enough for such an ultra tory, Londonderry had actually voted for Maynooth, and it is just possible, as *The Times* hinted, that there had been a bargain behind the scenes by which opposition to Maynooth was not to be pushed as far as rejection by the tory peers, if the government would shelve or modify the tenants' compensation bill. Certainly this might help to explain why the government ended by letting it die in the oblivion of a lords' select committee. I have not, though, found any confirmatory evidence of this, and, on the other hand, it may well have been the opposition of the marquis of Salisbury that weighed more heavily with the ministry. For the influential marquis told Wellington, no great enthusiast himself for the measure, that he thought the bill would establish the evil principle of government interference with the landowner's right to manage his own property, which might then be

[56] *Parl. deb.*, lxxx, cols 1160–1231, 1298–1374; lxxxi, 6–120. *The Times*, 7 June 1845, where the names of four pairs are given; Graham to Peel, 5 June 1845 (B.M., Add. MS 40451).

[57] *Parl. deb.*, lxxxi, cols 632–63; *The Times*, 18, 19 June 1845.

[58] *The Times*, 11 June 1845.

extended to England. He ended with the unpleasant threat that if the compulsory clauses were not omitted he would regretfully join ' the numerous body in the house of lords who have already withdrawn themselves from the active support of the government'. No wonder Wellington said the second reading debate was uncomfortable; the government's majority fell to 14, and might easily have vanished had not Stanley announced what was virtually the death sentence for the bill, its consignment to a select committee to examine the compulsory clauses. In effect the lords had won : there were limits beyond which they would not go even at the command of a conservative ministry.[59]

There remained the last part of Peel's programme for 1845, the colleges bill. Contemporaries seem to have been scarcely surprised that this received but slight attention in the lords. The explanation was, not that Peel's critics in the lords liked the bill—it is plain they did not—but with the whig peers supporting it, with no landlords' interest involved, and after the discouraging defeat on Maynooth, the high tory Irish and English peers knew there was no chance of vetoing or altering it.[60] The session of 1845, even though a victory had been won over the tenants' compensation bill, had shown that a section of the conservative forces in the lords was hopelessly at odds with the ministry. To the more violent of the ultra critics, there seemed no way of making their views prevail except by extra-parliamentary agitation. Hence at the end of the year the orange society was revived and reorganized. Graham's previous confidence and contempt for the ultra tories was turned to despair : to proceed against Enniskillen, the prime mover in this matter, might well lead to the mass resignation of the protestant magistrates in the north at a time when famine and rebellion filled the land.[61] This open breach between Peel and the ultra tories in 1845 was simply the logical consummation of the cleavage between them that runs all through the thirties. The truth of the matter was that no statesman of any calibre

[59] *Parl. deb.*, lxxxi, cols 1116–52, 1195–1205; lxxxii, col. 493; *The Times*, 7, 27 June 1845; Salisbury to Wellington, 20 June 1845 (B.M., Add. MS 40461); C. S. Parker, *Peel*, iii. 178.

[60] *Parl. deb.*, lxxxii, cols 729–90, 887–9; *Illustrated London News*, vii. 54; *The Times*, 4 June 1845.

[61] Graham to Peel, 11 Nov. 1845 (B.M., Add. MS 40452).

could or would carry out ultra tory policies. But the breach with them in 1845, coming as it did immediately after many conservative peers had come out into the open for the first time on agricultural policy by joining the ' anti-league ' of 1844, thus committing themselves to opposition to current governmental policy and to free trade, had its unpleasant repercussions for Peel and Wellington in 1846. In the corn law crisis Peel could not hope for many votes from English or Irish high tory peers and particularly those of pronounced evangelical sympathies. It is a significant fact that all but four of the seventy-three peers and bishops who voted against the second reading of the Maynooth bill, sided with the protectionists in 1846.

IV

After the fall of Peel's ministry when the peers reassembled in 1847 the famine had become so disastrous that as *The Times* said ' Ireland had once more become the British legislators' lenten exercise and humiliation '. The Russell government was compelled to ' open to the awestruck soul a perpetually increasing vista of misery, trouble, animosity and mismanagement ' before which all stood daunted.[62] Economic issues had driven all other questions from the field. Indeed leading protectionist peers such as Stanley and Richmond called for a ' truce to party politics until the great calamity had been got rid of '. Hence the temporary measures first of Peel and then of Russell to meet the situation were approved with little opposition in the lords. Even the orange leaders early in 1847 thanked the Russell ministry for their ' boons to Ireland ', while the Irish party that emerged as an opposition group in parliament in 1847 specifically distinguished between the ' temporary measures ' to which it offered no serious opposition in the lords and the ' permanent laws ' of which it disapproved.[63]

The first of the ' permanent laws ' to arouse a struggle in the lords was the poor relief bill of 1847. Nor was this surprising, for nearly ten years earlier the first introduction of poor laws for Ireland in the bill of 1838 had elicited the only

[62] *The Times*, 21, 26 Jan. 1847.
[63] *Parl. deb.*, lxxxix, cols 355–423; *The Times*, 2 Jan. 1847 (report of Richmond's speech at a Sussex protection meeting).

serious demonstration made by the 'Irish interest' as a whole in the lords in the thirties. This was in essence a rebellion by the Irish landlords, both whig and conservative, against the compromise by which Melbourne and the conservative leaders had agreed to bargain the appropriation clause against a poor law bill and a measure to reform the corporations. The rebels' temper was well indicated by the knight of Kerry in a fragmentary diary now in the National Library in which he wrote, 'the duke [i.e. Wellington] has involved himself under the false impression of men who know nothing of Ireland—the whole policy is one of compromise on all points at issue. They [i.e. the conservative leaders] attach too much importance to the appropriation clause and will in return sacrifice us in the poor law and municipal bill. The scheme at bottom is to clear away those troublesome measures which might upset a new ministry'. Even such a staunch Peelite peer as Lord Fitzgerald looked to his interests as a landlord first on the poor law issue and refused to follow his leaders. As the knight of Kerry tells us, Fitzgerald 'had a long and most painful conversation with the duke' who was 'very irritable and so harsh as to address him "my lord"' since they were at loggerheads on the poor law question'. Quite clearly the rebels who fought the bill to the end in the lords were deeply concerned with the effects of poor rates on their rentals. The chief amendment sponsored by them was the significant one to limit help to the poor by excluding relief in the workhouse to the able bodied poor as proposed in the bill.[64]

Between 1838 and 1847 intermittent criticism of the poor law administration in Ireland from both whig and tory Irish peers in the upper house showed that on such an issue, fundamentally one that affected the economic interests of the ascendancy, an Irish group was apt to disengage itself from the main party divisions. This occurred on the tenants' compensation bill in 1845. In 1847, with economic issues taking precedence over all others, the 'Irish interest' again made its presence felt in the lords. Early in February of that year a meeting of peers and M.P.s connected with Ireland, under the chairmanship of the whig lord Monteagle, was held in London. In the unsorted

[64] *Parl. deb.*, xliii, cols 1–71, 352–61, 472–501, 563–6, 895–8, 962–3; xliv, cols 11–30; knight of Kerry's fragmentary diary, 23 May 1838 (N.L.I., MS 2077).

portion of the Monteagle papers in the National Library there is a copy of resolutions adopted by that meeting in regard to the poor relief bill, regarded by the meeting evidently as the most dangerous of the ' permanent laws ' proposed by the government. Briefly the ' Irish interest ' objected first and foremost to any departure from the existing system in favour of gratuitous out-door relief for the able bodied poor through a relieving officer, and secondly to any increase in the size of areas on which the poor law assessment was levied. The objections were clearly motivated by fear that both steps would lead to increased poor rates and therefore to lower rentals. Larger areas, so the resolutions claimed, discourage the administration of relief with ' discrimination and economy ', and to give outdoor relief to the able bodied would be a blow to ' prosperity and subversive of social order ', while to allow a relieving officer to have the sole power of giving such relief would be ' most disastrous ', i.e. he would run up the poor rates at the landlords' expense by lavish relief. The resolutions were eventually signed by 87 peers and M.P.s. Among the peers were whigs such as the duke of Leinster, moderate conservatives such as Clare, and ultra tories such as Limerick, Westmeath, Farnham and Enniskillen. These resolutions formed the basis of an unavailing approach to Russell's government and of the subsequent attacks on the poor relief bill in parliament.[65]

In the lords the nature of the struggle over the bill was further revealed by impassioned speeches by Brougham as advocate for the city fathers of Liverpool, Glasgow, Hull and other cities inundated by a flood of starving Irish eating up the poor rates. On their behalf, Brougham assailed the absentee Irish landlords for neglecting their charitable duties, the resident landlords for using the famine as an opportunity for clearing their estates, and the whole landlord body for not supporting their own poor but allowing, even positively encouraging them, to come on the rates of English towns at a time when England was pouring out her substance to succour Ireland. Brougham was simply voicing for the first time in the lords the swing over of middle class opinion in England to holding the Irish landlords

[65] N.L.I., Monteagle papers, unsorted collection in box no. 81; *Annual Reg., 1847,* p. 40; Spencer Walpole, *Life of Lord John Russell,* i. 445.

responsible for the famine that had occurred in 1845. The remedy was a new poor law to make the Irish look after their own poor instead of eating up the English tax payers' money.[66] Listening to this and reading much the same in *The Times* enraged the Irish landlords in the upper house.[67] They hit back. Hard words were said about Liverpool shipping magnates profiting from the stimulus given to the provision trade by the famine. More than one of them argued that it was English misrule that had reduced Ireland to destitution and that she had a right to assistance from the people and legislature of England.[68] But their main case remained that of the resolutions referred to above. The poor relief bill would ruin the Irish landlords without helping anyone else for it would lead to a huge increase in the poor rates which were largely paid by themselves.

However the ' Irish interest ' had a stronger weapon than mere words at their disposal. In mid-February they had won the alliance of Lord Stanley and his large following of protectionist peers. Since the government could not command a majority simply among its own adherents in the lords the alliance of the ' Irish interest ' and the protectionists was in a position to dictate the fate of the poor relief bill in the lords unless enough Peelite peers could be found to come to the support of the whigs or the alliance should fall asunder. In other words a situation reminiscent of the thirties had been created in the lords. To begin with the alliance held together. When Stanley proposed a bargain with the ministry whereby the temporary famine relief measures would be accepted by the lords, he asked in return for amendments to the poor relief bill that were simply those outlined by the ' Irish interest ' at their meeting early in February.[69] In return the ' Irish interest ' in the lords demonstrated support for the protectionist scheme for Irish railway development.[70] The ministers were forced on to

---

[66] *Parl. deb.,* lxxxix, cols 501–3, 597–602, 612–4, 770–1, 1323–4; xc, cols 1004–12, 1133–4, 1228–35; xci, cols 544–5, 810–11.

[67] *The Times,* 1, 2, 3, 5 Feb. 1847; Londonderry complained of the paper and clashed with Brougham in the lords on the subject (*Parl. deb.,* xc, cols 387–91, 1004–12, 1073–9).

[68] e.g. Fitzwilliam, Mountcashel and Monteagle in a debate on the state of Ireland (*Parl. deb.,* lxxxix, cols 355–423).

[69] *Parl. deb.,* lxxxix, cols 1324–53.

[70] Ibid., lxxxix, cols 848–58, 932–7; xc, cols 665–76.

the defensive.　　Before the poor relief bill reached the lords they conceded that no relief should be given to anyone occupying more than quarter of an acre.　　During the committee stage in the lords they accepted a rewording of this clause to prevent any loopholes, to the disgust of the Peelite ex-chief secretary, St Germans, and to the joy of Roden.[71]　　Among the ministers, Lansdowne, who led for them in the lords, plainly sympathised with the 'Irish interest'.　He presented the poor relief bill as a 'palliative' not a 'permanent remedy', he went out of his way to denounce a 'general and permanent system of outdoor relief' as fatal to Ireland, and wooed his fellow Irish landlords with sweet words about the boons the government was conferring on them while acquitting them of any responsibility for the famine.[72]

It soon became clear, however, that the alliance was not going to provoke a political crisis by challenging the government on the principle of the bill.　　Instead the sting was to be taken out of it.　　Hence the 'Irish interest' and the protectionist peers mustered in great numbers and carried amendments to limit the outdoor relief provisions to one year's operation and to remove the proposal for union rating.　Both were received with absolute fury by *The Times,* taking upon itself to speak for the tax-paying industrial and commercial classes in England.　　The first amendment it described as 'an insult that would condemn England to go on paying for the Irish poor.　　Is England prepared to be fairly invaded, conquered and possessed by the Irish proprietors?' it indignantly demanded.　The second amendment evoked even shriller outbursts—it was 'a revolting outrage', a 'landlords' victory' in which Lord Stanley had 'paraded again his contempt for the great industrial interests'.[73]

[71] Ibid., xcii, cols 504–7.

[72] *Parl. deb.,* xcii, cols 60–126.

[73] *The Times,* 7, 8 May 1847.　The conflict of views over the union rating clause showed most clearly that the struggle in the lords over the poor relief bill was part of the lengthy battle between landlords and factory lords.　The bill proposed that when poor rates reached 2s. 6d. in the pound in an electoral district, the excess was to be taxed not only on the district concerned but on the whole union.　In the lords, Stanley argued the injustice of this, by citing his own case as an owner of lands in Ireland.　He possessed, he said, an estate of about 4000 acres which formed half of an electoral division rated at about £8,000–£9,000

The Russell ministry could not afford to be thus branded as an accomplice of the landlords by ignoring the amendments. Fortunately for it the alliance of protectionists and the 'Irish interest' was not so close knit as it seemed. In the commons, Bentinck, blindly vehement as usual, had sponsored a proposal to shift the burden of the Irish poor rate entirely on to the occupier. When Stanley, encouraged by his victories in the lords, abandoned his earlier caution on this matter, and took it up in the upper house he was forced to admit defeat. He had to withdraw a proposal to settle the Irish poor rate entirely upon the occupier. Why? First the 'Irish interest' would not go as far as this. Monteagle and Whately made it clear to Stanley they would not, arguing that it would raise a storm in Ireland. Secondly the Peelites came to the rescue. In the commons some of them had supported Bentinck, but when Stanley took the matter up in the lords where the protectionists were in a more powerful position, these Peelites changed their minds and the earl of Lincoln, the most prominent of them, circulated a message in the lords among Peelite friends there, telling them to vote against Stanley.[74] It was this check that encouraged the ministers to plan a counterstroke in the upper house. Gathering as many whig peers as possible, bringing up a dozen bishops, and successfully soliciting the votes of Peelite peers, such as the influential duke of Buccleuch, they just managed by thirteen votes, in a division in which nearly 200 peers cast a vote, to expunge the amendment that had limited the duration of the outdoor relief clauses to one year. Proxies were not allowed as the house was

of which he paid on about half. The pauperism on his lands however, so he said, amounted to only about one-fifteenth of all the pauperism in the division. Under the union rating clause he would be paying rates not only to support paupers in the rest of the electoral division but also in an additional area covering some 200,000–300,000 acres. What incentive was there in such circumstances for a landlord to keep down destitution on his own estate? *The Times* replied that Stanley's 'refusal to countenance the union rating principle amounted to sanctioning an express law for human drainage so that in every union there will be one or more great sinks of misery answering for the whole body of proprietors, which will then come on the treasury as had happened at Skibbereen. England would be saddled with paying taxes to relieve 130 Skibbereens' (*Parl. deb.*, xcii, cols 507–11; *The Times,* 15 May 1847).

[74] *Parl. deb.*, xcii, cols 555–98; during the debate Stanley objected to the circulation of the message from Lincoln.

in committee, but they were entered all the same—62 for the government and 42 for the opposition—so that it was clear that the government would carry their point on the third reading. On the other hand the narrowness of their victory and the labour it entailed meant that it was not possible fully to restore the bill to its original form.   The ' Irish interest ' had imposed its will on various portions of it by alliance with the protectionist peers, although in the end the poor relief bill came through the lords by the same means as the corn law bill of 1846.   The majority in 1847 that restored the outdoor relief clauses consisted of nearly all the whig peers and most of that section of the conservative peerage that had remained loyal to Peel in 1846.   The opposition was the serried ranks of those who had refused to follow the renegade in 1846.[75]

Down to the end of the 1849 session it was this opposition that continued to make itself felt in the lords in the moulding of Irish legislation whenever the Irish peers and the protectionists felt their interests to be menaced.   This was not the case generally in regard to the coercive measures sponsored by Russell's government or to the attitude of the Irish executive. Lord Lieutenant Clarendon's ' humanity and firmness ', as one prominent protectionist peer described his policy, was applauded in the lords, and measures such as the crime and outrage and crown and government security bills of 1848, the suspension of habeas corpus in 1848 and 1849, and the transportation for treason bill of 1849, passed the lords with scarcely more than a few grumbles that they had not been introduced soon enough or were not sufficiently stringent.[76]   This did not mean that the ' Irish interest ' was satisfied.   Earl Fitzwilliam, in moving a series of resolutions in the lords in June 1848, voiced their discontents most clearly.   The government's famine relief measures were hopelessly inadequate, their remedial legislation almost non-existent.   As for the Irish landlords, under ' the million and a half bill ' they had, he claimed, only received ' £200,000 to improve nineteen million acres ' and, staggering under the weight of the poor rates, they were in danger of

[75] *Parl. deb.*, xcii, cols 794–820; the government mustered 101 votes, the opposition 88; for the proxies see *The Times*, 17 May 1847.
[76] *Parl. deb.*, xcv, cols 594–7, 1123, 1182–1230, 1341–2; xcviii, cols 485–507, 534–7; c, cols 743–56; cii, cols 174–81, 1203–4; cvi, cols 158–63.

destruction. Surely, he asked, the house of lords did not intend this to happen for, if the Irish aristocracy disappeared, 'what was to stand between the English government and the Irish mob?'. But, as he ruefully admitted, in the lords he might be listened to with civility while pleading for his fellow-landlords, but outside there was general hostility to them.[77] In amending government measures to suit themselves the 'Irish interest' had to reckon with this hostility, yet such amendments were made and often carried through.

For example in 1848 a bill dealing with evictions was rewritten in the lords so that no provision was to be made for relieving an unfortunate evicted tenant until 'within a few hours of the occurrence of the calamity', to quote the ministerial spokesman in the upper house. A government attempt to reverse this decision on the third reading in the lords was beaten down by the 'Irish interest' with the help of Lord Stanley and his friends. Admittedly a compromise clause, stipulating that forty-eight hours' notice should be given to relieving officers before evictions took place, had to be accepted by Monteagle when the commons' amendments to the lords' amendments came back to the upper house, although he thought it 'extremely objectionable'. But Monteagle was able to congratulate himself that all the rest of his amendments had passed the commons.[78] Again in 1849 in regard to the poor law the opposition was able to leave its mark. The scheme to levy a rate in aid of the poverty-stricken unions in the south and west on the landed property of the whole country was bitterly fought by the 'Irish interest'. In the cabinet itself Lansdowne nearly resigned on the issue but consented to remain provided that he had only to defend a measure in the lords 'strictly limited to 6d in the pound for each of two years to come'. This only passed the lords on second reading by two votes over the protests of the Irish peers.[79] They had hoped that such a measure would not reach the lords

---

[77] *Parl. deb.*, xcix, cols 1057–1073.

[78] The bill was called the evicted destitute poor bill (*Parl. deb.*, xcix, cols 82–5, 996–1019, 1165–7; c, cols 1016–19). The government was beaten on its motion on the third reading by 78 votes to 67, including pairs.

[79] Spencer Walpole, *Life of Lord John Russell*, ii. 82–3; *Parl. deb.*, ciii, cols 234–5, 747–8, 1178–88; cv, cols 258–323; *The Times*, 14 May 1849, claimed that the ministers, however, had 'an overpowering reserve of proxies' which may have been true as proxies were not called.

at all for they had strongly supported the protectionist attempt
to throw out the repeal of the navigation laws in the lords which,
if successful, would have ended the Russell ministry.[80]   As it
was, the ' Irish interest ' had its revenge later in the session.   To
the anger of *The Times*, with the backing of the protectionists
the Irish peers were able to remodel the government's attempt
to amend the Irish poor law in a permanent fashion to such an
extent that the measure was rendered almost useless, and the
principle of aiding the poorer districts by rates on the more
prosperous was destroyed.   What was more, the lords' amendments actually infringed the commons' privileges in regard to
money bills and thus provided the government with an easy
weapon for persuading the lower house to reject the lords'
amendments.   But Lansdowne fought the ' Irish interest's '
battle in the cabinet once more : he told Russell that ' he should
feel it next to impossible to propose to the house of lords to
reconsider their decision on the subject '.   Russell bowed and
persuaded the commons to waive their privileges.[81]

Finally the opposition in the lords was able to make itself
felt in the shaping of the Russell ministry's one striking measure
in these years, the incumbered estates act.   Although no direct
opposition to the principle of either the abortive measure of
1848 or the revised version that became law in 1849 was offered
in the lords, there was considerable distrust of the scheme among
the Irish peers.   Few anticipated the rosy prospects held out by
the promoters of the bill.   Some of them thought the occasion
inopportune for such a scheme since land values had slumped in
the famine : estates would be driven into the market and sold
for absurdly low prices.   The idea, too, that English capitalists
would step into the shoes of the Irish landlords, while not
thought to be a very likely development by the Irish peers, was
scarcely attractive to them.   The opposition in the lords ended
in 1849, however, not by obstructing the passage of the bill, as
The Times feared, but by altering its provisions in a select
committee of the upper house.   The committee, clearly controlled

[80] *The Times,* 14 May 1849.

[81] *The Times*, 18 July 1849, ' just what was to be expected ', it
commented, and ' unless it is a mere formal protest we must consider
Irish poverty a permanent charge on the imperial treasury '; *Parl. deb.*,
cvii, cols 290–323, 364–397, 1120–28; Spencer Walpole, *Life of Lord
John Russell,* ii. 83–4.

by the opposition, led to amendments favourable to the Irish landlords.   Cheap methods of land transfer for them were inserted into the bill so that Stanley was able to say ' much good might be done by those portions of the bill that would enable owners of property to manage their estates more easily '.   Also against government opposition the old landlords were protected against the importunities of Irish mortgagees by a new provision ' that the sale of incumbered estates on their demand could be prevented on the application of the owner, unless half of the entire interest in the estate was . . . . swallowed up by the incumbrancer ', to quote Lord Campbell.[82]   In short the bill emerged, in part, as a compromise dictated by the strength of the opposition of the ' Irish interest ' and the protectionists in the lords.

But by the end of the 1849 session, within a year of Peel's death, a turning point was reached. The famine was subsiding, the queen was about to visit Ireland, a sign that outward peace reigned, but, most important of all, the legacy of hostility towards the Irish landlords had not died down either in Ireland or England. In Ireland tenant-right agitation made strides, and government after government in the fifties was obliged to make some sort of gesture in favour of tenant-right legislation. After Peel's death the ' Irish interest ' in the lords was really forced to fight a true rearguard action, just as the protectionist peers had slowly to retreat from the principle they had unsuccessfully fought for between 1846 and 1850.

[82] *Parl. deb.*, xcvi, cols 1242–53; xcviii, col. 758; c, cols 1019–41; cv, cols 1336–67; cvi, cols 709–14, 1040–2; *The Times,* 13 June 1849.

19

PEERAGE CREATIONS AND THE CHANGING
CHARACTER OF THE BRITISH NOBILITY, 1750-1850

MICHAEL W. McCAHILL

DURING the first three-quarters of the eighteenth century the size of the British peerage remained almost unchanged. New creations averaged two a year, a rate that was barely sufficient to offset losses due to the extinction of existing noble lines. Then suddenly in 1776 the parsimonious practices of previous decades were swept aside: over the next fifty-five years 209 new peerages were created, and the house of lords grew in size from 199 to 358.[1]

Modern historians have been at pains to stress that the new men were indistinguishable from those whom they joined in the lords. Neither George III, his successor nor their ministers were social radicals. Their peers were drawn from the traditional sources – from among the great landlords and, to a lesser degree, from the ranks of the more distinguished military commanders, judges and diplomats. According to Professor F. M. L. Thompson the new component in the outlook of the titled aristocracy at the end of the eighteenth century was a heightened preoccupation with rank. This sensitivity not only inflated the demand for titles of nobility; it also led men, already in the peerage, to request promotions up the noble hierarchy. Thus, as the nobility grew in size, its members began to differentiate themselves according to rank and wealth.[2]

In emphasizing continuity Thompson and others have obscured or belittled change. Between 1750 and 1830 a peerage which had been almost exclusively English came to represent all parts of the United Kingdom as large numbers of Scots and Irishmen took their seats in the house of lords on the same basis as Englishmen. Even as these noblemen from the celtic fringe reinforced the ranks of the territorial magnates within the nobility, land ceased to be the pre-eminent qualification for the peerage. The majority of the titles bestowed after 1801 went to active servants of the state: politicians, judges, military officers, diplomats or men of business. While some of these individuals were scions of landed families and possessed estates themselves, very few were magnates. Rather, their formidable presence demonstrates the degree to which a noble title, traditionally

---

1. A. S. Turberville, *The House of Lords in the XVIIIth Century* (Oxford, 1927), pp. 416–28; Turberville, *The House of Lords in the Age of Reform, 1784–1837* (London, 1958), pp. 42–43. Neither royal dukes nor eldest sons, elevated to the Lords in their fathers' baronies, are included as new peers in this study.

2. F. M. L. Thompson, *English Landed Society in the Nineteenth Century* (London, 1963), pp. 8–14. See also Turberville, *House of Lords in Age of Reform*, 42–45; G. C. Richards, 'The Creation of Peers Recommended by the Younger Pitt', *AHR*, xxxiv (1928), 47–54.

the certificate of membership in the élite group of great landlords, had become a reward for outstanding accomplishment.

Throughout the eighteenth century the ranks of landed magnates provided most of the new recruits for the peerage. Younger sons of the best endowed families, husbands of noble heiresses or men who were heirs through some near relative to families that had recently ornamented the peerage, all these demanded formal admission to a group of which they were, in a sense, already a part. Wealthy petitioners who lacked these aristocratic connections instead drew attention to the vast extent of their well-tended acres. But political factors weighed as heavily with ministers as rank or lineage. In the heated political atmosphere of the late eighteenth century the man who was fortunate enough to include a pocket borough in his patrimony possessed irresistable credentials: politicians were eager to strike a bargain with him.[1] Lacking such assets even the greatest landowners had not only to demonstrate their loyalty to the king and his ministers; many also required the intervention of some leading politician to carry their claims.

It was natural that great landlords should aspire to an honour for which they possessed all the established qualifications. Some, including George Pitt or the Scottish earl of Galloway, spent a substantial portion of their adult lives in pursuit of this goal.[2] The great majority of supplicants were less single-minded. Their pretensions were certainly as strong as Pitt's, but their applications were triggered by specific, immediately compelling factors. Thus, for a small number elevation to the upper chamber was the fitting conclusion to a long career in the Commons.[3] Others wished to escape rather than retire from the lower house: Lord Mulgrave longed to separate himself from men he hated and despised, while Lord Brudenell desired to be spared the 'trouble and fatigue' of attendance. The house of lords did offer the advantage of providing its members with a permanent seat at Westminster. A number of MPs who wanted to avoid expensive elections they were not confident of winning requested peerages, and a few even applied after failing to secure election to the Commons.[4] Increasingly, however, the main catalyst for applications from English country gentlemen was the galling spectacle of others' good fortune.

1. Fifty-six of the new peers controlled one or more borough seats in Great Britain as did forty-four of those who received a promotion.
2. L. Namier and J. Brooke, *History of Parliament: The House of Commons, 1754–90* (London, 1964), i. 99–101.
3. P[ublic] R[ecord] O[ffice], Dacres Adam Papers, P.R.O. 30/58/2, Sir J. Wodehouse to Pitt, 8 Sept. 1797; *The Later Correspondence of George III*, ed. A. Aspinall (Cambridge, 1970), iv. no. 3180.
4. P.R.O., Pitt Papers, P.R.O. 30/8/162, fo. 49, Mulgrave to Pitt, 24 May 1793; *The Correspondence of King George the Third, 1760–1783*, ed. J. Fortescue (London, 1928), v. no. 3128; *The Letters of King George IV, 1812–1830*, ed. A. Aspinall (Cambridge, 1938), i. no. 147; P.R.O., Pitt Papers, P.R.O. 30/8/152, fo. 125, Lewisham to Pitt, 10 Jan. 1796.

TABLE I. *English landowners raised to the British peerage 1750–1830*

	Eng. owners created	per cent. of total creations	Eng. with Heirs, etc. per cent. no. of total		Irish peerages per cent. no. of total		Country gents. per cent. no. of total	
1750–79	21	52.5	11	27.4	3	7.5	7	17.5
1780–1801	56	52.3	22	20.6	10	9.3	24	22.4
1802–30	20	21.7	9	9.8	2	2.1	9	9.8

'By making one Peer', Sir Archibald MacDonald remarked, 'ten enemies are made, & twenty claimants.'[1]

Even as the scramble for peerages became more hectic, the number of aspirants who actually attained the prize declined. The trend is apparent as early as 1780 after which a smaller portion of the whole group of new peers consisted of individuals who were heirs to families that had recently possessed a peerage. Pitt's lavish creations of country gentlemen and Englishmen with Irish titles temporarily obscured the effect of this development. But his successors refused to perpetuate Pitt's generous policies. Having remained steady from 1750–1800, the rate of creations of landed gentlemen began to decline precipitously after 1801.

The stinginess of Pitt's successors cannot be attributed to a slackening of demand within the group. Landed income continued to rise, at least until 1815, and the already prevalent preoccupation with rank appears only to have intensified during the first decade of the nineteenth century. Indeed, competition for new honours became so intense that the more ardent applicants were prepared to bribe, even to blackmail in order to achieve their object.[2]

The decline in the number of creations from the ranks of English landlords occurred because politicians consciously set aside their requests. By the end of the eighteenth century many concerned individuals had begun to apprehend the possibly damaging consequences of continuing, large-scale creations of peers. Of particular significance is their fear that extensive creations would demoralize

1. P.R.O., Granville Papers, P.R.O. 30/29/2/5, fos. 737–8, A. MacDonald to Lady Stafford, 24 July 1786. Lord Glastonbury claimed that he 'never thought of a peerage; but one day I took up the newspaper, and I read in it that Tommy [Charles] Townshend was made a peer. Confound the fellow! said I, what right had he to be a peer, I should like to know? So I resolved to write Pitt and tell him so. I wrote and was made a peer the following week.' G. E. C[okayne], *The Complete Peerage*, ed. Hon Vicary Gibbs *et al.* (London, 1926), v. 666, n.

2. *Letters of George IV*, ii. nos. 570, 576, 627; *The Journal of Mrs Arbuthnot, 1820–1832*, ed. F. Bramford and the duke of Wellington (London, 1950), i. 222, 224.

MPs and undermine the character of the house of commons. Thus, Lord Suffolk admonished George III that the removal of so many of its members was bound to degrade the lower house. Evidence of that degradation was already woefully apparent. Wilberforce complained that members willingly surrendered a portion of their independence in order to obtain the honours they coveted. Less high-minded observers shared his concern that the uncontrollable exodus of men of property was diminishing the stature and effectiveness of the commons. It was also transforming the character of that body, at least in the eyes of Lord Sheffield.

What chance has the landed interest here, when the system is to manage the considerable landed men by sending them to the House of Lords, after a very short service, not because they had public or other more useful talents than that of simple voting, but because they have landed property? – What chance have we, I say, when the House of Commons is filled with moneyed men, speculators, and underlings in office?[1]

Sheffield was overwrought; his fears were exaggerated. But the spectacle of English landowners moving *en masse* to the Lords was as distressing to the second earl of Liverpool as it was to Sheffield or to Wilberforce. The withdrawal of such men from the Commons imperilled the constitution, his lordship believed, because it was the landed aristocracy 'that makes the Ho. of Commons what it is in the British Constitution, & it is the want of such a Body that is the principal Reason why the British Constitution is inapplicable in every other Country. . . .'[2]

By the beginning of the nineteenth century it is clear that leading politicians not only appreciated these concerns but were also beginning to modify the extent and pattern of previous creations. They tried, at least intermittently, to limit the number of recommendations. From time to time they also entered into specific agreements with George III or the Prince Regent to impose a temporary moratorium on further creations.[3] Liverpool steadfastly refused to bestow peerages with special remainders to any but the greatest potentates.[4] Finally, and perhaps most significantly, these politicians began to

1. *The Journal of Elizabeth Lady Holland, (1791–1811)*, ed. earl of Ilchester (London, 1908), i. 191; R. and S. Wilberforce, *The Life of William Wilberforce* (London, 1838), i. 390–2; *Journals and Correspondence of William Lord Auckland*, ed. Bishop of Bath and Wells (London, 1862), iii. 356–7.

2. B[ritish] L[ibrary], Liverpool Papers, Add. MS. 38620, fos. 95–98, Liverpool to Wilbraham Bootle, 5 Nov. 1814 [draft]. *Cf. Quarterly Review*, xlii (1830), 325.

3. Berkshire Record Office, Braybrooke Papers, D/EZ 6CI, Braybrooke to J. Grenville, 7 Aug. 1797; *HMC, 13th R.*, iii, *Fortescue MSS*, viii. 1–2; *Dispatches, Correspondence and Memorials of Field Marshal Arthur, Duke of Wellington* (Millwood, N.Y., 1973), iv. 220; B.L., Liverpool Papers, Add. MS. 38260, fos. 95–98, Liverpool to Wilbraham Bootle, 5 Nov. 1814 [draft].

4. *Ibid.* Add. MS. 38261, fos. 239–43, Liverpool to Redesdale, 21 July 1815 [draft]; *The Correspondence of Charles Arbuthnot*, ed. A. Aspinall (London, 1941), 36–37.

attend closely to the applications of groups that hitherto had commanded relatively little attention. The strong claims of the peers of Ireland and Scotland along with those of the more prominent national servants began, after 1790, to receive unprecedented ministerial attention. The emergence of these groups at a time when politicians purportedly wished to limit the further growth of the peerage and stem the flow of English landlords into the nobility was bound to work to the latter's disadvantage.

Measured in numerical terms, the most substantial alteration to the traditional character of the peerage came as a result of the sudden introduction of large numbers of Scottish and Irish noblemen into its ranks. Between 1750 and 1780 the crown promoted six Irish peers to the British house of lords. During the same period the heirs to three Scottish peerages took their seats as peers of Great Britain: their fathers were prevented from enjoying the same honour by a standing order which remained in force until 1782.[1] However, over the next fifty years the traditional trickle became a flood: twenty-three Scots and fifty-nine Irish peers took their seats in the imperial parliament as peers of Great Britain or the United Kingdom. What was accomplished during these years was, in effect, the incorporation of the great lords of Scotland and Ireland into the British nobility. By 1830 the process was virtually completed: later governments bestowed peerages on individuals, but those were not noblemen of the first rank in terms of their landholdings or familial prestige.

Prior to 1782 a Scottish nobleman who wished to serve in Westminster generally had to secure election as one of his country's sixteen representative peers. Like members of the house of commons the representative peer stood for election at each new parliament. And to a greater degree than most borough contests, these peerage elections were controlled by the crown. Before an election the government released a list of its candidates and canvassed on their behalf. An impressive body of noblemen set out in 1770 to abolish this humiliating practice, but before 1790 the victorious peers were almost invariably those on the ministerial lists. Even the return of six independents in 1790 was insufficient to restore confidence in the representative system. As the dowager countess of Glasgow complained to Henry Dundas a year later:

the Peerage of Scotland is at Present upon a very disagreeable Footing. Born as they were to a hereditary seat in their own House before the Union they cannot but Feel the humiliating difference now when so few of their body can be Electing.[2]

1. For a discussion of the circumstances which induced the house of lords to adopt such an order, see G. S. Holmes, 'The Hamilton Affair of 1711–12: A Crisis in Anglo-Scottish Relations', above, 151-176.

2. S[cottish] R[ecord] O[ffice], Melville Castle MSS, S.R.O. GD 51/1a/15, Lady Glasgow to Dundas, 13 Aug. 1791; M. McCahill, 'The Scottish Peerage and the

Not surprisingly a system that seemed to symbolize their lowly status as well as their dependence was distasteful to the Scots. As early as 1784 several of the greatest peers refused to stand for election, 'not from any objection to parliamentary attendance, but from a feeling that they suffer in reputation, without gaining in consequence by it'. The men involved were enormously powerful and wealthy, but as Dundas explained to Pitt, they were no longer willing to endure an arrangement in which the greatest among them, on entering the house of lords, were forced to take their seats below the newest English baron.[1] For increasing numbers of Scots membership in the British peerage offered a means of escaping from a system that degraded their entire order.

If discontent with the representative system induced a number of Scots to think yearningly of a British peerage, many of these individuals also had positive and substantial claims on ministers. A few could demand a peerage in consequence of their notable military or diplomatic triumphs. The majority had equally compelling if less spectacular credentials. Their services in the counties and as local military commanders after 1792 testified to their loyalty and their territorial influence. Their political support enabled the Dundases to reign as the last of Scotland's great political managers.[2] As improving landlords they had at once increased their rents and helped to stimulate the rapid expansion of the Scottish economy. This last achievement was especially significant in their eyes: 'Scotch Peers of independent fortune feel their Situation more than ever', Lord Aboyne told Henry Dundas; 'having raised themselves by care & attention to ease and opulence, naturally they look to being placed in that state to which you allow they have every pretension.' Men who felt as Aboyne did bombarded ministers with their applications, all the more after colleagues whose claims were not better than their own received the coveted honour. Having helped to secure seven creations after 1783, Dundas still found in 1800 that his list of applicants included a marquis and twelve earls.[3]

In 1800 the Irish peerage was larger and more heterogeneous than

House of Lords in the late Eighteenth Century', *Scottish Historical Review*, li (1972), 172–96.; above, 283-307.

1. P.R.O., Pitt Papers, P.R.O. 30/8/157, fos. 351–4, Dundas to Pitt, 28 Jan. [1784].

2. S.R.O., Breadalbane Papers, GD 112/40/11, Breadalbane to ?, (no date); H. Furber, *Henry Dundas, First Viscount Melville, 1742–1811* (London, 1931), 182, 202–4.

3. For discussions of the nobility's role in eighteenth-century economic development see E. Richards, 'Structural Change in a Regional Economy; Sutherland and the Industrial Revolution, 1780–1830', *EcHR*, ns. xxvi (1973), 63–76; T. C. Smout, 'Scottish Landowners and Economic Growth, 1650–1800', *Scottish Journal of Political Economy*, xi (1964), 229–30; S.R.O., Melville Castle MSS, GD 51/1/55/3, Aboyne to Dundas, 31 May 1801; *ibid.* GD 51/1/55/2, Dundas to Aboyne, 29 May 1800 [copy].

TABLE 2. *Irish peers raised to the British nobility, 1750–1830*

	Total creations	Recipient British	Peerage awarded for service	Recipient Irish
1750–79	6	5(83.3%)	3	1
1780–1801	31	19(61.3%)	10	12
1802–30	22	6(27.3%)	5	16

its Scottish counterpart. The core of the group, of course, included the body of substantial Irish landowners. But many Irish peers were English landlords without an acre of Irish property, and it was common throughout the eighteenth century to reward prominent British crown servants with Irish titles. The factors which led increasing numbers of this amorphous body into the British peerage are, therefore, more varied and complex than those that would apply to the relatively homogeneous Scots.

Until 1801 the majority of the Irish noblemen elevated to the house of lords were, in fact, Englishmen. The large number among this group who earned their peerages as a result of public service will be discussed later. Most of the others were country gentlemen whose qualifications for admission were the standard ones – large estates, relatively eminent family, loyal support of government and, perhaps, a political interest. Most secured their honours as a result of the intervention of some important politician or magnate; a few, such as Melbourne or Lord Fife, were royal favourites.[1] Individually none of these men was so important that he could have carried his point by appealing directly to the minister. For these Englishmen the Irish peerage constituted a sort of middle passage. Even an Irish title conferred upon them a measure of dignity. It consoled them until they finally attained the great object of their ambitions – a British peerage. And, of course, governments dispensed Irish peerages in hopes of postponing this occasion as long as possible.[2]

It was Pitt who, despite his own prejudices and those of his colleagues, began introducing Irish members of that peerage into the house of lords.[3] He sent seven prior to 1800 and another four at the

1. See, for example, C. D. Yonge, *The Life and Administration of Robert Bankes, Second Earl of Liverpool* (London, 1868), iii. 379–80.
2. Namier and Brooke, *History of Parliament*, i. 101.
3. At the time of the Union Grenville made it clear that he wanted as few Irishmen as possible in the house of lords. P.R.O., Dacres Adam Papers, P.R.O. 30/58/2, Grenville to Pitt, 8 June 1800. Earlier Pitt explained that it was politically impossible to admit Irish applicants with no English property at a time when the multiplication of honours had already provoked an outcry. *Correspondence between the Right Honble. William Pitt and Charles, Duke of Rutland*, ed. Duke of Rutland (Edinburgh, 1890), 150–3.

Union. In the next twenty-eight years his successors sent sixteen more to the upper house. Like their English counterparts these men owed their honours primarily to their wealth, their loyalty and their political influence: after 1802 only three noble Irish landlords, Clancarty, Clanwilliam and Strangford, served in any official capacity with distinction. And, as the number of recruits from Ireland increased, fewer and fewer English members of that peerage found their way into the house of lords. Many, of course, had already attained their goal. Also, the Union and realities of early nineteenth-century Irish politics effectively barred more Englishmen from receiving Irish titles.[1]

Unlike the Scots the Irish had no insuperable objections to the representative system set up under the Act of Union. Competition for vacant seats was intense, all the more because the Irish did not have to stand for re-election at each new parliament. Once elected the Irish representative peer was a member of the lords for life, indistinguishable in most respects from British peers.[2] Haughty whigs might mock the submissiveness and questionable gentility of the representative peers,[3] but their sneers did not deter members of the nobility from bombarding the viceroy with pleas for the Castle's support at coming elections.

Still, it seemed to Liverpool that at times the entire Irish peerage was demanding admission to the nobility of the United Kingdom. And even while they inundated him with their petitions, they were also conniving to secure a promotion in their own order. Liverpool could only conclude that these men 'set a higher value in all Distinctions of this sort, than we do in this country'. This preoccupation with the symbols and ornaments of rank was not simply a figment of the English imagination. The Irish aristocracy was more conscious of

1. Shannon, Tyrone and Donegal were territorial magnates whose support the Castle required to maintain its hold on the Irish parliament. *HMC, 14th R.*, i. *Rutland MSS*, iii. 302–3, 322–3; *HMC, 13th R.*, iii. *Fortescue MSS*, i. 581. Macartney and Wellesley received their peerages on account of their services; Courtown was a courtier with extensive English connections; and Clare was probably raised to the English peerage because his services would be required to help carry the Union bill through parliament. For problems relating to the creation of the Union peers – Carysfort, Drogheda, Ely and Ormonde – see *Correspondence of Charles, First Marquis Cornwallis*, ed. C. Ross (London, 1859), iii. 32, 113, 244–5. Inchiquin, another royal favourite, apparently received his peerage because there was no room for him among the representative peers. *Later Correspondence*, iii. no. 2510.

2. Critics of the Scottish system had long lamented the necessity of the representative peers' standing for election at each new parliament. Elibank, *Considerations on the Present State of the Peerage of Scotland* . . . (London, 1771), 8–27; S.R.O., Morton Papers, GD 150/113, Selkirk to Morton, 7 Aug. 1786. The Irish system, established at the Union, was generally considered to be an improvement over the Scottish. B.L., Dropmore Papers, Add. MS. 59255, unfoliated, Darnley to Grenville, 24 Aug. 1800.

3. B.L., Holland House Papers, Add. MS. 51803, fos. 38–41, Leinster to Holland, 15 Mar. 1801.

caste, more sensitive to issues of this type than its British counterparts.[1]

'A Protestant gentry grew up, generation after generation, regarding ascendancy as their inalienable birthright; ostentatiously and arrogantly indifferent to the interests of the great masses of their nation, resenting every attempt at equality as a kind of infringement of the laws of nature.' The arrogance, the exaggerated sense of caste that Lecky excoriated were reinforced by events of the late eighteenth and early nineteenth centuries. On the one hand the Irish landlords enjoyed rising incomes which permitted them to rival the English in the lavishness of their expenditure and the grandeur of their style of living. But during these same years the mounting violence in Ireland rendered their position less secure. A great house, an additional title, even membership in the house of lords, these symbols were appealing in that they seemed to reinforce the illusion of unassailable eminence for an extraordinarily proud group that was increasingly under seige. 'The Mania of increasing Family honours,' Lady Londonderry explained to Pitt at the end of the century, 'seems to rise in proportion as they are threatened with extinction. . . .'[2] And as in the case of Scotland and England, the process of ennoblement was infectious: grants to one or more individuals generated demands from other noblemen able to present equally awesome credentials.[3]

As with the Scots, however, it was union which provided a compelling urgency and relevance to the Irish demands for British honours. For the Union created an anomaly: members of a nobility that had so recently possessed a house of its own found themselves free, after 1800, to sit in the commons at Westminster but unable to send more than twenty-eight of their fellows to the imperial house of lords. A hereditary body thus seemed to be in danger of becoming indistinguishable in many respects from commoners. The Scots had proclaimed this paradox for at least thirty years, and the Irish benefited from their endeavours. Indeed, Liverpool believed that the peculiarities of the union settlements gave Irish and Scottish lords strong grounds for claiming English titles.

The State of the Scotch & Irish Peerage have made a very great difficulty in the Question. For as some of them say with much reason, if we were Commons of old Family & large Property – we might doubt whether it was our Interest to be created Peers, but our anomalous Situation of

1. B.L., Liverpool Papers, Add. MS. 38290, fos. 176–7, Liverpool to C. Williams Wynne, 10 Dec. 1821 (copy); *ibid*. Add. MS. 38300, fos. 229–30, Liverpool to Bristol, 18 Oct. 1825. On some occasions Irish noblemen demanded British peerages after failing to get Castle support to fill a vacancy in the representative peerage. *Later Correspondence*, iii. no. 2515.

2. W. E. H. Lecky, *A History of Ireland in the Eighteenth Century*, ed. L. P. Curtis (Chicago, 1972), 80; L. M. Cullen, *An Economic History of Ireland since 1660* (New York, 1972), 82–3, 114–16; P.R.O., Pitt Papers, P.R.O. 30/8/153, fos. 13–14, Lady Londonderry to Pitt, 16 Sept.

3. *Ibid*. P.R.O. 30/8/165, fos. 38–39, Palmerston to Pitt, 2 Oct. 1798.

Scotch or Irish Peers with half the Privilege of the Peerage places us in an ambiguous & awkward Situation & makes us of course anxious to be invested with all the Privileges wch are considered belonging to our Rank.[1]

If the anomalous situation in which the nobilities of Ireland and Scotland were placed as a result of union gave a similar logic and urgency to their petitions for peerages, the groups' distinct experiences over the past hundred years caused them to raise the issue for very different reasons. The Scottish nobility of the mid-eighteenth century was, as a group, still relatively impoverished; two major rebellions within thirty years had also raised questions in English minds regarding its loyalty. By the end of the century the Scots had overcome these adversities: they were by then stalwart agents of the crown and the Dundases, and their wealth enabled them to live as splendidly as their counterparts. Understandably, they wished to establish themselves on an equal footing with the nobility of England.

The circumstances of the Irish nobility were rather different. That group did not experience the same degree of financial hardship. Though there was an Anglo–Irish patriotism in which even the greatest landlords participated, it never developed to the same extremes as Scottish Jacobitism. Not even the episode of Grattan and the Volunteers raised serious doubts about the ascendancy's attachment to the crown. Loyalty was the *raison d'être* of the Irish aristocracy. Its members justified their privileges on the ground that they were the security on which the English connection rested. The ascendancy's monopoly of power during the eighteenth century reinforced its arrogance while mounting violence after 1780 heightened its fortress-like mentality. Competing emotions gripped the mind of the aristocracy, and as they did so that Irish preoccupation with symbols was accentuated. Foremost amongst these was, of course, the peerage, and with the Union great Irish lords could optimistically aspire to an honour which formerly had been beyond their reach.

Finally, what impact did the introduction of Scots and Irishmen have on the character of the British nobility? In the first place the peerage and the house of lords received fresh accessions of talent. Cathcart and Aberdeen, along with the Irish earls of Clanwilliam, Clancarty and Strangford were competent diplomats; Dalhousie was an effective general and an ambitious viceroy in India; Lauderdale was a colourful, if eccentric political fixture; Clare was a tough if violent one; and Wellesley almost reached the first rank of statesmen. However, the outstanding quality of these new men was the extent of their properties and political interests. Their admission thus reinforced the nobility's landed character and influence. But it did so with a difference. The properties of these recruits were Scottish and Irish: relatively few had

1. B.L., Liverpool Papers, Add. MS. 38260, fos. 95–98, Liverpool to Wilbraham Bootle, 5 Nov. 1814 [draft].

sizeable English estates. Thus, as the nobility moved to embrace representatives from all portions of the United Kingdom, it had to throw aside traditional barriers. In the process it began to evolve a more cosmopolitan character. Differences of course remained. English parliaments, for example, continued to regard great Irish landlords with impatience and distaste for much of the nineteenth century. Still, there was a gradual commingling of the great aristocracies of the three kingdoms: not only did these individuals attend the same schools and universities and frequently intermarry; they came increasingly to see their political and economic interests in common.[1] The achievement of men such as Dundas, Pitt or Liverpool was to have facilitated this association by responding to legitimate concerns of the Scots and Irish. In the process they also eradicated some of the distinctions which changing conditions had rendered obsolete.

The fact that seventy per cent of the men elevated to the British peerage were scions of noble families or substantial landowners is, in a sense, misleading since it implies that land remained the pre-eminent qualification for admission to the nobility. In fact, forty per cent of the men who received peerages between 1750 and 1830 did so on account of their services to the crown. A quarter of these had large estates, but the remainder were neither blue-blooded nor immensely rich.

The state had always acknowledged great achievement with the bestowal of peerages. Lord chancellors, of necessity, were sent to the house of lords, often to be joined by the chief justice of the king's bench. Other public servants and politicians were likely towards the end of their careers to demand some substantial mark of royal approval of their accomplishments. Between 1750 and 1780 sixteen men, most of them politicians and lawyers, entered the nobility primarily because of their public achievements.[2]

Over the next fifty years the number of men sent to the house of lords as a reward for distinguished service increased dramatically: in fact, this group comprises fifty per cent of all peers created after 1801. Twenty years of war produced an array of generals, admirals and diplomats whose triumphs demanded recognition from the state. The Act of Union, by restricting the crown's right to create Irish peers, prevented ministers from following the traditional practice of rewarding English heroes with Irish honours: it also increased the number of judges who might expect to go to the house of lords.[3] Moreover,

---

1. The degree to which the aristocracies of the three kingdoms had amalgamated is reflected in the horrified reaction of English and Scottish landowners to the Irish land wars. See, for example, Argyll, 8th duke of, *Autobiography and Memoirs*, ed. dowager duchess of Argyll (New York, 1908), ii. 346–82.

2. Politicians: Chatham, Egmont, Hillsborough, Holland, Lyttleton and Melcombe. Judges: Bathurst, Camden, Mansfield, Northington and Thurlow. Military commanders: Amherst, Hawke, Ligonier. Diplomats: Grantham and Walpole.

3. Two Irish chancellors, Redesdale and Manners, were raised to the house of

Pitt, Addington and Liverpool consciously replenished the ranks of able, knowledgeable members in the upper house. The existing nobility produced few of the professional politicians or officials who conducted public affairs in this era. Instead, most of the important ministerial spokesmen in the Lords were recruited from the commons.[1]

But considerations such as these are insufficient to account for changes which occurred in the composition of the nobility after 1790. It is not only that more public servants were going to the house of lords. The new recruits included fewer politicians but a broader range of officials and military commanders than in the past, and most of these men were still active at the time of their creation. Before 1780 the grant of a peerage normally signified that the new lord's public career was at an end. Lord Chatham was but a shadow of William Pitt; Henry Fox retired quietly to the house of lords; even Bubb Dodington wished only for this one last mark of the king's favour. Ligonier and Lyttleton received their honours after being removed from office. Following his unexpected expulsion from the government of Virginia, Amherst was promised a title, though unlike the others his career extended for another twenty-five years.[2] For these men the peerage was an elaborate gold watch. In other instances it was no more than a bribe, one that enabled ministers to complete advantageous political arrangements or remove undesirable colleagues. Thus, De Grey, chief justice of the common pleas, was promised a peerage if he would make way for the ambitious Wedderburn, and North rid himself of the despised Lord George Germaine by dispatching him to the house of lords as Viscount Sackville.[3]

While later politicians also hastened the retirement of unwanted colleagues or officials by blandishing consolatory peerages, the majority of their new creations among this group went to men still in active service. Twenty-five of the thirty-three admirals and generals raised to the nobility after 1780 continued their careers as peers. So did twelve of the thirteen diplomats, and if a number of the men of

---

lords after 1801, as was William Plunkett, chief justice of the court of common pleas (I). The creation of the post of deputy speaker of the house of lords added another judge to that body. From time to time exceptional grants were made to very distinguished judges such as Sir William Scott, who presided over the admiralty court.

1. _Later Correspondence_, ii. no. 1626; M. McCahill, _Order and Equipoise: The Peerage and the House of Lords, 1783–1806_ (London, 1978), 128–9, 132–43.

2. _The Political Journal of George Bubb Dodington_, ed. J. Carswell and L. Dralle (Oxford, 1965), 397; R. Whitworth, _Field Marshal Lord Ligonier_ (Oxford, 1958), 376–8; M. Wyndham, _Chronicles of the Eighteenth Century_ (London, 1924), ii. 225–6; J. C. Long, _Lord Jeffrey Amherst: A Soldier of the King_ (New York, 1933), 200–13.

3. _Correspondence of George III_, iv. no. 2299: _ibid._ v. no. 3485. On the day Sackville was introduced to the house, a group of peers, led by the marquess of Carmarthen, introduced a motion condemning the authors of this peerage: the admission of a man who had been court-martialled would tarnish the dignity of the peerage and its house. B.L., Leeds Papers, Add. MS. 27918, fo. 56; Debrett, _Parliamentary Register_, viii. 217–28, 11 Feb. 1782.

TABLE 3. *Recruitment of politicians and state servants to the peerage, 1750–1830*

	1750–1779	1780–1801	1802–1830
Politicians	6	3	5
Men of Business		3	6
Diplomats	2	4	9
Armed Services	3	17	16
Judges	5	6	10
Governors		2	

business received their title upon retiring,[1] others, including Auckland and Liverpool, proved to be formidable members of the house of lords as well as important advisers of Pitt. A peerage, once the reward for a lifetime of brilliant achievement, was increasingly bestowed in recognition of specific outstanding triumphs or accomplishments.

Related to this change is another of greater importance: by the end of the eighteenth century vigorous politicians were able to go to the lords without jeopardizing their careers. Melville and Goderich occupied important posts after their elevation, and though he had reluctantly accepted a peerage that Pitt thrust upon him, Sidmouth remained a political figure of significance for fifteen years. More notable, however, were Lords Grenville and Hawkesbury, the latter of whom succeeded his father as earl of Liverpool in 1808. Neither of these men became politicians of the first rank until after they had entered the house of lords. Their careers convincingly demonstrate that acceptance of a peerage no longer constituted an act of political self-immolation.[2]

Melville, Grenville, Liverpool, these were the outstanding representatives of a new political élite that was gradually displacing the great landed potentate from his monopoly of power. Their claims to power rested on their detailed understanding of national problems and their familiarity with the operations of important government departments. These qualifications, not broad acres and extensive influence, became the prerequisites for high office, and their fortunate possessors could perform their administrative functions as well from the upper as from the lower house.[3]

1. *Arbuthnot Correspondence*, 36–37. Liverpool told Wellington's brother, Lord Maryborough, that he would never have asked him to retire from the Mint in 1823 if he had not obtained him a peerage three years earlier. B.L., Liverpool Papers, Add. MS. 39291, fos. 395–6, Liverpool to Maryborough, 18 Jan. 1823.
2. For a discussion of Grenville's career in the lords see McCahill, *Order and Equipoise*, 135–9. Cf. Namier and Brooke, *History of Parliament*, i. 102, which compares politicians in the upper house to dreadnoughts.
3. For discussions of the prominence of this new type of politician see W. Brock, *Lord Liverpool and Liberal Toryism: 1820 to 1827* (London, 1967), 78; J. E. Cookson, *Lord Liverpool's Administration: The Crucial Years, 1815–1822* (Edinburgh, 1975), 14–15; J. Ehrman, *The Younger Pitt: The Years of Acclaim* (New York, 1969), 323–6.

The prominence of these politicians in turn bolstered the claims of officials who previously had only rarely reached the upper house. Men of business, more akin to the modern civil servant than the politician, enjoyed a new prominence under Pitt. Several were among his closest advisors, and Pitt was really the first to honour them with peerages.[1] Diplomats constituted the other new group within the peerage. Between 1750 and 1785 only two ambassadors were advanced to the peerage; during the same period men already in the nobility tended to reject all but the most important embassies. In the last years of the century, however, the diplomatic service became decidedly more prestigious. Pitt began to heed the petitions of diplomats who argued that their stature in foreign capitals would be enhanced if they were peers, and Grenville made a concerted effort to raise the service's prestige by inducing English peers to accept missions to the lesser courts.[2]

As more and more public servants advanced to the house of lords, their colleagues naturally concluded that their own attainments merited similar acknowledgement. Sir Joseph Yorke, Sir Henry Wellesley and Sir Charles Stuart each claimed that his exploits were at least as notable as those of diplomats who had already received a peerage. Liverpool argued against conferring titles on diplomats precisely because such awards would only give rise to further demands, but he was able to resist neither their pleas nor those of England's military heroes.[3] The latter were as sensitive to considerations of rank and honour as any other men, and inter-service rivalries only inflated their claims for titles. The duke of York, for example, supported the grant of a peerage to the impoverished heir of General Abercrombie because he felt that the army was being ignored while peerages were showered on the navy. Twelve years later, however, Sir Sidney Smith complained that:

the *navy* has surely not the less merit for having worked itself out of employment by destroying all opposition on the coasts of the four quarters of the globe, & being the constant support of the Army in all its operations,

---

1. Pitt sent Auckland and Liverpool to the Lords; his successors ennobled Bexley, Colchester, Farnborough, Maryborough, Oriel and Wallace.
2. D. B. Horn, *The British Diplomatic Service, 1689–1789* (Oxford, 1961), 87–91; P.R.O., Pitt Papers, P.R.O. 30/8/100, fo. 195, Auckland to Pitt, 24 Dec. 1790; *HMC, 13th R*, iii. *Fortescue MSS*, v. 88–90.
3. B.L. Hardwicke Papers, Add. MS. 35372, fos. 397–400, J. Yorke to Hardwicke, 7 Sept. 1788; *Arbuthnot Correspondence*, 82–83; *Wellington's Dispatches*, iv. 165–7; B.L., Liverpool Papers, Add. MS. 38299, fos. 138–9, Liverpool to George IV, 11 Oct. 1824 [draft]. On the other hand Lord Dudley, Canning's foreign secretary, believed that the bestowal of a peerage on Sir William A'Court would 'operate as a salutary example to your Majesty's diplomatic servants and encourage them to display the same skill and fidelity in a profession to which must often be entrusted the interests of your Majesty's Crown'. *Correspondence of George IV*, iii. no. 1416.

without which support it would not have accomplished any one of the objects for which its distinguished officers are so deservedly rewarded.[1]

Ministers also had to take care that the rank bestowed corresponded to the magnitude of the individual's achievement. Was Cathcart's attack on Copenhagen comparable to the services of Viscount Lake and therefore deserving of the same reward? The Irish marquisate conferred on Lord Wellesley in acknowledgement of his victories in India provoked angry recriminations rather than effusions of gratitude: 'as I was confident there had been nothing *Irish* or *Pinchbeck* in my conduct, or in its result, I felt an equal confidence that I should find nothing *Irish* or *Pinchbeck* in my reward.'[2]

Such protestations increased the pressures on ministers, but their importance should not be exaggerated: by the end of the eighteenth century politicians were already giving priority to the claims of victorious military commanders, successful diplomats and knowledgeable men of business. Pitt apparently promised George III, who had been outraged by the size of recent creations, not to recommend any further persons after 1797 unless they had the strongest public claims. Nor were his priorities unique. In 1814 Liverpool told a petitioner that for the past eight years peerages had been granted only for professional reasons: the bestowal of these honours did not in any way obligate ministers to heed commitments to other applicants because the claims of public servants were independent of and prior to all others. Finally, Wellington, as minister, repeatedly reiterated his determination not to nominate peers 'unless some service of magnitude or public emergency should require it'.[3]

The prominence of the public servants among its ranks had a profound impact on the character of the nobility. In the first place a number of these talented recruits lacked the landed property which had been the essential prerequisite for membership in the peerage in the past. Suddenly it seemed to observers such as Lord Belgrave as if the nobility was being swamped by men whose heirs 'from the Inadequacy of their Fortunes, being seldom possessed of much landed Property, became naturally too dependent on the crown'. Eldon, whose progress from a blacksmith's shop to the woolsack did not prevent him from defending all that was traditional, lamented that so many of his legal colleagues accepted titles without having the

---

1. *HMC, Bathurst MSS*, 202, 204; *Later Correspondence*, iii. 278n; B.L., Liverpool Papers, Add. MS. 38258, fos. 147–50, Smith to Liverpool, 8 July 1812.
2. *Later Correspondence*, iv. no. 3544; P.R.O., Pitt Papers, P.R.O. 30/8/188, fos. 131–4, Wellesley to Pitt, 6 Oct. 1801.
3. B.L., Liverpool Papers, Add. MS. 38260, fos. 95–98, Liverpool to Wilbraham Bootle, 5. Nov. 1814 [draft]; *ibid*. Add. MS. 38258, fos. 74–76, Liverpool to Limerick, 20 June 1814; Berkshire Record Office, Braybrooke Papers, D/EZ 6CI, Braybrooke to J. Grenville, 17 Aug. 1797; *Wellington's Dispatches*, iv. 220, vi. 563–4; Liverpool Papers, Add. MS. 38285, fos. 94–95, Duncombe to Liverpool, 25 May 1820.

means to support them adequately. An impoverished peer lacked that lofty independence which was, theoretically, the hallmark of his class and the justification of the house of lords' role as the constitution's equipoise. Moreover, as more and more of these individuals entered the peerage, the supposedly healthy distinction between noblemen and commoners was blurred.[1] A few men did decline titles rather than diminish the stature of an order they were too poor to ornament.[2] Most, however, found themselves unable to resist the highest of honours when it was offered.

Forty-seven individuals, approximately twenty per cent of the peers created between 1750 and 1830, possessed less than three thousand acres at the time of their creation. Three such men (7.5 per cent of the men created between 1750 and 1779) found their way into the Lords before 1780 where they were joined by thirteen others (12.1 per cent of those created between 1780 and 1801) in the next two decades. The flood came after 1801. Thirty of the ninety-two men ennobled between 1802 and 1830 had little if any landed property at the time they were elevated to the peerage.[3] What made the difference between this and earlier periods was the number of peerages awarded for service: only two of the thirty were unable to point to some outstanding deed. Some of these public servants supported their new dignities with their salaries. Others had sizeable fortunes if little land. But about thirty depended on the state to support them in their new dignity by providing them with estates, sinecures or pensions. Indeed, Canning's widow refused to accept a proffered title until Goderich had endowed it with a pension.[4]

The number of noblemen who, by 1830, supported their dignity with public funds was unprecedented and highlights the altered character of peerage creations during the previous generation. Of course, the king and his ministers rejected a number of aspirants on account of their relative poverty and tried to dissuade men of modest estate from pressing their claims.[5] But, as governments tended more

1. P.R.O., Pitt Papers, P.R.O. 30/8/140, fos. 331–2, Belgrave to Pitt, 14 May 1804; H. Twiss, *The Public and Private Life of Lord Chancellor Eldon* (London, 1844), ii. 322–4; *Quarterly Review*, xlii (1830), 324.

2. *Later Correspondence*, iv. 157n.

3. This figure is based on research in *GEC*, among private correspondence and relevant secondary sources. Since these records are not precise, the figure itself cannot be definitive. 1750–79: Amherst, Chatham, Ligonier. 1780–1801: Abercromby, Auckland, Clare, Dorchester, Dover, Duncan, Grenville, Heathfield, Hutchinson, Hood, Nelson, St Helens, St Vincent. 1802–30: Arden, Beresford, Canning, Colchester, Collingwood, Cowley, Ellenborough, Erskine, Exmouth, Gambier, Gardner, Gifford, Granville, Harris, Hill, Lake, Lyndhurst, Lynedoch, Manners, Niddry, Plunkett, Seaford, Sidmouth, Stewart, Stuart, Tenterden, Bexley, Wellington, Whitworth, Wyndford.

4. *Correspondence of George IV*, iii. no. 1448.

5. *HMC, Bathurst MSS*, 212. George III protested that Nelson's lack of an estate disqualified him even from receiving a baronetcy, but, as a result of Lord Spencer's persistence, he finally agreed to raise the victor of the Nile to the peerage. *Later Correspondence*, iii. no. 1844, 1846.

and more to reward able officials and military commanders with titles of nobility, they found themselves obliged as well to provide some of their new peers with a measure of financial dignity.[1] The duke of Wellington's measure was lavish – a large pension and the great Stratfield Saye estate – and the impoverished heir of Nelson received an annual pension of five thousand pounds together with a grant of one hundred thousand more to be used for the purchase of an estate appropriate for an earl.[2] Lesser heroes contented themselves with pensions worth two or three thousand a year. Officials and diplomats received similar grants on their retirement, and in some instances these were extended to their heirs.[3] Belgrave's charge, therefore, had some substance. All too often the state found itself subsidizing the undistinguished and penurious heirs of these individuals. But ministers also took their precautions: a disproportionate number of the men who received a pension to support their new rank died without an heir to their peerage.[4]

As a general rule the nobleman of the eighteenth century possessed an estate of at least ten thousand acres. There were exceptions to this rule, but the degree to which it applied is reflected in the inconsiderable number of small landowners who found their way into the peerage before the end of the century. The creations of the next three decades were thus a marked departure from tradition: ministers were consciously ennobling men who lacked the most conspicuous characteristic of their new station. Claims of service now took precedence over land as the criterion for the peerage. The landless peer was no longer a freak, and as more and more of these individuals entered the nobility, standards for less outstanding claimants also relaxed. The peerage of the nineteenth century thus ceased to be the exclusive haven of the magnate. By the 1860s the genealogist Burke deemed an income of two thousand pounds a year as sufficient to

1. Liverpool told Wellington in 1814 that 'the Peerage has always been considered as the distinction & reward of the Service, and the Pension has only been given when it has been necessary to support the peerage'. B.L., Liverpool Papers, Add. MS. 38257, fos. 241–2, Liverpool to Wellington, 12 May 1814 (copy).

2. *A Peep at the Peers* (London, 1820), 24; B.L., Dropmore Papers, Add. MS. 59380, (unfoliated) Nelson to Grenville, 5 Mar. 1806; *Later Correspondence*, iv. no. 3242.

3. Examples include St Vincent, Abercromby's heir, Lake, Beresford and Hill. *Later Correspondence*, iii. no. 1685; G. Pelew, *The Life and Correspondence of the Right Hon. Henry Addington, First Viscount Sidmouth* (London, 1847), i. 394–5; *The Diary and Correspondence of Charles Abbot, Lord Colchester* (London, 1861), ii. 140, 497. When Speaker Abbot retired he received a peerage, a pension of £4000 and £2000 a year for his heir's life. *Ibid.* ii. 614, 616, 619. Granville Leveson-Gower, the diplomat, aspired to the peerage at least in part so he could receive the normal diplomatic pension of two thousand pounds, one which sitting MPs were barred from receiving. *Lord Granville Leveson-Gower (First Earl Granville) Private Correspondence, 1781–1821*, ed. Countess Granville (London, 1916), ii. 182–3.

4. P.R.O., Pitt Papers, P.R.O. 30/8/172, fos. 195–204, Memorandum to Pitt; *Later Correspondence*, v. no. 3607; B.L., Liverpool Papers, Add. MS. 38261, fo. 4, Hood to Liverpool, 2 Jan. 1814; *ibid.* Add. MS. 38294, fos. 93–94, Liverpool to St Vincent, 2 May 1823 [draft].

support a noble title. Few of the men ennobled after 1830 were actually landless, and ministers continued to scrutinize the financial and landed assets of candidates for the peerage. Still, the princely standards of the eighteenth century had been eroded: Burke's peer with two thousand a year was a pale replica of his eighteenth-century precursor.[1]

Despite their relative lack of landed wealth, the new peers were vitally important. Like the eighteenth-century grandee the new public officials among the peerage had complete confidence in their ability to govern. Unlike the grandees these men were professionals. Power was not theirs by right: they exercised it because they had the talents and expertise. Gradually magnates, who had dominated affairs for generations, found themselves displaced by a new political élite at the core of which stood those men elevated to the peerage after 1790 and their descendants. Whether Pitt set out consciously to submerge the old aristocracy, as Turberville implies, is open to question. It is clear, however, that the professional politicians, men of business, diplomats and outstanding military commanders he encouraged and rewarded came to dominate national affairs.[2]

Evidence to substantiate this conclusion is contained in Table 4 and 5. Table 4 demonstrates that over three twenty-four year periods the proportion of cabinet ministers who were peers declined from eighty per cent to just under fifty-three per cent. It is a mark of the talents and political importance of the new peers and their descendants that the rate of their participation at the cabinet level dropped less (20.5 per cent) during these years than that of the group as a whole (33.9 per cent). Indeed, Table 5 indicates that new peers and their heirs dominated the ranks of noble cabinet ministers with remarkable consistency after 1806. Many of the grandees retreated from the arena of national politics to manage their estates and adorn local government. That the aristocracy retained the influence it did during the nineteenth century is due in no small part to the fact that it quickly included within its ranks the most outstanding representatives of the new political and public service élites.[3]

Disoriented by massive new creations which challenged many of the time-honoured assumptions about the group they adorned, older members of the peerage inevitably tried to differentiate themselves from the new men by obtaining promotions in the nobility. Of course,

1. G. E. Mingay estimates that in order to meet the expenses of the London season, maintain a country house and use it as a centre of social and political influence without feeling a financial strain, a magnate required an income of at least ten thousand pounds. Mingay, *English Landed Society in the Eighteenth Century* (London, 1963), 19; Thompson, *Landed Society*, 60–63; J. Ridley, *Lord Palmerston* (New York, 1971), 504–5.

2. J. Holland Rose, *William Pitt and the Great War* (London, 1911), pp. 466–7; Turberville, *The Lords in the Age of Reform*, pp. 53–54.

3. For a discussion of the old aristocracy's gradual withdrawal from national politics, see D. Spring, 'The Role of the Aristocracy in the Late Nineteenth Century', *Victorian Studies*, v (1960–1), 58–59.

TABLE 4. *Noble members of cabinets, 1782–1855*

	1. Total number in cabinets	2. Peers in cabinets	3. New peers in cabinets	4. heirs of new peers in cabinets[1]	5. percentage of 3 and 4 in 1
1782–1805	90	72(80.0%)	31	5	40.0
1806–1830	121	75(62.0%)	29	19	39.7
1831–1855	138	72(52.9%)	24	20	31.9

George III, who regarded the English peerage 'as the most honourable of any country',[1] and several of his ministers endeavoured to prevent a serious disruption of the established noble hierarchy.[2] But their objections counted for little with men who saw individuals of lesser background advanced over their heads. The seventh earl of Salisbury, who reckoned that he stood among the first rank of peers, applied for a marquisate as soon as he discovered many junior peers had been put above him. Their lordships' sensibilities were particularly vulnerable to the promotion of a relative or neighbour. Lord Scarsdale requested an earldom after his younger brother received a viscountcy, and a number of his colleagues demanded similar honours for themselves as the only way to restore their prestige in neighbourhoods where upstart families of humble estate sported more exalted titles than their own.[3]

Yet, this was not primarily a struggle between the old peerage and the new. Fourteen of the 102 peers who were advanced between 1750 and 1830 could legitimately cite the antiquity of their line to support their pretensions.[4] On the other hand, forty-seven were themselves new peers, and twenty others were the heirs of such men.

The nobility in this period was also beginning to sort itself into a hierarchy in which rank was dictated by the extent of an individual's property. Applicants carefully noted that their incomes could support a more exalted title: the fact that he had provided for his younger children without burdening his estate and had, at the same time, invested £120,000 out of his income in roads and improvements

1. Only heirs of peers created after 1780 are included in column 4.

2. *Letters from George III to Lord Bute, 1756–1766*, ed. R. Sedgwick, (London, 1939), 231, 237; *Correspondence of George III*, iii. no. 1837; B.L., Liverpool Papers, Add. MS. 38300, fos. 266–75, Liverpool to Bristol, 4 Nov. 1825 [draft].

3. P.R.O., Pitt Papers, P.R.O. 30/8/175, fo. 60, Salisbury to Pitt, 17 June 1789. *Cf. ibid.* P.R.O. 30/8/129, fo. 266, Digby to Pitt, 6 Feb. 1790; B.L., Townshend Papers, Add. MS. 50011, fo. 132, de Ferrars to Townshend, 16 Apr. 1784; P.R.O., Dacres Adam Papers, P.R.O. 30/58/5, Scarsdale to Pitt, 23 May 1804; Earl of Cardigan, *The Wardens of Savernake Forest* (London, 1949), 294–5; P.R.O., Pitt Papers, P.R.O. 30/8/126, fos. 58–59, Courtenay to Pitt, 29 May 1796; B.L., Liverpool Papers, Add. MS. 38262, fos. 89–90, Falmouth to Liverpool, 1 Oct. 1815.

4. Abergavenny, Anglesey, Cornwallis, Craven, Delawarr, first Viscount and first earl of Dudley, Exeter, Maynard, Northampton, Northumberland, Salisbury, Uxbridge, Wentworth.

TABLE 5. *Proportion of noble cabinet members drawn from new peers and their heirs, 1782–1855*

	1 Total peers in cabinet	2 New peers and their heirs
1782–1805	72	36(50.0%)
1806–1830	75	48(64.0%)
1831–1855	72	44(62.5%)

seemed to Lord Bristol to justify his claim for a marquisate. For their part ministers tried to assure themselves that the recipient would be able to maintain a style of life commensurate with his new dignity.[1] But, as with rank, wealth was not the sole or even the primary qualification for promotion in many instances.

Thirty-nine of the peers advanced between 1750 and 1830 received those honours because of their services to the crown. The king periodically conferred additional honours upon his favourites and men in whom he had special confidence. Ministers did the same. In many instances promotion came as a matter of course: politicians might advance a rank on retiring, and five successive viceroys were advanced to honour their accomplishments in India.[2] Other servants demanded promotions as a mark of royal approbation of their recent accomplishments or services. And there is no evidence to show that ministers rejected petitions on the grounds that the applicant lacked the wealth to support his new position.

Ancient standing, large estate, meritorious service, all of these factors created a demand for and justified the bestowal of so many promotions. But it is misleading to overstress the importance of rational considerations in a process that was increasingly irrational. As ministers dispensed more and more peerages and promotions, more and more individuals decided that they were entitled to one of these rewards. Even the most indulgent politician could not begin to satisfy the demand. On the contrary, governments' attempts to meet and exploit the appetite for peerages only created an environment that encouraged further applications.

An earldom is very well worth having if it an't made the price of any business. If it were offered to my father I should certainly advise him to accept it, though my own immediate share of the honour would be rather unpleasant to me than otherwise. But I have not the presumption to despise those things which I see sought for so eagerly by persons so completely

1. B.L., Liverpool Papers, Add. MS. 38283, fos. 331–2, Bristol to Liverpool, 30 Sept. 1820. Liverpool and Bathurst debated for two weeks on the size of the grant that would have to accompany Wellington's marquessate. *HMC, Bathurst MSS*, 195–6. Cf. *Later Correspondence*, v. no. 3784.
2. *Some Official Correspondence of George Canning*, ed. E. J. Stapleton (London, 1887), ii. 228–30.

beyond all comparison my superiors. . . . There is a great deal of speculative philosophy on these matters, but when it comes down to the point I observe everybody takes all the honours he can honestly, and sometimes more. My father is, according to the usual 'tarif' a perfectly earlable man. . . .[1]

John Ward's father, the Viscount Dudley and Ward, was undoubtedly earlable. But as his son's letter makes clear, it was the atmosphere of the times as much as his personal qualifications and ambitions that would induce his lordship to lay his claims before the ministers. The yearning for titles had, in effect, become self-perpetuating.

The willingness of politicians to accede to the requests of so many applicants is, therefore, a matter of significance which demands explanation. Most ministers proclaimed their determination to limit further creations at some point in their careers, and for a while they did usually stem the flow. But in the long run none were able to resist so powerful a force which seemed to work so obviously to their political advantage. The relentless pressure of claimants, backed as they were in many cases by powerful magnates and royal princes, was particularly welcome at a time when the reserves of patronage were diminishing. Reform movements and parsimonious ministers had helped to sweep aside many of the sinecures and other douceurs which had once greased the political machine. The Union in 1800 eliminated the inexhaustible supply of Irish peerages which earlier politicians had dispensed so generously. In any case rising incomes freed the aristocracy, at least to a degree, from its financial dependence on the state. How convenient then to be able to retire useless colleagues, enhance the local prestige of a staunch ally, ingratiate slippery borough proprietors, even facilitate the management of representative peerage elections by dispensing an honour that was in demand yet which cost the treasury so little.

The lavish creation of peers that accompanied any major political arrangement or alliance attests to the usefulness of this particular reward. Pitt sought to prop his weak administration by making eleven new peers and by promoting eight existing noblemen during the early months of 1784. The Talents, many of whose members had chided Pitt for his extravagance on this occasion, bestowed the same number of new peerages along with four promotions in 1806. When the Portland whigs at last agreed to coalesce with Pitt in 1794, Lord Fitzwilliam reported that 'the King will mark his approbation of the junction by a creation of peers at the D. of Portland's recommendation'.[2] After so long an exile whigs rushed with almost unseemly

---

1. S. Romilly, '*Letters to Ivy' from the First Earl of Dudley* (London, 1905), pp. 300–1.

2. Wraxall believed that Pitt's early creations were an attempt to show the political world 'the facility with which he disposed of the honours of the crown, withheld by the sovereign from the Coalition, and consequently the rewards which might attend their early repairing to the royal standard'. N. Wraxall, *The Historical*

haste to share the fruits of power: four former members of the
opposition were advanced in rank between 1792 and 1796, and fifteen
others were elevated to the house of lords.[1] The number of awards
in this instance was exceptional, but ministers continued, if on a more
modest scale, to cement alliances in this manner. Liverpool ennobled
one and promoted another of Canning's cronies when the latter went
to Portugal in 1814, and two more of his candidates were included in
the first creation to take place after Canning took the foreign office.
Likewise, the government celebrated the union with the Grenvilles
by granting the Irish Lord Northland a British peerage and by conferring a dukedom on the head of the clan, Lord Buckingham.[2]

Broader political considerations necessitated the incorporation of
the upper portions of the Irish nobility into the British peerage.
Before 1800 Anglo-Irish nationalism and, more urgently, the exigencies of managing an independent Irish parliament forced ministers to
bestow innumerable Irish peerages and, for the great borough
proprietors, Shannon, Tyrone and Donegal, British titles. The latter,
with his four members, threatened to withdraw support from the
administration of Lord Westmorland unless he received an Irish
marquisate and an English barony.[3] The Union in no way diminished
Westminster's dependence on the ascendancy. The reduction in the
number of parliamentary boroughs only enhanced the power of those
who retained electoral influence. After the failure of Catholic Emancipation the government had no choice but to govern again in conjunction with the Anglo-Irish aristocracy. Since the most powerful
members of that group were 'inevitable politicians rather than
politicians by choice', London had continuously to dispense largesse
in order to maintain their active support. At the same time the
correspondence between Dublin and London indicates that English
statesmen were anxious to incorporate the loyal and powerful members of the Irish nobility into the parliament of the United Kingdom
by means of the representative peerage or a British title.[4]

In distributing peerages so freely ministers finally demonstrated to

---

and Posthumous Memoirs of Sir Nathaniel Wraxall, ed. H. Wheatley (London, 1884),
iii. 255. Whigs, such as Lord Palmerston, regarded these creations as no more than
bribes. B. Connell, *Portrait of a Whig Peer* (London, 1957), p. 147. North Riding
Record Office, Zetland Papers, ZNK X2, Fitzwilliam to Dundas, 7 July [1794].

1. Elevations: Dorchester, Hertford, Carnarvon, Bute. Creations: Upper Ossory,
Clive, Mendip, Bradford, Yarborough, Dundas, Gwydir, Brodrick, Newark,
Downe, Cawdor, de Dunstanville, Ribblesdale, Minto and Bayning.

2. W. Hinde, *George Canning* (London, 1973), 269; *Correspondence of George IV*,
ii. no. 989; iii. no. 1235; Yonge, *Life of Liverpool*, iii. 379–80.

3. *HMC, 14th R.*, i, *Rutland MSS*, iii. 302–3; *HMC, 13th R.*, iii, *Fortescue MSS*,
1. 581.

4. A. P. W. Malcomson, *John Foster: The politics of the Anglo-Irish Ascendancy*
(Oxford, 1978), 203–7; *The Correspondence of George, Prince of Wales 1770–1810*
(London, 1971), viii. 35n; B.L., Liverpool Papers, Add. MS. 38261, fos. 303–10,
Whitworth to Liverpool, 9 Aug. 1815; B.L., Wellesley Papers, Add. MS. 37304,
fos. 137–8, Goulburn to Wellesley, 27 May 1826; *Wellington's Dispatches*, v. 81–82.

the world that the king had confidence in their judgment. As long as the monarch retained substantial independent authority, these periodic manifestations of his sentiments had real significance. Pelham interpreted George II's offer of an earldom to Chancellor Hardwicke as 'a great proof of his present disposition'; and since he 'knew few things that would give greater *éclat* at present than this promotion', he insisted that the unenthusiastic chancellor accept the king's gracious offer. Similarly, Charles Fox suggested to Grenville in 1806 that the latter take an earldom because 'such a mark of Royal favour to you would be very useful to us at this time'. Fox's anxiety on this matter undoubtedly derived in part from his past experience: during his previous tenure in office in 1783, George III had proclaimed his distaste for the coalition by refusing to accept any of its recommendations for peerages.[1] Canning had no such difficulties: to the contrary, his opponents within the government interpreted the awards made at his recommendation in 1826 as a sign that he stood well with the king. Since the ageing Liverpool was bound to retire soon, Wellington and his friends were seriously alarmed.[2]

Yet, if the flow of peerages facilitated the consummation of a variety of political arrangements and publicized a particular government's good standing in the closet, the distribution of these honours only affected political loyalties in the short term. There were individuals such as the first Earl Grosvenor who, in spite of humiliations suffered at the hands of ministers, refused to oppose the king's government because his majesty had granted them their peerages. From time to time MPs transferred their political support in order to bolster their claims, and ministers certainly tried to lure powerful figures into their camp with promises of peerages or promotions.[3] It is also true that individuals who failed to secure their object sometimes withdrew their support from unworthy politicians. On the other hand, even so rapacious an individual as the first marquis of Hertford refused to succumb to the blandishments of his political leaders' adversaries.[4] In fact, peerages were generally conferred on men of proven loyalty; at most they served to reinforce bonds which were already firmly established. The influence derived from the dispersal of patronage, even in the form of a peerage, was insufficient to dictate or enforce political obedience. As Lord Rawdon told a correspondent, no new lord could be expected out of gratitude to ignore his private opinions

1. W. Coxe, *Memoirs of the Administration of Henry Pelham* (London, 1829), ii. 496–7; HMC, *13th* R., iii, *Fortescue MSS*, viii. 48–49; B.L., Fox Papers, Add. MS. 47579, fos. 23–24, Fox to Ossory, 12 Aug. 1783.

2. *Mrs Arbuthnot's Journal*, ii. 27–30.

3. HMC, *Various Collections*, *Knox MSS*, vi. 165; *Additional Grenville Papers*, *1763–1765*, ed. J. Tomlinson (Manchester, 1962), 69–70; *Life and Letters of Sir Gilbert Elliot*, ed. Countess of Minto (London, 1874), i. 180–2.

4. P.R.O., Pitt Papers, P.R.O. 30/8/119, fo. 9, Cadogan to ?, 16 Nov. 1798; B.L., Hertford Papers, Eg. 3262, fos. 118–9, Hertford to Beauchamp, 30 Nov. 1788.

or his duty as a citizen. New members of the nobility were certainly not the craven dependents of their benefactor: over half of the men Pitt ennobled or promoted during his first administration opposed him publicly on an important issue.[1]

Limited as the political effects of these creations were, they would have been more marginal still if the monarch had retained the control over their distribution which George III exercised in his prime. Throughout his life the king was a jealous defender of the nobility's good character. He scrutinized the claims of all candidates, rejecting those who did not meet his very traditional standards. In the face of his resistance ministers normally had to withdraw their candidates: Rockingham in 1766 and Fox in 1783 found that their obstinate and hostile sovereign refused to consider their recommendations.[2] Yet, even ministers in good standing only carried their candidates by giving way to the king's desires on others. Before 1783 George was in a very real sense the fountain of honour: not only did he determine who would receive titles, but he expected that peerages would be regarded by those who received them as obligations to the crown rather than to ministers.[3]

The decisive shift in power came during the first of Pitt's administrations. George III continued to raise men on his own authority; he rejected some ministerial candidates; he also objected to the size of Pitt's creations, in 1797 with some apparent effect. But the king's health was no longer robust; particularly after 1789 his interventions seem to have been more sporadic, less emphatic and authoritative than in earlier years. In any case he was dependent upon Pitt. In 1784 he had no choice but to accede to the latter's demands, and by the 1790s ministers easily overrode his objections.[4] Pitt's successors upheld and consolidated this authority. Thus, by 1820 Liverpool could inform the secretary to the new king that his royal master could only make commitments to bestow peerages 'through one of the regular & official responsible Channels', not on his own authority.

1. HMC, *Various Collections*, vi, *Knox MSS*, 204; McCahill, *Order and Equipoise*, 160–1.

2. Lord Holland complained that the king 'judged of the fitness for high station by rank rather than by talent. . . . Descent from an early enemy or obscurity of birth were in his eyes such offenses, that, with the exception of Mr Pitt and Mr Addington, he was seldom prevailed upon to pardon either. . . .' *Further Memoirs of the Whig Party, 1807–1821*, ed. Lord Stavordale (New York, 1905), 64. *Correspondence of George III*, i. no. 334; B.L., Fox Papers, Add. MS. 47579, fos. 23–24, Fox to Ossory, 12 Aug. 1783.

3. For example, George only consented to granting the barony of Malmesbury to Sir James Harris, the ambassador to Holland, on the condition that his friend, Sir Joseph Yorke, a previous ambassador also receive a peerage. The fact that Harris was distinguished and Yorke was not counted for little in his eyes. Earl Stanhope, *Life of the Rt. Honourable William Pitt* (London, 1879), i. 483. B.L., Robinson Papers, Add. MS. 37835, fo. 154. George III to Robinson, 5 Sept. 1780.

4. *Later Correspondence*, ii. no. 1500; iii. no. 1844, 1846; G. Bolton, *The Passing of the Irish Act of Union* (Oxford, 1962), 206–7.

After a brief display of independence during the early years of the Regency, George IV had abided by this standard. He accepted, if sometimes grudgingly, candidates referred to him and took care to consult Liverpool even before honouring his closest friends. Under these conditions politicians were free to dispose of honours as they wished and to claim for themselves the political goodwill that accompanied their dispersal.[1] Moreover, their ability to control access to the peerage insured that that group would adjust quickly to changing political realities.

It is this suppleness in the face of new trends that distinguishes the peerage during these years. As Scotland looked to establish itself as a partner, not a subordinate, of England and found in Henry Dundas a potent spokesman in Westminster, or as England endeavoured to bolster its troublesome position in Ireland by absorbing the Dublin parliament, large numbers of Scots and Irishmen obtained British peerages. The connection is not coincidental. Neither is it coincidental that as the age of Newcastle gave way to that of Liverpool, the bulk of new peerages went to politicians and public servants rather than to landed magnates.

The period 1790–1830 thus represents a major transition in the history of the nobility: what once had been the exclusive property of English grandees became a reward bestowed in recognition of distinguished public service. New recruits were not drawn from the worlds of commerce and industry.[2] Most owned estates but not of sufficient extent to uphold the princely standards of the eighteenth-century peerage. By the nineteenth century, land was insufficient in most instances to secure a petitioner his peerage. Unless he was an Irish grandee, he also had to be able to point to some major accomplishment to secure this honour.

The continuing leadership of the nobility throughout much of the nineteenth century derives from a variety of factors. Of not inconsiderable importance was the deferential character of the English populace.[3] Equally significant was the deftness with which an aristocratic leadership granted timely concessions that opened its institutions, one by one, to middle class recruits.[4] Nor were the radical denunciations of languid, rapacious or parasitic peers well-founded. Professor David Spring has shown that substantial portions of the aristocracy had become imbued with the spirit of Clapham by the

1. B.L., Liverpool Papers, Add. MS. 38289, fos. 249–50, Liverpool to Sir B. Bloomfield, 10 July 1821; Yonge, *Life of Liverpool*, iii. 379–80.

2. The one exception, Robert Smith, first Lord Carrington, was the scion of the Nottingham banking family. But Smith had extensive estates and a parliamentary interest.

3. J. G. A. Pocock, 'The Classical Theory of Deference', *AHR*, lxxxi (1976), 516–23; D. Spring, 'Walter Bagehot and Deference', *AHR*, lxxxi (1976), 524–31.

4. F. M. L. Thompson, 'Britain', in *European Landed Elites in the Nineteenth Century*, ed. D. Spring (Baltimore and London, 1977), pp. 22–44.

early nineteenth century.[1] Certainly the nobility included within its ranks a number of energetic and highly successful entrepreneurs.[2] Finally, the gradualism of reform and the movement of peers into political parties during the 1830s helped to sustain the political influence of the order.[3]

To these explanations of the nobility's enduring influence must be added the nature of the group's new recruits. The growth of towns, the expanded electorate, the enthusiasm with which radicals applied the standard of utility to measure the worthiness of institutions, these and other elements undermined traditional justifications for a nobility. In particular the argument that magnates ought to be the 'great Oaks that shade a country and perpetuate your benefits from Generation to Generation' had lost its force. The house of lords ceased after 1832 to be the balance of the constitution, and the nation no longer required or desired farsighted aristocrats to keep it on an even keel. Thus, nineteenth-century defenders of the peerage subtly altered Edmund Burke's defence: the repositories of public-spirited and principled conduct became instead living monuments that preserved and celebrated the glorious achievements of Britain's most distinguished sons. The peerage took on a more utilitarian character: at once it inspired Britons to preserve memories of a glorious past and induced them to labour in the public service so that they, by aiding their country, might even advance themselves into this awesome group.[4] It was the new creations after 1780 that endowed these apologies with some credibility. In this way as in others changes in the composition of the nobility helped to render that institution viable in a new age.

1. Professor Spring discusses the aristocracy's seriousness and the influence of Clapham on its behaviour in 'Aristocracy, Social Structure, and Religion in Early Victorian England', *Victorian Studies*, vi (1962–3), 263–80. Long before Victoria's accession popular journals were celebrating the diligence and social responsibility of certain great peers. See, for example, *Public Characters*, 1804–5, 443–5.

2. D. Spring, 'English Landowners and Nineteenth-Century Industrialism', in *Land and Industry: The Landed Estate and the Industrial Revolution* ed. J. T. Ward and R. G. Wilson (Newton Abbot, 1971), pp. 16–62.

3. J. Morgan Sweeney, 'The House of Lords in British Politics, 1830–41', D.Phil. dissertation (Oxford, 1974).

4. Palmerston not only told a South London audience that the peerage was an honourable roll of the nation's great public servants; he implied that if members of his audience worked hard enough, they too might join the nobility. G. Best, *Mid-Victorian Britain (1851–1875)* (New York, 1972), 234–5. *Cf.* G. Harris, *The Life of Lord Chancellor Hardwicke* (London, 1847), ii. 468–9, 521–2.

20

PEERS, PATRONAGE AND THE INDUSTRIAL REVOLUTION, 1760-1800[1]

MICHAEL W. McCAHILL

. . . My Thoughts always return to the *Necessity* of exercising Politicks in cultivating & protecting & extending our Manufactures as the principal Source for improving our Lands, multiplying our People & increasing & establishing our Commerce & Naval Force.

> Samuel Garbett to the Marquess of
> Lansdowne, 2 October 1786.

Students of the industrial revolution now generally admit what seemed obvious to Samuel Garbett, the Birmingham manufacturer and lobbyist, two hundred years ago; namely, that the state was an important participant in the early phases of the industrial revolution. Many scholars still emphasize the restraint of English government — a restraint which gave relatively free play to natural economic forces and to individual genius, a restraint which also aggravated the social repercussions of so momentous a transformation.[2] But they recognize that entrepreneurs could obtain legal sanction for enclosures, canals, and a myriad of other "improvements" easily and at moderate cost by means of a private act of parliament,[3] and they debate whether existing patent law stimulated invention by providing adequate rewards for the inventor or aimed primarily at discouraging stultifying monopoly.[4] Because

---

1. I wish to thank Professor Eric Robinson for reading and criticizing an earlier draft of this article, Mr. Arthur Westwood for allowing me to consult the Boulton Papers at the Birmingham Assay Office, and Earl Spencer for permission to quote from the Spencer Papers at Althorp.

2. M. W. Flinn, *Origins of the Industrial Revolution* (London, 1966), p. 93; P. Mathias, *The First Industrial Nation: An Economic History of Britain, 1700-1914* (New York, 1969), pp. 32-33, 43; H. Perkin, *The Origins of Modern English Society, 1780-1880* (London, 1969), pp. 63-67; W. W. Rostow, *Politics and the Stages of Growth* (Cambridge, 1971), pp. 83-84.

3. *Ibid.*, p. 84; Mathias, *The First Industrial Nation*, p. 35. Professors Holt and Turner not only exaggerate the state's importance but misapprehend the nature of private bill procedure in claiming that parliamentary approval of such acts constituted a decisive and conscious act of resource allocation on the government's part. R. T. Holt and J. E. Turner, *The Political Basis of Economic Development* (Princeton, 1966), pp. 250-53, 283, 310. For a discussion of private bill procedure and the expense involved in securing such acts, see Sheila Lambert, *Bills and Acts: Legislative Procedure in Eighteenth Century England* (Cambridge, 1971).

4. Mathias, *The First Industrial Nation*, p. 37; Rostow, *Politics and Growth*, p. 84; Witt Bowden, *Industrial Society towards the End of the Eighteenth Century* (London, 1965), pp. 24-51; Flinn, *Origins of the Industrial Revolution*, pp. 70-71; Eric Robinson, "James Watt and the Law of Patents," *Technology and Culture*, XIII (1972), 115-39.

the processes of growth in the last decades of the century were so fundamental and pervasive, fiscal, commercial, colonial, and foreign policies were bound to have an impact on the embryonic industrial economy. Whether government by its various acts encouraged or impeded growth is open to debate at a number of levels.[5] There can be no doubt, however, that politicians endeavored, if sometimes slowly and haphazardly, to adapt policy and law to changing conditions and that their decisions did affect the tempo and quality of growth.

This last is a vitally important point. Brewers were fortunate, indeed exceptional, in having between six and a dozen M.P.'s in the parliaments of the late eighteenth century.[6] Other manufacturers, despite their obvious interest in the formulation of public policy, were oddly averse to direct participation in political life. Few supported the reform movements of the period, and many proclaimed a distaste for the petty intricacies of party politics, preferring instead to immerse themselves in the problems of their business empires. Thus, in the 1780s the House of Commons had no representatives of Black Country ironmasters, West Riding woollen manufacturers, or Lancashire cotton magnates; only in 1790 did Robert Peel, the great cotton baron, purchase a seat at Tamworth and enter the House.[7]

Lacking direct representation, industrialists were instead forced to seek support from men who sat in parliament and from the king's ministers. Individual manufacturers such as Matthew Boulton or Josiah Wedgwood carried even the most controversial points because they were consummate lobbyists.[8] Of greater significance than the talents of these individuals, however, was the development of various industrial and commercial organizations. *Ad hoc* committees, regional or trade associations, finally the national Chamber of Manufacturers, these various groups embodied the manufacturers' increasingly mature and extensive efforts to

---

5. Mathias, *The First Industrial Nation*, pp. 34-48 and *The Brewing Industry in England, 1700-1830* (Cambridge, 1959), pp. 214-18, 330-38; Flinn, *Origins of the Industrial Revolution*, pp. 48-49, 60, 91-93; T. S. Ashton, *The Industrial Revolution, 1760-1830* (New York, 1964), pp. 8-9, 98-107; Phyllis Deane, *The First Industrial Revolution* (Cambridge, 1969), Ch. 13.

6. Mathias, *The Brewing Industry*, pp. 330-38.

7. Bowden, *Industrial Society*, pp. 162-64; Sir Lewis Namier and John Brooke, *History of Parliament: The House of Commons, 1754-90* (London, 1964), I, 138; S. D. Chapman, "The Peels in The Early English Cotton Industry," *Business History*, XI (1969), 77.

8. For a discussion of Boulton's lobbying skills, see Eric Robinson, "Matthew Boulton and the Art of Parliamentary Lobbying," *Historical Journal*, n.s. VII (1964), 209-30.

bring their collective pressure to bear on Westminster in order to shape policy. John Norris regards the Chamber of Manufacturers as a vital manifestation of the industrialists' sophistication and political expertise: in its aftermath local groups, organized for trade purposes, increasingly assumed the responsibility for industrial lobbying and became, in consequence, steadily more powerful and proficient.[9]

While admitting this point, it is essential also to stress the remarkable suppleness of contemporary political institutions. However adept industrial cajoling, however advanced the industrialists' organization, manufacturers still depended heavily on the good will of men who dominated England's political life. Neither parliament nor successive administrations were inert bodies from which wily lobbyists could extract whatever laws or policies they desired. The tightly knit political nation did cooperate with new industrial communities. Without such cooperation the accommodation of public policy to the needs of those areas would certainly have been slower and more difficult; it also would probably have been productive of considerable instability. That cooperation existed, that it brought about accommodation was due in no small part to the continuing effectiveness of the patronage system, especially as operated by members of the nobility.

This study focuses on the patronage activities of the peerage for two reasons. Innumerable landlords participated in enterprises which stimulated economic growth, and manufacturers of all types received political assistance from landowners in the country and from members at Westminster.[10] The peerage constitutes a small, well-defined portion of the larger landed class, one whose members resided throughout the country. The size of the nobility makes it possible to trace the activities of a substantial portion of its members very precisely. Its broad geographic distribution ensured that members would confront the full breadth and variety of contemporary economic development.

---

9. J. M. Norris, "Samuel Garbett and the Early Development of Industrial Lobbying in Great Britain," *Econ. Hist. Rev.*, second series, X (1958), 450-60. For discussions of trade organizations, see T. S. Ashton, *Iron and Steel in the Industrial Revolution* (Manchester, 1954), pp. 162-85; H. Heaton, *The Yorkshire Woollen and Worsted Industries* (Oxford, 1920), pp. 325-27, 418-37; Bowden, *Industrial Society*, pp. 165-69.

10. D. Spring, "The English Landed Estate in the Age of Coal and Iron," *Journal of Economic History*, XI, (1951), 3-24. For some recent discussion of the relation between M.P.'s and commercial or manufacturing centers, see G. Jackson, *Hull in the Eighteenth Century: A Study in Economic and Social History* (London, 1972), pp. 253, 257-58; R. G. Wilson, *Gentlemen Merchants: The Merchant Community in Leeds, 1700-1830* (Manchester, 1971), pp. 166-67.

Moreover, the peerage's position in society makes it a group of very special importance. Even in the late eighteenth century noblemen occupied the most exalted place on the social hierarchy. Vast properties formed the basis for the groups' privileged position; they also endowed peers with unrivalled economic and political resources. An examination of the manner in which these most prestigious and powerful representatives of an old order accommodated themselves to, even exploited, new economic forces and interests demonstrates the degree to which landed society shaped certain aspects of the industrial and political environment of this age.

II

According to one distinguished historian, the central accomplishment of the British industrial revolution was to convert the economy from "a wood and water basis to a coal and iron basis." Coal quickly replaced water or human power as the primary source of energy, while iron machinery and structural materials proved to be more durable and ultimately cheaper than counterparts made from England's dwindling supplies of wood.[11]

For lords of the soil a transition of this nature had profound and immediate repercussions. Since 1568 those men had enjoyed the right to exploit the mineral resources which lay under their domains. During the sixteenth and seventeenth centuries the great nobility of England and Scotland took a lead in mining the coal deposits of those kingdoms, and on a more limited basis they also extracted copper, iron, and lead.[12] Even in the second half of the eighteenth century a number continued to manage directly their mineral properties, to adopt the latest techniques in exploiting this wealth, indeed, to serve as models of modern entrepreneurial expertise.[13] But increasingly such noblemen were the exceptions within their order. Deeper pits required larger capital resources

---

11.   Deane, *The First Industrial Revolution*, pp. 129-30.

12.   For a general discussion of the aristocracy's mining ventures, see J. T. Ward, "Landowners and Mining" in *Land and Industry: The Landed Estate and the Industrial Revolution*, eds. J. T. Ward and R. G. Wilson (New York, 1971), pp. 63-116. For a detailed study of one noble estate, see T. J. Raybould, *The Emergence of the Black Country; A Study of the Dudley Estate* (Newton Abbott, 1973).

13.   Richard Reynolds, manager of the iron works at Coalbrookdale, said of the third Duke of Bridgewater's canals and coal works that "they are really amazing, and greater I believe than were ever before attempted, much less achieved by an individual and a subject." Hannah Rathbone (ed.), *Letters of Richard Reynolds with a Memoir of His Life* (London, 1852), pp. 93-94.

as well as more constant and expert supervision. Indifference, the unpleasant crudities of industrial strife, and a growing sense that the role of an industrial tycoon was incompatible with that of an aristocrat led nobles to withdraw. For these and other reasons partnerships or leasing agreements replaced direct exploitation ever more rapidly as the nineteenth century progressed.[14]

Whether a peer worked his mineral holdings or merely enjoyed the proceeds of others' labor, he still was bound to take some interest in measures which affected the prosperity of the coal or iron industries. By cutting transport costs, for example, turnpikes or canals expanded the market for coals and made it feasible to tap untouched resources. Not surprisingly, noble landlords served on committees and invested in ventures that would move their coal, iron, or limestone to hungry markets as cheaply as possible. It is remarkable, in fact, that whereas the nobility's investment in canals in general was not disproportionate to that group's share of the national wealth, peers did contribute more than their share to canals constructed especially to carry coal and other minerals.[15]

However, it is also significant that their political resources enabled lords to dictate the contents of canal legislation, even to determine whether appeals to parliament would be feasible. Nobles participated regularly in the preparation of such bills, often molding them to suit their individual needs.[16] Nor were canal projectors in a strong position to resist aristocratic interference, for they could hardly expect to carry such measures without the support of neighboring landowners. Thus, merchants and bankers of Leicester, who wished to make a cut from the town to the Loughborough Canal, saw their bill thrown out in 1786 at the instigation of a coalition headed by Lords Rawdon, Huntingdon, Stamford,

---

14. T. S. Ashton and J. Sykes, *The Coal Industry of the Eighteenth Century* (New York, 1967), p. 4; Ashton, *Iron and Steel*, p. 40; E. Richards, "The Industrial Face of a Great Estate: Trentham and Lilleshall, 1780-1860," *Econ. Hist. Rev.*, second series, XXVII (1974), 429; T. C. Smout, "Scottish Landowners and Economic Growth, 1650-1850," *Scottish Journal of Political Economy*, XI (1964), 251; F. M. L. Thompson, *English Landed Society in the Nineteenth Century* (London, 1963), pp. 264-66.

15. G. G. Hopkinson, "Road Development in South Yorkshire and North Derbyshire, 1700-1850," *Transactions of the Hunter Archaeological Society*, X, part 1 (1971), 25-29. J. R. Ward analyses the extent of landowners' investment in canals in *The Finance of Canal Building in Eighteenth Century England* (Oxford, 1974), pp. 73-74, 76, 157.

16. Hopkinson, "Road Development," *Hunter Archaeological Society*, X, part 1, 23-24; V. I. Tomlinson, "The Manchester, Bolton and Bury Canal Navigation and Railway Company, 1790-1845," *Transactions of the Lancashire and Cheshire Antiquarian Society*, LXXV-VI (1965-66), 257; Hopkinson, "The Development of Inland Navigation in South Yorkshire and North Derbyshire, 1697-1850," *Hunter Archaeological Society*, VII, part 5 (1956), 246.

and Ferrers. These peers, proprietors of coal mines and lime works, feared competition from Derby pits, competition which Leicester's cut would intensify. However, the plan did not die in the face of their opposition. Rawdon, who had taken the lead against the bill in the first instance, converted in 1790. His proselytizing efforts as well as certain modifications in the original plan overcame the objections of other magnates, and in 1791 legislation passed without difficulty.[17]

As this episode demonstrates, peers by their interventions influenced the outcome of proceedings on legislation which was sent up to London. Garbett and Josiah Wedgwood, the great potter, therefore rejoiced when Earl Gower consented to carry the Trent and Mersey Bill through parliament; indeed, Garbett felt that more depended on Gower's support than any other point,

> . . . and if He engages the Duke of Bridgewater, I don't see any alarming opposition; for all Arguments from common Landowners are no more than General Arguments against inland Navigation, and will be laugh'd at unless supported by a few such as Lord Gower and the Duke of Bridgewater, who have great ministerial weight. . . .[18]

In 1785 the proprietors of the Dudley Canal acknowledged a similar debt by voting special thanks to Lord Dudley for his "very powerfull and successfull Exertion in Parliament in support of the Extension of this Canal." Fitzwilliam remained till the end of the 1793 session because he felt obliged to supervise personally the passage of the Dearne and Dove Bill. Lord Moira, as Rawdon became on the death of his father in 1793, likewise assumed that no one but himself was competent to manage the passage of the Ashby Bill in 1794; and the committee of the Warwick and Birmingham Canal recorded in its minutes that the obtaining of

---

17. Charles Hadfield, *Canals of the East Midlands* (Newton Abbot, 1966), p. 80; *Victoria County History, Leicestershire*, III, pp. 94-96. See also S. R. Broadbridge, *The Birmingham Canal Navigations: I, 1768-1846* (Newton Abbot, 1974), pp. 25-26; Sheffield Public Library, Fitzwilliam to T. Beaumont, 18 Mar. 1793, Wentworth Woodhouse MSS, F68 (d)/18.

18. Eliza Meteyard, *The Life of Josiah Wedgwood* (London, 1865), I, 412-13. At a meeting on 30 Dec. 1765, Gower declared that he looked upon the proposed navigation,
> As of the utmost consequence to the manufacturers of that and adjacent counties, and to the kingdom in general; that ever since he had heard of the scheme, it had been his determination to support it with all his interest, both provincial and political; for he was satisfied that the landed and trading interest were so far from being incompatible, that they were the mutual support of each other.

John Phillips, *A General History of Inland Navigation, Foreign and Domestic* (London, 1795), p. 156.

their act was primarily due to Lord Warwick's "great Exertion in support of it."[19]

Why peers were so valuable is demonstrated in the correspondence of John Ward, agent for the Kennet and Avon Canal Bill, and Lord Ailesbury, one of the canal's noble supporters. Though he was a courtier of modest talents and no particular political aptitude, Ailesbury did enjoy access to all levels of the political hierarchy. Thus, he was dispatched by Ward to win over Lord Chancellor Loughborough, a powerful figure in private bill proceedings, and later to obtain a favorable procedural ruling from Lord Cathcart, chairman of the Lord's committees.[20] More importantly, Ailesbury helped to recruit supporters for the bill. Along with Lords Lansdowne, Carnarvon, and Craven he lent his name to an appeal soliciting M.P.s' support, and he was also pressed repeatedly to make personal applications to his friends in the lower and, later, the upper House. Indeed, Ward urged Ailesbury and his brother-in-law Moira to round up as many noble allies as possible even before the bill reached the House of Lords because he feared otherwise that uncommitted peers might be enlisted by rival canal companies.[21] Finally, the Earl utilized his local prestige in order to calm the unruly citizens of Marlborough. The latter, who jeopardized the passage of the bill by demanding at the last moment that a canal link be cut to their town, returned his lordship's nominees to parliament at every general election, and Ward expected they might also heed his admonitions in this instance.[22]

If their efforts in behalf of the various mineral canals constitute the nobility's most substantial political service for the coal and iron industries, peers did lend important support to other projects and demands presented by the leaders of these trades. Garbett and Dr. Roebuck, managers of the great Carron ironworks, complained to Lord Halifax, the Duke of Grafton, and other lords that Swedish manufacturers were conspiring to lure skilled artisans to emigrate with their equipment, and Halifax at least went to

---

19. Charles Hadfield, *Canals of the West Midlands* (Newton Abbot, 1966), p. 77; Northamptonshire Record Office, Lord Fitzwilliam to his wife [1793], Fitzwilliam Papers, Box 45; Wiltshire Record Office, Moira to Ailesbury, 30 Mar. 1794, Ailesbury Papers; Hadfield, *Canals of the East Midlands*, p. 165.

20. Wiltshire Record Office, J. Ward to Ailesbury, 29 Dec. 1793, 3, 5 Feb., 12 Mar. 1794, Ailesbury Papers.

21. *Ibid.*, Ward to Ailesbury, 5 Jan., 3, 9 Feb., 18 Mar. 1794, Ailesbury Papers. The practice of sending out cards was a common one. See, for example, PRO, Marlborough et al., to Pitt, 29 Dec. 1792, Pitt Papers, PRO 30/8/156, f. 37.

22. Wiltshire Record Office, J. Ward to Ailesbury, 30 Mar., 1, 4, 7, 13, 16, 22, 26 Apr. 1794, Ailesbury Papers.

rather absurd lengths to prevent such migrations.[23] Twenty years later, in 1786, Garbett asked that Pitt prevent one of his partners from establishing and managing an iron works in Russia: in addition to discussing the matter with the minister, Garbett also recommended to Pitt that he talk with Lord Dunmore, an old patron of the Carron Company and a magistrate dedicated to preventing illegal emigration.[24] The indefatigable ironmaster was also outraged that foreign producers were defrauding the customs by passing off plated iron as unwrought iron. Rockingham received at least one such complaint while he was in office, and following a visit to Birmingham, he recommended that Garbett take the matter up with the Duke of Grafton. In the meantime, Garbett drafted remedial legislation which he expected neighboring peers and M.P.'s to support. As he told William Burke, ". . . these old county familys look upon themselves as the Patrons of the trade of the Neighbourhood and really have great inclination to serve us when they distinctly understand the subject. . . ."[25]

While Garbett was undoubtedly correct in pointing out the public-spirited concern which landowners expressed for their neighborhoods, it is evident that economic self-interest at the very least gave urgency to, if it did not awaken, such sentiment in the minds of their lordships. Thus, Viscount Dudley, himself an ironmaster, joined with others of the trade to protest to the Treasury against the proposed coal tax in 1784. At the same time Richard Reynolds, manager of the Coalbrookdale iron works, complained of the tax and its probable consequences for the iron industry in a letter to Earl Gower, proprietor of the neighboring Lilleshall works and Lord President in Pitt's Administration.[26] His lordship, Reynolds expostulated, should give the measure all the opposition,

> . . . which thy abilities and thy station enable thee to give, and for which as a lover of thy country at large, as the protector of thy tenants, and as the hereditary patron of the

---

23. J. Redington (ed.), *Calendar of Home Office Papers, I (1760-65)*, (London, 1878), 414, 571, 605-6; J. Redington, *Calendar of Home Office Papers, II (1766-69)*, (London, 1879), 141-42.

24. R. Campbell, *Carron Company* (Edinburgh, 1961), pp. 148-51; PRO, Garbett to Pitt, 27 Sept. 1786, Pitt Papers, PRO 30/8/138, fols. 63-64. Dunmore, who leased his collieries to the Carron Company, induced George III to order a trial of the company's guns at Woolwich in 1779. In the wake of these trials came government contracts which established the company on a firm financial basis. Campbell, *Carron Company*, pp. 66, 93, 142.

25. Redington, *Calendar of Home Office Papers*, I, 637-38; *ibid.*, II, 27, 88, 141-42.

26. Norris, "Garbett and Industrial Lobbying," *Econ. Hist. Rev.*, second series, X, 453.

manufactories in this and the adjoining county, so many look up to thee with confidence, proportionate to their apprehensions of danger, and of thy disposition to save them from it.

While it is unclear what action Gower took on receiving this letter, Sir John Wrottesley, who was returned for Staffordshire in the Earl's interest, expressed his opposition to the tax on several occasions in the House of Commons.[27]

However, Pitt's speedy withdrawal of this controversial proposal was due not only to the protests of ironmasters and the interventions of their noble advocates. Owners of coal pits were themselves well represented in parliament. Being men of considerable importance and bitterly opposed to the tax, they were able, according to George III, to raise a loud and effective clamor against it.[28]

Self-interest and the needs of their localities also made effective lobbyists out of several leading copper magnates. During the 1780s and 1790s the industry's ability to find and maintain foreign markets remained a central problem. In the earlier decade overabundant supplies and falling prices dramatically pointed out the need for new customers. Thus, Viscount Falmouth went directly to Pitt with a request for permission to export copper and tin to India and the Far East. However, when the price of copper soared at the end of the 1790s, a meeting of the gentlemen and magistrates of Cornwall assembled specially to thank Lord de Dunstanville and four other peers and M.P.'s for preventing the Birmingham metal trades and their allies in the Government from curtailing or preventing exports which had become essential to the Cornish industry's prosperity.[29]

During these years peers also helped to secure and to protect the more immediate interests of the industry and its leading members. Only after he had entered into partnership with the Earl of Uxbridge was Thomas Williams, the dominant figure in the copper industry of the late eighteenth century, able to obtain legis-

27. Rathbone, *Reynolds Letters*, pp. 279-82; Stockdale, *Parliamentary Debates*, II, 212, 255 (30 June, 2 July 1784).

28. Ashton and Sykes, *The Coal Industry*, p. 1. For examples of the coal proprietors' opposition to the tax, see *Parliamentary History*, XXIV, 1034 (7 July 1784); Stockdale, *Parliamentary Debates*, II, 212, 245-255, 397 (30 June, 2, 7 July 1784).

29. PRO, Falmouth to Pitt, 13 Mar. 1789, Pitt Papers, PRO 30/8/134, f. 44; J. R. Harris, *The Copper King: A Biography of Thomas Williams of Llanidan* (Toronto, 1964), pp. 119, 127-30; PRO, "Resolutions of a Special Committee . . . of the Lieutenancy and Magistracy of the County of Cornwall," 21 July 1799, Pitt Papers, PRO 30/8/314, fols. 57-58.

lation remitting the duty on coals shipped by sea and begin smelting his ore in Anglesey. But the most vigorous and watchful advocate, particularly for the Cornish branch of the trade, was Lord de Dunstanville. No detail was too important to escape his lordship's attention. Thus, when a nervous Government ordered in 1798 that coastal vessels sail in convoy, he rushed to secure an exemption for Cornwall. Peculiar tidal conditions restricted opportunities for safe docking, and de Dunstanville pointed out that if vessels were not free to move with the tides, the mines' coal supplies would quickly be depleted.[30]

Though economic interest combined again and again with their sense of local responsibility to induce peers to speak in behalf of manufacturers' demands, it is significant that the nobility's industrial clientage extended beyond those trades in which their lordships had a direct or even a tangential economic stake. Throughout his career the second Marquess of Rockingham represented the interests of the Yorkshire woollen industry at Westminster: indeed, his first effort in the House of Lords was made in support of a bill favored by the trade, which would outlaw practices leading to the wastage of raw wool. Rockingham's solicitude derived in part from a sincere and well-founded conviction that trade was vital to the life of Yorkshire. However, his patronage also made sound political sense for one who constructed and maintained Yorkshire's dominant political interest between 1760 and 1780.[31] As old Horatio Walpole told the Marquess in 1752, a willingness to take up the business of woollen manufacturers, ". . . would give you credit both above & below as interesting yourself in matters of this sort & endeavoring to understand them. . . .I think it will spread thro' the kingdom a favourable impression of you. . . ."[32]

Along with the Wentworth properties, Earl Fitzwilliam inherited his uncle's paternal interest in the concerns of neighboring woollen manufacturers. The Earl extended his patronage to the industry, advising its leaders in 1785, for example, on how to present their case against Pitt's Irish propositions and later detailing

30. Harris, *The Copper King*, pp. 36-37; PRO, De Dunstanville to Lord ? , 25 May 1798, Pitt Papers, PRO 30/8/131, f. 117.

31. G. H. Guttridge, *The Early Career of Lord Rockingham, 1730-65* (Berkeley and Los Angeles, California, 1952), pp. 11, 16. P. Langford, *The First Rockingham Administration, 1765-1766* (Oxford, 1973), p. 112; C. Collyer, "The Rockinghams and Yorkshire Politics, 1742-61," *The Publications of the Thoresby Society*, XII, Part 4 (1953), 368.

32. R. J. S. Hoffman, *The Marquis: A Study of Lord Rockingham, 1730-1782* (New York, 1973), p. 12.

their specific objections in a speech delivered to the House of Lords.[33] However, Fitzwilliam was particularly attentive to the pleas of Pemberton Milnes, the whiggish head of Wakefield's leading mercantile family. Consequently, his interventions often reflected Milnes's point of view which was not necessarily that of the entire trade.[34]

In 1787-88 leaders of the Wiltshire and Somerset woollen industry introduced legislation to make more effective the prohibition on the export of raw wool.[35] While merchants and manufacturers of Leeds and other West Riding towns supported the measure, Milnes saw "some dark Black hidden work at the Bottom of this transaction." He feared, in fact, that west country manufacturers, jealous of Yorkshire's prosperity, were scheming to destroy their rival by barring coastal shipments of raw wool. Thus he urged Fitzwilliam and his friends to maintain a watch on the parliamentary machinations of the conniving west country men and to ensure that all those friendly to the needs of Yorkshire attended the House of Commons to oppose the bill. A meeting of merchants and manufacturers, held at Bradford in January, 1787, reiterated this plea, and through Fitzwilliam's intervention the Whig party committed its forces against the measure which failed to pass that session. Undaunted, the west country presented a new bill in the following session. Milnes again demanded resistance; in spite of modifications introduced to mollify the West Riding, in spite of Yorkshire's general support, Fitzwilliam therefore pressed for another postponement. Three years later the Earl again served as Milnes's spokesman, this time to oppose the Government's Russian policy and to repudiate its claims that the value of the woollen trade between the two countries was small.[36]

33. Sheffield Public Library, R. Parker to Fitzwilliam, 4 June 1785, Wentworth Woodhouse MSS, F65/26; *Parliamentary History*, XXV, 869-73 (18 July 1785).

34. T. Wemyss Reid, *The Life, Letters and Friendships of Richard Monckton Milnes, First Lord Houghton* (New York, 1891), I, 3, 5.

35. For more detailed discussion of the controversy surounding the proposals to permit the export of wool, see J. de L. Mann, *The Cloth Industry in the West of England from 1640 to 1880* (Oxford, 1971), pp. 268-70; J. H. Ramage, "The English Woollen Industry and Parliament, 1750-1830: A Study in Economic Attitudes and Political Pressure," (Ph.D. Thesis, Yale University, 1970), pp. 229-62; James Bischoff, *A Comprehensive History of the Woollen and Worsted Manufacturers* (London, 1842), I, 208-14, 241-44.

36. Northamptonshire Record Office, Milnes to Fitzwilliam, [1786], [Aug., 1786], 9 Nov. 1786, 10 Jan. 1787, Fitzwilliam Papers, Box 38; *ibid.*, Fitzwilliam to Portland, [undated], Fitzwilliam Papers, Box 38; *ibid.*, Portland to Fitzwilliam, 3 Feb. 1787, Fitzwilliam Papers, Box 38; *ibid.*, Milnes to Fitzwilliam, 20 Mar. 1788, Fitzwilliam Papers, Box 39; *Times*, June 12 1788; Sheffield Public Library, Milnes to Fitzwilliam, 29 Apr. 1791, Wentworth Woodhouse MSS, F65 (e)/70.

Ironically, however, Fitzwilliam's greatest electoral triumphs came only after he broke with larger merchants and manufacturers and rallied instead to the cause of the small clothiers. In 1802 weavers and cloth finishers in the west began a campaign to enforce the ancient corpus of legislation which regulated wages and the conditions of labor, a campaign which the clothiers of Yorkshire joined the next year. As a result of their efforts litigation blossomed, and large merchants and manufacturers, finding themselves deluged with suits, applied immediately for the repeal of these acts which were, in fact, suspended after 1802. Only in 1806, though, did the House of Commons begin seriously to confront the opposing demands; in that year a committee which included Yorkshire's members, William Wilberforce and Henry Lascelles, responded decisively in favor of repeal. The report in turn became the central issue at the Yorkshire elections of 1806 and 1807. Wilberforce was returned without difficulty, but Lascelles, who had been unsympathetic to the small clothiers from the start, lost two contests, the first to the independent William Fawkes, the second to Lord Milton, Fitzwilliam's son. At each election Fitzwilliam overcame the combined forces of the Harewood and manufacturing interests by exploiting the fierce resentment of the small producers.[37]

If Fitzwilliam's powerful presence proved to be a mixed blessing for the leading elements of the Yorkshire woollen industry, Staffordshire potters were fortunate in finding a number of loyal and adept aristocratic patrons. North and some of his colleagues were generally prepared to serve the trade,[38] but one minister in particular, Granville, Earl Gower, proved to be a most efficient spokesman. Gower, Staffordshire's leading political potentate, was on friendly terms with the county's foremost potter, Josiah Wedgwood. Political interest, territorial bonds, and personal friendship produced a fruitful partnership between his lordship and leaders of the local trade.[39] Thus, in 1767 Gower arranged that the attorney

37. R. G. Wilson, *Gentlemen Merchants*, pp. 169-71; E. A. Smith, "The Yorkshire Elections of 1806 and 1807; A Study in Electoral Management," *Northern History*, II (1967), 62-90.

38. R. A. Roberts (ed.), *Calendar of Home Office Papers, III (1770-72)* (London, 1888), 425; R. A. Roberts (ed.), *Calendar of Home Office Papers, IV (1773-75)* (London, 1889), 21-22; V. W. Bladen, "The Association of Manufacturers of Earthenware (1784-86)," *Economic History*, I (1928), 357.

39. Granville, Earl Gower (1721-1803), cr. Marquess of Stafford, 1786; Lord Lieutenant of Staffordshire, 1755-1800; Lord President of the Council, 1767-79, 1783-84; Lord Privy Seal, 1784-94. Namier and Brooke, *History of Parliament*, I, 374. According to one of his biographers, Wedgwood rode constantly to Trentham to visit his lordship. Meteyard, *Life of Wedgwood*, II, 177.

general of South Carolina, one of his nominees, would procure that colony's special clays for the potteries. Seven years later, when Wedgwood failed to modify Richard Chamberlain's bill extending a patent for fourteen years in the Commons, Gower and Lord Rockingham added amendments in the Lords which permitted Staffordshire to use the new process and the coveted Cornish clays. Finally, the Earl quickly settled a duty on Meissen porcelain in 1776 so that merchants could send out their commissions as early as possible.[40]

In addition to Gower, the potters, particularly the forceful Wedgwood, had a number of other noble supporters. "Many good and Able Lords," Wedgwood informed Matthew Boulton, were prepared to aid manufacturers in their struggle against the Irish commercial resolutions in 1785. On the eve of William Eden's departure to open negotiations with the French, Wedgwood "had very free, & pretty long conversations on the intended treaty with the D. of Portland & Ld. Stormont . . .," two Whig leaders who later opposed the results of Eden's diplomacy; and he corresponded with the ambassador about details affecting the potteries while the latter was in France.[41] Important potters were, in fact, among the most persistent advocates of new trade policies in the last decades of the eighteenth century, and Dr. McKendrick asserts that Wedgwood relied heavily upon his noble connections to secure the commercial arrangements he desired with Ireland, France, and later Sweden.[42]

Finally, in assessing the range and significance of the nobility's patronage it is important to examine the group's relationships not only with particular trades but also with major industrial centers. Among the latter Birmingham was, of course, one of the most important, and it had in Garbett and Matthew Boulton two of the most skillful industrial lobbyists of the age. But Birmingham and

---

40. A. Finer and G. Savage (eds.), *The Selected Letters of Josiah Wedgwood* (New York, 1965), pp. 55-56, 177-80, 199; Bladen, "Manufacturers of Earthenware," *Economic History*, I, 357-58. Rockingham's opposition to Chamberlain's bill probably arose from the fact that a small pottery, predecessor of the celebrated Rockingham works, had exploited the fine clays on his Swinton estate since 1745. B. and T. Hughes, *English Porcelain and Bone China, 1743-1850* (New York, 1968), pp. 233-34.

41. Assay Office Library, Birmingham, Wedgwood to Boulton, 31 May 1785, Boulton Papers; Lady Farrer (ed.), *Correspondence of Josiah Wedgwood: 1781-1794* (London, 1906), pp. 32-34; Bishop of Bath and Wells (ed.), *The Journal and Correspondence of William, Lord Auckland* (London, 1861), I, 133-36.

42. Bladen, "Manufacturers of Earthenware," *Economic History*, I, 356-67; N. McKendrick, "Josiah Wedgwood: An Eighteenth-Century Entrepreneur in Salesmanship and Marketing Techniques," *Econ. Hist. Rev.*, second series, XII (1960), 431.

its leaders also benefited immeasurably from the support of lords who espoused the whole range of projects that emerged from this creative, exuberant industrial metropolis.

Among these patrons, William, second Earl of Dartmouth, was perhaps the most active and useful. More than most men of his age the Earl was moved by a strong sense of territorial responsibility. During the 1760s and 1770s he was an important politician of the second rank, holding office in Rockingham's first Administration and later serving under his step-brother, Lord North.[43] His coal mines and canal ventures also brought him into contact with members of the Midlands industrial community, but he was most remarkable for his deep religious fervor — one which broadened and enriched his acquaintanceship and reinforced his abiding desire to assist his neighbors and friends by contributing "to the success of their designs."[44]

Impelled, then, by an obligation to his community as well as by his political and economic interests, Dartmouth gave substantial political assistance to the manufacturers of the Midlands. During the campaign against the Stamp Act, a campaign which received extensive support from industrial communities, the Earl worked with Samuel Garbett to mobilize opposition in and around Birmingham. It was to Dartmouth that Garbett wrote explaining the economic consequences of the Act, and the Earl was entrusted with a draft of the town's petition for relief in order that he might use it to convince others of the need for repeal. In 1772 Dartmouth helped to secure the passage of the Birmingham Canal Bill for its committee, and the next year he actively supported Matthew Boulton during the latter's drive to pass legislation authorizing the establishment of assay offices at Birmingham and Sheffield.[45]

Throughout the 1770s Boulton, in particular, received frequent and invaluable assistance from the Earl. Dartmouth not only rallied support for the bill to extend Watt's patent; on Boulton's instructions he also applied to North for his powerful backing. When a Mr. Jones of Bristol applied to the Privy Council to take

---

43. William, second Earl of Dartmouth (1731-1801), First Lord of Trade, 1765-66 and 1772-75; Secretary of State for Colonies, 1772-75; Lord Privy Seal, 1775-82; Lord Steward of the Household, 1783.

44. *Public Characters* (1798-99), p. 222; *H.M.C., Dartmouth MSS*, III, 189-90; Arthur Westwood, *The Assay Office at Birmingham, Part I: Its Foundation* (Birmingham, 1936), p. 25.

45. Langford, *The Rockingham Administration*, pp. 123-24; *H.M.C., Dartmouth MSS*, II, 32, 46-47; S. Broadbridge, "Monopoly and Public Utility: The Birmingham Canals, 1767-72," *Transport History*, V (1973), 235; Westwood, *The Assay Office*, p. 11.

out a patent on a machine which raised water by steam, his lordship immediately informed his friend. Though there was nothing
he could do to stop the application, he wished to apprise Boulton
of this potential competitor at the first possible opportunity.[46] Even
when Boulton applied for a licence to export steam engines to
France, with whom England happened to be at war, Dartmouth
was undaunted. Since the request would "undoubtedly require a
little serious consideration," he did not immediately commit himself. Still, the Earl professed to see no insuperable obstacles in
Boulton's way, and he promised, if the latter sent him a copy of
the memorial in advance, that he would ". . . talk with the Lord
President, & some of the members of the Council upon it, &
will advise you whether I think it will be complied with or not."
Clearly Boulton, and also other industrialists, had a most helpful
advocate in Dartmouth.[47]

Birmingham, however, never relied solely on Dartmouth's support, even while he remained in office. Boulton, who perceived
the political advantages which would accrue from an extensive
aristocratic acquaintanceship, cultivated peers at every opportunity. Eric Robinson has demonstrated that in lobbying for the
extension of Watt's patent Boulton ignored political affiliations in
his search for potential sources of support: the fifteen peers to
whom he applied for assistance constituted a rather mixed array
of Midland magnates, colliery owners, and Scottish associates of
Watt.[48] Moreover, once he had established valuable connections,
Boulton did not permit them to languish. To the contrary, old
allies were called upon again and again to serve Boulton or his
friends. Even as late as 1806 he applied to ten peers to support
the passage of a bill presented by the Birmingham Canal Company, and seven years earlier he had helped another friend to pass
a controversial enclosure bill by rounding up enough members to
outvote the measure's twenty-one opponents in the Lords' committee.[49]

But perhaps Boulton's greatest lobbying effort was one of his

---

46. Assay Office Library, Birmingham, Boulton to Dartmouth, 26 June 1773
(copy), 21 Feb. 1775, Boulton Papers; *ibid.,* Dartmouth to Boulton, 3 Jan. 1777,
Boulton Papers.

47. Birmingham Reference Library, Boulton to Dartmouth [1779], Boulton-
Watt Papers; *ibid.,* Dartmouth to Boulton, 6 Apr. 1779, Boulton-Watt Papers.

48. Eric Robinson, "Boulton and Parliamentary Lobbying," *Historical Journal,*
n.s. VII, 209-30.

49. Assay Office Library, Birmingham, Galton to Boulton, 13 June 1806,
Boulton Papers; *ibid.,* Notebook, 1806, fol. 14, Boulton Papers; *ibid.,* N. Edwards
to Boulton, 12 Mar., 12 July, 19 Nov. 1800, 1, 13 June 1801, Boulton Papers.

earliest — in support of a bill which would establish assay offices at Birmingham and Sheffield. As early as 1766 Lord Shelburne noted after a visit to Boulton's Birmingham establishment that an assay office would be of "infinite advantage" to the community. Five years later Shelburne received a more concrete reminder of Birmingham's needs: careless packing at the Chester office resulted in severe damage to candlesticks destined for his own table. Under such circumstances Boulton hardly needed to point out to his lordship the difficulties that stood in the way of one who aspired to be a great silversmith. The only solution, as he informed another illustrious peer, the Duke of Richmond, was to establish an assay office at Birmingham, and in 1773 Boulton presented the necessary legislation.[50]

The introduction of the Assay Office Bill naturally intensified the pace of Boulton's lobbying, but to a remarkable degree he concentrated on members of the peerage. Thus, at a conference in late December, 1772, he reported that the King and "many of the nobility" had expressed their support for his measure. Within a month Sheffield joined Birmingham with a petition of its own, and Boulton, who already had a powerful ally in Lord Dartmouth, gained two new advisers, the Marquess of Rockingham and the Duke of Norfolk. Even with these new adherents opposition mounted by the goldsmiths and silversmiths of London forced Boulton to continue his canvassing. While the bill was still in the Commons, he reported that he had twice as large an interest in the upper House, a considerable asset given the influence of some of his noble allies. Lord Derby, for example, took Boulton during the final stages of proceedings in the Commons "to several ministerial members pressing them to serve us." Moreover, when the Bill went up to the Lords, Boulton set aside all other business and concentrated his whole energies on canvassing the lords spiritual and temporal — forty of them according to a list in his papers.[51]

Even Boulton did not exhaust the supply of noblemen willing to serve Birmingham's interests. During the summer of 1784 Lord Rawdon twice intervened in behalf of Samuel Garbett and the Birmingham Metal Company. Despite his lack of parliamentary experience that peer was able, as a result of his maiden speech in

---

50. H. W. Dickinson, *Matthew Boulton* (Cambridge, 1937), pp. 64-65; Assay Office Library, Birmingham, Boulton to Richmond, 4 Dec. 1772, Boulton Papers.

51. Westwood, *The Assay Office, passim*; Robinson, "Boulton and Parliamentary Lobbying," *Historical Journal*, n.s. VII, 217-20; Assay Office Library, Birmingham, Notebook 10, fols. 7-8, Boulton Papers.

the House of Lords, to defeat a bill to permit the export of brass which Garbett and his allies had been unable to stop in the Commons. Vigorous canvassing also enabled Rawdon to outmaneuver Lord Effingham, the sponsor of the Sheffield Plate Bill, and to amend that measure in such a manner as to make it palatable to Garbett.[52]

Throughout the momentous struggles of 1785 Garbett continued to seek support among the peerage. Early in the year copies of a resolution against the excise, drafted by the Commercial Committee of Birmingham, were dispatched to Lords Dartmouth, Effingham, Ferrers, Hertford, Huntingdon, and the Bishop of Llandaff in hopes of enlisting their parliamentary support. Garbett also took great pains to induce Lord Dudley to oppose Pitt's propositions. Not only did he stress his lordship's close ties to Birmingham; he also pointed out that the nail workers tenanted on Dudley's estates might suffer severely if the measure carried. Thus, that peer, though normally a supporter of the Administration, opposed this controversial proposal.[53]

The range of their lordships' patronage extended beyond the industries and communities already discussed. Leaders in the chemical industry, who wished to manufacture alkali from salt but found themselves impeded by high duties, relied in part upon Lord Dudley to convince North of the wisdom of lowering the salt tax.[54] Bottle makers from the north of England delegated Lord Delaval, himself the proprietor of a large bottle works, to explain the peculiar problems of that trade to Pitt,[55] while Scottish distillers repeatedly expressed their gratitude to members of the nobility for endeavoring to relax the burden of repressive, iniquitous duties.[56] Even well-represented brewers appealed for assistance from local peers: brewing M.P.'s were, on the whole, drawn from the ranks of the London trade, and provincial brewers could

---

52. Birmingham Reference Library, Garbett to Lansdowne, 2 Oct. 1784, Garbett-Lansdowne Correspondence, I, fols. 64-65; Assay Office Library, Birmingham, Garbett to Boulton, 19 July 1784, Boulton Papers; H. Hamilton, *The English Brass and Copper Industries to 1800* (London, 1926), pp. 224-25.

53. Birmingham Reference Library, Garbett to Lansdowne, 9, 13 Feb. 1785, Garbett-Lansdowne Correspondence, I, fols. 131-32, 134-36; Assay Office Library, Birmingham, Garbett to Boulton, 8 June 1785, Boulton Papers; *Parliamentary History*, XXV, 835 (8 July 1785).

54. E. Robinson and D. McKie (eds.), *Partners in Science; Letters of James Watt and Joseph Black* (Cambridge, Mass., 1970), p. 99; A. and N. Clow, *The Chemical Revolution* (London, 1952), pp. 96-97.

55. PRO, Delaval to Pitt, 23 Feb. 1794, Pitt Papers, PRO 30/8/129, f. 85.

56. *Scots Magazine*, XLVI (1784), 551-52; *ibid.*, XLVII (1785), 203-4, 516-17; *ibid.*, XLVIII (1786), 47, 95, 357-58; *ibid.*, L (1788), 72-73, 251; Stockdale, *Parliamentary Debates*, III, 246-50, (18 Feb. 1785).

logically expect neighboring landowners, who provided them with their barley and malt, to be at least as sympathetic to and understanding of their problems as any Londoner.[57] Over the course of the late eighteenth century peers extended their patronage, if rather unevenly, across the face of industrial England, to new trades and old, to small producers and the greatest of the factory owners.

III

Over the past twenty years our perception of the nobility's role in the growing economy of the eighteenth century has broadened and been redefined. Peers, whose preoccupation with agriculture was overstressed by earlier historians, were not responsible in most instances for the discovery or diffusion of new techniques.[58] On the other hand, H. J. Habakkuk underestimates their importance when he suggests that the unpremeditated repercussions of large landowners' activities may have had the most decisive economic consequences.[59] Many noble lords had large capital resources, and a number used them productively — financing agricultural improvements, encouraging the expansion of mining and transport, developing urban areas.[60] Measured in economic terms, the ventures of large landlords at the very least helped to prepare the way for the industrial revolution; in areas such as North Wales, parts of Scotland, and the north of England, they provided the essential catalyst for this transformation.[61] At the same time the economic activities of the peerage and the larger gentry set an example for the community as a whole, helping thereby to legitimize the pursuit of wealth.[62] Finally, the peers' participation in

57. Mathias, *The Brewing Industry*, p. 337; Northumberland County Record Office, Northern Brewers to Delaval [no date], Delaval [Waterford] MSS, 2/DE 49/1.

58. G. E. Mingay, *English Landed Society in the Eighteenth Century* (London, 1963), pp. 163-88.

59. H. J. Habakkuk, "Economic Functions of Landowners in the Seventeenth and Eighteenth Centuries," *Explorations in Entrepreneurial History*, VI (1953), 99.

60. Mingay, *English Landed Society*, 189-201; Perkin, *The Origins of Modern English Society*, pp. 74-78; D. Spring, "English Landowners and Nineteenth-Century Industrialism" in *Land and Industry*, pp. 16-62.

61. A. H. Dodd, *The Industrial Revolution in North Wales* (Cardiff, 1971), p. 109; E. Richards, "Structural Change in a Regional Economy; Sutherland and the Industrial Revolution, 1780-1830," *Econ. Hist. Rev.*, XXVI (1973), 63-76; Smout, "Scottish Landowners and Economic Growth," *Scottish Journal*, XI, 229-30; E. Hughes, *North Country Life: Cumberland and Westmorland, 1700-1830* (London, 1965), *passim*.

62. D. Landes, *The Unbound Prometheus: Technological Change and Industrial Development in Western Europe from 1750 to the Present* (Cambridge, 1969), pp. 68-70; Perkin, *Origins of Modern English Society*, pp. 63-67; Wilson, *Gentlemen Merchants*, pp. 232-33; "Introduction", *Land and Industry*, p. 13.

industrial enterprises enabled them to rise above the parochial aspects of their own environment and to appreciate the qualities and aspirations of the leaders of commerce and industry.[63]

Historians of the British industrial revolution have argued that new manufacturers were fortunate to work in a generally friendly environment: instead of encountering hostile suspicion they received support, even encouragement. This accommodation between established interests and the new industrial communities had its political as well as its economic aspects. Time and again pioneers of the industrial revolution looked to Westminster to modify existing policies or to embark in directions more conducive to the needs of a growing economy. Time and again institutions dominated largely by landlords responded to those needs, in part because a large portion of the peerage intermittently lent its weight in support of the demands of the developing communities.[64]

Of course, members of the peerage were not single-minded champions of industrialists. The peers' patronage, extensive as it was, did not extend equally to all industries or into all parts of the country: unlike Birmingham, Lancashire and its cotton trade, for example, found relatively few noble advocates in these years.[65] Moreover, the cotton and other industries were sometimes thwarted by the petulant, even foolish opposition of lords.[66] Samuel Garbett, who received aid from so many peers, could still complain in 1784 that "from the Bulk of those Gentlemen who

---

63. Earl Spencer, for example, told his mother that a meeting of the committee of the Grand Junction Canal had enabled him to,

> become acquainted with an entire new set of People whose conversation is very entertaining & instructive in its way, but who are very much like a sort of amphibious Animal, as they are never easy without they can be dabbling in some Water Work or other, and are into the Bargain some of the greatest Jobbers in the Kingdom.

Althorp, Spencer to Dowager Countess Spencer, 6 June 1793, Spencer Papers, Box 12.

64. We know of at least sixty peers who maintained contacts with various industrial communities during these years. However, since this figure more accurately reflects the sources we consulted than contemporary realities, it is not a very reliable indicator of the incidence of this type of patronage within the group.

65. Even his rivals acknowledged that the twelfth Earl of Derby's criticisms of the Irish propositions in 1785 were impressive and forceful (*H.M.C., Rutland MSS*, III, 229-30). Yet, while he took part in local canal ventures and had his own cotton enterprises, he did not on any other occasion distinguish himself as the advocate of local economic interests.

66. For examples of their lordships' obstruction of canal legislation, see W. Addison, *Audley End* (London, 1953), pp. 141-43; J. R. Harris, "Early Liverpool Canal Controversies", in *Liverpool and Merseyside,* ed., J. R. Harris (London, 1969), p. 91; W. T. Jackman, *The Development of Transportation in Modern Britain* (London, 1962), p. 403; Malet, *The Canal Duke,* pp. 92-93.

compose the Landed Interest I do not expect Liberal Extensive
Comprehension. . . ."[67]

To understand these limitations as well as the strengths of the
nobility's industrial patronage, it is essential to appreciate what
factors and forces induced peers to espouse the causes of manufacturers. Among these, the skill and persistence of the industrialists themselves was an element of considerable importance.
Trade associations developed increasingly skillful lobbying techniques during the late eighteenth century, and outstanding manufacturers such as Garbett, Wedgwood, or Boulton were masters
of the art of persuasion. Groups as well as individuals cultivated
peers with whom they had business dealings, and the great industrialists all established personal ties with individual members of
the peerage.

However, peers had their own very potent reasons for responding to manufacturers' appeals. Most acknowledged some
obligation to advance projects which would benefit their neighborhoods. More importantly, the nobility shared economic interests in common with important industrial groups. Both united to
promote projects such as canals which would be mutually beneficial. Owners of extensive mineral resources were bound to be
somewhat sympathetic to the needs and well-being of their industrial customers, and a portion of the aristocracy maintained
industrial establishments themselves.

Of course, the nobility also expected to reap political advantages from its services. A rising politician such as Rockingham
believed that by demonstrating an understanding of and a sympathy for the needs of industrialists he would enhance his national political stature. His nephew, Fitzwilliam, and other Whig
peers eagerly supported manufacturers whenever they opposed
Pitt's policies as a means of extending the influence and prospects
of their party. Similarly, politicians in office attended closely to
the requests of important manufacturers who in turn provided
substantial, even invaluable support for the governments in which
they served.[68] Peers also assumed that their ability to protect local
industries would enlist new allies and reinforce old bonds, thereby
strengthening family political interests. Finally, a number of these

---

67. Birmingham Reference Library, Garbett to Lansdowne, 28 Aug. 1784,
Garbett-Lansdowne Correspondence, I, fols. 54-55.

68. In 1775, for example, Boulton was largely responsible for raising a
petition from Birmingham in support of the American War. He did so at least
partly at the instigation of his friend and patron, Lord Dartmouth. Assay Office
Library, Birmingham, Dartmouth to Boulton, 19 Jan. 1775, Boulton Papers.

men hoped that their effective performance as patrons would preserve the "standard of true aristocracy" and with it the constitution which accorded them such enormous power.[69]

Very often these territorial, economic, or political considerations were mutually reinforcing. The paternal duties of a landlord
corresponded in many instances with the responsibilities of a
borough patron and an active entrepreneur. Completely disinterested patronage, in fact, was almost non-existent: over the long
term patrons derived substantial economic and political benefits
from their activities. Moreover, while peers may have wished to
maintain a relatively harmonious balance between their needs and
those of the surrounding community, they did not feel bound on
all occasions to accept the advice of neighbors or supporters.
Economic self-interest induced some noblemen to sponsor enclosures, canals, drainage bills, or other projects which provoked considerable local opposition. To minimize potential damage to their
electoral interests, these peers argued, and not always ingenuous-
ly, that very real advantages would accompany the implementa-
tion of their proposals.[70] Capitalism did not in their minds involve
a repudiation of paternal responsibility. But in cases of conflict,
the political needs of a family interest usually gave way to the
economic requirements of the family patrimony.

It was the very diversity of the peers' interests which made
them less than totally reliable agents for Garbett and other industrialists. Even public-spirited peers like Dartmouth lacked the
single-minded commitment which would enable them to champion
all the causes of a particular trade. Whereas a businessman was
concerned primarily for the prosperity of his enterprises, peers
had to weigh the diverse needs of their estates, families, and neighbors, the demands of their political interests, even the directives
of political leaders in London. Therefore, manufacturers had to
expect that when their proposals encountered opposition from

69. The Duke of Portland told Earl Fitzwilliam that if the latter was not
in a position to provide direct answers to the applications of the various interests
of Yorkshire, representatives of those interests would not look upon the Earl as
a powerful figure. In consequence Fitzwilliam would lose much of his authority
within the county, an authority which Portland felt it was essential to preserve in
the mid-1790s. Sheffield Public Library, Portland to Fitzwilliam, 19 June 1794,
Wentworth Woodhouse MSS, F31 (b)/19.

70. The third Earl of Hardwicke, for example, carried the Eau Brink Drainage
Bill over the opposition of many of his tenants and political supporters. BM, C.
Yorke to Hardwicke, 23 Nov. 1795, Hardwicke Papers, Add. MS 35,392, fols.
255-56. His success was the result of compromise and skillful advocacy. BM, W.
Creasy to Hardwicke, 4 Nov. 1792, Hardwicke Papers, Add. MS 25,685, fols.
311-12; *ibid.*, Hardwicke to Sir Martin Holker, 2 Dec. 1794, Hardwicke Papers,
Add. MS 35,686, fols. 113-14.

other trades or communities, peers whom they had formerly regarded as their protectors might for personal, territorial, economic,
or political reasons support their rivals. The small number of
noblemen who themselves maintained large scale enterprises could
be counted upon to comprehend, if not always to uphold, the
principal interests of their fellow producers. But a man like Fitzwilliam supported or obstructed the projects of the more dynamic
segments of Yorkshire's industrial and mercantile communities at
least in part to promote the cause of his party and his personal
electoral interest, and his adversaries acted in a similar manner.[71]

If the need for consistent, informed spokesmen led to the formation of trade organizations, peers continued to render valuable
services for individual manufacturers as well as various trade
groups. The multitude of interests which sometimes made them
less than reliable spokesmen for industrial communities still probably enabled noblemen to be more attuned and responsive than
lesser landowners to the needs of developing industries. During
these years peers were active in exploiting their economic resources and in extending their political empires. Indeed, wealth
and power combined at once to make members of the nobility
both sensitive to the aspirations of manufacturers and knowledgeable, effective patrons. Time and again they were able not only
to secure for their clients the cooperation of government and parliament but also to ensure, as no trade organization could ensure,
that those institutions legislated or modified policy according to
the needs of the communities they served. In so doing the nobility helped to bridge the gap between the traditional eighteenth-
century political nation and the new industrial communities.

To look beyond the reality of the nobility's patronage and
measure its economic consequences is impossible save in the most
general manner. Economic historians continue to debate whether
major acts of state advanced or impeded economic growth. Yet,
it would be far more difficult to ascertain with any precision the

71. At the general election of 1790 Fitzwilliam was able to return Lord Burford as a member for Hull in part because of his alliance with the proprietors of
the local dock. In 1787 the Earl had helped to defeat a bill which would have
had the town take over that facility, and during the 1790s he joined with the proprietors in opposing the extension of the dock. Northamptonshire Record Office,
W. Hammond to Fitzwilliam, 5 May 1787, Fitzwilliam Papers, Box 34; *ibid.*,
Burford to Fitzwilliam, 12 Feb. 1794, *ibid.*, Box 46; *ibid.*, H. Ethrington to
Burford, 15 Sept. 1794, *ibid.*, Box 46; Jackson, *Hull*, pp. 250-58. Those who
wished to extend the dock facilities received support from the fifth Duke of Leeds
who even carried the case to Pitt. BM, Leeds to Pitt, 23 May 1795 (copy),
Egerton MSS, Eg. 3506, f. 46; Northamptonshire Record Office, Leeds to Fitz-
william, 14 Feb. 1794, Fitzwilliam Papers, Box 46.

impact of the host of minor measures sponsored by members of the peerage, particularly since gains achieved by one trade might be made at the expense of others.

On balance, however, it is probably true that peers advanced more often than they impeded the goals of industrialists. Projects were sometimes obstructed because of their lordships' opposition, but as a body the nobility lent impressive support to the whole range of issues raised by leading manufacturers. Peers helped to secure the passage of much important legislation — measures such as the Birmingham Assay Office Bill which encouraged local trades or, on another level, the multitude of canal acts which, when taken together, formed an essential underpinning for that vital, new transport network. They labored to rearrange the details as well as the broader scope of commercial policy, to modify the ancient labor code, and to prevent increases in the excise on raw materials and finished products. Modern historians may dismiss many of the acts or policy changes noblemen helped to obtain as being insignificant in economic terms, but for contemporary manufacturers such measures often seemed vital to the future prosperity of their trades. Thus, the accessibility of noble politicians and territorial magnates to men such as Garbett, Boulton, or Wedgwood, and their ability to arrange matters quickly and to their clients' tastes, enormously facilitated the operation of large scale business enterprises.

Ultimately, however, the political significance of the peers' patronage may have outweighed its economic consequences. In supporting some of the manufacturers' important demands, peers demonstrated the vitality at once of the eighteenth-century patronage system and the political institutions which rested upon it. Their activities belie the notion, expressed by some historians, that parliament was hostile or at best indifferent to the needs and interests of new industrial communities.[72] Their involvement in the political business of manufacturers and their demonstrated capacity to shape policy according to the latter's needs also contradicts John Ehrman's claim that the governing classes had a low opinion of the competence of industrialists to offer sound economic advice, particularly as it affected their own trades.[73] In the end

---

72. Bowden argued that governments were biased against new industries, at least before 1785 (Bowden, *Industrial Society,* pp. 141-93). Dr. Schofield simply assumed that parliament was indifferent to or suspicious of manufacturers' claims (R. E. Schofield, *The Lunar Society of Birmingham* (Oxford, 1963), p. 9).

73. J. Ehrman, *The British Government and Commercial Negotiations with Europe* (Cambridge, 1962), pp. 183-84.

statesmen determined what national policy would be, but the peers' advocacy of a variety of industrial interests helped to ensure that policy would consider those interests. An efficient patronage network thus enabled parliament to transcend some of the more obvious defects of the late eighteenth-century representative system.

THE GROWTH OF DEMOCRACY
1860 – 1911

BIBLIOGRAPHICAL NOTE

THE GROWTH OF DEMOCRACY (1860-1911)

[The numbers in brackets refer to items in the bibliography, above pp xvii-xxix. Chapter numbers refer to the essays printed below.]

Despite the fact that the Prime Minister sat in the Lords for over a third of Victoria's reign, we still await a definitive study of the Victorian house. An excellent brief account has been written by Le May (162).

Attention has largely been devoted to the membership of the house. Pumphrey studied the changes in the social structure of the aristocracy both through internal adjustment as well as by the creation of new peerages without landed wealth (169-170). The peers who departed from the Liberal Party over Home Rule are the subject of an article by Phillips who argues that their voting patterns show they formed, for a number of years, a separate force in the House before they merged into the Conservative Party (172). The attempt to create life peers is examined by Anderson who concludes that the failure of the government's proposal reflected a lack of management rather than an indication of the conservative power of the Lords (159-60). The only reform in the Lords during this period was the abandonment of proxy voting (146).

Relations between a Conservative House of Lords and a Liberal House of Commons led Lord Salisbury to develop the doctrine that the Lords had the duty to insist on referring a measure to the electorate when there were grounds for believing that the Commons lacked a mandate. Weston argues that this doctrine had a major influence on defeating Liberal measures and appears to have strengthened the Lords (chapter 21). This view is largely confirmed by Le May (162). The resolution of the dispute between the Lords and Commons over Irish disestablishment and which led to the Salisbury doctrine has been described by Fair (168); this article is reprinted in his *British Interparty Conferences* (Oxford, 1980).

Le May suggests that the influence of the Salisbury doctrine eventually led to the rejection of the budget of 1909. The most detailed account of the conflict between the two houses during Asquith's government is *Mr Balfour's Poodle* by Roy Jenkins, a study based on printed sources (176). Shorter accounts have been written by Cromwell (177) and Le May (178); the latter's sources include documents in the Royal Archives.

The right-wing section of the Conservative opposition has been exhaustively studied by Phillips (179-181) who argues that the 'die-hards', the 112 peers who voted against the third reading of the Parliament Bill, were not 'backwoodsmen' but were active politicians. Phillips has produced a valuable account of a section of the peerage but his attempt to define their beliefs as radical conservative rather than reactionary is not convicing. The influence of the 'die-hards' on the Conservative party is analysed by Fanning (182).

Weston describes the differences among the Liberal leadership over the method of limiting the Lords' veto (chapter 22). Thirty-seven Conservative peers voted with the government for the Parliament Bill; they are usually known as the 'rats' or the 'Judas group'. It was believed that Lord Curzon persuaded these peers to vote with the government as the Conservative leadership in the Lords was determined to avoid a mass creation of peers. Southern argues that this important role was played by Lord Newton, a backbencher, who was chosen by the leadership to save them from an impossible situation and to conceal their own actions (chapter 23). Weston and Kelvin agree with Southern that the opposition leadership were well in control of events during the crisis. However, they award the crucial role in forming the 'Judas group' to Lord Cromer (chapter 24).

Despite the wealth of sources, especially a reasonably accurate account of debates in the Lords, the publication of research on the history of the House of Lords between the Reform Act of 1832 and the Parliament Bill of 1911 has been disappointing. We have already indicated that a number of valuable dissertations have been written and it is hoped that the results of this research will be made more generally available.

21

SALISBURY AND THE LORDS,

1868-1895 *

CORINNE COMSTOCK WESTON

During the period from the Reform Act of 1832 to the early 1880s, when a change set in, the house of lords was perceptibly weaker than the house of commons.[1] The prevailing view of its position, accepted for the most part even

* This research was supported (in part) by a grant from the Faculty Research Award Program of the City University of New York.

[1] H. J. Hanham, *The nineteenth century constitution, 1815-1914* (Cambridge, 1969), p. 172. The Reform Act of 1832 introduced a new era in the history of the house of lords, partly because of its provisions but also because of the manner in which it passed. When Lord Grey threatened the house of lords with a large creation of peers if it continued to oppose the Reform Bill, he dealt a body blow to the prevailing theory of mixed government which held that the house of lords was a co-ordinate estate with an independent legislative power. To be sure, no new peers were created, but enough peers abstained on the critical vote for the measure to become law, and it was evident that the Grey government and the house of commons had won a great victory while the king and the house of lords had suffered a great defeat. The peers' anguish deepened when the reformed electorate returned a large reforming majority of Whigs and Radicals in the general election of 1832-3; and the house of lords, seeking to reassert its legislative independence, now adopted an obstructionist course in its dealings with the reformed house of commons. The situation was full of danger to the house of lords, and it even seemed for a time as if the Whigs would be compelled to reform that house. That this was not the outcome was due to the emergence of the organized two-party system, in particular to the growing co-operation between Sir Robert Peel and the duke of Wellington, who commanded the Conservative forces in their respective houses. The political necessities of party overrode the combative instincts of the house of lords, and by the middle of the 1830s the peers had found more subtle ways of asserting their independence. The house of lords became passive after Peel took office in 1841. Though the harmony between the two houses was threatened in 1846, when repeal of the Corn Laws was at issue, the peers accepted Peel's measure at the instance of the leadership in both political parties. Lord John Russell held office between 1846 and 1851, at a time when the Conservative party was in disarray, but the scenes of the post-1832 period were not repeated, perhaps because Whig reforming zeal had slackened. No great political issues divided the parties after 1846, and the house of lords now sank into the somnolence to which contemporary observers called attention at mid-century. Norman Gash, *Reaction and reconstruction in English politics 1832-1852* (Oxford, 1965), chapters II and v. See also Olive Anderson, 'The Wensleydale Peerage Case and the position of the house of lords in the mid-nineteenth century', *English Historical Review*, LXXXII, 324 (July 1967), 486-502, for denial that the behaviour of the house of lords in 1856 constituted a reassertion of that house's political strength and 'its re-emergence as a redoubtable Conservative stronghold'. Not the revival of the house of lords but such factors as ministerial ineptitude and carelessness explain why life peers were not added at this time to the house of lords. That house displayed signs of a renewed energy once more in 1860 by rejecting Gladstone's Paper Duties Bill, only to be circumvented in 1861 when he consolidated all taxation measures in a single Finance Bill that the peers felt obliged to accept (G. H. L. Le May, *The Victorian constitution: conventions, usages and contingencies* (London, 1979), pp. 132-3). By 1869 the two houses were in opposition on the Irish church question, and to this subject it is necessary to return at a later stage in this article.

by the peers themselves, was expressed in Walter Bagehot's highly influential *English constitution* (1867, rev. 1872), where the house of lords is described as safe from rough destruction but not from inner decay, the danger coming not so much from assassination as atrophy, not from abolition but decline. This description drew on Bagehot's distinction between the dignified and efficient parts of the constitution. The house of lords belonged to the first category: that house in its dignified capacity inspired a reverence in the people that attached them to the government. Yet, paradoxically, in view of the great respect for the aristocracy, the house of lords had been subordinate as a legislative chamber to the house of commons even before the Reform Act of 1832; and since then this subordination had grown ever more pronounced.[2]

Not that the theory of the constitution – to Bagehot, a literary theory – took stock of the political reality. That theory treated the house of lords as a co-ordinate estate of the realm, equal in rank to the house of commons. So far was this from being the case that a capital excellence of the English constitution was its provision for an upper house, not of equal authority with the lower house but yet with some authority. The flaw in a system of two co-ordinate houses was that a single house might stop legislation and bring the machine of government to a standstill. Fortunately, this danger had been averted in England where the cabinet, its power based on the powerful house of commons, had the means of making final decisions. 'There ought to be in every constitition an available authority somewhere,' wrote Bagehot, and this 'sovereign power must be come-at-able.'[3] That the English government possessed this salient characteristic had received public demonstration during the passing of the Reform Bill of 1832 when the Grey government, in concert with the king and the house of commons, compelled the house of lords to accept that measure. Since then the function of the house of lords had altered. Earlier, 'if not a directing chamber, at least a chamber of directors', it was now 'a revising and suspending house'. Bagehot spelled out its limited legislative power:

It can alter bills; it can reject bills on which the house of commons is not yet thoroughly in earnest – upon which the nation is not yet determined. Their veto is a sort of hypothetical veto. They say, 'We reject your bill for this once or these twice, or even these thrice: but if you keep on sending it up, at last we won't reject it.'[4]

A revising and leisured house of this type was very useful, if not quite necessary.[5]

To this description was added an account of Wellington as the politician-statesman who had presided over the constitutional change with a minimum of damage to the country. In the pages of the *English constitution* appeared the celebrated letter written by the duke to Lord Stanley (later fourteenth earl of Derby and prime minister), relating how he had persuaded hostile peers to stay away from the house of lords so that the Reform Bill could become law, and

[2] *The English constitution* (Ithaca, New York, 1966), pp. 121, 125–6, 128, 132, 149.
[3] Ibid. pp. 126–7.   [4] Ibid. p. 128.   [5] Ibid. p. 134.

had afterwards worked to lessen conflict between his house and the reformed house of commons. He had guided the peers to what Bagehot considered their true position. In this way the house of lords had become 'a chamber with (in most cases) a veto of delay with (in most cases) a power of revision, but with no other rights or powers'.[6]

Both Wellington and Bagehot assumed that the house of lords must take its direction from the house of commons as the nation's spokesman. Until the early 1880s, when the lords became noticeably more assertive,[7] Liberals and Conservatives alike accepted this description; and the Liberal party continued to subscribe to it long afterward, acting on this premise in passing the Parliament Act of 1911.[8] But not the Conservative party. Its members by this time preferred the very different view of the house of lords advanced by Lord Salisbury, the Conservative peer of distinguished lineage who was thrice prime minister in late Victorian England. Whenever his party was in opposition he relied on what may be called a referral or referendal theory to cripple Liberal legislation.[9] According to its tenets, the house of lords had a referendal function: it had the duty of referring measures to the electorate or nation whenever important questions arose and there was ground for believing that the government, resting on the house of commons, lacked a mandate for its measures. Only if a mandate was forthcoming would or should the house of lords permit a disputed measure on a vital question to pass into law. The most

---

[6] Ibid. pp. 129–31. Wellington's letter circulated widely in the well-known biographies of the duke written by A. H. Brialmont and George Gleig and published in the 1850s and 1860s. Brialmont's work appeared in French in 1856 and between 1858 and 1860 in Gleig's translation. In 1862 the latter published his own study of Wellington, which went through a people's edition. *The life of Arthur first duke of Wellington* (London, 1862), pp. 569–72.

[7] Hanham, *The nineteenth century constitution*, p. 173.

[8] It underlay the provisions of the Parliament Act of 1911. See also Prime Minister Asquith's speech of 2 Dec. 1909 after the house of lords rejected the Finance Bill. *Parliamentary debates* (commons), fifth series, XIII, 556–7 and his speech of 21 Feb. 1911 introducing the Parliament Bill. Ibid. XXI, 1748–9.

[9] One sees references to the referendal authority, the referendal function, and the referendal capacity of the house of lords. The 'referendal theory of the house of lords' seems not to have been used but is logical. See, for example, J. A. R. Marriott, *English political institutions* (Oxford, third edition, 1925), XII, 164. Among the few modern scholars who have recognized the importance of this subject are Robert Taylor, *Lord Salisbury* (London, 1975), pp. 34, 39, 76–7 and, more fully, Le May, *Victorian constitution*, pp. 133–45. The subject is not discussed in such modern works as Lord Blake's lecture on Salisbury in his *Conservative party from Peel to Churchill* (London, 1970), pp. 131–66; Paul Smith's introduction to his *Lord Salisbury on politics: A selection from his articles in the Quarterly Review, 1860–1883* (Cambridge, 1972), pp. 1–109 and Peter Marsh, *The discipline of popular government: Lord Salisbury's domestic statecraft, 1881–1902* (Sussex, 1978). Smith does note the presence of this kind of reasoning in Salisbury's last article ('Disintegration') in the *Quarterly Review* but underestimates its importance and as a consequence devotes very little attention to it: *Lord Salisbury on politics*, p. 102. Basic materials are in Lady Gwendolen Cecil, *Life of Robert marquis of Salisbury* (London, 1921), II, 23–7. Hanham has reprinted the key portion of Salisbury's important speech of 17 June 1869, but his interpretation is seriously misleading: *The nineteenth century constitution*, pp. 172, 183–5. See also Sidney Low, *The governance of England* (London, 1919), pp. 224–6. Low considered that this usage left the peers with only a limited and suspensory veto. Ibid. p. 223. This was not Salisbury's opinion. Low's *Governance of England*, published originally in 1904, went through five editions by 1919.

striking aspect of the referendal theory was the insistence that the political barometer for the peers to watch was not the house of commons – so central to Wellington and Bagehot – but the nation itself. To the nation the house of lords should look for guidance and direction; and only to the nation's will, as registered at the polls, would that house bow. But that it would bow to the nation's will was stated over and over again. 'This may be taken to be a settled convention', wrote Sir William Anson, 'on which the house of lords will act, in contrast to their action in 1832.'[10]

Salisbury developed the theory in a series of speeches, delivered over a generation of politics, sometimes at Westminster but at other times before large audiences in the industrial cities. The style of his argument appears from his speech of 8 July 1884 in the house of lords, recommending the rejection of the third Reform Bill ostensibly on the ground that Gladstone had failed to couple the extension of the franchise with a redistribution of seats in the house of commons. The issue should go to the electorate for settlement. To the peers he declared:

In the presence of such vast proposals we appeal to the people... If it is their judgment that there should be enfranchisement without redistribution, I should be very much surprised: but I should not attempt to dispute their decision. But now that the people have in no real sense been consulted, when they had, at the last general election [in 1880], no notion of what was coming upon them, I feel that we are bound, as guardians of their interests, to call upon the goverment to appeal to the people, and by the result of that appeal we will abide.[11]

Such a house of lords was unknown to Wellington and Bagehot.

Despite the unblushing partisanship with which the referendal theory was exercised, the house of lords now had at hand, for the first time, a democratic rationale for its legislative veto. Here was a truly indispensable acquisition, one well suited to the age of mass politics that followed the second Reform Act; and it opened up new possibilities for the house of lords, especially after the Irish question became prominent in English politics. Skilfully exploited by Conservative politicians, the referendal theory goes far to explain the increasingly aggressive spirit that Conservative peers displayed in late Victorian England. Among the contemporary observers who remarked on the striking change in the house of lords was J. A. Hobson when he wrote in 1909: 'No English Liberal of the 'seventies would have deemed it possible that so evidently obsolescent an organ of government as the house of lords should, within a single generation, have come to show so vigorous a spirit of

---

[10] *The law and custom of the constitution* (Oxford, 4th edn, 1909), I, 286. Although Anson was a Conservative partisan in the struggle over the Parliament Bill and the third Home Rule Bill, his statement was by this time a commonplace in political literature: William Sharp McKechnie, *The reform of the house of lords* (Glasgow, 1909), pp. 19, 20.

[11] *Hansard*['s *parliamentary debates*], third series, ccxc, 468–9. Salisbury was working in 1884 for a dissolution of parliament and a general election: Corinne Comstock Weston, 'The royal mediation in 1884', *English Historical Review*, LXXXII (1967), 296–322. See also Salisbury's article 'Disintegration' (1883), reprinted in Paul Smith, *Lord Salisbury on politics*, pp. 335–76, in particular, 101–3, 345–70.

encroachment.'[12] It was, then, a legislative chamber with an outlook and attitude very different from the one in Bagehot's *English constitution* that harassed the Liberal house of commons after 1906.

II

Any satisfactory account of Salisbury's reasons for taking up the referendal theory, and the circumstances in which he did so, must take into consideration the qualities of personality, temperament and intellect that made him so formidable a political figure in late Victorian England. A strong will, an intense emotional commitment to the house of lords extending over a long career in politics, a combativeness of temperament approaching recklessness, at least in his early political career, and a high intelligence, critical and questioning in its nature – qualities such as these made it impossible for Salisbury, after fourteen years in the house of commons, to sit in the elegant and empty house of lords without making a strenuous effort to strengthen its power and authority. At the same time Gladstone's mastery of the house of commons, in contemporary esteem so much the more powerful house, could only have rankled with him and added impetus to his drive to elevate the position of the house of lords.[13]

[12] *The crisis of liberalism: new issues of democracy* (London, 1909), p. vii. The Liberals contrasted Wellington's leadership with Salisbury's, to the latter's disadvantage: H. H. Asquith, *Fifty years of British parliament* (Boston, 1926), I, 239; Le May, *The Victorian constitution*, pp. 136–7; and the remarks in 1888 of Lord Granville, for more than a generation the Liberal leader in the house of lords. Granville also noted that Lord Aberdeen and Lord Beaconsfield (Disraeli) had been animated by a different spirit from Salisbury: *Hansard*, third series, cccxxiii, 1602. Salisbury defended the partisanship with which the referendal theory was used. See, for example, his speech at Liverpool, reported in *The Times* (14 Apr. 1882), p. 6. The Conservative attachment to the referendal theory in the early twentieth century can be seen in the formula that Lord Lansdowne used in moving the rejection of Lloyd George's Finance Bill in the lords on 22 Nov. 1909. He moved 'that this house is not justified in giving its consent to the Bill until it has been submitted to the judgment of the country'. The subject is discussed by Neal Blewett, *The peers, the parties and the people* (Toronto, 1972), pp. 98–9. The formula was very carefully prepared: ibid. p. 99; J. S. Sandars to Lansdowne, 6 Nov. 1909, Balfour papers, Add. MS 49730, fos. 21–6; Lansdowne to Arthur Balfour, 10 Nov. 1909, fos. 27–8; Balfour to Lansdowne, telegram, 11 Nov. 1909, fo. 29; and Lansdowne to Balfour, 13 Nov. 1909, fos. 30–1. For a similar formulation see the official opposition amendments in 1913 and 1914, intended to explain the lords' rejection of the third Home Rule Bill: *Parl. deb.* (lords), fifth series, xiv, 869, 881, 965; xv, 12. Also, Asquith, *Fifty years of British parliament*, II, 149.

[13] To Lord Blake, Salisbury was 'the most formidable intellectual figure that the Conservative party has ever produced': *Disraeli* (London, 1966), p. 499. Smith considers that Salisbury's combative instincts at times exceeded reasonable bounds: *Lord Salisbury on politics*, p. 8. Smith's study should also be consulted for its analysis of Salisbury's political thought, in particular his view of politics as class struggle. No attempt has been made to deal with the matter here. For Salisbury's longstanding distrust of Gladstone see L. P. Curtis, *Coercion and conciliation in Ireland* (Princeton, 1963), pp. 67–8. See in addition note 60 below. Also to be noted is Salisbury's attitude towards the house of commons, which he left reluctantly in 1868 on the death of his father, and proceeded thereafter to treat with an air of great contempt. According to Henry Lucy, 'whenever in debate he was compelled to allude to it, he managed to throw into his tone a note of contempt that greatly amused commoners thronging the bar, or privy councillors standing on the steps of the throne'. Lucy thought this attitude one of pure affectation: *Memories of eight parliaments*

Salisbury's attempt to strengthen the house of lords gained momentum after 1880, especially when home rule for Ireland became the leading question in politics. But the particular form that his attempt would take was determined much earlier in his career, as early in fact as his experience at Westminster in the immediate years after the Derby–Disraeli government, to his deep displeasure, passed the Reform Act of 1867. In the post-1867 era – at a time when Salisbury was at odds with the leadership of his party – Gladstone sponsored two controversial measures: the first of these, the Suspensory Bill of 1868, which did not become law; the other, the Irish Church Bill, based on the Suspensory Bill, which disestablished the Irish church in 1869. Out of the party struggles over the Irish church came the referendal theory that distinguished the late Victorian house of lords; and when Salisbury, at this juncture, made a decisive and important contribution not only to it formulation but also to its future credibility, he made that theory to all intents and purposes his own.

The antecedents of the Suspensory Bill, which throw much light on the emergence of the new theory, are found in the months between the passing of the second Reform Bill into law in August 1867 and the general election of November 1868. Midway through the period Derby resigned as prime minister and was replaced by Disraeli, his faithful lieutenant, as the head of what was essentially a caretaker government. Handicapped by having only a minority support in the house of commons, he was determined nevertheless to persist in office until a general election could be held under the new electoral arrangements. The second Reform Act applied only to England, and similar legislation still pended for Ireland and Scotland. Once this was enacted and the voting registers prepared, the Conservatives planned to brave the electoral waters and learn who would govern England. Meanwhile, its labours incomplete, the Disraeli government clung to office.

From this unusual situation came the Suspensory Bill and not long afterwards the referendal theory. In fact, the whole sequence of events is pertinent. A few days after Disraeli took office, an Irish member moved to draw attention to the state of Ireland; and Disraeli, playing for time, responded with

(London, 1908), p. 121. But this was not the opinion of Sir Michael Hicks Beach, an experienced politician with ample opportunity to observe Salisbury. He considered that the latter had 'small respect for the opinions of the house of commons, and constantly chafed against his obligation as prime minister to support in the lords proposals to which his colleagues in the commons had been obliged to agree': cited in Hanham, *The nineteenth century constitution*, p. 68. Another contemporary, Lord Stanley, later fifteenth earl of Derby, wrote of Salisbury shortly after he entered the house of lords that he 'seems to feel himself at home in the lords, which he never did altogether in the commons': *Disraeli, Derby and the Conservative party: journals and memoirs of Edward Henry, Lord Stanley 1849–1869*, ed. John Vincent (New York, 1978), p. 335. There is also relevant comment in A. L. Kennedy, *Salisbury, 1830–1903: portrait of a statesman* (London, 1953), p. 75. But Kennedy's statement that Salisbury had no desire to strengthen the house of lords in relationship to the house of commons is mistaken, as is his comment that Salisbury was willing to accept the will of the house of commons as supreme. Contemporaries dated a change in the house of lords from Salisbury's entrance: *The Times* (9 June 1869), p. 9; *The Saturday Review*, xxvii (26 June 1869), 829

the denial that the present house of commons was morally competent to deal with a question that had not been placed before the electorate in 1865. That is, it had no mandate. 'This objection', according to Erskine May, 'raised an important constitutional issue; and by a singular inversion of parts Mr Disraeli now appeared as the champion of the democratic theory of the mandate, while Mr Gladstone, perceiving an obstacle in his path and eager to overthrow it, maintained with his customary passionate eagerness, the uncontrolled right of parliament to deal with what subjects it pleased.'[14] After Gladstone introduced several resolutions preparatory to disestablishing the Irish church, including a resolution affirming the desirability of an immediate disestablishment, Disraeli sponsored a temporizing amendment, known as the Stanley amendment, to the effect that the house of commons, while admitting that considerable modifications in the temporalities of the Irish church might after the impending inquiry appear to be expedient, was 'of opinion that any proposition tending to the disestablishment or disendowment of that church ought to be reserved for the decision of a new parliament'.[15]

It was Gladstone, however, not Disraeli, who shaped the course of events at this point. Rejecting the Stanley amendment, the house of commons approved Gladstone's resolutions and thus opened the way for the Suspensory Bill, which suspended appointments to the Irish church for a year. As political defeat once more loomed, while the need to gain time remained imperative, Disraeli decided to pass the Bill through the house of commons and leave rejection to the house of lords. After clearing the house of commons with impressive majorities, the Suspensory Bill went to the house of lords; and that house, basing itself on the democratic rationale so conveniently supplied by Disraeli, now fulfilled its assigned role. It rejected the Suspensory Bill, but only after a series of speakers had enunciated the main lines of a referendal function for the house of lords.

Conspicuous in their ranks was Salisbury, newly arrived in the house of lords. In his speech of 26 June 1868, which commanded much contemporary attention, he crisply advised the rejection of the Suspensory Bill. His fellow peers should disregard the majorities in the house of commons and reject this crude and violent measure, despite the warning from the Liberal Lord Clarendon that they should pay closer attention to public opinion and to those majorities. He then proceeded to separate the house of commons from the country at large and to advance the daring proposition that on a given occasion the house of lords might be more representative of public opinion than the house of commons. Dismissing Clarendon's warning contemptuously, Salisbury wondered aloud whether the Liberal leader had ever considered the purpose for which the house of lords existed. To become 'a mere echo and tool of the house of commons was slavery'. To be sure, the house of lords must yield its

---

[14] *May's constitutional history of England*, ed. and cont. to 1911 by Francis Holland (London, 1912), III, 206-7. For Salisbury's view in 1892 see Marsh, *The discipline of popular government*, p. 222, and Curtis, *Coercion and conciliation*, p. 398.

[15] *Hansard*, third series, CXCI, 507.

opinion when the sustained convictions of the country clearly favoured a particular course, but this was a very different action from echoing the house of commons. It was not easy to ascertain the country's opinion, and it was conceivable that the house of lords might be more successful in this respect than the house of commons. And he then recalled that thirty years earlier, with the tide running against the Irish church, the house of commons had sent measures to the house of lords reflecting this hostility. But after the house of lords rejected these measures, the nation had become apathetic on the question. 'In course of time it turned out that you were right,' Salisbury told the peers triumphantly. 'You knew the opinion of the nation better than the house of commons.' This example demonstrated the necessity of determining the nation's opinion before acting in favour of the Bill, and it was the lords' duty to take a course marked no less by firmness than prudence.[16]

The last speaker for the Conservatives was Lord Chancellor Cairns, an intimate friend of Disraeli and Conservative leader in the house of lords during the parliamentary session of 1869. An Ulsterman, who had earlier sat for Belfast in the house of commons, he made at this time a long speech defending the Irish church and attacking the Suspensory Bill that was printed, widely distributed, and much admired. Urging the peers to reject the Suspensory Bill as an attack on property, the supremacy of the crown, the interests of protestantism, and peace in Ireland, Cairns concluded on this significant note:

My lords, these are the vast issues involved in this Bill. These are the issues involved in your lordships' decision now, and they are the issues yet to be presented to the country in the great appeal to its enlarged constituencies...In that appeal...the government will stand as the defenders of all that this Bill and the policy of its promoters would seek to overthrow.

By the result of the appeal to the constituencies the government would abide.[17]

The rejection came on 29 June 1868, the peers sending the Suspensory Bill to the country with generously worded pledges to accept the electoral results. According to *The Times*, the house of lords had remitted 'the question of the Irish church to the constituencies of the kingdom'.[18] Little wonder that late Victorian Englishmen, harking back to this episode, considered that the house of lords had deliberately and self-consciously acted out the tenets of the referendal theory in rejecting the Suspensory Bill.[19] Yet the theory was at this time only in the process of gestation, its appearance almost accidental. It was, as has been seen, the product of a fortuitous combination of circumstances

---

[16] Ibid. CXCIII, 88–90. Writing in the *Central Literary Magazine* (1903–4), p. 150, Isaac Bradley described the part of Salisbury's speech where it was said the peers would yield their opinion when the country's sustained convictions favoured a course as 'the celebrated statement, now accepted, practically, by all parties, as to the true position of the upper house'.

[17] *Hansard*, third series, CXCIII, 288.

[18] *The Times* (30 June 1868), p. 11. 'The defenders as well as the opponents of the Irish establishment...appeal to the nation', ran another passage.

[19] Bradley, *Central Literary Magazine*, pp. 149–50. There is a Victorian interpretation of the events of 1868–9, published between the third Reform Act and the first Home Rule Bill, in F. S. Pulling, *The life and speeches of the marquis of Salisbury* (London, 1885), I, 125–9.

arising out of the minority position of the Conservative party in the post-1867 house of commons and the politics of improvisation as Disraeli sought to lengthen his tenure of office and enhance his party's electoral prospects.

The only important issue in the election was the disestablishment of the Irish church, and Gladstone won a ringing endorsement from the newly enlarged electorate when the Liberals were returned to Westminster with the impressive majority of 112. Recognizing the significance of the electoral result and fully aware of his government's choice of language before the general election,[20] Disraeli resigned before parliament met, taking his dismissal as it were from the electorate rather than the house of commons and thus inaugurating a new era in politics. According to Erskine May, it was 'the first open acknowledgment of the truth that a ministry in reality derives its commission from the electorate'.[21] Gladstone now acted swiftly to carry out the electoral commitment. The Irish Church Bill, based on the Suspensory Bill, passed early in the session with remarkable celerity and by large majorities through the house of commons; and on 14 June 1869 the second reading began in the house of lords. The peers must now match their words with deeds. Yet it was no easy matter to muster the self-discipline to carry out the pledges so freely given before the general election. In *The Spectator*'s words, 'the great vote was on the very subject on which of all others average Conservative peers felt most strongly'.[22] Whatever their misgivings, they could ill afford the luxury of yielding to them, if they were to use this particular language again in dealings with the house of commons. Should the Irish Church Bill fail the second reading in the house of lords, after the profuse professions of its members that they would respect the results of the general election, they must wreck the emergent referendal theory at the outset. Conversely, reading the Bill a second time, as was done on 19 June, must constitute a milestone of the Victorian house of lords. Such self-restraint under the most trying circumstances could be treated as convincing evidence for the proposition that the house of lords would not defy the nation's will, after that will had been expressed at the polls, regardless of the manner in which that house dealt with the house of commons.[23] That is, the case of the Irish Church Bill, once the controversy was successfully resolved, could be used thereafter to legitimate a leading tenet of the referendal theory – indeed, its most important tenet. If this tenet was accepted, the more likely it was that other tenets would carry conviction.

The passage of the Irish Church Bill was, then, the testing time of the referendal theory. Yet it was not apparent for some time that the Bill would in fact receive a second reading, and for a time it even seemed as if Salisbury would play no part in the outcome. Meetings were under way to determine Conservative policy before the Bill reached the lords; and major obstacles to passage were evident as early as the meeting of 8 May at Lambeth palace,

[20] Alfred Erskine Gathorne-Hardy. *Gathorne Hardy, first earl of Cranbrook* London, 1910, I. 286.
[21] *May's constitutional history of England*, III, 75.
[22] *The Spectator*, XLII (26 June 1869), 753.
[23] Leonard Courtney, *The working constitution of the United Kingdom* New York, 1901, pp. 101-2.

arranged at Disraeli's suggestion by the archbishop of Canterbury, Archibald Campbell Tait.[24] When Tait proposed that the peers vote for the second reading, to be followed by amendments in committee, Lord Grey – the only Liberal peer present – was amenable; but Salisbury seems to have been non-committal, as was Cairns, who held the balance of power in the party.[25] Lord Derby, the ex-premier, to whom the peers had long looked for leadership, was not even present. A zealous champion of protestant ascendancy throughout the United Kingdom, he is said to have asserted at this time that no consideration on earth could induce him to compromise on the Irish Church Bill,[26] a position to which he steadily adhered.

Meanwhile Disraeli had retired to the sidelines: he was very quiet during this session and the two following sessions. The Liberal victory in 1868 had weakened his position by suggesting that the Conservative sponsorship of parliamentary reform in the preceding year had brought the party no political gain; and it is by no means clear that he was in any position to influence events in the house of lords.[27] His place as a possible mediator passed to Queen Victoria, who was impressed by the electoral verdict of 1868 and by the large majorities for the Irish Church Bill in the newly elected house of commons. She was soon in close touch with the principals, with important consequences.[28] As early as 4 June she urged Tait to exercise a moderating influence, and two days later he reported that Derby had apparently won the support of the Conservative rank and file.[29] A meeting of 140 peers, on 5 June, at the duke of Marlborough's house, had voted for rejection; and this time Cairns had joined forces with Derby, making a long speech against giving the Bill a second reading. One of the few peers to resist was Salisbury. Considering the passage of the Irish Church Bill to be only a question of time and pressure, so he said, he would not vote for rejection; nor would his close friend and ally, Lord Carnarvon. But they were in the minority. When Derby denounced the Irish Church Bill as 'revolutionary and abominable', he spoke for the meeting.[30]

---

[24] Randall Thomas Davidson and William Benham, *Life of Archibald Campbell Tait, archbishop of Canterbury* (London, 1891), II, 18–19.

[25] Cairns felt very strongly on the Irish church question, saying at one point that if the Irish church went, the English would follow in twenty years. Yet as late as 8 Apr. 1869 he told the shadow cabinet that the lords would not throw out the Irish Church Bill on the second reading though they might amend it in detail: *Disraeli, Derby and the Conservative party*, pp. 328, 331, 340. See also note 30, below.

[26] Wilbur Devereux Jones, *Lord Derby and Victorian conservatism* (Oxford, 1956), p. 345, note; P. M. H. Bell, *Disestablishment in Ireland and Wales* (Church Historical Society 90, 1969), p. 143. Cf. John D. Fair, 'The Irish disestablishment conference of 1869', *The Journal of Ecclesiastical History*, XXVI, 4 (Oct. 1975), 385.

[27] Blake, *Disraeli*, pp. 516, 520–1; E. J. Feuchtwanger, *Disraeli, democracy and the Tory party* (Oxford, 1968), pp. 1–16.

[28] Fair, 'The Irish disestablishment conference', pp. 383–7.	[29] *Life of Tait*, II, 25.

[30] *The Times* (7 June 1869), p. 5; Fair, 'The Irish disestablishment conference', pp. 386–7; Sir Arthur Hardinge, *The Life of...earl of Carnarvon* (London, 1925), II, 9–10. According to *The Times*, however, Salisbury was undecided about the best course to be followed. Cairns's attitude is explained in Fair, 'The Irish disestablishment conference', p. 386, note 2 and in Bell, *Disestablishment in Ireland*, p. 143. See also note 25 above.

Even Salisbury's position was by no means firm. On 3 June, before the meeting at Marlborough's house, Lord Granville – the Liberal leader of the house of lords and Gladstone's chief political associate – reported a conversation with Lord Grey. 'Grey told me', he wrote, 'that he was afraid there was a chance of the rejection, & that Salisbury to his surprise, had become shaky.'[31] Six days later, on 9 June, Granville wrote of another conversation, this one with Carnarvon. It appeared that Salisbury would refrain from voting on the Irish Church Bill. 'He [Carnarvon]', wrote Granville, 'has still some hopes of getting Salisbury to vote, and of persuading other peers, but he is always over sanguine in this matter.'[32] Yet Carnarvon had it right. While Salisbury hesitated, Tait wrote optimistically, on 7 June, to the queen that the majority against the Bill had dwindled to twenty. He considered this too small a margin for rejection and forecast that the Conservative majority would allow a second reading and insist on amendments later.[33] He then asked Disraeli to advise his friends to adopt this policy.[34] By this time the Liberals, responding to the queen, were more conciliatory; and as the debate began Granville announced the government's willingness to consider alterations in the Bill's details.[35]

To *The Times* the Irish Church Bill was now safe,[36] but other observers found the turning point in Salisbury's speech on the night of 17 June. They agreed with *The Spectator* that it was 'the main influence which induced the conservatives to desert their leader, Lord Cairns, and their ex-leader, Lord Derby, and sustain the government'.[37] Derby spoke in debate before Salisbury. Pale and ill, his voice feeble, he disappointed an attentive audience despite his strenuous attempt to justify his unwillingness to accept the results of the general election. Urging the rejection of the Irish Church Bill, he denied that the question of disestablishment had been adequately submitted to the voters. 'The bill now before...[the house of lords] never was before the country', he declared. Indeed, it appeared that the ministers and their chief supporters had studiously held back many of its provisions in their declarations.[38]

[31] *The political correspondence of Mr Gladstone and Lord Granville, 1868-1876*, ed. Agatha Ramm (London, 1952), I, 26.

[32] Ibid. I, 27.

[33] *Life of Tait*, II, 26-7; Carnarvon to Salisbury, 7 June 1869: Hatfield MSS 3M/Class E. I am grateful to the present marquess of Salisbury for permission to consult the papers of the third marquess and to quote from them.

[34] *Life of Tait*, II, 27-8.

[35] Fair, 'The Irish disestablishment conference', p. 387.

[36] *The Times* (14 June 1869), p. 8. *The Spectator* noted, however, that until the night of 14 June it was believed that Derby held the house in his hand: ibid. XLII (26 June 1869), 753.

[37] Ibid. (17 July 1869), 387; Lord Granville to Queen Victoria, 17 June 1869, *Letters of Queen Victoria*, ed. G. E. Buckle (London, 1926), second series, I, 610-11; Lord Edmond Fitzmaurice, *The life of...second earl of Granville* (London, 1905), II, 10; Pulling, *The life and speeches of...Salisbury*, I, 128-9. 'The Nature of Democracy', *The Quarterly Review* (October 1884), p. 329, note. The author is said to have been Sir Henry Maine. See also P. T. Marsh, *The Victorian church in decline* (London, 1969), p. 35; Bell, *Disestablishment in Ireland*, pp. 116-7. Bell implies that Disraeli, with Cairns, opposed a second reading of the Irish Church Bill in the house of lords.

[38] *Hansard*, third series, CXCVII, 37. Sir Ivor Jennings seems to suggest that Derby's speech marks the beginning of the mandate on a regular basis in English politics. This was not in fact the case:

Disagreeing with Derby, Salisbury recommended reading the Bill a second time and amending it later; and he now offered a discourse on the constitution, destined to have much influence, that would allow the peers to vote gracefully for the second reading. He found the position of the house of lords to be high, indeed the equal of the commons', but stressed that both houses were subordinate to the nation. But what of the widespread assumption that the house of commons as the representative of the nation was supreme in lawmaking? That proposition was completely unacceptable to Salisbury. Granted that in 99 cases out of 100 the house of commons theoretically represented the nation, this was so only in theory. In an equal number of cases the nation took no interest in politics, following out its usual avocations and viewing the political scene with detachment. When the nation was not directly concerned, the house of lords was equal in all essentials to the house of commons. In fact, the two houses were co-ordinate in lawmaking. 'In all of these cases I make no distinctions – absolutely none', Salisbury stated, 'between the prerogative of the house of commons and the house of lords.' Yet a few cases existed where the voices of the two houses were less important – where 'the nation must be called into council and must decide the policy of the government'. That is, direct democracy must operate. This happened when grounds existed for believing that the house of commons was misinterpreting the opinion of the nation. On such occasions the house of lords must insist that the nation be consulted. How was that house to know when intervention was required? Salisbury's advice was more general in 1869 than later in the century. It was 'a matter of feeling and judgment'. The peers must decide by all they saw around them and by events. Each must decide for himself upon his conscience and to the best of his judgement in exercising 'that tremendous responsibility which at such a time each member of this house bears – whether the house of commons does or does not represent the full, the deliberate, the sustained convictions of the nation'.[39] If the peers decided that the house of commons and the nation were one, the vocation of the house of lords, except in very exceptional cases, passed away. That house must devolve the responsibility upon the nation and accept its conclusion. In so acting the peers would not be accepting the commons' verdict, not at all, but rather that of the nation acting as the arbiter of the issue. The nation had decided in the general election against the protestant ascendancy in Ireland – the opinion of Scotland, Ireland, and Wales was passionately in favour of this measure of disestablishment, and England, too, favoured it though more doubtfully and languidly – and Salisbury was certain that 'this house would not be doing its duty if it opposed itself further against the will of the nation'.[40]

Cabinet government (London, second edition, 1951), p. 467, note 6. See the rather different view in C. S. Emden, *The people and the constitution: being a history of the development of the people's influence in British government* (Oxford, second edition, Oxford Paperbacks, 1962), pp. 216-18. The best modern study of the mandate is Patricia Kelvin's 'The development and use of the concept of the electoral mandate in British politics, 1867 to 1911', unpublished Ph.D. dissertation, University of London, 1977.   [39] *Hansard*, third series, cxcvii, 83-4.

[40] Ibid. 85; Le May, *The Victorian constitution*, pp. 135-6.

Two days later he was as good as his word when he, and Carnarvon too, took the extreme step of voting for the second reading alongside the Liberals in the house of lords.[41] He did so despite a strong personal piety, a deep attachment to traditional institutions, and a devotion to the principle of establishment – that is, with sympathies much like Derby's. When the momentous vote was taken at three o'clock in the morning of 19 June, in the fullest house in living memory and before crowded galleries, 36 conservative peers voted with the government, providing a winning margin of 33 in the vote of 179 to 146. Salisbury had even led the contingent of Conservative peers into the lobby in favour of the second reading, while Cairns and Derby voted with the minority.[42]

It was a remarkable performance. So conservative in his political opinions as to elicit from the Liberals the witty epithet 'Young Sarum' and described variously in his lifetime as a 'feudal baron', a 'capital fossil', even as an 'Elizabethan relic', Salisbury seems to have been sufficiently self-controlled at this juncture to avoid a course of conflict with the newly elected house of commons that could jeopardize the future usefulness of the house of lords. Perhaps he considered it but a question of time and pressure before the Irish Church Bill became law, the position maintained at Marlborough's house, or perhaps felt bound by the peers' promise to accept Irish disestablishment if the electors voted for it in the general election. But it is also possible that the motivation for his final decision was more complex. This was not the first occasion on which he had publicly defied the party leadership, and his biographers agree that he had not as yet recovered from the trauma of 1867. At that time he and Carnarvon (with General Peel) had resigned from the Derby–Disraeli government rather than accept a reform bill providing for household suffrage; and as recently as March 1868, while still in the house of commons as Lord Cranborne, he had refused to follow his party's lead on the Stanley amendment, urging instead a forthright rejection of Gladstone's resolutions regarding the Irish church. This defiance was coupled with a vitriolic personal attack on Disraeli for his role in carrying the second Reform Act.[43] Earlier that month Salisbury had written to Carnarvon of his mistrust of Disraeli as a leader: the latter enjoyed 'the old game of talking green in the house and orange in the lobby'.[44] The comments of Disraeli's supporters were equally revealing. Writing to Gathorne Hardy, on 1 April – after Salisbury's attack on Disraeli in the house of commons – Cairns remarked: 'Cranborne's ardour for the Irish church has remained dormant until he found he could use it as a means of expressing his hatred to D.'[45]

---

[41] *Hansard*, third series, CXCVII, 305.

[42] Fitzmaurice, *Granville*, II, 10; *Hansard*, third series, CXCVII, 304–7.

[43] Ibid. CXCI, 532–41. The speech was given on 30 Mar. 1868. See the comment in Blake, *Disraeli*, pp. 498–500 and in S. H. Jeyes, *The life and times of…the marquess of Salisbury* (London, 1895), I, 119. Lord Stanley considered Salisbury more conciliatory after he went to the lords but still unwilling to act with Disraeli: *Disraeli, Derby and the Conservative party*, pp. 335, 340, 345.

[44] Cited in Curtis, *Coercion and conciliation*, p. 8. The letter is dated 6 Mar. 1868.

[45] Gathorne-Hardy, *Cranbrook*, I, 268. See also ibid. p. 266.

Now, a year after refusing to support the Stanley amendment, Salisbury broke publicly with Cairns and Derby on the course to be adopted on the second reading of the Irish Church Bill. While Disraeli's position at this point is by no means clear, Salisbury in adopting a different policy from Cairns seems to have been striking at Disraeli. After all, Cairns was Disraeli's choice as Conservative leader in the house of lords, though he could not select him for the post; and he was not only a colleague whom Disraeli thoroughly trusted but also an intimate friend and close political associate.[46] Disraeli had made Cairns lord chancellor in 1868. And Derby was of course the prime minister who had presided over the passing of the second Reform Act. In his famous article in the *Quarterly Review*, describing what he saw as the Conservative surrender to the pressure for parliamentary reform, Salisbury censured Derby, as well as Disraeli, though in his view the latter's influence was paramount in what was done.[47]

The course adopted was of consequence for the house of lords. Salisbury's speech of 17 June, coupled with his earlier speech recommending the rejection of the Suspensory Bill, supplied the major elements of the referendal theory in late Victorian England, while his response to the general election of 1868, made independently of Cairns and Derby, gave that theory viability for the future. Thanks to Salisbury's leadership the house of lords, if it chose to act again on such a theory, would enjoy a large measure of credibility. In fact, though this was not apparent for some time, the speech of 17 June provided the house of lords with an astonishing propaganda victory. This is to say a great deal, since that house had in effect lost the general election of 1868 and as a consequence had to swallow the bitter medicine of the Irish Church Bill. But no defeated house, in the wake of a political disaster, ever received a more effective ideological gloss than Salisbury imparted in 1869. His argument for giving the Irish Church Bill a second reading was remembered as long as the referendal theory was associated with the house of lords.[48] Salisbury himself recalled it to the public in 1895 in a letter to *The Times* to which it will be necessary to return, and in 1906 Lord Lansdowne (who would be the Conservative leader in the lords during the debates on the Parliament Act) reminded the peers of Salisbury's words. The latter had once described the house of lords 'as an instrument for reserving on all great and vital questions a voice for the electors and the people of this country'.[49] In the following year

[46] Ibid. I, 281; Feuchtwanger, *Disraeli, democracy and the Tory party*, p. 5; Blake, *Disraeli*, p. 544; William F. Monypenny and George E. Buckle, *The life of Benjamin Disraeli, earl of Beaconsfield* (New York, 1929), pp. 378, 427, 434, 451–2, 513.

[47] Smith, *Lord Salisbury on politics*, pp. 256–7, 263–6, 272–3, 276, 277, etc.

[48] C. H. K. Marten, 'The marquess of Salisbury', *The political principles of some notable prime ministers of the nineteenth century*, ed. F. J. C. Hearnshaw (London, 1926), p. 280; Cecil, *Life of Salisbury*, II, 24–6. See also the *D.N.B.* article on Salisbury, written by his nephew, Algernon Cecil. The latter refers to Salisbury's speech of 26 June 1868, as laying down, in words often quoted since, what he considered the function of the peers in the modern state. And he adds that Salisbury reaffirmed the doctrine in an impressive speech after the general election of 1868, advising the peers to pass the second reading of the Irish Church Bill.

[49] *Parl. deb.* (lords), fourth series, CLXVI, 702.

the duke of Devonshire – formerly leader of the Conservative party in the lords and at this time one of the most respected men in English pubic life – quoted at length from Salisbury's speech, telling his fellow peers: 'So long as this house accepts that canon for its conduct I do not believe it can go far wrong.'[50]

The conduct of the house of lords in 1869, with which Salisbury was so closely associated, seemed to contemporaries to introduce a new era in its history. In September 1893, as the second reading of the second Home Rule Bill for Ireland got under way in the house of lords, *The Times* urged rejection on the ground that the electorate should give the verdict. Should a general election take place on the issue, the peers would accept the outcome. To be sure, their course of action had been very different in 1832 when they defied the electoral verdict for the Reform Bill in the general election of the preceding year and brought the country to the brink of revolution. But this constitutional mistake had been corrected a generation later. The opportunity to correct it had come after the peers rejected Gladstone's Suspensory Bill, despite its having been carried by a majority of 65 votes in the house of commons. When the appeal to the constituencies revealed the nation's mind on the issue, they had accepted the disestablishment of the Irish church.[51] Here, then, was the illustration *par excellence* of the relationship between the house of lords and the post-1867 electorate.[52] But if the peers bowed to the people, it was obviously much less necessary for them to do so in their dealings with the house of commons – so many an observer reckoned.

III

With the passage of the Irish Church Bill into law, the circumstances vanished that had spawned the referendal theory; and it looked for a time as if no more would be heard of it. Its abandonment was probably due to its association with failure. The peers' rhetoric had led to a statute for which they had no sympathy, and they must have seen in the reference to the people a dangerous policy that would not bear repetition. Not even Salisbury was ready at this point to make systematic use of the referendal theory. Yet by February 1872 he had brushed aside his doubts and was seeking a consistent principle to govern the acceptance or rejection of legislative measures by the house of lords – such a principle, it must be understood, as would permit the house of lords to exercise its legislative power with a minimum of risk to that house and

[50] Ibid. CLXXIV, 15–16. This portion of Devonshire's speech was quoted by Bernard Henry Holland in a political biography of the duke published in 1911, the year of the Parliament Act: *The life of Spencer Compton, eighth duke of Devonshire* (London, 1911), II, 406–7. In Devonshire's view, the action of the house of lords in 1869 provided convincing proof that the peers did not hesitate to defer to the will of the electorate even when that will was contrary to their own: ibid. II, 406. See also the speech of Lord Robertson, about the same time, in *Parl. deb.* (lords), fourth series, CLXXIII, 1264. Robertson was a law lord and faithful member of the Conservative (Unionist) party.

[51] *The Times* (5 Sept. 1893), p. 7.

[52] Jeyes, *Salisbury*, I, 120. Jeyes wrote: 'The Irish church was emphatically a case in point.' See also Earl Cadogan's speech on 7 July 1884: *Hansard*, third series, CCXC, 185.

to its freedom of action. Mindful of the events of 1868–9, he now turned to the referendal theory that had emerged from the controversy over the Irish church.

His doing so was crucial for the Victorian house of lords. There were earlier parliamentary episodes in which questions were raised about the competence of parliament to handle a given question and the cry raised that there must be an appeal to the constituencies for a decision, notably during the crisis over catholic emancipation in 1829 and again in 1846 when the repeal of the Corn Laws was before parliament.[53] But in their wake no political leader of Salisbury's stature had come forward, determined to use such a theory persistently to elevate the house of lords. That the aftermath of the Irish church controversy was different in this respect is still another reason for stressing its distinctive role in developing the referendal theory. At this time Salisbury's personal qualities assumed a particular importance. He was too proud, too spirited, too combative, even too pugnacious to stand by passively as evidence mounted that the house of which he was a leading member was incapable of dealing effectively with Gladstone. Depressed by the lords' failure to staunch Liberal reform legislation and irritated in turn by this situation, he wrote on 20 June 1870 to Carnarvon:

I send you a leader of Maguire's [in the *Cork Examiner*] which will illustrate what I mean in saying, that in point of power and public weight, the h. of lords is dying of rapid decline. I give only one instance of observations that I have heard in every direction. I feel convinced that if we make any substantial retreat from the very moderate position we have taken up, our future position in the constitution will be purely decorative.[54]

One year later that house's weakness was publicly exhibited in a dispute with Gladstone over abolishing the purchase of army commissions. The manner in which he handled the dispute proved more than ordinarily humiliating to the house of lords, and very probably this episode led a thoroughly resentful Salisbury to adopt the referendal theory as consistent policy in dealing with Liberal legislation.

The Gladstonian manoeuvre that ended army purchase came after the peers voted, 17 July 1871, by a margin of twenty-five votes, to set aside the Army Regulation Bill until a larger reform scheme was produced. The action was tantamount to rejection and the vote so close as to suggest a divided house, and in fact much soul-searching had preceded the adoption of a policy of rejection. But not on the part of Salisbury, who early insisted on rejection and carried other members of his party with him. 'He was evidently influenced by

---

[53] Michael Brock, *The Great Reform Act* (London, 1973), p. 57; Betty Kemp, 'Reflections on the repeal of the Corn Laws', *Victorian Studies* (March, 1962), pp. 201–4. For the debates on catholic emancipation see *Hansard*, new series, xx, 437–8 (Gascoyne), 787 (O'Neill), 854 (Blandford), 1170–1 (Sadler), 1288 (Peel); xxi, 271 (earl of Guilford). For the debates on the corn laws, see ibid., third series, LXXXIII, 941 and LXXXVI, 1174–5 (Lord Stanley); LXXXIV, 253–4, 261–2 (Bankes), etc. The speakers' willingness to carry out their implied promises went untested since there were no general elections in 1829 and 1846.

[54] Hatfield MSS 3M/D31/22, typescript copy. See Salisbury to Carnarvon as late as 1 Jan. 1882: ibid. 3M/D31/81; and 19 Jan. 1883, ibid. 3M/D31/88; Cecil, *Salisbury*, II, 27.

the old feeling of irritation at the humiliating position in which he thought the house of lords was placed, and was by no means averse to a conflict with the house of commons,' so Lord Carnarvon's biographer concluded.[55] Both Carnarvon and Cairns had favoured a more pacific course, but waived their objections in deference to strong opinions within the party. As tension mounted after the rejection, Gladstone announced that a royal warrant, signed by Queen Victoria on ministerial advice, had ended army purchase. If army officers were to receive compensation for their losses, the peers would have to reverse their action on the Army Regulation Bill; and this was what happened. Insistence by the Liberals that the queen had acted, not on the basis of her prerogative but of power conferred by a statute of George III, met with scepticism; and in the house of commons Disraeli denounced Gladstone's action as 'part of an avowed and shameful conspiracy against the undoubted privileges of the other house of parliament'.[56]

An angry house of lords censured the Gladstone government for what the peers perceived as an abuse of power and a breach of faith. In a speech urging this course of action, described by the duke of Argyll as one of the bitterest and narrowest party speeches in his memory,[57] Salisbury reproached the government for bringing forward the abolition of purchase as a question subject to parliamentary jurisdiction, only to withdraw it in the face of a hostile reaction. It was as if the Liberals had said: 'We snap our fingers in your face against your decision, and will decide for ourselves in spite of you.' The government had treated the house of lords in a way that no private individual would treat another. When Salisbury now asserted that the government had acted emotionally because it was being thwarted by the house of lords, Granville cheered; and Salisbury responded with a cutting statement: 'I can sympathize with the noble earl who thus cheers me,' he said, 'for he has been the instrument – I have no doubt the most reluctant instrument – of insulting the order to which he belongs.'

Assigning to Granville the doctrine that it was the whole duty of the house of lords to obey the house of commons, Salisbury traced that doctrine to Wellington. It was the duke, he observed sarcastically, who had 'raised this house to its present high pitch of authority'. Salisbury now foreshadowed the position he would take in February 1872 and thereafter. He recognized, he said, that the house of lords ought to pay earnest attention to the party in power and the opinion current in the country; but such considerations were by no means paramount. For example, the vote in the house of commons deserved to be taken less seriously when extremism was ascendant among the Liberals. If the majority in that house was used to enforce the opinion of a radical element, the peers must 'reserve for the opinion of the constituencies measures passed by the house of commons under that pressure'.[58]

Before summer was over, Salisbury was encouraged by a visible sign that

---

[55] Hardinge, *Carnarvon*, II, 24.
[56] *Annual Register*, N.S. (1871), p. 77; Hardinge, *Carnarvon*, II, 24.
[57] Described in the *Annual Register*, N.S. (1871), p. 79.
[58] *Hansard*, third series, CCVIII, 475–80.

the country was tiring of Gladstone's reforming zeal. A by-election in East Surrey, on 24 August, administered to the government its first serious setback when a Conservative was victorious by 1,163 votes. The Liberal majority in 1868 had been 384.[59] Less than six months later Salisbury was writing to Carnarvon, urging the necessity of adopting a consistent principle to govern the acceptance or rejection of bills and recommending for this purpose the referendal theory. It would give the house of lords a genuine legislative independence, whatever the outward appearance. If the tone of the letter suggests expediency on Salisbury's part, elements of the theory he was advocating are discernible at a much earlier stage of his political career, indeed long before the Irish church controversy;[60] and on public occasions he had often asserted an independent legislative power in the house of lords. Urging the rejection of the Ballot Bill on the second reading, Salisbury explained his position at length, writing:

I am strongly for rejecting the Bill on the second reading, for this reason. It appears to me of vital necessity that our acceptance of bills to which we are opposed should be regulated on some principle. If we listen to the Liberals we should accept all important bills which had passed the house of commons by a large majority. But that in effect would be to efface the house of lords. Another principle – which is, so far as I can gather, what commends itself to Derby [the fifteenth earl] – is to watch newspapers, public meetings and so forth, and only to reject when 'public opinion' thus ascertained, growls very loud. This plan gives a premium to bluster and will bring the house into contempt. The plan which I prefer is frankly to acknowledge that the nation is our master, though the house of commons is not, and to yield our own opinion only when the judgement of the nation has been challenged at the polls and decidedly expressed.

This doctrine, he continued, had a number of advantages. It was '(1) theoretically sound, (2) popular, (3) safe against agitation, and (4) so rarely applicable as practically to place little fetter upon our independence'. Not that he was so hostile to the ballot, though he plainly disliked it, but that he favoured resistance as 'part of a general principle'. On this ground he was urging the duke of Richmond, at that time the Conservative leader in the house of lords, to resist the second reading even though Disraeli favoured acquiescence. A postscript to the letter harked back to the last general election, often in Salisbury's mind when he thought of politics. 'I forgot to note – as to ballot',

---

[59] Smith, *Lord Salisbury on politics*, p. 339.

[60] See Salisbury's extraordinary speech of 6 May 1861, on the resolution for the repeal of the paper duties. Assigning a high importance to extra-parliamentary opinion, it foreshadows the better-known speeches of 1868, 1869 and 1872, from which the referendal theory came, and suggests that Salisbury (at the time Lord Robert Cecil) had, as early as this, strong personal objections to Gladstone as a political leader: Pulling, *Salisbury*, I, 44–9. See also Lucy's comment on Salisbury's attitude towards Gladstone in *Memories of eight parliaments*, p. 116, and Salisbury's earlier views on the house of lords in the *Saturday Review*, XII (3 Aug. 1861), 113–14; XVII (7 May 1864), 547, 548; XX (8 July 1865), 44–5. That Salisbury wrote these articles may be seen in Michael Pinto-Duschinsky, *The political thought of Lord Salisbury, 1854–1868* (London, 1967), pp. 162–88.

he wrote, 'that at the election of 1868 the chief of the present ministry appeared as anti-ballot man: so that the nation has not been consulted.'[61]

Salisbury's speech on the Ballot Bill (10 June 1872) is a suitable companion piece to his speeches on the Suspensory Bill and the Irish Church Bill from which so much of the political language of the referendal theory sprang. By 1872 he was more exact. Thus the word 'mandate' has crept in; and there is an insistence, as in the letter to Carnarvon, that the house of lords in deciding on a given measure, look directly to the results of a general election if its members were to learn the nation's wishes. Although the general election of 1868 was foremost in his mind on the night of 17 June 1869, he had not at that time singled out the electorate as the source of authority, saying only: 'We must decide each for himself, upon our consciences and to the best of our judgment.'

Otherwise his speech on the Ballot Bill bears a marked resemblance to the speeches of 1868 and 1869. This time, too, he carefully distinguished between the house of commons and the nation: for the most part they were separate entities, and it was to the nation alone that the house of lords should look for direction when important questions arose. 'I draw the widest possible distinction between the opinions of the house of commons and the opinions of the nation,' he asserted, as he excoriated the view that the house of commons represented the nation. It was a constitutional fiction convenient for practical purposes to respect but literally true only on certain occasions and subjects, as when a question was being discussed on which the house of commons had been elected. At other times that house represented the nation only in theory. As he said, when four years had elapsed and the memory of all the questions on which the house was elected had passed away and when change had overtaken many opinions of the government, which the house of commons was elected to support, that house represented only theoretically and not literally the nation's opinion.[62] If reason existed for believing that a measure before the house of lords lacked a mandate, it was the lords' duty to reject the measure until the electorate gave its verdict. This was such an occasion: there was no mandate for the Ballot Bill. Those now advocating the ballot had been non-ballot politicians in the general election of 1868. That is, 'the country has never had a fair opportunity of considering whether it likes the ballot or not'. Under these circumstances the house of lords must act as the agents of the nation, seeing to it that the house of commons 'in thus tampering with the laws under which it was itself elected, has not transgressed the mandate it received'.[63]

Despite the letter to Carnarvon, Salisbury did not take up the referendal theory steadily until 1880. The need to do so disappeared after the passage of the Ballot Act. There were no bills of major importance in 1873, and as

---

[61] The letter is published, without the postscript, in Cecil, *Salisbury*, II, 25–6. A typescript copy of the complete letter is at Hatfield House. Salisbury to Carnarvon, 20 Feb. 1872, Hatfield MSS 3M/D31/23.

[62] *Hansard*, third series, CCXI, 1493–4.

[63] Ibid. 1495.

by-elections turned against the Liberals it became apparent that Gladstone's government was entering its last stage. When the house of lords rejected measures, it did so without referring to such a theory. After 1874 the Conservatives were in power for a six-year span. Salisbury and Disraeli were reconciled; and the former entered the government, first as secretary for India and then as foreign secretary. Then came the great Midlothian campaigns of 1879–80, in which Gladstone's oratorical campaign against the government's Eastern policy gave a new impetus to direct democracy. The election of 1880 was held against a background of deepening depression, and the country returned Gladstone to office with a record majority. One year later the death of Disraeli (now Lord Beaconsfield) led to Salisbury's becoming the leader of the Conservatives in the house of lords and also of the Conservative party, a post shared, however, until 1885, with Sir Stafford Northcote.

He was now in a position to put his ideas into effect; and, indeed, only two months after most of the polls were declared in the general election of 1880 Salisbury made it apparent, in a speech at Hackney, that the referendal theory topped his list of priorities. It was of paramount importance that the house of lords assert its independence. Not that the peers should maintain positions different from the mature convictions of the nation at large. That was impossible, but he was asserting the doctrine that the house of lords should represent the permanent as opposed to the passing feeling of the nation; and in a speech at Liverpool, two years later, he added the corollary that the lords must see to it that no permanent and irrevocable change took place in political institutions until the people had the opportunity to learn about it and form a mature and solemn decision on the subject.[64] Gladstone's Midlothian campaigns may have influenced the timing of Salisbury's decision to revive the referendal theory and bring it forward. He could hardly have dismissed their impact. Gladstone had dramatically carried his political message to the electorate, holding the attention of the whole country and deeply impressing Salisbury.[65]

In opposition Salisbury made tireless use of the referendal theory. A new opportunity for doing so was at hand after Gladstone introduced clôture and

[64] Both speeches are quoted in Arthur Leach, 'House of Lords', *Fortnightly Review*. xxxviii, old series (1882), 358–60. Gladstone's response was that the house of commons, not the house of lords, represented the country's solid and permanent opinion. That opinion was Liberal, as could be seen from the parliaments elected since the Reform Act. Hanham, *The nineteenth century constitution*, p. 203.

[65] Smith, *Lord Salisbury on politics*, p. 338; Salisbury at Sheffield, reported in *The Times* (23 July 1884), p. 10; Taylor, *Lord Salisbury*, p. 79. Very probably Salisbury also took note when a strong segment of public opinion rallied to the house of lords after its appellate jurisdiction was ended by Gladstone's Judicature Act of 1873. Although this was a Liberal measure, the product of Lord Chancellor Selborne, it had the support of Disraeli and Cairns. After the general election of 1874 a group of Conservative backbenchers forced a reversal of policy on their leaders and secured the restoration of the lords' appellate jurisdiction in the Judicature Act of 1876: Robert Stevens, *Law and politics. The house of lords as a judicial body, 1800–1976* (Chapel Hill, 1978), pp. 44–67. Stevens writes that 'the real purpose of the pressure groups behind the bill [of 1876] had been to bolster the peers as a branch of the legislature.' Ibid. p. 67.

the guillotine to offset the obstructionist tactics of the Parnellites in the house of commons. One side-effect, probably unintended, was to strengthen the cabinet in relationship to the house of commons. A favourite practice with Salisbury was to contrast the house of commons of his day with that found earlier in English history, much to the former's disadvantage. That house had lost its once proud position and was being ground down between the contending pressures of an autocratic prime minister and the caucus, that is, the party machinery and organization that had developed outside parliament since 1867. Denouncing what he called wire-pullers, Salisbury declared at Liverpool in 1882: 'A house of commons, enslaved by the caucus, and muzzled by the clôture, would be a very different body from that which has hitherto been the glory of English history.' The only solution, and an unsatisfactory one at that, was to replace the existing Septennial Act with a provision for triennial or even annual parliaments if the house of lords for any reason was unable to carry out its referendal function and so keep the electorate within the political process.[66] On another occasion he described the house of commons as 'the most servile house of commons – servile to the minister, servile to the caucus – that the palace of Westminster has ever seen'.[67]

These themes were elaborated in speeches before large audiences in the midlands, the north, and Scotland; and the speeches in turn were faithfully printed in the newspapers of the day. In the years between 1881 and 1885, as Salisbury's grip tightened on the leadership of his party, he delivered some seventy speeches outside Westminster, which the national press fully reported. Many of them were given during the constitutional crisis over the Reform Bill of 1884 when he defended the legislative independence of the house of lords in important speeches at Manchester, Glasgow and Sheffield and spoke to deputations from Conservative associations in London and Middlesex. This activity demonstrates that Salisbury had as much skill as Gladstone and Joseph Chamberlain – a recent scholar describes him as being more skilled – in exploiting the techniques of the new democratic politics.[68] Everywhere he carried his message about the referendal function of the house of lords as he shaped its tenets to reflect the issues of the day and fit the mood of his audience. To one observer, Salisbury's favourite formula was that the peers must throw themselves into the breach whenever the house of commons had no mandate from the people.[69] By this time the referendal theory was securing a popular

[66] In this speech, which was given wide circulation as a publication of the National Union, Salisbury made his argument from direct democracy even more explicit when he declared that 'the direct action of the people is superseding the indirect action of its representatives': Pulling, *Salisbury*, II, 117–18. See Curtis, *Coercion and conciliation*, p. 411, for an account of how Salisbury in 1893 exploited, for propaganda purposes, the government's control over proceedings in the house of commons and Marsh, *The discipline of popular government*, pp. 200–2 for a description of the propaganda of the National Union.

[67] Salisbury at Sheffield, *The Times* (23 July 1884), p. 10. See also his speech at Glasgow, *The Times* (2 Oct. 1884), p. 7; Kelso, 12 Oct. 1884, *Speeches of the marquis of Salisbury*, ed. William Henry Lucy (London, 1895), pp. 142–4; Dumfries, 22 Oct. 1884, ibid. pp. 151–3; and the Junior Constitutional Club, *The Times* (8 July 1893), p. 12.   [68] Taylor, *Lord Salisbury*, pp. 76–7.

[69] *The last function of the house of lords* (London, 1884), p. 30.

base. It proved useful to the house of lords in the debates over the third Reform Bill in 1884[70] and again in 1893 when it was invoked to reject Gladstone's second Home Rule Bill for Ireland.[71] After Gladstone took up home rule, the theory acquired a large following outside parliament. Such publications as *The Times* and *The Spectator*, hitherto sympathetic to Gladstone, shifted their allegiance to the Conservatives; and their editorial columns reflected Salisbury's ideological arguments.[72]

If the house of lords insisted on a mandate for a measure before accepting it, was it also claiming the right to determine when parliament was to be dissolved? This issue was prominent in 1884 when Gladstone charged Salisbury with taking this position. To Gladstone such a doctrine had no place in the constitution. He would rather abandon the Reform Bill than cease for a single moment to protest against such an innovation.[73] Denying that the house of lords claimed this power, Salisbury made it clear, nevertheless, that the government in power would have to decide between withdrawing a vital measure that lacked a mandate and submitting it to the people in a general election.[74] Such a position came close to advocating a referendum – a word now increasingly heard in English politics – and to this position he eventually came.[75]

IV

The referendal theory was further refined in the 1890s when Salisbury applied the concept of the 'predominant partner' to the Irish question in the course

[70] *Hansard*, third series, ccxc, 124 (Cairns); 149, 153 (Balfour of Burleigh); 155–6 (Stanhope); 185 (Cadogan); 384–5 (Carnarvon); 425 (Rutland), 438 (Wemyss). See also the *Annual Register* (1884), pp. 98–9, 207.

[71] *Parl. deb.* (lords), fourth series, xvii, 26–31 (Devonshire); 238–9 (Playfair commenting on Devonshire); and 296–7 (Ripon on Devonshire). See also 70–1 (Cowper) and 204–5 (Argyll).

[72] See, for example, *The Times* on 24, 29, and 31 July 1884 and on 5 Sept. 1893, p. 7. By the end of the nineteenth century G. Lowes Dickinson was writing: 'The peers no longer stand upon their rights as an independent and co-ordinate estate [the language used during the parliamentary debates on the Reform Bill of 1832]; they recognize that the "will of the people," when once it has been really pronounced, must be law; and if they oppose the commons, they do so ostensibly on the ground that the representative house is misrepresenting the nation.' 'This position', he added, 'has become so familiar to us that we hardly pause to observe that it implies a revolution in the theory of the constitution.' *The development of parliament during the nineteenth century* (London, 1895), pp. 98–9.

[73] *Political speeches delivered in August and September 1884 by W. E. Gladstone* (Edinburgh, n.d.), p. 20. See also Gladstone's speech at the foreign office on 10 July 1884, reprinted in *The Times* (11 July 1884), p. 10; Hanham, *The nineteenth century constitution*, p. 189; *The Times* (16 July 1884), p. 9.

[74] Pulling *Salisbury*, ii, 223; *The Times* (29 July 1884), p. 10. Salisbury was addressing deputations from the various Conservative associations of London and Middlesex.

[75] Salisbury wrote to A. V. Dicey on 26 Nov. 1892: 'I fully concur in your opinion that some form of the referendum is the solution towards which we are tending, and indeed the only one by which a termination can be put to the entire divergence of view which has grown up between the two houses of parliament. I am rather doubtful whether you do not exaggerate the speed with which we are likely to reach that end. My own impression is that there will be a good deal of troubled water to pass through first': Hatfield MSS 3M/C7/486. See also the account of Salisbury's speech at the Junior Constitutional Club, *The Times* (8 July 1893), p. 12, and Marriott, *English political institutions*, p. 228, for the latter's belief that the referendum was the logical outcome of the insistence on a mandate.

of his successful campaign to defeat the second Home Rule Bill. England – and Scotland, too – as the predominant partner in the United Kingdom must agree before Ireland could receive home rule. The point was the more telling because Gladstone had failed to win England and Scotland in the general election of 1892. His majority was only 40 in the house of commons, where he was dependent on his Irish allies. Gladstone's problems were complicated by other factors. Despite his close association with home rule since 1886, the Liberals had not been able to agree on the details of a home rule bill before the general election and as a consequence had kept their electoral commitment purposely vague. Further, concerned lest their electoral programme seem too limited, they had added the Newcastle programme, described perjoratively by F. A. Channing as a 'stereotyped but rather hackneyed list of disestablishment, local option, registration and taxation, each appealing only to special groups' and based on 'the log-rolling which faddists like'.[76] The situation was made to order for Salisbury, and the Conservatives could also draw encouragement from the dwindling majorities for the second Home Rule Bill as it moved through the house of commons. Introduced in February 1893, it received a second reading by a margin of 43 votes and a third reading on 1 September by 34. One week later the house of lords refused a second reading by the overwhelming vote of 419 to 41.[77] Unable to persuade his cabinet to dissolve on the issue of the house of lords, Gladstone stayed on a few months, giving way in March 1894 to Lord Rosebery.

An early statement from Rosebery angered the Liberals while delighting the Conservatives. In his first speech as premier on the queen's address he quoted from Salisbury and endorsed these words: 'Before Irish home rule is conceded by the imperial parliament,. England as the predominant member of the partnership of the three kingdoms will have to be convinced of its justice and equity.' On the following day John Morley defended Rosebery's statement; but John Redmond, the leader of the Parnellite faction among the home rulers, would have none of it. Rosebery's statement made an already serious situation intolerable. It was preposterous and insulting to suggest that Ireland must have a majority of English votes when she had a parliamentary majority, implying that Irish votes were not equal to English votes. 'If Lord Rosebery was right about the English majority, the lords were right in rejecting the bill.'[78] Two

---

[76] Quoted in D. A. Hamer, *Liberal politics in the age of Gladstone and Rosebery* (Oxford, 1972), p. 174. See also ibid. pp. 156–61. Gladstone was aware before the general election that the referendal theory would be resurrected to deny legitimacy to his legislative proposals if he was returned to office: Asquith, *Fifty years of British parliament*, 1, 269.

[77] Marsh believes that Salisbury wanted the rejection of the second Home Rule Bill to take place in the house of lords 'in order to demonstrate that, at least on the great issue of home rule, the house of lords represented British opinion in the new parliament better than the house of commons': *The discipline of popular government*, p. 225. The same idea is in Curtis, *Coercion and conciliation*, p. 412. But this is to take Salisbury's rhetoric at face value. See also Marsh's account of Salisbury's elaborate preparation for the lords' veto: *The discipline of popular government*, pp. 226–7.

[78] Rosebery's statement is in *Parl. deb.* (lords), fourth series, XXII, 32. See also R. C. K. Ensor, *England since 1870* (Oxford, 1960 edn), p. 216; Marquess of Crewe, *Lord Rosebery* (London, 1931), II, 444–5. According to *The Times*, he had at one blow shattered the fabric of Liberal policy (cited ibid. p. 445); *Annual Register*, N.S. (1894), pp. 68–73. In Cranbrook's opinion, Rosebery had

days after Rosebery's pronouncement, the government was defeated on an amendment to the address; and it was then withdrawn and a new one substituted.

That the new concept posed a threat to home rule explains the reaction from Rosebery's supporters; but surely they were also alienated by his choice of language. It was part and parcel of the referendal theory from which Salisbury had drawn so much advantage in his attacks on the Liberal house of commons in the 1880s. Following the general election in 1892, he had cast about for a means of justifying a rejection of home rule despite Gladstone's electoral victory. Slim that victory might be in nineteenth-century terms, but it was a victory all the same. As W. T. Stead pointed out,

For sixty years it had come to be regarded as part of the unwritten law of the constitution that the house of lords should bow to the will of the nation upon any measure after that will had been ascertained by an appeal to the country. In 1893 the house of commons, fresh from a general election which turned upon the question of home rule, sent up a home rule bill to the house of lords, which promptly threw it out by a majority of 419 to 41.[79]

The concept of the predominant partner solved this dilemma for Salisbury. Not that he would grant that his usual argument did not meet the situation. According to him Gladstone had not received a mandate for home rule in the general election. As he said, in a much-read article on constitutional revision in 1892, it was 'notorious that the Welsh voted for radical candidates not for their love of home rule, but for their aversion towards the Welsh church. The crofters of the Scottish highlands and the peasants of Norfolk were full of agrarian projects and aspirations', and so on. In the din of confused voices, no single solid support was evidenced for home rule, a project of profound constitutional revision. If it were to be argued that the election had indeed turned on home rule, it would have to be recognized that England and Scotland had voted against the project. Without their consent no project of constitutional revision of this scope should take place. The lords must ensure that 'no such fundamental change shall be introduced into our ancient polity unless England and Scotland are assenting parties to it'. Granted the anomalies of that house's constitution, here was the only means in the constitutional system of providing that the nation would be honestly consulted on a question of such fundamental change and its voice faithfully obeyed.[80] Strangely, in view

'distinctly varied the home rule condition by expressing his concurrence with Salisbury that England must be converted before it could be adopted' (Gathorne-Hardy, *Cranbrook*, II, 344). Asquith followed Rosebery's lead in 1901. See the latter's remarks as prime minister on 14 Feb. 1912, in the debate on the address before the introduction of the third Home Rule Bill. Asquith declared: 'We have now what we had not in 1893 – we have got a majority for home rule in Great Britain': *Parl. deb.* (commons), fifth series, xxxiv, 34.

[79] William T. Stead, *Peers or people? The house of lords weighed in the balance and found wanting* (London, 1907), p. 3. See also Le May, *The Victorian constitution*, p. 145.

[80] 'Constitutional revision', *National Review*, no. 117 (Nov. 1892), pp. 295–6, 297, 299. According to Alfred Austin, editor of the *National Review*, Salisbury's article made a very deep impression: Austin to Salisbury, 26 Sept. 1893, Hatfield MSS 3M/Class E. See also Roy Jenkins,

of its appropriateness, almost no mention of the concept of the predominant partner was made in the speech with which Salisbury completed the debates in the house of lords on the second Home Rule Bill. But it was expounded in his speech on the address in 1894, from which Rosebery borrowed. By now, Salisbury had dropped Scotland from the concept: he had only one predominant partner in mind, and that was England.[81]

Salisbury's last important pronouncement on the referendal theory is in a letter to *The Times*, dated 4 April 1895. It was printed on the eve of the general election of that year and was written, of course, with an eye to that election. As will be seen, the letter integrated his concept of the predominant partner with the main lines of his celebrated speech on the Irish Church Bill. Noting that such prominent Liberals as Sir William Harcourt, the leader of the house of commons, and H. H. Asquith, the home secretary, were citing his support of that Bill to suggest inconsistency on his part if he opposed the disestablishment of the Welsh church, a subject before the house of commons, Salisbury offered an interpretation of the events of 1868–9 that gave succinctly his final version of the lords' referendal function. In his speech of 17 June he had noted that all parts of the United Kingdom had agreed in the general election of 1868 to the disestablishment of the Irish church; but the point was then relatively unimportant to him, and his reference to it was almost in passing. England had agreed to disestablishment, although more doubtfully and languidly than other parts of the United Kingdom – this was his phrasing, and he did not return to the subject elsewhere in the speech. Twenty-six years later his letter to *The Times* stressed that in 1868 large majorities had voted in all parts of the United Kingdom for disestablishment. The contention appears in several places, without any mention of hesitation on England's part. That is, the predominant partner had agreed and had done so, it was implied, without reservations.

Thus the referendal theory received its perfected form in the letter of 1895. It contains Salisbury's mature reflexions on that theory, or at least the view of it that he wished to leave with contemporaries, and is for this reason well worth reading. Key portions of it, to which a few italics have been added, are printed below. He wrote:

In 1868, when the Suspensory Bill was sent up to the house of lords, I spoke against it, and voted with the majority by which it was thrown out. Its rejection showed that there was a profound difference of opinion between the two houses upon a question of the first importance. This difference was duly submitted to the electors for their decision. The dissolution took place in the same year, and the constituencies were fully aware that the disestablishment of the Irish church was the question which the election was to determine. No attempt was made to distract their minds by raising several other vital issues at the same time, or by deferring the election till the matter in controversy was forgotten. The question was put to the electors honestly and plainly. *The result was*

Mr Balfour's poodle: An account of the struggle between the house of lords and the government of Mr Asquith (London, 1954, rep. 1968), pp. 33–4; Le May, *The Victorian constitution*, pp. 140–2.

[81] *Parl. deb.* (lords), fourth series, XVII, 640; XXII, 22–5.

a verdict adverse to the Irish church from all parts of the United Kingdom. The view of the house of commons was sustained by large majorities in England, Scotland, and Ireland. Effect was given in the following year – 1869 – to this decision. The house of lords in effect reversed their former vote by passing the second reading of the Bill; and I spoke and voted in that sense. I did not do so because I had changed my opinion on the measure; but, as I stated at the time, because a higher authority than the house of lords had spoken. I still thought that the Bill was founded on dangerous principles, and would lead to the gravest evils. But *it was perfectly manifest that a contrary judgment had been formed by a large majority of the nation in all its main divisions.*[82]

Similar sentiments were expressed in a speech at Bradford, reported in *The Times* on 23 May 1895. Looking back to the years 1868–9 once more, he noted that Gladstone had brought forward his Irish Church Bill only after he had secured 'a large majority, in all parts of the country'. Though the latter had on more than one occasion proposed measures of vast scope affecting the organic integrity of the empire and the interests of great classes, not until 1893 did he do so without 'an enormous majority at his back'.[83]

To contemporaries, the general election of 1895 – the greatest electoral triumph since 1832 – ratified the action of the house of lords in rejecting the second Home Rule Bill, and the results were seen as reaffirmed when the Conservatives were again victorious in 1900. As an anonymous writer in the *Quarterly Review* put it, the last two general elections had revealed conclusively how deeply the public mind was impressed by Salisbury's defence of the house of lords as 'a democratic necessity' and as 'the only alternative to triennial or even annual parliaments' and by 'his practical demonstration of this proposition when, at his instance, the house [of lords] saved Great Britain from Irish dictation by rejecting the home rule bill'. And he described the rehabilitation of the house of lords as a striking illustration of the vast scope of Salisbury's labours as a political leader.[84] Another equally cogent observation might have been made about Salisbury's labours as a political leader – one that calls to mind once more the controversy over the Irish church. In his speech on the Suspensory Bill he had urged rejection on the ground, novel at the time, that the peers were just as capable of judging the nation's will as the house of commons, and in support of this point had evoked the lords' successful opposition in the 1830s to a series of measures hostile to the Irish church that the house of commons favoured. In the event the nation had proved indifferent

---

[82] Printed in *The Times* (8 Apr. 1895), p. 9.

[83] Ibid. (23 May 1895), p. 6. The ideas of 1868–9 were also revived in 1895 when the barrister S. H. Jeyes published a biography of Salisbury. Jeyes gave the speech on the Suspensory Bill extensive coverage, finding its language as relevant in 1895 as it had been earlier: *Salisbury*, I, 113–20. See also Sir Spencer Walpole's *The history of twenty-five years* (London, 1904), II, 366. This four-volume work, published in the years from 1904 to 1908, is still the fullest history of the period from 1856 to 1880. Discussing the Irish church controversy, Walpole writes of Salisbury as seeing 'rightly or wrongly, [that] the fate of the Irish church had been referred to the constituencies in 1868, *and that, in every part of the kingdom, the electors had given a reply which could not be misinterpreted by the dullest intellect* [italics added]'. And he added that Salisbury was 'too wise to refuse assent to its [the Irish Church Bill's] principle'. See also Le May, *The Victorian constitution*, p. 141.

[84] *The Quarterly Review*, CXCVI (July–Oct. 1902), 652–3.

on the question. 'In course of time it turned out that you were right,' Salisbury told the peers in 1868. 'You knew the opinion of the nation better than the house of commons.' To numerous observers in the 1890s, this was the great lesson of the events from 1892 to 1895, though it is not clear how many of them traced this kind of argument to Salisbury. As a Victorian diarist recorded, 'for the first time in history the lords represented the feeling of the people of England & the commons did not'.[85]

Salisbury himself considered that he was leaving the house of lords stronger than he had found it. In the wake of the general election of 1895 he wrote to a long-time political ally: 'Whatever happens to us, I think the position of the house of lords is considerably strengthened.'[86] Significantly, Arthur Balfour, his nephew and successor in the leadership of the Conservative party, concurred in this assessment. In his well-known letter to Lansdowne, outlining the opposition strategy for dealing with the post-1906 house of commons, Balfour assigned the house of lords a central role when he wrote:

I do not think the house of lords will be able to escape the duty of making serious modifications in important government measures, but, if this be done with caution and tact, I do not believe that they will do themselves any harm. On the contrary, as the rejection of the home rule bill undoubtedly strengthened their position, I think it quite possible that your house may come out of the ordeal strengthened rather than weakened by the inevitable difficulties of the next few years.[87]

This optimistic forecast, as Balfour's words reveal, was rooted in Salisbury's success in checkmating Liberal governments by means of the house of lords – a success to which the referendal theory had made an indispensable contribution. Little wonder that the post-Salisbury Conservative party embraced that theory eagerly and committed the house of lords to the political wars, apparently without a clear recognition until too late that a very different outcome was possible.

---

[85] *A Victorian diarist: extracts from the journals of Mary, Lady Monkswell, 1873–1895*, ed. E. C. F. Collier (London, 1944), pp. 238–9. See also Stead, *Peers or people?*, pp. 3–5; W. E. H. Lecky, *Democracy and liberty* (London, 1896), I, 438; McKechnie, *The reform of the house of lords*, pp. 18–19; and note 77 above.

[86] Gathorne-Hardy, *Cranbrook*, II, 351–2. This is an entry in Cranbrook's diary, dated 23 July 1895. See also Sidney Low, 'The house of lords as a constitutional force', *The New Review*, X, 58 (Mar. 1894), 257–64. This was a Conservative publication. For a rather different estimate of the lords' position at this time see *The Spectator*, LXXVII (1 Aug. 1896), 132–3 and Le May, *The Victorian constitution*, pp. 144–5.

[87] The letter, dated 13 Apr. 1906, was originally published in Lord Newton, *Lord Lansdowne: a biography* (1929) and is reprinted in Hanham, *The nineteenth century constitution*, p. 192.

8. The Home Rule debate in the House of Lords, 1893.

A painting by Dickinson and Foster, by courtesy of the House of Lords Record Office.

The Lord Chancellor, Lord Herschell, is about to put the question at the end of the debate on Gladstone's second Home Rule Bill on 9 September 1893. The bill was rejected. Dickinson and Foster published a key plate to the portrait and this identifies 180 peers and officials as well as 39 peeresses and ladies in the Gallery. There is a companion portrait which shows the other side of the chamber at the time the Marquess of Salisbury was speaking in the debate.

22

THE LIBERAL LEADERSHIP AND THE LORDS' VETO, 1907-10

CORINNE COMSTOCK WESTON

I

THE official biographers of H. H. Asquith believed that his sole difference of any importance with Sir Henry Campbell-Bannerman in the period when Asquith served as his principal lieutenant rose in connexion with the Trade Disputes Act of 1906.[1] In fact, another important difference divided them in the following spring, this one rising out of their respective views on the proper mode of limiting the veto of the house of lords. That of Campbell-Bannerman is well known. He sponsored a plan of suspensory veto that could conceivably limit the period in which the lords' veto operated to little more than six months. Under its terms a bill sent up to the house of lords would go to a small conference representing each house equally when the two houses were in disagreement. Should the conference fail, the bill or another like it could be reintroduced in the house of commons after an interval of at least six months, passed under drastic closure, and sent once more to the house of lords. The impasse continuing, a second conference might be held; and a second failure at this juncture could entail a repetition of the whole process. But if a third conference proved unsuccessful, the bill could become law without the consent of the house of lords. Known subsequently as the C-B veto plan, it was made public by the Prime Minister in a speech in the house of commons, on 24 June 1907, when he also introduced and carried by a large majority a resolution asserting that the power of the house of lords to alter or reject bills should be so restricted by law as to secure that the decision of the house of commons should prevail within the limits of a single parliament. At the same time Campbell-Bannerman recommended shortening the legal duration of parliament from seven to five years in order, he explained, to prevent the strengthened house of commons from acting arbitrarily in an ageing parliament.[2] He took no further action towards limiting the lords' veto; but just before Campbell-Bannerman's death in 1908, Asquith became prime minister and

---

[1] J. A. Spender and Cyril Asquith, *The Life of Herbert Henry Asquith, Lord Oxford and Asquith* (London, 1932), I, 184. Roy Jenkins, *Asquith* (London, 1964), p. 171. Nor does J. A. Spender's account of the evolution of Liberal policy on the lords' veto in 1907 ascribe to Asquith a viewpoint different from the Prime Minister's. Spender, *The Life of the Right Hon. Sir Henry Campbell-Bannerman* (London, 1923), II, 348–57. Interestingly, Randolph S. Churchill pointed out in the biography of his father that 'Campbell-Bannerman's talk of a suspensory veto was probably considered too drastic by Asquith'. But no elaboration is offered. *Winston S. Churchill* (Boston, 1967), II, 311.

[2] *Parliamentary Debates*, fourth series, CLXXVI, columns 909–26. Spender, II, 357.

as such carried into law three years later the highly controversial Parliament Act that contained both a modified version of the C-B veto plan and a provision for quinquennial parliaments.

Yet Asquith, the official author of the Parliament Act, held in 1907, and for some time thereafter, a view very different from Campbell-Bannerman's as to the proper mode of limiting the lords' veto. Some months before the C-B veto plan was disclosed to the house of commons Asquith and a few colleagues formulated within the privacy of the Cabinet a more moderate plan that was almost immediately labelled in a misleading way the Ripon plan, a name derived from Lord Ripon, lord privy seal and leader of the house of lords in the Campbell-Bannerman Government. It provided that in the event of difference between the two houses the disputed measure would be finally settled in the following parliamentary session by a joint vote in which the house of commons would sit as a body but the house of lords would be represented by a delegation of 100 members. The delegation would include all the members of the Government who were peers, not exceeding 20, and other peers sufficient to make up the number of 100, whom the house of lords would choose. Assuming a Unionist-dominated house of lords, it followed that no Liberal Government could carry a really contentious measure without a substantial majority in the house of commons. Back of the Ripon plan was a sound historical precedent. Had it prevailed, the pattern by which the great majority of peers had informally withdrawn from the judicial sphere leaving the exercise of their judicial powers to a few law lords would have been extended by law to the legislative sphere whenever deadlock gripped the two houses.

If the Ripon plan on first sight presents a somewhat exotic appearance, its solid features nevertheless attracted important support in high Liberal circles in the years from 1907 to 1910. At the very beginning of this period it was the only formidable rival there to the C-B veto plan, commanding support so powerful that had it not been for Campbell-Bannerman's determination the principles of the Ripon plan, and not those of the suspensory veto, would have been announced to the house of commons as the basis of Liberal policy towards the house of lords. The Ripon plan was not forgotten after the great setback of 1907. Perhaps the most significant sign of the continued interest was its reappearance during the Constitutional Conference of 1910, where the Liberal delegation headed by Asquith sponsored it as a vital part of a far-reaching settlement by consent of the constitutional question. This reappearance strongly suggests that the Ripon plan had constituted for the political heirs of Campbell-Bannerman their preferred solution to the question of the house of lords in the years after 1907, and this suggestion receives reinforcement from an examination of the beginnings of the Ripon plan and the circumstances in which it first assumed political importance.[3]

[3] This line of thought is not pursued by Spender and Asquith or by Jenkins, either in his *Asquith* or in his earlier *Mr. Balfour's Poodle: An Account of the Struggle between the House*

II

The Ripon plan made its political début in the report of an important Cabinet Committee that was appointed early in the spring of 1907 after a struggle between the Liberal Government and the house of lords over education and plural voting bills. It was composed of leading members of the Campbell-Bannerman Government. The chairman was Lord Chancellor Loreburn, a veteran of Liberal politics whose outlook closely resembled Campbell-Bannerman's; and other members included the ailing Ripon, who was almost eighty at the time; Asquith, chancellor of the exchequer, already marked out as Campbell-Bannerman's successor in the premiership; the Earl of Crewe, lord president of the council, who assisted Ripon in the leadership of the house of lords and succeeded to that post early in the Asquith Government; and David Lloyd George, president of the board of trade and a rising figure in the left wing of the party. If the other members may be less certainly stated, they probably were Lord Haldane, secretary for war and an intimate of Sir Edward Grey, both members of the Asquith circle in the Cabinet, and Lewis Harcourt, who had only recently entered the Cabinet as commissioner of works.[4] Empowered 'to consider the mode that may be adopted to redress

---

of Lords and the Government of Mr. Asquith (London, 1954). Nor is it to be found in Emily Allyn, *Lords versus Commons* (New York, 1931). R. C. K. Ensor linked Lord Ripon with the joint-sitting scheme discussed at the Constitutional Conference but made no reference to the events of 1907. *England: 1870–1914* (Oxford, 1936), p. 423.

[4] Campbell-Bannerman to Lord Knollys, 25 Mar. 1907, Campbell-Bannerman Papers, Brit. Mus. Add. MS. 41,208, fos. 30–31v. This letter, a copy, has been collated with the original, which is in the Royal Archives, Windsor Castle. Acknowledgement is due and is gratefully made to the gracious permission of Her Majesty Queen Elizabeth II to make use of materials from the Royal Archives. All references to these materials have the prefix RA. For Campbell-Bannerman's letter, see RA R28/33. Campbell-Bannerman stated that Loreburn was chairman of the Cabinet Committee, and this is substantiated by a notation on the typed copy of their report that is in the Asquith Papers. Apparently written by Asquith's secretary, Vaughan Nash, it reads: 'Copy of the Lord Chancellor's suggested scheme for modifying relations of the two Houses'. MS. Asquith 102, fos. 140–5. The Asquith Papers have been used with the kind permission of Mr Mark Bonham Carter. I am also grateful to Mr D. S. Porter, Department of Western Manuscripts, Bodleian Library, where the Asquith Papers are deposited. The membership of the Cabinet Committee is given in a memorandum listing reform proposals affecting the house of lords that was prepared for the use of the House of Lords Committee appointed in 1921. House of Lords Committee, MS. Fisher 11, item 4. The Fisher Papers are in the Bodleian Library. The memorandum errs in listing Lord Ripon as chairman and leaving out Loreburn's name, not altogether a surprising mistake. The House of Lords Committee, after an unsuccessful attempt to secure a copy of the Cabinet Committee's report, were compelled to rely upon the recollections of a former member, Lloyd George, who was Prime Minister in 1921. That Lloyd George was a member is also suggested by the survival in his papers of one of the rare copies of the Cabinet Committee's report, which he was unable to locate in 1921. Private Papers of David, Earl Lloyd George of Dwyfor, B/2/2. These papers, cited hereafter as the Lloyd George Papers, are in the Beaverbrook Library. Access to the Lloyd George Papers was kindly granted by the Trustees of the Beaverbrook Foundations. A more accessible copy of the Cabinet Committee's report is in the Public Record Office. See P.R.O., Cab. 37/87/38 or Cab. 37/101/136. The Public Record Office has assembled printed Cabinet memoranda for the period from 1880 to 1914, many of them from private collections. These have been photographed, and the photographic copies now form

the mischief arising from the present relations between the two Houses of Parliament', the Cabinet Committee interpreted their charge as one of dealing with the lords' veto but not with the reform of the house of lords. Their work was harmoniously completed by 19 March;[5] and four days later the Cabinet, after discussing fully the Cabinet Committee's report, accepted their plan—the Ripon plan—as the basis of the Liberal policy on the lords' veto.[6]

The following numbered propositions embody the principles of the Cabinet Committee's plan:

1. When either House has refused to pass a Bill, or has insisted on amendments to a Bill sent to it from the other House, the consideration of the Bill shall stand adjourned till the next Session.

2. On motion made next Session the House shall reconsider its refusal or its amendments, as the case may be, and if it insists then the other House shall be entitled to claim a joint vote.

3. For the purpose of such joint vote the House of Lords shall be represented by 100 Members, consisting of all the members of the Government who are Peers, not exceeding 20, and of other Peers sufficient to make up the number of 100, who shall be chosen by the House.

4. Thereupon the Peers representing the House of Lords and the House of Commons shall deliberate and vote together on the points of difference between the two Houses, and their decision shall be binding on both Houses.

5. Nothing herein is to affect any practice or privilege as to money Bills.

Uncertain as to how Liberal circles would receive this plan, since nothing of the kind had received a public discussion, the Cabinet Committee noted on the positive side its distinctive merit of 'being the line of least resistance': the house of lords would retain its privileges except that in a joint sitting the peers would count as 10 to 67 compared with members of the house of commons. The net effect, it was estimated, was the addition of 60 Unionist votes from the house of lords to that vote in the house of commons. If somewhat hesitant about its reception, the Cabinet Committee had no doubt of the intrinsic superiority of their plan to that of the suspensory veto, which, as it was

part of a class (Cab. 37) in the Cabinet Office group of records. The documents cited above are in this class, to which an index has been supplied in *List of Cabinet Papers 1880–1914* (London, 1964).

[5] Ripon received the completed report by 19 March. Ripon to Crewe (copy), 19 Mar. 1907, Ripon Papers, Brit. Mus. Add. MS. 43,552, fos. 132–3. These are cited hereafter as the Ripon Papers. The printer's date on the copy of the report of the Cabinet Committee in the Lloyd George Papers is 20 Mar. 1907. Their charge is in their report. The Committee pointed out that it precluded any scheme for reconstructing the house of lords. Any change in its composition, they added, would tend to strengthen it and increase its powers. 'Accordingly', the report ran, 'no proposals in this direction can be made.'

[6] Campbell-Bannerman to Lord Knollys, 25 Mar. 1907, Campbell-Bannerman Papers, Brit. Mus. Add. MS. 41,208, fos. 30–31v. Crewe to Ripon, 21 Mar. 1907, Ripon Papers, fos. 134–5.

being canvassed, would have left the house of lords a delaying power of only six months. They stated simply: 'We think it is the preferable of the two methods.'[7]

Almost at once the plan of the Cabinet Committee was attributed to Lord Ripon. 'The parent of it was Ld. Ripon', wrote Campbell-Bannerman to one of the King's secretaries, Lord Knollys, in a letter intended to inform Edward VII of the progress being made by the Cabinet Committee.[8] If he knew, the Prime Minister gave no intimation that the main authorship was Asquith's and Crewe's, particularly the latter's. For Ripon was an absentee member of the Cabinet Committee. Old and ill, he was in residence at Studley Royal, Ripon, during their deliberations, and a letter from him to Crewe, written on 19 March after receiving the Cabinet Committee's completed report, reveals the very limited nature of his role. 'If the report of the Cabinet Committee is discussed at Cabinet before I return to London', wrote Lord Ripon, 'you are quite at liberty to say that I acquiesce in it.'[9] The attribution of authorship is explicable in terms of Ripon's support for the provision of a joint sitting as a means of ending deadlock, a procedure that he deemed 'greatly preferable' to the plan of restricting the lords' veto to one session. He wrote: 'I see great objections [to the suspensory veto] the more I think of it.'[10] Yet Ripon's role was minimal. The burden of leading the house of lords in these months had fallen to Crewe, as Ripon himself recognized when he wrote to Asquith on resigning the leadership a year later because of age and infirmities. 'Unselfish as Crewe may be,' Ripon declared, 'it is not fair to him to let him take almost all the work and give him none of the honour.'[11]

It was Crewe working with Asquith who formulated the Ripon plan. The beginnings of their activity are to be found in a highly influential memorandum, printed 8 March 1907, in which Crewe stated for his colleagues on the Cabinet Committee the various possible solutions of the problem of the house of lords without adopting any one of them but also without concealing his

[7] P.R.O., Cab. 37/87/38. At Harcourt's suggestion Loreburn later wrote to Campbell-Bannerman proposing an alteration in the second proposition so that only the house of commons could claim a joint vote. Lorebure to Campbell-Bannerman, 6 May 1907, Campbell-Bannerman Papers, Brit. Mus. Add. MS. 41,222, fo. 206. Sir Almeric Fitzroy, clerk to the privy council, recorded that the Cabinet Committee met on 16 March to decide between a plan of joint sittings and one for a suspensory veto by which the peers could delay legislation for two years. *Memoirs* (London, 1925), I, 317. But the surviving letters of the principals and the Cabinet Committee's report offer no support for the idea that this type of suspensory veto ever received serious consideration.

[8] Campbell-Bannerman to Lord Knollys, 25 Mar. 1907. Campbell-Bannerman Papers, Brit. Mus. Add. MS. 41,208, fos. 30–31v.

[9] Ripon to Crewe (copy), 19 Mar. 1907, Ripon Papers, fos. 132–3. Same to same (copy), 22 Mar. 1907, ibid. fo. 138. *Journals and Letters of Reginald Viscount Esher*, ed. Maurice V. Brett (London, 1934), II, 227–8.

[10] Ripon to Crewe (copy), 19 Mar. 1907, Ripon Papers, fos. 132–3.

[11] Lucien Wolf, *Life of the First Marquess of Ripon* (London, 1921), II, 296. Ripon offered to resign on 10 March 1907 at the height of the Cabinet Committee's activity, but Campbell-Bannerman persuaded him to remain. Ibid. pp. 286–7.

individual preference.[12] After reading the March memorandum Asquith expressed admiration and then offered a suggestion that fundamentally altered Crewe's preferred plan. It was this plan, first propounded by Crewe and then transformed by Asquith, that the Cabinet Committee considered and adopted and the Cabinet as a whole approved on 23 March. Since the Cabinet Committee's action implied their acceptance of the line of reasoning in Crewe's March memorandum, its contents require a rather lengthy exploration.

Crewe's approach was one of examining and discarding a number of plans until he reached his individual preference, though he made no claim of having reached a final conclusion. He first listed four plans as either utterly unacceptable or practically unattainable. These were the following: 1, a single chamber; 2, an elected senate as the second chamber; 3, the plan known as 'Home Rule all round'; and 4, the referendum. Only the last drew further comment, and Crewe's opposition to it was complete. Indeed, a major reason for not adopting the suspensory veto, advanced later in the memorandum, was that its operation might accidentally open the door to the referendum. The house of commons, it might be said, ought to display more care in preparing a measure when anticipating the lords' veto since the country would give close attention to any suspended measure. 'The weakness of this argument', Crewe warned, 'seems to be in the admission of a kind of informal referendum, alien to our English theory of a representative House. Introduce the principle and you are in sight of the real referendum and a maimed House of Commons.' The Cabinet Committee also rejected the referendum though for a different reason: it would place the two houses 'on terms of absolute equality', an outcome intolerable to Liberal opinion.

The emphasis in the March memorandum, however, was on the respective merits or otherwise of the suspensory veto plan and that of the joint sitting as a means of ending deadlocks. Somewhat surprisingly, Crewe found scarcely more acceptable than the referendum the plan of a suspensory veto by which the lords' veto would be limited to a year or a session (about six months in 1907). Its effect, so he later stated, seemed to him tantamount to abolishing the lords' veto, a viewpoint that he never abandoned and one that the Cabinet Committee also expressed. Neither he nor the Cabinet Committee in their report suggested lengthening the period in which the lords' veto would operate. The March memorandum revealed the reasons for Crewe's antipathy. He would grant that limiting the veto in this way seemed the most obvious policy for a Liberal Government and that it was the one most favoured by the Liberal

[12] 'Memorandum on Various Expedients for Adjusting the Relations between the Two Houses of Parliament', P.R.O., Cab. 37/101/137. There was no ring of previous consultation with Ripon when Crewe wrote on 11 March 1907: 'I am sending under another cover a short memorandum which states the various House of Lords solutions as I understand them. I hope you may agree generally with the preferences I express...' Crewe to Ripon, Ripon Papers, fo. 128.

party in so far as thought had been given to methods of ending deadlocks. Yet the plan had grave disadvantages. The peers would resist it to the last, and it could only be carried by measures close to revolution that Crewe could not countenance. He condemned the idea of creating 500 peers as a desperate measure, highly distasteful to the King and vulnerable to possible counter-moves from the house of lords. Nor did Crewe believe that the plan of a suspensory veto would draw popular support, a doubt that the Cabinet Committee's report echoed. This was the key question: 'Would the limited veto commend itself to the great majority of the people of this country as a sufficient check on hasty legislation?' He thought not. Whereas experienced observers of parliament would agree that the delay imposed by the suspensory veto could be a real check when the mind of the country was not made up, this conclusion was less obvious to the average critic; and even the first group might adduce the contrary argument. Nor would the operation of the suspensory veto commend itself. It would be concluded that it was better to 'rely at once on the necessary caution of a single Chamber than invent a paper check which might lull the country into false security'. If it were argued, on the other hand, that the house of commons would give greater attention to a measure likely to encounter the lords' veto, the disliked referendum was in sight. Crewe also forecast difficulties for an overworked house of commons from the apparent necessity of sending up a bill on a second occasion in a precisely identical form.

Crewe now reached his preferred plan that when modified by a suggestion from Asquith provided the foundation of the Ripon plan. He proposed limiting the lords' veto to a year or even a session. But on the second arrival of a disputed bill in the house of lords, if it were again rejected or amended, the two houses would sit or vote as one, the verdict of the majority being final. Recognizing that a small house of lords would be required, Crewe considered a number of possibilities including the idea of a reduced edition of the existing house of lords. Perhaps 150 hereditary peers, their numbers reflecting the balance of political parties, ought to be selected on the basis of their experience as privy councillors, chairmen of county councils, etc.[13] This portion of Crewe's plan was abandoned almost at once as the direct result of a terse suggestion from Asquith. Writing on 11 March, three days after the printing of the March memorandum, the latter expressed a strong admiration for its contents but recommended a change that virtually transformed Crewe's plan. 'I have

---

[13] P.R.O., Cab. 37/87/38; Cab. 37/101/137. Crewe's hostility towards the referendum persisted long after the period in which the Parliament Act was born. He was directly responsible for the portion of the Bryce Report that explained why the Conference on the Reform of the Second Chamber in 1918 had rejected the referendum as a means of adjusting differences between the two houses. Crewe to G. F. M. Campion, 5 April 1918; Crewe to Lord Bryce, 8 April 1918, 'Uncalendared Bryce Papers Box P.14'. The unpublished Crewe letters in the Bryce Papers have been used with the kind permission of the Bodleian Library and Mary, Duchess of Roxburghe, who is the daughter of Lord Crewe.

just read your admirable memorandum on H of Lords, and find myself in almost complete agreement', wrote Asquith. His recommendation, phrased as a question, suggested that he was either more cautious on the lords' question than Crewe or else more ingenious. 'But have you considered, and, if not, will you consider', Asquith asked, 'whether it might not be easier to leave the H. of L. exactly as it is for all normal purposes; and only to bring into existence the *delegacy*, in the comparatively rare cases when, after a two sessions' difference, the two Houses were in irreconcilable collision?'[14] Crewe's plan, altered so as to incorporate Asquith's idea of a delegation from the lords, proved attractive to the Cabinet Committee. 'We were practically unanimous on the Committee that this plan offers the best path out of the thicket', Crewe reported to Ripon.[15]

From the first, however, one indispensable element of support was missing: that of the strong-willed Campbell-Bannerman, whose viewpoint regarding the lords' veto differed markedly from both the Cabinet Committee and the Cabinet. He had earlier sought a general election on the issue of the house of lords, only to acquiesce in the appointment of the Cabinet Committee; and he was keenly disappointed by their report. Writing two days after the Cabinet adopted the Ripon plan, the Prime Minister informed Lord Knollys: 'One or two (myself included among them) rather hanker after the more drastic method of the one year's veto and fear that this milder scheme is too artificial & complicated.'[16] On another occasion he apparently described it graphically as 'too much in the spirit of the Abbé Sieyès'.[17] Yet for some time he held his peace. As late as 6 May, about six weeks after the Cabinet adopted the Ripon plan, Loreburn assumed that it would provide the basis of Liberal policy towards the lords' veto when it was made public.[18] About this time Campbell-Bannerman bestirred himself, undertaking first to block the Ripon

[14] Asquith to Crewe (copy), 11 Mar. 1907, MS. Asquith 46, fo. 161. Crewe's Papers, which are in the University Library, Cambridge, cannot be consulted until 1973. But there is no doubt that the Asquith letter reached Crewe. James Pope-Hennessy used it in his biography of the Liberal leader. *Crewe* (London, 1955), p. 112.

[15] Crewe to Ripon, 21 Mar. 1907, Ripon Papers, fo. 134. The Prime Minister stated that the Cabinet Committee were unanimous in their report. Campbell-Bannerman to Lord Knollys, 25 Mar. 1907, Campbell-Bannerman Papers, Brit. Mus. Add. MS. 41,208, fos. 30–31v.

[16] Ibid. Yet the Prime Minister saw some advantage to the Ripon plan, in particular that it left the house of lords untouched.

[17] Loreburn seemed to attribute this expression to Campbell-Bannerman when he wrote on 5 June 1907: 'My view was that the Committee's proposal would be effective but if you think it too much in the spirit of the Abbé Sieyès or would not meet the legitimate grievance I shall have no sort of difficulty in supporting a suspensory veto as I have in fact always done.' Loreburn to Campbell-Bannerman, Campbell-Bannerman Papers, Brit. Mus. Add. MS. 41,222, fo. 208.

[18] Loreburn to Campbell-Bannerman, 6 May 1907, ibid. fo. 206. See also Lord Cawdor to A. J. Balfour, 17 June 1907, Balfour Papers, Brit. Mus. Add. MS. 49,709, fos. 34v–35v. Writing after Campbell-Bannerman entered on the notice paper on 14 June the resolution that he moved ten days later, Cawdor declared: 'It really seems incredible that any 6 men of ordinary common sense should be able to put their hand to anything so silly. The amusing

plan and then to replace it with a suspensory veto plan. In doing so he carried out virtually by himself a sweeping reversal of a Cabinet policy that had been adopted by the leading members of his Government after a process of discussion and due deliberation. The Prime Minister's first step was to take what Asquith's biographers described as 'the strong and rather unusual course of issuing a memorandum to his colleagues against the scheme of his own Cabinet Committee'.[19] At this juncture he turned to Courtenay Ilbert (later Sir Courtenay), clerk of the house of commons and an authority on parliament, who supplied the Prime Minister with the desired ammunition for a reversal of the Cabinet policy. According to Ilbert, writing in 1911 after the house of lords accepted the Parliament Bill, the Prime Minister, who was not 'quite satisfied' with the Cabinet Committee's report, had asked him to examine it and convey confidentially his thoughts about it. Ilbert after raising some objections to their plan had proposed an alternative course for the Prime Minister's consideration. Campbell-Bannerman, so Ilbert wrote, 'liked my memorandum, had it printed & circulated to the Cabinet (without my initials), and adopted it as his own, & persuaded the Cabinet to adopt it instead of that to which they had previously agreed'. It 'became the foundation of the resolutions of the following June & through them of the Parliament Bill'.[20]

Ilbert, then, was the author of the anonymous memorandum of 31 May 1907 that J. A. Spender believed so important as to warrant giving it fully in his life of Campbell-Bannerman. It contained three objections in principle to the Cabinet Committee's plan. The first was to the principle of a delegation from the house of lords. Not only was the proposed 100 peers too generous a representation of the house of lords, the principle itself would puzzle the plain man. He would find it difficult to believe that a vote in which the whole of one house and a fraction of the other were entitled to share could be described properly as a joint vote of two bodies. Yet a plan capable of obtaining general assent should be easily intelligible to the plain man. A second objection was to the principle of joint sittings, which was described as a return with modifications to the old plan of formal conferences between the two houses. But an assembly of 770 persons would be too large for a conference: it would

and also incredible thing is that the Lord Chancellor should have told B. of B. [Balfour of Burleigh?] before Whitsuntide [19 May], that they had some weeks before decided on their resolution, and that it was so moderate, that he was sure we should be quite ready to accept it—& yet, that it had been so framed that it would be acceptable to their extreme friends!—they must be mad!'

[19] Spender and Asquith, I, 191. Compare Spender, *Life of Campbell-Bannerman*, II, 351. The comment in Spender and Asquith is couched in stronger language. In view of the fact that Crewe read much of their manuscript and contributed 'most valuable comment and criticism', it is tempting to believe that Crewe's opinion on this point was being expressed.

[20] Ilbert to Lord Bryce, 12 Aug. 1911, MS. Bryce 14, fos. 34v–35. Ilbert's statement is confirmed by his earlier letter to Bryce, 22 July 1907, ibid. 13, fos. 124v–5. The Ilbert letters have been used with the kind persmission of the Bodleian Library and Mrs Mary Bennett, Principal of St Hilda's College, Oxford, who is Ilbert's granddaughter.

be a mob. Negotiation and deliberation would be impossible, and only a strict party vote could take place. The final objection on principle was that the scheme would prove unworkable whenever the Government's working majority was less than 70: a Government in this situation would be worse off than at present because the peers would insist on using the new machinery. Apart from the objections on principles, Ilbert also advanced difficulties of detail that he discussed.

He then proposed the alternative plan for limiting the lords' veto that became the C-B veto plan. Noting that 'the most serious objection to what has been called the suspensory veto proposal, namely, the proposal that the power of the House of Lords to throw out a Bill should be restricted to a single Session' was that it practically abolished the legislative power of the house of lords, Ilbert proposed to meet it by introducing a conference between the two houses that would provide an opportunity for reflexion, deliberation, and negotiation. But no decisions taken in the proposed conference were to be binding on the house of commons, and the conference itself could be held only if the Government were willing.[21] What, then, were the views of Campbell-Bannerman's colleagues, who had already considered the plan of a suspensory veto at some length, only to reject it in favour of the Ripon plan? Would the injection of Ilbert's proposed conference make the plan of a suspensory veto more attractive? No surmise is needed. That the proposed conference inspired little confidence in Campbell-Bannerman's colleagues is evident from the fact that the number of conferences tripled in the three weeks between the appearance of the Ilbert memorandum and the public statement of the Liberal plan in Campbell-Bannerman's speech of 24 June. After the Prime Minister's statement was made, Harcourt, who was later the most ardent supporter of the C-B veto plan in the Asquith Government, wrote to congratulate him on his 'splendid' speech. Harcourt's comment on the number of conferences now proposed must have amused Campbell-Bannerman, who had reached the same conclusion. 'You suggested *three* conferences', wrote Harcourt in some surprise. The number was higher than he had anticipated or believed necessary, but he added: 'There is no harm in them'.[22] The viewpoint of the Cabinet Committee may have been expressed by Crewe, writing in 1909 at a time when the Liberal policy on the lords' veto was undergoing review. He still believed the proposed suspension of the lords' veto in the C-B veto plan 'tantamount to its abolition'. In his opinion, which

---

[21] 'Relations of the Two Houses', P.R.O., Cab. 37/101/136. Spender, *Life of Campbell-Bannerman*, II, 351–5. Asquith reprinted the Cabinet Committee's report and the Ilbert memorandum, with a prefatory note, in 1909.

[22] Harcourt to Campbell-Bannerman, 24 June 1907, Campbell-Bannerman Papers, Brit. Mus. Add. MS. 41,220, fo. 218. Ilbert may have opposed multiplying the number of conferences. He wrote: 'The plan sketched out at the end of the speech was taken [from?] my memorandum though I had opposed [three?] conferences.' Ilbert to Bryce, 22 July 1907, MS. Bryce 13, fos. 124v–5.

Lord Ripon had shared, 'the suggested conferences would be altogether illusory'.[23]

That Campbell-Bannerman encountered resistance from the Cabinet when he undertook to establish his own plan for limiting the lords' veto also appears from his reports to Edward VII. The King learned, for example, that a new plan had been introduced to the Cabinet on 5 June, simpler than the other, but that no decision was reached.[24] Thereafter Edward VII apparently received no more detailed information about the new plan until it was disclosed to the house of commons on 24 June, probably because the Cabinet remained divided until very late about their plan. A report of 11 June explained that progress had been made in formulating the June resolution but that the plan to accompany it was still under discussion.[25] Three days later the Cabinet adopted the final form of the resolution, but Campbell-Bannerman's further comment was ambiguous: 'The particulars of the plan contemplated for carrying out the Resolution will be stated on Monday the 24th.'[26] Nor was the report of 19 June, five days before the disclosure of the Liberal plan, any more precise. The Cabinet had been mainly occupied with 'the statement to be made in the House of Commons on Monday next, as to which the Prime Minister has already had the honour of communicating with your Majesty...'.[27]

Some further details of the Cabinet struggle may be gleaned from the comments of the leading participants. Loreburn, the chairman of the Cabinet Committee, readily accepted the Prime Minister's strong lead. Writing to Campbell-Bannerman on 5 June, the Lord Chancellor stated that in his judgement the Cabinet Committee's plan would have been effective but that he found no difficulty in supporting the suspensory veto, as in fact he had always done. Yet the pressure of judicial business would keep him from attending the Cabinet meeting on the business of the house of lords unless Campbell-Bannerman should expressly send for him.[28] Thereafter Loreburn was one of

[23] In October 1909 Asquith reprinted the rival plans of 1907, and at the same time Crewe reissued two memoranda that he had circulated in 1907. His revealing observations are in a prefatory statement dated 6 Oct. 1909. It looks very much as if Asquith and Crewe were engaged in a common enterprise in 1909. P.R.O., Cab. 37/101/137.

[24] Campbell-Bannerman to the King, 5 June 1907, RAR28/54.

[25] Campbell-Bannerman to the King, 11 June 1907, RAR28/57.

[26] Campbell-Bannerman to the King, 14 June 1907, RAR28/58.

[27] Campbell-Bannerman to the King, 19 June 1907, RAR28/60. Spender, *Life of Campbell-Bannerman*, II, 355. T. E. May, *The Constitutional History of England*, ed. and cont. Francis Holland (London, 1912), III, 348.

[28] Loreburn to Campbell-Bannerman, 5 June 1907, Campbell-Bannerman Papers, Brit. Mus. Add. MS. 41,222, fo. 208. They were old friends, bound together by memories of their disagreement with Lord Salisbury's Government on the events leading to the Boer War, and perhaps this tie helps explain the ease with which Loreburn changed sides. On the other hand, Asquith, Haldane, and Grey (who favoured the Ripon plan) had been of the Chamberlain–Milner persuasion; and Loreburn may have disliked being found on the question of the lords' veto on the side of the former Liberal Imperialists. Spender, *Life of Campbell-Bannerman*, I, 244–5, 264, 384. For the split in the Liberal leadership during and after the Boer War, see Jenkins, *Asquith*, chaps. IX–XI. But Ripon, to whom much the same reasoning could be applied, did not change his mind.

the very few members of the Asquith Government who wrote positively in support of the C-B veto plan, though his language was never glowing. Two years later, at a time when Liberal policy on the lords' veto was being reappraised, he circulated to the Cabinet his opinion that no better plan had been proposed if the relations of the two houses were to be treated apart from other pressing problems.[29]

On first sight Asquith's position seems more equivocal, perhaps because so little substantial information has survived regarding his personal opinions at times of important policy-making. Not only was he a reticent man, who destroyed valuable papers because of a reluctance that his biography be written, he was also compelled by party loyalty to mask in public his difference with Campbell-Bannerman. Speaking in the house of commons on 26 June, after the Prime Minister had made his veto plan public, Asquith described himself as 'a slow and, to some degree, even a reluctant convert to the necessity of this particular method of dealing with the problem'.[30] Yet it is difficult to conceive of his being a convert at all. Only a few months earlier he had privately expressed a deep admiration for Crewe's March memorandum, which had rejected the plan of the suspensory veto after a minute exploration of its implications. In addition he had formulated one of the genuinely distinctive features of the Ripon plan. It seems incredible that either the Ilbert memorandum or Campbell-Bannerman's argument in the Cabinet could have illuminated advantages of the plan of suspensory veto that had eluded the politically sophisticated Cabinet. How much more likely that Asquith had retained his initial preference for the Ripon plan while publicly adhering to the Prime Minister's policy! That this was the case is surely suggested by Asquith's advocacy of the Ripon plan during the Constitutional Conference as well as by his action, taken in October 1909, at a time when it was anticipated, correctly as it proved, that the house of lords would reject Lloyd George's Finance Bill and precipitate a constitutional crisis that would compel the Liberals to deal with the lords' veto. At this time Prime Minister and master in his own house, Asquith demonstrated that the June resolution of 1907 had not permanently bound the political heirs of Campbell-Bannerman when he arranged for reprinting and recirculating to his colleagues the report of the Cabinet Committee of 1907 and the hostile Ilbert memorandum.[31]

[29] P.R.O., Cab. 37/101/140. The memorandum is dated 25 Oct. 1909. If the lords' veto were to be considered in relationship to other pressing questions, Loreburn now favoured the plan known as 'Home Rule all round' that Crewe had dismissed without a discussion.

[30] *Parliamentary Debates*, fourth series, CLXXVI, column 1507. Asquith's biographers, while recognizing that he was not the originator of the C-B veto plan, credit him with using his influence to unify the Cabinet behind it but supply no substantiating details. Spender and Asquith, I, 191; Jenkins, *Asquith*, p. 173. Jenkins follows Spender, *Life of Campbell-Bannerman*, II, 355, in asserting that the Cabinet discussed the possibility of adopting the referendum after the Ilbert memorandum, in Jenkins' words, 'effectively killed the joint session plan of the Cabinet committee'. This is very unlikely.

[31] The pertinent papers are in MS. Asquith 102, fos. 137–53. See also P.R.O., Cab. 37/101/136.

In reopening the controversy on the lords' veto Asquith may have responded to Crewe's advice, which he highly valued. A colleague of the two Liberal leaders described Crewe's position in the Cabinet during the Asquith years in these words: 'Lord Crewe held an unique position in the Cabinet. This was not on account of any pre-eminence in Parliament, or in the country, or in the counsels of the Party, but through an almost uncanny soundness of judgment. In any difficult situation, where pros and cons were nicely balanced, it was Crewe, more than any other colleague, that the Prime Minister was accustomed to consult'.[32] No conjecture is necessary about Crewe: he was never a convert to the C-B veto plan or to the modified version in the Parliament Act. But it is perhaps some measure of the weakness in Campbell-Bannerman's position that Crewe was able, though only what he called 'a humble member of the Cabinet' in 1907, to insist successfully on a major price for his acquiescence in the C-B veto plan. This was the provision for quinquennial parliaments that the Prime Minister proposed on 24 June as an accompaniment to his plan of a suspensory veto and that later appeared in the Parliament Act. After Campbell-Bannerman had circularized the Cabinet with the Ilbert memorandum, Crewe wrote a second memorandum, this one for the Cabinet meeting of 5 June that he was not going to attend. It contained the remarks that he would have made if present. In it he not only strongly defended the Cabinet Committee's plan but also frankly expressed the fear that if the Liberals were to take up the plan of a suspensory veto while retaining septennial parliaments, the Unionist opposition would 'ride off on the Referendum'. However much the Unionists disliked the referendum they would greatly prefer its adoption to the abolition of the lords' veto.[33] He insisted subsequently on quinquennial parliaments. Recalling these events in 1909, he wrote that he had agreed 'though with reluctance, to the plan of the suspensory veto afterwards announced to the House of Commons, in consideration of the provision for shortening the life of Parliament'.[34] This statement is confirmed by a comment of Ilbert, written in July 1907, that Crewe was the author of the provision for quinquennial parliaments proposed by Campbell-Bannerman: he had written the proposal on a copy of the Ilbert memorandum.[35]

If Asquith in reviving the plans of 1907 had in mind replacing the C-B veto plan with the Ripon plan, the project had to be discarded in the emergency created by the lords' rejection of the Finance Bill. Even before the rejection Crewe had recognized that it might now be necessary to adhere to the C-B veto plan, but just the same he had reprinted his memoranda of 1907 and re-

[32] Quoted in Pope-Hennessy, *Crewe*, pp. xi–xii. The words are Herbert L. Samuel's. See also ibid. p. 64.
[33] P.R.O., Cab. 37/101/137. Crewe to Campbell-Bannerman, 3 June 1907. Campbell-Bannerman Papers, Brit. Mus. Add. MS. 41,213, fo. 341. Pope-Hennessy described Crewe's deep dislike of the Parliament Act. *Crewe*, pp. 124–5.
[34] P.R.O., Cab. 37/101/137. See the prefatory statement.
[35] Ilbert to Bryce, 22 July 1907, MS. Bryce 13, fos. 124v–125.

circulated them to the Cabinet with a statement of his belief that the suspensory veto would increase greatly the difficulties of Liberal ministers in the conduct of bills in the house of commons and, in effect, abolish the veto of the house of lords.[36] Loreburn in reply foreshadowed the Liberal action in the early months of 1910. Admitting the force of Crewe's critique of the C-B veto plan, he followed his admission with the statement that if the lords rejected the Finance Bill and a general election followed, the situation would require a simple, direct proposal regarding the house of lords. For this purpose, the Lord Chancellor concluded, 'none better than Sir H. Campbell-Bannerman's seems forthcoming, whatever its defects may be'.[37] Loreburn's position was reinforced when the general election of January 1910, by destroying the great Liberal majority in the house of commons, rendered the Asquith Government dependent for survival upon the support of John Redmond's Irish Nationalists. Home rule for Ireland loomed as the Irish pressed for the destruction of the last important barrier, the lords' veto. The Liberal dilemma was evident in Asquith's letter of 10 February to the King describing another letter, this one from the Irish leader T. P. O'Connor, 'stating as a certain fact that the Irish party led by Mr. Redmond would vote against the Budget unless they were assured that the passing of a Bill dealing with the Veto of the House of Lords was guaranteed during the present year'.[38] Even if no guarantees were forthcoming, the Asquith Government were in no position to bring forward an entirely new plan for dealing with the lords' veto; and Harcourt's anxiety was unwarranted when he wrote to Asquith, on 7 February, in words reminiscent of Campbell-Bannerman: 'I don't now discuss what our ultimate anti-veto policy is to be, but I hope it will not take the form of fanciful schemes (like the Abbé de Sieyès) for a new heaven & a new earth'.[39] In an atmosphere fraught with uncertainty about their continuance in office, the Asquith Government formulated their policy towards the lords' veto; and only one result was politically feasible. The product of a Cabinet Committee of which Loreburn was chairman, the veto resolutions introduced by Asquith at the end of March rested squarely on the C-B veto plan, as did the Parliament Bill that he produced a few weeks later. But perhaps out of deference for Crewe the

[36] P.R.O., Cab. 37/101/137.   [37] P.R.O., Cab. 37/101/140.

[38] Spender and Asquith, I, 272. Lloyd George Papers, C/6/10/3. Fitzroy, I, 395–8. The changed position of the Irish Nationalists is discussed by J. C. Beckett, *The Making of Modern Ireland* (London, 1966), pp. 422–3.

[39] Harcourt to Asquith, 7 Feb. 1910, MS. Asquith 12, fos. 114–15. According to the chief Liberal whip, the Master of Elibank, Harcourt was 'part author with Ilbert of the famous C. B. resolutions'. He also described him as the most irreconcilable of the vetoists but lacking in the persistence required for forcing his opinions through the conflicting views of others. Arthur C. Murray, *Master and Brother: Murrays of Elibank* (London, 1945), pp. 38 and 40. Despite Harcourt's close association with Campbell-Bannerman during the appropriate months of 1907 and his later ardent advocacy of the C-B veto plan in the Asquith Government where such ardour was rare, there seems to be no substantiating evidence for the Master of Elibank's statement of Harcourt's co-authorship. The diary and letters of Harcourt himself are closed to scholars until 1972. *English Historical Review*, LXXVII, no. 304 (July 1962), 491.

conferences that he and Ripon had disliked were deleted, and Asquith's own views may well have been reflected when the period in which the lords' veto could delay legislation was lengthened to two years.[40]

Roy Jenkins, the most recent authority on the passing of the Parliament Act, described the Asquith Government as divided in these months between vetoists such as Harcourt and would-be reformers of the house of lords such as Grey, who next to Crewe was Asquith's closest political associate.[41] Perhaps a more helpful division could be drawn between two types of vetoists: those like Harcourt and Loreburn who accepted the C-B veto plan and the more conservative elements in the Cabinet like Crewe, Grey, and very probably Asquith who much preferred the Cabinet Committee's plan of 1907. It was only after political realities compelled the abandonment of the Ripon plan that Grey insisted publicly on the reform of the house of lords, this insistence leading to the preamble in the Parliament Act that recites its authors' intention of placing the house of lords at some future date on a popular basis. A letter from Grey to Asquith, dated 25 March 1910, supports this idea. Writing in opposition to the second veto resolution—'in form the so-called C-B. resolution bare & simple'—to which he had objected, so he said, before the general election and also at the beginning of the present parliamentary session, Grey stated his position. He could vote readily, he wrote, 'for the first plan of the C.B. Cabinet, that of a joint sitting between the two Houses in case of deadlock...whether it stood alone or were coupled with the reconstitution of the Second Chamber, or would necessarily have led to reconstitution, when once it was passed'. As for the C-B veto plan, he could vote for it only if it were 'preparatory to reconstitution and...a means of carrying it', a position that he subsequently softened.[42]

These comments are a reminder that the Ripon plan was still a formidable rival to the C-B veto plan in high Liberal circles when the unexpected death of Edward VII and the accession of a new monarch, George V, created a widespread feeling that the political parties ought to find a compromise on the constitutional question. The result was the Constitutional Conference, unprecedented in scope and duration, that began on a hopeful note on 17 June but ended in failure on 10 November after twenty-two sittings. Asquith's Liberal delegation also included Crewe who had urged a conference; Lloyd George, who opposed the policy as unwise; and Augustine Birrell, the chief secretary for Ireland, who proved, perhaps unexpectedly, an active participant at crucial moments in the Conference's proceedings.[43] They met with a Union-

---

[40] Spender and Asquith, I, 277. Jenkins, *Asquith*, p. 208. Asquith to the King, 26 Feb., 9 Mar., and 11 Mar. 1907. MS. Asquith 5, fos. 194–8v. Pope-Hennessy, *Crewe*, pp. 124–5.

[41] *Asquith*, pp. 205–6, 270. *Mr. Balfour's Poodle*, pp. 82–3.

[42] Grey to Asquith, 25 Mar. 1910, MS. Asquith 23, fos. 82–82v. G. M. Trevelyan, *Grey of Fallodon* (London, 1937), pp. 171–3.

[43] Alfred M. Gollin, *The Observer and J. L. Garvin 1908–1914* (London, 1960), pp. 190–1.

ist delegation drawn from the Shadow Cabinet; headed by Arthur Balfour, it also included Lords Lansdowne and Cawdor and Austen Chamberlain. Though no official records were kept and at Liberal insistence no public statement issued that disclosed the course of negotiations or the reasons for their termination, Chamberlain kept notes of each sitting, which Lansdowne later read and supplemented from his own records; and their accounts make it possible to delineate with some precision the course of negotiations affecting the Ripon plan.[44] The breakdown of the Conference was due, however, not to disagreement over this plan, which the Liberal delegation sponsored, but to the inability of the two delegations to agree on the special treatment to be accorded home rule bills. It appears that the Ripon plan was one more casualty resulting from the intrusion of the Irish question into English politics, but the final result was by no means a foregone conclusion when the Constitutional Conference assembled in the summer of 1910.

III

At the beginning of the Constitutional Conference Balfour presented a memorandum (dated 22 June), in which he divided legislation into three categories —ordinary, financial, and constitutional—and offered reasons for believing that these required separate consideration and different treatment if the constitutional question were to be satisfactorily settled. These categories, though unacceptable to the Liberal delegation, have typically provided the framework for discussing the Conference's proceedings. Expressed in Balfourian terms, the hope sustaining the Liberal delegation almost until the end was that both sides could agree on a procedure regulating the lords' veto so mutually satisfactory as to render unnecessary a separate consideration and different treatment of constitutional legislation. In this category home rule bills for

[44] The House of Lords Reform Committee of 1921 concluded that there were no available official papers on the subject of the Constitutional Conference. And Austen Chamberlain's, *Politics from Inside* (London, 1936), pp. 289–90, contains a letter, dated 22 August 1912, in which Lansdowne wrote: 'I am...reminded of a conversation with you on the subject of the Constitutional Conference of 1910. We were both shocked at the absence of all record of its proceedings, and I think we both believed that from the notes which we had made...it might be possible and desirable to draw up a kind of *procès verbal* of great value for historical purposes.' The notes made by Chamberlain and Lansdowne are in the Chamberlain Papers, which have been used in this article with the kind permission of the Librarian, Birmingham University Library, on behalf of the Chamberlain Trustees. Chamberlain's notes, under the title 'Notes of Conference on the Constitutional Question', are found in the Chamberlain Papers Ac 10/2/35–Ac 10/2/64. Lansdowne's notes, under the title 'Constitutional Conference 1910: Notes on A. C.'s record by L.', are listed as Chamberlain Papers Ac 10/2/65. The Lansdowne notes have been used in this article with the kind permission of the present Lord Lansdowne. The materials in the Chamberlain Papers supersede the accounts found in the standard biographies of the participants, which have provided historians with the main lines of what took place but have left many puzzling gaps. See the comment in Jenkins, *Mr. Balfour's Poodle*, pp. 102–6.

Ireland loomed large.[45] As an earnest of their good faith the Liberals proved willing during the Conference to make an impressive concession in the category of financial legislation, but the problem first facing the Conference was primarily one of settling on a procedure for regulating the lords' veto that would satisfy both parties to the extent contemplated by the Liberal delegation.

Several procedures were possible but by no means equally feasible since each had its own disabilities. One was the suspensory veto as it had appeared in Asquith's controversial Parliament Bill, even if it was unlikely. Another was the referendum, bitterly disliked by Crewe and the Cabinet Committee of 1907 but undeniably attractive to the Unionist delegation. Still a third possibility was the system of joint sittings as provided in the Ripon plan, which was eminently acceptable to the Liberal delegation but unknown to the Unionists when the proceedings began. Of the three, the plan of the suspensory veto commanded the least support, perhaps none at all. Neither Chamberlain's nor Lansdowne's notes contain a single reference to what the political world viewed as the official policy of the Asquith Government on the lords' veto. But the referendum was an entirely different matter, and initially it occupied more of the Conference's time than the Ripon plan.

For some months before the Conference the Unionists had pondered the advisability of combining the reform of the house of lords with the referendum as a response to the Liberals' Parliament Bill; and they came to the bargaining table prepared to insist upon setting up a category of constitutional legislation, to which it would be applied. A practical reason for their taking up the referendum was that its adoption would leave the house of lords, reformed or not, with its legislative power unaltered and its position at the same time relatively immune to criticism whenever constitutional questions were at issue between the two houses. The theoretical position of the Unionists was expounded by Balfour in the June memorandum when he asserted a firm belief in the predominance of the house of commons in the province of legislation, of administration, and of finance but insisted that redefining its position would entail making special provision for certain constitutional interests. The papers circulated by the Prime Minister at the Conference appeared to show that every important constitution in countries other than the United Kingdom had been safeguarded by precautions against hasty change. Only in the United Kingdom

---

[45] Balfour, 'A Note on the Constitutional Question', P.R.O., Cab. 37/102/23. Lansdowne recorded Asquith's suggestion on 23 June that special safeguards for constitutional legislation might prove to be unnecessary if a satisfactory procedure were devised for ordinary legislation. 'Constitutional Conference 1910', Chamberlain Papers Ac 10/2/65. On the importance attached to agreement on home rule legislation see, for example, second sitting, 23 June 1910, 'Notes of Conference', Chamberlain Papers Ac 10/2/30; eleventh sitting, 26 July 1910, ibid. Ac 10/2/45; thirteenth sitting, 28 July 1910, ibid. Ac 10/2/47; sixteenth sitting, 13 Oct. 1910, ibid. Ac 10/2/50; seventeenth sitting, 14 Oct. 1910, ibid. Ac 10/2/51; and eighteenth to twenty-first sittings, 1–4 Nov. 1910, ibid. Ac 10/2/52–Ac 10/2/61. There is pertinent comment in Sir Charles Petrie, *The Life and Letters of Austen Chamberlain* (London, 1939), I, 254.

was it possible to destroy ancient institutions by a procedure identical with that employed for the simplest public measures.[46] The safeguard that would satisfy the Unionists, so they later stated, was the use of the referendum under these conditions: if a bill effecting a change in the constitution were twice rejected by the house of lords, it should be referred to the electorate and proceeded with only if approved by the majority of the electorate voting.[47] At first, however, they simply inquired as to whether the Liberals had considered the referendum, and they abandoned the subject temporarily when it proved divisive. It split both delegations. In favour were Balfour, Lansdowne, and Birrell; opposed were Chamberlain (at this point), Lloyd George, Asquith, and Crewe. Cawdor was silent. With this route blocked the Constitutional Conference turned seriously to the Ripon plan.[48]

It certainly appears that the Asquith Government had very early decided on the Ripon plan and undertaken to win the support of the Unionists. The first task was to acquaint them with the pertinent details; and this was accomplished when a treasury clerk, at Lloyd George's instance, prepared for the use of the conferees a memorandum summarizing recent proposals affecting the house of lords. There is little doubt that the details of the Ripon plan printed in it had originated with the Liberal delegation. Following a statement that the late Lord Ripon had privately circulated the plan, the memorandum presented its details by giving without further attribution the numbered propositions that had appeared in the secret report of the Cabinet Committee of 1907.[49] The Unionists were given no clues to the past history of the Ripon plan beyond Asquith's statement on 27 June, after Lloyd George called attention to the Ripon plan, that it had been 'very carefully considered by Campbell-Bannerman's Cabinet and found some favour at the time'.[50] But the Unionist delegation were soon aware of the Government's keen interest. After listening to the discussion of 15 July, when a whole sitting was for the first time devoted to it, Lansdowne concluded that the Government's goal consisted of adopting the Ripon plan and postponing the reform of the house of lords.[51] As the sitting ended Asquith promised to bring in a paper that would reflect their discussion, and on 19 July he produced and read 'A Suggested Scheme for

[46] 'A Note on the Constitutional Question', P.R.O., Cab. 37/102/23. Lansdowne to J. S. Sandars, 25 Feb. 1910, Balfour Papers, Brit. Mus. Add. MS. 49,730, fos. 65–7. Lansdowne to Balfour, 27 Mar. 1910, ibid. fos. 68–70v. The Unionist interest in the referendum at this stage of the party's history was due essentially to the activity of Lord Selborne.

[47] Sixteenth sitting, 13 Oct. 1910, 'Notes of Conference', Chamberlain Papers Ac 10/2/50.

[48] Third sitting, 27 June 1910, ibid. Ac 10/2/37. See also the account of the first sitting, 17 June 1910, ibid. Ac 10/2/35.

[49] Lloyd George made his suggestion at the first sitting, ibid. The memorandum was compiled by a Mr Hawtrey. P.R.O., Cab. 37/103/24.

[50] Third sitting, 27 June 1910, 'Notes of Conference', Chamberlain Papers Ac 10/2/37.

[51] Eighth sitting, 15 July 1910, ibid. Ac 10/2/41. Lansdowne's comment is in 'Constitutional Conference 1910', ibid. Ac 10/2/65.

Dealing with Deadlocks', on which the Liberal delegation had been at work since the beginning of the month.[52]

Asquith's paper brought the Ripon plan to the very centre of the Conference's deliberations, where it stayed during the remainder of the summer sittings. Based on that plan and reflecting its principles, the 'Suggested Scheme' combined a limited veto for the lords with detailed procedures by which a contentious bill that had twice passed the house of commons would go to a joint sitting of the two houses for a final determination. This would happen at once if the bill were rejected on the second reading in the house of lords, but an amended bill would make its way to the joint sitting only after an attempt at agreement in an obligatory conference had failed. Asquith described the joint sitting as one in which the house of commons sat as a body, the house of lords through 'a delegation of x members', the whole deliberating and voting together. The decision of the majority in the joint sitting—where much cross-voting was anticipated—would be final and conclusive. Asquith's concessions to the Unionists were very limited, if he thought that his paper contained the main lines of a final settlement. Though he left x, the number and composition of the lords' delegation, open for negotiation, the Prime Minister had chosen to ignore the Unionist contention that a separate category of constitutional legislation was needed. Nor did he mention finance, which he doubtless viewed as different from legislation and perhaps as a subject for further negotiation. The effect of the 'Suggested Scheme' was to send all disputed legislation to the joint sitting for settlement; and this remained Asquith's objective, if not necessarily that of his Liberal colleagues, to the end of the Conference.

It was not to be expected that the Unionist delegation would easily acquiesce, and its members readied a memorandum for Asquith by 26 July that stated explicitly the points wherein they found the 'Suggested Scheme' defective. This July memorandum grew out of a private meeting of the Unionist delegation on 18 July, that had pondered the Ripon plan even before Asquith brought in his paper, and of a meeting of the Shadow Cabinet at Lansdowne House. Its contents may be briefly stated. The Unionist delegation would accept a version of the Ripon plan, subject to the qualification that the number of the lords' delegation and the method of choice were still open questions,

---

[52] The 'Suggested Scheme' is in P.R.O., Cab. 37/103/34. Dated 21 July 1910, it has on its face a statement written by Chamberlain: 'Produced & Read by Mr. Asquith at our 9th meeting, July 19th'. See also ninth sitting, 19 July 1910, 'Notes of Conference', Chamberlain Papers Ac 10/2/43 and ibid. Ac 10/2/78. Early versions of the 'Suggested Scheme' dated 7 July 1910 may be seen in MS. Asquith 104, fos. 90–90v. The Asquith Papers also contain a handwritten 'Suggested Scheme', to which the Prime Minister had given his personal attention. The title was written by Asquith himself as were the word 'Secret' at the top and various emendations throughout the paper (as, for example, the introduction of the words 'First Session', the substitution of 'Obligatory Conference' for 'Joint Sitting', etc.). Otherwise the paper is in someone else's writing, perhaps that of an amanuensis. I am indebted for this analysis to Mr Porter, Department of Western Manuscripts, Bodleian Library.

but only for what Balfour called 'ordinary' legislation and as part of a general settlement with special securities for financial and constitutional legislation, the latter including home rule bills. At the meeting of 18 July Lansdowne and Cawdor had favoured pressing for the reform of the house of lords, and the July memorandum also covered this point.[53]

By the last week of July, then, the lines had been drawn from which the two delegations might negotiate; but it appeared for some time on 28 July, the last summer meeting of the Conference before the parliamentary recess, that no further progress was possible. On that day Lloyd George, independently of his delegation, produced his own version of the concessions that could be granted in response to the Unionist memorandum and then, unexpectedly, turned it into an ultimatum to the Unionists that almost disrupted the Conference. Lloyd George's paper presupposed the adoption of the Ripon plan, with Asquith's x defined in its terms, in return for which he offered a concession regarding finance and a category of what he labelled constitutional questions that would be given special treatment. If his definition of constitutional questions was purposefully narrow, the procedure represented a decided concession in principle to the Unionists. Bills affecting (a) the existence of the throne or the succession, (b) the reconstruction of the house of lords, or (c) altering or amending the Conference's settlement should not be carried into law until they had been submitted to the electorate either by referendum or at a general election after having passed either or both houses of parliament.[54] Lloyd George's paper was unacceptable to the Unionist for a whole series of reasons. They had not agreed to defining x in terms of the Ripon plan, and above all they were opposed to establishing a category of constitutional questions that excluded home rule bills unless a compensatory arrangement were forthcoming. They were also insisting on a reform of the house of lords as part of the Conference's work, perhaps for tactical reasons;[55] and to this issue Lloyd George had made no meaningful reference.

[53] 'Note', 19 July 1910, 'Notes of Conference', Chamberlain Papers Ac 10/2/42. See also eleventh sitting, 26 July 1910, ibid. Ac 10/2/45. The Unionist memorandum is not in the Chamberlain Papers, but the main points may be surmised from Chamberlain's 'Note' and his account of the eleventh sitting.

[54] Document A ('Joint Session'), 'Notes of Conference', Chamberlain Papers Ac 10/2/81. Lloyd George expressed his view of the referendum at the nineteenth sitting, 2 Nov. 1910, 'Notes of Conference', Chamberlain Papers Ac 10/2/53. Regarding it as 'a good means for preventing things being done', he would apply it to the monarchy and the constitutional pact coming out of the Constitutional Conference, which he wished to remain unchanged.

[55] 'Note', 19 July 1910, ibid. Ac 10/2/42. A private meeting of the Unionist delegation had earlier (18 July) considered whether to insist upon a reconstruction of the house of lords. The main obstacle, as Balfour noted, was that the Government would ask the Unionists for their plan and they had none on which they were agreed. The matter was then left for settlement at a Shadow Cabinet meeting at Lansdowne House, where the decision was taken to insist upon the reform of the house of lords, or so it would appear from Lansdowne's tone at the eleventh sitting, 26 July 1910, ibid. Ac 10/2/45. But Lansdowne had been perfectly willing for a time to abandon this item of the Unionist programme. Lansdowne to Balfour, 'Note on suggested scheme for dealing with Deadlocks', 25 July 1910, Balfour Papers, Brit. Mus. Add. MS. 49,729, fos. 89–96. He wrote at one point: 'If...H.M. Government take the

Crisis set in when Balfour asked Asquith whether he planned on making any statement in the house of commons before the parliamentary recess about the Conference's proceedings. When Lloyd George interjected that such a statement should be definite in nature, the Unionists replied that any conclusions so far reached were only provisional. The situation was tense for about an hour. According to Chamberlain's account, Balfour stayed out of the quarrel and Crewe wanted peace. The active participants for the Liberals were Lloyd George and Birrell; Cawdor, Lansdowne, and Chamberlain for the Unionists. 'Ll.G and Birrell seemed to me to be heading straight for a break-up of the Conference there and then unless we accepted the terms in Ll. G.'s paper', wrote Chamberlain. The latter passed a note to Balfour: 'It seems to me that this is an ultimatum to us—give up Home Rule or we break off.' Balfour agreed but wondered whether he had made a mistake in hurrying. 'It is clear to me', Balfour added, 'that Asquith and L. G. are on different sides.' Notes were again exchanged. Chamberlain wrote: 'Gov't terms are (*a*) that questions like Home Rule, Disestablishment & franchise can have no special safeguards: (*b*) that treatment of legislation must be settled independently of & before reform of the H of L.' These terms were unacceptable, as Balfour noted, writing: 'Of course we can't agree. But I am not sure that Asquith does not want to go on!' Tension subsided as suddenly as it had arisen when Chamberlain asked Asquith directly whether the Liberals were planning to exclude reform of the house of lords from the final settlement. The Prime Minister's reply was reassuringly explicit: 'Oh no, no, certainly not.' Crisis averted, the Conference adjourned for the summer months after drawing up the innocuous statement that Asquith read on the following day to the house of commons.[56] But aware that a breakdown had been imminent, the Liberal delegation returned to the bargaining table in the fall with an extraordinary concession regarding finance and the house of lords that went far towards giving that house new powers. They were obviously prepared to pay a high price for an agreed settlement, to which the Ripon plan remained one key.

After the Constitutional Conference reconvened on 11 October, both delegations centred their efforts on evolving a formula that would leave money bills the sole business of the house of commons while permitting the house of lords to reject or amend measures that were technically but not purely financial. On this subject very important progress was made. Despite the difficulty of legal definition Asquith evolved a formula that became part of the Liberal terms at the end of the Conference; and even though the Unionists evolved

responsibility of asking the Conference to deal with the question of Deadlocks (Conferences plus Joint Sittings) leaving House of Lords Reform for further consideration, I would offer no opposition, although we ought, I think, to place it upon record that we are in favour of House of Lords reform and shall take up the question ourselves should we have an opportunity of doing so.' Ibid. fo. 94.

[56] Thirteenth sitting, 28 July 1910, 'Notes of Conference', Chamberlain Papers Ac 10/2/47.

one of their own, they could have accepted Asquith's. It provided that in cases of what was called 'equitable tacking', even if taxation were involved, such legislation would be treated as ordinary legislation, subject in case of deadlock to the joint sitting. A joint committee of the two houses with the speaker of the house of commons in the chair would decide when equitable tacking existed in the light of this definition: 'Finance is the sole business of the H. of C. provided that if it appears that any provision of a Bill though dealing with taxation would effect important social or political changes through expropriation or differentiation against any class of owners or property these provisions shall not be treated for the purposes of this Act as provisions dealing with taxation.'[57] Roy Jenkins believed it inconceivable that the Liberal delegation accepted so sweeping an exclusion.[58] But they not only accepted it, they took the lead in its elaboration as part of a general settlement and in doing so acted with full awareness of the implications of the Asquith formula. At the time Crewe observed that the financial proviso being elaborated by the Conference impaired the financial position of the house of commons, which the Liberal party expected their leaders to maintain. Admitting the truth of the charge, Asquith asserted: 'We are prepared to face that if we can get a formula sufficiently broad but not too broad'.[59] And on 10 November, when a public statement was under advisement that would give the course of the negotiations and the reasons for their failure, the Liberals opposed it, largely on the ground that it would make known their attitude on finance. If this happened, they would, in Asquith's words, 'go about with a halter round their necks'. Warm in support, Lloyd George added that 'no Liberal Ministers would ever be allowed to enter into a conference again unpledged'.[60]

No comparable progress was made on the constitutional front. On 14 October Asquith reported to George V that the Conference was adjourning for

[57] 'Copy of Sir R. Finlay's Notes of the Meeting of the Unionist Leaders to hear Balfour's Report of the Proceedings at the Constitutional Conference', in Chamberlain, *Politics from Inside*, p. 295. This was the Lansdowne House meeting of 8 November 1910, which by rejecting Liberal terms for a settlement played a part in bringing the Constitutional Conference to a close. Finlay's 'Notes' are also in 'Notes of Conference', Chamberlain Papers Ac 10/2/57; Ac 10/2/63. See also eleventh sitting, 26 July 1910, ibid. Ac 10/2/45; fourteenth sitting, 11 Oct. 1910, ibid. Ac 10/2/48; fifteenth sitting, 12 Oct. 1910, ibid. Ac 10/2/49; twenty-first sitting, 4 Nov. 1910, ibid. Ac 10/2/61; Document D ('Parliament'), ibid. Ac 10/2/79; and Document C ('Parliament'), ibid. Ac 10/2/83. The comments on the financial settlement should be seen in the memorandum that Balfour prepared at the ending of the Conference for George V, to which Asquith added marginal notes. 'The Constitutional Conference: Memorandum by Mr. Balfour with marginal comments by the Prime Minister', 14 Nov. 1910, MS. Asquith 104, fos. 183–5 v.

[58] *Asquith*, p. 214. *Mr. Balfour's Poodle*, p. 103. This would have been easier for Jenkins to accept if he had consulted the full copy of Finlay's notes in *Politics from Inside*, pp. 295–7, rather than relying on the limited version in Lord Newton's *Lord Lansdowne* (London, 1929), pp. 402–3.

[59] Fifteenth sitting, 12 Oct. 1910, 'Notes of Conference', Chamberlain Papers Ac 10/2/49. 'Constitutional Conference 1910', ibid. Ac 10/2/65.

[60] Twenty-second sitting, 10 Nov. 1910, 'Notes of Conference', Chamberlain Papers Ac 10/2/64.

a fortnight. 'The point of divergence which has been reached', wrote the Prime Minister, 'is the question whether organic & constitutional changes (such e.g. as Home Rule, the franchise, redistribution) should be excepted from the procedure of joint sessions, which, it is agreed, should be applicable to deadlocks between the two Houses, in regard to ordinary legislation; and should (in case of such difference) be submitted to a popular *referendum ad hoc*.'[61] The Liberal delegation had weakened on this point: first in Lloyd George's July paper, where he had conceded the principle even if his concession was meagre, and then during the October sittings. Balfour believed in early November that a tentative agreement had been reached with regard to reform bills, the monarchy and the Protestant succession, and the act embodying the results of the Conference.[62] By the Conference's end the Liberals had agreed to establishing a category of constitutional questions, to be exempt from the joint sitting, that included all the items mentioned by Balfour except for reform bills.[63] But they had scored a minor victory on the nature of the safeguards. The procedure to be used was very different from the referendum as advocated by the Unionists and more just to the Liberals. If the two houses differed on a constitutional question, it would be dropped; only if they agreed would it go to the electorate. After the Constitutional Conference was over, Balfour expressed his dislike of the proposed procedure when he wrote: 'The Referendum is intended as a method of settling deadlocks between the two Houses when they differ, not as a means of upsetting the decision of the two Houses when they agree.'[64] Yet the Unionists would have been satisfied with the arrangement as a whole if home rule bills had been included in the category of constitutional questions.[65] This the Liberals would not grant.

The Liberals were willing, however, to deal with home rule as a special case; and on this crucial point the Constitutional Conference came closer to agreement than has been realized. The Liberal offer, which originated with Lloyd George, provided that a general election should intervene on the next occasion on which a home rule bill, having once passed the house of commons, met rejection in the house of lords, but only on this one occasion.[66]

---

[61] Asquith to the King, 14 Oct. 1910, Spender and Asquith, I, 290. MS. Asquith 23, fos. 136–136v.

[62] Balfour to Asquith, 3 Nov. 1910, ibid. fos. 142–3v. Chamberlain Papers Ac 10/2/60.

[63] 'Copy of Sir R. Finlay's Notes', *Politics from Inside*, p. 296.

[64] Balfour to Chamberlain, 28 Nov. 1910, ibid. p. 303. Balfour to Chamberlain, 13 Dec. 1910, ibid. p. 306. To arrange for a referendum on constitutional legislation only at such times as the two houses were in disagreement penalized the Liberals. Whenever the Unionists were in office, the two houses worked in unison. This was the nub of the matter.

[65] Seventeenth sitting, 14 Oct. 1910, 'Notes of Conference', Chamberlain Papers Ac 10/2/51. See also Chamberlain's Document E, ibid.

[66] Eighteenth sitting, 1 Nov. 1910, 'Notes of Conference', Chamberlain Papers Ac 10/2/52. Lloyd George actually advanced three proposals, of which only the one mentioned above received serious consideration from the Unionists. But the third of these proposals is of particular interest in view of his abortive attempt outside the Conference to form a coalition government that would carry an agreed home rule bill. Lloyd George proposed an agreed

The Unionist delegation wanted the arrangement to be permanent. What proved to be the final Unionist counter-offer came on 3 November when Balfour stated that his party would accept the Liberal offer, with or without the referendum, if it were made permanent. Chamberlain described Balfour as asking why the Government could not agree to this. The Unionists recognized that the Liberals had to consider the Irish, as Asquith had earlier stated; but Balfour wondered aloud whether the Irish, if they were ready to accept this condition for the next struggle—the one on which all their hopes and attention were concentrated and to which they looked to settle the question— would mind its being applied also to any future struggle. Surely, he argued, they would not care about what might happen ten or fifteen years hence.[67] At this crucial juncture Balfour received support from an entirely unexpected quarter. On this point both Birrell and Crewe were on his side. Much to Lloyd George's anger, Birrell, appealed to by Asquith, stated that he rather agreed with Balfour: the Irish would concentrate their attention on the next great struggle. They would not think much of what might happen later. When Lloyd George differed from him, the Irish Secretary continued: 'The Irish as men of business would concentrate on x [the number of lords in the joint sitting].' Birrell considered, so Chamberlain recorded, that 'if they had a good x, they would be satisfied; if not, the reverse'.[68] Crewe felt similarly.[69] Asquith's position is unclear, but his final decision was foreshadowed in a comment made after Lloyd George spoke. At one point in this sitting the Prime Minister had stated that whatever was decided with regard to home rule ought, in his opinion, to apply to all constitutional legislation; but after listening to Lloyd George, he repeated his earlier objection to drawing any distinction at all between constitutional and other legislation.[70] There was no mistaking Lloyd George's stand. His dissent from Birrell was vehement. 'I don't know', he said, 'whether Birrell has changed his mind. I have not changed mine. I have always objected to this proposal & I certainly shall not assent to it.'[71] No

home rule bill or an agreed alternative. Chamberlain wrote that this proposal was not again mentioned but left an interesting exchange of notes about it. He asked Balfour: 'Do you mean to ask Lloyd George to develop his third alternative i.e. that we should see whether we could not agree upon Home Rule or some alternative?' Balfour replied: 'I rather thought *not*: but am not sure that my instinct is right.' Lloyd George's attempt at coalition-making is described in Ensor, p. 424, and in Jenkins, *Asquith*, pp. 215–17.

[67] Nineteenth sitting, 2 Nov. 1910, 'Notes of Conference', Chamberlain Papers Ac 10/2/53; twentieth sitting, 3 Nov. 1910, ibid. Ac 10/2/54. During the nineteenth sitting Asquith stated that the Liberals could not accept home rule as a suitable subject for a referendum. They had to think of those with whom they worked, and the Irish would never accept it.

[68] Twentieth sitting, ibid.

[69] 'Constitutional Conference 1910', Chamberlain Papers Ac 10/2/65.

[70] Ibid. Twentieth sitting, 3 Nov. 1910, 'Notes of Conference', Chamberlain Papers Ac 10/2/54.

[71] Ibid. Writing to Lloyd George before the Liberal offer regarding home rule was formulated, Winston Churchill complained of the obstacles in the way of carrying home rule if such an arrangement were made. Since the new machinery contemplated by the Constitutional Conference was to work only after another election, the Liberals would need to win four elections in succession before home rule became law. Churchill to Lloyd George, 14 Oct.

further progress proved possible at this sitting, and it ended with an agreement to meet on the following day.

In the interval a letter from Asquith to Balfour, on the afternoon of 3 November, revealed that Lloyd George's viewpoint had won. The Liberal delegation had decided to retain his suggestion regarding home rule bills, without accepting the Unionist amendment, and to abide by their financial concession. But otherwise they had reverted to the position of 19 July when Asquith brought in his 'Suggested Scheme for Dealing with Deadlocks' and before Lloyd George's July paper had opened the first crack in the Liberal position by setting up a category of constitutional questions. Asquith's letter of 3 November stated flatly that no such category could be established in view of the extensive financial concession that had been made, although the case of home rule would be dealt with on the lines of Lloyd George's suggestion. 'To defend it [the financial concession] at all [to Liberal supporters]', he explained, 'would we feel become an impossibility if it were accompanied by the exclusion from the new machinery for preventing deadlocks of what is called organic or constitutional legislation.' An exemption of this type would render the new system inapplicable to a large number of proposed changes to which the supporters of the Government attached the greatest value. 'We do not feel', Asquith concluded, 'that we can maintain our weakened position in regard to Finance unless (a) the new machinery is made applicable to all legislation and (b) we can come to a satisfactory agreement in regard to the interpretation of x.'[72] The Liberal delegation subsequently restored the category of constitutional questions after Balfour objected that it was already the subject of a provisional agreement,[73] but Asquith otherwise stood firm. At the turning-point in the Constitutional Conference he had sided with Lloyd George against Crewe and Birrell.

In so doing Asquith had destroyed the prospect of the Ripon plan's re-

1910, Lloyd George Papers C/3/15/2. Accordingly, it would have been very difficult for him and Lloyd George to contemplate accepting the Unionist counter-offer. On the other hand Crewe and Birrell had felt differently; and it is worth remembering that Lord Rosebery in 1894, at the time Prime Minister, had imposed a more drastic restriction on home rule bills than the one proposed by the Unionists in 1910. He had stated that 'before Irish Home Rule is concluded by the Imperial Parliament, England as the predominant member of the membership of the Three Kingdoms will have to be convinced of its justice and equity. The Marquess of Crewe, *Lord Rosebery* (London, 1931), II, 444–5.

[72] MS. Asquith 23, fos. 141–141 v. This is a copy of a letter that the Prime Minister sent to Balfour, which as Jenkins observes, was 'most uncharacteristically undated but presumably written towards the end of the conference'. *Mr. Balfour's Poodle*, p. 103. Some help in dating it is provided by Balfour's answering note, also in the Asquith Papers, which is dated 3 Nov. 1910. Balfour wrote that he had 'just received' Asquith's letter and circulated it to his three colleagues. MS. Asquith 23, fos. 142–143 v. Chamberlain kept his copies of the Asquith letter, dated 3 Nov. 1910, Balfour's reply, similarly dated, and Balfour's covering note, also dated 3 Nov. 1910, that reads: 'Mr. Balfour encloses copies of letters which have passed between the Prime Minister & himself this afternoon'. 'Notes of Conference', Chamberlain Papers Ac10/2/58; Ac10/2/59; Ac10/2/60.

[73] Ibid. MS. Asquith 23, fos. 142–143 v. 'Copy of Sir. R. Finlay's Notes', *Politics from Inside*, p. 296.

placing the C-B veto plan. It was only in the last stage of the Conference that the Liberal delegation defined x as in the Ripon plan, a course foreshadowed, however, in Lloyd George's July paper. After Asquith sent his letter to Balfour, the Unionist leader stated, on 4 November, that his delegation could not improve upon their counter-offer made at the last sitting; but they thought it well to report the situation to their Unionist colleagues before definitely closing the Conference. For this purpose the Liberals would need to clarify their terms, including their version of x. Balfour stressed that it was not the main point between the two sides or the one on which the impasse had been reached. Asquith replied: 'Ripon's number 100, 20 to be members of the Gov't & the other 80 to be elected in proportion to the strength of Parties in the H. of Lords'. Their calculation was that these figures would give 28 Liberals to 72 Unionists or a net Unionist vote of 44. But the Cabinet Committee of 1907 had concluded that these figures would yield 60 Unionist votes, a disparity suggesting that the Asquith Government in a continued negotiation might have offered more lenient terms. Indeed, this was Chamberlain's conclusion though for another reason. Observing the Prime Minister in the discussion that followed, Chamberlain thought him inclined to 'spring' a little. If so, it meant little since Lloyd George was once more adamant: 44 was the maximum.[74] So the negotiations ended, and the Conference was soon over. Four days later the Unionist delegation met their colleagues at Lansdowne House and when asked gave their opinion for rejection. According to Chamberlain, all their colleagues concurred in this decision.[75] After the result was communicated to Asquith, the Liberal delegation considered but decided against asking George V to intervene; and the Conference ended.[76] Not long afterwards Asquith explained to the King the reasons for the failure. The Conference were unable to agree on two points: 1, the separate treatment of constitutional questions; and 2, the number and composition of the lords' delegation to the joint sitting. In regard to the first the Government had offered a suggestion for the exceptional treatment of home rule, which failed to satisfy the opposition. In regard to the second, the opposition had criticized the Government's scheme but had offered no counter-proposal of their own.[77]

---

[74] Twenty-first sitting, 4 Nov. 1910, 'Notes of Conference', Chamberlain Papers Ac 10/2/61.

[75] *Politics from Inside*, p. 298. The comment is dated 13 Nov. 1910. See also 'Copy of Sir R. Finlay's Notes', ibid. p. 296. The account in Gollin, *The Observer and J. L. Garvin*, pp. 231–2, implies that the decision remained in doubt as late as the Lansdowne House meeting, but this is misleading. See also 'Memo. (Between 21st and 22nd Sitting)', 'Notes of Conference', Chamberlain Papers Ac 10/2/62. Lord Esher apparently saw Balfour not long after the Lansdowne House meeting and described him as caught between elements of his own party and Asquith's failure to make sufficient concessions on the other side. *Journals and Letters of...Esher*, ed. Oliver, Viscount Esher (London, 1938), III, 30. The comment is dated 9 Nov. 1910.

[76] Lloyd George Papers C/6/11/8. Asquith to Sir Arthur Bigge, 10 Nov. 1910, RAGV K2552(1)/38. MS. Asquith 23, fo. 150.

[77] RAGV K2552(1)/43.

IV

The failure of the Constitutional Conference meant that the Ripon plan would not replace the C-B veto plan at the centre of Liberal policy on the lords' veto. Expressing the ideas of a small but highly influential group of Liberal leaders, it had displayed an astonishing vitality in the years before the Parliament Act, only to be set aside at important turning-points, in 1907 because of Campbell-Bannerman's dislike and distrust, in 1910 because of entanglement with the troublesome Irish question.

Campbell-Bannerman's activity in 1907 will be variously judged. But it may be remarked that his reversing in this way a policy on which the Cabinet had decided after a full discussion and in which he himself had acquiesced for six weeks is extraordinary even when viewed within the context of the Prime Minister's growing power versus his colleagues by the early twentieth century.[78] Moreover, Campbell-Bannerman almost alone had formulated a radical policy on the lords' veto for the Liberal party at a time when it was very likely that the difficult and disagreeable task of carrying it into law would fall to his younger, more conservative colleagues. He knew full well that their preference, independently expressed, was the Ripon plan. On the day that he introduced his plan in the house of commons, the Prime Minister suffered a heart attack, perhaps brought on by the struggle in the Cabinet; and less than a year later he was dead. There were no signs in the intervening period of an attempt to follow up the plan of 1907 with a Parliament Bill of 1908.[79] It could be said, of course, that Campbell-Bannerman's qualms about the practicality of the Ripon plan compelled him as a responsible leader to impose his judgement on his colleagues; but this creates a temptation to question the quality of his judgement. In this connexion it may be noted that two veterans of English politics, long in close association with Campbell-Bannerman, explicitly rejected his assessment. Loreburn had believed that the Ripon plan would be effective, and Lord Ripon took a similar stand in a letter to Campbell-Bannerman after the Cabinet had adopted the plan of the Cabinet Committee. 'It is not an ideal scheme,' Ripon admitted, 'but I believe that it is under all the circumstances of the case the most practical one that we could have proposed.'[80] Precedent supported this view. The proposal that the great majority of peers withdraw from lawmaking whenever deadlock developed between the two houses was analogous, as was noted earlier, to the voluntary withdrawal of the main body of peers from the judicial sphere. Interestingly, Ilbert, writing before Campbell-Bannerman delivered his 24 June speech, thought it conceivable that the peers would make a voluntary renunciation of this type. 'If

---

[78] John P. Mackintosh, *The British Cabinet* (London, 1962), chap. 11.

[79] Jenkins, *Asquith*, p. 177.

[80] Ripon to Campbell-Bannerman, 25 Mar. 1907, Campbell-Bannerman Papers, Brit. Mus. Add. MS. 41,225, fo. 206 v. Wolf, *Life of Ripon*, II, 303. Spender, *Life of Campbell-Bannerman*, II, 284–6.

the H. of L. should propose to delegate their legislative functions, as they have delegated their judicial functions, to a limited number of their own body,' he wrote, 'the Cabinet Committee scheme would assume a different aspect.'[81]

The situation was more complex in 1910 because the Irish question had returned to the forefront of politics. In the first months of the year any idea of replacing the C-B veto plan with the Ripon plan had to be abandoned when the Liberals became dependent upon Irish support as a result of the January election. By the end of the year it was again put aside because of the failure in the Constitutional Conference to secure agreement on the treatment of home rule bills, to which adoption of the Ripon plan had become ancillary. Had the Liberal delegation accepted Balfour's counter-offer, the way would have been cleared for consideration of x, which to Asquith was the other important question that explained the final breakdown. Whether agreement was possible cannot be stated certainly. But the Ripon plan had much to commend it.[82] And a limited adjustment of its terms, which Asquith conceivably could have yielded,[83] might well have rendered it acceptable to the Unionist delegation who, satisfied with the provision regarding home rule, had reasons of their own for settling the embarrassing question of the house of lords before the next general election. Nor does it appear that reform of that house was an essential precondition for settling the lords' veto according to the Liberal plan. Neither Lansdowne, at one point in the negotiations, nor the Liberal delegation thought it was.[84]

[81] Ilbert to Arthur Ponsonby, Campbell-Bannerman Papers, Brit. Mus. Add. MS. 41,239, fo. 276. The letter though not dated appears to have been written just before the Prime Minister's speech. Ponsonby was principal secretary to Campbell-Bannerman.

[82] Ensor, p. 423.

[83] Chamberlain had thought Asquith inclined to give a little, and there was the disparity between the estimates of 1907 and 1910. Moreover, Winston Churchill at one time adopted the Ripon plan and even recommended a delegation of 120 peers with the aim of reducing dependence upon the Irish vote. His memorandum, printed 10 Nov. 1909, is in MS. Asquith 102, fos. 185–7v. The importance of his advocacy of an enlarged lords' delegation lies in the fact that he was a leader in the left wing of the party, in close communication with Lloyd George. If Churchill could contemplate with equanimity an enlargement of the lords' delegation, so could other Liberals. Lloyd George's position in opposition to such a concession is understandable in the light of his rejection of the Unionist condition regarding home rule bills. Presumably the two were interdependent. But it is difficult to believe that a Lloyd George overruled on home rule bills would have held out on this point. Some notion of what the Unionists would have asked can be gleaned from Lansdowne's private memorandum of 10 Sept. 1910. After stating that Lord Ripon's figures were inadequate, he proposed pressing for 150 peers in the lords' delegation but settling for less. Lansdowne to Balfour, 16 Sept. 1910, Brit. Mus. Add. MS. 49,729, fo. 110. See also Balfour's 'The Constitutional Conference', MS. Asquith 104, fos. 183–5v for the arguments that were prepared for the King.

[84] See notes 5 and 55 in this article. Jenkins concluded that agreement on the reform of the house of lords was a precondition for determining the nature and composition of the lords' delegation to the joint sitting. *Mr. Balfour's Poodle*, p. 104; *Asquith*, p. 215. Yet the assumption of the Liberal delegation was the contrary. Its members entered the Conference with the intention of carrying the Ripon plan without the reform of the house of lords: they shared the viewpoint of the Cabinet Committee of 1907, of which three of them had been members. At one point in the Conference Asquith stated explicitly that he was 'not a Grey man' and that he regarded reform of the house of lords as a second chapter. And Lloyd George

The failure of the Constitutional Conference to reach agreement on home rule bills, according to R. C. K. Ensor, was due finally to Lansdowne, whose 'views about Ireland remained narrow and obstinate, being those of a Southern Irish landlord who had never forgotten the Land League'. Had a more flexible leader been in charge, this authority concludes, the Constitutional Conference would have succeeded.[85] Just why Lansdowne should have been singled out in this fashion is unclear. The Unionist delegation as a group had informed the Liberal delegation on 4 November that they could not improve upon their counter-offer regarding home rule, and they concurred in recommending rejection of the Liberal terms to the Lansdowne House meeting. Nor is there any reason for believing that Balfour was more pliable on the Irish question than Lansdowne. He was quoted as asserting during the period of the Conference that 'his whole history forbade his being a party to any form of Home Rule, though younger men less involved in the controversies of '86 and '93 might be free to contemplate what he could not accept'.[86] Moreover, Chamberlain's and Lansdowne's accounts surely suggest that responsibility for the outcome lay ultimately with Lloyd George, despite Jenkins' comment that the Liberal leader 'gave the impression of searching almost feverishly for compromise'.[87] Possessing little respect for the traditions and formalities of the British system of politics and in particular for the house of lords, Lloyd George had initially opposed the idea of a conference. If he accepted the policy, once the Cabinet had adopted it, declaring that his best efforts would be given to its success,[88] still his July ultimatum had jeopardized the continuance of the Conference when its work was only beginning. Finally, in the last stage he had strenuously and successfully opposed the Unionist condition regarding home rule bills, a condition acceptable to two members of the Liberal delegation, one of them chief secretary for Ireland.[89] A different response from Lloyd George could have saved the Constitutional Conference. It is conceivable, to be sure, that Asquith might have overruled his colleagues in a fashion remini-

asserted that if the question of deadlocks or veto were satisfactorily settled, the reform of the house of lords would take care of itself, indicating that the reduction of numbers and exclusion of those who really took no part in that house's work would be a sufficient reform. One rather suspects that Balfour and Lansdowne, who disliked the idea of an elective element in that house, found cogency in Lloyd George's argument. Another point to be remembered is implicit in Asquith's statement that a later reform of the house of lords would result in a readjustment in the lords' delegation. 'Constitutional Conference 1910', Chamberlain Papers Ac 10/2/65. Eighteenth sitting, 1 Nov. 1910, 'Notes of Conference', Chamberlain Papers Ac 10/2/52. Balfour, 'The Constitutional Conference', MS. Asquith 104, fos. 183–5 v. Walter Long, for one, wanted the question of the house of lords settled outside the party arena. Sir Charles Petrie, *Walter Long and His Times* (London, 1936), p. 144.

[85] Ensor, pp. 423–4.

[86] Chamberlain, *Politics from Inside*, p. 293. The occasion was Balfour's breaking off of the negotiations for a coalition that were being conducted outside the Conference.

[87] *Asquith*, p. 215.   [88] Gollin, *The Observer and J. L. Garvin*, p. 190.

[89] Ensor believed that Birrell in these months provided a liaison between the Liberal delegation and the Irish Nationalists. Ensor, p. 422, note 1. But too much should not be made of this since Lloyd George was likewise in touch with the Irish leadership.

scent of Campbell-Bannerman; but this is doubtful in view of his unique contribution to the Ripon plan, which was the next order of business after the Irish question was settled, and his strong desire for the success of the Constitutional Conference, which was repeatedly displayed during the proceedings.[90] In any event, it was all over; and the Liberal leaders were confronted with the grim task of limiting the lords' veto without an agreed settlement. Their situation may be simply stated. They had been the prisoners of the C-B veto plan since 1907, and they knew without joy that it was now the turn of the lords.

[90] Asquith told Sidney Low in 1913 that almost the greatest disappointment of his life was the breakdown of the Constitutional Conference in the autumn of 1910. Major Desmond Chapman-Huston, *The Lost Historian: A Memoir of Sir Sidney Low* (London, 1936), pp. 245–6.

23

LORD NEWTON, THE CONSERVATIVE PEERS AND THE PARLIAMENT ACT OF 1911

DAVID SOUTHERN

THE Parliament Act of 1911 substituted a suspensory for the house of lords' absolute power of veto. When the bill had its final reading in the house of lords a small group of opposition conservative peers tipped the balance by voting in favour of the government measure. Their action averted the mass creation of peers, to which the liberal government would otherwise have resorted in order to overcome the resistance of the conservative-dominated house of lords. The two most recent biographies of Asquith share a notable misapprehension about the circumstances in which the Parliament Bill was passed by the house of lords. Roy Jenkins writes: 'Apart from the great bulk of the Unionist peers, who in the final division abstained with Lansdowne, Curzon persuaded a decisive 37 to follow him in voting for the Government.'[1] Stephen Koss – clearly depending on Jenkins' account – writes: 'A preponderance of Unionist peers followed Lansdowne's example and abstained, while Curzon played Pied Piper and led a pack of thirty-seven "rats" into the Government lobby.'[2] These two passages contain a simple factual error. In the crucial division on 10 August 1911 Curzon did not vote with the Government but abstained, as the division list in the house of lords reveals. Moreover, these two authors impute to Lord Curzon a role which was in fact played by Lord Newton. This note seeks to illuminate the modest but vital part played by the second Lord Newton as revealed by the passing into law of the Parliament Act in 1911.

The second Lord Newton was born in 1857, son and heir of an ancient landed family, the Leghs of Cheshire. His father, William Legh, was a long-serving conservative MP for the South Lancashire division who in 1892 accepted a peerage in preference to incurring the expense of becoming High Sheriff.[3] His son, Thomas, secured election as conservative MP for Newton in 1886, in which capacity he served obscurely until succeeding to his father's title in 1898. In the upper house he came to specialize in the question of house of lords reform. As a fair-minded, reasonable man, he perceived and sought to remedy the anomalous part played by the upper house in

---

This note is based on the diary of the 2nd Lord Newton, which has been used and quoted from by kind permission of the present (4th) Lord Newton.

1. Roy Jenkins, *Asquith* (revised edition, London, 1978), p. 229.
2. Stephen Koss, *Asquith* (London, 1976), p. 128.
3. Lord Newton, *Retrospection* (London, 1941), p. 67. Thomas Wodehouse Legh, 2nd Lord Newton (1857–1942): educated Eton and Christ Church, Oxford; diplomatic service 1879–86; paymaster-general 1915–16; controller of prisoners of war department 1916–19.

the nation's political system. 'It was overgrown . . .', he recollected in his memoirs, 'unrepresentative, and had a huge Conservative majority permanently encamped there. . . . The treatment of this Tory stronghold by successive Conservative governments was often both narrow and foolish. When they were in office they showed little but contempt for it . . . and when in opposition they left to the peers the thankless task of throwing out Liberal bills regardless of the consequences.'[1] He could be very scathing about his fellow conservative peers, on one occasion referring in his private diary to 'pig-headed imbeciles' who were 'so grossly ignorant that they went into the wrong lobby'.[2] The lords' veto of the Education Bill of 1906 was, he said, a 'ridiculous exhibition of [a] majority consisting of igno-ramuses'.[3]

There were two approaches to the reform of the house of lords: to strengthen it by changing its composition; or to weaken it by reducing its powers. Newton unequivocally recommended the former approach. He held that a strong second chamber would be necessary to restrain the socialism of the house of commons. Of the 1906 general election he commented: 'One thing to be thankful for is that there are not more Labour candidates. Fact is that working classes have at last recognized their power.'[4] He notes that Lord Rosebery, with whom he co-operated over lords reform, was 'very anxious to set up an effective check on commons, and considers it only way of fighting socialism'.[5] In 1907 he introduced a house of lords reform bill, proposing that the composition of the upper house should be altered so that it consisted of hereditary peers and life peers appointed by the government of the day. Newton's principal interest for the historian, however, lies in his role in securing the passage of the Parliament Act in 1911. This can be illuminated from three sources: his biography of Lord Lansdowne (1929),[6] his autobiography (1941),[7] and his unpublished diaries. Historians have neglected, because he himself chose to conceal, his true part in the crisis over the Parliament Act, which is only revealed by the study of his diaries.

The Parliament Bill had its first reading in the commons on 14 April 1910. The events leading to this measure, its provisions, and the course of politics in 1910–11 are well known.[8] On 16 November 1910 Asquith secured a pledge from George V that, if a liberal government were returned in the general election, the king would exercise his

1. *Retrospection*, p. 154.
2. Diary, vol. VII, 14 July 1909.
3. Diary VI, 30 Oct. 1906.
4. Diary VI, 16 Jan. 1906.
5. Diary VII, 11 Feb. 1908.
6. Lord Newton, *Lord Lansdowne: A Biography* (London, 1929).
7. Above, p. 519, n. 3.
8. See: Roy Jenkins, *Mr. Balfour's Poodle* (London, 1968); Neal Blewett, *The Peers, the Parties and the People: The General Elections of 1910* (London, 1972).

prerogative to create sufficient liberal peers to secure the enactment of the Parliament Bill. The general election of December 1910 substantially reproduced the result of the January election. Asquith's liberal government retained office and reintroduced the bill.

Many conservatives remained indifferent to the threat of a mass creation. As the bill went through its parliamentary stages Asquith wrote to Balfour and Lansdowne, informing them that the government would – as a last resort – advise the king to create liberal peers in numbers which would ensure the passage of the bill in its original form and that the king would feel bound to act in accordance with that advice. This letter helped to persuade the conservative leadership to follow Wellington's precedent of 1832 and propose a policy of abstention. On 24 July Lansdowne wrote to Unionist peers, requesting them to support him by withholding their votes when the Parliament Bill returned from the commons with the lords' amendments. Lord Curzon, hitherto a protagonist for the rejection of the bill, had now come to the conclusion that 'it would be fatal to the best interests of the country to force the hand of the Government by standing out any longer against the Parliament Bill'.[1] On his prompting, Balfour gave Lansdowne support by writing a letter to *The Times* – published on 26 July – cast in the form of a public reply to 'a perplexed peer who required advice'. To his surprise, Lord Newton was selected as this 'imaginary correspondent'.[2] He recorded in his diary on 25 July: 'In the evening rung up by Curzon, seems A.J.B. means to publish important manifesto backing up Lansdowne giving his reasons. Said I had no objection.'[3]

The conservative leadership however had too long applied the accelerator to be able now to apply the brake. The conservative peers split into two groups. The 'Hedgers' were prepared to follow Lansdowne in abstaining in the crucial division. The 'Ditchers' (or Die-Hards) – led by Lord Halsbury and Lord Willoughby de Broke – were resolved to vote against the Parliament Bill whatever the consequences. The strength of the Ditchers was such that they could outvote the government peers and their supporters. On 31 July Morley had come to the conclusion that the bill could not pass unless upwards of forty Unionist peers voted with the government. Hence the official policy of the opposition could not save the bill and avoid the consequences of its defeat. The front-bench conservative peers – including Curzon and Lansdowne – were unwilling to vote for the bill themselves and so could scarcely ask others to do so. They feared that any overt attempt to persuade conservatives to support the bill would drive others to vote against it. As Newton wrote in his diary on 4 August 1911: 'No organised support of Government should be

1. Earl of Ronaldshay, *The Life of Lord Curzon* (London, 1928), iii. 56.
2. *Lansdowne*, p. 425.
3. Diary VII, 25 July 1911.

given . . . as soon as it is known that our people are going to vote with Government other peers will at once join Halsbury party.'[1] The conservative leaders required someone who would recruit a band of conservative peers to vote for the measure, thereby sparing them the dangers of a rejection of the bill. They needed, in short, a stooge. They turned to Lord Newton.

Newton himself thought that an alternative solution was possible: a limited creation. He recorded in his diary on 26 July: 'Conference about how we are to vote when division comes: suggested by Cromer that certain number should sacrifice themselves by voting for bill, to save Lansdowne and Front Bench. Am inclined to think now best solution would be for few peers to be made.'[2] However, Lansdowne and the front bench, unable to conquer, unwilling to perish, wanting to retreat, but unwilling to give the order, recognized that this was not a possibility. On 27 July Curzon spoke to Newton on behalf of Lansdowne: 'tackled by Curzon about asking peers to vote for bill, Lansdowne having suggested I should do it, promised to write to a lot, although rather unpleasant job.'[3] Accordingly, on 28 July Newton 'wrote to lot of people (about 20) asking them to vote if necessary'.[4] The first crop of replies arrived on 30 July. He noted in his diary: 'Heard from various peers agreeing to vote – also from Curzon.'[5] He added the names of nine peers 'collected up to date'. On the next day he 'heard from about 12 peers promising to vote if necessary'.[6] On 1 August Newton reported to Lansdowne 'who was afraid that I had used his name in letters'.[7] Lord Newton himself was more relaxed: 'situation altogether highly entertaining and sorry to leave town.'[8] The reason for his good spirits was that he, like many others, greatly underestimated the number of Ditchers. On 2 August he put the total number of Ditchers at about 78: 'Probably an outside estimate and nothing like that number will vote.'[9]

The Bill returned from the commons with the lords' amendments deleted on 9 August for a two-day debate before the crucial division on 10 August. The outcome of this vote was uncertain to the last moment. For the bill were about eighty government peers and most of the bishops – in the event thirteen out of fifteen. The relative strength of the three sections of conservatives – Hedgers abstaining, Ditchers voting against and the crucial group voting for the Bill – was a profound mystery. If necessary, some Hedgers would vote for the government, but if they did so, other Hedgers would vote for the Die-Hards out of disapproval of Unionist support for the bill. The

1. Diary VII, 4 Aug. 1911.   2. Diary VII, 26 July 1911.
3. Diary VII, 27 July 1911.   4. Diary VII, 28 July 1911.
5. Diary VII, 30 July 1911.   6. Diary VII, 31 July 1911.
7. Diary VII, 1 Aug. 1911.   8. Diary VII, 4 Aug. 1911.
9. Diary VII, 2 Aug. 1911. On 31 July he wrote: 'Impossible to find out how many ditchers there are as they will not say. Impression is that they are less than 50 and therefore no danger.'

Ditchers concealed their strength to gain surprise. When the division took place it seemed that the Ditchers might carry the day. Newton reacted promptly: 'Things looking desperate, persuaded myself 5 or 6 to vote with Government. Surprise was that Ditchers had managed to collect so many, and most of them probably quite unknown obscurities.'[1] Amid great tension, the Parliament Bill was passed by a majority of seventeen – 131 votes to 114. Estimates of the number of conservative peers voting with the Government varied from 38 (*Liberal Magazine*), 37 (Lord Morley), 35 (*Globe*) to 29 (*Observer*). Newton estimated that between 25 and 30 conservative peers voted for the Parliament Act. Newton, on the evidence of his diary, recruited about 26 of this number, and was thereby instrumental in securing the passage of the Parliament Bill.

All historians of this episode share with Jenkins and Koss the view that it was Curzon who secured this outcome. R. C. K. Ensor writes: 'Curzon induced a number of Unionist peers headed by Lord Winchelsea and Lord Camperdown to sacrifice themselves when the need should arise by voting for the Bill.'[2] This view is highly misleading. On the authority of Newton's diaries it is clear that Lansdowne, although he had written to *The Times* on 1 August to say that he wanted no conservative peer to vote with the government, was both cognizant with and approved of the recruitment of a covert band of Unionist peers to vote for the government: indeed, there was no alternative if Lansdowne wanted both to abstain and to let the Bill through. While Curzon persuaded Lansdowne to authorize this step, Curzon – like Lansdowne – could not himself vote for the bill: he was a member of the shadow cabinet and could not pursue a different policy to that of the conservative party in the house of commons. If Curzon could only in public advocate,abstention, he could hardly in private persuade peers to vote with the government. Curzon had in turn to rely on Newton to recruit a band of conservative peers to vote for the bill, thereby making themselves the unconscious agents of Lord Lansdowne's covert policy. If Newton had failed in this task, the Ditchers would have won and the Bill, to which the government had committed all its prestige and authority and for which it had sacrificed its towering majority of 1906, been lost. Therefore the credit for inducing the crucial group of conservative peers to support the government must be given to Lord Newton.

That Newton's action should pass unnoticed at the time was a condition of its success. It has remained unknown because he himself chose to conceal it when he later came to write about the constitutional crisis of 1911. In his notable biography of Lord Lansdowne – published in 1929 – he records evasively that it 'became necessary to take

1. Diary VII, 10 Aug. 1911.
2. R. C. K. Ensor, *England 1870–1914* (Oxford, 1936), pp. 429–30; Ronaldshay, *Curzon*, iii. 56–58.

the unpleasant step of ascertaining whether a sufficient number of peers were prepared if necessary to sacrifice themselves by voting with the government'.[1] In his volume of memoirs, *Retrospection* (1941), he writes more revealingly: 'As it was difficult to estimate the probable number of Die-hards, precautions had to be taken to secure the promise of a certain number of self-sacrificing Unionist peers who would be prepared to save the Bill, if necessary, and these people, who really showed more courage than anyone else we discovered with some difficulty.'[2]

There were two reasons for his reticence. In the first place, he felt a little ashamed of himself because, while persuading over twenty of his colleagues to vote with the government, he himself had abstained. He was not of the blood of martyrs. If his opinions were somewhat advanced, that was the more reason for his actions to be strictly orthodox. Surveying his fellow conservative peers, he knew that they had drunk from the same cup, supped from the same table, and joined in the same pastimes. If those nominally responsible for the leadership of the conservative party would not take the responsibility of voting for the bill, he would not incur odium for himself to spare them from it. As he wrote on 30 July 1911: 'I should not feel bound to vote unless opposition Front Bench did so also. Do not see why I should be utilised to save their face.'[3] Yet he recognized with characteristic honesty and fair-mindedness that the action of those conservatives who voted in favour of the Bill was more courageous: 'Result taken with good humour at the time, but on going to Carlton afterwards with Galway latter was received with shouts of Judas. As a matter of fact, he and other peers who voted with Government deserve great credit.'[4] Likewise he observed in his autobiography that 'this action was in reality more satisfactory than that of the great mass of peers like myself, who had abstained'.[5] Second, Newton wished his biography of Lansdowne to be laudatory. It reflected adversely on the conservative leader that he had hidden behind a back-bench peer, when his own strength of decision failed. The only overt criticism which Newton allows himself in print comes when he comments that 'the impression left upon me . . . was that – for once in a way – Lord Lansdowne showed some slight deficiency in the art of leadership'.[6] Lord Newton's diaries, in contrast, are filled with acrid comments on Lansdowne:

No sign whatever that it is his duty to lead. Either he and his friends have something up their sleeve or (much more likely) have no plan whatsoever.[7]

1. *Lansdowne*, p. 427.
2. *Retrospection*, p. 185.
3. Diary VII, 30 July 1911.
4. Diary VII, 10 Aug. 1911.
5. *Retrospection*, p. 187.
6. *Lansdowne*, p. 423.
7. Diary VII, 20 June 1911.

Everyone agreed that Lansdowne had bungled things, and that his last letter had made it practically impossible for people to vote with Government.[1]

In particular, Newton records a conversation with Walter Long which, besides reflecting on Lansdowne, also confirms all that we know about Balfour: 'W. Long . . . says Lansdowne was strongly urged by his colleagues to put his foot down. Agrees that if he had, we should have had no trouble with ditchers. Says some difficulty with A.J.B., and a lot of bother to get letter written to me. A.J.B. actually told several supporters that he saw no harm in their going to Halsbury banquet.'[2]

It remains to be considered why Newton was selected by Lansdowne and Curzon for the discharge of this delicate and responsible task. Newton had no existing connection with either Lansdowne or Curzon. On the contrary, he ascribed his disappointment over office in 1905, when he had hoped to become under-secretary for India in Balfour's government, to Lansdowne's intervention against him.[3] In the circumstances of 1911, however, only a back bencher could save the party leadership. The leaders of the party in the lords were committed to the policy of abstention, and had to summon up all their influence and that of their immediate supporters to persuade some Ditchers to hedge. The conservative leadership as a whole faced extreme discontent within the party following its defeat in three successive elections, and any hint that a conservative peer who voted for the government would have the blessing of Lansdowne would have split the party and caused the fall of the leadership. Most back-bench peers, however, were too partisan or too obscure to be of any utility in inducing Hedgers to support the government. It was Newton's long advocacy of house of lords reform which had given him sufficient prominence to make him influential within the party in this connection. He was a reliable party man detached from immediate faction. He recognized the dilemma of the leadership and could be persuaded to rescue it.

The leadership of Balfour and Lansdowne did not long survive the passing of the Parliament Act. Nevertheless the unity of the party was preserved. More important, a mass creation of peers, which would have imposed an additional strain on a political system approaching its critical load, was successfully averted by the activity of a then little-known and now largely forgotten conservative peer. Lord Newton, it can justly be claimed, was a minor figure who made a small yet crucial contribution towards smoothing the advance of democracy in Britain.

1. Diary VII, 4 Aug. 1911.   2. Diary VII, 28 July 1911.
3. Diary VI, 20 Jan. 1905, 30 Jan. 1905.

24

THE 'JUDAS GROUP' AND THE PARLIAMENT
BILL OF 1911*

PATRICIA KELVIN, CORINNE COMSTOCK WESTON

WAS Lord Curzon's the decisive role on the Unionist side in passing the Parliament Bill of 1911? Contemporaries thought it was, and until recently modern scholars have echoed the judgment uncritically. It is usually said that Curzon persuaded thirty-odd Unionist peers, whom their political enemies called 'the Judas group', to save the Bill by voting with the Asquith government. And he is even described as leading the Judas group into the government lobby. The idea that Curzon voted for the Parliament Bill seems to have originated in a misreading of a passage in Sir Robert Ensor's *England: 1870–1914* (1936) and has been propagated by Roy Jenkins and Stephen Koss.[1] As David Southern has noted, it is easily dispelled by referring to the Lords' division list, which reveals that Curzon did not in fact vote for the Bill.[2] But there are other points to be settled. Did Curzon, for example, although he did not vote with the Judas group, persuade its members to support the government and organize them for this purpose, or find an agent who would do these things for him? If he was not their leader, even in this restricted sense, who was? And what was the relationship between the Unionist leadership, which included Curzon, and the Judas group? Were its members only an arm of that leadership, or was the group an entity in its own right, pursuing an independent course on the Parliament Bill until the tally was complete?

Southern is the first scholar to confront these questions squarely. Demolishing the belief that Curzon led the Judas group into the government lobby, he holds, nevertheless, that the Unionist leaders successfully controlled the sequence of events on their side of the house until the final vote. Within this context he discusses what he sees as the modest but vital role of the second Lord Newton in the passage of the Parliament Bill. Southern's main contribution is to show incontrovertibly that at one stage of the constitutional crisis Newton was actively engaged in pressing fellow Unionist peers to vote with the government and that at the time he was working closely with Curzon and with Lord Lansdowne, the Unionist leader in the Lords. In doing so he relies on new evidence supplied by unpublished

* This research was supported (in part) by grant number 12936 from the PSC-CUNY Research Award Program of The City University of New York.

1. Ensor, *England: 1870–1914* (Oxford, 1936, reprinted 1960), pp. 429–30; Jenkins, *Asquith* (London, 1964), p. 229; Koss, *Asquith* (London, 1976), p. 128.

2. 'Lord Newton, the conservative peers and the Parliament Act of 1911', see above, p. 519; see also p. 523.

and hitherto unknown diaries kept by Newton.[1] Southern writes that the Unionist front bench in the Lords, unwilling to vote for the Parliament Bill and in no position to encourage openly any Unionist support for it, yet painfully aware that it would have to pass to avoid a peerage creation, solved their dilemma by turning to Newton. As a backbencher and loyal party member, he could recruit Unionist votes without further dividing the party and jeopardizing the leaders' position. Southern concludes roundly that Lansdowne and Curzon, working together, relied on Newton to secure the Unionist votes needed for the Bill's passage and thus made the members of the Judas group 'the unconscious agents of Lord Lansdowne's covert policy'.[2]

It is urged here, however, that the leader of the Judas group was not Newton but Lord Cromer. His very different gifts, outlook, experience, and even relations with the Unionist leadership made him a much more independent figure than Newton. A distinguished proconsul whose strength of character, self-reliance, and autocratic tendencies have often been remarked, Cromer had a career in imperial government, first in India and then in Egypt, that brought him reputation as a brilliant administrator and financier. Returning to England, he became the leader of the free-trade elements in the Lords at a time when tariff reformers were ascendant in the Unionist party; and isolated from the official party and its leadership, he took up his seat on the cross-bench. In short, Cromer was hardly the kind of individual who does the bidding of others in a party struggle, and his relations with the Unionist leaders were not conducive to such an arrangement. If he was indeed the head of the Judas group, it was in all probability autonomous.

Newton's and Cromer's roles in the summer of 1911 are only understandable in terms of the part played by the Unionist leaders. As is well known, the party leaders were united in opposition to the Parliament Bill but divided on tactics with respect to it; and these divisions came to a head at a meeting of the shadow cabinet on 21 July, after Balfour learned from Asquith that the King had promised

1. The copyright in the Newton diaries belongs to the fourth Lord Newton, who has made them available only to Southern. The latter has graciously responded to a series of questions prepared by us that grew out of his account of Lord Newton and the Parliament Act. His responses, contained in a letter to Patricia Kelvin, 22 July 1982, are in the form of verbatim extracts from the diaries. Since the present Lord Newton is unwilling for any extracts to be reproduced except in so far as Southern has printed from them, they are not quoted unless Southern has already quoted them. Material from them has been used, however; and the reference is 'Southern to Kelvin, 22 July 1982'. We wish to thank Southern for allowing us to see the verbatim extracts in question when we were preparing this note.

2. See above, 523. See in general, above, pp. 521-4, 525. Newton was a relatively minor peer who is remembered today as Lansdowne's biographer; he received recognition at the time as the author of a much-discussed plan to reform the House of Lords.

to create the necessary peers if the Lords rejected the Bill.[1] There was at this stage no question of voting for the Bill. The alternatives were simply 'abstention' (*i.e.* 'surrender') or 'resistance', and the majority of the shadow cabinet followed the leaders in choosing abstention. Jack Sandars (Balfour's private secretary) listed those 'for resistance' (8) and 'against resistance' (14).[2] Curzon's name appears directly after Balfour's and Lansdowne's among those 'against resistance', and very early his energy and aggressiveness made him a leading spokesman for the 'hedger' majority. The formal beginnings of the 'ditchers' are also traceable to the events of 21 July. Despite being out-voted the minority persisted with the policy of resistance under Lord Halsbury. Their success with back-bench Unionist peers meant that the policy of abstention could be self-defeating: abstention alone would not ensure the passage of the Bill. In this way the question of Unionist support for the Bill came to the front: at least a few Unionist peers might need to go into the government lobby if the creation of peers was to be averted.

There were Unionist peers who had already faced this unpleasant possibility and were prepared to make the required sacrifice. As early as 13 July, Cromer in a letter to Lord Midleton (described at the time as Curzon's 'henchman') contemplated the need for 'voting with this infernal government to prevent its own defeat'.[3] And Lord Monteagle, on 24 July, expressed the hope to Cromer that Lansdowne would carry his decision for abstention to its logical conclusion 'even to the length of voting with the government should this become necessary'.[4] The Unionist leaders resisted this logic. They willed the end – preventing the creation of peers, but not the means – voting with the government. It was not clear for some time however that this would be their position, and Curzon at first encouraged other Unionists to support the Parliament Bill. Southern demonstrates conclusively that on 27 July he pressed Newton to recruit Unionist peers to this end[5] although after 1 August, as will be seen, Curzon abandoned this kind of activity. As for Lansdowne, he certainly recognized that a number of Unionist peers would have to vote with the government; and in close association with Curzon he

1. Balfour Papers, British Library, Add. MS 49767, fos. 203–4 (pp. 19–20). This is from Sandars, 'A Diary of the Events and Transactions in connection with the passage of the Parliament Bill of 1911 through the House of Lords', fos. 184–236. It is also paginated as 1–52, and both sets of numbers are used here. The 'Diary' is dated 12 Aug. 1911.

2. Balfour Papers, Add. MS 49767, fo. 204 (p. 20).

3. Cromer Papers, Public Record Office, FO 633/34–3079, Cromer to Midleton, 13 July 1911. The letters from Cromer in his papers are copies. C. C. Weston would like to record her appreciation to Dr Stephen Levine of New York City, who first called her attention to the Cromer Papers and the light they shed on the passing of the Parliament Act.

4. *Ibid.* Monteagle to Cromer, 24 July 1911.

5. Above, p. 522.

too was engaged in lining up Unionist votes for the Bill.[1] But not Balfour, who rejected the idea as early as 22 July in a memorandum suppressed at Lansdowne's and Curzon's insistence.[2] Balfour's view prevailed at a decisive meeting with Lansdowne on 31 July, attended by other Unionist leaders but not by Curzon. Directly afterwards there was published in *The Times*, on 1 August, a letter from Lansdowne to Lord Camperdown, a Unionist peer who had made public his intention of voting with the government. Recommending the policy of abstention on the final vote on the Parliament Bill, Lansdowne now deprecated any tendency on the part of his following to imitate Camperdown. He took the action despite a plea, on 31 July, from Cromer, who had asked him not to take this stand publicly.[3] From the abstention policy as now stated, with its important corollary that the hedgers were not to vote with the Asquith government, Lansdowne never wavered. And, it is contended here, this policy once it was public received Curzon's unswerving support despite his earlier activity. Nor is there evidence that Newton, as Curzon's agent, continued to recruit Unionist support after Lansdowne's letter appeared. On the night of 10 August the great majority of Unionist peers, including Curzon and Newton, abstained from voting on the critical Lansdowne amendment. Their abstention explains the smallness of the final vote if not the outcome of the constitutional struggle.

The reasons for this potentially self-defeating course on the part of the Unionist leadership need a separate consideration going beyond the context of this discussion. Two things emerge, however, from Sandars' diary: (i) that it was Balfour who insisted on Lansdowne's public disavowal of those prepared to vote with the government, and (ii) that Cromer was seen by the Unionist hierarchy as a leader of these peers. Sandars describes the 31 July meeting thus:

Attention was . . . drawn to the development of a policy among Unionists, headed by [Lord] St Aldwyn and Cromer and others, to vote with the

1. *Ibid.*
2. Balfour Papers, Add. MS 49767, fo. 207 (p. 23). See also *ibid.* fo. 208 (p. 24).
3. Cromer Papers, Lansdowne to Cromer, 30 July 1911; to Edmund Gosse, 12 Aug. 1911. Gosse, the librarian of the House of Lords, helped Cromer put Unionist peers into the government lobby on 10 Aug. On 15 Aug. Lansdowne wrote to Cromer that he was still unrepentant about the letter to Camperdown; *ibid.* 15 Aug. 1911. For Balfour's pressure on Lansdowne and the letter to Camperdown, see Balfour Papers, Add. MS 49767, fos. 223–6 (pp. 39–42). The Lansdowne letter is on p. 9 of *The Times*. But if Lansdowne did not succumb until 31 July, he grew more cautious before that date. He wrote to Curzon on 29 July: 'The cooperation of the bishops with H.M. Gov't won't hurt us, but I hope no considerable number of lay Unionist peers will join them. I do not say for a moment that they would not be justified in taking such a course in view of the line which has been taken by the "ditchers", but I am sure it would be a misfortune for our party if any of us were to take that course ourselves or encourage our friends to take it. There is an extraordinary amount of bitterness about, and we must not let it eat in too far'; Curzon Papers, MSS Eur. F. 112/89. These papers are in the India Office Library, which is part of the British Library.

government on the Bill. Mr Balfour pointed out to Lord Lansdowne that this was as much opposed to his policy as was the action of the Halsbury group, and that he ought to express his disapproval of this action. Lord Lansdowne exhibited much reluctance to intervene, but took with him a draft of a letter which Mr Balfour thought might serve the purpose.[1]

This 'draft' became the letter that Lansdowne addressed to Camperdown. As earlier noted, the Lansdowne policy at this stage took shape without Curzon's participation. He was not present at the meeting of 31 July, and had he been there he must have resisted a policy whereby the majority of the shadow cabinet lost its power to influence decisively the outcome of the constitutional crisis. Unlike Balfour, who was willing to have a small creation of peers, Curzon was resolutely opposed to the creation of even a single peer. He surely knew that to lose control of events in early August was to risk a peerage creation.[2]

Whatever his personal feelings, Curzon at this point abandoned any systematic attempt to recruit Unionist peers to vote with the government. His correspondence with St Loe Strachey on 1 August reveals his attitude. Strachey feared a large creation of peers, believed it was essential for some Unionists to vote for the Bill, and asked Curzon to take the lead so as to save the party from destruction.[3] Curzon's response, also on 1 August, reflected a new sense of constraint: any action now must come from leadership outside the Unionist front bench:

The situation can only be retrieved not by isolated action by any individual, least of all anyone on the front bench, but by concerted action of those who are not upon it. Lord Cromer has this in hand, and if it is not talked about too much is quite likely to succeed. For the moment I am better employed in preventing further backsliding among our leaders to which there have been many leanings. . . . But Lord Cromer or I will let you know of any developments calling for assistance. For the moment the thing is to produce the conscience peers but to say as little about it as possible.[4]

Presumably 'backsliding' was an allusion to Lansdowne's letter, which Curzon thought 'unnecessary and regrettable'. The tenor of his

1. Balfour Papers, Add. MS 49767, fo. 225 (p. 41).
2. *Ibid.* fos. 213 (p. 29); 230–1 (pp. 46–47). Midleton complained to Sandars about Lansdowne's letter of 1 Aug., stating that if any peers were created, he and many others would probably vote with the ditchers; *ibid.* fo. 226 (p. 42).
3. The letter is in the Curzon Papers, MSS Eur. F. 112/89. Strachey, who edited the influential Unionist publication, *The Spectator*, was a long-time ally of Cromer's.
4. Curzon's letter is in the Strachey Papers, Record Office, House of Lords, S/4/17/12. Curzon's expression 'conscience peers' is explicable when it is realized that the Judas group was referred to as 'conscience men'. The expression appears in an unsigned letter to Curzon, 10 Aug. 1911, Curzon Papers, MSS Eur. F. 112/89. Cromer also sent out a circular to several peers on 2 Aug. in which he wrote: 'It is clear from Lord Lansdowne's recently published letter that if any further steps are to be taken to prevent the creation of peers, they must be initiated by the spontaneous action on the part of the independent members of the Unionist party'; Cromer Papers, 2 Aug. 1911. On the same day he wrote to St Aldwyn that Lansdowne's letter 'has had a very deplorable effect'; *ibid.*

own letter is clear enough. As a front-bench man, Curzon was no longer in a position to encourage Unionist peers to go into the government lobby, though he had been doing this before 1 August; and just as clearly, he was at this time backing Cromer's initiative. To be sure, he referred to himself as well as to Cromer when he promised Strachey that 'Lord Cromer *or I* [italics added] will let you know of any developments calling for assistance'. But given the context of the remark, it would appear that he had in fact abandoned the leadership of the Judas group to Cromer. This assumption is borne out by Curzon's emphatic denial at a later date that he had ever trafficked with the Judas group. In an undated but signed memorandum in his papers, he declared:

Our policy was that of abstention in the final division: and we did not in any way traffic with or encourage those Unionist peers who for conscientious reasons ultimately decided – in far greater numbers than was ever anticipated – to vote for the Bill rather than see the house of lords flooded and the constitution turned into ridicule.[1]

This is not a true description of his actions before 1 August but is accurate for his position after Lansdowne's letter appeared in *The Times*.

As important as the effect of that letter on Curzon was its impact on those to whom it was most particularly addressed: that is, on the Unionist peers who contemplated voting with the government. It is these men whose leadership and whose independent existence as an organized group are in dispute. The ambiguities surrounding the group are due partly to the later unwillingness of certain peers to acknowledge their association with the group. This was true of Newton, as Southern makes clear, and also of Curzon, whose memorandum tells so much about his attitude. They were also due to the imperatives of the moment, which made this group reluctant to proclaim itself at the time. The great fear was that hitherto neutral peers would be driven to join the ditchers. Another source of difficulty in interpretation rises out of the political situation at the time. It changed rapidly, and many adjustments were made in a relatively short span of time.

There seem to be three phases in the coming together of a body of Unionist peers willing to take the distasteful step of voting with the government to save the Parliament Bill. The first, which may be considered as beginning with Cromer's letter to Midleton (13 July), ended with the publication of Lansdowne's letter on 1 August. It saw a growing recognition by a small number of Unionist peers that it might be necessary to support the government if the creation of peers

1. The memorandum introduces a portion of the Curzon Papers entitled 'Correspondence on the Parliament Bill and Crisis of 1911, July–Aug. 1911'. MSS Eur. F. 112/89.

was to be averted. Precisely because this action ran so much against the grain they sought the reassurance of mutual support and a leader who commanded respect in his own right. Cromer was such a man. Although his independent status as a cross-bencher may have left some Unionist peers hesitant, this was offset by the support of St Aldwyn, with the impeccable party credentials of an ex-Unionist cabinet minister (as Sir Michael Hicks Beach). In this first phase Cromer was occupied in writing letters, sounding out friends, and answering questions from his followers. Evidence of Cromer's primacy in these activities at this stage appears in Curzon's comment to Strachey: 'Lord Cromer has this in hand', and in Sandars' reference to 'a policy among Unionists, headed by St Aldwyn and Cromer and others, to vote with the government on the Bill'.[1]

In the first days of August the activities of the Cromer group passed into a middle phase. Characterized by uncertainty and backsliding, it lasted until the night of 9 August, the first of the final two days of debate in the House of Lords. Lansdowne's letter of 1 August, which forced several of Cromer's recruits back to the hedgers,[2] was primarily responsible for this. But a letter from the duke of Norfolk to *The Times* on 3 August also shaped events. Norfolk threatened to go over, with his followers, to the ditchers if any organized body of Unionist peers voted with the government. These factors forced a shift in Cromer's plans, and a change in government tactics at this time gave him the opportunity to relax his pressure for an organized group. Cromer had been having secret talks with Lord Crewe, the leader of the Liberal peers, trying to persuade the government to hold off creating peers in return for a promise of a specified number of Unionist votes in the division. Crewe suggested that fifty Unionists, including the bishops, would need to go into the government lobby: in return for a guarantee of such a number, the government would

---

1. Cromer Papers, Cromer to Midleton, 13, 14, 15 July 1911; Monteagle to Cromer, 24, 31 July 1911; Blythswood to Cromer, 28 July 1911. The main work of organization seems to have fallen to Cromer rather than to St Aldwyn, perhaps because he sat on the cross-bench and so many of the Judas group were recruited from there; Cromer Papers, Lord Heneage to Cromer, 10, 13 Aug. 1911. Heneage also mentioned recruiting Liberal Unionists. On the other hand, it was St Aldwyn whom the King summoned to meet with him on 25 July about the business of a Unionist vote with the government. St Aldwyn promised to try to persuade Lansdowne to take this course but did not expect success; Lady Victoria Hicks Beach, *Life of Sir Michael Hicks Beach* (London, 1932), ii. 268–9; Balfour Papers, Add. MS 49767, fo. 222 (p. 38). There were references in the press to St Aldwyn's movement; *Life of Sir Michael Hicks Beach*, ii. 271. This was in fact the heading of the account in *The Times*, 5 Aug. 1911, p. 6, of the meeting at Lord Bath's house. St Aldwyn was in the chair, and Cromer was the only other peer listed by name as addressing the group. He had summoned the meeting and wrote about it afterwards to Curzon, Lansdowne, and Lord Crewe.

2. Cromer Papers, Faber to Cromer, 1 Aug. 1911; Lichfield to Cromer, 1 Aug. 1911; Cromer to Gosse, 12 Aug. 1911. See also Sandars' account of Bath's attitude; Balfour Papers, Add. MS 49767, fo. 233 (p. 49). In the end Bath abstained.

delay the creation of peers.[1] Up to this time both Unionists and
Liberals seem to have assumed that creation would precede the
division despite the known reluctance of the King to create peers
until the Parliament Bill had been in fact defeated. The government
was under pressure from its own, its Irish, and its Labour supporters
to ensure the unquestioned passing of the Bill by immediate creation,
and could not afford the loss of time that would ensue from a possible
defeat in the House of Lords and the need to create peers. On 3
August, however, the government changed its mind. It would risk
the Bill without a prior creation of peers and without any prior pledge
of support in the final vote. Cromer described the turnabout to
Lansdowne as 'a very considerable point gained' and to Curzon as a
point that changed the situation 'very greatly' for the Unionist peers.[2]
He now briefly swung around to the policy of abstention so as to
avoid friction within the party and prevent the Norfolk faction within
it from siding with the ditchers.[3] The decision to adopt the hedger
policy came at a meeting of his supporters on 4 August at Lord Bath's
house, 29 Grosvenor Square. Cromer summoned it, and a notice of
the change in policy was inserted in *The Times* and sent directly to
Norfolk. The peers in attendance agreed that they might in the end be
compelled to vote with the government, depending on what was said
in the forthcoming debates of 9/10 August in the Lords; but they
decided for the time being to disband their organization. The purpose
was to keep Norfolk in the hedger ranks by convincing him that
Camperdown's activity was confined to a very few unorganized,
independent peers.[4] Camperdown cooperated on this point by
stressing during the debate on 10 August that he was acting alone.[5]
When Norfolk, ignoring these reassurances, went over that night to
the ditchers, his action provided a signal to the watchful Judas group,
which promptly abandoned the hedger policy that they had adopted
only six days earlier at Lord Bath's house.

The third phase of their association began, then, with the final
debate already underway in the House of Lords. By denying
themselves the advantages of organization during the crucial middle
phase, its members had created serious tactical problems for

1. Cromer Papers, Cromer to St Aldwyn, 2 Aug. 1911.
2. *Ibid.* Cromer to Lansdowne, 3 Aug. 1911; to Curzon, 3 Aug. 1911.
3. *Ibid.* This letter is also in the Curzon Papers, MSS Eur. F. 112/89.
4. Cromer Papers, 'Circular sent to several Peers', 2 Aug. 1911. Cromer to Lansdowne, 3 Aug. 1911; to Curzon, 3 Aug. 1911; Lansdowne to Cromer, 4 Aug. 1911; 'Letter sent to a few Peers', 4 Aug. 1911; Cromer to Crewe, 4 Aug. 1911; to Gosse, 12 Aug. 1911.
5. *Parliamentary Debates*, Lords, fifth series, ix. 1017. Ensor writes of Camperdown and Lord Winchilsea working with Curzon to win passage for the Parliament Bill; *England: 1870–1914*, p. 430. His account suggests a concerted action on Camperdown's part that the latter contradicted when he described himself as acting alone, and Winchilsea did not speak in the final stage of the debates. He was in close touch with Cromer and voted with the Judas group; Cromer Papers, Winchilsea to Cromer, 15 Aug. 1911.

themselves. Lord Fortescue had written to Cromer the day after the meeting at Lord Bath's house, pointing out the need for a whip to give last-minute advice to those who shared Cromer's views and suggesting that Cromer and St Aldwyn try to arrange this; alternatively, he suggested, one of them should speak toward the close of the debate to give a lead to their following.[1] The latter course was adopted but threatened to come apart as debate began on 9 August. At issue was the Lansdowne amendment, which would have changed the Bill in a fundamental respect. Not to insist upon the amendment was to vote with the Asquith government for the Parliament Bill. By this time Cromer was convinced that Norfolk fully intended to join the ditchers though he had not as yet taken this action, and acting on this conviction Cromer wrote to St Aldwyn asking him to give the Judas group a strong lead in his speech to be given that night. That St Aldwyn should do so was the more necessary since Cromer himself had been suddenly incapacitated by the gout and could not take his seat in the Lords. St Aldwyn, however, had been persuaded by Curzon that as an ex-front bench man, his presence in the government lobby would accentuate divisions within the party. 'I am all the more sorry that you are ill,' he wrote to Cromer, 'because I could not make the speech you suggested in your letter after seeing Curzon. I thought I had indicated that to you already'.[2] In the final hours before the vote Cromer was left to manage affairs as best he could from his sickbed. His surrogate, hastily appointed on 10 August, was Lord Heneage, who had not planned to speak. Acting with him were Lords Lytton, Blythswood, Cobham and Lichfield. From outside the House, Strachey, who also had links with Heneage, worked with Cromer. With the latter's permission Heneage informed the peers that if Cromer were present he would vote with the government for the Parliament Bill and encourage other peers to do so, and he sent Cromer a detailed account of the events in the last hour before the vote. Among other things he promised Lord Rosebery, who had hung back until then from supporting the government, that if he voted with the Cromer group he would have twenty Unionist peers to support him.[3]

Cromer's papers afford firm evidence that his leadership, exercised

1. *Ibid.* Fortescue to Cromer, 5 Aug. 1911; Curzon Papers, MSS Eur. F. 112/89, Cromer to Curzon, 4 Aug. 1911.

2. *Ibid.* Cromer to Curzon, enclosing a copy of St Aldwyn's letter to him, 10 Aug. 1911; Cromer Papers, 9 Aug. 1911. See also *ibid.* Heneage to Cromer, 10 Aug. 1911; Strachey to Cromer, 10 Aug. 1911; Cromer to Gosse, 12 Aug. 1911; to Lord Blythswood, 12 Aug. 1911. Cromer considered that St Aldwyn had fought shy at the last moment. L. P. Curtis, Jr has an appraisal of St Aldwyn, then Hicks Beach, much like Cromer's in *Coercion and Conciliation in Ireland* (Princeton, 1963), pp. 25–26. See Sir Almeric Fitzroy, *Memoirs* (London, n.d.), i. 386. Cromer was also critical of the leaders of the Unionist party; Cromer Papers, Cromer to Blythswood, 12 Aug. 1911.

3. *Ibid.* Heneage to Cromer, 11, 13 Aug. 1911. At the end Heneage considered that he had thirty supporters. Rosebery brought with him Lords Cadogan and Minto.

independently of Curzon, determined the line of action taken by the
Judas group on 10 August: from 21 July to 10 August Cromer had
been in almost daily communication with Unionist peers who feared
the effects of creation enough to contemplate voting against their
own party to save a Bill they hated. Of the 29 Unionist peers listed by
Sandars as voting with the government, the names of 15 are present in
the Cromer Papers.[1] Moreover, Cromer stated categorically that he
had urged the peers to vote with the government and had
commissioned Heneage to make this clear to the House of Lords.[2]
On the night of 10 August Heneage did so, declaring:

Personally I had no intention of taking part in this debate because I knew
that . . . Lord Cromer was most desirous of speaking, and his views and mine
are identical. *But unfortunately he is ill today and unable to be here to make the speech
he intended to make urging his friends to vote as I am going to vote and as he would have
voted if he had been here, for not insisting upon this amendment.* [italics added][3]

To vote for 'not insisting upon this amendment [the Lansdowne
amendment]' was, as noted earlier, to vote for the Parliament Bill.

There is no evidence in the Cromer papers, which are unusually full
on this episode, or in the Curzon papers at the India Office, which are
very skimpy, that Cromer's cue came from Curzon; and the signs are
plentiful that his path was independent and voluntary although he
kept Curzon and Lansdowne informed.[4] To put a substantial number
of Unionist peers into the government lobby, given their great
distaste for the Parliament Bill and dislike of voting with the Asquith
government, required a thoroughgoing organization. If Curzon
headed such an organization, signs of it would be present in his[5] or

1. Balfour Papers, Add. MS 49767, fo. 236 (p. 52). See also Cromer Papers,
Blythswood to Cromer, 11 Aug. 1911.
    2. *Ibid.* Cromer to Blythswood, 12 Aug. 1911. See also *ibid.* Cromer,
'Memorandum in Connection with the Passing of the Parliament Bill', 11 Aug. 1911.
At one point he also authorized Camperdown to speak for him, but this authorization
seems to have been withdrawn. This is not strange under the circumstances; Curzon
Papers, MSS Eur. F. 112/89, Cromer to Curzon, 10 Aug. 1911.
    3. *Parliamentary Debates*, Lords, fifth series, ix. 1062.
    4. Thus he informed Curzon of the conversations with Crewe, the planned
meeting at Lord Bath's house on 4 Aug., and his keen disappointment when St
Aldwyn defected. As for the Cromer group being independent of Curzon, it might
be noted that Lansdowne writing to Norfolk referred to 'Cromer's group'; Cromer
Papers, 4 Aug. 1911. It is also meaningful that Curzon expected the ditchers to win
when the debate began on 10 Aug., hardly the view of Cromer and his group; Cromer
Papers, Heneage to Cromer, 13 Aug. 1911. Lansdowne may have shared Curzon's
pessimism; *ibid.* Lansdowne to Cromer, 15 Aug. 1911. See also *ibid.* Strachey to
Cromer, 8 Sept. 1911.
    5. In the memorandum on the Parliament Bill that Curzon left behind he describes
his activity during the crisis of 1911 in these terms: 'I threw myself energetically into
the fray – and organized the forces which ultimately enabled Lord Lansdowne to
prevail. Every day for a fortnight a Committee met in my house (1 Carlton House
Terrace). Lord Lansdowne constantly attended. The more active spirits were duke of
Devonshire, Lord Dunmore, Lord Hindlip, & myself'. There is no reference in the
list to Cromer, St Aldwyn, or Newton – the three peers who have been suggested as
leaders of the Judas group – although Cromer and Newton were working with

Cromer's papers. But the signs that exist point to the equally experienced and forceful Cromer. It was left to him, working closely with Heneage, to secure the passage of the Bill without a large creation of peers. An independent Unionist peer outside the shadow cabinet with little popularity in his party because of his free-trade views, Cromer could exercise under ordinary circumstances only a peripheral influence on Unionist policy. The paradox was complete when illness kept him from the House of Lords on the night of 10 August. He was not even present when the critical vote was taken though the outcome was due ultimately to his management and his leadership. What Curzon may have succeeded in doing, albeit unwittingly, was to serve as a decoy that drew ditcher attention away from the real source of danger to the group's cause. Distracted by their distrust of Curzon and Midleton, whose activity in late July had been so noticeable, they failed to perceive that Cromer was moving into a position to determine the final result. As Curzon remarked to Strachey in the wake of Lansdowne's letter, Cromer had the situation in hand and 'if it is not talked about too much is quite likely to succeed'. The words were percipient, but this is all that can be said of Curzon's role in the final stage of the crisis over the Parliament Bill. Balfour and Lansdowne had seen to that.

What then of Lord Newton's role in the passing of the Parliament Bill? Southern claims that 'the credit for inducing the crucial group of conservative peers to support the government must be given to Lord Newton . . .. Newton, on the evidence of his diary, recruited about 26 of [these peers].'[1] The figure of 26 is Southern's, not Newton's. It seems to have been arrived at in the following manner: on 28 July Newton 'wrote to lot of people (about 20) asking them to vote if necessary'; on 30 July he recorded names of 8 out of 9 peers 'collected up to date'; the next day he 'heard from about 12 peers promising to vote if necessary' and in the division itself, with 'things looking desperate, persuaded myself 5 or 6 to vote with the government'.[2] Southern has added the 9, the 12, and the 5, to give a total of 26. But another reading of these diary entries points to Newton's own estimate of his 'persuasions' as the '5 or 6' to whom he spoke at the division. Nothing reported by Southern, at least, suggests that these few were additional to the replies to his letters of 28 July. Moreover, it is likely that Newton was preaching to the converted – some of his letters were to Cromer's correspondents, and one went to Cromer himself.[3] The whole episode of Newton's activity on behalf of the

---

Curzon in the period before 1 Aug. and Cromer, at least, was in communication with Curzon until the end of the crisis; Curzon Papers, MSS Eur. F. 112/89.

1. Above, p. 523.   2. Above, pp. 522-3.

3. Cromer Papers, Newton to Cromer, 27 (*sic*) July 1911; and Southern to Kelvin, 22 July 1982. Cromer, Heneage, Blythswood and Lord Gough (an ally to Cromer) were on Newton's list of 30 July, Blythswood and Gough on his list of 10 Aug.

Parliament Bill seems to belong to the period before the Lansdowne letter of 1 August. He attended the meeting at Lord Bath's house on 4 August, where he welcomed the decision to disband the Judas group, and not long afterwards left town.[1] In the debate itself, he spoke on 9 August, not on 10 August, and then made no reference to the Judas group, not even to defend their integrity.[2] As earlier noted, he abstained in the division, along with Curzon. While there is no doubt that Newton, at Curzon's instigation, wrote a batch of letters on 28 July asking about 20 peers to vote for the Bill, there is no evidence of a more sustained role of this kind; nor of his cooperation with others in organizing a group; nor of his being seen by anyone as the leader or organizer of such a group.[3]

By contrast Cromer's followers referred to him as the leader of the Judas group, as did Curzon, Sandars, and Lansdowne. Cromer and Lansdowne wished to prevent the creation of peers, but their positions forced them to employ different methods. Cromer had the standing to lead his group independently of the front-bench Unionists, and also the freedom, denied to them, to negotiate and, in the last resort, to co-operate with the government. His relationship with Lansdowne, unlike Newton's with Curzon, was one of equality. In one exchange of letters, Lansdowne referred to 'deserters from my camp', expanding this subsequently, as follows: '[I refer] not to peers who left my flock in order to join yours, but to peers who left my flock in order to join the "ditchers".'[4] The existence of three Unionist groups could not be clearer. And equally clear was Lansdowne's

1. Southern to Kelvin, 22 July 1982; and see above, p. 522. Blythswood reported to Cromer on 5 Aug. that Newton had written to say he would not vote with the government; Cromer papers, 5 Aug. 1911. This was the day after the meeting at Lord Bath's house. Since Blythswood was not at the meeting, his information presumably rested on a different basis, probably reflecting Newton's own reaction to the Lansdowne letter of 1 Aug.

2. *Parliamentary Debates*, Lords, fifth series, ix. 949–55. To be sure, Cromer had planned for St Aldwyn to give the Judas crowd their lead on 9 Aug., but until the attack of gout intervened he expected to speak on 10 Aug.; Cromer Papers, Cromer to Gosse, 12 Aug. 1911.

3. Indeed the evidence points to the opposite conclusion. In two separate letters written on 13 Aug., Heneage recorded his dismay at the lack of support from Newton in the final stage of the debate, grouping him in this respect with Lord Galway (unfairly, as it happens) and the duke of Montrose. Thus he wrote to Strachey: 'Lords Galway and Newton & d. of Montrose should feel very small now and it is no wonder our private peers were distrustful of each of them when they were so unreliable'; Strachey Papers, S/17/2/15. That Galway (as Lord Moncton) voted with the Judas group can be seen in the division list. See also Cromer Papers, Heneage to Cromer, 13 Aug. 1911.

4. *Ibid.* Lansdowne to Cromer, 2 Aug. 1911. See also *ibid.* Blythswood to Cromer, 14 Sept. 1911 (probably 14 Aug. 1911). There is one further point to be made in discussing the respective roles of Cromer and Newton in this period. Crewe had dealt with Cromer in the negotiations of early August; and George V, on the question of Unionist peers voting with the government, had consulted Cromer's close associate at the time, that is St Aldwyn. But in no case does Newton seem to have been accorded this kind of recognition as leader of the Judas group.

understanding that it was Cromer who headed what was soon to be called the 'Judas group'.[1]

1. The epithet was in use as soon as the debate closed. Newton wrote: 'Result taken with good humour at the time, but on going to Carlton afterwards with Galway latter was received with shouts of Judas'; Southern, p. 839. The name originated with Hugh Cecil; Sandars to Balfour, 11 Aug. 1911, Balfour Papers, Add. MS 49767, fo. 152. During the debates on the Second Home Rule Bill in 1893 the Irish benches had applied the epithet to Joseph Chamberlain.

INDEX

Abbot, George, archbishop of Canterbury, 46
Abercorn, James Hamilton, 8th earl of, 274, 275, 311-14, 317
Abercorn, John James Hamilton, 1st marquess of, 300, 319, 320
Abercrombie, general, heir of, 420
Aberdeen, George Gordon, 3rd earl of, 302, 314
Aberdeen, George Gordon, 4th earl of, 242, 244, 381, 383, 416
Abergavenny, George Nevill, lord, 194
Abingdon, James Bertie, 1st earl of, 94
Abingdon, Montagu-Venables Bertie, 2nd earl of, 144, 159, 192
Aboyne, Charles Gordon, 4th earl of, 412
Act, ballot (1872), 479
—, corporation (1661), repeal of, 357
—, controverted elections (1770), 331; (1788), 328
—, county elections (1788), 335-7, 339; (1790), 337
—, election of MPs (1786), 328
—, election of Scottish representative peers (1847), 323; (1851), 323; (1879), 324
—, electoral rights of English peers with Scottish titles (1708), 136
—, Habeas Corpus (1679), 103
—, incumbered estates (1849), 404
—, Jewish naturalization (1753), 336
—, Parliament (1911), 463, 490, 501, 503, 519-39 passim
—, polls (1785), 328
—, reform (1867), 466, 473, 474
—, septennial (1716), 481
—, stamp (1765), 446; repeal of, 266
—, Test (1678), 324; repeal of, 357
—, trade disputes (1906), 489
—, triennial (1641), 64
—, union with Scotland (1707), 139, 151-76 passim, 310
—, union with Ireland (1800), 414, 417
Addington, Henry, see Sidmouth, 1st viscount
Addison, Joseph, 190
Address in reply, 208-10
Adelaide, queen consort of William IV, 253
Admiralty, first lord of, 237
Ailesbury (Aylesbury), Charles Brudenell-Bruce, 1st marquess of, 355, 356
Ailesbury, Thomas Bruce, 1st earl of, 439
Ailesbury, Thomas Bruce, 2nd earl of, 80, 81, 86, 88, 91, 93-103; division lists of, 79-110; father of, 80
Aislabie, John, 190
Albemarle, Christopher Monck, 2nd duke of, 98, 99; wife of, 99
Albemarle, William Charles Keppel, 4th earl of, 251
Althorp, viscounts, 350
Amherst, Jeffrey, 1st lord, 237, 240, 418
Andover, Hants., borough of, 356
Andover, Charles Howard, styled viscount, see Howard of Charlton, lord
Anglesey, 442
Anglesey (Anglesea), Arthur Annesley, 4th earl of, 192
Anglesey, James Annesley, 2nd earl of, 86, 100
Annandale, William Johnston, 1st marquess of, 138, 145, 156
Anne, queen, princess, 84, 116, 121, 122, 134, 161, 163, 164, 166, 173, 178
Annual Register, 352
Anson, Thomas Anson, viscount, 349
Anstis (Anslis), George, 121
Arbuthnot, Charles, 242, 244
Argyll, Archibald Campbell, 3rd duke of, earl of Islay, 156, 159, 163, 169, 172, 278, 284
Argyll, George Douglas Campbell, 8th duke of, 477
Argyll, George William Campbell, 6th duke of, 351
Argyll, John Campbell, 2nd duke of, 135, 136, 152, 186, 192
Argyll, John Campbell, 5th duke of, 300, 303, 304, 351
Argyllshire, 351
Arundel, Sussex, borough of, 349
Arundel, Thomas Howard, 14th earl of, 9, 16, 17, 23-29, 43, 65
Ashburnham, John Ashburnham, 2nd earl of, 250
Asquith, H.H., 485, 489-91, 493, 495, 496, 500-21, 528
Astley (Ashley), Jacob, 3rd lord, 86, 87
Atholl, James Murray, 2nd duke of, 318
Atholl, John Murray, 1st duke of, 164
Atholl, John Murray, 4th duke of, Lord Strange, 277, 279, 287, 289, 312, 315, 316, 356
Atterbury, Francis, bishop of Rochester, 189, 192

Auckland, William Eden, 1st lord, 219, 419
Aylesford, Heneage Finch, 4th earl of, 252
Aylmer, John, bishop of London, 54

Bacon, Francis, 9
Bagehot, Walter, 462-5; *English Constitution*,
    462, 464
Bagshaw, Henry, 59
Baillie of Jerviswood, George, 135, 155
Balcarres, Alexander Lindsay, 6th earl of, 299,
    302, 305, 315
Balfour, Arthur J., 487, 504, 506, 508, 509,
    511-14, 517, 521, 525, 528-31
Balmerino, John Elphinstone, 4th lord, 156,
    159
Bandon, Francis Bernard, 1st earl of, 246
Barlow, Thomas, bishop of Lincoln, 81, 91
Barrington, Sir Thomas, 51, 59, 69
Bath, Henry Bourchier, 5th earl of, 59, 60,
    72
Bath, John Granville, 1st earl of, 95, 98, 99
Beach, Sir Michael Edward Hicks, *see* St
    Aldwyn, viscount
Bearcroft, Edward, 334
Beauclerk, James, bishop of Hereford, 264
Beaufort, Henry Somerset, 1st duke of, 87
Beaw, William, bishop of Llandaff, 91, 98
Bedchamber, lords of 252, 254
Bedford, Francis Russell, 4th earl of, 15,
    50-52, 55, 59-61, 64, 66-69, 72
Bedford, John Russell, 6th duke of, 354
Bedford, John Russell, 7th duke of, 269
Beecher, Charles, 99-100
Belasyse, Henry, 59
Belgrave, viscount, *see* Grosvenor, 1st earl
Belhaven, Robert Montgomery Hamilton,
    8th lord, 243, 244
Belmore, Somerset Lowry-Corry, 2nd earl,
    376
Bentinck, Lord George, 401
Beresford, viscount, *see* Tyrone, earl of
Beresford, William, archbishop of Tuam, 382
Berkeley, G.C., captain, 337
Berkeley (Berkley), George Berkeley, 1st
    earl of, 80, 88, 91, 94, 100
Berkeley of Stratton, William, 4th lord, 143,
    161
Berkshire, Henry Bowes Howard, 4th earl of,
    144
Bill, arms (1843), 391
-, army regulation (1871), 476, 477
-, Ashby (1794), 438
-, attainder of Earl of Strafford (1641), 67,
    68
-, assay office (1773), 448, 455

-, ballot (1872), 478, 479
-, Birmingham Canal (1772), 446; (1806),
    447
-, bribery (1784), 331
-, charitable bequests (1844), 392
-, corn (1846), 257
-, county elections (1774), 329; (1778-9),
    329; (1783), 329-30; (1785), 329,
    331, 337; (1786), 329, 332, 333,
    337; (1787), 333; (1788), 329,
    333-5, 338
-, Dearne and Dove (1793), 438
-, disfranchising service personnel (1786), 328
-, dissenters' relief (1772-3), 265, 271, 277
-, duke of Norfolk's divorce (1692-3), 79-81,
    96-98, 101, 102; (1700), 97
-, East India Company dividend (1768), 267,
    277
-, ecclesiastical estates (1765), 266
-, education (1906), 520
-, election expenses (1782), 329-30
-, encumbered estates (1848-9), 404-5
-, evictions (1848), 403
-, finance (1909), 500-2
-, forfeited estates (1784), 305
-, French commerce (1713), 178
-, frequent Parliaments (1641), 64
-, house of lords reform (1907), 520
-, India (1783), 233, 247, 294
-, Irish church (1869), 466, 469-75, 479, 485,
    486
-, Irish church and tithe (1837), 379
-, Irish church temporalities (1833), 381-4
-, Irish coercion (1833), 380
-, Irish colleges bill (1845), 395
-, Irish corporations (1836-40), 379, 389
-, Irish drainage (1842), 390
-, Irish home rule (1893), 475, 482, 483,
    486
-, Irish poor law (1837-8), 379, 396; (1847),
    396, 399, 400
-, Irish tenants' compensation (1845), 394,
    395
-, Irish tithe (1833-4), 381, 389
-, Kennet and Avon Canal (1793-4), 439
-, male suffrage and annual parliaments (1780),
    328, 337
-, Maynooth (1845), 392-6
-, Mersey and Trent, 438
-, municipal corporations (1835), 389
-, mutiny (1717), 186
-, occasional conformity (1702), 112; (1704),
    111-25
-, pains and penalties (1820), 246
-, Parliament (1911), 497, 502, 505, 519-39
    passim

–, peerage (1719), 309; (1780), 309
–, place (1692-3), 79-81, 92-94, 104
–, polls (1782-3), 210
–, poor (1765), 266, 276
–, reform (1830-2), 243, 244, 246, 249, 253, 352, 356, 357, 360, 363, 462; (1884), 464, 481, 482
–, regency (1765), 266; (1788), 233; (1811), 359
–, repeal of County Elections Act (1789), 336
–, restricting Scottish distillers (1788), 305
–, Roman Catholics and dissenters in ·the armed forces, 240
–, Roman Catholic relief (1813), 359
–, royal marriage (1772), 271, 280
–, Scottish episcopalians relief (1792), 305
–, suspensory (1868), 466-9, 474, 479, 485, 486
–, Titus Oates (1689), 79, 80, 90, 101
–, to extend Richard Chamberlain's patent, 445; James Watt's patent, 446
–, toleration (1712), 170, 171
–, to prevent dissolution of Long Parliament (1641), 72
–, to remove bishops from the Lords (1641), 63
–, to repeal Naturalization Act (1712), 169
–, triennial (1641), 62
–, wool export (1787-8), 443
–, Yorkshire woollen industry, 442
Billingsley, Captain, 68, 71
Bill of rights, 35, 36, 42
Birmingham, Warws., 440, 445-9, 451; Commercial Committee of, 449
Birmingham Canal Company, 448
Birmingham Metal Company, 448
Birrell, Augustine, 503, 506, 509, 512, 513
Bisse, Philip, bishop of Hereford, 192
Black Book (1820), 347
Blackburn, Lancelot, bishop of Exeter, 192
Blackstone, Sir William, 241
Blackwood's Edinburgh Magazine, 348
Blandford, George Spencer-Churchill, *styled* marquess of, 356
Blenheim, battle of, 116
Blenheim Palace, Oxon., 349; archives of, 111, 114
Blomfield, Charles James, bishop of London, 248
Blythswood, Archibald Campbell Campbell, lord, 535
Bodmin, Cornwall, borough of, 349, 355
Bolingbroke, Oliver St John, 1st earl, 15
Bolton, Charles Powlett, 1st duke of, 90, 91
Bothmer, John Caspar, baron von, 178, 187

Boulton, Matthew, 434, 445-8, 452, 455
Boyle, Henry, 118, 120
Bradford, Yorks., 443, 486
Brandon, 1st duke of, *see* Hamilton, 4th duke of
Breadalbane, John Campbell, 3rd earl of, 278, 290, 291
Breadalbane, John Campbell, 4th earl of, 299, 302
Brewer (Bruer), John, 114, 121
Bridgwater (Bridgewater), Som., borough of, 356
Bridgwater, Francis Egerton, 3rd duke of, 438
Bridgwater, John Egerton, 1st earl of, 37
Bridgwater, John Egerton, 3rd earl of, 80, 91, 93
Bridgwater, Scroop Egerton, 4th earl of, 144
Bristol, Frederick William Hervey, 5th earl of, 219
Bristol, Frederick William Hervey, 8th earl of, 426
Bristol, John Digby, 1st earl of, 45, 46, 60, 64, 66-68, 73
Bromley (Bromly), William, 114, 118, 124, 188, 190, 191
Brooke, Fulke Greville, 5th lord, 102
Brooke, Robert Greville, 2nd lord, 50, 52, 55, 56, 59-61, 65
Brougham, Henry, 1st lord, 384, 391, 398
Bruce, James, 121
Bruce, Robert, 121
Brudenell, James, lord, 408
Buccleuch, dukes of, 351
Buccleuch, Henry Scott, 3rd duke of, 290-2, 300, 303, 351
Buccleuch, Walter Francis Scott, 5th duke of, 240, 401
Buchan, David Steuart Erskine, 11th earl of, 290, 291
Buckhounds, master of, 250
Buckingham, George Villiers, 1st duke of, 6, 9-12, 23-29, 33, 37-39, 44, 45, 52
Buckingham, John Sheffield, 1st duke of, 192, 195
Buckingham, Richard Temple, 1st duke of, 2nd marquess of, 348, 353-6, 428
Buckinghamshire, 350
Bulkeley, Thomas James Bulkeley, 7th viscount, 354
Burdett, Sir Francis, 354
Burges, Cornelius, 53, 71
Burke, Edmund, 233; *Thoughts on the Cause of the Present Discontents*, 233
Burke, John, 423
Burke, William, 440
Burlington, Richard Boyle, 1st earl of, 85, 100

Burnet, Gilbert, bishop of Salisbury, 89, 90, 91, 95, 97, 98, 112, 113, 140, 141, 160, 163, 171; wife of, 119, 124

Burroughs, Jeremiah, 52

Burton, Henry, 60

Bute, John Stuart, 3rd earl of, 214, 275, 278, 279

Byron, George Anson Byron, 7th lord, 253

Cabinet, 134, 491-4, 496, 499, 501, 502, 515

Cabinet Committee (1907), 491-8, 500-3, 505, 506, 515

Cabinet Council, 116, 121

Cadogan, William, lieutenant-general, 178

Caesar (Ceasar), Charles, 118

Cairns, Hugh McCalmont Cairns, 1st lord, lord chancellor, 468, 470, 471, 473, 474, 477

Caledon, Du Pre Alexander, 2nd earl of, 348

Caledonian Mercury, 312

Calne, Wilts., borough of, 354

Cambridge, Cambs., borough of, 348

Camden, John Jeffreys Pratt, 2nd earl, 255

Camelford, Cornwall, borough of, 348

Campbell, Lord Frederick, 323

Campbell, John, 1st lord, 405

Campbell-Bannerman, Sir Henry, 489, 496-502, 515, 518

Campden, Baptist Hicks, 1st viscount, 33

Camperdown, Robert Adam Philips Haldane, 3rd earl of, 523, 530, 531, 534

Canning, George, 242, 246, 254, 256, 351, 428, 429; widow of, 422

Capel, Arthur, 57

Cardiff, John Stuart, lord, 315

Carleton, Henry Boyle, lord, 188, 189

Carlisle, Cumb., borough of, 354

Carlisle, Edward Howard, 2nd earl of, 86, 87

Carlton Club, 524

Carlyle, Alexander, 285

Carmarthen, Thomas Osborne, marquess of, earl of Danby, 82-85, 87-91, 93, 94, 100, 207

Carnarvon, Charles Dormer, 2nd earl of, 87, 88, 94, 100

Carnarvon, Henry Herbert, 1st earl of, 251, 439

Carnarvon, Henry Howard Molyneux Herbert, 4th earl of, 470, 471, 473, 476-9

Carnarvon, James Brydges, earl of, 188, 196

Caroline, queen consort of George IV, 360

Carrington, Robert Smith, 1st lord, 331, 356

Carteret, John, 2nd lord, 212

Cartwright, John, 351

Cassillis, David Kennedy, 10th earl of, 301

Castleton, James Saunderson, viscount, 192

Cathcart, William Schaw Cathcart, 10th lord, 294, 295, 298, 299, 320, 321, 416, 421

Catherine of Braganza, queen dowager, 91

Cawdor, Frederick Archibald Vaughan Campbell, 3rd earl of, 504, 506, 508, 509

Chamberlain, Austen, 504-6, 509, 512, 514, 517

Chamberlain, Joseph, 481

Chamber of Manufacturers, 435

Chancellor, lord, 210, 237, 250, 255, 293

Chancery, clerk of the crown, 323

Chancery, court of, 99

Chandos, James Brydges, 8th lord, 179

Chandos, Richard Plantagenet Temple, *styled* marquess of, 351, 353

Channing, F.A., 483

Charles I, king, prince, 10, 11, 16-18, 23-29, 31, 33-35, 38-42, 45-49, 53, 56, 60-73

Chatham, William Pitt, 1st earl of, 418

Chester, Cheshire, assay office, 448; borough of, 348

Chesterfield, Philip Dormer Stanhope, 4th earl of, 213

Chesterfield, Philip Stanhope, 2nd earl of, 81, 85, 91, 100

Chetwynd, Walter, 122

Cheyne, William, 2nd lord, 188

Chippenham, Cambs., 194

Cholmondeley, Hugh Cholmondeley, 1st earl of, baron, 95

Churchill, George, 121

Churchill, lord, *see* Marlborough, duke of

Clancarty, William Power Keating Trench, 1st earl of, 414, 416

Clanwilliam, Richard Charles Francis Christian Meade, 3rd earl of, 393

Clanwilliam, Richard Meade, 2nd earl of, 414, 416

Clare, John FitzGibbon, 2nd earl of, 393, 398, 416

Clare, John Holles, 1st earl of, 15, 27, 37

Clare, John Holles, 2nd earl of, 60

Clare, John Holles, 4th earl of, 91, 99

Clarendon, Edward Hyde, 1st earl of, 50, 51

Clarendon, Edward Hyde, 3rd earl of, 192, 194

Clarendon, George William Frederick Villiers,

4th earl of, lord lieutenant of Ireland, 392, 393, 402, 467

Clarendon, Henry Hyde, 2nd earl of, 80, 84-87

Clarke (Clark), George, 121

Cleveland, William Harry Vane, marquess of, 3rd earl of Darlington, 348, 356

Clotworthy, Sir John, 57, 58, 69, 72

Cobham, Charles George Lyttelton, 8th viscount, 535

Coke, Sir Edward, 37, 41, 46, 54

Colepeper, John, 3rd lord, 95, 177

Commissioners for prizes, 121

Commissioners on the municipal corporations, 352

Committee for Customs and Privileges, 9, 16

Committee for Petitions, 9, 16

Committee of privileges, 320

Committee of the Whole House, 42, 167-9

Committee on Petitions, 16

Committees of both Houses, joint meeting of, 68

Committee system, 15

Commons, House of, bar of, 91

—, committee of supply, 119

—, committee on charges against earl of Strafford (1640), 58

—, committee on state of the kingdom (1640), 58

—, members of, 7

—, protestation (1641) of, 69-72

—, remonstrance against duke of Buckingham, 23, 26-29, 33 (n. 7)

Compton, George, Speaker of the House of Commons, 190

Compton, Henry, bishop of London, 83, 84, 87, 88, 91, 100

Conference between the two Houses, 38, 113

Congleton, Henry Brooke Parnell, 1st lord, 256

Coningsby, Thomas, lord, 134

Constitutional Conference (1910), 490, 500, 503-18

Conyers, Thomas, 121, 123

Conyngham, Henry Conyngham, 1st marquess, 246, 376

Copenhagen, 421

Cork Examiner, 476

Cornwall, 442

Cornwallis, Charles, 3rd lord, 80, 93

Cornwallis, Charles Cornwallis, 2nd earl, 237

Cornwallis, Charles Cornwallis, 2nd marquess, 251

Cornwallis, Frederick, archbishop of Canterbury,

264

Cottenham, Charles Christopher Pepys, 1st earl of, 258

Cottington, Francis, lord, 59

Coventry, Thomas, 1st lord, lord keeper, 37, 39

Coventry, Thomas, 5th lord, 85, 87, 88, 100

Cowper, William, lord, lord chancellor 142, 143, 187, 192, 195

Cranborne, lord, *see* Salisbury, 3rd marquess of

Craven, William, 7th lord, 439

Craven, William Craven, earl of, 95

Crawford, George Lindsey Crawford, 21st earl of, 290

Creevey, Thomas, 242

Crew (Crewe), John, 59

Crew, Nathaniel, bishop of Durham, 85-87, 141, 192

Crewe, Robert Offley Ashburton Milnes, earl of, 491, 493-6, 498, 500-3, 505, 506, 509, 510, 512-14, 533

Cricklade, Wilts., borough of, 327

Croker, J.W., 349, 351

Cromer, Evelyn Baring, 1st earl of, 522, 528-39 *passim*

Crown, offer of, 79, 80, 82-88

Culpepper, Sir John, 54, 59

Cumberland, Ernest Augustus, duke of, 377, 380-3, 386, 387

Cumberland, Richard, bishop of Peterborough, 141, 192

Curzon, George Nathaniel, lord, 519, 521-3, 525, 527-38

Daer, Basil William Douglas, *styled* lord, 321

Dalhousie, George Ramsay, 8th earl of, 320

Dalhousie, George Ramsay, 9th earl of, 416

Dalhousie, James Andrew Ramsay, 10th earl of, 257

Dalrymple, Sir David, 139

Dalrymple, Sir James, 139

Daly, Robert, bishop of Cashel, 392

Danby, earl of, *see* Carmarthen, marquess of

Darlington, 3rd earl of, *see* Cleveland, marquess of

Dartmouth, William Legge, 1st earl of, 2nd lord, secretary of state, 143, 144, 152, 154, 161, 162, 164, 165, 188

Dartmouth, William Legge, 2nd earl of, 446-9, 453

Dawes, William, archbishop of York, bishop of Chester, 141, 192

Declaration of Rights, 89

De Dunstanville, Francis Basset, lord, 349, 355, 441, 442

De Grey, Sir William, 418

Delamer (Delamare), Henry Booth, 1st lord, 91

Delaval, John Hussey, lord, 449

Delawarr, John West, 15th lord, 194

Denbigh, Basil Fielding, 4th earl of, 95, 144, 178

Denbigh, Basil Fielding, 6th earl of, 318

Denbigh, William Basil Percy Fielding, 7th earl of, 253

Derby, Edward Geoffrey Stanley, 14th earl of, *styled* Lord Stanley, 246, 391, 393-6, 399-401, 403, 405, 462, 466, 470-4

Derby, Edward Henry Stanley, 15th earl of, 478

Derby, Edward Stanley, 11th earl of, 448

Derby, William George Richard Stanley, 9th earl of, 95, 102

Dering, Sir Edward, 61

Devon, 350

Devon, William Courtenay, 2nd earl of, 394

Devonshire, duke of, 349

Devonshire, Spencer Compton, 8th duke of, 475

Devonshire, William Cavendish, 2nd duke of, 138, 186, 194

Devonshire, William Cavendish, 4th duke of, 213

Devonshire, William Cavendish, 4th earl of, 80, 93, 94, 97 ·

Devonshire, William George Spencer Cavendish, 6th earl of, 259, 376

D'Ewes, Sir Simonds, 62, 63

Digby, George, lord, 58, 66

Disraeli, Benjamin, 467, 468, 471, 474, 477, 478, 480

Dod, Charles R., 352

Doddington, Bubb, 418

Donegal, Arthur Chichester, 1st marquess of, 428

Dormer, Robert, 118

Dorset, Charles Sackville, 6th earl of, 93

Dorset, George Frederick Sackville, 3rd duke of, 252

Dorset, Lionel Cranfield Sackville, 7th earl of, 143

Dorset, Richard Sackville, 3rd earl of, 8, 15, 38

Dover, dukes of, *see* Queensberry, dukes of

Downes, Ulysses Burgh, 2nd lord, 246, 376

Downton, Wilts., borough of, 354

Drummond, Robert Hay, archbishop of York, 268

Drummond, Thomas, 385

Dryden, John, 89

Dudley Canal, proprietors of, 438

Dudley and Ward, John Ward, 1st viscount, 427

Dudley and Ward, John Ward, 2nd viscount, 438, 440, 449

Dumfries, Patrick Macdowall-Crichton, 6th earl of, 320

Duncombe, Henry, 331, 332

Dundas, Henry, 356; *see also* Melville, 1st viscount

Dundas, Robert, *see* Melville, 2nd viscount

Dundas, Sir Thomas, 295

Dunmore, John Murray, 4th earl of, 276, 305, 315, 440

Dupplin, viscount, *see* Hay, lord

Dysart, Lionel Tollemache, 5th earl of, 275, 290, 291

Earle, Sir Walter, 50, 58, 66

East, Sir Edward Hyde, 355

East Retford, Notts., borough of, 349

East Surrey, by-election (1872), 478

Ebrington, viscounts, 350

Eden, William, 445

Edgcumbe, Richard, 186

Edinburgh, Midlothian, 291; Holyrood House, 309; Register House, 289

Edinburgh Advertiser, 316

Edward VII, king, 493, 495, 499, 503

Effingham, Thomas Howard, 2nd earl of, 262, 449

Egerton, John, bishop of Bangor, 269

Eglinton (Eglintoun), Alexander Montgomerie, 9th earl, 156

Eglinton, Alexander Montgomerie, 10th earl of, 277

Eglinton, Archibald Montgomerie, 11th earl of, 290, 302, 317

Egremont, Charles Wyndham, 2nd earl of, 214

Ehrman, John, 455

Eldon, John Scott, 1st earl of, 421

Elgin, Thomas Bruce, 7th earl of, 299, 305

Elibank, George Murray, 6th lord, 290-2

Eliot, Sir John, 36

Elphinstone, Charles, 10th lord, 290

Elphinstone, John, 12th lord, 296

Elphinstone, John, 13th lord, 243, 244

England, 125

Enniskillen, William Willoughby Cole, 3rd earl of, 395, 398

Ensor, R.C.K., 517, 523, 527

Errol, George Hay, 18th earl of, 243

Erskine, Sir Alexander, 170

Erskine, Henry, 295

Erskine, Sir James, brother of 6th earl of Mar, 162

Essex, Algernon Capel, 2nd earl of, 93
Essex, Robert Devereux, 3rd earl of, 15, 18, 46, 50, 52, 59-61, 64, 68, 69, 72
Eugene, prince, of Savoy, 178
Eure (Ewer), Ralph, 7th lord, 91
Evelyn, John, 97
Ewer, John, bishop of Bangor, 271

Falkland, Lucius Bentinck Cary, 10th viscount of, 243, 244
Falkland, Lucius Carey, 2nd viscount of, 54, 69
Falmouth, Edward Boscawen, 1st earl of, 355
Falmouth, George Evelyn Boscawen, 3rd viscount, 441
Farnham, John Maxwell-Barry, lord, 377, 398
Fauconberg, Thomas Belasyse, lord, 59
Fauconberg, Thomas Belasyse, 2nd viscount, 83, 84, 87, 88, 100
Fawkes, William, 444
Fellowes, Newton, 356
Fenwick, Sir John, 97
Ferguson, W., professor, 351
Ferrers, Robert Shirley, 1st earl, lord, 85, 100, 102, 167, 192
Ferrers, Robert Shirley, 6th earl, 438, 449
Feversham, Louis de Duras, 2nd earl of, 80
Fiennes, Nathaniel, 50-52, 63, 69, 72
Fife, James Duff, 2nd earl, 413
Firth, Charles, 31, 32, 46
Fitzgerald, Henry Vescy-Fitzgerald, 3rd lord, 397
Fitzgerald, Maurice, knight of Kerry, 397
Fitzwalter, Charles Mildmay, 18th lord, 177, 179
Fitzwilliam, Charles William Wentworth-Fitzwilliam, 3rd earl, 376, 402
Fitzwilliam, Thomas Fitzwilliam, 9th viscount, 356
Fitzwilliam, William Fitzwilliam, 2nd earl, 427, 438, 442-4, 452, 454
Fleetwood, Sir Miles, 59
Fleetwood, Nicholas, bishop of Ely, 192
Flood, Henry, 328
Folkestone, William Pleydell-Bouverie, *styled* viscount, 354
Forbes, Duncan, 187, 189
Fortescue, earls, 350
Fortescue, Hugh Fortescue, 2nd earl, 257
Fortescue, Hugh Fortescue, 4th earl, 535
Fountain Tavern, 117
Fox, Charles, 238, 239, 247, 251, 294, 296, 329-31, 429, 430
Fox, Henry, 418
Fraser's Magazine, 385

Fuller, Rose, 329
Furber, Holden, professor, 300

Galloway, John Stewart, 7th earl of, 288, 300, 315, 338, 408
Galway, George Edmund Milnes Monckton-Arundel, 7th viscount, 524
Garbett, Samuel, 433, 438-40, 445, 446, 448, 449, 451, 452, 455
Gardiner, Samuel Rawson, 5, 46, 49
Gash, N., professor, 349
Gastrell, Francis, bishop of Chester, 188, 192
Gatton, Surrey, borough of, 348
Gazette, 116
General election (1710), 152; (1774), 293; (1820), 349; (1868), 485; (1906), 520; (1910), 520, 521
Georg Ludwig, elector of Hanover, *see* George I, king
George, prince of Wales, 186, 191, 193, 195; *see also* George IV, king
George I, king, 177-80, 185, 186, 191, 195, 196
George III, king, 213-16, 240, 247, 248, 250-2, 275, 276, 280, 407, 410, 421, 425, 427, 430, 441, 448
George IV, king, prince of Wales, Prince Regent, 239, 248-52, 254, 302, 315, 410, 430, 431; brothers of, 302
George V, king, 503, 510, 514, 520, 521, 528, 534
George of Denmark, prince, consort of Queen Anne, 94, 112, 115, 121, 122, 134
Germain, John, 81, 96
Germaine, Lord George, 418
Gibbs, Vicary, 174
Gifford, William, 121
Gilbert, Davies, 355
Gilbert, W.S., 256
Gisborne, Thomas, 241
Gladstone, W.E., 465-7, 469, 476, 477, 480-4, 486
Glasgow, David Boyle, 1st earl of, 138, 156
Glasgow, Elizabeth Boyle, dowager countess of, 411
Glasgow, Lanarkshire, 481; corporation of, 398
Glencairn, William Cunningham, 13th earl of, 290
Globe, 523
Glow, Lotte, 73
Glynne, John, 69
Goderich, John Frederick Robinson, viscount, 248, 419
Godolphin, Sidney, 1st earl, lord, lord

treasurer, 85, 111-25, 133-5, 137, 139, 140, 142, 145, 166, 208

Gordon, Alexander Gordon, 4th duke of; earl of Norwich, 277, 287, 289, 300, 303, 315, 317, 318

Goring, George, lord, 38

Gosford, Archibald Acheson, 2nd viscount, 245

Gower, George Granville Leveson-Gower, *styled* lord, *see* Sutherland, 2nd duke of

Gower, Granville Leveson-Gower, 2nd earl, lord president of the council, 438, 440, 441, 444, 445, 447

Grafton, Augustus Henry Fitzroy, 3rd duke of, 214, 215, 263, 270, 271, 439, 440

Grafton, Charles Fitzroy, 2nd duke of, 142, 144

Graham, David Graham, earl, son of 2nd duke of Montrose, 175

Graham, James Graham, *styled* marquess of, 386, 392, 395

Graham, Thomas, colonel, 356

Grange, James Erskine, lord, 139

Grantham, Henry d'Auverqueque, earl of, 179

Granville, George, 123

Granville, Granville George Leveson-Gower, 2nd earl, 471, 477

Granville, John, lord, 95

Granville of Lansdowne, Charles, *styled* lord, 91

Grattan, Henry, 359

Greenhill, William, 52

Grenville, George, 214-16, 239

Grenville, Thomas, 240

Grenville, William Wyndham Grenville, lord, 217, 240, 256, 258, 319, 331, 419, 420, 429

Greville, Charles Cavendish Fulke, 220, 233, 247

Grey, Charles Grey, 2nd earl, 238, 243, 248, 252, 253, 256, 258, 348, 353, 364, 383, 384, 388

Grey, Edward, bishop of Hereford, 249

Grey, Sir Edward, 503

Grey, Henry Grey, 3rd earl, 470, 471

Grey of Warke, William, 1st lord, 42

Grimston, Harbottle, 51, 57, 58

Grosvenor, Richard Grosvenor, 1st earl, *styled* Viscount Belgrave, 421, 423, 429

Grosvenor, Robert Grosvenor, 2nd earl, 348

Guernsey, Heneage Finch, lord, 158

Guilford, Francis North, 2nd lord, 144

Gunpowder plot, 39

Guy, John, 122

Habakkuk, H J., 450

Hackney, Midd., 480

Haddington, Thomas Hamilton, 7th earl of, 290

Hailes, David Dalrymple, lord, 322

Haldane, Richard Burdon Haldane, viscount, 491

Hales, Sir Thomas, 123

Halifax, Charles Montagu, lord, 119, 158

Halifax, George Montague-Dunk, 2nd earl of, 214, 439

Halifax, George Savile, 1st marquess of, 80, 84, 89, 90, 93, 94

Hall, Timothy, bishop of Oxford, 85, 87

Halsbury, Hardinge Stanley Gifford, 1st earl of, 511, 529

Hamilton, Lord Archibald, 146

Hamilton, Douglas Hamilton, 8th duke of, 175, 299-300, 311

Hamilton, Elizabeth Hamilton, duchess of, 171

Hamilton, James Hamilton, 4th duke of, 1st duke of Brandon, 135, 136, 139, 142-6, 151-76 *passim*, 177, 312

Hamilton, James Hamilton, 5th duke of, 318

Hampden, John, 50, 51, 58, 66, 69, 72

Hampden, Richard, 191

Hanover, 186

Hansard, 234

Harcourt, Sir Lewis, 491, 498, 502, 503

Harcourt, Sir Simon, 1st lord, solicitor-general, 119, 124, 140, 144, 161, 187, 188, 191, 192, 194, 195

Harcourt, Sir William, 485

Hardwicke, Philip Yorke, 1st earl of, lord chancellor, 429

Hardwicke, Philip Yorke, 3rd earl of, 350

Hardy, Gathorne, 473

Harley, Lord Edward, 189

Harley, Robert, *see* Oxford and Mortimer, 1st earl of

Harley, Sir Robert, 59, 61, 69

Harrington, William Stanhope, 1st earl of, 212, 213, 237

Harrowby, Dudley Ryder, 1st earl of, 356

Harsnett, Samuel, bishop of Norwich, 37, 46

Hartington (Hartenton), William Cavendish, lord, 118

Harvey, A.D., 361

Haselrig, Sir Arthur, 66

Hatherton, Edward John Littleton, 1st lord, 259

Hatton, Christopher Hatton, 1st viscount, 85, 100, 102
Haversham, John Thompson, 1st lord, 120
Hawkesbury, lord, *see* Liverpool, 2nd earl of
Hawles (Holles), Sir John, 118
Hay, George, lord, *styled* Viscount Dupplin, son of earl of Kinnoull, 175, 188, 189
Heath, Sir Robert, 36, 37
Hedges, Sir Charles, secretary of state, 120-3
Heneage, Edward, 1st lord, 535-7
Hertford, Francis Charles Seymour-Conway, 3rd marquess of, 349
Hertford, Francis Seymour-Conway, 1st marquess of, earl of, 429
Hertford, Francis Seymour-Conway, 5th marquess of, 251
Hertford, William Seymour, 2nd earl of, 59, 60, 64, 67, 68
Heyman, Sir Peter, 59
Hinchinbrook, John Montagu, *styled* viscount, 251
History of Parliament: the House of Commons, 1754-90, 352
Hoadley, Benjamin, bishop of Bangor, 192
Hobart, Robert, lord, 217-19
Hobson, J.A., 464
Hobson (Hibson), Sir Thomas, 121
Holborne, Robert, 63
Holland, 125
Holland, Henry Richard Vassall, 3rd lord, 243, 257
Holles, Denzil, 50, 58, 59, 63, 69, 72
Holloway, Sir Richard, 89
Holt, Sir John, chief justice, 90, 96
Home, Alexander Home, 7th earl of, 172
Home, Alexander Home, 9th earl of, 290
Home Secretary, 215
Hooper, George, bishop of Bath and Wells, 192
Hopetoun, James Hope, 3rd earl of, 293, 294, 298, 302, 305, 318, 319, 338
Hopetoun, John Hope, 2nd earl of, 290
Hopetoun House, West Lothian, 285
Horner, Francis, 348, 354
Horse, master of, 251
Hotham, Sir John, 50
Hough, John, bishop of Coventry and Lichfield, 192
Howard of Charlton, Charles, lord, *styled* Viscount Andover, 65, 72
Howard of Effingham, Francis, 5th baron, 80, 93
Howard of Escrick, Charles, 4th lord, 144
Howard of Escrick, Edward, 1st lord, 37, 72

Howard of Escrick, William, 3rd lord, 87, 102
Howe (How), John, 114
Howe, Richard William Penn Curzon, earl, 253
Howley, William, archbishop of Canterbury, 388
Hull, Yorks., corporation of, 398
Hume, David, 285
Hume, John, bishop of Salisbury, 269
Hungerford, John, 118
Hunsdon, Robert Carey, 7th lord, 95, 192
Hunsdon, William Ferdinand Carey, 8th lord, 192
Huntingdon (Huntington), Francis Hastings, 10th earl of, 437, 449
Huntingdon, Henry Hastings, 5th earl of, 8, 15
Huntingdon, Theophilus Hastings, 7th earl of, 86-88, 91, 100
Huntingford, George Isaac, bishop of Worcester and of Hereford, 247
Hurd, Richard, bishop of Coventry and Lichfield, and of Worcester, 247
Hussey, Sir Edward, 92
Hyndford, John Carmichael, 4th earl of, 290

Ilbert, Courtenay, 497, 498, 501, 515
India, 443
Infanta, Spanish, 10
Inverary Castle, Argyllshire, 285
Ireland, 186, 405
Ireland, Church of, disestablishment of, 469, 475, 485
Ireland, lord lieutenant of, 257
Ironside, Gilbert, bishop of Hereford, 98
Irvine, Charles Ingram, 9th viscount, 274
Islay (Ilay), earl of, *see* Argyll, 3rd duke of

James, prince of Wales, 83
James I, king, 17, 33
James II, king, 82, 83, 87, 88
Jeffreys, George, lord chief justice, 81, 88, 89
Jekyll, Joseph, 355
Jekyll, Sir Joseph, 191
Jenkins, Roy, 503, 510, 517, 519, 523, 527
Jermyn, Thomas, 2nd baron, 80
Jersey, Edward Villiers, 1st earl of, 116
Jersey, George Bussy Villiers, 4th earl of, 250-1
Jones, Mr, of Bristol, 446
Journals, 234, 235

Keeler, Mary Frear, 59
Kellie, Charles Erskine, 7th earl of, 305
Kellie, Thomas Alexander Erskine, 6th earl

of, 290, 291

Kellie, Thomas Erskine, 9th earl of, 296, 298

Kent, Anthony Grey, 10th earl of, 88, 100

Kent, Henry Grey, duke of, 143, 195

Kenyon, George, 2nd lord, 393

Keppel, Frederick, bishop of Exeter, 270, 271

Ker, Robert Ker, earl, son of 1st duke of Roxburghe, 175

Key to Both Houses of Parliament, A, 352

Kimbolton, Edward Montagu, lord, *styled* Viscount Mandeville, 15, 50, 56, 59, 60, 64, 65, 72

King, Sir Peter, 139

King's Bench, court of, 34, 96

King's Bench prison, 89

King's speech, 212

Kingston-upon-Hull, Robert Pierrepoint, 1st earl of, 59

Kinnaird, George, 7th lord, 295, 302, 305, 317, 318, 320, 322

Kinnaird, William George Fox, 9th lord, 243

Kinnoulle, Robert Auriol Hay-Drummond, 10th earl of, 300, 303

Kinnoulle, Thomas Hay, 9th earl of, 299, 300

Kirkcudbright, stewartry of, 321

Kirton, Edward, 59

Kirkwall, Thomas John Hamilton, *styled* viscount, 245

Knatchbull, Edward, 121

Knollys, Francis, 1st lord, 493, 496

Koss, Stephen, 519, 523, 527

Lake, George Lake, 1st viscount, 421

Lambeth palace, Surrey, 50, 469

Lancashire, 451

Lancaster, duchy of, chancellor of, 237

Land tax commissioners, 334

Langford, Hercules Langford Rowley, 2nd lord, 376

Lansdowne, Henry Charles Keith Petty, 6th marquess of, 474, 487, 504-6, 508, 509, 516, 517, 519, 521-5, 527-38

Lansdowne, Henry Petty, 3rd marquess of, 220, 258, 354, 359, 376, 403, 404

Lansdowne, John Henry Petty, 2nd marquess of, 355

Lansdowne, William Petty, 1st marquess of, 433, 439

Lansdowne, *see also* Granville of Lansdowne, lord

Lascelles, Henry, 444

Laud, William, archbishop of Canterbury (previously bishop of St David's and of Bath and Wells), 52, 53, 61

Lauderdale, James Maitland, 7th earl of, 287

Lauderdale, James Maitland, 8th earl of, 296, 298, 303, 316, 416

Lawsuits, Ashby v. White, 119-20

–, Darnell's Case (1626), 34, 37

–, Montagu v. Bath, 79-81, 98-99, 102

Leeds, Francis Godolphin Osborne, 5th duke of, 215-17

Legh, William, 519

Leicester, Leics., 437

Leicester, John Sydney, 6th earl of, 144

Leicester, Thomas William Coke, 1st earl of, 256

Leinster, Augustus Frederick Fitzgerald, 3rd duke of, 376, 393, 398

Leominster, William Fermor, 1st lord, 97

Lewis, Erasmus, 187

Lewis, Thomas Frankland, 354

Lexinton (Lexington), Robert Sutton, 2nd baron, 86, 87, 95

L'Hermitage, René de Sauniers, Dutch agent in London, 169, 179

Liberal Magazine, 523

Lichfield (Litchfield), Staffs., borough of, 349

Lichfield, George Henry Lee, 3rd earl of, 251

Lichfield, Thomas Francis Anson, 3rd earl of, 535

Ligonier, John Louis Ligonier, 1st earl, 418

Limerick, William Tenison Pery, 2nd earl of, 398

Lincoln, Edward Clinton, 5th earl of, 86, 87

Lincoln, Henry Clinton, 7th earl of, 144, 177

Lincoln, Henry Fiennes Clinton, 9th earl of, 269

Lincoln, Henry Pelham Clinton, *styled* earl of, 401

Lincoln, Theophilus Clinton, 4th earl of, 12, 15, 46

Lindsey, Robert Bertie, 3rd earl of, 83, 84, 87, 88, 94

Lismore, Cornelius O'Callaghan, 1st viscount, 376

Liverpool, Lancs., 481; corporation of, 398

Liverpool, Charles Jenkinson, 1st earl of, 219, 220, 41

Liverpool, Robert Bankes Jenkinson, 2nd earl of, Lord Hawkesbury, 215, 219, 220, 242, 246, 248, 249, 251, 252, 258, 374, 375, 410, 415, 417-21, 428, 429-31

Lloyd, William, bishop of St Asaph, and of Coventry and Lichfield, and of Worcester, 87, 98, 102, 192

Lloyd George, David, 491, 503, 506, 508-14, 517

Lockhart of Carnwarth, George, 153, 162, 170

London, 34, 67, 72, 178, 300, 397, 481, 493

–, Aldgate, 89

–, Apsley House, 257

—, Bath House (29 Grosvenor Square), 534, 535, 538

—, Lansdowne House, 507

—, Marlborough House, 470, 471, 473

—, Newgate, 89

—, Tower of, 58, 68, 71, 185, 188, 189, 191

Londonderry, Charles William Stewart, 3rd marquess of, 380, 387, 394

Londonderry, Frances Stewart, countess of, 415

Long, Walter, 525

Lonsdale, Henry Lowther, 3rd viscount, 194

Lonsdale, William Lowther, 1st viscount, 354

Lords, House of, antechamber of, 40; bar of, 65, 89, 103, 191; chamber next to, 39; clerk assistant of, 103; doorway of, 39; tellers of, 103

Lords' Journals, 297, 298, 319, 331

Loreburn, Robert Threshie Reid, lord, lord chancellor, 491, 496, 499, 502, 503, 515

Lothian, William Henry Kerr, 4th marquess of, 274

Lothian, William John Kerr, 5th marquess of, 302

Lothian, William Kerr, 2nd marquess of, 138, 145

Loudoun, Hugh Campbell, 3rd earl of, 138, 159

Loughborough, Alexander Wedderburn, lord, lord chancellor, 314, 439

Loughborough Canal, 437

Louis XIV, king of France, 125

Lovelace, John, 3rd lord, 95

Lowndes, William, 114, 121, 123

Lowth, Robert, bishop of London, 271

Lushington, James Law, 354

Luttrell, Narcissus, 95

Lyndhurst, John Singleton Copley, lord, 360, 378

Lyttelton, Charles, bishop of Carlisle, 270

Lyttelton, William Henry, 1st lord, 418

Lytton, Victor Alexander George Robert Bulwer-Lytton, 2nd earl of, 535

Macaulay, T.B., 354

McCahill, M.W., 273, 315, 324

Macclesfield, Charles Gerard, 1st earl of, 95

Macclesfield, Charles Gerard, 2nd earl of, estate of, 143

Macclesfield, George Parker, 4th earl of, 252

MacDonald, Sir Archibald, 409

MacHale, John, Roman Catholic archbishop of Tuam, 387

McKendrick, N., Dr, 445

Mackenzie, James Stuart, 278, 284

Mackenzie, John, 139

Mackworth, Sir Humphrey, 118

Magna Carta, 47

Manchester, Lancs., 481

Manchester, Charles Montagu, 4th earl of, 80, 99, 143, 187

Manchester, Henry Montagu, 1st earl of, lord president of the council, 37, 65

Manley, John, 121, 123

Manningham, Thomas, 192

Mansell (Mansil), Thomas, 118

Mansfield, David Murray, 2nd earl of, 7th Viscount Stormont, 215, 216, 287, 293, 294, 298, 300, 301, 305, 312-19, 321, 330, 445

Mansfield, William Murray, 1st earl of, 316

Mar, John Erskine, 6th earl of, 139-41, 153, 154, 156, 159, 162-5, 168, 169, 172

March, James Stuart, 2nd earl of, 72

Marchmont, Hugh Hume-Campbell, 3rd earl of, 274, 275, 279

Marchmont, Patrick Hume, 1st earl of, 136, 138

Marlborough, Wilts., borough of, 80, 439

Marlborough, George Spencer, 4th duke of, 349

Marlborough, George Spencer, 5th duke of, 349

Marlborough, John Churchill, 1st duke of, earl of, Lord Churchill, 84, 91, 93, 94, 111-13, 115, 116, 124, 125, 142, 177-79, 185

Marlborough, John Ley, 1st earl of, lord treasurer, 37

Marlborough, Sarah Churchill, duchess of, 119, 121, 122, 124, 125, 179

Marshall, Stephen, 53

Marsham, Charles, 328

Martin, Henry, 69

Mary II, queen, princess of Orange, 79, 82-84, 97, 98, 100

Maryborough, William Wellesley, lord, 251

Massachusetts Bay Company, 51; council of, 277

May, Erskine, 467, 469

Maynard, John, 69

Maynard, William, 1st baron, 45

Melbourne, Peniston Lamb, 1st viscount, 413

Melbourne, William Lamb, 2nd viscount,

238, 256, 258, 388, 389, 396
Melville, Henry Dundas, 1st viscount, 241,
    283, 284, 286-90, 293-8, 300, 303,
    304, 311, 411, 412, 417, 419, 431
Melville, Robert Dundas, 2nd viscount,
    241, 242, 244
Methuen, Paul, 186, 194
Middlesex, 481
Midleton, William St John Fremantle
    Brodrick, 9th viscount, 529, 532, 537
Midlothian campaigns, 480-1
Milnes, Pemberton, 443
Miltown, Joseph Leeson, 4th earl of, 377
Mint, master of, 237
Mirror, The, 234
Mitchell, Cornwall, borough of, 355
Mohun, Charles, 4th lord, 139, 143,
    144, 173
Mohun, John, 1st lord, 38
Moira, Francis Rawdon-Hastings, earl of,
    Lord Rawdon, 233, 238, 429, 437-9,
    448, 449
Monck, Christopher, 99
Monck, Henry, 99
Monmouth, earl of, *see* Peterborough, 3rd
    earl of
Monson, John, 5th lord, 348
Montagu, George Brudenell, duke of, 250,
    251
Montagu, John Montagu, 2nd duke of, 194
Montagu, Ralph Montagu, earl of, 86, 87,
    93, 94, 97, 99
Monteagle, Thomas Spring Rice, 1st lord,
    397, 401, 403
Monteagle, Thomas Spring Rice, 2nd lord,
    529
Montgomery family, 351
Montrose, James Graham, 1st duke of,
    137, 138, 152, 156
Montrose, James Graham, 3rd duke of, 251,
    254, 300
Montrose, William Graham, 2nd duke of,
    299, 300
Moray, Francis Stuart, 9th earl of, 290,
    291, 300, 315
Mordaunt, 2nd viscount, *see* Peterborough,
    3rd earl of
Morley, Edmund Robert Parker, 4th earl of,
    521, 523
Morley, John, 483
Morrice, Roger, 83, 86, 91
Morton, George Douglas, 16th earl of, 294,
    296, 299, 300, 314, 317, 338
Mountcashell, Stephen Moore, 2nd earl,
    245

Mount Edgecumbe, George Edgecumbe, 1st earl
    of, 251
Mulgrave, Edmund Sheffield, 1st earl of, 15
Mulgrave, Henry Phipps, 3rd lord, 408
Mulgrave, John Sheffield, 3rd earl of, 91-93

Napier, William John, 9th lord, 243, 244
Neile, Richard, bishop of Durham, 52
Nelson, William Nelson, 1st earl, 423
Nethersole, Sir Francis, 38
Newark, Notts, borough of, 348
Newcastle-under-Lyme, Staffs., borough of, 349
Newcastle-under-Lyne, Henry Pelham
    Pelham, 4th duke of, 348, 349, 353,
    355, 356
Newcastle-upon-Tyne, Northumb., 138
Newcastle-upon-Tyne, Henry Cavendish,
    2nd duke of, 99
Newcastle-upon-Tyne, Thomas Pelham-Holles,
    1st duke of, 213, 214, 268-70
Newcome, Richard, bishop of St Asaph,
    270
Newmarket, Suff., 186, 193
Newport, Francis Newport, viscount, 93
Newport, Mountjoy Blount, 1st earl of, 71
Newton, Thomas, bishop of Bristol, 270
Newton, Thomas Wodehouse Legh, 2nd lord,
    519-32 *passim*, 537, 538; *Retrospection*,
    524
New Woodstock, Oxon., borough of, 349,
    356
Nicholas, Edward, 121
Nicolson (Nicholson), William, bishop of
    Carlisle, 113, 124, 192, 193
Norfolk, Bernard Edward Howard, 12th duke
    of, 349
Norfolk, Bernard Marmaduke Fitzalan-Howard,
    16th duke of, 533-5
Norfolk, Edward Howard, 9th duke of, 448
Norfolk, Henry Howard, 7th duke of, 81, 93,
    96-98
Norfolk, Mary Howard, duchess of, wife of
    7th duke, 81, 96-98
Norris, John, 435
North, Brownlow, bishop of Winchester, 249
North, Dudley, 3rd lord, 15
North, Edward North, *styled* lord, 216, 247,
    253, 255, 256, 270, 271, 418, 446, 449
Northampton, George Compton, 4th earl
    of, 83, 84, 87, 88, 91, 190
Northamptonshire, 350
North and Grey, Charles North, 5th lord, 101
North and Grey, William North, 6th lord, 191, 19
Northcote, Sir Stafford, 480
Northland, Thomas Knox, 2nd viscount, 428

Northumberland, Algernon Percy, 4th earl of, 59

Northumberland, George Fitzroy, duke of, 91, 143, 144

Northumberland, Hugh Smithson, earl of, 213

Norwich, earl of, *see* Gordon, 4th duke of

Nottingham, Daniel Finch, 2nd earl of, 84, 90, 93, 94, 115, 116, 191, 192

Nugent, George Temple, *styled* lord, 353

Oates, Titus, 81, 88-91, 100; *The Case of Titus Oates*, 89

Observer, 523

O'Connell, Daniel, 385, 387, 390, 391

O'Connor, T.P., 502

Oldfield, T.H.B., 349, 352; *The Entire and Complete History, Political and Personal, of the Boroughs of Great Britain*, 352; *The Representative History of Great Britain and Ireland*, 351, 352

Old Sarum, Wilts., borough of, 348

Ordnance, master general of, 237

Orford, Edward Russell, earl of, 133-5, 186, 194

Orkney, George Hamilton, earl of, 144

Ormond, James Butler, 2nd duke of, 95, 102

Osborne, Lord Francis Godolphin, 350

Ossulston, Charles Bennet, 2nd baron, 144

Ottley, Adam, bishop of St David's, 192

Oxford, Aubrey de Vere, 20th earl of, 80, 95, 101

Oxford and Mortimer, Robert Harley, 1st earl, of, Speaker of the House of Commons, 111, 113, 114, 116-20, 122-4, 133, 142, 152-4, 156, 160, 165-71, 175, 177-80, 185-205 *passim*, 208, 309

Paget (Pagett), William, 6th lord, 15, 45, 50, 65, 72

Paley, William, archdeacon of Carlisle, 241

Palmer, Geoffrey, 59, 63

Pares, Richard, 263

Parker, Sir Philip, 61

Parker, Sir Thomas, 139

Parker, Thomas, 1st lord, 192

Parliament (1621), 8, 9; (1624), 6, 10; (1626), 23, 28, 33; (1628), 33, 34; (1640), 'Long', 51, 53, 54, 58, 60, 73; (1640), 'Short', 54, 56, 60; (1689), Convention, 82, 88; (1702), 110-25 *passim*; (1705), elections to, 125; (1715), 187

Parliamentary Debates, 347, 357, 359, 364

Parliamentary History, The, 234

Parliamentary Register, The, 234

Patrick, Simon, bishop of Ely, 98

Paulet, Vere, 356

Pearce, Zachary, bishop of Rochester, 265

Peard, George, 59

Peebleshire, 351

Peel, general 473

Peel, Robert, 434

Peel, Sir Robert, 220, 246, 253, 376-93, 395-7, 402

Pelham, George, bishop of Exeter, 248

Pelham, Thomas, 1st lord, 215, 217-19, 258, 429

Pembroke, Thomas Herbert, 8th earl of, 84, 93, 94, 101, 133, 134, 144, 161, 187, 194

Pembroke, William Herbert, 3rd earl of, lord steward, 37, 59

Pennington, alderman of London, 60, 69

People's Book, The, 352

Perceval, Spencer, 240, 241, 245

Perthshire, 356

Peter, Hugh, 52

Peterborough, Charles Mordaunt, 3rd earl of, earl of Monmouth, 2nd Viscount Mordaunt, 80, 86, 93, 94, 97, 142

Petition of grievances (1641), 67, 68

Petition(s), root and branch, 60, 61, 63

Petition of Right, 9, 11, 17, 31-37, 41-48

Petty, Lord Henry, 241

Phillpotts, Henry, bishop of Exeter, 382, 387, 388

Pierrepont, William, 59

Pitt, George, 408

Pitt, William, the younger, 216, 217, 238, 239, 248, 252, 256, 287, 296, 302, 327-9, 331, 332, 334, 337, 409, 412, 413, 417-21, 424, 427, 430, 440-2, 449

Plunket, William Conyngham, 348, 354

Plymouth, Other Windsor, 3rd earl of, 178

Poker Club, 286, 291

Poley (Polly), Henry, 124

Polwarth, Alexander Hume-Campbell, *styled* lord, 155

Popish Plot, 81, 89

Porritt, E., 352

Portland, Hans Willem Bentinck, 1st earl of, 91, 93, 94

Portland, William Henry Cavendish Cavendish-Bentinck, 3rd duke of, 215, 217-19, 240, 241, 245, 251, 258, 330, 427, 445

Portsmouth, John Charles Wallop, 3rd earl of, 356

Postmaster(s) general, 237

Potter, Barnabas, bishop of Carlisle, 71
Potter, John, bishop of Oxford, 192
Poulett (Poulet), John Poulett, 1st earl, 160, 188, 195
Poulett, John Poulett, 4th earl, 356
Powis, Thomas, 329
Powys, Sir Thomas, 157-60
Pratt, John, serjeant, 139, 157
President, lord, 210, 237
Preston, John, 52
Prince Regent, *see* George IV, king
Privy Council, 34, 38, 45, 64, 446
Privy Council, clerk of, 56
Privy seal, lord, 210, 237
Proceedings in Committees on Private Bills, 298
Providence Island Company, 51
Proxy, 24, 25, 66, 267; reforms (1626) of, 8, 11, 23, 24
Prynne, William, 60
Pulteney, John, 123
Pulteney, William, 186
Pym, John, 50-52, 57, 58, 66, 68-72

Quarterly Review, 474, 486
Queensberry (Queensbury), dukes of, 351
Queensberry (Queensburgh), Charles Douglas, 3rd duke of, 2nd duke of Dover, 179, 318
Queensberry, James Douglas, 2nd duke of, 1st duke of Dover, 133, 135-46, 152, 158, 164, 174
Queensberry, William Douglas, 4th duke of, 243, 244, 252, 287, 289, 294, 311-15, 317-20

Radnor, Charles Bodvile Roberts, 2nd earl of, 177
Radnor, Jacob Pleydell-Bouverie, 2nd earl of, 354
Rawdon, lord, *see* Moira, earl of
Reay, Eric Mackay, 7th lord, 243
Redesdale, John Thomas Mitford, 2nd lord, 244, 256
Redmond, John, 483, 502
Relf, Frances Helen, 31, 37, 46
Reynolds, Richard, 440
Richmond, Charles Henry Gordon-Lennox, 6th duke of, 478
Richmond, Charles Lennox, 1st duke of, 142
Richmond, Charles Lennox, 3rd duke of, 217, 313, 319, 328, 337, 448
Richmond, Charles Lennox, 5th duke of, 396
Ridpath, George, 179
Ripon, George Frederick Samuel Robinson, marquess of, 490, 491, 493, 496, 499, 506, 515
Rivers, Richard Savage, 4th earl, 142, 143
Robartes, John, 2nd lord, 59, 60
Robinson, Eric, 449
Robinson, John, bishop of London, 192
Rochester, Laurence Hyde, 1st earl of, 81, 85, 90, 93, 98, 113, 124, 125
Rochford, Frederick Nassau de Zuylestein, 3rd earl of, 194
Rockingham, Charles Watson-Wentworth, 2nd marquess of, 215, 252, 270, 276, 430, 440, 442, 445, 448, 452
Rockingham, Lewis Watson, 3rd lord, 97, 101
Roden, Robert Jocelyn, 3rd earl of, 377, 380, 391, 400
Roe, Sir Thomas, 63
Roebuck, Dr, 439
Rosebery, Archibald Philip Primrose, 5th earl of, 483-5, 520, 535
Rosebery, Archibald Primrose, 1st earl of, 163
Ross, William, 12th lord, 138
Rosse, William Parsons, 3rd earl of, 393
Rosslyn, James Erskine, 2nd earl of, 256, 382, 387
Rossmore, Warner William Westenra, 2nd lord, 377
Roxburghe, John Ker, 3rd duke of, 300, 303
Roxburghe, John Ker, 1st earl of, 135, 145
Rudyard, Sir Benjamin, 57, 59
Ruigh, Robert, 6
Russia, 440
Russell, Conrad, 51
Russell, Lord John, 389, 396, 404
Rutherford, John Anderson, *called* lord, 294, 320, 322
Rutland, John Henry Manners, 5th duke of, 348
Rutland, John Manners, 2nd duke of, 194
Rutland, John Manners, 3rd duke of, 250
Rutland, John Manners, 9th earl of, 91
Ryder, Richard, 356

St Albans, Charles Beauclerk, 1st duke of, 95, 179; wife of, 179
St Aldwyn, Sir Michael Edward Hicks Beach, viscount, 530, 533, 535
St Germains, Edward Granville Eliot, 3rd earl of, 257, 400
St John, Henry, 118, 119
St John, Oliver, 50, 58, 66, 68
St Loe (Lo), George, 121

St Mawes, Cornwall, borough of, 348, 354, 355

St Quintin, Sir William, 186

Salisbury, James Brownlow William Cecil, 2nd marquess of, 394

Salisbury, James Cecil, 7th earl of, 425

Salisbury, Robert Arthur Talbot Cecil, 3rd marquess of, *styled* Lord Cranborne, 463-87 *passim*

Salisbury, William Cecil, 2nd earl of, 15, 36, 59

Sandars, Jack, 529, 530, 533, 536, 538

Sandwich, John Montagu, 4th earl of, 330, 333

Savile, Thomas, 2nd lord, 59, 60, 64, 66, 67

Saybrook Company, 51

Saye (Say) and Sele, Lawrence Fiennes, 5th viscount, 178

Saye and Sele, William Fiennes, 1st viscount, 15, 37, 38, 40, 45, 46, 50-52, 54, 55, 59-61, 64, 65, 68, 72

Scarborough, Richard Lumley, 1st earl of, 94, 194

Scarlett, Sir James, 356

Scarsdale, Nathaniel Curzon, 2nd lord, 425

Scarsdale, Nicholas Leke, 5th earl of, 144

Schomberg, Meinhardt Schomberg, 2nd duke of, 94-95, 143

Schütz, baron von, 178, 187

Scotland, burghs, 328

–, Clerks of the session, 138

–, Register, lord (clerk), 138, 320, 323, 324

–, representative peers of, election of, 309; election (1708), 135-7; (1710), 152, 162; (1770), 290; (1780), 293; (1787), 295, 302; (1788), 295, 320; (1790), 296, 319; (1803), 296

Seafield, James Ogilivy, 1st earl of, 135, 142

Secker, Thomas, archbishop of Canterbury, 268

Secretaries of state, 56, 210, 215, 258

Selden, John, 59, 69

Select committee, 404-5

Select Society, 291

Selkirk, Dunbar Hamilton, 4th earl of, 290, 292, 295, 299, 302, 317, 320

Session, court of, 280

Seymour, Sir Edward, 116, 118, 119

Seymour, Sir Francis, 57, 59

Shadow Cabinet, 504, 507

Shaftesbury, Dorset, borough of, 348

Shannon, Richard Boyle, 2nd earl of, 428

Sharp, John, archbishop of York, 102

Sheffield, Yorks., 446, 448, 481

Sheffield, John Holroyd, lord, 410

Shelburne, William Petty, 2nd earl of, 215, 448

Sheridan, Richard Brinsley, 328

Shipley, Jonathan, bishop of St Asaph, 247, 272

Shrewsbury, Charles Talbot, duke of, 12th earl of, 86, 91, 142, 144, 188, 189, 193

Sidmouth, Henry Addington, 1st viscount, 217-19, 238-40, 418, 419

Sidney, Robert, lord, 91

Sieyès, abbé de, 496, 502

Skinner, Robert, bishop of Bristol, 71

Sligo, Howe Peter Browne, 2nd marquess of, 370

Smalridge, George, bishop of Bristol, 188, 191, 192

Smith, John, 118

Smith, Robert, 356

Smith, Robert, *see also* Carrington, 1st lord

Smith, Sir Sidney, 420

Smith, Sir Thomas, 54

Snow, Vernon, professor, 18, 24, 25

Society for Constitutional Reform, 328

Society of the Friends of the People, 352

Somers (Summers), John, lord, 133, 134, 137, 138, 191

Somerset (Somersett), Charles Seymour, 6th duke of, 116, 142, 171

Somerville, John Southey, 14th lord, 288, 296

Southampton, Henry Wriothesley, 3rd earl of, 8, 15

South Carolina, attorney general of, 444-5

Southern, David, 527-9, 532, 537

Spanish ambassador, lodgings of, 68

Spectator, The, 469, 471, 482

Spencer, earls, 350

Spencer, William, 2nd baron, 15, 37

Spencer-Churchill, Lord John, 356

Spender, J.A., 497

Spring, David, professor, 431

Stafford, George Granville Leveson-Gower, 2nd marquess of, 349, 351, 355, 356

Stafford, Granville Leveson-Gower, 1st marquess of, 238, 314

Stafford, William Howard, lord, 81

Stair, John Dalrymple, 5th earl of, 277, 279, 290

Stamford, George Harry Grey, 5th earl of, 437

Stamford, Henry Grey, 1st earl of, 15, 71

Stamford, Thomas Grey, 2nd earl of, 177, 179

Stamford, Sir William, 37
Stanhope, Charles Stanhope, 3rd earl, lord Mahon, 310, 318, 321, 322, 327-35, 336-9
Stanhope, James Stanhope, 1st earl, viscount, 186, 189, 193, 211, 212
Stanhope, Thomas, 118
Stanley, John Thomas, 1st lord, 256
Stanley, lord, *see* Derby, 14th earl of
Stapleton, Sir Philip, 69, 73
Staunton, George Thomas, 355
Stawell, William, 3rd lord, 178
Stead, W.T., 484
Stillingfleet, Edward, bishop of Worcester, 102
Stockbridge, Hants., borough of, 348
Stole, groom of, 250
Stone, Lawrence, 49
Stormont, 7th viscount, *see* Mansfield, 2nd earl of
Strachey, St Loe, 531-3, 535, 537
Strafford, Thomas Wentworth, 1st earl of, 58, 59, 64-69, 71-73
Strange, lord, *see* Atholl, 4th duke of
Strangford, Percy Clinton Sydney Smythe, 6th viscount, 414, 416
Strangways, Sir John, 59
Stratfield Saye, Hants., 387
Stratford, Nicholas, bishop of Chester, 95
Strode, William, 50, 58, 59, 66, 69, 72
Stuart, Sir Charles, 420
Stuart, James Edward Francis, the pretender, 135, 155
Studley Royal, near Ripon, Yorks., 493
Suckling, Sir John, 68, 69
Suffolk, John Howard, 15th earl of, 410
Sugden, Sir Edward B., 355
Sunderland, Charles Spencer, 3rd earl of, 113-15, 133, 137, 143, 145, 158, 161, 178, 185, 186, 192, 193, 195, 196, 208, 210-12
Sussex, Thomas Lennard, earl of, 177
Sutherland, 349, 351
Sutherland, Elizabeth Sutherland, countess of, 349
Sutherland, George Granville Leveson-Gower 2nd duke of, *styled* Lord Gower, 259, 359
Sutherland, John Sutherland, 16th earl of, 138
Sydney (Sidney), Thomas Townshend, 1st lord, home secretary, 215, 217, 258, 314, 318, 331-3, 337, 338
Sykes, Norman, 263

Tain Burghs, 351
Tait, Archibald Campbell, archbishop of Canterbury, 470

Talbot, William, bishop of Oxford and of Salisbury, 113, 192
Talbot, William Talbot, 1st earl, 250
Tamworth, Staffs., borough of, 434
Tavistock, Francis Russell, *styled* lord, 360
Tenison, Thomas, archbishop of Canterbury, bishop of Lincoln, 98, 116
Teynham, Henry Roper, 8th lord, 194
Thanet, Thomas Tufton, 5th earl of, 80, 87, 88, 99, 100
Thomond, William O'Bryen, 2nd marquess of, 245
Thompson, Christopher, 52
Thompson, F.M.L., professor, 407
Thurlow, Edward, 1st lord, lord chancellor, 216, 258, 305, 313, 314, 318, 322, 331-4, 337, 338
Times, The, 391, 393, 394, 399, 400, 404, 468, 471, 474, 475, 482, 485, 486, 521, 523, 530, 533, 534
Tiverton, Devon, borough of, 356
Tomline, Sir George Pretyman, bishop of Winchester, 247
Townshend, Charles Townshend, 2nd viscount, 185, 186, 189, 190, 192, 193, 195, 212
Townshend, Thomas, Hon., 212
Trade, board of, president of, 237
Treasury, the, 85, 440
Treasury, first lord of, 210, 215
Trelawny (Trelawney), Jonathan, bishop of Bristol and of Winchester, 83-85, 87, 88, 144, 192, 193
Trevon, Thomas, lord, 188, 190, 192, 196
Trevor, Richard, bishop of Durham, 270
Trimnell, Charles, bishop of Norwich, 192
Turberville, A.S., 352, 353, 424
Turner, Francis, bishop of Ely, 84
Tweeddale, George Hay, 6th marquess of, 290
Twiss, Horace, 360
Tyacke, Nicholas, 53
Tyburn, Midd., 89
Tyler, John, bishop of Llandaff, 192
Tyrone, George de la Poer Beresford, 2nd earl of, Viscount Beresford, 382, 428

Uxbridge, Henry Paget, 1st earl of, 441

Vane, Sir Henry, the younger, 50, 63
van Mildert, William, bishop of Durham, 382
Vaughan, John, 69
Vaughan, Robert Bertie, baron, 94, 97
Veitch, G.S., 335, 336
Victoria, queen, 220, 248, 405, 470, 471, 477

Villiers, John Charles, 355

Wake, William, archbishop of Canterbury, bishop of Lincoln, 139, 141, 192, 193
Walpole, Horace, 270
Walpole, Horace, brother of Robert, 186
Walpole, Horatio, 442
Walpole, Robert, 139, 185-7, 189, 190, 193, 195, 196
Walsingham, Thomas de Grey, 2nd lord, 237
Ward, John, 439
Warner, John, bishop of Rochester, 71
Warren, John, bishop of Bangor, 333, 334
Warrington, Henry Booth, 1st earl of, 93, 94
Warwick, George Greville, 2nd earl of, 439
Warwick, Robert Rich, 2nd earl of, 15, 46, 50-53, 60, 64, 65, 72
Warwick and Birmingham Canal, committee of, 438
Watson, Richard, bishop of Llandaff, 247, 449
Wedderburn, Alexander, 418
Wedgwood, Josiah, 434, 438, 444, 445, 452, 455
Wellesley, Sir Henry, 420
Wellesley, Richard Wellesley, marquess of, 359, 416, 421
Wellington, Arthur Wellesley, 1st duke of, 215, 220, 237, 243, 244, 246, 248, 253, 254, 256, 258, 375-88, 393-7, 421, 423, 429, 462, 463, 464, 477
Wemyss, David Wemyss, 4th earl of, 138
Wentworth, Peter, 137, 157, 163
Wentworth, Sir Thomas, 36
Westmeath, George Thomas John Nugent, 1st marquess of, 246, 398
Westminster, 50, 67, 69; Duke St, 257
Westminster, Palace of, painted chamber, 113
Westminster Hall, 66, 68, 191, 194, 195
Westmorland, John Fane, 11th earl of, 237, 242, 251
Westmorland, Thomas Fane, 6th earl of, 142
Weston, Richard, lord, 37-39, 43
Weymouth, Thomas Thynne, 1st viscount, 85, 100
Wharncliffe, James Archibald Stuart-Wortley, 1st lord, 391
Wharton, Philip, 4th lord, 50, 59, 60, 72, 94
Wharton, Thomas, 5th lord, 133, 134, 137, 145, 161, 167
Whateley, Richard, archbishop of Dublin, 382, 394, 401

Whitehall palace, banqueting house, 62
–, Cockpit, 166, 211
Whitfield, Walter, 121
Wicklow, William Howard, 4th earl of, 393
Widdrington, Sir Thomas, 59
Wilberforce, William, 329, 331-3, 410, 444
William, prince of Orange, *see* William III, king
William III, king, prince of Orange, 79, 82-84, 87, 92, 93, 97-100
William IV, king, 246, 248, 253
Williams, John, bishop of Chichester, 141
Williams, John, bishop of Lincoln, 37, 46, 60, 65
Williams, Thomas, 441
Willis, Richard, bishop of Gloucester, 192
Willoughby de Broke, Richard Greville Verney, 19th lord, 521
Willoughby of Parham, Edward, 2nd lord, 177, 179
Willoughby of Parham, Thomas, 1st lord, 95, 177, 179-80
Wilson, Joshua, *Biographical Index to the Present House of Commons*, 351
Winchester, Hants., borough of, 355
Winchilsea (Winchelsea), Charles Finch, 4th earl of, 178, 180
Winchilsea, George William Finch-Hatton, 10th earl of, 386, 387, 393
Winchilsea, Henry Stormont Finch-Hatton, 13th earl of, 523
Windham, William, 348
Winthrop, John, 54, 55
Wray, Sir Cecil, 329
Wray, Sir Christopher, 59
Wright, Sir Nathan, lord keeper, 122
Wrottesley, Sir John, 441
Wynford, William Draper Best, 1st lord, 387
Wynne, John, bishop of St Asaph, 192
Wythens, Francis, 89
Wyvill, Christopher, 329, 333, 335, 337

Yarmouth, William Paston, 2nd earl of, 85, 177, 178
Yelverton, Sir Henry, 9
Yeomen of the guard, captain of, 252
York, Yorks., 50, 56
York, Frederick, duke of, 420
York House Conference (1626), 52
Yorke, Sir Joseph, 420

Zagorin, Perez, 6